NFT™

Not For Tourists™ Guide to **WASHINGTON DC**

Get more on
notfortourists.com

Keep connected with:
Twitter:
twitter/notfortourists

Facebook:
facebook/notfortourists

iPhone App:
nftiphone.com

www.notfortourists.com

Not For Tourists Inc

011

Published and designed by:
Not For Tourists, Inc.
NFT,—Not For Tourists, Guide to Washi
www.notfortourists.com

Publisher
Jane Pirone

City Ed
Magda
Rachel

Information Design
Jane Pirone
Rob Tallia
Scot Covey

Writin
Amber
Magda Nakassis
Rachel Tepper
Rin-rin Yu

Director
Stuart Farr

Research
Michael Dale
Susan Lee
Keely B. Hild
Zachary Wilson
John-Paul Anthony

Managing Editors
Craig Nelson
Rob Tallia

Production Manager
Aaron Schielke

Database Manager
Michael Dale

Graphic Design & Production
Annika Koski
Aaron Schielke
Sarah Wyman

Information Systems Manager
Juan Molinari

Proofreader
Scott Sendrow

Printed in China
ISBN# 978-0-9795339-0-7 $21.99
Copyright © 2010 by Not For Tourists, Inc.

Every effort has been made to ensure that the information in this book is as up-to-date as possible at press time. However, many details are liable to change—as we have learned. The publishers cannot accept responsibility for any consequences arising from the use of this book.

Not For Tourists does not solicit individuals, organizations, or businesses for listings inclusion in our guides, nor do we accept payment for inclusion into the editorial portion of our book; the advertising sections, however, are exempt from this policy. We always welcome communications from anyone regarding ANYTHING having to do with our books; please visit us on our website at www.notfortourists.com for appropriate contact information.

Dear NFT User,

If 2010 has been any indication, this new decade is going to be a doozy for DC. The Commander in Chief's first year in this famously Democratic city continues to work everyone into a tizzy, and the liberal populace doesn't seem to be settling down anytime soon. Whether or not politicians share Washingtonians' enthusiasm is another question. Though Obamafever continues to rage, other big things have happened, too: January and February saw record snowfalls, appropriately named Snowpocalypse and Snowmageddon, which practically shut down the entire metropolitan area; MTV began airing episodes of The Real World: Washington DC, thus exposing the world to drunken hookup spots the city over; and in March, DC joined the ranks of New Hampshire, Connecticut, Iowa, Massachusetts and Vermont by recognizing same-sex marriages.

And things keep changing on the neighborhood front. Once terrifying parts of DC continue to transform into places you'd be comfortable strolling around after daylight—and maybe even paying rent in. Areas hit hard by the recession are starting to see restaurants and business coming back, much to the relief of Washingtonians. Our new 2011 guidebook includes up-to-date listings of all our favorite coffee shops, clubs, comic book shops, and more. Pithy, snarky blurbs will help you discern where you might dine on Friday night, or meet a friend for an al fresco cocktail. And detailed pages on parks, monuments, transit, and arts & entertainment will help you navigate your way to the closest dog park, Wi-Fi spot, library, post office, Art Deco movie theater, gourmet supermarket, train station, or bowling alley…essentially, everything your laminated, fold-out tourist map doesn't cover.

But as 21st-century DC, Maryland, and Virginia residents, we know you straddle the line between overeducated bookworm and tech-savvy geek. In the land of high-speed Internet and smart phones, you're probably updating your blog, Facebook status, and Twitter feed—simultaneously, right now. And so in tandem with this printed artifact, Not For Tourists has launched its very own iPhone app for The Beltway, so that you can access our infinite, irreverent wisdom on the go. Satellite stalkers in the sky can geo-locate you and immediately inform you of all the restaurants, nightlife, shopping, and landmarks in your vicinity. And if you don't (yet) have an iPhone, our website is constantly expanding, and has been souped up so that you can create a profile, write reviews, upload photos, make maps, and submit new listings.

In short, we demand that our books, website, and mobile applications be the definitive, go-to source for all things DC. So add to our endless listings produced by and for locals, and join our sassy, know-it-all urban army.

Here's to us!

Magda, Rachel, Rob, Jane, and Craig

Table of Contents

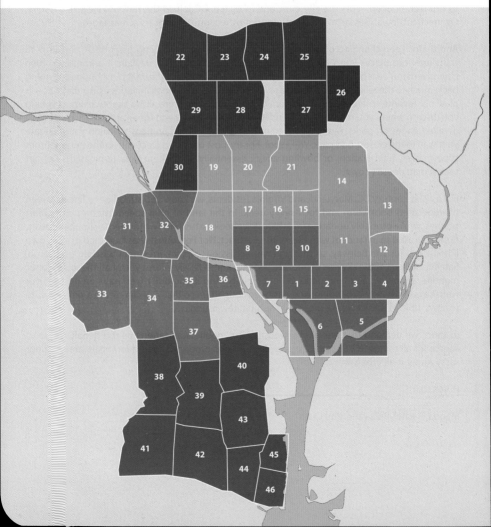

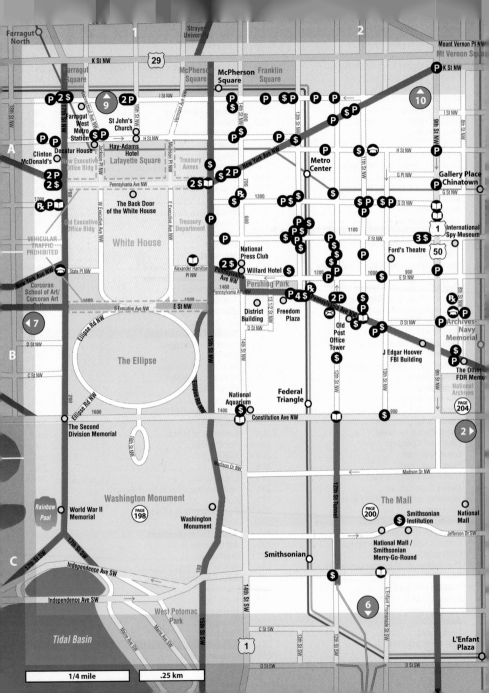

Essentials

Here you'll find pretty much every reason DC is a top tourist destination—The White House, the Washington Monument, the Declaration of Independence, etc. If you didn't see them on a school trip, try to check them out on the weekdays. The Mall, on weekends, especially in warm weather, is a mob scene. Tip: When you've had enough of the white marble, photocopy this map and let it substitute as the tour guide when relatives arrive.

Map 1

$ Banks

- **Bank of America** · 1001 Pennsylvania Ave NW
- **Bank of America** · 1501 Pennsylvania Ave NW
- **Bank of America** · 700 13th St NW
- **Bank of America** · 888 17th St NW
- **BB&T** · 601 13th St NW
- **BB&T** · 815 Connecticut Ave NW
- **Chevy Chase** · 1200 F St NW
- **Chevy Chase** · 1299 Pennsylvania Ave NW
- **Chevy Chase** · 1717 Pennsylvania Ave NW
- **Chevy Chase (ATM)** · 1000 Jefferson Dr SW
- **Chevy Chase (ATM)** · National Museum of Natural History
  · 10th St NW & Constitution Ave NW
- **Chevy Chase (ATM)** · 1100 Pennsylvania Ave NW
- **Chevy Chase (ATM)** · 1200 Independence Ave SW
- **Chevy Chase (ATM)** · 1300 Pennsylvania Ave NW
- **Chevy Chase (ATM)** · 1400 I St NW
- **Chevy Chase (ATM)** · 14th St & Constitution Ave NW
- **Chevy Chase (ATM)** · 302 12th St NW
- **Chevy Chase (ATM)** · 555 13th St NW
- **Chevy Chase (ATM)** · 607 13th St NW
- **Chevy Chase (ATM)** · 815 14th St NW
- **Citibank** · 1400 G St NW
- **Citibank** · 435 11th St NW
- **Independence Federal Savings** · 1006 E St NW
- **Industrial** · 1317 F St NW
- **M&T** · 555 12th St NW
- **Mercantile Potomac** · 1100 H St NW
- **PNC** · 1331 Pennsylvania Ave NW
- **PNC** · 1503 Pennsylvania Ave NW
- **PNC (ATM)** · 1101 New York Ave NW
- **PNC (ATM)** · 1300 New York Ave NW
- **PNC (ATM)** · 1455 Pennsylvania Ave NW
- **PNC (ATM)** · Courtyard Marriott · 900 F St NW
- **Sun Trust** · 1100 G St NW
- **Sun Trust** · 1445 New York Ave NW
- **Sun Trust** · 900 17th St NW
- **United** · 1001 G St NW
- **United** · 1275 Pennsylvania Ave NW
- **Wachovia** · 1300 I St NW
- **Wachovia** · 1301 Pennsylvania Ave NW
- **Wachovia** · 1310 G St NW
- **Wachovia** · 1700 Pennsylvania Ave NW
- **Wachovia** · 740 15th St NW
- **Wachovia** · 801 Pennsylvania Ave NW
- **Wachovia (ATM)** · 1201 G St NW
- **Wachovia (ATM)** · 529 14th St NW

⊙ Landmarks

- **The Clinton McDonald's** · 750 17th St NW
- **The Back Door of The White House** ·
  1600 Pennsylvania Ave
- **Decatur House** · 1610 H St NW
- **District Building** · 1350 Pennsylvania Ave NW
- **Farragut West Metro Station** · 17th St NW & I St
- **Ford's Theatre** · 511 10th St NW
- **Freedom Plaza** · 1300 Pennsylvania Ave NW
- **Hay-Adams Hotel** · 16th St & H St NW
- **International Spy Museum** · 800 F St NW
- **J Edgar Hoover FBI Building** · 935 Pennsylvania Ave NW

- **National Aquarium** · Constitution Ave NW & 14th St NW
- **National Mall** · 3rd St SW & Jefferson Dr SW
- **National Mall/Smithsonian Merry-Go-Round** ·
  1000 Jefferson Dr SW
- **National Press Club** · 529 14th St NW, 13th Fl
- **Old Post Office Tower** · 1100 Pennsylvania Ave NW
- **The Other FDR Memorial** ·
  Pennsylvania Ave NW, b/w 7th St NW & 9th St NW
- **The Second Division Memorial** · 17th St NW &
  Constitution Ave NW
- **Smithsonian Institution Building (The Castle)** ·
  1000 Jefferson Dr SW
- **St John's Church** · 16th St NW & H St NW
- **Washington Monument** · 15 St NW
- **Willard Hotel** · 1401 Pennsylvania Ave NW
- **World War II Memorial** ·
  15th St SW and Independence Ave SW

Libraries

- **Dibner Library** · Constitution Ave NW & 12th St NW
- **Martin Luther King Jr Memorial Library** · 901 G St NW
- **National Endowment for the Humanities Library** · 1100
  Pennsylvania Ave NW
- **Office of Thrift Supervision Library** · 1700 G St NW
- **Robert S Rankin Memorial Library** ·
  624 9th St NW, Rm 600
- **Treasury Library** · 1500 Pennsylvania Ave NW, Rm 1314
- **US Department of Commerce Library** ·
  1401 Constitution Ave NW
- **US Department of Energy Library** ·
  1000 Independence Ave SW, RM GA-138

P Parking

Rx Pharmacies

- **CVS** · 1275 Pennsylvania Ave NW
- **CVS** · 1716 G St NW
- **CVS** · 435 8th St NW
- **CVS** · 717 14th St NW

 Post Offices

- **Benjamin Franklin** · 1200 Pennsylvania Ave NW

Schools

- **Corcoran College of Art + Design
  (Downtown Campus)** · 500 17th St NW
- **Marriott Hospitality Public Charter** · 410 8th St NW

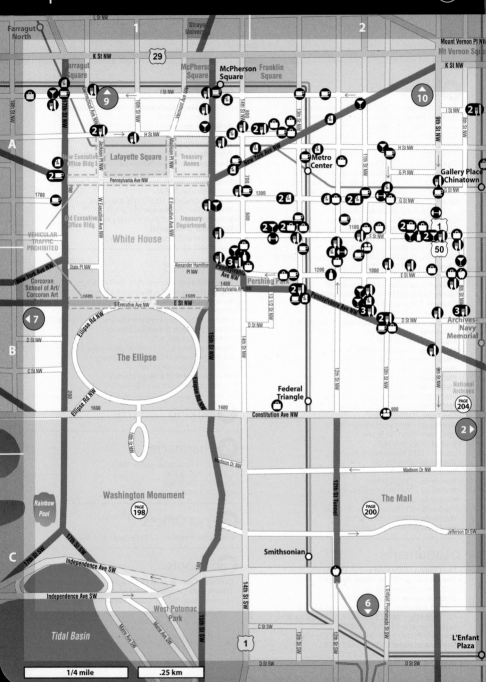

Map 1 • **National Mall**

This neighborhood caters mostly to tourists and office types during working hours. If you need to find a Starbucks or an Au Bon Pain, just look across the street. After five, The Mall clears out and action migrates downtown, where happy hours kick in at dozens of bars and restaurants—new hyper-trendy places seem to open weekly. What else? Catch an indie flick at the Landmark E Street Cinema to build up an appetite

Coffee

- **Bucks County Coffee** · 1300 Pennsylvania Ave NW
- **Caribou Coffee** · 1701 Pennsylvania Ave NW
- **Caribou Coffee** · 601 13th St NW
- **Coffee Espress** · 1250 H St NW
- **Cosi** · 1001 Pennsylvania Ave NW
- **Cosi** · 1333 H St NW
- **Cosi** · 1700 Pennsylvania Ave NW
- **Cosi** · 700 11th St NW
- **Firehook Bakery & Coffee House** · 555 13th St NW
- **Firehook Bakery & Coffee House** · 912 17th St NW
- **Gelatissimo** · 1300 Pennsylvania Ave NW
- **ME Swing** · 1702 G St NW
- **Sip of Seattle** · 1120 G St NW
- **Solar Café** · 1300 I St NW
- **Starbucks** · Grand Hyatt · 1000 H St NW
- **Starbucks** · 1301 Pennsylvania Ave NW
- **Starbucks** · 1401 New York Ave NW
- **Starbucks** · 555 11th St NW
- **Starbucks** · 700 14th St NW
- **Starbucks** · 701 9th St NW
- **Starbucks** · 901 15th St NW
- **Wally's World Coffee** · 1225 I St NW

Copy Shops

- **Ace Press** · 910 17th St NW
- **Advanced Printing** · 1201 New York Ave NW
- **Alpha Graphics Printshop** · 1325 G St NW
- **Document Technology** · 1300 Pennsylvania Ave NW
- **FedEx Kinko's** · 1350 New York Ave NW
- **FedEx Kinko's** · 419 11th St NW
- **Ikon Office Solutions** · 1120 G St NW
- **John Bar Printing** · 1308 G St NW
- **Metro Press** · 1444 I St NW
- **Penn Press II** · 750 17th St NW
- **Reliable Copy** · 555 12th St NW
- **Sir Speedy Printing** · 1212 G St NW
- **Sir Speedy Printing** · 1429 H St NW
- **Staples** · 1250 H St NW
- **Superior Group** · 1401 New York Ave NW

 Farmers Markets

- **Penn Quarter Freshfarm (Apr–Nov, Thurs 3pm–7pm)** · 8th St NW & E St NW
- **US Dept of Agriculture Farmers Market (Jun-Oct, Fri 10 am -2 pm)** · 12th St SW & Independence Ave SW

Gyms

- **Club Fitness at Washington Center** · 1001 G St NW
- **Fitness Co** · 555 12th St NW
- **Washington Sports Clubs** · 1345 F St NW
- **YWCA Fitness & Aquatics Center (women only)** · 624 Ninth St NW

Liquor Stores

- **Central Liquor Store** · 917 F St NW
- **Press Liquors** · 527 14th St NW
- **Washington Wine & Liquor** · 1200 E St NW

Movie Theaters

- **Landmark E St Cinema** · 555 11th St NW
- **Samuel C Johnson IMAX Theater·** Museum of Natural History · Constitution Ave NW & 10th St NW

Nightlife

- **Capitol City Brewing Company** · 1100 New York Ave NW
- **Eyebar** · 1716 I St NW
- **Gordon Biersch Brewery** · 900 F St NW
- **Grand Slam Sports Bar** · 1000 H St NW
- **Harry's Restaurant and Saloon** · 436 11th St NW
- **Home** · 911 F St NW
- **Le Bar** · 806 15th St NW
- **Old Ebbitt Grill** · 675 15th St NW
- **Round Robin Bar** · The Willard Intercontinental Hotel · 1401 Pennsylvania Ave NW
- **Shelly's Back Room** · 1331 F St NW
- **Society of Wine Educators** · 1319 F St NW, Ste 303
- **Ultrabar** · 911 F St NW

Restaurants

- **Asia Nine Bar and Lounge** · 915 E St NW
- **Aria Trattoria** · 1300 Pennsylvania Ave NW
- **Bistro D'Oc** · 518 10th St NW
- **BLT Steak Bistro Laurent Tourondel** · 1625 I St NW
- **Bourbon Steak** · 2800 Pennsylvania Ave NW
- **Café Asia** · 1720 I St NW
- **Café Atlantico** · 405 8th St NW
- **Café Mozart** · 1331 H St NW
- **Caucus Room** · 401 9th St NW
- **Cedar** · 822 E St NW
- **Ceiba** · 701 14th St NW
- **Central Michel Richard** · 1001 Pennsylvania Ave NW
- **Chef Geoff's** · 1301 Pennsylvania Ave NW
- **Dangerously Delicious** · 1339 H St NW
- **Ella's Wood Fired Pizza** · 901 F St NW
- **Equinox** · 818 Connecticut Ave NW
- **ESPN Zone** · 555 12th St NW
- **Gerard's Place** · 915 15th St NW
- **Harry's Restaurant and Saloon** · 436 11th St NW
- **High Noon** · 1311F St NW
- **J & G Steakhouse** · 515 15th St NW
- **Lia's** · 1401 Pennsylvania Ave NW
- **Loeb's Perfect New York Deli** · 832 15th St NW
- **Maggie Moo's** · 1001 Pennsylvania Ave NW

- **Meiwah** · 1401 Pennsylvania Ave NW
- **minibar** · 405 8th St NW
- **Occidental** · 1475 Pennsylvania Ave NW
- **Off the Record** · 16th St NW & H St NW
- **Old Ebbitt Grill** · 675 15th St NW
- **Ollie's Trolley** · 425 12th St NW
- **Potenza** · 1430 H St NW
- **PS7s** · 777 I St NW
- **Teaism** · 400 8th St NW
- **Teaism** · 800 Connecticut Ave NW
- **TenPenh** · 1001 Pennsylvania Ave NW
- **Willard Room** · Willard InterContinental · 1401 Pennsylvania Ave NW
- **Yogen Fruz** · 825 14th St NW
- **Zaytinya** · 701 9th St NW
- **Zola** · International Spy Museum · 800 F St NW

Shopping

- **American Apparel** · 1090 F St NW
- **Banana Republic** · 601 13th St NW
- **Barnes & Noble** · 555 12th St NW
- **Café Mozart** · 1331 H St NW
- **Celadon Spa** · 1180 F St NW
- **Central Liquor Store** · 917 F St NW
- **Coup de Foudre Lingerie** · 1001 Pennsylvania Ave NW
- **Cowgirl Creamery** · 919 F St NW
- **Ecco** · 714 7th St NW
- **Fahrney's Pens** · 1317 F St NW
- **Filene's Basement** · 529 14th St NW
- **H&M** · 1025 F St NW
- **International Spy Museum Gift Shop** · 800 F St NW
- **Macy's** · 1201 G St NW
- **Mia Gemma** · 933F St NW
- **Nancy Flower Shop** · 1300 Pennsylvania Ave NW
- **Penn Camera** · 840 E St NW
- **Political Americana** · 1331 Pennsylvania Ave NW
- **Ristorante Tosca** · 1112 F St NW
- **Roses Flower Delivery Service** · 601 13th St NW
- **Utrecht Art & Drafting Supplies** · 1250 I St NW
- **Washington DC Signs** · 775 12th St NW
- **White House Gift Shop** · 529 14th St NW

Map 2 • **Chinatown / Union Station**

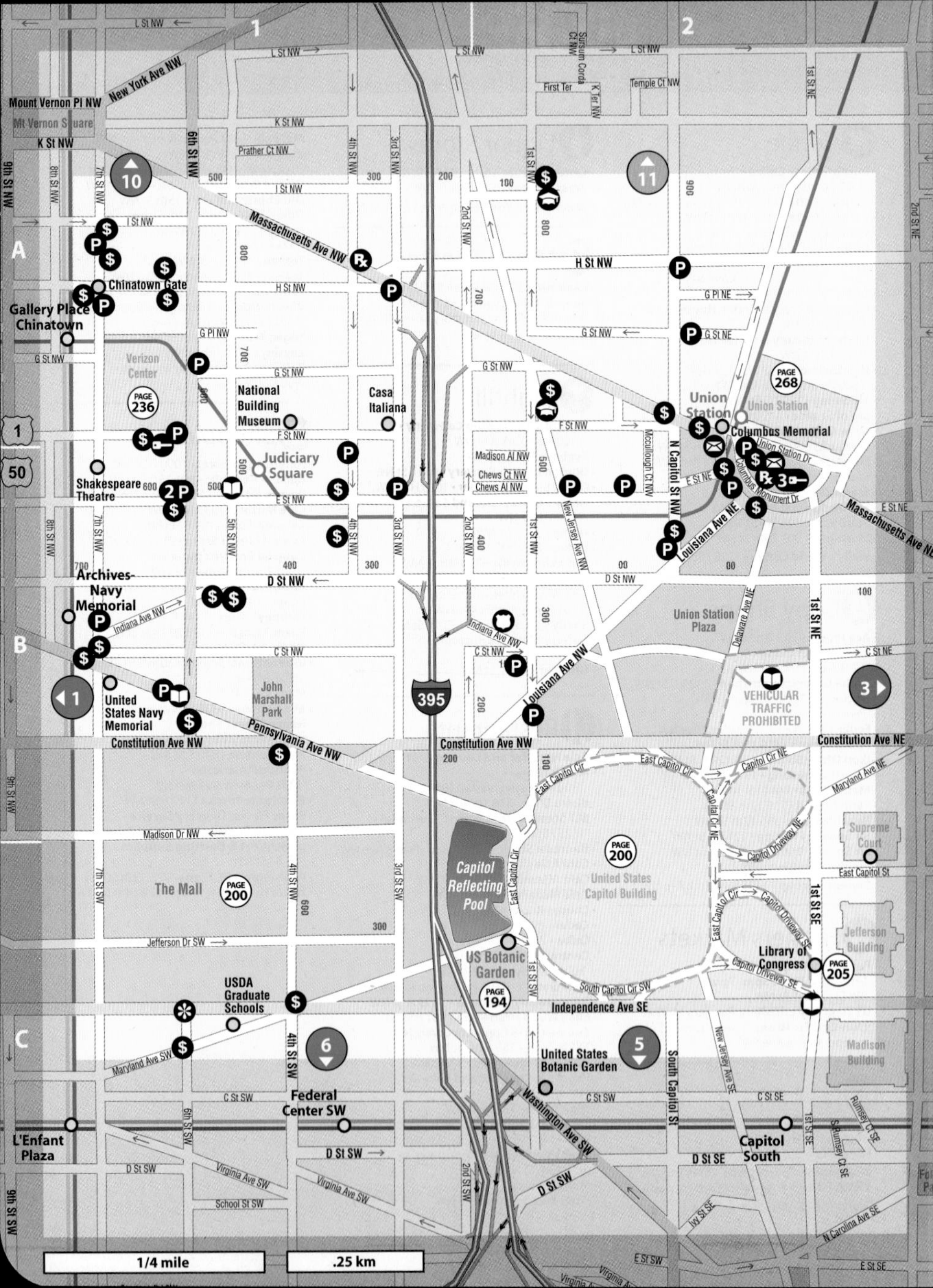

N

L St NW
L St NW
L St NW
L St NW
Sursum Corda
First Ter
L St NW
Temple Ct NW
L St NW

New York Ave NW
Mount Vernon Pl NW
Mt Vernon Square
K St NW

6th St NW
K St NW
Prather Ct NW
K St NW

4th St NW
3rd St NW
2nd St NW
1st St NW

10

500
300
200
100
800

I St NW

K Ter NW

H St NW
G Pl NE

900

11

Chinatown Gate
I St NW
H St NW
G St NW
700

800

1st St NE
2nd St NE

A

Gallery Place
Chinatown

G St NW
G Pl NW
G St NW

G St NE
G St NE

1
50

Verizon Center

PAGE 236

National Building Museum

Casa Italiana

F St NW

Union Station

PAGE 268

Union Station

Shakespeare Theatre

Judiciary Square

Madison Al NW
Chews Ct NW
Chews Al NW

500

McCollough St NW

Columbus Memorial
Union Station Dr

PAGE 3

Massachusetts Ave NW

2

600
500
400
300

E St NW
D St NW

3rd St NW
2nd St NW

400
300
200

New Jersey Ave NW

D St NW

Louisiana Ave NE

E St NE
Columbus Circle NE

00

100

B

Archives-Navy Memorial

Indiana Ave NW
C St NW
Indiana Ave NW
C St NW

300

Union Station Plaza

Delaware Ave NE

1st St NE

United States Navy Memorial
Constitution Ave NW

John Marshall Park
Pennsylvania Ave NW

395

200

Louisiana Ave NW

VEHICULAR TRAFFIC PROHIBITED

Constitution Ave NE

1

Constitution Ave NW
200

100

Capitol Cir NE

3

East Capitol Cir

Capitol Cir NE

Maryland Ave NE

Supreme Court

Madison Dr NW

The Mall

PAGE 200

300

Capitol Reflecting Pool

PAGE 200

United States Capitol Building

East Capitol Cir

Capitol Driveway NE

East Capitol St

1st St SE

Jefferson Building

Jefferson Dr SW

US Botanic Garden

South Capitol Cir SW

Library of Congress

PAGE 205

USDA Graduate Schools

PAGE 194

Independence Ave SE

Capitol Driveway SE

Madison Building

C

Maryland Ave SW

6

5

L'Enfant Plaza

Federal Center SW

C St SW

United States Botanic Garden

New Jersey Ave SE
South Capitol St

C St SW
C St SE

Capitol South

4th St SW

D St SW

D St SW

Washington Ave SW

2nd St SW

D St SW

D St SE
D St SE

N Carolina Ave SE

9th St SW

Virginia Ave SW
School St SW

Virginia Ave SW

Virginia Ave SW

Pennsylvania Ct SE
Schumbarg Ct SE

E St SE

1/4 mile
.25 km

Mostly white-collar business by day, Chinatown, Judiciary Square, Union Station, and the Capitol are full of politicians, lobbyists, lawyers, and other Washington fat cats. Expect to pause for motorcades and see suits feasting on sirloin steaks during weekday power lunches. Still, Chinatown is always bustling with credit-card-happy consumers encumbered with bags full of clothes.

Map

$ Banks

- **Adams National** • 50 Massachusetts Ave NE
- **Adams National** • 802 7th St NW
- **BB&T** • 614 H St NW
- **BB&T (ATM)** • 707 7th St NW
- **Chevy Chase** • 650 F St NW
- **Chevy Chase** • 701 Pennsylvania Ave NW
- **Chevy Chase (ATM)** •
  National Air and Space Museum •
  4th St SW & Independence Ave SW
- **Chevy Chase (ATM)** • National Gallery of Art •
  600 Constitution Ave NW
- **Chevy Chase (ATM)** • 600 Maryland Ave SW
- **Industrial (ATM)** • DC Superior Court • 409 E St NW
- **Industrial (ATM)** • 441 4th St NW
- **Industrial (ATM)** • 500 Indiana Ave NW
- **PNC** • 301 7th St NW
- **PNC** • 833 7th St NW
- **PNC (ATM)** • National Gallery of Art • 4th St NW &
  Constitution Ave NW
- **PNC (ATM)** • 600 New Jersey Ave NW
- **PNC (ATM)** • 601 E St NW
- **PNC (ATM)** • 820 1st St NE
- **Sun Trust** • 2 Massachusetts Ave NW
- **Sun Trust (ATM)** • 30 Massachusetts Ave NE
- **Sun Trust (ATM)** • 624 H St NW
- **Wachovia** • 444 N Capitol St NW
- **Wachovia** • 600 Maryland Ave SW
- **Wachovia (ATM)** • 50 Massachusetts Ave NE

Car Rental

- **Alamo** • 50 Massachusetts Ave NE • 202-842-7454
- **Budget** • 50 Massachusetts Ave NE • 202-289-5373
- **National** • 50 Massachusetts Ave NE • 202-842-7454
- **Thrifty** • 601 F St NW • 202-371-0485

✱ Community Gardens

◎ Landmarks

- **Casa Italiana** • 595 1/2 3rd St NW
- **Chinatown Gate** • H St NW & 7th St NW
- **Columbus Memorial** •
  Massachusetts Ave & First St (near Union Station)
- **National Building Museum** • 401 F St NW
- **Shakespeare Theatre** • 450 7th St NW
- **Supreme Court of the United States** • 1st St NE
  b/w E Capitol St SE & Maryland Ave NE
- **United States Botanic Garden** • 245 1st St SW
- **United States Navy Memorial** •
  701 Pennsylvania Ave NW
- **US Botanic Garden** • 100 Maryland Ave SW
- **US Library of Congress** • 101 Independence Ave SE
- **USDA Graduate Schools** • 600 Maryland Ave SW

Libraries

- **Federal Trade Commission Library** •
  600 Pennsylvania Ave NW
- **National Research Council Library** • 500 5th St
  NW, Room 304
- **US Library of Congress** • 101 Independence Ave SE
- **US Senate Library** • Russell Senate Office Bldg, B15

P Parking

Rx Pharmacies

- **CVS** • 400 Massachusetts Ave NW
- **Tschiffely Pharmacy** • 50 Massachusetts Ave NE

Police

- **MPDC Headquarters** • 300 Indiana Ave NW

✉ Post Offices

- **National Capitol** • 2 Massachusetts Ave NE
- **Union Station** • 50 Massachusetts Ave NE

Schools

- **Georgetown University Law Center** •
  600 New Jersey Ave NW
- **Gonzaga College High** • 19 I St NW

Once defined by its ethnic and culinary connections to China, a yuppie influx encouraged by the popularity of the Verizon Center has made Chinatown (aka the Penn Quarter) a haven for mid-career types looking to blow a wad on food, drink, and residence. Eat American at Matchbox, try Indian at Rasika, or down hundreds of beers at RFD.

Coffee

- **Bucks County Coffee** · 50 Massachusetts Ave NE
- **Café Renee** · 50 Massachusetts Ave NE
- **Camiles Sidewalk Café** · 650 F St NW
- **Chinatown Coffee Company** · 475 H St SW
- **Cosi** · 601 Pennsylvania Ave NW
- **Dunkin' Donuts** · 100 F St NE
- **Dunkin' Donuts** · 601 F St NW
- **Firehook Bakery & Coffee House** · 441 4th St NW
- **Juan Valdez Cafe** · 675 E St NW
- **Starbucks** · 325 7th St NW
- **Starbucks** · 443-C 7th St NW
- **Starbucks** · 600 Maryland Ave SW
- **Starbucks** · 800 7th St NW

Copy Shops

- **FedEx Kinko's** · 325 7th St NW
- **Minuteman Press** · 555 New Jersey Ave NW

Gyms

- **Wah Shing Kung-Fu** · 815 7th St NW
- **Washington Sports Clubs** · 783 7th St NW

Liquor Stores

- **Kogod Liquors** · 441 New Jersey Ave NW
- **Union Wine & Liquors Store** · 50 Massachusetts Ave NE

Movie Theaters

- **Lockheed Martin IMAX Theater** ·
  National Air and Space Museum ·
  601 Independence Ave SW
- **Regal Gallery Place Stadium** · 707 7th St NW

Nightlife

- **Bar Louie** · 701 7th St NW
- **Capitol City Brewing Company** ·
  2 Massachusetts Ave NE
- **The Dubliner** · Phoenix Park Hotel · 4 F St NW
- **Fado Irish Pub** · 808 7th St NW
- **Irish Channel Pub** · 500 H St NW
- **Iron Horse Tap Room** · 507 7th St NW
- **Kelly's Irish Times** · 14 F St NW
- **Lucky Strike Lanes** · 701 7th St NW
- **My Brother's Place** · 237 2nd St NW
- **Poste Moderne Brasserie** · 555 8th St NW
- **RFD Washington** · 810 7th St NW
- **Rocket Bar** · 714 7th St NW

Restaurants

- **701** · 701 Pennsylvania Ave NW
- **America** · 50 Massachusetts Ave NE
- **Art and Soul** · 415 New Jersey Ave NW
- **B Smith's** · 50 Massachusetts Ave NE
- **Billy Goat Tavern & Grill** · 500 New Jersey Ave NW
- **Bistro Bis** · 15 E St NW
- **Burma** · 740 6th St NW
- **Capital Q** · 707 H St NW
- **Capitol City Brewing Company** ·
  2 Massachusetts Ave NE
- **Center Café at Union Station** · 50 Massachusetts Ave NE
- **Charlie Palmer** · 101 Constitution Ave NW
- **Chinatown Express** · 746 6th St NW
- **District Chophouse** · 509 7th St NW
- **The Dubliner** · Phoenix Park Hotel · 4 F St NW
- **Eat First** · 609 H St NW
- **Fado Irish Pub** · 808 7th St NW
- **Full Kee** · 509 H St NW
- **Jaleo** · 480 7th St NW
- **Jerk Chicken Wrap Cart** · 4th St NW & E St NW
- **Johnny's Half Shell** · 400 N Capitol St NW
- **Kelly's Irish Times** · 14 F St NW
- **La Tasca** · 722 7th St NW
- **Matchbox** · 713 H St NW
- **Mitsitam Native Foods Café** ·
  National Museum of the American Indian ·
  4th St SW & Independence Ave SW
- **My Brother's Place** · 237 2nd St NW
- **Nando's Peri-Peri** · 819 7th St NW
- **Pizza Bistro Med** · 736 6th St NW
- **Poste Moderne Brasserie** · 555 8th St NW
- **Rasika** · 633 D St NW
- Red Velvet Cupcakery · 675 E St NW
- **Rosa Mexicano** · 575 7th St NW
- **Sei** · 444 7th St NW
- **Tony Cheng's Mongolian Restaurant** ·
  619 H St NW, downstairs
- **Tony Cheng's Seafood Restaurant** ·
  619 H St NW, upstairs
- **Zengo** · 781 7th St NW

Shopping

- **Alamo Flags** · 50 Massachusetts Ave NE
- Ann Taylor Loft · 707 7th St NW
- **Appalachian Spring** · 50 Massachusetts Ave NE
- **Apple Seed Boutique** · 115 S Columbus St
- **Aveda Institute** · 713 Seventh St NW
- **Bed Bath and Beyond** · 709 7th St NW
- **Comfort One Shoes** · 50 Massachusetts Ave NE
- **Godiva Chocolatier** · 50 Massachusetts Ave NE
- **National Air and Space Museum Shop** ·
  Independence Ave & 4th St SW
- **Pua Naturally** · 701 Pennsylvania Ave NW
- **Red Velvet Cupcakery** · 675 E St NW
- **Tangy Sweet** · 675 E St NW
- **Urban Outfitters** · 737 7th St NW

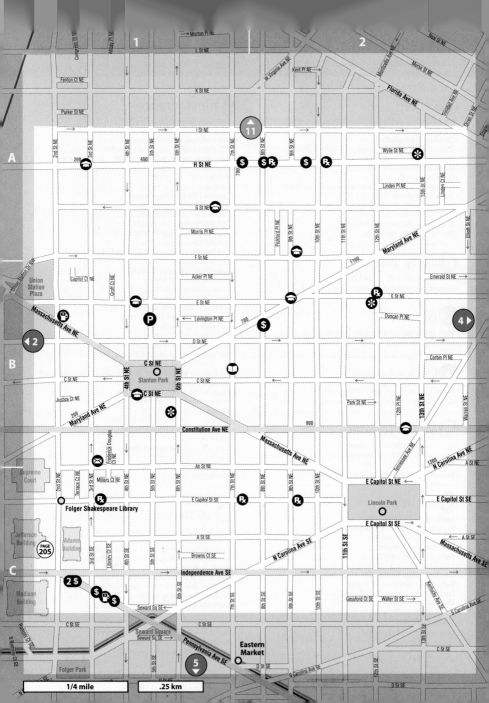

Few make it to the top, and when you get there, you're broke, unless you're a lobbyist. This area is home to an eclectic collection of so-called political gurus: international moguls, young professionals, rowdy interns, and working stiffs. The controlling political party may change, but they all complain about the rising property taxes and rent in this quaint, historic neighborhood.

Banks

- **Bank of America** · 201 Pennsylvania Ave SE
- **Bank of America** · 722 H St NE
- **Bank of America (ATM)** · 961 H St NE
- **Chevy Chase** · 336 Pennsylvania Ave SE
- **Citibank (ATM)** · 7-Eleven · 407 8th St NE
- **PNC** · 800 H St NE
- **Sun Trust** · 300 Pennsylvania Ave SE
- **Wachovia** · 215 Pennsylvania Ave SE

Community Gardens

Gas Stations

- **Exxon** · 200 Massachusetts Ave NE
- **Exxon** · 339 Pennsylvania Ave SE

Landmarks

- **Folger Shakespeare Library** · 201 E Capitol St SE
- **Lincoln Park** · E Capitol St SE b/w 11th & 13th St SE
- **Stanton Park** · C St NE & Maryland Ave NE

Libraries

- **Northeast Neighborhood Library** · 330 7th St NE

 Parking

Pharmacies

- **CVS** · 500 12 St SE
- **Grubb's CARE Pharmacy & Medical Supply** · 326 E Capitol St NE
- **Morton's CARE Pharmacy** · 724 E Capitol St NE
- **Rite Aid** · 801 H St NE
- **Robinson's Apothecary** · 922 E Capitol St NE
- **Super CARE Pharmacy** · 1019 H St NE

Post Offices

- **Fort McNair** · 300 A St NE

Schools

- **Cornerstone Community** · 907 Maryland Ave NE
- **Ludlow-Taylor Elementary** · 659 G St NE
- **Maury Elementary** · 1250 Constitution Ave NE
- **Options Middle** · 800 3rd St NE
- **Peabody Elementary** · 425 C St NE
- **Prospect Learning Center** · 920 F St NE
- **Stuart-Hobson Middle** · 410 E St NE

Wine connoisseurs dine at Sonoma and the grunge crowd heads to the Atlas District at 13th & H. Weeknights, Hill staffers share bar space with other office drones at Lounge 201 and Hawk and Dove. These kids work hard and they play hard, so don't underestimate the potency of a night out on the Hill.

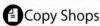

☕ Coffee

- **Belga Cafe** · 514 8th Street, SE
- **Cosi** · 301 Pennsylvania Ave SE
- **Ebenezers** · 201 F St NE
- **Firehook Bakery & Coffee House** · 215 Pennsylvania Ave SE
- **Le Bon Café** · 210 2nd St SE
- **Neb's Café** · 201 Massachusetts Ave NE
- **Sidamo Coffee and Tea** · 417 H St NE
- **SOVA Espresso & Wine** · 1359 H St NE
- **Starbucks** · 237 Pennsylvania Ave SE

🖨 Copy Shops

- **FedEx Kinko's** · 208 2nd St SE

🍎 Farmers Markets

- **H Street Freshfarm Market (May–Oct, Sat 9 am–12 pm)** · 624 H St NE

🏋 Gyms

- **Willpower Health & Fitness Studio** · 1005 H St NE

🔨 Hardware Stores

- **Park's Hardware** · 920 H St NE

🍾 Liquor Stores

- **Family Liquors** · 710 H St NE
- **Gandel's Liquors** · 211 Pennsylvania Ave SE
- **H Street Liquor Store** · 303 H St NE
- **Hayden's Liquor Store** · 700 North Carolina Ave SE
- **Jumbo Liquors** · 1122 H St NE
- **Schneider's of Capitol Hill** · 300 Massachusetts Ave NE

🍸 Nightlife

- **Capitol Lounge** · 229 Pennsylvania Ave SE
- **Granville Moore's** · 1238 H St NE
- **H Street Country Club** · 1335 H St NE
- **Hawk and Dove** · 329 Pennsylvania Ave SE
- **Lounge 201** · 201 Massachusetts Ave NE
- **Palace of Wonders** · 1210 H St NE
- **Pour House** · 319 Pennsylvania Ave SE
- **Rock & Roll Hotel** · 1353 H St NE
- **Sonoma** · 223 Pennsylvania Ave SE
- **The Majestic** · 1368 H St NE
- **The Pug** · 1234 H St NE
- **Top of the Hill** · 319 Pennsylvania Ave SE
- **Toyland** · 421 H St NE
- **Tune Inn** · 331 1/2 Pennsylvania Ave SE

🍴 Restaurants

- **Belga Cafe** · 514 8th St SE
- **Bistro Cacao** · 320 Massachusetts Ave NE
- **Café Berlin** · 322 Massachusetts Ave NE
- **Ethiopic** · 401 H St NE
- **Good Stuff Eatery** · 303 Pennsylvania Ave SE
- **Hawk and Dove** · 329 Pennsylvania Ave SE
- **Horace & Dickie's** · 809 12th St NE
- **Kenny's Smokehouse** · 732 Maryland Ave NE
- **La Loma Mexican Restaurant** · 316 Massachusetts Ave NE
- **The Liberty Tree** · 1016 H St NE
- **Locanda Cucina Meditalia** · 633 Pennsylvania Ave SE
- **Pete's Diner** · 212 2nd St SE
- **Sonoma** · 223 Pennsylvania Ave SE
- **Spy Diner** · 900 F St NE
- **Sticky Rice** · 1224 H St NE
- **Union Pub** · 201 Massachusetts Ave NE
- **Wellness Cafe** · 325   Pennsylvania Ave SE
- **White Tiger** · 301 Massachusetts Ave NE
- **Zest** · 735 8th St NE

🛍 Shopping

- **Capitol Hill Poultry** · 255 7th St SE
- **Dangerously Delicious Pies** · 1339 H St NE
- **George's Place Limited** · 1001H St NE
- **S&S Shoe Repair** · 1126 H St NE

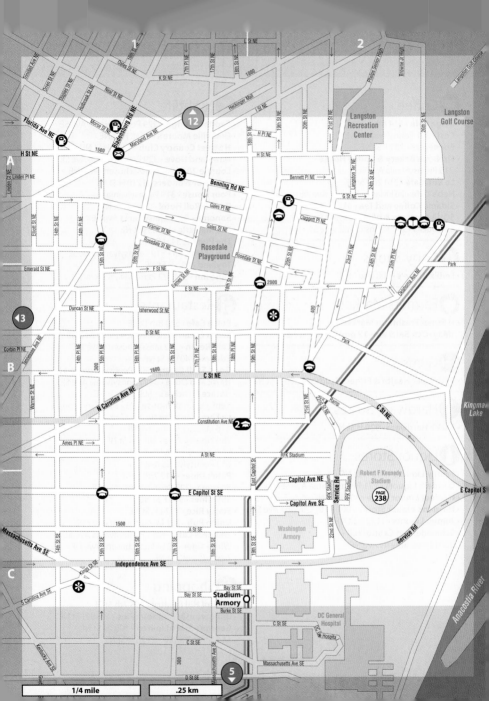

It used to be the home of the Skins, then the home of the Nats, and now DC United soccer fans finally have a stadium of their own. Feel free to join in for tailgating, samba music, and a heavy does of Spanish. The Metro conveniently has a stop here for those looking for something to do after a game. A word of warning: parts of the area can be on the sketchy side, so look aware and walk in pairs.

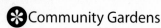 Community Gardens

 Gas Stations
- **Amoco** • 1396 Florida Ave NE
- **Amoco** • 1950 Benning Rd NE
- **Amoco** • 814 Bladensburg Rd NE
- **Exxon** • 2651 Benning Rd NE

 Libraries
- **Langston Community Library** •
  2600 Benning Rd NE

Pharmacies
- **Sterling CARE Pharmacy** • 1647 Benning Rd NE

Post Offices
- **Northeast** • 1563 Maryland Ave NE

Schools
- **The Academy for Ideal Education Upper** •
  702 15th St NE
- **Browne Center Special Education** •
  1830 Constitution Ave NE
- **Eastern High** • 1700 E Capitol St NE
- **Eliot Junior High** • 1830 Constitution Ave NE
- **Friendship Edison: Blow Pierce Campus** •
  725 19th St NE
- **Gibbs Elementary** • 500 19th St NE
- **Holy Comforter-St Cyprian** • 1503 E Capitol St SE
- **Miner Elementary** • 601 15th St NE
- **Spingarn Center** • 2500 Benning Rd NE
- **St Benedict of the Moor** • 320 21st St NE

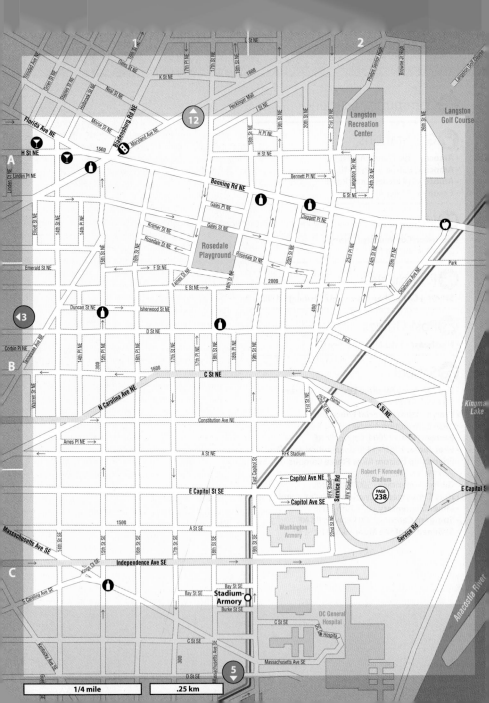

Visit one of the many liquor stores in the daylight hours to plot your house parties. If you're searching for evening activities out and about, the best options revolve around the far end of H Street, including mini golf at H Street Country Club (Map 3) or hanging with the locals at The Argonaut. Dining options are very limited in this area, so plan ahead.

Farmers Markets

- **Open Air Farmers Markets
 (May–Dec, Tues, Thurs & Sat, 7 am–4 pm;
 Jan–Apr, Thurs & Sat 7 am–4 pm)** ·
 Oklahoma Ave NE & Benning Rd NE

Nightlife

- **The Argonaut** · 1433 H St NE
- **Rose's Dream Bar & Lounge** · 1370 H St NE

Liquor Stores

- **Capitol Liquors** · 1835 Benning Rd NE
- **Madison Liquors** · 1806 D St NE
- **New York Liquor Store** · 1447 Maryland Ave NE
- **S&J Liquor Store** · 1500 Massachusetts Ave SE
- **Silverman's Liquor** · 2033 Benning Rd NE
- **Viggy's Liquors** · 409 15th St NE

Video Rental

- **Blockbuster** · 1555 Maryland Ave NE

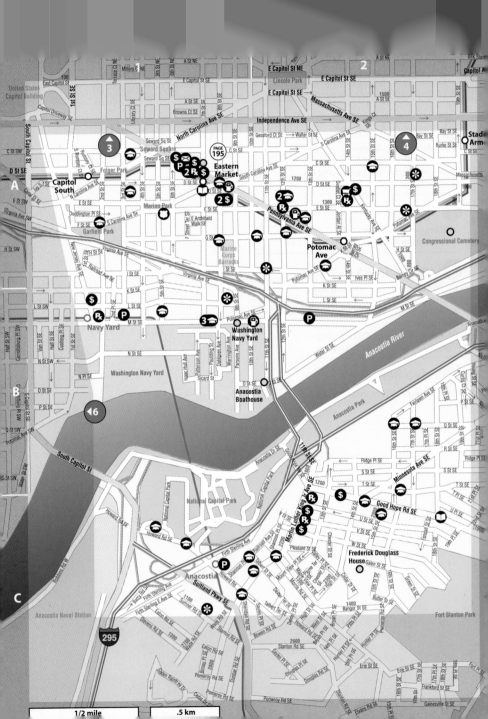

A microcosm of America itself, here you'll find life snippets ranging from urban decay to disturbin' decadence, with a splash of semi-suburban simplicity a stone's skip away from Anacostia. Congressional Cemetery is a lesser-known jewel in a city crowned with famous landmarks, where you can visit the final resting places of many forgotten congressmen from previous centuries and enjoy views of the river.

$ Banks

- **Bank of America** · 2100 Martin Luther King Jr Ave SE
- **Chevy Chase** · 1100 New Jersey Ave SE
- **Chevy Chase (ATM)** · 401 8th St SE
- **Citibank** · 600 Pennsylvania Ave SE
- **Citibank (ATM)** · 7-Eleven · 429 8th St SE
- **PNC** · 2000 Martin Luther King Jr Ave SE
- **PNC** · 650 Pennsylvania Ave SE
- **Sun Trust** · 1340 Good Hope Rd SE
- **Sun Trust (ATM)** · Safeway · 415 14th St SE

 Community Gardens

Gas Stations

- **Amoco** · 823 Pennsylvania Ave SE
- **Exxon** · 1022 M St SE
- **Exxon** · 1201 Pennsylvania Ave SE
- **Sunoco** · 1248 Pennsylvania Ave SE

Landmarks

- **Anacostia Boathouse** · 1105 O St SE
- **Congressional Cemetery** · 1801 E St SE
- **Eastern Market** · 225 7th St SE
- **Frederick Douglass House** · 1411 W St SE
- **Washington Navy Yard** · 9th St SE & M St SE

Libraries

- **Anacostia Interim Library** · 1800 Good Hope Rd SE
- **Southeast Neighborhood Library** · 403 7th St SE

P Parking

- **Central Parking** · 1201 M St SE

Rx Pharmacies

- **Capitol Hill CARE Pharmacy** · 650 Pennsylvania Ave SE
- **CVS** · 1100 New Jersey Ave SE
- **CVS** · 500 12th St SE
- **CVS** · 661 Pennsylvania Ave SE
- **Neighborhood CARE Pharmacy** · 1932 Martin Luther King Jr Ave SE
- **Safeway** · 415 14th St SE
- **State CARE Pharmacy** · 2041 Martin Luther King Jr Ave SE

 Police

- **MPDC 1st District Substation** · 500 E St SE

Post Offices

- **Southeast** · 600 Pennsylvania Ave SE

Schools

- **Ambassador Baptist Church Christian Academy** · 1412 Minnesota Ave SE
- **Anacostia Bible Church Christian** · 1610 T St SE
- **Anacostia High** · 1601 16th St SE
- **Birney Elementary School** · 2501 M L King Jr Ave SE
- **Brent Elementary** · 301 North Carolina Ave SE
- **Capitol Hill Day** · 210 S Carolina Ave SE
- **Cesar Chavez Public Charter** · 709 12th St SE
- **Clara Muhammad** · 2313 Martin Luther King Jr Ave SE
- **Eagle Academy** · 770 M St SE
- **Friendship Edison: Chamberlain Campus** · 1345 Potomac Ave SE
- **Hine Junior High** · 335 8th St SE
- **Holy Temple Christian Academy** · 439 12th St SE
- **Howard Road Academy** · 701 Howard Rd SE
- **Ketcham Elementary** · 1919 15th St SE
- **Kipp DC/Key Academy** · 770 M St SE
- **Kramer Middle** · 1700 Q St SE
- **Payne Elementary** · 305 15th St SE
- **Rose Elementary** · 821 Howard Rd SE
- **Sasha Bruce Middle** · 745 8th St SE
- **Savoy Elementary** · 2400 Shannon Pl SE
- **St Peters Interparish** · 422 3rd St SE
- **Thurgood Marshall Academy** · 2427 Martin Luther King Jr Ave SE
- **Tyler Elementary** · 1001 G St SE
- **Van Ness Elementary** · 1150 5th St SE
- **Washington Math Science Technology High** · 770 M St SE
- **Watkins Elementary** · 420 12th St SE

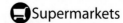 Supermarkets

- **Safeway** · 415 14th St SE

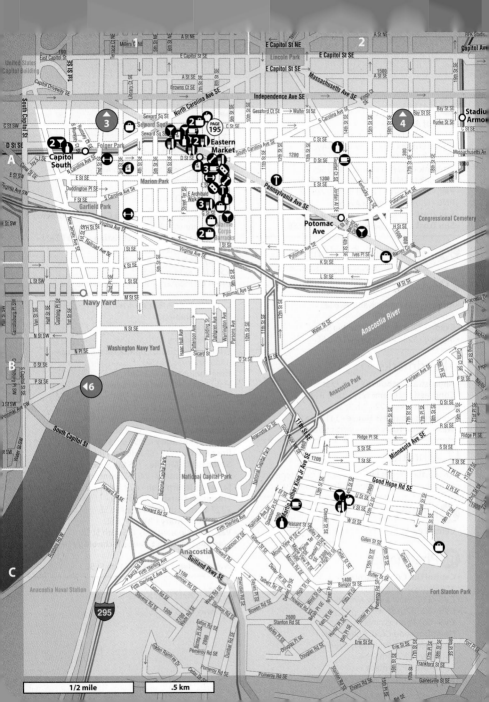

Eighth Street (Barracks Row) is a nightlife epicenter that offers a variety of restaurants, bars, and a smattering of live music options. Check out Eastern Market on the weekends for arts and crafts outside and a mind-boggling selection of sausages inside. Feeling adventurous? Go explore Anacostia and see the Frederick Douglass house. Although it's improving, Anacostia is still known as a place you don't want to be after daylight hours.

Map

Coffee

- **Big Chair Coffee** • 2122 Martin Luther King Jr Ave SE
- **Dunkin' Donuts** • 801 Pennsylvania Ave SE
- **Peregrine Espresso** • 660 Pennsylvania Ave SE
- **Starbucks** • 401 8th St SE
- **Starbucks** • 415 14th St SE

Copy Shops

- **FedEx Kinko's** • 715 D St SE
- **UPS Store** • 611 Pennsylvania Ave SE

Farmers Markets

- **Anacostia Farmers Market (Jun–Nov, Wed 3 pm–7 am)** • 14th St SE b/w U St SE & V St SE
- **Eastern Market Outdoor Farmers Market (Sat & Sun, 7 am–4 pm)** • 7th St SE b/w C St SE & North Carolina Ave SE

Gyms

- **Curves (women only)** • 407 8th St SE
- **Results the Gym** • 315 G St SE
- **Washington Sports Clubs** • 214 D St SE

Hardware Stores

- **District Lock & Hardware** • 505 8th St SE
- **Frager's Hardware** • 1115 Pennsylvania Ave SE

Liquor Stores

- **Albert's Liquor Store** • 328 Kentucky Ave SE
- **Big K Liquors** • 2252 Martin Luther King Jr Ave SE
- **Chat's Liquors** • 503 8th St SE
- **Congressional Liquors** • 404 1st St SE
- **JJ Mutts Wine & Spirits** • 643 Pennsylvania Ave SE

Nightlife

- **Bullfeathers** • 410 1st St SE
- **Mr Henry's Capitol Hill** • 601 Pennsylvania Ave SE
- **Patty Boom Boom** • 1359 U St SE
- **Remingtons** • 639 Pennsylvania Ave SE
- **Tortilla Coast** • 400 1st St SE

- **Trusty's** • 1420 Pennsylvania Ave SE
- **Tunnicliff's Tavern** • 222 7th St SE
- **The Ugly Mug** • 723 8th St SE

Pet Shops

- **Chateau-Animaux** • 524 8th St SE
- **Pawticulars Gourmet Pet Boutique** • 407 8th St SE

Restaurants

- **Banana Café & Piano Bar** • 500 8th St SE
- **Belga Cafe** • 514 8th St SE
- **Bistro La Bonne** • 1340 U St SE
- **Bread & Chocolate** • 666 Pennsylvania Ave SE
- **Cava** • 527 8th St SE
- **Jordan's 8** • 523 8th St SE
- **La Plaza** • 629 Pennsylvania Ave SE
- **Locanda Cucina Meditalia** • 633 Pennsylvania Ave SE
- **Matchbox** • 521 8th St SE
- **Montmartre** • 327 7th St SE
- **Pizza Boli's** • 417 8th St SE
- **Starfish** • 539 8th St SE
- **Tortilla Coast** • 400 1st St SE

Shopping

- **AM Wine Shoppe** • 2122 18th St SE
- **Backstage Inc** • 545 8th St SE
- **Capitol Hill Bikes** • 709 8th St SE
- **Capitol Hill Books** • 657 C St SE
- **Capital Hill Sporting Goods & Apparel** • 727 8th St
- **Eastern Market** • 225 7th St SE
- **Greenworks Florist** • 1455 Pennsylvania Ave SE
- **Ipso Crafto** • 733 8th St SE
- **Marvelous Market** • 303 7th St SE
- **Red Door Gallery & Lounge** • 1129 Pennsylvania Ave SE
- **Woven History & Silk Road** • 311 7th St SE

Video Rental

- **Blockbuster** • 400 8th St SE
- **Capitol Video Sales** • 514 8th St SE

National Ballpark! DC's baseball stadium is the real deal. But as exciting as that is, the rest of this concrete tundra is where fun comes to die. Luckily, word on the street is that this area may not be a black hole for fun much longer; the Waterfront has been selected to be the next round of DC redevelopment projects.

Banks

- **Bank of America** · 401 M St SW
- **PNC** · 935 L'Enfant Plz SW
- **Sun Trust** · 965 L'Enfant Plz SW

Car Rental

- **Enterprise** · 970 D St SW · 202-554-8100
- **Rent-A-Wreck** · 1252 Half St SE · 202-408-9828

Car Washes

- **Splash the Car Wash** · 10 I St SE

Community Gardens

Gas Stations

- **Amoco** · 1244 S Capitol St SE
- **Exxon** · 1001 S Capitol St SW
- **Sunoco** · 50 M St SE

Landmarks

- **Arena Stage** · 1101 6th St SW
- *The Awakening* **Statue** · Tip of Hains Point, East Potomac Park
- **Bureau of Engraving and Printing** · 14th St SW & C St SW
- **Ft Lesley J McNair** · 4th St SW & P St SW
- **Gangplank Marina** · 600 Water Street SW
- **Nationals Park** · 1500 South Capitol St SE
- **Odyssey Cruises** · 6th St SW & Water St SW
- **Spirit of Washington** · 6th St SW & Water St SW
- **Thomas Law House** · 1252 6th St SW
- **Tiber Island** · 429 N St SW
- **USS Sequoia** · 6th St SW & Maine Ave SW

Libraries

- **DOT Law Library, Coast Guard Branch** · 2100 2nd St SW, Rm B726
- **NASA Headquarters Library** · 300 E St SW
- **Southwest Neighborhood Library** · 900 Wesley Pl SW
- **US Housing & Urban Development Library** · 451 7th St SW

Parking

Pharmacies

- **CVS** · 401 M St SW
- **CVS** · 433 L'Enfant Plz SW
- **CVS** · 500 C St SW

Police

- **MPDC 1st District Station** · 415 4th St SW

Post Offices

- **L'Enfant Plaza** · 437 L'Enfant Plz SW
- **Southwest** · 45 L St SW

Schools

- **Amidon Elementary** · 401 I St SW
- **Bowen Elementary** · 101 M St SW
- **Jefferson Junior High** · 801 7th St SW
- **National Defense University** · 300 5th Ave
- **Southeastern University** · 501 I St SW

Supermarkets

- **Safeway** · 401 M St SW

Map 6 · **Waterfront**

Sundries / Entertainment

Flanked by tourist buses, the fortress-like restaurants along the Waterfront's main drag—Water Street—are as dull and inhospitable as they look. But there are some worthy destinations, and there's always a beer waiting in the newly opened beer garden, the Bullpen.

Map 6

Coffee

- **Olympic Espresso** · 955 L'Enfant Plz SW
- **Starbucks** · 409 3rd St SW
- **Starbucks** · 550 C St SW

Farmers Markets

- **US Dept of Transportation Farmers Market (May–Nov, Tues 10 am–2 pm)** · 400 7th St SW

Gyms

- **Gold's Gym** · 409 3rd St SW
- **Metro Fitness** · 480 L'Enfant Plz SW
- **Waterside Fitness & Swim Club** · 901 6th St SW

Liquor Stores

- **Bernstein's Reliable Liquor Store** · 39 M St SW
- **Cap Liquors** · 1301 S Capitol St SW
- **Shulman's Southwest Liquor** · 1550 1st St SW

Nightlife

- **The Bullpen** · 1299 Half St SE
- **Cantina Marina** · 600 Water St SW
- **Zanzibar on the Waterfront** · 700 Water St SW

Restaurants

- **Cantina Marina** · 600 Water St SW
- **CityZen** · 1330 Maryland Ave SW
- **H2O** · 800 Water St SW
- **Jenny's Asian Fusion** · 1000 Water St SW
- **Phillip's Flagship** · 900 Water St SW
- **Pier 7** · 650 Water St SW

Shopping

- **Maine Avenue Fish Market** · 1100 Maine Ave SW
- **Safeway** · 401 M St SW

Map 7 · **Foggy Bottom**

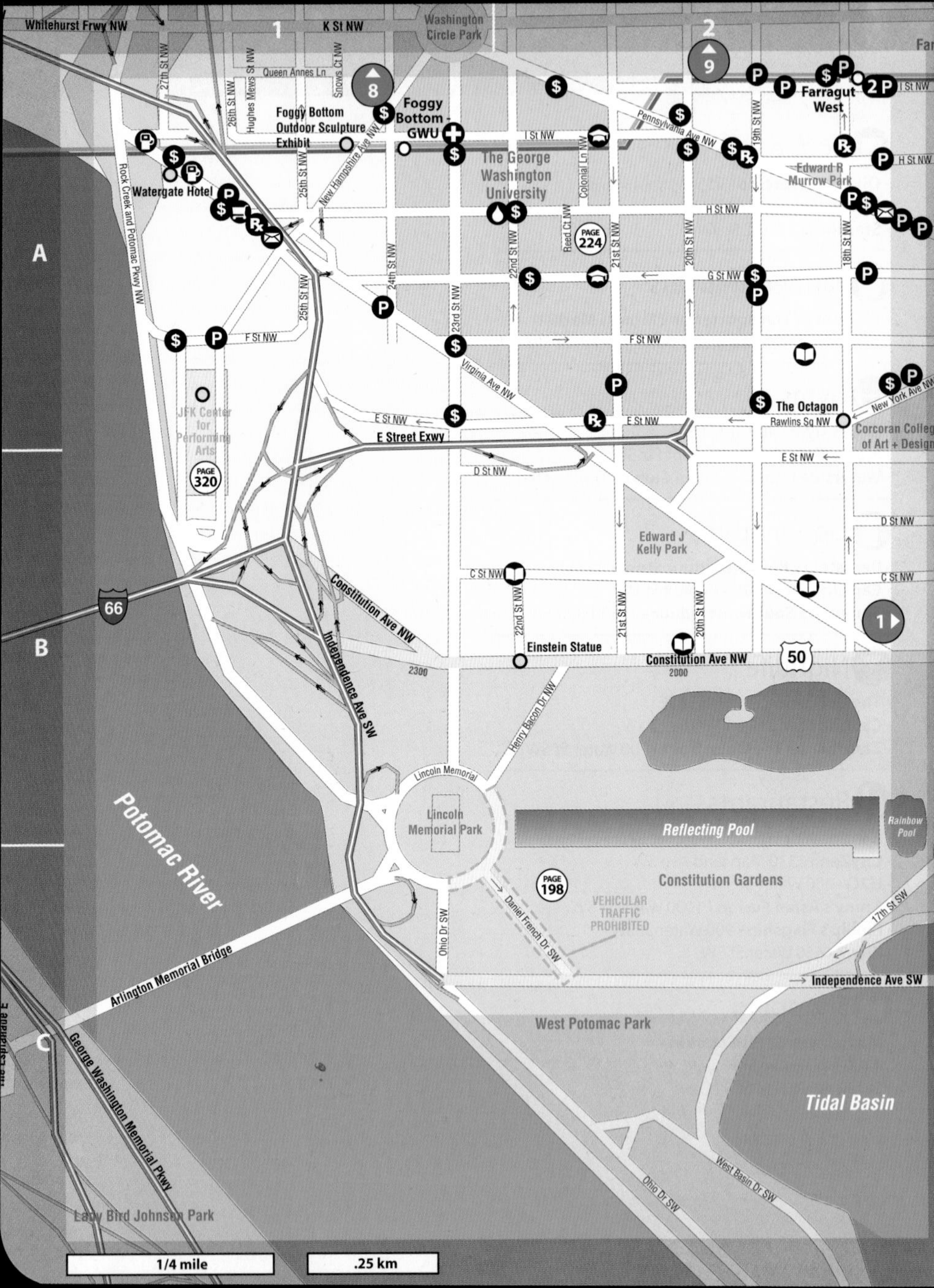

N

Whitehurst Frwy NW

K St NW

Washington Circle Park

1

Far

2
9

Queen Annes Ln

Hughes Mews St NW

Shows Ct NW

26th St NW

27th St NW

25th St NW

Pennsylvania Ave NW

P P

P P 2 P

Farragut West

8

Foggy Bottom Outdoor Sculpture Exhibit

Foggy Bottom-GWU

I St NW

19th St NW

Edward R Murrow Park

H St NW

Rock Creek and Potomac Pkwy NW

Watergate Hotel

New Hampshire Ave NW

25th St NW

The George Washington University

Colonial Ln NW

PAGE
224

21st St NW

20th St NW

18th St NW

A

24th St NW

23rd St NW

22nd St NW

Read Ct NW

H St NW

G St NW

P

JFK Center for Performing Arts

F St NW

Virginia Ave NW

F St NW

New York Ave NW

The Octagon

Rawlins Sq NW

Corcoran College of Art + Design

PAGE
320

E St NW

E Street Exwy

E St NW

E St NW

66

Constitution Ave NW

Independence Ave SW

D St NW

Edward J Kelly Park

D St NW

D St NW

C St NW

C St NW

22nd St NW

21st St NW

20th St NW

1

Einstein Statue

Constitution Ave NW
2000

50

2300

Potomac River

Arlington Memorial Bridge

Lincoln Memorial

Lincoln Memorial Park

Ohio Dr SW

Daniel French Dr SW

PAGE
198

Reflecting Pool

Constitution Gardens

VEHICULAR TRAFFIC PROHIBITED

Rainbow Pool

17th St NW

George Washington Memorial Pkwy

C

Independence Ave SW

West Potomac Park

Tidal Basin

Lady Bird Johnson Park

West Basin Dr SW

Ohio Dr SW

| 1/4 mile | .25 km |

This neighborhood is populated by a mix of George Washington University students, government employees, and "old money" Washingtonians who think the Watergate is the 21st century version of the Ritz. Nevertheless, there isn't much entertainment, but at least there's a plethora of high-end restaurants for those Federal employees looking to impress dignitaries.

Banks

- **Bank of America** · 2001 Pennsylvania Ave NW
- **Bank of America (ATM)** · GW-Thurston Hall · 1900 F St NW
- **Bank of America (ATM)** · GWU · 801 22nd St NW
- **Chevy Chase (ATM)** · 2000 Pennsylvania Ave NW
- **Chevy Chase (ATM)** · GWU - Acute Care Center · 2150 Pennsylvania Ave NW
- **Chevy Chase (ATM)** · GWU - Duques Hall · 2201 G St NW
- **Chevy Chase (ATM)** · 2301 I St NW
- **Chevy Chase (ATM)** · 900 18th St NW
- **Citibank** · 1775 Pennsylvania Ave NW
- **Citibank (ATM)** · 7-Eleven · 514 19th St NW
- **Citibank (ATM)** · 7-Eleven · 912 New Hampshire Ave NW
- **PNC** · 1919 Pennsylvania Ave NW
- **PNC** · 2600 Virginia Ave NW
- **PNC (ATM)** · Kennedy Center · 2700 F St NW
- **PNC (ATM)** · 606 23rd St NW
- **Sandy Spring (ATM)** · Chevron · 2643 Virginia Ave NW
- **Sun Trust** · 1750 New York Ave NW
- **Sun Trust (ATM)** · GWU--Thurston Hall · 1900 F St NW
- **United** · 1875 I St NW
- **Wachovia** · 502 23rd St NW

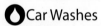 Car Washes

- **Nab Auto Appearance Salon** · 2211 H St NW

 Emergency Rooms

- **George Washington University Hospital** · 900 23rd St NW

 Gas Stations

- **Chevron** · 2643 Virginia Ave NW
- **Exxon** · 2708 Virginia Ave NW

Landmarks

- **Einstein Statue** · Constitution Ave NW & 22nd St NW
- **Foggy Bottom Outdoor Sculpture Exhibit** · New Hampshire Ave NW
- **Kennedy Center** · 2700 F St NW
- **The Octagon** · 1799 New York Ave NW
- **The Watergate Hotel** · 2650 Virginia Ave NW

Libraries

- **Federal Reserve Board Research & Law Libraries** · 20th St NW & Constitution Ave NW
- **General Services Administration Library** · 1800 F St NW, RM 1033
- **Ralph J Bunch Library** · Dept of State · 2201 C St NW, Room 3239
- **US Department of the Interior Library** · 1849 C St NW

 Parking

Pharmacies

- **CVS** · 1901 Pennsylvania Ave NW
- **CVS** · 2125 E St NW
- **CVS** · 2530 Virginia Ave NW
- **Foer's CARE Pharmacy** · 818 18th St NW

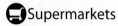 Post Offices

- **McPherson** · 1750 Pennsylvania Ave NW
- **Watergate** · 2512 Virginia Ave NW

Schools

- **George Washington University** · 2121 I St NW
- **School Without Walls** · 2130 G St NW

Supermarkets

- **Safeway** · 2550 Virginia Ave NW

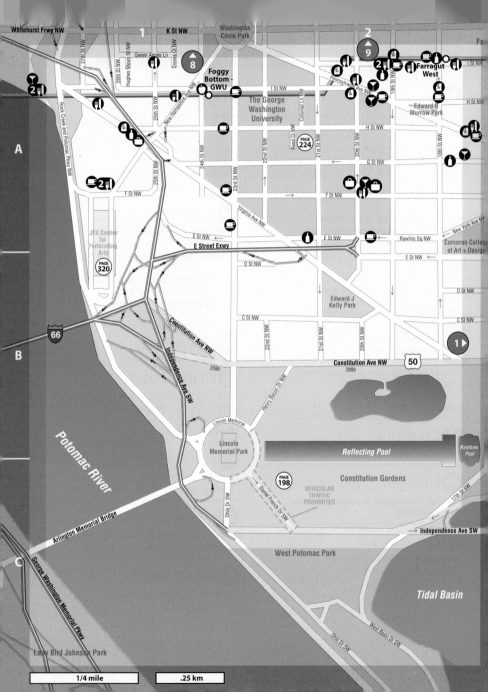

The mix of upscale and college dives is obvious. Notti Bianche, 600 Restaurant at the Watergate, and Dish are reserved for the power players and parents visiting GW students. If you forgot your jacket, grab a beer with students drowning their tuition sorrows at McFadden's, duck into a gyro joint, or head for the nearest neon window to mingle with the co-ed crowd.

Coffee

- **Casey's Coffee Inc** · 508 23rd St NW
- **Cup'a Cup'a** · 600 New Hampshire Ave NW
- **Dunkin Donuts** · 616 23rd St NW
- **Karma** · 1900 I St NW
- **Starbucks** · 1730 Pennsylvania Ave NW
- **Starbucks** · 1825 I St NW
- **Starbucks** · 1919 Pennsylvania Ave NW
- **Starbucks** · 1957 E St NW
- **Starbucks** · 2130 H St NW
- **Starbucks** · 801 18th St NW
- **Starbucks** · 900 23rd St NW

Copy Shops

- **B&B Duplicators** · 818 18th St NW
- **Discovery Copy** · 2001 Pennsylvania Ave NW
- **Fast Copying & Printing** ·
  1745 Pennsylvania Ave NW
- **U Nik Press** · 900 19th St NW
- **UPS Store** · 2000 Pennsylvania Ave NW

Farmers Markets

- **Foggy Bottom Freshfarm**
  (Apr–Nov, Wed, 2:30pm–7pm) ·
  I St NW & 24th St NW

Liquor Stores

- **McReynold's Liquors** · 1776 G St NW
- **Pan Mar Wine & Liquors** · 1926 I St NW
- **Riverside Liquors** · 2123 E St NW
- **S&R Liquors** · 1800 I St NW
- **Watergate Wine & Beverage** ·
  2544 Virginia Ave NW

Nightlife

- **19th** · 1919 Pennsylvania Ave NW
- **The Exchange** · 1719 G St NW
- **Froggy Bottom Pub** · 2142 Pennsylvania Ave NW
- **Funxion** · 1309 F St NW
- **McFadden's** · 2401 Pennsylvania Ave NW
- **Nick's Riverside Grill** · 3050 K St NW

Restaurants

- **600 Restaurant at the Watergate** ·
  600 New Hampshire Ave NW
- **Aquarelle** · Watergate Hotel ·
  2650 Virginia Ave NW
- **Bread Line** · 1751 Pennsylvania Ave NW
- **Cabanas** · 3050 K St NW
- **Dish** · The River Inn · 924 25th St NW
- **Finemondo** · 1319 F St NW
- **Karma** · 1900 I St NW
- **Kaz Sushi Bistro** · World Bank · 1915 I St NW
- **Kinkead's** · 2000 Pennsylvania Ave NW
- **Nick's Riverside Grill** · 3050 K St NW
- **Notti Bianche** ·
  George Washington University Inn ·
  824 New Hampshire Ave NW
- **Pret a Manger** · 1825 I St NW
- **Primi Piatti** · 2013 I St NW
- **Roof Terrace Restaurant and Bar** ·
  Kennedy Ctr · 2700 F St NW
- **Taberna Del Alabardero** · 1776 I St NW

Shopping

- **Acacia Flowers** · 1427 H St NW
- **Peruvian Connection** · 950 F St NW

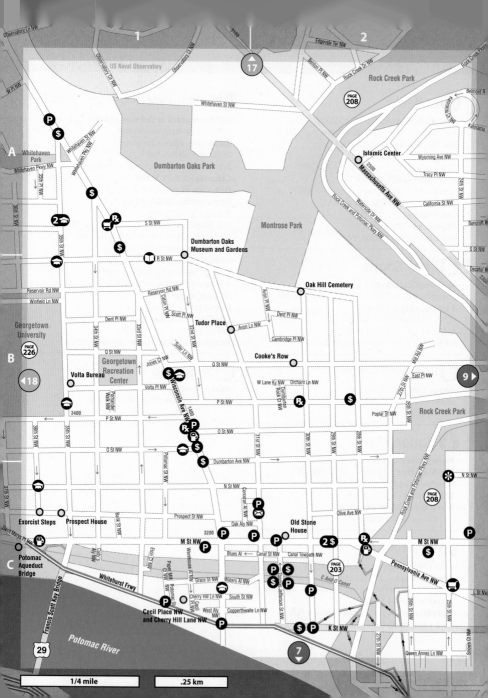

Precious townhouses and stately mansions, cobblestone streets and garden tours—yes, this is very Washington indeed. The peons cluck though the main drags of M and Wisconsin searching for trendy outfits and the traffic is jam-packed by car and foot day and night. Leave your heels at home as the cobblestones will gobble them right up.

Banks

- **Adams National** · 1729 Wisconsin Ave NW
- **Bank of America** · 1339 Wisconsin Ave NW
- **BB&T** · 1365 Wisconsin Ave NW
- **Chevy Chase** · 1545 Wisconsin Ave NW
- **Chevy Chase (ATM)** · 1055 Thomas Jefferson St NW
- **Chevy Chase (ATM)** · 3222 M St NW
- **Citibank** · 1901 Wisconsin Ave NW
- **Citibank (ATM)** · 7-Eleven · 2617 P St NW
- **PNC** · 1201 Wisconsin Ave NW
- **PNC** · 2550 M St NW
- **PNC (ATM)** · Holiday Inn Georgetown · 2101 Wisconsin Ave NW
- **PNC (ATM)** · 3050 K St NW
- **Provident** · 1055 Thomas Jefferson St NW
- **Sun Trust** · 2929 M St NW
- **Wachovia** · 2901 M St NW

Community Gardens

Gas Stations

- **Amoco** · 2715 Pennsylvania Ave NW
- **Exxon** · 1601 Wisconsin Ave NW
- **Exxon** · 3607 M St NW

Landmarks

- **Cecil Place NW and Cherry Hill Lane NW** · Cecil Pl NW & Cherry Hill Ln NW
- **Cooke's Row** · 3009 Q St NW
- **Dumbarton Oaks Museum and Gardens** · 1703 32nd St NW
- *Exorcist* **Steps** · 3600 Prospect St NW
- **Islamic Center** · 2551 Massachussetts Ave NW
- **Oak Hill Cemetery** · 30th St NW & R St NW
- **Old Stone House** · 3051 M St NW
- **Potomac Aqueduct Bridge** · 3530 Water St NW
- **Prospect House** · 3508 Prospect St NW
- **Tudor Place** · 1644 31st St NW
- **Volta Bureau** · 1537 35th St NW

Libraries

- **Georgetown Library** · 3260 R St NW

Parking

Pharmacies

- **CVS** · 1403 Wisconsin Ave NW
- **CVS** · 2819 M St NW
- **Morgan CARE Pharmacy** · 3001 P St NW
- **Safeway** · 1855 Wisconsin Ave NW

Post Offices

- **Georgetown** · 1215 31st St NW

Schools

- **Corcoran School of Art + Design**
  - 1801 35th St NW
- **Ellington School of the Arts** · 3500 R St NW
- **Fillmore Arts Center Elementary** · 1819 35th St NW
- **Georgetown Montessori** · 1041 Wisconsin Ave NW
- **Georgetown Visitation Preparatory** · 1524 35th St NW
- **Holy Trinity** · 1325 36th St NW
- **Hyde Elementary** · 3219 O St NW
- **Montessori of Washington** · 1556 Wisconsin Ave NW

 Supermarkets

- **Safeway** · 1815 Wisconsin Ave NW
- **Trader Joe's** · 1101 25th St NW

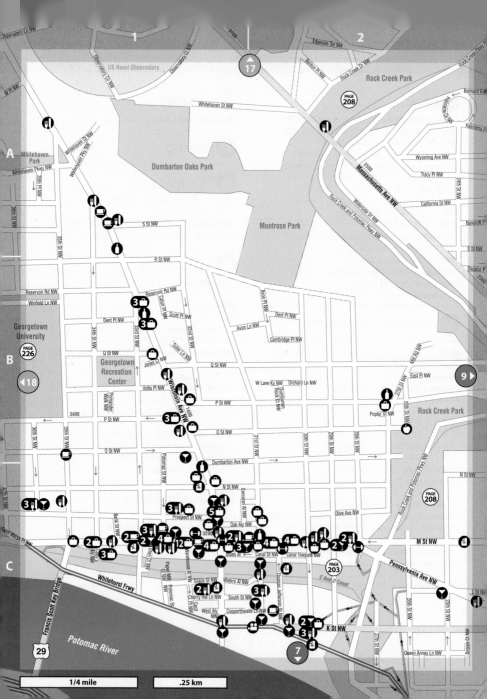

Hands-down, the most comprehensive shopping strip in the city is here. Once the sun sets, the human traffic jams continue as Georgetown plays host to a predominantly preppy and collar-popping nightlife scene. Garrett's, Old Glory, and The Tombs are college kid madness. Blues Alley, Mie N Yu, and Maté are hot spots. And Morton's, 1789, and Café Milano will set you back a few hundred each.

Coffee

- **Baked & Wired** • 1052 Thomas Jefferson St NW
- **Café Europa** • 3222 M St NW
- **Dean & DeLuca** • 3276 M St NW
- **Saxbys Coffee** • 3500 O St NW
- **Starbucks** • 1810 Wisconsin Ave NW
- **Starbucks** • 1855 Wisconsin Ave NW
- **Starbucks** • 3122 M St NW

Copy Shops

- **ABC Imaging** • 1155 21st St NW
- **Document Technology** • 1300 Pennsylvania Ave NW
- **FedEx Kinko's** • 1002 30th St NW
- **FedEx Kinko's** • 3329 M St NW
- **National Reprographics Inc** • 3210 Grace St NW
- **UPS Store** • 3220 N St NW
- **Westend Press** • 2445 M St NW
- **Zap Copies & Communications** • 1052 Thomas Jefferson St NW

Farmers Markets

- **Georgetown Market in Rose Park (Apr–Oct, Wed, 4 pm–7 pm)** • 26th St NW & O St NW

Gyms

- **Definitions** • 1070 Thomas Jefferson St NW
- **Four Seasons Fitness Club** • 2800 Pennsylvania Ave NW
- **Washington Sports Clubs** • 3222 M St NW, Ste 140

Liquor Stores

- **Bacchus Wine Cellar** • 1635 Wisconsin Ave NW
- **Georgetown Wine & Spirits** • 2701 P St NW
- **Potomac Wines and Spirits** • 3100 M St NW
- **Towne Wine & Liquors** • 1326 Wisconsin Ave NW
- **Wagner's Liquor Shop** • 1717 Wisconsin Ave NW

Movie Theaters

- **AMC Loews Georgetown 14** • 3111 K St NW

Nightlife

- **51st State Tavern** • 2512 L St NW
- **Blue Gin** • 1206 Wisconsin Ave NW
- **Blues Alley** • 1073 Wisconsin Ave NW
- **Chadwicks** • 3205 K St NW
- **Champions** • 1206 Wisconsin Ave NW
- **Clyde's** • 3236 M St NW
- **Fahrenheit & Degrees** • 3100 South Street NW
- **Garrett's** • 3003 M St NW
- **The Guards** • 2915 M St NW
- **L2 Lounge** • 3315 Cady's Alley NW

- **Martin's Tavern** • 1264 Wisconsin Ave NW
- **Maté** • 3101 K St NW
- **Mendocino** • 2917 M St NW
- **Mie N Yu** • 3125 M St NW
- **Modern** • 3287 M St NW
- **Mr Smith's** • 3104 M St NW
- **Old Glory** • 3139 M St NW
- **Paper Moon** • 1073 31st St NW
- **Rhino Bar & Pumphouse** • 3295 M St NW
- **Riverside Grill** • 3050 K St NW
- **Sequoia** • 3000 K St NW
- **Third Edition** • 1218 Wisconsin Ave NW
- **The Tombs** • 1226 36th St NW
- **Tony and Joe's** • 3000 K St NW

Restaurants

- **1789** • 1226 36th St NW
- **Aditi** • 3299 M St NW
- **Amma Vegetarian Kitchen** • 3291 M St NW
- **Bangkok Joe's** • 3000 K St NW
- **Birreria Paradiso** • 3282 M St NW
- **Bistrot Lepic** • 1736 Wisconsin Ave NW
- **Booeymonger** • 3265 Prospect St NW
- **Café Bonaparte** • 1522 Wisconsin Ave NW
- **Café Divan** • 1834 Wisconsin Ave NW
- **Café La Ruche** • 1039 31st St NW
- **Café Milano** • 3251 Prospect St NW
- **Chadwick's** • 3205 K St NW
- **Ching Ching Cha** • 1063 Wisconsin Ave NW
- **Citronelle** • Latham Hotel • 3000 M St NW
- **Clyde's** • 3236 M St NW
- **Crisp & Juicy** • 4533 Wisconsin Ave NW
- **Fahrenheit & Degrees** • Ritz Carlton 3100 South Street NW
- **Furin's** • 2805 M St NW
- **HomeMade Pizza Co.** • 4857 Massachusetts Ave NW
- **Hook** • 3241 M St NW
- **Il Canale** • 1063 31st St NW
- **J Paul's** • 3218 M St NW
- **La Chaumiere** • 2813 M St NW
- **La Madeleine** • 3000 M St NW
- **The Landmark** • Melrose Hotel • 2430 Pennsylvania Ave NW
- **Martin's Tavern** • 1264 Wisconsin Ave NW
- **Mendocino** • 2917 M St NW
- **Morton's of Georgetown** • 3251 Prospect St NW
- **Mr Smith's** • 3104 M St NW
- **Old Glory** • 3139 M St NW
- **Peacock Cafe** • 3251 Prospect St NW
- **Prince Café** • 1042 Wisconsin Ave NW
- **Puro Cafe** • 1529 Wisconsin Ave NW
- **Riverside Grill** • 3050 K St NW
- **Café Romeo's** • 2132 Wisconsin Ave NW
- **Sequoia** • 3000 K St NW
- **Smith Point** • 1338 Wisconsin Ave NW
- **Sweetgreen** • 3333 M St NW
- **The Third Edition** • 1218 Wisconsin Ave NW
- **The Tombs** • 1226 36th St NW
- **Tony and Joe's** • 3000 K St NW
- **Wisemiller's** • 1236 36th St NW
- **Wisey's** • 1440 Wisconsin Ave NW

Shopping

- **Abercrombie & Fitch** • 1208 Wisconsin Ave
- **Ann Sacks** • 3328 M St NW
- **Anthropologie** • 3222 M St NW

- **Banana Republic** • 3200 M St NW
- **Barnes & Noble** • 3040 M St NW
- **BCBGMAXAZRIA** • 3210 M St NW
- **bebe** • 1211 Wisconsin Ave NW
- **Betsey Johnson** • 1319 Wisconsin Ave NW
- **Blue Mercury** • 3059 M St NW
- **Blink** • 1776 18th St NW
- **BoConcepts** • 3342 M St NW
- **Commander Salamander** • 1420 Wisconsin Ave NW
- **CUSP** • 3030 M St NW
- **Dean & DeLuca** • 3276 M St NW
- **Design Within Reach** • 3307 Cadys Alley
- **Diesel** • 1249 Wisconsin Ave NW
- **Dolcezza** • 1560 Wisconsin Ave NW
- **Express** • 3222 M St NW
- **Georgetown Cupcake** • 1209 Potomac St NW
- **Georgetown Running Company** • 3401 M St NW
- **Georgetown Tobacco** • 3144 M St NW
- **Georgetown Wine & Spirits** • 2701 P St NW
- **H&M** • 3222 M St NW
- **Hu's Shoes** • 3005 M St NW
- **The Hattery** • 3222 M St NW
- **Illuminations** • 3323 Cady's Aly NW
- **Intermix** • 3222 M St NW
- **J Crew** • 3222 M St NW
- **J Mclaughlin** • 3278 M St NW
- **Jaryam** • 1631 Wisconsin Ave NW
- **Jinx Proof Tattoo** • 3285 M St NW
- **Kate Spade** • 3061 M St NW
- **The Keith Lipert Gallery** • 2922 M St NW
- **Ligne Roset** • 3306 M St NW
- **lil' thingamajigs** • 3222 M St NW
- **Lush** • 3066 M St NW
- **MAC** • 3067 M St NW
- **Marvelous Market** • 3217 P St NW
- **Old Print Gallery** • 1220 31st St NW
- **Paper Source** • 3019 M St NW
- **papyrus** • 1300 Wisconsin Ave NW
- **Patisserie Poupon** • 1645 Wisconsin Ave NW
- **The Phoenix** • 1514 Wisconsin Ave NW
- **Pottery Barn** • 3077 M St NW
- **Proper Topper** • 3213 P St NW
- **Puma** • 1237 Wisconsin Ave NW
- **Ralph Lauren Polo Shop** • 1245 Wisconsin Ave NW
- **Relish** • 3312 Cadys Aly
- **Restoration Hardware** • 1222 Wisconsin Ave NW
- **Revolution Cycles** • 3411 M St NW
- **Sassanova** • 1641 Wisconsin Ave NW
- **Secret Garden** • 3222 M St NW
- **See** • 1261 Wisconsin Ave NW
- **Sephora** • 3065 M St NW
- **Sherman Pickey** • 1647 Wisconsin Ave NW
- **Smith & Hawken** • 3077 M St NW
- **Sugar** • 1633 Wisconsin Ave NW
- **Thomas Sweet Ice Cream** • 3214 P St NW
- **Toka Salon** • 3251 Prospect St NW
- **Up Against the Wall** • 3219 M St NW
- **Urban Chic** • 1626 Wisconsin Ave NW
- **Urban Outfitters** • 3111 M St NW
- **Victoria's Secret** • 3222 M St NW
- **The White House/Black Market** • 3103 M St NW
- **Zara** • 1238 Wisconsin Ave NW

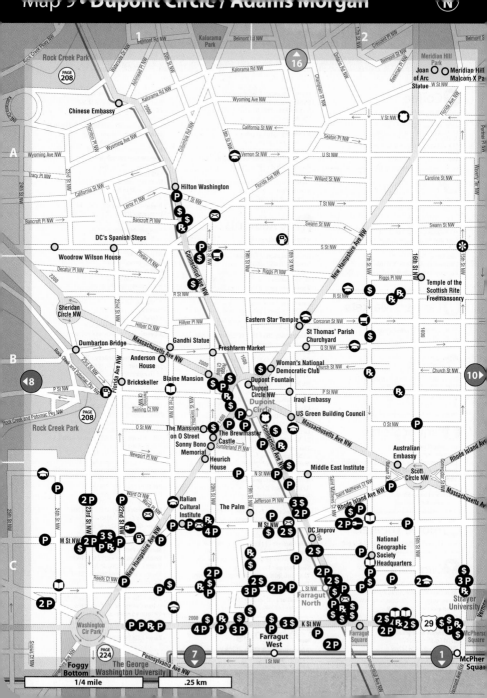

Neither tourist trap nor chain-store stuffed, boutique-filled Dupont is a standard destination for locals. North and east of the circle, toward club-crazed Adams Morgan and the trendy Logan Circle/U Street areas, is where the scene really is: shops, cafes, and great people-watching. Dupont is a little too settled to be considered bohemian or edgy any more, though, and anywhere south of the circle is office territory.

Map 9

$ Banks

- **Adams National** · 1130 Connecticut Ave NW
- **Adams National** · 1501 K St NW
- **Adams National** · 1604 17th St NW
- **Bank of America** · 1801 K St NW
- **Bank of America** · 3 Dupont Cir NW
- **Bank of America (ATM)** · 1612 K St NW
- **BB&T** · 1730 Rhode Island Ave NW
- **BB&T** · 1909 K St NW
- **Chevy Chase** · 1100 17th St NW
- **Chevy Chase** · 1700 K St NW
- **Chevy Chase** · 1800 M St NW
- **Chevy Chase** · 1850 K St NW
- **Chevy Chase** · 2400 M St NW
- **Chevy Chase (ATM)** ·
  1001 Connecticut Ave NW
- **Chevy Chase (ATM)** ·
  1050 Connecticut Ave NW
- **Chevy Chase (ATM)** · 1525 20th St NW
- **Chevy Chase (ATM)** ·
  1743 Connecticut Ave NW
- **Chevy Chase (ATM)** · 1800 K St NW
- **Citibank** · 1225 Connecticut Ave NW
- **Citibank** · 2101 L St NW
- **Citibank (ATM)** · 7-Eleven · 1700 17th St NW
- **Commerce** · 1753 Connecticut Ave NW
- **Eagle** · 1228 Connecticut Ave NW
- **Eagle** · 2001 K St NW
- **HSBC** · 1130 Connecticut Ave NW
- **Independence Federal Savings** ·
  1229 Connecticut Ave NW
- **M&T** · 1680 K St NW
- **M&T** · 1899 L St NW
- **Mercantile Potomac** · 1629 K St NW
- **PNC** · 1101 15th St NW
- **PNC** · 1800 M St NW
- **PNC** · 1815 Connecticut Ave NW
- **PNC** · 1875 Connecticut Ave NW
- **PNC** · 1913 Massachusetts Ave NW
- **PNC** · 1920 L St NW
- **PNC (ATM)** · 1333 New Hampshire Ave NW
- **Presidential Savings** · 1660 K St NW
- **Sun Trust** · 1020 19th St NW
- **Sun Trust** · 1150 Connecticut Ave NW
- **Sun Trust** · 1369 Connecticut Ave NW
- **Sun Trust** · 2240 M St NW
- **Sun Trust** · 2250 M St NW
- **United** · 1667 K St NW
- **United** · 2301 M St NW
- **United (ATM)** · Jurys Washington Hotel ·
  1500 New Hampshire Ave NW
- **Wachovia** · 1100 Connecticut Ave NW
- **Wachovia** · 1300 Connecticut Ave NW
- **Wachovia** · 1510 K St NW
- **Wachovia** · 1800 K St NW
- **Wachovia** · 1850 M St NW
- **Wachovia** · 2000 L St NW
- **Washington First** · 1025 Connecticut Ave NW
- **Washington First** · 1146 19th St NW
- **Washington First** · 1500 K St NW

Car Rental

- **Avis** · 1722 M St NW · 202-467-6585
- **Enterprise** · 1221 22nd St NW · 202-872-5790

Community Gardens

Gas Stations

- **BP/Amoco** · 1800 18th St NW
- **Exxon** · 2150 M St NW
- **Sunoco** · 2200 P St NW

Landmarks

- **Andeson House** ·
  2118 Massachusetts Ave NW
- **Australian Embassy** ·
  1601 Massachusetts Ave NW
- **Blaine Mansion** ·
  2000 Massachusetts Ave NW
- **The Brewmasters Castle** ·
  1307 New Hampshire Ave NW
- **The Brickskeller** · 1523 22nd St NW
- **Chinese Embassy** ·
  2300 Connecticut Ave NW
- **DC Improv** · 1140 Connecticut Ave NW
- **DC's Spanish Steps** · S St NW & 22nd St NW
- **Dumbarton Bridge** · 23rd St NW & Q St NW
- **Dupont Fountain** · Dupont Cir
- **Eastern Star Temple** ·
  1618 New Hampshire Ave NW
- **Farragut Square** · K St NW & 17th St NW
- **Freshfarm Market** ·
  20th St NW near Q St NW
- **Gandhi Statue** ·
  Massachusetts Ave NW & 21st St NW
- **Heurich House** ·
  1307 New Hampshire Ave NW
- **Hilton Washington** ·
  1919 Connecticut Ave NW
- **Iraqi Embassy** · 1801 P St NW
- **Italian Cultural Institute** · 2025 M St NW
- **Joan of Arc Statue** · Meridian Hill Park
- **The Mansion on O Street** · 2020 O St NW
- **Meridian Hill/Malcolm X Park** · 16th St NW
  b/w W St NW & Euclid St NW
- **Middle East Institute** · 1761 N St NW
- **National Geographic Society
  Headquarters** · 1145 17th St NW
- **The Palm** · 1225 19th St NW
- **Sonny Bono Memorial** ·
  20th St NW & New Hampshire Ave NW
- **St Thomas' Parish Churchyard** ·
  1772 Church St NW
- **Temple of the Scottish Rite of
  Freemasonry** · 1733 16th St NW
- **US Green Building Council** ·
  1800 Massachusetts Ave NW
- **Woman's National Democratic Club** ·
  1526 New Hampshire Ave NW
- **Woodrow Wilson House** · 2340 S St NW

Libraries

- **Arthur R Ashe Jr Foreign Policy Library** ·
  1629 K St NW, Ste 1100
- **Foundation Center** · 1627 K St NW, 3rd Fl
- **National Geographic Society Library** ·
  1145 17th St NW
- **Polish Library in Washington** ·
  1503 21st St NW
- **Jeannette Rankin Library -
  US Institute of Peace** ·
  1200 17th St NW, Ste 200

- **West End Neighborhood Library** ·
  1101 24th St NW

Parking

Pharmacies

- **Alpha Drugs** · 1638 R St Nw
- **CVS** · 1025 Connecticut Ave NW
- **CVS** · 1500 K St NW
- **CVS** · 1637 P St NW
- **CVS** · 1990 K St NW
- **CVS** · 2000 L St NW
- **CVS** · 2000 M St NW
- **CVS** · 2240 M St NW
- **CVS** · 6 Dupont Cir NW
- **Foer's CARE Pharmacy** · 2141 K St NW
- **Pharmacare** · 1517 17th St NW
- **Rite Aid** · 1034 15th St NW
- **Rite Aid** · Universal Building ·
  1815 Connecticut Ave NW
- **Tschiffely Pharmacy** · 1145 19th St NW
- **Tschiffely Pharmacy** ·
  1330 Connecticut Ave NW

Police

- **MPD Gay & Lesbian Liaison Unit** ·
  1369 Connecticut Ave NW
- **MPDC 3rd District Station** · 1620 V St NW

Post Offices

- **Farragut** · 1800 M St NW
- **Temple Heights** ·
  1921 Florida Ave NW
- **Twentieth St** · 2001 M St NW
- **Ward Place** · 2121 Ward Pl NW
- **Washington Square** ·
  1050 Connecticut Ave NW

School

- **Academy for learning Through the Arts** ·
  2100 New Hampshire Ave NW
- **Adams Elementary** · 2020 19th St NW
- **Emerson Preparatory** · 1324 18th St NW
- **Francis Junior High** · 2425 N St NW
- **Rock Creek International Upper** ·
  1621 New Hampshire Ave NW
- **Ross Elementary** · 1730 R St NW
- **School for Arts in Learning** ·
  1100 16th St NW
- **Stevens Elementary** · 1050 21st St NW
- **Strayer University (Washington Campus)** ·
  1133 15th St NW

Supermarkets

- **Safeway** · 1701 Corcoran St NW
- **Safeway** · 1800 20th St NW

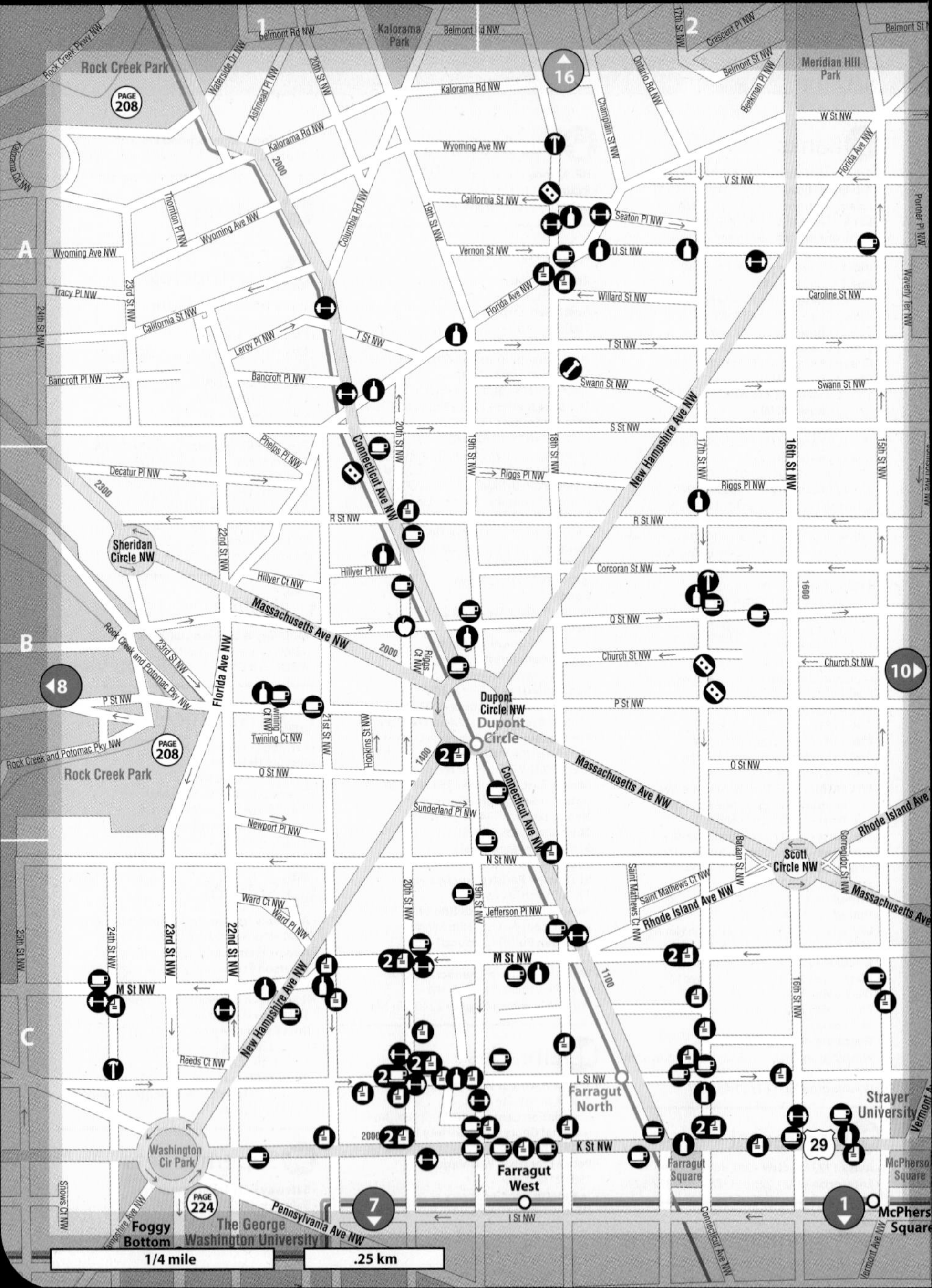

Map 9 · **Dupont Circle / Adams Morgan**

N

1

Rock Creek Park

PAGE
208

Belmont Rd NW

Kalorama
Park

Belmont Rd NW

2

Meridian Hill
Park

16

Kalorama Rd NW

W St NW

Wyoming Ave NW

V St NW

California St NW

Seaton Pl NW

Vernon St NW

U St NW

Caroline St NW

A

Willard St NW

Florida Ave NW

Wyoming Ave NW

Tracy Pl NW

T St NW

T St NW

Leroy Pl NW

Swann St NW

Swann St NW

Bancroft Pl NW

Bancroft Pl NW

S St NW

Decatur Pl NW

Phelps Pl NW

R St NW

Riggs Pl NW

R St NW

Sheridan
Circle NW

Riggs Pl NW

Hillyer Ct NW

Hillyer Pl NW

Corcoran St NW

B

Massachusetts Ave NW

Q St NW

Church St NW

Church St NW

8

P St NW

P St NW

Twining Ct NW

Q St NW

Newport Pl NW

Sunderland Pl NW

Dupont
Circle NW

Dupont
Circle

Massachusetts Ave NW

Q St NW

Scott
Circle NW

10

PAGE
208

Rock Creek Park

N St NW

Jefferson Pl NW

Rhode Island Ave NW

Scott
Circle NW

Ward Ct NW
Ward Pl NW

M St NW

M St NW

Reeds Ct NW

C

Strayer
University

Farragut
North

L St NW

McPherson
Square

Washington
Cir Park

PAGE
224

K St NW

Farragut
Square

29

Foggy
Bottom

Pennsylvania Ave NW

7

Farragut
West

1

McPherson
Square

The George
Washington University

I St NW

1/4 mile

.25 km

This is about as complete a neighborhood as you can find in DC. Just a short walk down the street will put you in reach of a tofu wrap, Advil for the hangover, and a copy of the London Daily Mirror, all on the same block. All Dupont needs is a three-story Ikea and the yuppies would never have to leave.

Coffee

- **Azela Coffee Shop** · 2118 18th St NW
- **Caribou Coffee** · 1101 17th St NW
- **Caribou Coffee** · 1156 15th St NW
- **Caribou Coffee** · 1800 M St NW
- **Casey's Coffee** · 2000 L St NW
- **Coffee Espress** · 2001 L St NW
- **Coffee Espress** ·
  1101 Connecticut Ave NW
- **Coffee & the Works** ·
  1627 Connecticut Ave NW
- **Cosi** · 1350 Connecticut Ave NW
- **Cosi** · 1501 K St NW
- **Cosi** · 1647 20th St NW
- **Cosi** · 1875 K St NW
- **Cosi** · 1919 M St NW
- **Cozy Café** · 1828 L St NW
- **Dupont Coffee Shop** · 1234 19th St NW
- **Filter Coffeehouse** · 1726 20th St NW
- **Firehook Bakery & Coffee House** ·
  1909 Q St NW
- **Foster Brothers Coffee** · 1003
  Connecticut NW
- **Ily Cafe** · 1143 New Hampshire Ave NW
- **Java Green** · 1020 19th St NW
- **Java House** · 1645 Q St NW
- **Jolt'n Bolt Coffee & Tea House** · 1918
  18th St NW
- **Krispy Kreme** · 1350 Connecticut Ave NW
- **LA Café II** · 1825 K St NW
- **Locolat** · 1781 Florida Ave NW
- **Love Café** · 1506 U St NW
- **Soho Tea & Coffee** · 2150 P St NW
- **Starbucks** · 1001 Connecticut Ave NW
- **Starbucks** · 1205 19th St NW
- **Starbucks** · 1301 Connecticut Ave NW
- **Starbucks** · 1500 21st St NW
- **Starbucks** · 1501 Connecticut Ave NW
- **Starbucks** · 1600 K St NW
- **Starbucks** · 1600 U St NW
- **Starbucks** · 1700 Connecticut Ave NW
- **Starbucks** · 1734 L St NW
- **Starbucks** · 1900 K St NW
- **Starbucks** · 2101 P St NW
- **Starbucks** · 2175 K St NW
- **Starbucks** · 2400 M St NW
- **Steam Café** · 1700 17th St NW

Copy Shops

- **ABC Imaging** · 1147 20th St NW
- **ABS Complete Printing** ·
  1150 Connecticut Ave NW
- **Commercial Duplicating Service** ·
  1920 L St NW
- **Copy Cats** · 1140 17th St NW
- **Copy General** · 2000 L St NW
- **Deadline Press** · 1020 19th St NW
- **Document Technology** · 2000 M St NW
- **Dupont Circle Copy** · 11 Dupont Cir NW

- **Eagle Printing** · 1156 15th St NW
- **EZ Business Services** · 1929 18th St NW
- **FedEx Kinko's** · 1 Dupont Cir NW
- **FedEx Kinko's** · 1029 17th St NW
- **FedEx Kinko's** · 1123 18th St NW
- **FedEx Kinko's** · 1612 K St NW
- **FedEx Kinko's** · 1825 K St NW
- **FedEx Kinko's** · 2020 K St NW
- **FedEx Kinko's** · 2400 M St NW
- **Huff Printing & Ad Specialties** ·
  1100 17th St NW
- **Ikon Office Solutions** · 1120 20th St NW
- **Imagenet** · 2000 M St NW
- **Impress Print & Copy** · 2001 L St NW
- **MBC Precision Imaging** · 1200 18th St NW
- **Minuteman Press** · 2000 K St NW
- **National Reprographics Inc** ·
  1705 Desales St NW
- **NRI** · 1705 Desales St NW
- **Park Press** · 1518 K St NW
- **Press Express Copy & Printing** ·
  1015 18th St NW
- **Print Time** · 1714 20th St NW
- **Printer** · 1803 Florida Ave NW
- **Pronto Press** · 1133 20th St NW
- **Reprographic Technologies** ·
  2000 L St NW
- **Sequential** · 1615 L St NW
- **Service Point USA** · 1129 20th St NW
- **Sir Speedy Printing** · 1025 17th St NW
- **Sir Speedy Printing** ·
  1300 Connecticut Ave NW
- **Sir Speedy Printing** · 2134 L St NW
- **Staples** · 1901 L St NW
- **UPS Store** · 1718 M St NW
- **UPS Store** · 2100 M St NW
- **US Printing & Copying** · 1725 M St NW

Farmers Markets

- **Dupont Circle Freshfarm**
  (Apr–Dec, 9 am–1 pm;
  Jan–Mar, 10am–1pm) ·
  20th St NW & Q St NW

Gyms

- **Bally Total Fitness** · 2000 L St NW
- **Capital City Club and Spa** · Hilton ·
  1001 16th St NW
- **Curves (women only)** ·
  1710 Rhode Island Ave NW
- **Fitness First** · 1075 19th St NW
- **Gold's Gym** · 1120 20th St NW
- **Mint** · 1724 California St NW
- **Results the Gym** · 1612 U St NW
- **Sports Club/LA** · 1170 22nd St NW
- **Third Power Fitness** · 2007 18th St NW
- **Washington Hilton Sport Club** ·
  1919 Connecticut Ave NW

- **Washington Sports Clubs** ·
  1211 Connecticut Ave NW
- **Washington Sports Clubs** ·
  1835 Connecticut Ave NW
- **Washington Sports Clubs** ·
  1990 K St NW
- **Washington Sports Clubs** ·
  1990 M St NW
- **West End Executive Fitness Center** ·
  2401 M St NW

Hardware Stores

- **Adams Morgan Hardware** ·
  2200 18th St NW
- **Candey Hardware** · 1210 18th St NW
- **District True Value Hardware** ·
  2003 P St NW
- **True Value on 17th** · 1623 17th St NW

Liquor Stores

- **Barmy Wine & Liquor** · 1912 L St NW
- **Bell Liquor & Wine Shoppe** ·
  1821 M St NW
- **Benmoll Liquors** · 1700 U St NW
- **Best Cellars (wine only)** ·
  1643 Connecticut Ave NW
- **Cairo Wine & Liquor Store** ·
  1618 17th St NW
- **Connecticut Avenue Liquors** ·
  1529 Connecticut Ave NW
- **DeVino's** · 2001 18th St NW
- **Downtown Spirits & Deli** · 1522 K St NW
- **Imperial Liquor** · 1050 17th St NW
- **La Salle Liquors** · 1719 K St NW
- **Martin's Wine & Spirits** ·
  1919 Florida Ave NW
- **Rosebud Liquors** · 1711 17th St NW
- **State Liquors** · 2159 P St NW
- **Universal Wine & Spirits** ·
  2018 Florida Ave NW
- **Virginia Market** · 1776 U St NW
- **The Wine Specialists** · 2115 M St NW

Pet Shops

- **Doggie Style Bakery, Boutique and Pet Spa** · 1825 18th St NW

Video Rental

- **Blockbuster** · 1639 P St NW
- **Capitol Video Sales** ·
  1729 Connecticut Ave NW
- **Capitol Video Sales** · 2028 P St NW
- **Video Americain** · 2104 18th St NW
- **The Video Rack** · 1511 17th St NW

Dupont is where DC bubbles over with nightlife options. Although frequently labeled the hub of DC's gay community, even Evangelicals can find a place to party here. From beer-soaked sports bars to clubs that are so painfully hip that their name is their address…in Roman numerals, Dupont is still a vibrant singles 'hood. But despite Bistrot du Coin, no one will ever mistake Connecticut Avenue for the Champs-Elysées.

Movie Theaters

- **Carnegie Institution** · 1530 P St NW
- **Loews Dupont Circle 5** · 1350 19th St NW

Nightlife

- **Andalu** · 1214 18th St NW
- **Bar Rouge** · Hotel Rouge · 1315 16th St NW
- **Beacon Bar & Grill** · Beacon Hotel 1615 Rhode Island Ave NW
- The **Big Hunt** · 1345 Connecticut Ave NW
- **Black Fox Lounge** · 1723 Connecticut Ave NW
- **Black Rooster Pub** · 1919 L St NW
- **Bravo Bravo** · 1001 Connecticut Ave NW
- **The Brickskeller** · 1523 22nd St NW
- **Buffalo Billiards** · 1330 19th St NW
- **Café Citron** · 1343 Connecticut Ave NW
- **Café Japone** · 2032 P St NW
- **Camelot Show Bar** · 1823 M St NW
- **Chi-Cha Lounge** · 1624 U St NW
- **Childe Harold** · 1610 20th St NW
- **Cobalt/30 Degrees** · 1639 R St NW
- **Dan's Café** · 2315 18th St NW
- **DC Improv** · 1140 Connecticut Ave NW
- **Dragonfly** · 1215 Connecticut Ave NW
- **Eighteenth Street Lounge** · 1212 18th St NW
- Elephant & Castle · 900 19th St NW
- **Firefly** · 1310 New Hampshire Ave NW
- **The Fireplace** · 2161 P St NW
- **Floriana Mercury Bar** · 1602 17th St NW
- **Fly Lounge** · 1802 Jefferson Pl NW
- **Fox and Hounds Lounge** · 1537 17th St NW
- **The Front Page** · 1333 New Hampshire Ave NW
- **Gazuza** · 1629 Connecticut Ave NW
- **James Hoban's** · 1 Dupont Cir NW
- **Josephine Lounge** · 1008 Vermont Ave NW
- **JR's** · 1519 17th St NW
- **Kramerbooks & Afterwords Café** · 1517 Connecticut Ave NW
- **La Frontera Cantina** · 1633 17th St NW
- **Lauriol Plaza** · 1835 18th St NW
- **Local 16** · 1602 U St NW
- **Lucky Bar** · 1221 Connecticut Ave NW
- **Maddy's Bar and Grille** · 1726 Connecticut Ave NW
- **Madhatter** · 1321 Connecticut Ave NW
- **McClellan's** · Hilton · 1919 Connecticut Ave NW
- **McFadden's** · 2401 Pennsylvania Ave NW
- **Omega** · 2122 P St NW
- **Ozio** · 1813 M St NW
- **Recessions** · 1823 L St NW
- **Rumors** · 1900 M St NW
- **Russia House Restaurant and Lounge** · 1800 Connecticut Ave NW
- **Science Club** · 1136 19th St NW
- **Sign of the Whale** · 1825 M St NW
- **Soussi** · 2228 18th St NW
- **Steve's Bar** · 1337 Connecticut Ave NW
- **Stetson's Famous Bar & Restaurant** · 1610 U St NW
- **Tabard Inn Restaurant** · 1739 N St NW
- **Topaz Bar** · Topaz Hotel · 1733 N St NW
- **Town & Country** · Mayflower Renaissance Hotel · 1127 Connecticut Ave NW
- **Townhouse Tavern** · 1637 R St NW
- **Twist Dupont Restaurant and Lounge** · 1731 New Hampshire Ave NW

Restaurants

- **15 Ria** · Washington Terrace Hotel · 1515 Rhode Island Ave NW
- **Al Tiramisu** · 2014 P St NW
- **Annie's Paramount** · 1609 17th St NW
- **Bagels, Etc.** · 2122 P St NW

- **Bistro Bistro** · 1727 Connecticut Ave NW
- **Bistrot du Coin** · 1738 Connecticut Ave NW
- **Blue Duck Tavern** · Park Hyatt Hotel · 1201 24th St NW
- **The Brickskeller** · 1523 22nd St NW
- **Bua** · 1635 P St NW
- **Café Citron** · 1343 Connecticut Ave NW
- **Café Luna** · 1633 P St NW
- **Chi-Cha Lounge** · 1624 U St NW
- **Daily Grill** · 1200 18th St NW
- **Darlington House** · 1610 20th St NW
- **Duplex Diner** ·l2004 18th St NW
- **Eye Street Grill** · 1575 I St NW
- Ezmè · 2016 P St NW
- **The Front Page** · 1333 New Hampshire Ave NW
- **Hank's Oyster Bar** · 1624 Q St NW
- **Henry's Soul Cafe** · 1704 U St NW
- **I Ricchi** · 1220 19th St NW
- **Komi** · 1509 17th St NW
- **Kramerbooks & Afterwords Café** · 1517 Connecticut Ave NW
- **La Tomate** · 1701 Connecticut Ave NW
- **Lauriol Plaza** · 1835 18th St NW
- **Levante's** · 1320 19th St NW
- **Local 16** · 1602 U St NW
- **Love Café** · 1506 U St NW
- **Luna Grill & Diner** · 1301 Connecticut Ave NW
- **Mackey's Public House** · 1823 L St NW
- **Malaysia Kopitiam** · 1827 M St NW
- **Marcel's** · 2401 Pennsylvania Ave NW
- **Marrakesh Palace** · 2147 P St NW
- **McCormick and Schmick's** · 1652 K St NW
- **Meiwah** · 1200 New Hampshire Ave NW
- **Mimi's** · 2120 P St NW
- **Mixt Greens** · 1200 19th St NW
- **Mourayo** · 1732 Connecticut Ave NW
- **Nage** · Scott Circle Marriott Hotel · 1600 Rhode Island Ave NW
- **Nirvana** · 1810 K St NW
- **Nooshi** · 1120 19th St NW
- **Obelisk** · 2029 P St NW
- **Olives** · 1600 K St NW
- **Palette** · 1177 15th St NW
- **The Palm** · 1225 19th St NW
- **Peacock Grand Cafe** · 2020 K St NW
- **Pesce** · 2002 P St NW
- **Pizzeria Paradiso** · 2003 P St NW
- **The Prime Rib** · 2020 K St NW
- **Public Bar** · 1214 18th St NW
- **Raku** · 1900 Q St NW
- **Restaurant Nora** · 2132 Florida Ave NW
- **Rogue States** · 1300 Connecticut Ave NW
- **Rosemary's Thyme** · 1801 18th St NW
- **Sacrificial Lamb** · 1704 R St NW
- **Sam and Harry's** · 1200 19th St NW
- **Sette Osteria** · 1666 Connecticut Ave NW
- **Skewers** · 1633 P St NW
- **Smith and Wollensky** · 1112 19th St NW
- **Straits of Malaya** · 1836 18th St NW
- **Sushi Taro** · 1503 17th St NW
- **Sweetgreen** · 1512 Connecticut Ave NW
- **Tabard Inn Restaurant** · 1739 N St NW
- **Teaism** · 2009 R St NW
- **Teatro Goldoni** · 1909 K St NW
- **Thai Chef** · 1712 Connecticut Ave NW
- **Thaiphoon** · 2011 S St NW
- **Tomatillo Taqueria** · 1347 Connecticut Ave NW
- **Veritas Wine Bar** · 2031 Florida Ave NW
- **Vidalia** · 1990 M St NW
- **Westend Bistro** · 1190 22nd St NW
- **Yee Hwa** · 1009 21st St NW

Shopping

- **Andre Chreky, the Salon Spa** · 1604 K St NW
- **Ann Taylor** · 1140 Connecticut Ave NW
- **Ann Taylor Loft** · 1611 Connecticut Ave NW
- **Bang Salon** · 1612 U St NW

- **Beadazzled** · 1507 Connecticut Ave NW
- **Best Cellars (wine only)** · 1643 Connecticut Ave NW
- **Betsy Fisher** · 1224 Connecticut Ave NW
- **Blink** · 919 18th St NW
- **Blue Mercury** · 1619 Connecticut Ave NW
- **Books-A-Million** · 11 Dupont Cir NW
- **Borders** · 18th St NW & L St NW
- **Brooks Brothers** · 1201 Connecticut Ave NW
- **Burberry** · 1155 Connecticut Ave NW
- **CakeLove** · 1506 U St NW
- **Caramel** · 1603 U St NW
- **Chocolate Moose** · 1743 L St NW
- **Comfort One Shoes** · 1607 Connecticut Ave NW
- **Comfort One Shoes** · 1630 Connecticut Ave NW
- **Commonwealth** · 1781 Florida Ave NW
- **Custom Shop Clothiers** · 1033 Connecticut Ave NW
- **DeVino's** · 2001 18th St NW
- **Doggie Style Bakery, Boutique and Pet Spa** · 1825 18th St NW
- **Downs Engravers & Stationers** · 1746 L St NW
- **Drilling Tennis & Golf** · 1040 17th St NW
- **Dupont Market** · 1807 18th St NW
- **Emma Mae Gallery** · 1515 U St NW
- **Filene's Basement** · 1133 Connecticut Ave NW
- **Gap** · 1120 Connecticut Ave NW
- **Ginza** · 1721 Connecticut Ave NW
- **Godiva Chocolatier** · 1143 Connecticut Ave NW
- **Greater Good** · 1626 U St NW
- **The Grooming Lounge** · 1745 L St NW
- **The Guitar Shop** · 1216 Connecticut Ave NW
- **Habitat Home Accents & Jewelry** · 1512 U St NW
- **Human Rights Campaign** · 1640 Rhode Island Ave NW
- **J Press** · 1801 L St NW
- **Jos A Bank** · 1200 19th St NW
- **Junction** · 1510 U St NW
- **The Kid's Closet** · 1226 Connecticut Ave NW
- **Kramerbooks & Afterwords Café** · 1517 Connecticut Ave NW
- **Larry's** · 1633 Connecticut Ave NW
- **Leather Rack** · 1723 Connecticut Ave NW
- **Legendary Beast** · 1520 U St NW
- **Lucky Brand Dungarees** · 1739 Connecticut Ave NW
- **Marvelous Market** · 1511 Connecticut Ave NW
- **Meeps Vintage Fashionette** · 2104 18th St NW
- **Melody Records** · 1623 Connecticut Ave NW
- **Millennium Decorative Arts** · 1528 U St NW
- **Nana** · 1528 U St NW
- **National Geographic Shop** · 1145 17th St NW
- **Pasargad Antique and Fine Persian** · 1217 Connecticut Ave NW
- **Pleasure Place** · 1710 Connecticut Ave NW
- **Proper Topper** · 1350 Connecticut Ave NW
- **Radio Shack** · 1150 Connecticut Ave NW
- **RCKNDY** · 1515 U St NW
- **Red Onion Records & Books** · 1901 18th St NW
- **Reiter's Scientific & Professional Books** · 1990 K St NW
- **Rizik's** · 1100 Connecticut Ave NW
- **Salon Cielo** · 1741 Connecticut Ave NW
- **Second Story Books & Antiques** · 2000 P St NW
- **Secondi** · 1702 Connecticut Ave NW
- Shake Your Booty · 2206 18th St NW
- **Shoe Fly** · 1520 U St NW
- **Sisley** · 1666 Connecticut Ave NW
- **Skynear and Co** · 2122 18th St NW
- **Tabletop** · 1608 20th St NW
- **Thomas Pink** · 1127 Connecticut Ave NW
- **Tiny Jewel Box** · 1147 Connecticut Ave NW
- **United Colors of Benetton** · 1666 Connecticut Ave NW
- **The Wine Specialists** · 2115 M St NW

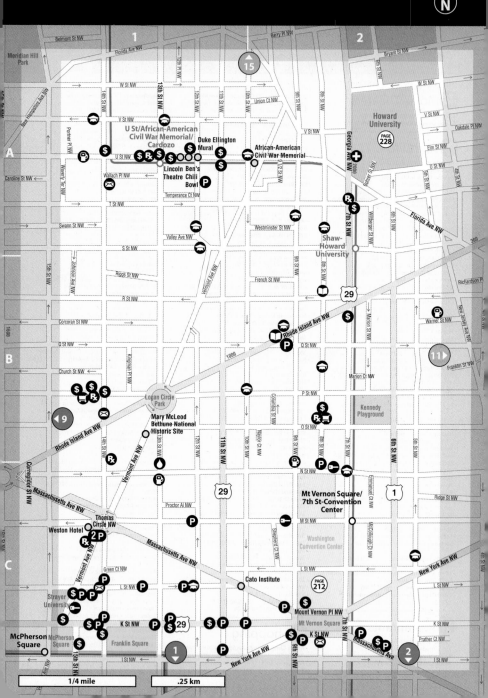

It's a river of bars, restaurants, and shops in this culturally vibrant part of town. U Street is up-and-coming and a great place for indie rockers, hip-hoppers, and street-stoppers. Thanks to an eye turned toward the past—once called Black Broadway, jazz joints that once famously lined the streets in the '20s are making a comeback.

$ Banks

- **Bank of America** · 1090 Vermont Ave NW
- **Bank of America** · 635 Massachusetts Ave NW
- **BB&T** · 1316 U St NW
- **Chevy Chase** · 901 New York Ave NW
- **Chevy Chase** · 925 15th St NW
- **Chevy Chase (ATM)** · 1414 8th St NW
- **Citibank** · 1000 Vermont Ave NW
- **Citibank (ATM)** · 7-Eleven · 1115 U St NW
- **Citibank (ATM)** · 7-Eleven · 1622 7th St NW
- **Eagle** · 1425 K St NW
- **Industrial** · 2000 11th St NW
- **Industrial** · 2000 14th St NW
- **Industrial (ATM)** · Ben's Chili Bowl · 1213 U St NW
- **Industrial (ATM)** · DC Convention Center · 801 Mt Vernon Pl NW
- **PNC** · 1306 U St NW
- **PNC** · 1400 K St NW
- **PNC** · 1405 P St NW
- **PNC (ATM)** · 1413 P St NW
- **Sun Trust** · 1250 U St NW
- **Sun Trust** · 1275 K St NW
- **Wachovia** · 1150 K St NW
- **Wachovia** · 1447 P St NW
- **Wachovia** ·1901 7th St NW

Car Rental

- **Enterprise** · 1029 Vermont Ave NW · 202-393-0900
- **Enterprise** · 760 N St NW · 202-289-4707
- **Rent-A-Wreck** · 910 M St NW · 202-408-9828

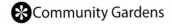 Car Washes

- **Mr Wash** · 1311 13th St NW

 Community Gardens

 Emergency Rooms

- **Howard University Hospital** · 2041 Georgia Ave NW

Gas Stations

- **Amoco** · 1301 13th St NW
- **Amoco** · 1317 9th St NW
- **Chevron** · 4200 Burroughs Ave NE
- **Sunoco** · 1442 U St NW

Landmarks

- **African-American Civil War Memorial** · 1000 U St NW
- **Ben's Chili Bowl** · 1213 U St NW
- **Cato Institute** · 1000 Massachusetts Ave NW
- **Duke Ellington Mural** · 1200 U St NW
- **Lincoln Theatre** · 1215 U St NW
- **Mary McLeod Bethune National Historic Site** · 1318 Vermont Ave NW
- **Westin Washington DC City Center** · 1400 M St NW

Libraries

- **Watha T Daniel Branch Library** · 945 Rhode Island Ave NW

Pharmacies

- **BioScrip Pharmacy** · 1325 14th St NW
- **CVS** · 1199 Vermont Ave NW
- **CVS** · 1418 P St NW
- **CVS** · 1900 7th St NW
- **Giant Food Pharmacy** · 1414 8th St NW
- **Rite Aid** · 1306 U St NW

Post Offices

- **Martin Luther King Jr** · 1400 L St NW
- **T Street** · 1915 14th St NW
- **Techworld** · 800 K St NW

Schools

- **Children's Studio** · 1301 V St NW
- **Cleveland Elementary** · 1825 8th St NW
- **FLOC Learning Center** · 1816 12th St NW
- **Garnet-Patterson Middle** · 2001 10th St NW
- **Garrison Elementary** · 1200 S St NW
- **Immaculate Conception** · 711 N St NW
- **Maya Angelou Public Charter** · 1851 9th St NW
- **Seaton Elementary** · 1503 10th St NW
- **Shaw Junior High** · 925 Rhode Island Ave NW
- **St Augustine** · 1419 V St NW
- **Sunrise Academy** · 1130 6th St NW
- **Thomson Elementary** · 1200 L St NW
- **Ujima Ya Ujamaa** · 1554 8th St NW

 Supermarkets

- **Giant Food** · 1414 8th St NW
- **Whole Foods Market** · 1440 P St NW

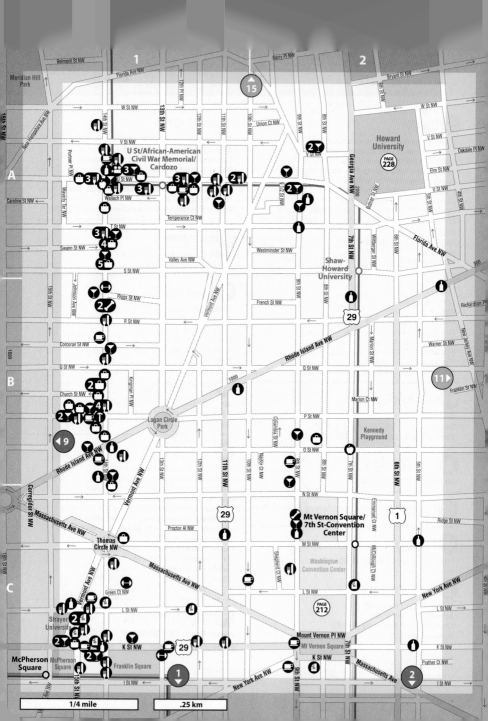

The current surge of activity hearkens back to U Street's heyday as an African-American cultural destination. Also in the mix are Mediterranean joints like Tabaq Bistro, upscale coffee shops like Busboys and Poets, the all-organic Viridian, and party spots like DC 9, the Black Cat, and Café St. Ex.

Coffee

- **The 14U Café** · 1939 14th St NW
- **Azi's Café** · 1336 9th St NW
- **Busboys and Poets** · 2021 14th St NW
- **Café Cozy Corner** · 1117 10th St NW
- **Caribou Coffee** · 1400 14th St NW
- **Cosi** · 1275 K St NW
- **Starbucks** · 1110 Vermont Ave NW
- **Starbucks** · 1250 U St NW
- **Starbucks** · 1425 P St NW
- **Starbucks** · 1455 K St NW
- **Starbucks** · 801 Mt Vernon Pl NW
- **Starbucks** · 901 New York Ave NW

Copy Shops

- **Barrister Copy Solutions** · 1090 Vermont Ave NW
- **FedEx Kinko's** · 1400 K St NW
- **FedEx Kinko's** · 800 K St NW
- **Miller Copying Service** · 1123 7th St NW
- **Print Express** · 1101 14th St NW
- **Sir Speedy Printing** · 1025 Vermont Ave NW
- **UPS Store** · 1220 L St NW

Farmers Markets

- **14th & U Farmers Market** (Jun–Oct, Wed 4 pm–8 pm) · 14th St NW & U St NW
- **Shaw Community Farm Stand** (Jun–Oct; Sat, 9 am–12 pm) · 7th St & O St NW

Gyms

- **One World Fitness** · 1738 14th St NW
- **Renaissance Swim & Fitness** · 941 9th St NW
- **Thomas Circle Sports Club** · 1339 Green Ct NW

Hardware Stores

- **Logan Hardware** · 1416 P St NW

Liquor Stores

- **A-1 Wine & Liquor** · 1420 K St NW
- **Barrel House** · 1341 14th St NW
- **Bestway Liquors** · 2011 14th St NW
- **Caplan Joe Liquor** · 1913 7th St NW·
- **Continental Liquors** · 1100 Vermont Ave NW
- **District Liquors** · 1211 11th St NW
- **Good Libations** · 1201 5th St NW
- **Grape Legs** · 1905 9th St NW
- **Guilford Liquors** · 446 Rhode Island Ave NW

- **Log Cabin Liquors** · 1748 7th St NW
- **Logan Circle Liquors** · 1018 Rhode Island Ave NW
- **Modern Liquors** · 1200 9th St NW
- **S&W Liquors** · 1428 9th St NW
- **Sav-On-Liquors** · 1414 14th St NW
- **Serv U Liquors** · 1935 9th St NW
- **Subway Liquors II** · 500 K St NW

Movie Theaters

- **Busboys and Poets** · 2021 14th St NW

Nightlife

- **9:30 Club** · 815 V St NW
- **Bar Pilar** · 1833 14th St NW
- **Black Cat** · 1811 14th St NW
- **Busboys & Poets** · 2021 14th St NW
- **Café Saint-Ex** · 1847 14th St NW
- **Cork Wine Bar** · 1720 14th St NW
- **DC9** · 1940 9th St NW
- **Dickson Wine Bar** · 903 U St NW
- **EFN Lounge** · 1318 9th St NW
- **The Gibson** · 2009 14th St NW
- **Helix Lounge** · Hotel Helix 1430 Rhode Island Ave NW
- **HR-57 Center for the Preservation of Jazz and Blues** · 1610 14th St NW
- **Josephine Lounge** · 1008 Vermont Ave
- **K Street Lounge** · 1301 K St NW
- **Lotus Lounge** · 1420 K St NW
- **Old Dominion Brewhouse** · DC Convention Center · 1219 9th St NW
- **The Park at Fourteenth** · 920 14th St NW
- **The Saloon** · 1207 U St NW
- **Solly's U Street Tavern** · 1942 11th St NW
- **The Space** · 903 N St NW
- **Tabaq Bistro** · 1336 U St NW
- **Tattoo Bar** · 1413 K St NW
- **Titan** · 1337 14th St NW
- **Twins Jazz** · 1344 U St NW
- **Vegas Lounge** · 1415 P St NW
- **Velvet Lounge** · 915 U St NW
- **Warehouse** · 1021 7th St NW

Pet Shops

- **Green Pets** · 1722 14th St NW
- **Wagtime** · 1232 9th St NW

Restaurants

- **Acadiana** · 901 New York Ave NW
- **Al Crostino** · 1324 U St NW
- **Ben's Chili Bowl** · 1213 U St NW
- **Brasserie Beck** · 1101 K St NW
- **Busboys and Poets** · 2021 14th St NW
- **Café Saint-Ex** · 1847 14th St NW
- **Cafe Salsa** · 1712 14th St NW
- **Chix** · 2019 11th St NW
- **Coppi's** · 1414 U St NW

- **Corduroy** · 1122 9th St NW
- **Creme Café** · 1322 U St NW
- **DC Coast** · 1401 K St NW
- **Dukem** · 1114 U St NW
- **Eatonville** · 2121 14th St NW
- **Georgia Brown's** · 950 15th St NW
- **Great Wall Szechuan House** · 1527 14th St NW
- **Juice Joint Cafe** · 1025 Vermont Ave NW
- **Il Mulino New York** · 1110 Vermont Ave NW
- **Lima** · 1401 K St NW
- **Logan Tavern** · 1423 P St NW
- **Marvin** · 2007 14th St NW
- **Next Door** · 1211 U St NW
- **Oohhs and Aahhs** · 1005 U St NW
- **Policy** · 1904 14th St NW
- **Polly's Café** · 1342 U St NW
- **Post Pub** · 1422 L St NW
- **Posto** · 1515 14th St NW
- **Rice** · 1608 14th St NW
- **The Saloon** · 1207 U St NW
- **Siroc** · 915 15th St NW
- **Sweetgreen** · 1471 P St NW
- **Tabaq Bistro** · 1336 U St NW
- **Thai Tanic** · 1326 14th St NW
- **U-topia** · 1418 U St NW
- **Ulah Bistro** · 1214 U St NW
- **Vinoteca** · 1940 11th St NW
- **Viridian** · 1515 14th St NW
- **Zentan** · 1155 14th St NW

Shopping

- **13th & U Street Flea Market** · Corner of 13th St NW & U St NW
- **Artfully Chocolate** · 1529 14th St NW
- **Ayers Variety and Hardware** · 10 Thomas Cir NW
- **Blink** · 1431 P St NW
- **Dekka** · 1338 U St NW
- **Gallery Plan B** · 1530 14th St NW
- **Garden District** · 1740 14th St NW
- **Giant Food** · 1414 8th St NW
- **Go Mama Go!** · 1809 14th St NW
- **Good Wood** · 1428 U St NW
- **Haunted House** · 1830 14th St NW
- **Home Rule** · 1807 14th St NW
- **HomeMade Pizza Co.** · 1522 14th St NW
- **INARI Salon & Spa** · 1425 K St NW
- **Logan Hardware** · 1416 P St NW
- **Muleh** · 1831 14th St NW
- **Pink November** · 1231 U St NW
- **Pulp** · 1803 14th St NW
- **Redeem** · 1734 14th St NW
- **Reincarnations** · 1401 14th St NW
- **Ruff & Ready Furnishings** · 1908 14th St NW
- **Treasury Vintage Boutique** · 1843 14th St NW
- **Urban Essentials** · 1330 U St NW
- **Universal Gear** · 1529 14th St NW
- **Vastu** · 1829 14th St NW
- **Whole Foods Market** · 1440 P St NW
- **The Written Word** · 1427 P St NW

Map 11 • **Near Northeast**

Ledroit Park and Bloomingdale are at the edge of the gentrification craze pushing east from Shaw, which is predicted to be the next Dupont Circle, and historic homes are being restored block by block. Unfortunately, the huge swath of railroad tracks slicing through does little for unification or aesthetics, however, and certain areas require an extra bit of caution.

Banks

- **Bank of America** · 915 Rhode Island Ave NE
- **Chevy Chase (ATM)** · 1050 Brentwood Rd NE
- **Citibank** · 1060 Brentwood Rd NE
- **PNC** · 1348 4th St NE
- **PNC (ATM)** · 800 Florida Ave NE
- **Sun Trust** · 410 Rhode Island Ave NE

Gas Stations

- **Amoco** · 1231 New York Ave NE
- **Amoco** · 306 Rhode Island Ave NW
- **Amoco** · 400 Rhode Island Ave NE
- **Amoco** · 45 Florida Ave NE
- **Auster Inc** · 22 Florida Ave NW
- **Citgo** · 1905 Ninth St NE
- **Exxon** · 1 Florida Ave NE
- **Hess** · 1739 New Jersey Ave NW
- **Sunoco** · 101 New York Ave NE

Community Gardens

Landmarks

- **Crispus Attucks Park** · b/w V St NW & U St NW
- **Florida Avenue Market** ·
  Florida Ave NE b/w 2nd St NE & 6th St NE

Libraries

- **LeDroit Park** ·
  Rhode Island Ave NW & Florida Ave NW
- **National Transportation Library** ·
  1200 New Jersey Ave NW
- **Northwest One Neighborhood Library** ·
  155 L Street NW
- **Washington Coliseum** · 1140 3rd St NW

Parking

Pharmacies

- **CVS** · 660 Rhode Island Ave NE
- **Giant Food Pharmacy** · 1050 Brentwood Rd NE
- **Safeway** · 514 Rhode Island Ave NE

Post Offices

- **Le Driot Park** · 416 Florida Ave NW
- **Washington Main Office** · 900 Brentwood Rd NE

Schools

- **Calvary Christian Academy** ·
  806 Rhode Island Ave NE
- **Center for Life Enrichment** · 120 Q St NE
- **City Lights** · 62 T St NE
- **Cook Elementary** · 30 P St NW
- **Cooke Elementary** · 300 Bryant St NW
- **DC Preparatory Academy** · 701 Edgewood St NE
- **Dunbar High** · 1301 New Jersey Ave NW
- **Emery Elementary** · 1720 1st St NE
- **Gage Eckington Elementary** · 2025 3rd St NW
- **Gallaudet University** · 800 Florida Ave NE
- **Hamilton Center Special Education** ·
  1401 Brentwood Pkwy NE
- **Hardy Middle** · 1401 Brentwood Pkwy NE
- **HD Cooke** · 300 Bryant St NW
- **Holy Name** · 1217 West Virginia Ave NE
- **Holy Redeemer** · 1135 New Jersey Ave NW
- **Hope Community Public Charter** · 2917 8th St NE
- **Hyde Leadership** · 101 T St NE
- **Kendall Demonstration Elementary/Model Secondary** · 800 Florida Ave NE
- **McKinley High** · 151 T St NE
- **Model Secondary** · 800 Florida Ave NE
- **Montgomery Elementary** · 421 P St NW
- **Noyes Elementary** · 2725 10th St NE
- **Pre-Engineering Senior High** ·
  1301 New Jersey Ave NW
- **Shaed Elementary** · 301 Douglas St NE
- **Terrell Junior High** · 100 Pierce St NW
- **Tree of Life Community Elementary** ·
  800 3rd St NE
- **Two Rivers Elementary** · 1227 4th St NE
- **Walker-Jones Elementary** · 100 L St NW
- **Washington Career High** · 27 O St NW
- **William E Doar Jr Elementary** ·
  705 Edgewood St NE
- **Wilson Elementary** · 660 K St NE

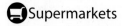 Supermarkets

- **Giant Food** · 1050 Brentwood Rd NE
- **Safeway** · 514 Rhode Island Ave NE

A couple years ago, there was only Home Depot, Giant, and a legion of liquor stores. But now the area has a host of cafés (including the truly wonderful Big Bear) and bars (including FUR, for the club kids) to diversify one's quality of life.

Coffee
- **Dunkin Donuts** · 1739 New Jersey Ave NW
- **Big Bear Café** · 1700 1 St NW
- **Pound Coffee** · 1300 2nd St NE

Copy Shops
- **Blueboy Document Imaging** · 214 L St NE

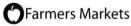Farmers Markets
- **DC Farmers Market**
  (Tue, 7 am–5:30 pm; Sat, 7 am–6 pm;
  Sun, 7 am–2 pm) ·
  1309 5th St NE
- **Florida Avenue Farmers' Market** · 500 Neal Pl NE
- **North Capitol Neighborhood Farmers Market**
  (Jun–Oct; Sun, 10am–1pm) ·
  1626 N Capitol St NE
- **Rhode Island Flea and Farmers Market**
  (May–Oct; Sat, 10 am–5 pm) ·
  Rhode Island Ave NE & 4th St NE

Gyms
- **Curves** · 1334 N Capitol St NW

Hardware Stores
- **Home Depot** · 901 Rhode Island Ave NE
- **W S Jenks** · 953 V St NE

Liquor Stores
- **Big Ben Liquor Store** · 1300 N Capitol St NW
- **Bloomingdale Liquor** · 1836 1st St NW
- **Brentwood Liquors** · 1319 Rhode Island Ave NE
- **Brother's Liquor** · 1140 Florida Ave NE
- **Coast-In Liquors** · 301 Florida Ave NE
- **Edgewood Liquor Store** · 2303 4th St NE
- **J&J Liquor Store** · 1211 Brentwood Rd NE
- **JB Liquorette** · 1000 Florida Ave NE
- **Mac's Wine & Liquor** · 401 Rhode Island Ave NE
- **Metro Ice & Beverage** · 50 Florida Ave NE
- **Moon Liquor** · 322 Florida Ave NW
- **Northeast Liquors** · 1300 5th St NE

- **Super Liquors** · 1633 N Capitol St NE
- **Walter Johnson's Liquor Store** ·
  1542 N Capitol St NW

Nightlife
- **Fur Nightclub** · 33 Patterson St NE
- **Lux Lounge** · 649 New York Ave NE

Restaurants
- **Divinely Decadent Desserts** · 2703 12th St NE
- **Kushi** · 465 K St NW
- **Scion** · 2100 P St

Shopping
- **A. Litteri, Inc.** · 517 Morse St NE
- **Anna's Linen** · 1060 Brentwood Rd NE
- **Brass Knob Back Door Warehouse, Inc** ·
  57 N St NW
- **Capitol Hill Premium Cigars & Tobacco** · 1006
  Florida Ave NE
- **Giant Food** · 1050 Brentwood Rd NE
- **Home Depot** · 901 Rhode Island Ave NE
- **Windows Café** · 101 Rhode Island Ave NW

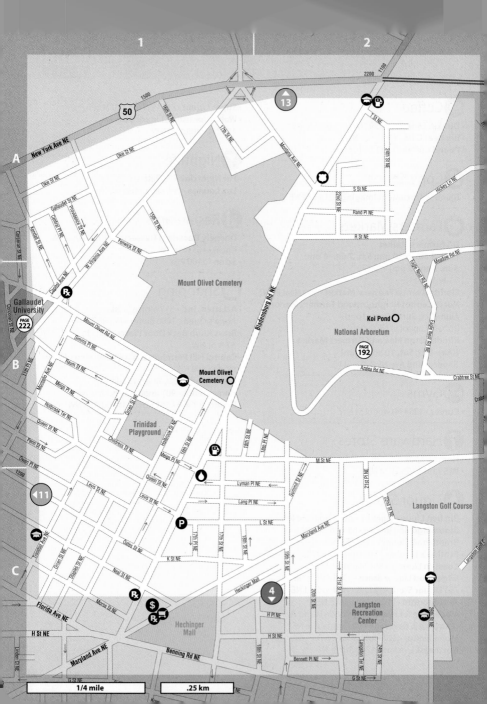

On the NE outskirts of the District, Trinidad is one of DC's last affordable neighborhoods... and it shows. But outside speculators are coming in with business concepts that longtime residents would rather fend off, and between Mount Olivet Cemetery and the National Arboretum, green spaces are plentiful.

Banks
- **Sun Trust (ATM)** · Hetchinger Mall Safeway · 1601 Maryland Ave NE

 Car Washes
- **Smoke Detail Hand Carwash** · 1161 Bladensburg Rd NE

 Gas Stations
- **Amoco** · 1201 Bladensburg Rd NE
- **Exxon** · 1925 Bladensburg Rd NE

⊙ Landmarks
- **Koi Pond** · National Arboretum
- **Mount Olivet Cemetery** · 1300 Bladensberg Rd NE

Ⓟ Parking

Ⓡ Pharmacies
- **CVS** · 845 Bladensburg Rd NE
- **Mt Olivet CARE Pharmacy** · 1809 West Virginia Ave NE
- **Safeway** · 1601 Maryland Ave NE

Police
- **MPDC 5th District Station** · 1805 Bladensburg Rd NE

Schools
- **Browne Junior High** · 850 26th St NE
- **New School for Enterprise and Development** · 1920 Bladensburg Rd NE
- **Webb Elementary** · 1375 Mt Olive Rd NE
- **Wheatley Elementary (temporarily closed)** · 1299 Neal St NE
- **Young Elementary** · 820 26th St NE

Supermarkets
- **Safeway** · 1601 Maryland Ave NE

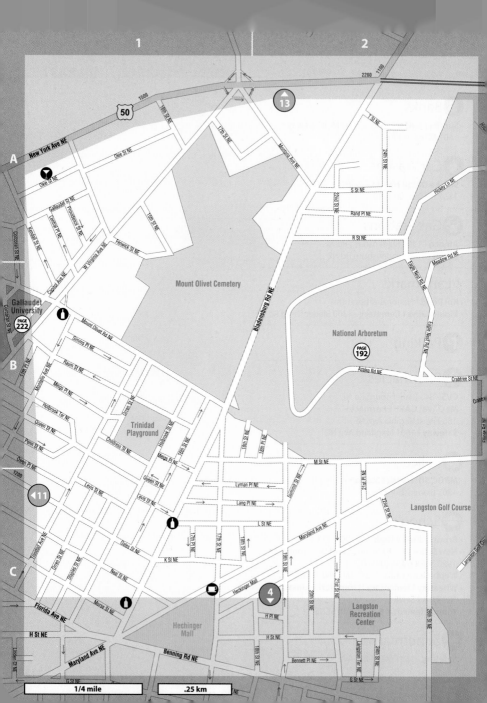

Map 12

The two hotspots here are the gorgeous Arboretum, which keeps its beauty gated away from the neighborhood, and a huge destination nightclub, Love (formerly known as Dream). Apart from peonies and Patron, there's not much else to do in this primarily residential neighborhood.

Coffee

• **Starbucks** • 1601 Maryland Ave NE

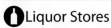Liquor Stores

• **Kovaks Liquors** • 1237 Mt Olivet Rd NE
• **Rose's Liquor** • 830 Bladensburg Rd NE
• **Stanton Liquors** • 1044 Bladensburg Rd NE

Nightlife

• **Love Nightclub** • 1350 Okie St NE

Map 13 • **Brookland / Langdon**

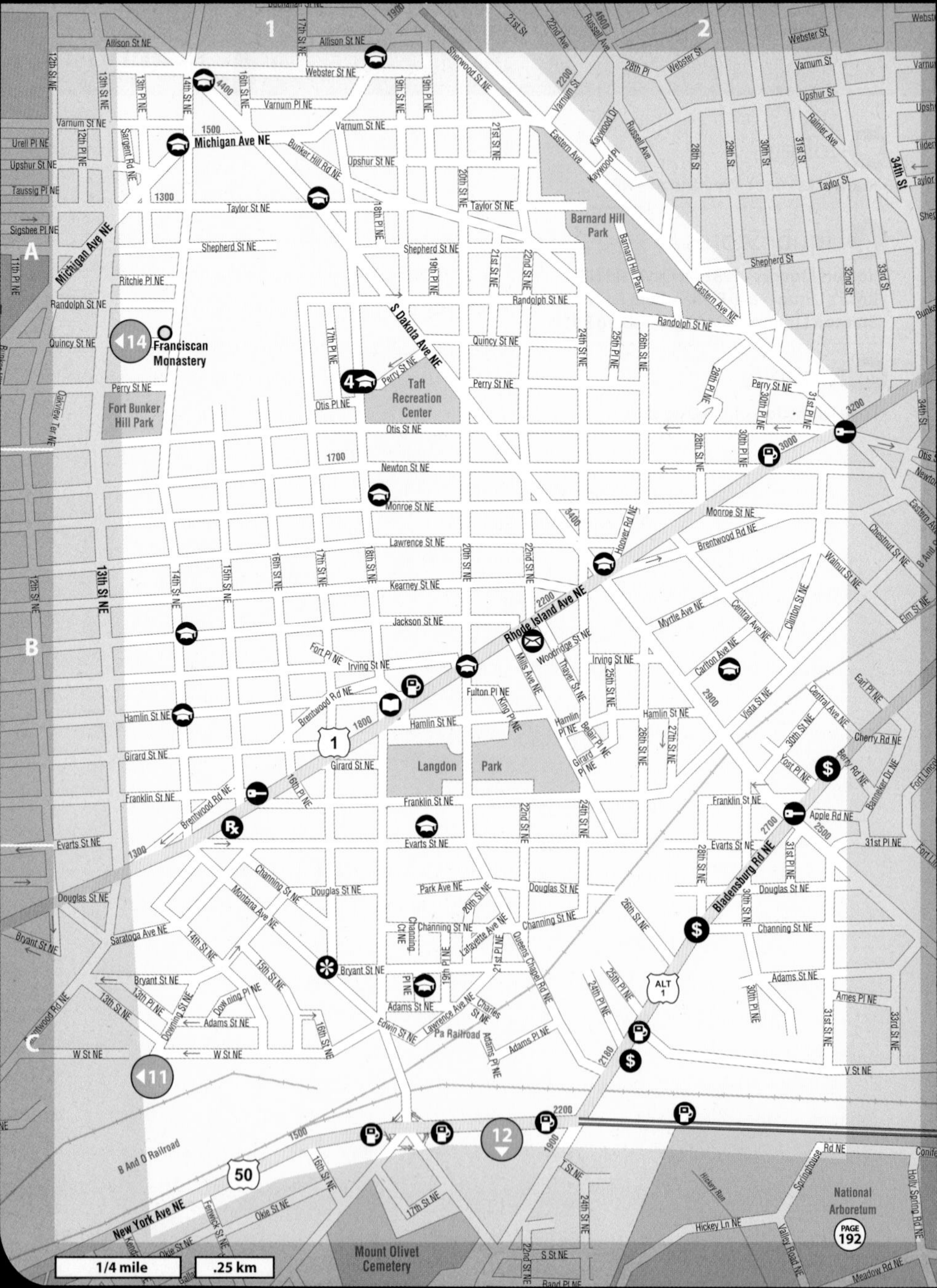

1

2

N

Buchanan St NE

Allison St NE

21st St NE

22nd St NE

Russell Ave

28th Pl

Webster St NE

Allison St NE

Webster St NE

Shirewood St NE

Varnum St NE

Upshur St NE

Rainier Ave NE

34th St.

Allison St NE

4400

18th St NE

19th St NE

19th Pl NE

Varnum St NE

Eastern Ave

Kaywood Dr

Kaywood Pl

29th St NE

30th St NE

31st St NE

32nd St

33rd St

Varnum Pl NE

Webster St NE

Varnum St NE

Michigan Ave NE

1500

Bunker Hill Rd NE

18th Pl NE

Upshur St NE

Taylor St NE

Eastern Ave NE

Shepherd St

1300

Barnard Hill Park

A

Taylor St NE

Shepherd St NE

Shepherd St NE

21st St NE

22nd St NE

24th St NE

25th Pl NE

Barnard Hill Park

Shepherd St NE

32nd St

33rd St

Ritchie Pl NE

Randolph St NE

Quincy St NE

19th St NE

Randolph St NE

Randolph Ave NE

Michigan Ave NE

S. Dakota Ave NE

Quincy St NE

24th St NE

25th Pl NE

26th St NE

Perry St NE

30th Pl NE

31st St NE

2200

◄14 Franciscan Monastery

17th Pl NE

18th St NE

Perry St NE

Perry St NE

28th St NE

3000

Otis St NE

4 Taft Recreation Center

30th St NE

Newton St NE

Otis St NE

Fort Bunker Hill Park

1700

Newton St NE

28th St NE

Otis St NE

Monroe St NE

Monroe St NE

Brentwood Rd NE

Chestnut St NE

Lawrence St NE

28th St NE

22nd St NE

3rd Service Rd

Walnut St NE

13th St NE

14th St NE

15th St NE

16th St NE

17th Pl NE

18th St NE

Kearney St NE

Jackson St NE

Myrtle Ave NE

Irving St NE

Carlton Ave NE

B

Fort Pl NE

Irving St NE

Rhode Island Ave NE

2200

Woodbridge St NE

Thayer St NE

25th St NE

Vista St NE

2000

Hamlin St NE

Fulton Pl NE

Hamlin St NE

26th St NE

27th St NE

Central Ave NE

Central Ave NE

3600 St NE

Cherry Rd NE

Hamlin St NE

King Pl NE

Bates St NE

Girard Pl NE

Fort Lincoln Dr NE

$

Apple Rd NE

2500

1

Girard St NE

Langdon Park

Franklin St NE

22nd St NE

Franklin St NE

2700

Evarts St NE

31st Pl NE

Franklin St NE

Brentwood Rd NE

18th St NE

Evarts St NE

26th St NE

Rx

1300

Channing St NE

Douglas St NE

Park Ave NE

20th St NE

Channing St NE

Douglas St NE

$

Bladensburg Rd NE

Douglas St NE

Channing St NE

Adams St NE

Evarts St NE

Douglas St NE

Merrill Ave NE

Channing Ct NE

21st St NE

Lafayette Ave NE

25th St NE

26th St NE

Ames Pl NE

31st St NE

33rd St NE

Bryant St NE

15th St NE

Downing Pl NE

✳

Bryant St NE

3rd St NE

Queens Chapel Rd NE

ALT 1

25th St NE

$

30th Pl NE

C

Adams St NE

13th St NE

14th St NE

Adams St NE

Lawrence St NE

Charles Pl NE

Adams St NE

2100

$

V St NE

◄11

W St NE

W St NE

Edwin St NE

Pa Railroad

Adams Pl NE

Bryant St NE

B And O Railroad

1500

1800

12 ▼

Springside Rd NE

W St NE

National Arboretum

50

Okie St NE

17th St NE

S St NE

24th St NE

Hickey Ln NE

Bond St NE

Rand Pl NE

Meadow Rd NE

PAGE 192

1/4 mile

.25 km

New York Ave NE

Mount Olivet Cemetery

Plenty of schools near leafy streets and bigger lots will provide you with a cheaper, scruffier alternative to the quiet streets and single-family living of your suburban friends while allowing you to keep you DC address. Life outside of an apartment building will mean plenty of mowing, raking, and snow shoveling—what better way to keep your mind off the fact that there's nothing else to do?

Banks

- **Citibank (ATM)** · 7-Eleven · 2850 Bladensburg Rd NE
- **First Horizon** · 2808 Douglas St NE
- **Wachovia** · 2119 Bladensburg Rd NE

Car Rental

- **A&D Auto Rental** · 2712 Bladensburg Rd NE · 202-832-5300
- **Enterprise** · 1502 Franklin St NE · 202-269-0300
- **Thrifty** · 3210 Rhode Island Ave · 301-890-3600

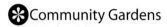 Community Gardens

 Gas Stations

- **Amoco** · 2210 Bladensburg Rd NE
- **Citgo** · 2420 New York Ave NE
- **Exxon** · 2230 New York Ave NE
- **Hess** · 1801 New York Ave NE
- **Shell** · 1765 New York Ave NE
- **Shell** · 1830 Rhode Island Ave NE
- **Shell** · 3101 Rhode Island Ave NE

○ Landmarks

- **Franciscan Monastery** · 1400 Quincy St NE

Libraries

- **Woodridge Library** · 1801 Hamlin St NE

Pharmacies

- **Rite Aid** · 1401 Rhode Island Ave NE

Post Offices

- **Woodridge** · 2211 Rhode Island Ave NE

Schools

- **Bunker Hill Elementary** · 1401 Michigan Ave NE
- **Burroughs Elementary** · 1820 Monroe St NE
- **Choice Middle Program** · 1800 Perry St NE
- **DC Alternative Learning Academy/West** · 1800 Perry St NE
- **Friendship Edison: Woodridge Campus** · 2959 Carlton Ave NE
- **Langdon Elementary** · 1900 Evarts St SE
- **Lincoln Middle** · 1800 Perry St NE
- **Potomac Lighthouse Public Charter** · 1600 Taylor St NE
- **Rhema Christian Center** · 1825 Michigan Ave NE
- **Slowe Elementary** · 1404 Jackson St NE
- **St Anselm's Abbey** · 4501 S Dakota Ave NE
- **St Francis de Sales** · 2019 Rhode Island Ave NE
- **Taft** · 1800 Perry St NE
- **Tree of Life Community Public Charter** · 2315 18th Pl NE
- **Washington Science and Technology** · 2420 Rhode Island Ave NE
- **Youthbuild Public Charter** · 3014 14th St NE

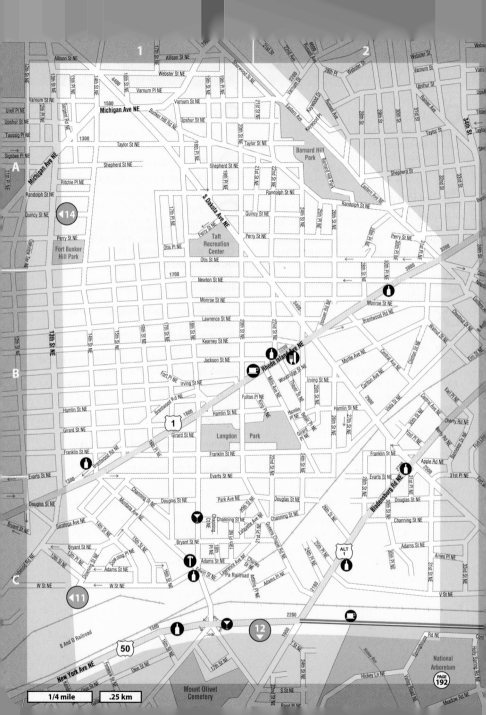

No one moves to Brookland for the nightlife. But it's a nice walk through the Franciscan Monastery grounds, with 44 acres of gardens and replicas from the Holy Land, including Roman catacombs and the garden where Jesus was arrested. And be sure to wake up from your suburban slumber for the annual neighborhood home tour—who doesn't love a great Sears bungalow or Queen Anne?

Coffee

• **Dunkin Donuts** • 2420 New York Ave NE

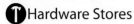 Hardware Stores

• **Blaydes Industries Inc** • 2335 18th St NE

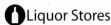 Liquor Stores

• **Good Ole Reliable Liquor** •
  1513 Rhode Island Ave NE
• **Montana Liquors** • 1805 Montana Ave NE
• **National Wine & Liquors** •
  2310 Rhode Island Ave NE
• **Peacock Liquor** • 1625 New York Ave NE
• **Sammy's Liquor** • 2725 Bladensburg Rd NE
• **Stop & Shop Liquors** • 3011 Rhode Island Ave NE
• **Syd's Drive-In Liquor Store** •
  2325 Bladensburg Rd NE
• **Woodridge Vet's Liquors** • 1358 Brentwood Rd NE

Nightlife

• **Aqua** • 1818 New York Ave NE
• **District** • 2473 18th St NE

Restaurants

• **Rita's** • 2318 Rhode Island Ave NE

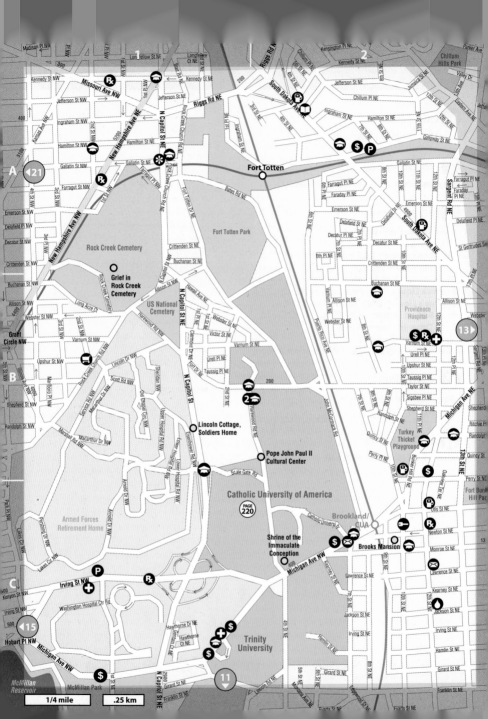

Welcome to Little Vatican, where it's easy to genuflect, particularly at the largest church in the western hemisphere, the Basilica of the National Shrine of the Immaculate Conception. It's named not for the birth of Jesus, but for the divinely blessed conception of Jesus' mother Mary in JC's grandma's womb. At least the coeds have a short walk to the confessional if they fall short of the Blessed Virgin's example.

$ Banks

- **Chevy Chase** · 210 Michigan Ave NE
- **Chevy Chase (ATM)** · Children's Hospital Center · 111 Michigan Ave NW
- **Chevy Chase (ATM)** · 1150 Varnum St NE
- **Chevy Chase (ATM)** · 550 Galloway St NE
- **Chevy Chase (ATM)** · 620 Michigan Ave NE
- **PNC** · 3806 12th St NE
- **PNC (ATM)** · 125 Michigan Ave NE

Car Rental

- **Enterprise** · 3700 10th St NE · 202-635-1104

Car Washes

- **McDonald Custom Car Care** · 3221 12th St NE

Community Gardens

Emergency Rooms

- **Children's National Medical Center** · 111 Michigan Ave NW
- **Providence Hospital** · 1150 Varnum St NE
- **Washington Hospital Center** · 110 Irving St NW

Gas Stations

- **Amoco** · 3701 12th St NE
- **Amoco** · 4925 S Dakota Ave NE
- **Exxon** · 1020 Michigan Ave NE
- **Exxon** · 5501 South Dakota Ave NE

Landmarks

- **Brooks Mansion** · 901 Newton St NE
- **Grief in Rock Creek Cemetery** · Rock Creek Church Rd NW & Webster St NW
- **Lincoln Cottage, Soldiers Home** · 3700 N Capitol St NW
- **Pope John Paul II Cultural Center** · 3900 Harewood Rd NE
- **Shrine of the Immaculate Conception** · 400 Michigan Ave NE

Libraries

- **Lamond-Riggs Neighborhood Library** · 5401 S Dakota Ave NE

Parking

Pharmacies

- **CVS** · 128 Kennedy St NW
- **CVS** · 3601 12th St NE
- **Ensign** · 106 Irving St NW
- **New Hampshire CARE Pharmacy** · 5001 New Hampshire Ave NW
- **Wellington Pharmacy** · 1160 Varnum St NE

Post Offices

- **Brookland** · 3401 12th St NE
- **Catholic University** · 620 Michigan Ave NE

Schools

- **Academia Bilingue de la Comunidad Public Charter** · 209 Upshur St NW
- **Archbishop Carroll** · 4300 Harewood Rd NE
- **Backus Middle** · 5171 S Dakota Ave NE
- **Brookland Elementary** · 1150 Michigan Ave NE
- **Catholic University of America** · 620 Michigan Ave NE
- **JOS-ARZ Academy** · 220 Taylor St NE
- **Kennedy Institute Lower** · 801 Buchanan St NE
- **Maime Lee Elementary** · 100 Gallatin St NE
- **Metropolitan Day** · 1240 Randolph St NE
- **Moore Academy** · 1000 Monroe St NE
- **Roots Public Charter** · 15 Kennedy St NW
- **Rudolph Elementary** · 5200 2nd St NW
- **St Anthony** · 12th St NE & Lawrence St NE
- **Tri-Community Public Charter School** · 3700 N Capitol St NW
- **Trinity University** · 125 Michigan Ave NE
- **Universal Ballet Academy** · 4301 Harewood Rd NE
- **Washington Jesuit Academy** · 900 Varnum St NE

Supermarkets

- **M&S Market** · 213 Upshur St NW

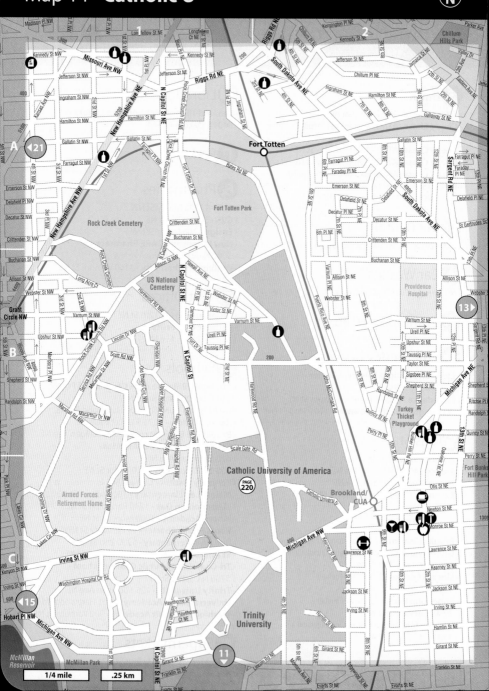

Map 14 · **Catholic U**

Catholic's founders moved outside the old city for more space and cooler, cleaner, perhaps more saintly, air. The 12th Street business corridor is known as "The Village." With its hardware store, post office, and friendly taverns, it can feel a bit Mayberry. But hey, let the U Street hipsters scoff—after a few pints at Colonel Brooks' Tavern, who cares that you're not downtown?

Coffee

- **Café Sureia** · 3629 12th St Ne

Copy Shops

- **Quality Printers** · 301 Kennedy St NW

◯ Farmers Markets

- **Historic Brookland Farmer's Market (May–Oct; Sun, 10 am–2 pm; Jun–Oct; Tues, 4 pm–7 pm)** · 12th St NE & Newton St NE

⊕ Gyms

- **Excel Movement Studios** · 3407 8th St NE

⊤ Hardware Stores

- **Brookland True Value** · 3501 12th St NE

◯ Liquor Stores

- **Dakota Liquors** · 5510 3rd St NE
- **Fair Liquors** · 5008 1st St NW
- **Kennedy Liquors** · 5501 1st St NW
- **Michigan Liquor Store Receiver** · 3934 12th St NE
- **Northwest Liquors** · 300 Kennedy St NW
- **Riggs Wine & Liquors** · 5581 S Dakota Ave NE
- **University Wine and Spirits** · 333 Hawaii Ave NE
- **Whelan's Liquors** · 3903 12th St NE

◯ Nightlife

- **Colonel Brooks' Tavern** · 901 Monroe St NE

◯ Restaurants

- **Colonel Brooks' Tavern** · 901 Monroe St NE
- **El Limeno** · 201 Upshur St NW
- **The Hitching Post** · 200 Upshur St NW
- **Murry and Paul's** · 3513 12th St NE
- **Pete's New Haven Style Apizza** · 1400 Irving St
- **San Antonio Bar and Grill** · 3908 12th St

Map 15 · **Columbia Heights**

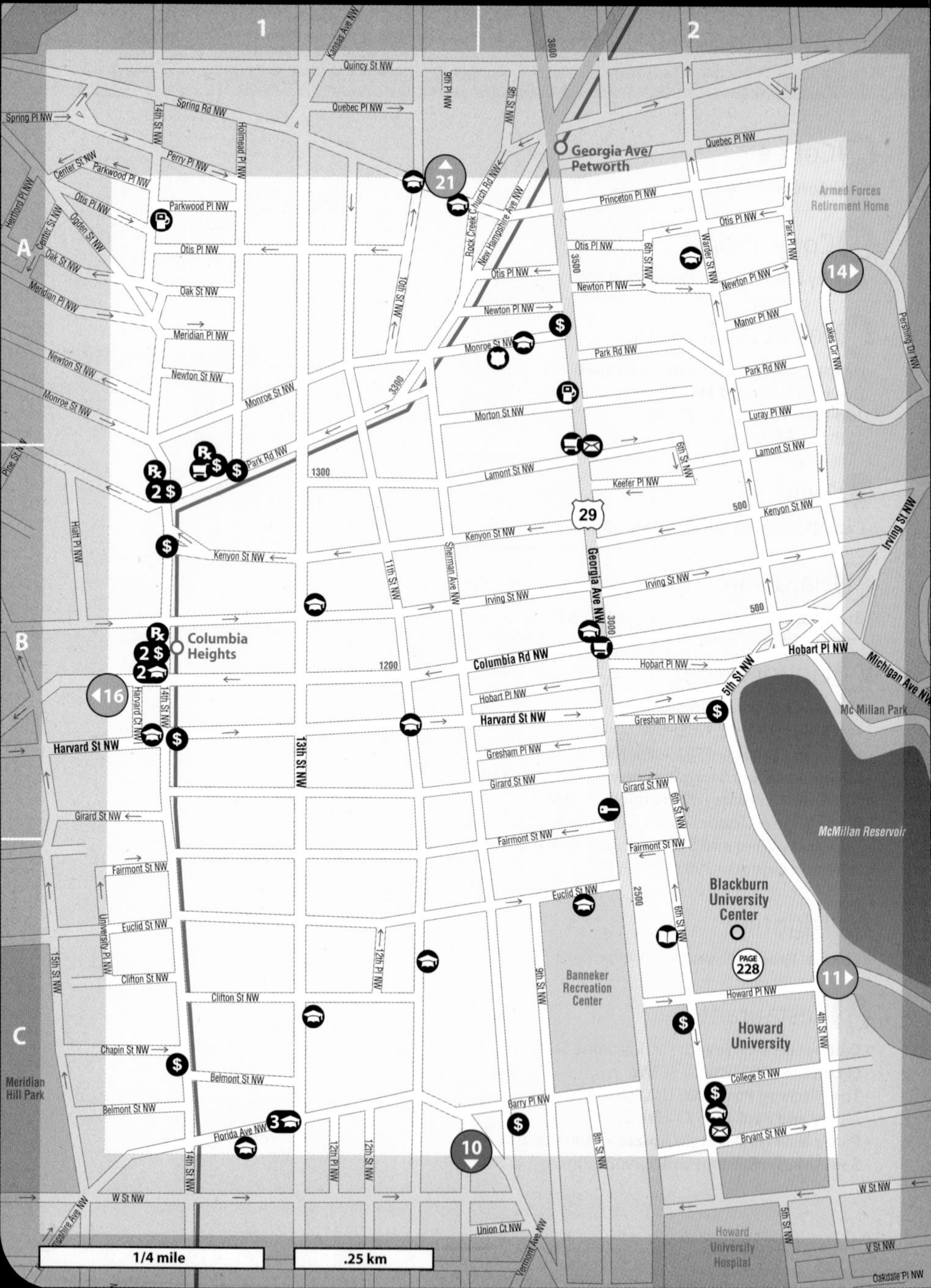

N

1   2

Kansas Ave NW

Quincy St NW

Spring Rd NW

Spring Pl NW

9th Pl NW

Quebec St NW

Quebec St NW

Rock Creek Church Rd NW

14th St NW

Holmead Pl NW

Spring Pl NW

Perry Pl NW

Parkwood Pl NW

Center St NW

Parkwood Pl NW

New Hampshire Ave NW

○ **Georgia Ave/ Petworth**

21

Princeton Pl NW

Armed Forces Retirement Home

A

Cedar St NW

Hemlock Pl NW

Cedar St NW

Oak St NW

Otis Pl NW

Otis Pl NW

Otis Pl NW

6th St NW

Warder St NW

Otis Pl NW

Park Pl NW

Newton Pl NW

Meridian Pl NW

Oak St NW

3600

Newton Pl NW

Manor Pl NW

Luray Pl NW

14

Newton St NW

Meridian Pl NW

Newton St NW

Monroe St NW

$

Park Rd NW

Park Rd NW

Lakes Ct NW

Perishing Dr NW

Monroe St NW

Pine St NW

Monroe St NW

Park Rd NW

Morton St NW

℗

Luray Pl NW

Lamont St NW

6th St NW

Lamont St NW

Hiatt Pl NW

1300

3300

Kenyon St NW

Keefer Pl NW

500

Kenyon St NW

Sherman Ave NW

Kenyon St NW

11th St NW

29

Irving St NW

Irving St NW

500

B

Columbia Heights

16 ◄

1200

Columbia Rd NW

Hobart Pl NW

Georgia Ave NW

3000

Hobart Pl NW

Michigan Ave NW

Mc Millan Park

Harvard Dr NW

Hobart Pl NW

Harvard St NW

$

13th St NW

Gresham Pl NW

$

Gresham Pl NW

5th St NW

Irving St NW

Harvard St NW

Girard St NW

Girard St NW

6th St NW

McMillan Reservoir

Girard St NW

Fairmont St NW

Fairmont St NW

Fairmont St NW

University Pl NW

Euclid St NW

Clifton St NW

12th Pl NW

Euclid St NW

2500

Blackburn University Center ○

15th St NW

Clifton St NW

Banneker Recreation Center

9th St NW

📖

PAGE 228

11 ►

C

Chapin St NW

$

Belmont St NW

Howard Pl NW

$

Howard University

4th St NW

Meridian Hill Park

Belmont St NW

12th Pl NW

12th St NW

3

College St NW

$$

14th St NW

Florida Ave NW

Barry Pl NW

$

Bryant St NW

✉

Spring Pl NW

W St NW

Union Ct NW

8th St NW

W St NW

10

9th St NW

5th St NW

V St NW

Vermont Ave NW

Howard University Hospital

Oakdale Pl NW

1/4 mile   .25 km

Columbia Heights has a well-earned reputation as a hipster mecca and vegan ghetto. It's true, there's no shortage of skinny jeans, fixies or soy cheese here. Traveling outside of the main drags will reveal that the neighborhood's transformation isn't yet complete.

$ Banks

- **Bank of America** · 3500 Georgia Ave NW
- **Bank of America (ATM)** · 1345 Park Rd NW
- **Bank of America (ATM)** · HU—West Tower · 2251 Sherman Ave NE
- **Bank of America (ATM)** · HU—Blackburn Bldg · 2397 6th St NW
- **Bank of America (ATM)** · HU—Admin Bldg · 2400 6th St NW
- **Bank of America (ATM)** · 3031 14th St NW
- **Bank of America (ATM)** · HU—Drew Hall · 511 Gresham Pl NW
- **Chevy Chase (ATM)** · 1345 Park Rd NW
- **Chevy Chase (ATM)** · 3030 14th St NW
- **Citibank** · 3241 14th St NW
- **Citibank (ATM)** · 7-Eleven · 1401 Columbia Rd NW
- **PNC** · 3300 14th St NW
- **Wachovia** · 3325 14th St NW

Car Rental

- **Enterprise** · 2730 Georgia Ave NW · 202-332-1716

Gas Stations

- **Amoco** · 3426 Georgia Ave NW
- **Exxon** · 3540 14th St NW

○ Landmarks

- **Blackburn University Center** · 2400 6th St NW

Libraries

- **Howard University School of Business Library** · 2600 6th St NW

Pharmacies

- **Columbia Heights CARE Pharmacy** · 3316 14th St NW
- **CVS** · 3031 14th St NW
- **Giant Food Pharmacy** · 1345 Park Rd NW

Police

- **MPDC 3rd District Substation** · 750 Park Rd NW

Post Offices

- **Columbia Heights Finance** · 3321 Georgia Ave NW
- **Howard University Post Office** · 2400 6th St NW

Schools

- **Banneker High** · 800 Euclid St NW
- **Booker T Washington Public Charter** · 1346 Florida Ave NW
- **Bruce-Monroe Elementary** · 3012 Georgia Ave NW
- **Cardozo High** · 1200 Clifton St NW
- **Carlos Rosario High** · 1100 Harvard St NW
- **DC Bilingual Public Charter** · 1420 Columbia Rd NW
- **EL Haynes Elementary** · 3029 14th St NW
- **Howard University Public Charter Middle** · 2731 Georgia Ave NW
- **Latin American Youth Bilingual Montessori Public Charter School** · 1419 Columbia Rd NW
- **Meridian Public Charter** · 1328 Florida Ave NW
- **Meyer Elementary** · 2501 11th St NW
- **Next Step/El Proximo Paso** · 1419 Columbia Rd NW
- **Park View Elementary** · 3560 Warder St NW
- **Paul Robeson Center Elementary** · 3700 10th St NW
- **Raymond Elementary** · 915 Spring Rd NW
- **Sankofa Fie** · 770 Park Rd NW
- **Tubman Elementary** · 3101 13th St NW

Supermarkets

- **Everlasting Life Community Grocery** · 2928 Georgia Ave NW
- **Giant Food** · 1345 Park Rd NW
- **San Cipriano** · 3304 Georgia Ave NW

Chicks in granny glasses and guys with sleeve tattoo chow down on vegan eats at Sticky Finger Bakery or diving into delights at Julia's Empanadas. Catch them washing all it with a beer at Wonderland Ballroom.

Coffee

- **Columbia Heights Coffee** · 3416 11th St NW
- **Dunkin' Donuts** · 2750 14th St NW
- **Starbucks** · 2225 Georgia Ave NW
Tynan Coffee and Tea 1400 Irving St NW

Copy Shops

- **General Services Notary and Copy Services** · 3613 Georgia Ave NW
- **UPS Store** · 1380 Monroe St NW

Farmers Markets

- **Columbia Heights Community Marketplace (Jun–Oct; Sat, 9 am–2 pm)** · 14th St NW & Irving St NW

Gyms

- **Washington Sports Club** · 3100 14th St NW

Liquor Stores

- **Cavalier Liquor Shop** · 3515 14th St NW
- **CC Liquor** · 3401 14th St NW
- **D'Vines** · 3103 14th St NW
- **Florida Liquors** · 2222 14th St NW
- **Harvard Wine & Liquor Store** · 2901 Sherman Ave NW
- **Lion's Liquor** · 3614 Georgia Ave NW
- **Petworth Liquors** · 3210 Georgia Ave NW

Nightlife

- **Chuck & Billy's Bar and Carry-Out** · 2718 Georgia Ave NW
- **Room 11** · 3234 11th St NW
- **The Wonderland Ballroom** · 1101 Kenyon St NW

Restaurants

- **Brown's Caribbean Bakery** · 3301 Georgia Ave NW
- **CommonWealth** · 1400 Irving St NW
- **El Pollo Sabroso** · 1434 Park Rd
- **El Rinconcito II** · 1326 Park Rd NW
- **Five Guys** · 1400 Irving St NW
- **Florida Ave Grill** · 1100 Florida Ave NW
- **The Heights Restaurant and Bar** · 3115 14th St NW
- **Julia's Empanadas** · 3239 14th St NW
- **Looking Glass Lounge** · 3634 Georgia Ave NW
- **Negril** · 2301 Georgia Ave NW
- **Panda Express** · 3100 14th St NW
- **Pollo Campero** · 3229 14th St NW
- **RedRocks** · 1036 Park Rd NW
- **Rita's West Indian Carry-Out** · 3322 Georgia Ave NW
- **Ruby Tuesday** · 3365 14th St NW
- **Rumberos** · 3345 14th St NW
- **Soul Vegetarian and Exodus Café** · 2606 Georgia Ave NW
- **Taqueria Distrito Federal** · 3463 14th St NW
- **Thai Tanic II** · 3462 14th St NW

Shopping

- **Mom & Pop's Antiques** · 3534 Georgia Ave NW
- **Palace 5IVE** ·2216 14th St NW
- **Rita's** · 3237 14th St NW
- **Sticky Fingers Bakery** · 1370 Park Rd NW
- **Target** · 3100 14th St NW

Map 16 • Adams Morgan (North) / Mt Pleasant Ⓝ

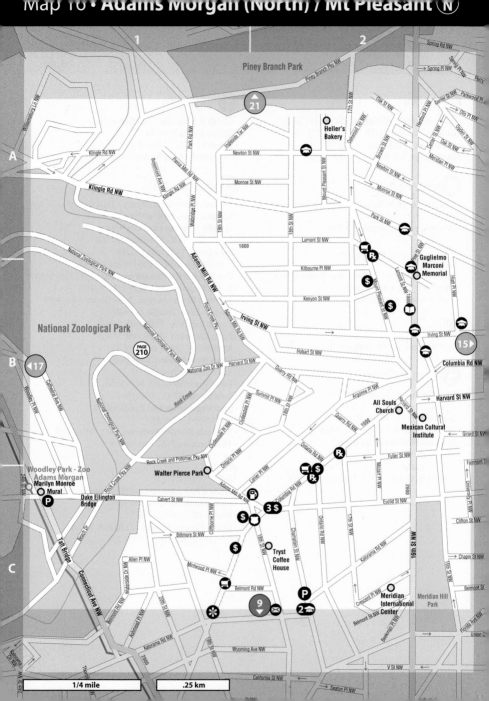

From the Salvadoran pupuserias to the glut of Ethiopian eats to the frat house scene along 18th Street, these two neighborhoods are where different races and ethnicities mix most in DC. Adams Morgan is the nightlife destination, especially for those who like to scream on sidewalks. Mount Pleasant has fewer offerings, but those there are laid-back sanctuaries.

Map

$ Banks

- **Bank of America** · 1835 Columbia Rd NW
- **Bank of America** · 3131 Mt Pleasant St NW
- **BB&T** · 1801 Adams Mill Rd NW
- **Citibank** · 1749 1/2 Columbia Rd NW
- **Citibank (ATM)** · 7-Eleven · 3146 Mt Pleasant St NW
- **PNC** · 1779 Columbia Rd NW
- **Sun Trust** · 1800 Columbia Rd NW
- **Wachovia** · 1804 Adams Mill Rd NW

⛽ Gas Stations

- **Exxon** · 1827 Adams Mill Rd NW

❋ Community Gardens

○ Landmarks

- **All Souls Church** · 1500 Harvard St NW
- **Guglielmo Marconi Memorial** · 16th & Lamont Sts NW
- **Heller's Bakery** · 3221 Mt Pleasant St NW
- **Marilyn Monroe Mural** · Connecticut Ave NW & Calvert St NW
- **Meridian International Center** · 1630 Crescent Pl NW
- **Mexican Cultural Institute** · 2829 16th St NW
- **Tryst Coffee House** · 2459 18th St NW
- **Walter Pierce Park** · 2630 Adams Mill Rd NW

📖 Libraries

- **Mt Pleasant Neighborhood Library** · 3160 16th St NW

P Parking

℞ Pharmacies

- **CVS** · 1700 Columbia Rd NW
- **Mt Pleasant Care Pharmacy** · 3169 Mt Pleasant St NW
- **Safeway** · 1747 Columbia Rd NW

👮 Police

- **3rd District Latino Liaison Unit** · 1800 Columbia Rd NW

✉ Post Offices

- **Kalorama** · 2300 18th St NW

🎓 Schools

- **Bancroft Elementary** · 1755 Newton St NW
- **Bell Multicultural High** · 3145 Hiatt Pl NW
- **Capital City Public Charter Elementary** · 3047 15th St NW
- **Elsie Whitlow Stokes Community Freedom** · 3200 16th St NW
- **Lincoln Middle** · 3101 16th St NW
- **Marie Reed Elementary** · 2200 Champlain St NW
- **Reed Learning Center** · 2200 Champlain St NW
- **Sacred Heart** · 1625 Park Rd NW

🛒 Supermarkets

- **Bestway** · 3178 Mt Pleasant St NW
- **Harris Teeter** · 1631 Kalorama Rd NW
- **Metro K IGA** · 1864 Columbia Rd NW
- **Safeway** · 1747 Columbia Rd NW

Map 16 • Adams Morgan (North) / Mt Pleasant Ⓝ

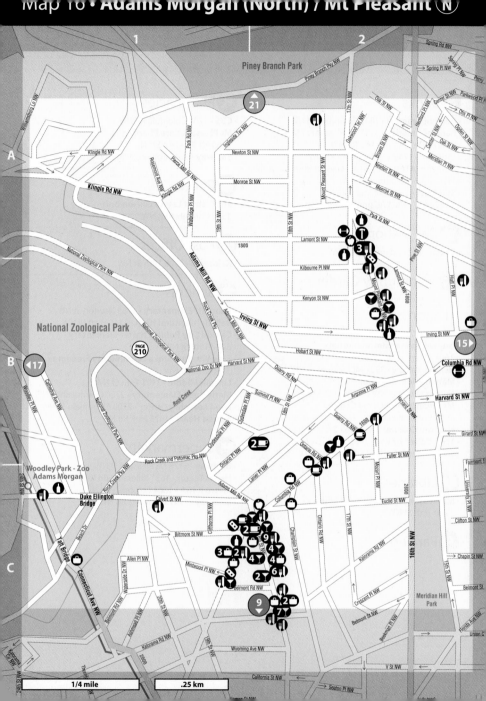

Piney Branch Park

National Zoological Park

PAGE 210

Woodley Park - Zoo
Adams Morgan

Duke Ellington
Bridge

Taft Bridge

Meridian Hill
Park

| 1/4 mile | .25 km |

Start your day by jockeying for a window seat (or a seat) at Tryst, where you can linger over a cup of joe. Save your appetite for the legendary food of Meskerem Ethiopian Restaurant. After your meal, you'll be ready the live music at Madam's Organ, where red heads always drink half price, before heading to one of the neighborhood pizza joints at bar time, for a requisite jumbo slice.

Coffee

- **Crumbs & Coffee** ·
  1737 Columbia Rd NW
- **Potter's House** ·
  1658 Columbia Rd NW
- **Starbucks** · 1801 Columbia Rd NW
- **Tryst Coffee House** · 2459 18th St NW
- **Tryst Coffee House Bar and Lounge** ·
  2453 18th St NW

Farmers Markets

- **Adams Morgan
  (May–Dec, 8 am–2 pm)** ·
  18th St & Columbia Rd NW
- **Mt Pleasant Farmers Market
  (May–Dec)** ·
  17th St NW & Lamont St NW

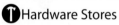Gyms

- **BETA Academy** ·
  1459 Columbia Rd NW
- **Curves (women only)** ·
  3220 17th St NW

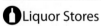Hardware Stores

- **Pfeiffer's Hardware** ·
  3219 Mt Pleasant St NW

Liquor Stores

- **AB Liquor** · 1803 Columbia Rd NW
- **Bestway (wine and beer only)** ·
  3178 Mt Pleasant St NW
- **Lee Irving Liquors** ·
  3100 Mt Pleasant St NW
- **Metro Liquors** · 1726 Columbia Rd NW
- **Sherry's Wine & Liquor** ·
  2315 Calvert St NW
- **Sportsman's Wine & Liquors** ·
  3249 Mt Pleasant St NW

Nightlife

- **Adams Mill Bar and Grill** ·
  1813 Adams Mill Rd NW
- **Angles Bar and Billiards** · 2339 18th
  St NW
- **Asylum** · 2471 18th St NW
- **Bedrock Billiards** ·
  1841 Columbia Rd NW
- **The Black Squirrel** · 2427 18th St NW
- **Bossa** · 2463 18th St NW

- **Brass Monkey** · 2317 18th St NW
- **Bukom Café** · 2442 18th St NW
- **Chief Ike's Mambo Room** ·
  1725 Columbia Rd NW
- **Columbia Station** · 2325 18th St NW
- **District Bar and Grille** · 2473 18th
  St NW
- **Draft Plx** · 2450 18th St NW
- **Grand Central** · 2447 18th St NW
- **Leftbank** · 2424 18th St NW
- **Madam's Organ** · 2461 18th St NW
- **Meze** · 2437 18th St NW
- **Pharmacy Bar** · 2337 18th St NW
- **The Raven** · 3125 Mt Pleasant St NW
- **The Reef** · 2446 18th St NW
- **Rumba Café** · 2443 18th St NW
- **Timehri International** ·
  2439 18th St NW
- **Toledo Lounge** · 2435 18th St NW
- **Tom Tom** · 2333 18th St NW
- **Tonic** · 3155 Mt Pleasant St NW

Restaurants

- **Adam's Express** ·
  3211 Mt Pleasant St NW
- **Amsterdam Falafel** · 2425 18th St NW
- **Angelico** · 3205 Mt Pleasant St NW
- **Astor Mediterranean** ·
  1829 Columbia Rd NW
- **Bardia's New Orleans Café** ·
  2412 18th St NW
- **Bukom Café** · 2442 18th St NW
- **Cashion's Eat Place** ·
  1819 Columbia Rd NW
- **The Diner** · 2453 18th St NW
- **Don Jaime** · 3209 Mt Pleasant St NW
- **Dos Gringos** · 3116 Mt Pleasant St NW
- **El Pollo Sabroso** ·
  3153 Mt Pleasant St NW
- **Grill From Ipanema** ·
  1858 Columbia Rd NW
- **Haydee's** · 3102 Mt Pleasant St NW
- **Heller's Bakery** ·
  3221 Mt Pleasant St NW
- **Himalayan Heritage** · 2305 18th
  St NW
- **Julias Empanadas** · 2452 18th St NW
- **La Fourchette** · 2429 18th St NW
- **Leftbank** · 2424 18th St NW
- **The Little Fountain Café** ·
  2339 18th St NW, downstairs
- **Mama Ayesha's** · 1967 Calvert St NW
- **Marx Café** · 3203 Mt Pleasant St NW
- **Meskerem Ethiopian Restaurant** ·
  2434 18th St NW
- **Millie & Al's** · 2440 18th St NW
- **Mixtec** · 1792 Columbia Rd NW

- **Pasta Mia** · 1790 Columbia Rd NW
- **Perry's** · 1811 Columbia Rd NW
- **Pho 14** · 1436 Park Rd NW
- **Pica Taco** · 1629 Columbia Rd NW
- **Radius Pizza** ·
  3155 Mt Pleasant St NW
- **Rumba Café** · 2443 18th St NW
- **Savour and Sutra** · 2408 18th St NW
- **Sawah Diner** · 2222 18th St NW
- **Shawarma King** ·
  1654 Columbia Rd NW
- **Tonic** · 3155 Mt Pleasant St NW
- **Tono Sushi & Asian Cuisine** ·
  2605 Connecticut Ave NW
- **Tryst Coffee House** · 2459 18th St NW

Shopping

- **Beauty 360** ·
  1350 Connecticut Ave NW
- **Brass Knob Architectural Antiques** ·
  2311 18th St NW
- **City Bikes** · 2501 Champlain St NW
- **Crooked Beat Records** ·
  2318 18th St NW
- **Demian** · 2427 18th St NW
- **Design Within Reach** ·
  1838 Columbia Rd NW
- **Dollar Star** · 3129 Mt Pleasant St NW
- **Fleet Feet** · 1841 Columbia Rd NW
- **Idle Time Books** · 2467 18th St NW
- **Little Shop of Flowers** ·
  2421 18th St NW
- **Miss Pixie's Furnishing and
  What-Not** · 2473 18th St NW
- **Radio Shack** · 3100 14th St NW
- **Radio Shack** · 1767 Columbia Rd NW
- **Smash** · 2314 18th St NW
- **So's Your Mom** ·
  1831 Columbia Rd NW
- **Sticky Fingers Bakery** ·
  1370 Park Rd NW
- **Trim** · 2700 Ontario Rd NW
- **Yes! Natural Gourmet** ·
  1825 Columbia Rd NW

Video Rental

- **Blockbuster** · 1805 Columbia Rd NW
- **Lamont Video** ·
  3171 Mt Pleasant St NW
- **Video King** · 1845 Columbia Rd NW

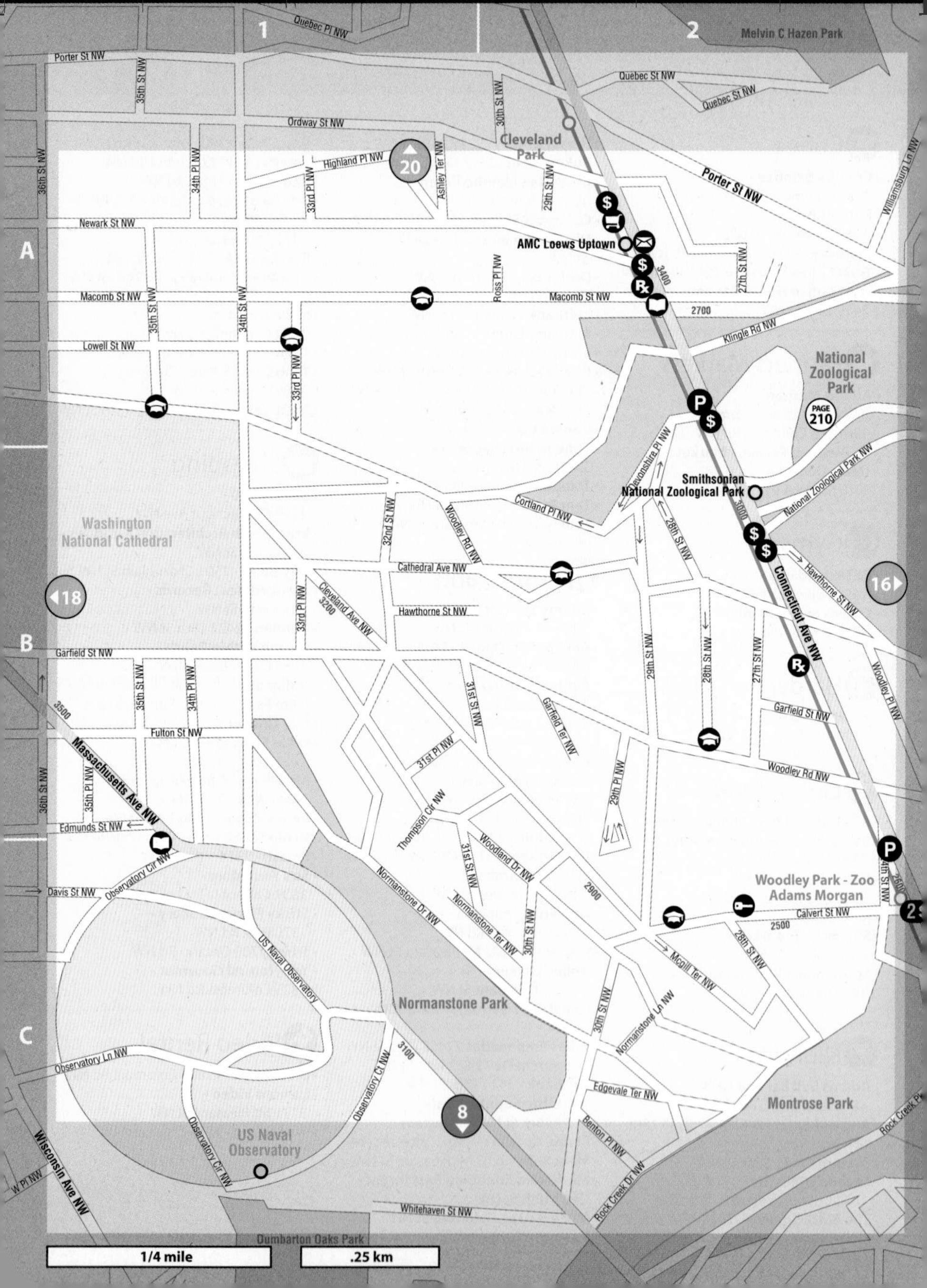

Map 17 · Wood... Park N

1 2

Quebec Pl NW

Melvin C Hazen Park

Porter St NW

Quebec St NW

Quebec St NW

Ordway St NW

Highland Pl NW

Cleveland Park

Porter St NW

34th Pl NW

33rd Pl NW

Ashley Ter NW

29th St NW

30th St NW

27th St NW

Wittenberg Pl NW

36th St NW

35th St NW

34th St NW

Newark St NW

AMC Loews Uptown

$

A

Ross Pl NW

$

Rx

3100

Klingle Rd NW

Macomb St NW

35th St NW

34th St NW

33rd Pl NW

Macomb St NW

2700

National Zoological Park

Lowell St NW

Massachusetts Pl NW

P

$

PAGE 210

Washington National Cathedral

32nd St NW

Woodley Rd NW

Cortland Pl NW

Smithsonian National Zoological Park

National Zoological Park NW

28th St NW

$

$

Connecticut Ave NW

Hawthorne St NW

◄18

33rd Pl NW

Cleveland Ave NW 3200

Cathedral Ave NW

Hawthorne St NW

29th St NW

28th St NW

27th St NW

Woodley Pl NW

16►

B

Garfield St NW

31st Pl NW

Garfield Ter NW

Rx

3500

Fulton St NW

35th St NW

34th Pl NW

Garfield St NW

Woodley Rd NW

Massachusetts Ave NW

36th St NW

35th Pl NW

31st Pl NW

Thornton Cir NW

Woodland Dr NW

31st St NW

28th Pl NW

26th St NW

Edmunds St NW

Observatory Cir NW

Normanstone Dr NW

Normanstone Ter NW

2500

Woodley Park - Zoo Adams Morgan

P

Davis St NW

Calvert St NW

2500

2◄

McGill Ter NW

36th St NW

Normanstone Ln NW

Normanstone Park

US Naval Observatory

Observatory Ln NW

Observatory Cir NW

3100

Montrose Park

C

8

Observatory Ln NW

Edgevale Ter NW

Benton Pl NW

Wisconsin Ave NW

W Pl NW

US Naval Observatory

Rock Creek Dr NW

Rock Creek Pkwy

Whitehaven St NW

Dumbarton Oaks Park

1/4 mile .25 km

Woodley Park and Cleveland Park have long stood proud as safe, residential neighborhoods with good retail. Sandwiched between the imposing National Cathedral and the screaming mating calls of monkeys at the National Zoo, the gorgeous single-family homes of the 21st century cost a pretty penny.

Banks

- **Bank of America** · 2631 Connecticut Ave NW
- **Bank of America** · 3401 Connecticut Ave NW
- **Chevy Chase (ATM)** · National Zoological Park · 3001 Connecticut Ave NW
- **Chevy Chase (ATM)** · 3133 Connecticut Ave NW
- **Citibank (ATM)** · 7-Eleven · 3000 Connecticut Ave NW
- **M&T** · 2620 Connecticut Ave NW
- **Sun Trust (ATM)** · 3435 Connecticut Ave NW

Car Rental

- **Enterprise** · 2601 Calvert St NW · 202-232-4443

Landmarks

- **Smithsonian National Zoological Park** · 3001 Connecticut Ave NW
- **AMC Loews Uptown** · 3426 Connecticut Ave NW
- **US Naval Observatory** · Massachusetts Ave NW & Observatory Cir NW

Libraries

- **Cleveland Park Neighborhood Library** · 3310 Connecticut Ave NW
- **James Melville Gilliss Library** · 3450 Massachusetts Ave NW

Parking

Pharmacies

- **Cathedral CARE Pharmacy** · 3000 Connecticut Ave NW
- **CVS** · 3327 Connecticut Ave NW

Post Offices

- **Cleveland Park** · 3430 Connecticut Ave NW

Schools

- **Aidan Montessori** · 2700 27th St NW
- **Beauvoir-The National Cathedral Elementary** · 3500 Woodley Rd NW
- **Eaton Elementary** · 3301 Lowell St NW
- **Maret** · 3000 Cathedral Ave NW
- **Oyster Elementary** · 2801 Calvert St NW
- **Washington International (Tregaron Campus)** · 3100 Macomb St NW

Supermarkets

- **Brookville Supermarket** · 3427 Connecticut Ave NW

Map 17 · **Woodley Park / Cleveland Park**

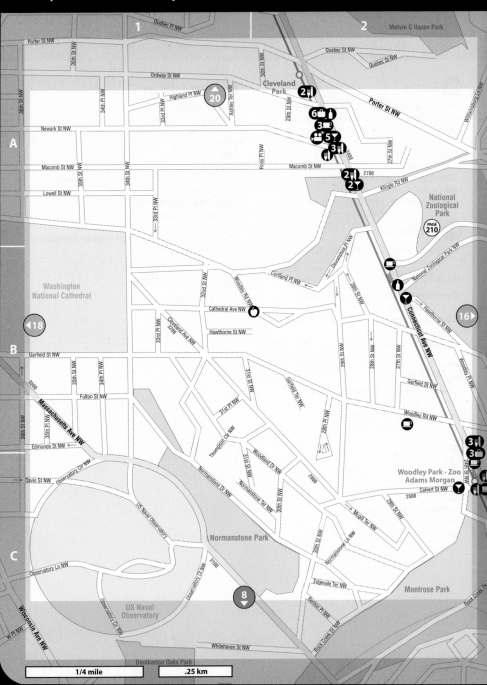

This stretch of Connecticut Avenue has commercial clusters surrounding Metro stations that can provide you with basic necessities. As for nightlife, the strip boasts a number of top-notch restaurants that cater to a variety of palates, a few hopping bars, and the Art Deco Uptown Theater, a single-screen DC institution. Arrive early to get a front-and-center balcony seat at the latest high-grossing blockbuster.

Coffee

- **Café International** · 2633 Connecticut Ave NW
- **Firehook Bakery & Coffee House** · 3411 Connecticut Ave NW
- **Open City** · 2331 Calvert St NW
- **Starbucks** · 3000 Connecticut Ave NW

Farmers Markets

- **Twin Springs Fruit Farm** **(May–December; Sat, 8:30 am–12:30 pm)** · Woodley Rd & Cathedral Ave NW

Liquor Stores

- **Cathedral Liquors** · 3000 Connecticut Ave NW
- **Cleveland Park Liquor & Wines** · 3423 Connecticut Ave NW

Movie Theaters

- **AMC Loews Uptown 1** · 3426 Connecticut Ave NW

Nightlife

- **Aroma** · 3417 Connecticut Ave NW
- **Atomic Billiards** · 3427 Connecticut Ave NW
- **Bardeo** · 3311 Connecticut Ave NW
- **Cleveland Park Bar & Grill** · 3421 Connecticut Ave NW
- **Ireland's Four Fields** · 3412 Connecticut Ave NW
- **Murphy's of DC** · 2609 24th St NW
- **Nanny O'Brien's** · 3319 Connecticut Ave NW
- **The Zoo Bar Cafe** · 3000 Connecticut Ave NW

Restaurants

- **Alero** · 3500 Connecticut Ave NW
- **Ardeo** · 3311 Connecticut Ave NW
- **Byblos Deli** · 3414 Connecticut Ave NW
- **The Cereal Bowl** · 3420 Connecticut Ave NW
- **Dino** · 3435 Connecticut Ave NW
- **Four Green Fields** · 3412 Connecticut Ave NW
- **Fresh Med** · 3313 Connecticut Ave NW
- **Lavandou** · 3321 Connecticut Ave NW
- **Lebanese Taverna** · 2641 Connecticut Ave NW
- **Mr Chen's Organic Chinese Cuisine** · 2604 Connecticut Ave NW
- **Nam Viet** · 3419 Connecticut Ave NW
- **Open City** · 2331 Calvert St NW
- **Petits Plats** · 2653 Connecticut Ave NW
- **Sabores** · 3435 Connecticut Ave NW
- **Sake Club** · 2635 Connecticut Ave NW
- **Sorriso** · 3518 Connecticut Ave NW
- **Spices** · 3333A Connecticut Ave NW

Shopping

- **All Fired Up** · 3413 Connecticut Ave NW
- **Allan Woods Flowers** · 2645 Connecticut Ave NW
- **Antiques Anonymous** · 2627 Connecticut Ave NW
- **Bombe Chest** · 2629 Connecticut Ave NW
- **Guitar Gallery** · 3400 Connecticut Ave NW
- **Manhattan Market** · 2647 Connecticut Ave NW
- **Transcendence-Perfection-Bliss of the Beyond** · 3428 Connecticut Ave NW
- **Vace** · 3315 Connecticut Ave NW
- **Wake Up Little Suzie** · 3409 Connecticut Ave NW
- **Yes! Organic Market** · 3425 Connecticut Ave NW

Map 18 · Glove

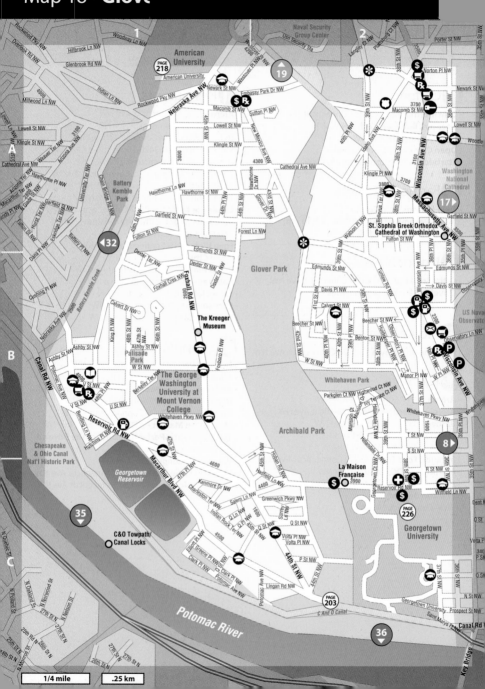

Bordering one of DC's most unappreciated green spaces, Glover Park is populated largely by well-heeled couples. The Palisades, which hugs the river, is off in its own little world of twee front porches. But Foxhall, on the extreme and unapologetic end, is so exclusive that it's completely inaccessible by public transportation.

$ Banks

- **Chevy Chase** · Leavey Center · 3800 Reservoir Rd NW
- **PNC (ATM)** · 3800 Reservoir Rd NW
- **PNC (ATM)** · 4100 Reservoir Rd NW
- **Sandy Spring (ATM)** · Chevron · 2450 Wisconsin Ave NW
- **Sun Trust** · 3301 New Mexico Ave NW
- **Sun Trust** · 3440 Wisconsin Ave NW
- **Wachovia** · 3700 Calvert St NW

Car Rental

- **Alamoot Rent A Car** · 3314 Wisconsin Ave NW · 202-390-7544

✳ Community Gardens

➕ Emergency Rooms

- **Georgetown University Hospital** · 3800 Reservoir Rd NW

Ⓟ Gas Stations

- **Chevron** · 2450 Wisconsin Ave NW
- **Exxon** · 4812 MacArthur Blvd NW
- **Georgetown Chevron** · 2450 Wisconsin Ave NW

○ Landmarks

- **C&O Towpath/Canal Locks** · Canal Rd NW
- **The Kreeger Museum** · 2401 Foxhall Rd NW
- **La Maison Française** · 4101 Reservoir Rd NW
- **National Cathedral** · Massachusetts Ave NW & Wisconsin Ave NW
- **Saint Sophia Greek Orthodox Cathedral of Washington** · Massachusetts Ave NW & 36 St NW

📖 Libraries

- **Palisades Neighborhood Library** · 4901 V St NW

Ⓟ Parking

Pharmacies

- **CVS** · 2226 Wisconsin Ave NW
- **CVS** · 4859 MacArthur Blvd
- **Giant Food** · 3406 Wisconsin Ave NW
- **Rite Aid** · 3301 New Mexico Ave NW

🚔 Police

- **MPDC 2nd District Station** · 3320 Idaho Ave NW

✉ Post Offices

- **Calvert** · 2336 Wisconsin Ave NW

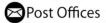 Schools

- **Annunciation** · 3825 Klingle Pl NW
- **The Field School** · 2301 Foxhall Rd NW
- **George Washington University at Mount Vernon College** · 2100 Foxhall Rd NW
- **Georgetown Day Lower** · 4530 MacArthur Blvd NW
- **Georgetown University** · 37th St NW & O St NW
- **Lab School of Washington** · 4759 Reservoir Rd NW
- **Mann Elementary** · 4430 Newark St NW
- **National Cathedral** · 3612 Woodley Rd NW
- **National Cathedral School** · 3612 Woodley Rd NW
- **Our Lady of Victory** · 4755 Whitehaven Pkwy NW
- **River** · 4880 MacArthur Blvd NW
- **Rock Creek International Lower** · 1550 Foxhall Rd NW
- **St Albans** · 3665 Massachusetts Ave NW
- **St Patrick's Episcopal Day** · 4700 Whitehaven Pkwy NW
- **Stoddert Elementary** · 4001 Calvert St NW
- **Washington International Primary** · 1690 36th St NW

🛒 Supermarkets

- **Giant Food** · 3336 Wisconsin Ave NW
- **Giant Food** · 3406 Wisconsin Ave NW
- **Safeway** · 4865 MacArthur Blvd NW
- **Whole Foods Market** · 2323 Wisconsin Ave NW

This area of DC is home to some of the finest eats in the city, including 2 Amys' heavenly Neapolitan pizza pies and Sushi-Ko's delectable sashimi. Of course, there are more exotic options here too, including one of the city's most popular strip clubs, Good Guys.

Coffee

- **Starbucks** · 2302 Wisconsin Ave NW
- **Starbucks** · 3301 New Mexico Ave NW
- **Starbucks** · 3430 Wisconsin Ave NW

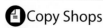 Copy Shops

- **UPS Store** · 1419 37th St NW

Gyms

- **Curves (women only)** · 3414 Idaho Ave NW
- **Washington Sports Clubs** · 2251 Wisconsin Ave NW

Hardware Stores

- **Glover Park Hardware** · 2251 Wisconsin Ave NW

Liquor Stores

- **Ace Beverage** · 3301 New Mexico Ave NW
- **Burkas Wine & Liquor Store** · 3500 Wisconsin Ave NW
- **MacArthur Beverages** · 4877 MacArthur Blvd NW
- **Papa's Liquor** · 3703 Macomb St NW
- **Pearson's Liquor & Wine Annex** · 2436 Wisconsin Ave NW

 Nightlife

- **Alliance Tavern** · 3238 Wisconsin Ave NW
- **Blue Ridge** · 2340 Wisconsin Ave NW
- **Bourbon** · 2348 Wisconsin Ave NW
- **Breadsoda** · 2233 Wisconsin Ave NW
- **The Deck** · Savoy Suites · 2505 Wisconsin Ave NW
- **Gin & Tonic** · 2408 Winsconsin Ave
- **Good Guys Restaurant** · 2311 Wisconsin Ave NW
- **Grog and Tankard** · 2408 Wisconsin Ave NW

Restaurants

- **2 Amys** · 3715 Macomb St NW
- **BlackSalt** · 4883 MacArthur Blvd NW
- **Cactus Cantina** · 3300 Wisconsin Ave NW
- **Café Deluxe** · 3228 Wisconsin Ave NW
- **Chef Geoff's** · 3201 New Mexicio Ave NW
- **Figs Fine Foods Cafe** · 4828 MacArthur Blvd NW
- **Heritage India** · 2400 Wisconsin Ave NW
- **Jetties** · 1609 Foxhall Rd NW
- **Kavanagh's Pizza Pub** · 2400 Wisconsin Ave NW
- **Kitchen** · 2404 Wisconsin Ave NW
- **Kotobuki** · 4822 MacArthur Blvd NW, 2nd floor
- **Makoto Restaurant** · 4822 MacArthur Blvd NW
- **Max's Best Ice Cream** · 2416 Wisconsin Ave NW
- **Old Europe** · 2434 Wisconsin Ave NW
- **Palisades Pizzeria & Clam Bar** · 4885 Macarthur Blvd NW
- **Rocklands** · 2418 Wisconsin Ave NW
- **Something Sweet** · 3706 MAcomb St NW
- **Surfside** · 2444 Wisconsin Ave NW
- **Sushi Sushi** · 3714 Macomb St NW
- **Sushi-Ko Glover Park** · 2309 Wisconsin Ave NW
- **Town Hall** · 2218 Wisconsin Ave NW
- **Z Burger** · 2414 Wisconsin Ave NW

 Shopping

- **Ann Hand Collection** · 4885 Macarthur Blvd NW
- **Encore Resale Dress Shop** · 3715 Macomb St NW
- **Inga's Once Is Not Enough** · 4830 MacArthur Blvd NW
- **The Kellogg Collection** · 3424 Wisconsin Ave NW
- **Marvelous Market** · 4885 Macarthur Blvd NW
- **Sullivan's Toy Store** · 3412 Wisconsin Ave NW
- **Theodore's** · 2233 Wisconsin Ave NW

Video Rental

- **Potomac Video** · 4828 MacArthur Blvd NW

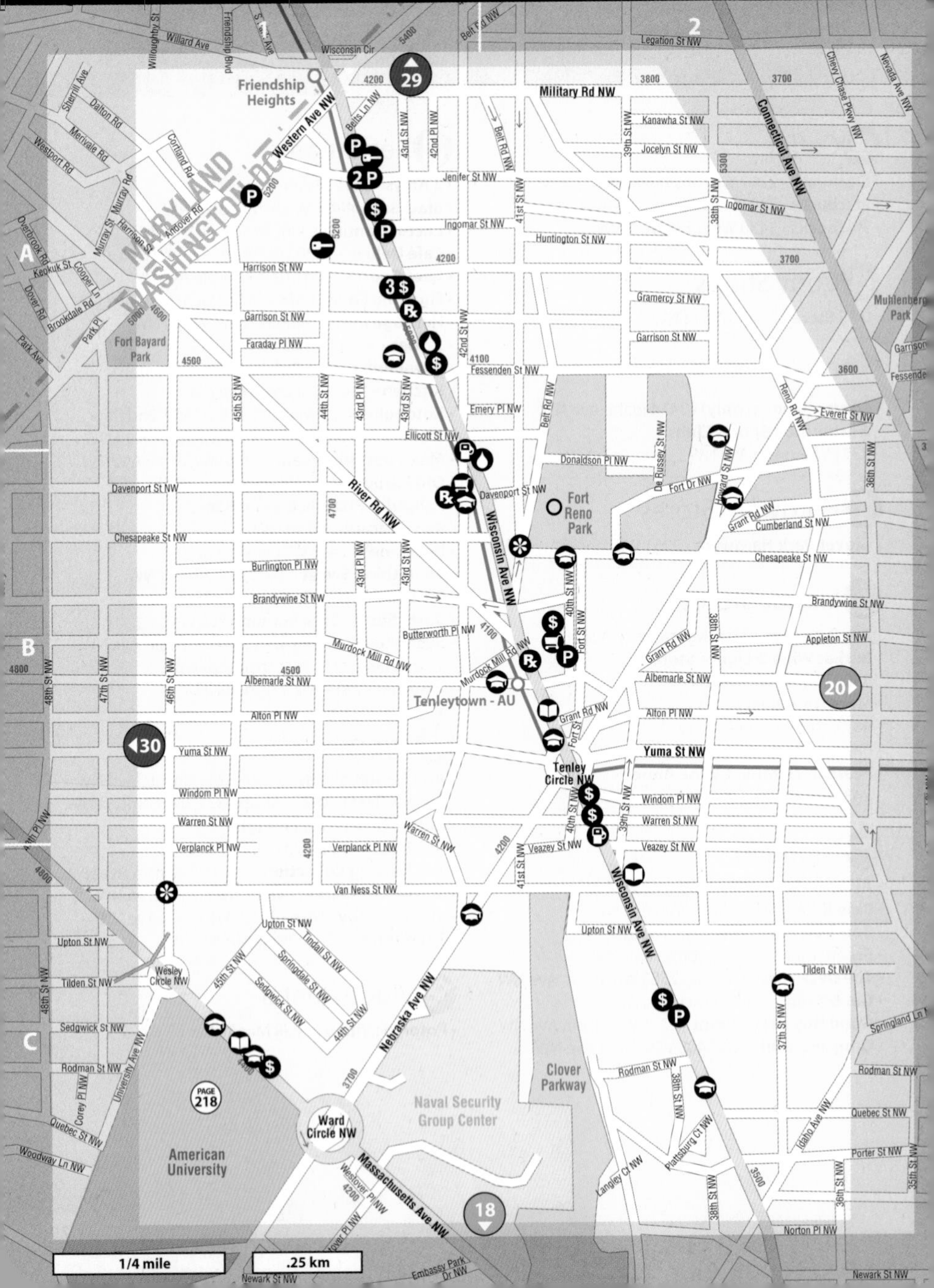

Map 19 · Tenle

Legation St NW

2

Military Rd NW

3800   3700

Wisconsin Cir

4200   29

Friendship
Heights

Western Ave NW

Belt Rd NW

43rd St NW

42nd Pl NW

39th St NW   Kanawha St NW

Jocelyn St NW

Ingomar St NW

Jenifer St NW   41st St NW

Ingomar St NW   Huntington St NW

3700

Harrison St NW

4200

A

Gramercy St NW

Garrison St NW

Garrison St NW

Faraday Pl NW

Muhlenberg
Park

Fort Bayard
Park   4500

Garrison
Fessende

3600

Fessenden St NW

Emery Pl NW

Everett St NW

3

Ellicott St NW

Donaldson Pl NW

Davenport St NW

River Rd NW

Davenport St NW

De Bussey St NW   Dor Dr NW

Grant Rd NW

Cumberland St NW

Fort Reno
Park

Chesapeake St NW

B

4800

Chesapeake St NW

Burlington Pl NW

Brandywine St NW

Brandywine St NW

Appleton St NW

Butterworth Pl NW

Murdock Mill Rd NW

Grant Rd NW   Albemarle St NW

20

Albemarle St NW

Murdock Mill Rd NW

Tenleytown - AU

Alton Pl NW

Alton Pl NW

Grant Rd NW

Yuma St NW

30

Yuma St NW

Fort St NW

Yuma St NW

Windom Pl NW

Tenley
Circle NW

Windom Pl NW

Warren St NW

Warren St NW

Verplanck Pl NW

4200   Verplanck Pl NW

Veazey St NW   Veazey St NW

Van Ness St NW

Upton St NW

Upton St NW   Tindall St NW

Upton St NW   Tilden St NW

Wesley
Circle NW

Somerset St NW

Tilden St NW

Springland Ln

Sedgwick St NW

Sedgwick St NW

C

Rodman St NW

PAGE
218

Clover
Parkway

Rodman St NW   Rodman St NW

Quebec St NW

Quebec St NW

Corey Pl NW

Ward
Circle NW

American
University

Naval Security
Group Center

Rodman St NW   38th St NW

Porter St NW

Woodway Ln NW

Massachusetts Ave NW

18

Norton Pl NW

Embassy Park
Dr NW

Newark St NW

Newark St NW

1/4 mile   .25 km

MARYLAND
WASHINGTON DC

If you want the feel of a wealthy suburb without sacrificing your DC address, this is your neighborhood. Upscale retail and casual dining line the major streets, while the close proximity of the neighborhoods allows you to easily get around on foot. This area proves you can live inside the city and still enjoy as bland an existence as any other God-fearing American suburbanite.

Banks

- **Bank of America** · 5201 Wisconsin Ave NW
- **BB&T** · 5200 Wisconsin Ave NW
- **Chevy Chase** · 4000 Wisconsin Ave NW
- **Chevy Chase** · American U · 4400 Massachusetts Ave NW
- **Citibank** · 5001 Wisconsin Ave NW
- **Citibank (ATM)** · 7-Eleven · 4319 Wisconsin Ave NW
- **PNC** · 4249 Wisconsin Ave NW
- **PNC** · 5252 Wisconsin Ave NW
- **PNC (ATM)** · Whole Foods · 4530 40th St NW
- **Wachovia** · 5100 Wisconsin Ave NW

Car Washes

- **H&C Car Wash** · 4837 Wisconsin Ave NW
- **Wash & Shine** · 5020 Wisconsin Ave NW

Community Gardens

Gas Stations

- **Amoco** · 4900 Wisconsin Ave NW
- **Exxon** · 4244 Wisconsin Ave NW

Landmarks

- **Fort Reno** · Ft Reno Park

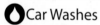 Libraries

- **American University Library** · 4400 Massachusetts Ave NW
- **Tenley-Friendship Library** · 4200 Wisconsin Ave NW

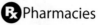 Parking

Pharmacies

- **CVS** · 4555 Wisconsin Ave
- **Rodman's** · 5100 Wisconsin Ave NW
- **Safeway** · 4203 Davenport St NW

Schools

- **American University** · 4400 Massachusetts Ave NW
- **Deal Junior High** · 3815 Fort Dr NW
- **Georgetown Day Upper** · 4200 Davenport St NW
- **Hearst Elementary** · 3950 37th St NW
- **Janney Elementary** · 4130 Albermarle St NW
- **National Presbyterian** · 4121 Nebraska Ave NW
- **Potomac College** · 4000 Chesapeake St NW
- **Potomac Massage Training Institute** · 5028 Wisconsin Ave NW
- **Rose** · 4820 Howard St NW
- **Sidwell Friends** · 3825 Wisconsin Ave NW
- **St Ann's Academy** · 4404 Wisconsin Ave NW
- **Wesley Theological Seminary** · 4500 Massachusetts Ave NW
- **Wilson High** · 3950 Chesapeake St NW

Supermarkets

- **Safeway** · 4203 Davenport St NW
- **Whole Foods Market** · 4530 40th St NW

Friendship Heights drank your provincial milkshake long ago, with its mall-style shopping (J. Crew, Pottery Barn) and speciously upscale dining (Cheesecake Factory, Maggiano's). Tenleytown fought big-box stores for years, but tired of Chinese takeout and mattress outlets, went with the niche shops (Hudson Trail Outfitters, Container Store) and eateries that at least sound owner-operated (Guapo's, Angelico's, Morty's).

Coffee

- **Cosi** · 5252 Wisconsin Ave NW
- **Mazza Café** · 5300 Wisconsin Ave NW
- **Starbucks** · 4513 Wisconsin Ave NW
- **Starbucks** · 5335 Wisconsin Ave NW

Copy Shops

- **FedEx Kinko's** · 5225 Wisconsin Ave NW
- **Kwik Kopy Printing** · 4000 Wisconsin Ave NW
- **UPS Store** · 4200 Wisconsin Ave NW
- **UPS Store** · 4410 Massachusetts Ave NW

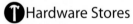 Gyms

- **Embassy Suites** · 4300 Military Rd NW
- **Tenley Sport & Health Club** · 4000 Wisconsin Ave NW
- **Sport & Health Clubs** · 4001 Brandywine St NW
- **Washington Sports Clubs** · 5345 Wisconsin Ave NW
- **Yong Studios** · 4445 Wisconsin Ave NW

 Hardware Stores

- **Ace** · 4500 Wisconsin Ave NW

 Liquor Stores

- **Paul's Wine & Liquors** · 5205 Wisconsin Ave NW
- **Rodman's** · 5100 Wisconsin Ave NW
- **Tenley Mini Market** · 4326 Wisconsin Ave NW
- **Tenley Wine & Liquors** · 4525 Wisconsin Ave NW

Movie Theaters

- **AMC Mazza Gallerie** · 5300 Wisconsin Ave NW
- **Wechsler Theatre** · 4400 Massachusetts Ave NW

Nightlife

- **Guapo's** · 4515 Wisconsin Ave NW
- **Maggiano's** · 5333 Wisconsin Ave NW
- **The Dancing Crab (aka Malt Shop)** · 4615 Wisconsin Ave NW

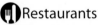 Pet Shops

- **Metro Pet** · 4220 Fessenden St NW

Restaurants

- **4912 Thai Cuisine** · 4912 Wisconsin Ave NW
- **Angelico Pizzeria & Cafe** · 4529 Wisconsin Ave NW
- **Bambule** · 5225 Wisconsin Ave NW
- **Café of India** · 4909 Wisconsin Ave NW
- **Café Ole** · 4000 Wisconsin Ave NW
- **The Dancing Crab** · 4611 Wisconsin Ave NW
- **Froyo** · 5252 Wisconsin Ave NW
- **Guapo's** · 4515 Wisconsin Ave NW
- **Maggiano's Little Italy** · 5333 Wisconsin Ave NW
- **Marvelous Market** · 4800 Wisconsin Ave NW
- **Matisse** · 4934 Wisconsin Ave NW
- **Morty's Delicatessen** · 4620 Wisconsin Ave NW
- **Murasaki** · 4620 Wisconsin Ave NW
- **Murphy's Law** · 4624 Wisconsin Ave NW
- **Osman's and Joe's Steak 'n Egg Kitchen** · 4700 Wisconsin Ave NW
- **Ruby Tuesdays** · 4200 Wisconsin Ave NW
- **Z Burger** · 4321 Wisconsin Ave NW

Shopping

- **Bloomingdale's** · 5400 Wisconsin Ave
- **Borders** · 5333 Wisconsin Ave NW
- **The Container Store** · 4500 Wisconsin Ave NW
- **Elizabeth Arden Red Door Salon & Spa** · 5225 Wisconsin Ave NW
- **Hudson Trail Outfitters** · 4530 Wisconsin Ave NW
- **Johnson's Florist & Garden Centers** · 4200 Wisconsin Ave NW
- **Loehmann's** · 5333 Wisconsin Ave NW
- **Neiman Marcus** · 5300 Wisconsin Ave NW
- **Pottery Barn** · 5345 Wisconsin Ave NW
- **Roche Bobois** · 5301 Wisconsin Ave NW
- **Rodman's** · 5100 Wisconsin Ave NW
- **Serenity Day Spa** · 4000 Wisconsin Ave NW
- **Tempo Book Store** · 4905 Wisconsin Ave NW
- **Tenley Wine and Liquor** · 4525 Wisconsin Ave NW

Self-satisfied liberals unite! These blocks are dominated by well-meaning professionals who carry their own bags to the organic market, shun fancy restaurants for Vietnamese, and enjoy the debates at Politics & Prose. But don't get too radical; they like their coffeehouses sans the grunge.

$ Banks

- **Bank of America** · 4201 Connecticut Ave NW
- **Chevy Chase** · 3519 Connecticut Ave NW
- **Chevy Chase** · 4455 Connecticut Ave NW
- **PNC (ATM)** · 4000 Connecticut Ave NW
- **Sun Trust** · 5000 Connecticut Ave NW
- **Wachovia** · 4302 Connecticut Ave NW

Car Rental

- **Avis** · 4400 Connecticut Ave NW · 202-686-5149

Car Washes

- **Connecticut Avenue Brushless** ·
  4432 Connecticut Ave NW

Community Gardens

Gas Stations

- **Amoco** · 5001 Connecticut Ave NW
- **Exxon** · 3535 Connecticut Ave NW
- **Exxon** · 5030 Connecticut Ave NW
- **Shell** · 4500 Connecticut Ave NW
- **Shell** · 4940 Connecticut Ave NW

Landmarks

- **Hillwood Estate, Museum & Gardens** ·
  4155 Linnean Ave NW
- **Pierce Mill** · 2401 Tilden St NW
- **Rock Creek Park Nature Center and Planetarium** ·
  5200 Glover Rd NW

P Parking

Rx Pharmacies

- **CVS** · 4309 Connecticut Ave NW
- **CVS** · 5013 Connecticut Ave NW

Schools

- **Auguste Montessori** · 3600 Ellicott St NW
- **Coeus International School** · 4401 Connecticut Ave NW
- **Edmund Burke** · 2955 Upton St NW
- **Franklin Montessori** · 4473 Connecticut Ave NW
- **Montessori of Chevy Chase** · 5312 Connecticut Ave NW
- **Murch Elementary** · 4810 36th St NW
- **Sheridan** · 4400 36th St NW
- **University of the District of Columbia** · 4200 Connecticut Ave NW

Supermarkets

- **Giant Food** · 4303 Connecticut Ave NW

The upper NW stretch of Connecticut has plenty of reasons to make the trek. Politics & Prose is easily the city's best bookstore and regularly hosts major-league literati; the upscale beer, wine, and liquor stores have the best selection in the District; and beauty abounds—from the trails of Rock Creek Park to the exquisite 17th-century furniture and parterres at Hillwood Museum & Gardens.

Coffee

- **Politics & Prose** · 5015 Connecticut Ave NW

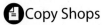 Copy Shops

- **Office Depot** · 4455 Connecticut Ave NW
- **UPS Store** · 4401 Connecticut Ave NW

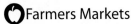 Farmers Markets

- **New Morning Farm Market**
  (Jun–Mar; Sat, 8 am–1 pm;
  Jun–Sept; Tue, 4:30–8 pm) ·
  36th St NW & Alton Pl NW

Gyms

- **City Fitness Gym** · 3525 Connecticut Ave NW
- **Gold's Gym** · 4310 Connecticut Ave NW

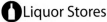 Liquor Stores

- **Calvert Woodley Liquors** ·
  4339 Connecticut Ave NW
- **Sheffield Wine & Liquor Shoppe** ·
  5025 Connecticut Ave NW
- **Van Ness Liquors** · 4201 Connecticut Ave NW

Nightlife

- **Comet Ping Pong** · 5037 Connecticut Ave NW

Pet Shops

- **Pet Pantry** · 4455 Connecticut Ave NW
- **Petco** · 3505 Connecticut Ave NW

Restaurants

- **Acacia Bistro** · 4340 Connecticut Ave NW
- **Buck's Fishing & Camping** ·
  5031 Connecticut Ave NW
- **Delhi Dhaba** · 4455 Connecticut Ave NW
- **Indique** · 3512 Connecticut Ave NW
- **Palena** · 3529 Connecticut Ave NW
- **Paragon Thai** · 3507 Connecticut Ave NW
- **Yanni's Greek Taverna** · 3500 Connecticut Ave NW

Shopping

- **Calvert Woodley Liquors** ·
  4339 Connecticut Ave NW
- **Marvelous Market** · 5035 Connecticut Ave NW
- **Politics & Prose** · 5015 Connecticut Ave NW

Map 21 • **16th Street Heights / Petworth**

It was only a matter of time before the neighborly charm of Petworth's ticky-tack rowhouses was "discovered" by upstarts. This incursion has led to spiking real estate costs and some grumbling from the old timers. But come on, where are all the liberals priced out of Logan Circle and Dupont supposed to go?

$ Banks

- **Industrial** · 4812 Georgia Ave NW
- **PNC** · 5600 Georgia Ave NW

Car Rental

- **Enterprise** · 927 Missouri Ave NW · 202-726-6600

Car Washes

- **Car Wash Express** · 5758 Georgia Ave NW

Community Gardens

Gas Stations

- **Exxon** · 4501 14th St NW
- **Shell** · 4000 Georgia Ave NW
- **Shell** · 4140 Georgia Ave NW

Libraries

- **Petworth Library** · 4200 Kansas Ave NW

Rx Pharmacies

- **CVS** · 5227 Georgia Ave NW
- **Rite Aid** · 5600 Georgia Ave NW
- **Safeway** · 3830 Georgia Ave NW

Post Offices

- **Petworth** · 4211 9th St NW

Schools

- **The Academy for Ideal Education Lower** · 1501 Gallatin St NW
- **Barnard Elementary** · 430 Decatur St NW
- **Brightwood Elementary** · 1300 Nicholson St NW
- **British School of Washington** · 4715 16th St NW
- **Clark Elementary** · 4501 Kansas Ave NW
- **Community Academy** · 1300 Allison St NW
- **High Road** · 1246 Taylor St NW
- **Ideal Alternative** · 5331 Colorado Ave NW
- **Kingsbury Day** · 5000 14th St NW
- **Latin American Montessori Bilingual** · 1375 Missouri Ave NW
- **Macfarland Middle** · 4400 Iowa Ave NW
- **Parkmont** · 4842 16th St NW
- **Paul Junior High** · 5800 8th St NW
- **Powell Elementary** · 1350 Upshur St NW
- **Roosevelt High** · 4301 13th St NW
- **Sharpe Health** · 4300 13th St NW
- **St Gabriel** · 510 Webster St NW
- **Tots Developmental** · 1317 Shepherd St NW
- **Truesdell Elementary** · 800 Ingraham St NW
- **West Elementary** · 1338 Farragut St NW

Supermarkets

- **Safeway** · 3830 Georgia Ave NW

Map 21 • **16th Street Heights / Petworth**

N

1

Rock Creek Park
Golf Course

Somerset Pl NW

Sheridan St NW

Rittenhouse St NW

Somerset Pl NW

2

Tuckerman St NW

R Dakota

Roxboro Pl NW

Rittenhouse St NW

Quintana St NW

Quintana Pl NW

Quackenbos St NW

Powhatan St NW

Fort Stevens Dr NW

Military Rd NW

Joyce Rd NW

Beach Dr NW

Morrow Dr NW

Missouri Ave NW

Oglethorpe St NW

Manchester Ln NW

Nicholson St NW

Nicholson St NW

Peabody St NW

A

Rock Creek Park

PAGE
208

Ross Dr NW

Rock Creek

Montague St NW

Madison St NW

Kennedy Pl NW

27

Missouri Ave NW
900

Marietta Pl NW

Shepherd Rd NW

Oneida Pl NW

Oglethorpe St NW

Nicholson St NW

Marietta Pl NW

Madison St NW

Madison St NW

Longfellow St NW
500

Kennedy St NW

Jefferson St NW

Ridge Rd NW

16th St

3500

William
Fitzgerald
Tennis
Stadium

Colorado Ave NW

Iowa Ave NW
4900

13th St NW

Illinois Ave NW

8th St NW

Ingraham St NW
400

Hamilton St NW

B

Broad Branch

20

12th St NW

18th St NW

Blagden Ter NW

Crittenden St NW

Blagden Ave NW

15th St NW

Piney Branch Rd NW

Arkansas Ave NW

Iowa Ave NW

Delafield Pl NW

Farragut St NW

Emerson St NW

Georgia Ave NW

Decatur St NW

Crittenden St NW

Buchanan St NW

7th St NW

Gallatin St NW

Farragut St NW

Emerson St NW

Delafield Pl NW

14

New Hampshire Ave NW

4700

Allison St NW

Webster St NW

Varnum St NW

4200

Beach Dr NW

Mathewson Dr NW

Argyle Ter NW

Webster St NW

Varnum St NW

1700
Upshur St NW

Taylor St NW

Shepherd St NW

18th St NW

Crestwood Dr NW

Randolph St NW

Quincy St NW

16th St NW

4200

Special Ed. Ctr.

Upshur St NW

Taylor St NW

Shepherd St NW

Kansas Ave NW

8th St NW

Allison St NW

5th St NW

Varnum St NW

4400

Randolph St NW

Quincy St NW

New Hampshire Ave NW

3600

US Soldiers' &
Airmen's Hm.

C

Rock Creek

Williamsburg
Ln NW

Tilden St NW

Rock Creek and Potomac

Piney Branch Park

16

Piney Branch Pkwy

3600

14th St NW

Spring Pl NW

Spring Pl NW

Spring Rd NW

Sherwood

Perry Pl NW

Quebec Pl NW

Quebec Pl NW

15

Georgia Ave–
Petworth

Princeton Pl NW

Randolph St NW

Quincy St NW

Park Pl NW

Otis Pl NW

Quebec Pl NW

Klingle Rd NW

Adams Mill

Ingleside Ter NW

Newton St NW

Monroe St NW

12th St NW

Oak St NW

Mount Pleasant St NW

Glenwood Cem.

Center St NW

Sparkwood

Parkwood Pl NW

Cedar St NW

Otis Pl NW

Oak St NW

Meridian Pl NW

Newton St NW

Holmead

9th St NW

Otis Pl NW

Newton St NW

Park Rd NW

Newton St NW

3500

Park Rd NW

Luray Pl NW

Manor Pl NW

Pershing Dr NW

Lakes Pl NW

Williamsburg
Ln NW

Rosemount

Pierce Mill Rd NW

Walbridge Pl NW

Adams Mill Rd NW

Klingle Rd NW

Monroe St NW

Meridian Pl NW

Monroe St NW

Morton St NW

Park Rd NW

Kenyon St NW

Kilbourne Pl NW

Lamont St NW

Lamont St NW

Lamont St NW

Keefer Pl NW

1/4 mile

.25 km

In rapidly gentrifying 16th Street Heights, Domku offers mismatched furniture and Scandinavian/Slavic food and drink nearly invisible elsewhere in the city. Sweet Mango's jerk chicken rates the best food near the Metro, at least until a nearby retail development arrives to ruin this solid neighborhood's old-time character.

Coffee

· **Mocha Hut** · 4706 14th St NW

Farmers Markets

· **14th St Heights Community Market (May–Oct; Sat, 10 am–2 pm)** · 14th St NW & Crittenden St NW

Gyms

· **Curves (women only)** · 5521 Colorado Ave NW
· **DC Boxing and Fitness Center** · 5505 5th St NW

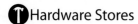Hardware Stores

· **Capitol Locksmith** · 3655 Georgia Ave NW

Liquor Stores

· **Colony Liquor & Groceries** · 4901 Georgia Ave NW
· **Herman's Liquor Store** · 3712 14th St NW
· **J-B Liquors** · 3914 14th St NW
· **Jefferson Liquor Store** · 5307 Georgia Ave NW
· **LA Casa Morata** · 5421 Georgia Ave NW
· **Lucky Stars Liquors Inc** · 620 Kennedy St NW
· **Rocket Liquors** · 900 Kennedy St NW
· **Target Liquor** · 500 Kennedy St NW
· **Three Way Liquor Store** · 4823 Georgia Ave NW

Nightlife

· **Red Derby** · 3718 14th St NW
· **San Gria Café** · 3636 16th St NW

Restaurants

· **Beverage Mania** · 849 Upshur St NW
· **Colorado Kitchen** · 5515 Colorado Ave NW
· **Domku** · 821 Upshur St NW
· **El Torogoz** · 4231 9th St NW
· **Fusion** · 4815 Georgia Ave NW
· **Safari DC** · 4306 Georgia Ave NW
· **Sweet Mango Café** · 3701 New Hampshire Ave NW

Shopping

· **Flip It Bakery** · 4530 Georgia Ave NW

Video Rental

· **Woodner Video** · 3636 16th St NW

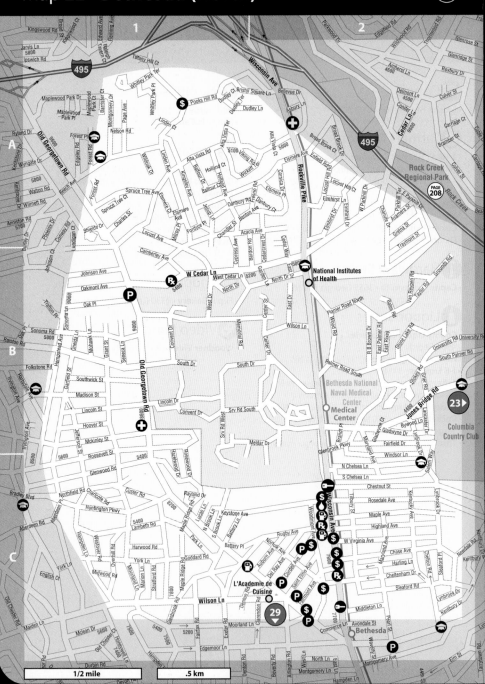
Map 22 · Bethesda (North)

Don't fear the unknown. Bethesda may seem like a bourgie wonderland of homeowners and SUVs, but it's really where Washingtonians go to grow up... and avoid sending their kids to DC public schools. Even the single, childless ones have found a better standard of living and a parking spot.

Banks

- **Chevy Chase** · 4825 Cordell Ave
- **Chevy Chase** · 7700 Old Georgetown Rd
- **Citibank** · 8001 Wisconsin Ave
- **Citibank (ATM)** · 7-Eleven · 7820 Wisconsin Ave
- **Eagle** · 7815 Woodmont Ave
- **Sandy Spring (ATM)** · Texaco · 8240 Wisconsin Ave
- **Sun Trust (ATM)** · 5225 Pooks Hill Rd
- **Wachovia** · 7901 Wisconsin Ave

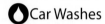 Car Rental

- **Enterprise** · 7725 Wisconsin Ave · 301-907-7780

 Car Washes

- **Texaco** · 8240 Wisconsin Ave

Emergency Rooms

- **National Naval Medical Center** · 8901 Rockville Pike
- **Suburban Hospital** · 8600 Old Georgetown Rd

Gas Stations

- **Amoco** · 8101 Wisconsin Ave
- **Exxon** · 7975 Old Georgetown Rd
- **Texaco** · 8240 Wisconsin Ave

Landmarks

- **L'Academie de Cuisine** · 5021 Wilson Ln
- **National Institutes of Health** · 9000 Rockville Pike

Parking

Pharmacies

- **CVS** · 7809 Wisconsin Ave
- **Foer's CARE Pharmacy** · 8218 Wisconsin Ave
- **Village Green CARE Apothecary** · 5415 W Cedar Ln

Schools

- **Bethesda Country Day** · 5615 Beech Ave
- **Bradley Hills Elementary** · 8701 Hartsdale Ave
- **French International** · 7108 Bradley Blvd
- **Glenmont** · 8001 Lynnbrook Dr
- **Lycee Rochambeau** · 9600 Forest Rd
- **Stone Ridge** · 9101 Rockville Pike
- **Uniformed Services University** · 4301 Jones Bridge Rd

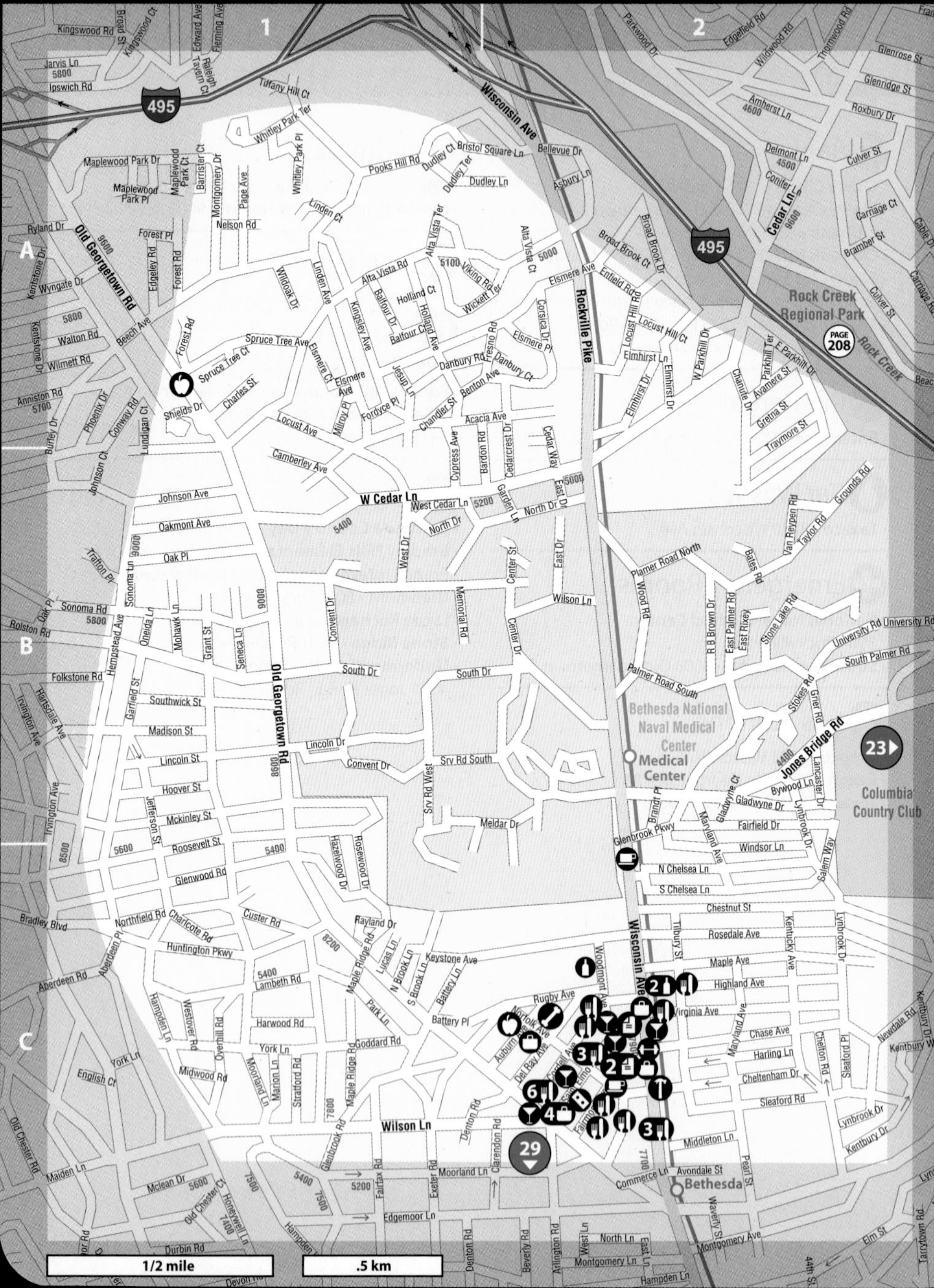

Map 22 • Bethesda (North)

N

1

2

495

Wisconsin Ave

495

Kingswood Rd
Kingswood Ct
Edward Ave
Fleming Ave
Broad St
Jarvis Ln
5800
Ipswich Rd
Tiffany Hill Ct
Whitley Park Pl
Whitley Park Ter
Glenrose Rd
Glenridge Rd
Roxbury Dr

Maplewood Park Dr
Maplewood Park Ct
Maplewood Park Pl
Barrister Dr
Montgomery Dr
Page Ave
Pooks Hill Rd
Dudley Ct
Bristol Square Ln
Bellevue Dr
Dudley Ter
Dudley Ln
Asbury Dr
Delmont Ln
4500
Conifer Ln
Cedar Ln
Carriage Ct
Culver St

Old Georgetown Rd
Ryland Dr
Forest Ln
Edgeley Rd
Forest Pl
Forest Rd
Nelson Rd
Linden Ct
Alta Vista Rd
Alta Vista Ter
5100 Viking Rd
Wicket Ln
Broad Brook Dr
Broad Brook Ct
Elsmere Ave
Enfield Rd
Amherst Ln
Conifer Ln
A
Wyngate Dr
Beach Ave
Forest Rd
Linden Ave
Windsor Ln
Balfour Dr
Kingsley Ave
Holland Ct
Corsica Dr
Elsmere Pl
Locust Hill Ct
W Parkhill Dr
Chandler Dr
Traymore St
Rock Creek
Regional Park
PAGE
208
Rock Creek

Wilmett Rd
Anniston Rd
5700
Prospect Ln
Conway Rd
Lundigan Ave
Shields Dr
Spruce Tree Ave
Spruce Tree Cir
Charles St
Locust Ave
Fordyce Ave
Elsmere Ave
Jessup Rd
Danbury Rd
Benton Ave
Acacia Ave
Cedarcrest Dr
Cedar Way
Elmhirst Dr
W Parkhill Dr
Avamere St
Greina St
Traymore St

Johnson Ct
Johnson Ave
Oakmont Ave
Oak Pl
Camberley Ave
W Cedar Ln
West Cedar Ln 5200
North Dr
North Dr
Cypress Ave
Harrison Rd
Cedarcrest Dr
East Dr
5000
Van Dusen Rd
Taylor Rd
Grounds Rd

B
Rolston Rd
Folkstone Rd
Triton Pl
Olinda Ln
Hempstead Ave
Mohawk Ln
Grant St
Seneca Ln
West Dr
Memorial Rd
Center Dr
Wilson Ln
Center Dr
Palmer Road North
R B Brown Dr
East Palmer Rd
East Rixey
Bates Rd
Stone Lake Rd
University Rd
University Rd
South Palmer Rd

Southwick St
Madison St
Lincoln St
Lincoln Dr
Convent Dr
South Dr
South Dr
Srv Rd South
Palmer Road South
Bethesda National
Naval Medical
Center
Medical
Center
Stones Rd
Grier Rd
Jones Bridge Rd
23

Irvington Ave
Jefferson St
Hoover St
Mckinley St
Hazelwood Dr
Rosewood Dr
Convent Dr
Srv Rd West
Meldar Dr
Branch Ave
Montana Ave
Gladwyne Dr
Bywood Ct
Fairfield Dr
Windsor Dr
Lancaster Rd
Columbia
Country Club

5600
Roosevelt St
Glenwood Rd
Glenbrook Pkwy
N Chelsea Ln
S Chelsea Ln
Chestnut St
Rosedale Ave
Kentbury Ave
Lynbrook Ave

Bradley Blvd
Northfield Rd
Charlcote Rd
Custer Rd
5200
Rayland Dr
Lucas Ln
N Brook Ln
Keystone Ave
Maple Ave
Highland Ave
Chase Ave
Harling Ln
Cheltenham Dr
Kentbury Dr
Chelton Rd

Aberdeen Rd
Huntington Pkwy
5400
Lambeth Rd
Maple Ridge Rd
N Brook Ln
Battery Pl
Rugby Ave
Virginia Ave
2
Chase Ave
Harling Ln
Sleaford Rd

C
York Ln
English Ct
Midwood Rd
Marion St
Overhill Rd
Moreland Rd
Stratford Rd
York Ln
Goddard Rd
Park Ln
Del Ray Ave
Battery Pl
Rugby Ave
3
2
1
3
Middleton Ln
Avondale St
Lynbrook Ct
Kentbury Dr

Wilson Ln
Old Chester Rd
Maiden Ln
Mclean Dr
5600
Denton Rd
Fairfax
5200
Exeter Rd
Moorland Ln
Clarendon Rd
Tilbury St
Wisconsin Ave
Commerce Ln
29
Bethesda
Commerce Ln
North Ln
East Ln
Elm St
44th St

1/2 mile

.5 km

This suburban city can feel staged or overly self-selected, but residences in the apartments along the Woodmont Avenue corridor have made Bethesda livelier. There's always Rock Bottom Brewery, as well as a wide selection of restaurants such as Javan (Persian), Matuba (Japanese), or Faryab (Afghan). If it all feels a bit too fancy, head to the Tastee Diner for Aquanet hairdos and meatloaf.

Coffee
- **Dunkin' Donuts** · 8901 Wisconsin Ave
- **Starbucks** · 7700 Norfolk Ave

 Copy Shops
- **MBC Precision Imaging** · 7902 Woodmont Ave
- **Minuteman Press** · 7758 Wisconsin Ave
- **Reprographic Technologies** · 7902 Woodmont Ave

 Farmers Markets
- **Bethesda Farmers Market (May–Oct; Tues, 10am–2pm)** · Norfolk Ave & Auburn Ave
- **YMCA Farmers Market (Year round; Tue, 10 am–3pm)** · 9401 Old Georgetown Rd

Gyms
- **Fitness First** · 7900 Wisconsin Ave NW

Hardware Stores
- **Union Hardware** · 7800 Wisconsin Ave

Liquor Stores
- **Bethesda Beer & Wine** · 8015 Wisconsin Ave
- **Dunmor's (wine only)** · 8013 Woodmont Ave
- **World Market** · 8125 Wisconsin Ave

Nightlife
- **Caddie's on Cordell** · 4922 Cordell Ave
- **Flanagan's Harp and Fiddle** · 4844 Cordell Ave
- **Rock Bottom Brewery** · 7900 Norfolk Ave
- **Saphire Cafe** · 7940 Wisconsin Ave
- **Union Jack's** · 4915 St Elmo Ave

Pet Shops
- **Posh Pooch** · 8009 Norfolk Ave

Restaurants
- **Bacchus** · 7945 Norfolk Ave
- **BlackFinn Restaurant & Saloon** · 4901 Fairmont Ave
- **Cafe Prezzo** · 4867 Cordell Ave
- **Delicias Carry Out** · 4708 Highland Ave
- **Faryab** · 4917 Cordell Ave
- **Grapeseed** · 4865 Cordell Ave
- **Haandi** · 4904 Fairmont Ave
- **Javan** · 7710 Wisconsin Ave
- **La Miche** · 7905 Norfolk Ave
- **Louisiana Kitchen & Bayou Bar** · 4907 Cordell Ave
- **Matuba** · 4918 Cordell Ave
- **Mia's Pizzas** · 4926 Cordell Ave
- **Olazzo** · 7921 Norfolk Ave
- **Passage to India** · 4931 Cordell Ave
- **Peter's Carry Out** · 8017 Wisconsin Ave
- **Tastee Diner** · 7731 Woodmont Ave
- **The Original Pancake House** · 7700 Wisconsin Ave
- **Tako Grill** · 7756 Wisconsin Ave
- **Tragara** · 4935 Cordell Ave
- **Zelaya** · 4940 St Elmo Ave

 Shopping
- **Big Planet Comics** · 4908 Fairmont Ave
- **Daisy Too** · 4940 St Elmo Ave
- **Design Within Reach** · 4828 St Elmo Ave
- **Promise For the Savvy Bride** · 4931 St Elmo Ave
- **Ranger Surplus** · 8008 Wisconsin Ave
- **Wiggle Room** · 4914 Del Ray Ave

Video Rental
- **Version Francaise (French only)** · 4930 St Elmo Ave

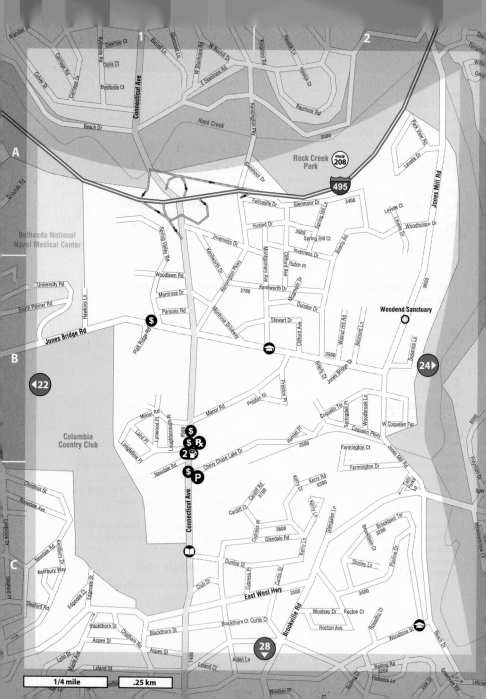

You might as well be on location at a Smith & Hawken catalog shoot. The fussy homes and landscaping here make Maryland's side of Chevy Chase a sought-after, practically unreachable suburb. Your kids will go to one of the area's best public school…But of course you would never send them to public school.

Banks

- **Chevy Chase** · 8401 Connecticut Ave
- **Chevy Chase (ATM)** · Giant Food Store · 8531 Connecticut Ave
- **Sun Trust** · 8510 Connecticut Ave
- **Wachovia (ATM)** · Howard Hughes Medical Institute · 4000 Jones Bridge Rd

Gas Stations

- **Citgo** · 8505 Connecticut Ave
- **Sunoco** · 8500 Connecticut Ave

○Landmarks

- **Woodend Sanctuary** · 8940 Jones Mill Rd

Libraries

- **Chevy Chase Library** · 8005 Connecticut Ave

Ⓟ Parking

Ⓡ Pharmacies

- **Chevy Chase Care Pharmacy** · 8531 Connecticut Ave

Schools

- **Lycee Rochambeau** · 3200 Woodbine St
- **North Chevy Chase Elementary** · 3700 Jones Bridge Rd

Map 23 · **Chevy Chase (North)**

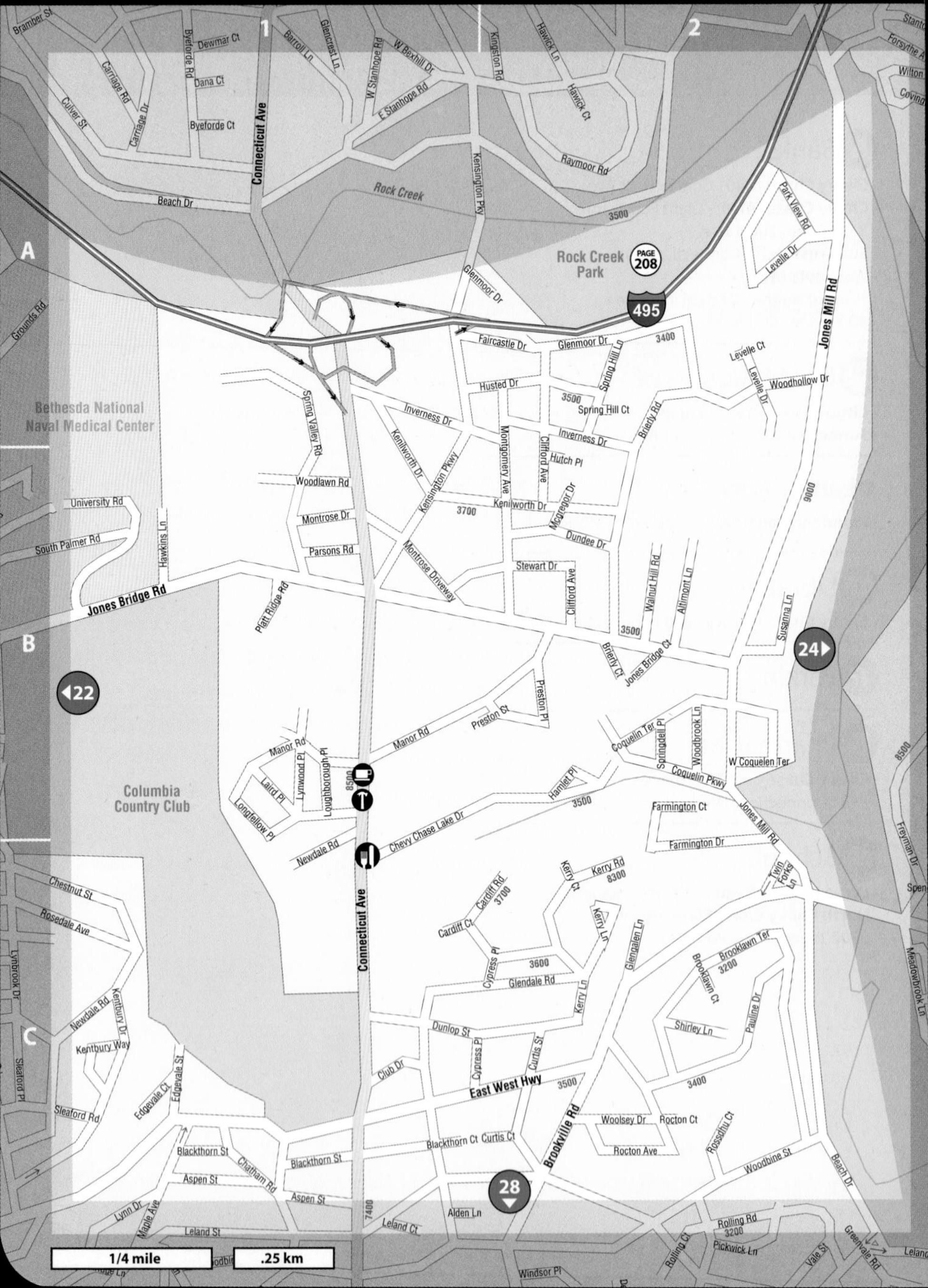

N

1

2

Bramber St
Dewmar Ct
Byeforde Rd
Dana Ct
Carriage Rd
Carver St
Carriage Dr
Carfagno Dr
Byeforde Ct

Barroll Ln
Glenmoor Rd
W Stanhope Rd
E Stanhope Rd
Kingston Rd

Hamlet Ln
Hamlet Ct
Raymoor Rd

Stani
Forsythe R
Wilton
Covina

Beach Dr
Rock Creek
Kensington Pkwy

Connecticut Ave

3500

Park View Rd

Rock Creek Park
PAGE 208

Levelle Dr

A

Grounds Rd

495

Levelle Ct
Levelle Dr
Woodhollow Dr

Jones Mill Rd

Faircastle Dr
Glenmoor Dr
3400
Spring Hill Ln

Glenmoor Dr
Husted Dr
3500
Spring Hill Ct

Bethesda National
Naval Medical Center

Spring Valley Rd

Inverness Dr
Kenilworth Dr
Kensington Pkwy
Montgomery Ave
Clifford Ave
Inverness Dr
Hutch Pl
Brierly Rd

9000

Woodlawn Rd
Montrose Dr
3700
Kenilworth Dr
Dundee Dr

Susanna Ln

University Rd
South Palmer Rd
Hawkins Ln
Parsons Rd
Montrose Driveway
Stewart Dr
Clifford Ave

Walnut Hill Rd
Allmont Ln

Jones Bridge Rd
Platt Ridge Rd

3500
Jones Bridge Ct

24

B

22

Manor Rd
Lynwood Pl
Loughborough Pl
Laird Pl
Longfellow Pl
Manor Rd
Preston Rd

Preston Pl

Coquelin Ter
Springdell Pl
Woodbrook Ln
Coquelin Pkwy
W Coquelin Ter

8500

Columbia
Country Club

Newdale Rd
Chevy Chase Lake Dr
Hamlet Pl
3500
Farmington Ct
Farmington Dr

Jones Mill Rd
Twin Ln

Chestnut St
Rosedale Ave

Newdale Rd
Kerry Rd
Cardiff Rd
3700
Kerry Rd
8300

Brooklawn Ln

Cardiff Ct
Cypress Pl
Cardiff Ct
Kerry Ln
Glenglen Ln

Brooklawn Ter
3200
Brooklawn Ct
Pauline Dr

C

Lynbrook Dr
Kentbury Dr
Edgevale St
Edgevale Ct
3600
Glendale Rd
Kerry Ln
Shirley Ln
Rossdhu Ct

Kentbury Way
Dunlop St
Cypress St

3400
Woodbine St

Sleaford Rd
Sleaford Rd
Blackthorn St
Chatham Rd
Blackthorn St
Aspen St
Aspen St
Club Dr
East West Hwy
3500
Blackthorn Ct Curtis Ct

Woolsey Dr
Rocton Ct
Rocton Ave

Beach Dr

Brookville Rd

Rolling Rd
3200

Lynn Dr
Maple Ave
Leland St
7400
Leland Ct
28
Alden Ln

Windsor Pl
Rolling Ct
Pickwick Ln
Vale St
Greenvale Rd
Leland

Spen
Meadowbrook La

| 1/4 mile | .25 km |

Ironically, there's few spaces to spend your money in exceedingly wealthy Chevy Chase, Maryland. Was it careful saving that landed these folks in million-dollar homes? Food for thought, but don't bring it up at the country club. Just soak in the WASP-y beauty of your brick colonial and white picket fence.

Coffee
• **Starbucks** • 8542 Connecticut Ave

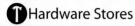Hardware Stores
• **Thomas W Perry** • 8519 Connecticut Ave

Restaurants
• **Tavira** • 8401 Connecticut Ave

Map 24 • Uppe

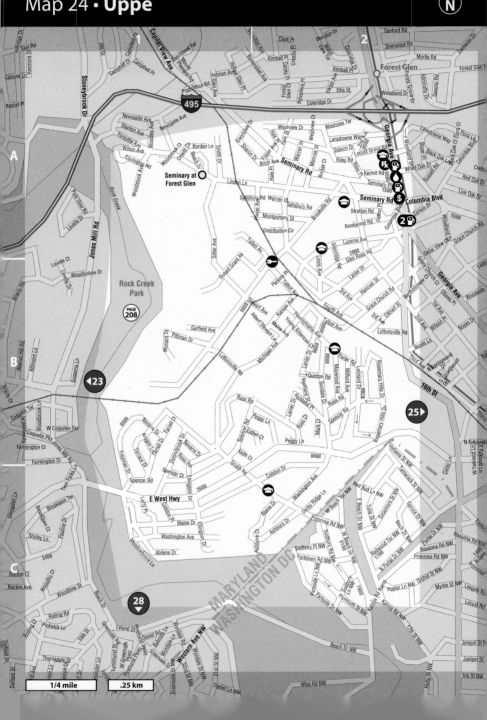

If you ever follow Rock Creek Park to its northern end, you'll stumble upon a quiet sanctuary of beautiful homes, seemingly far away from the gritty city. Sandwiched between the Beltway and the District line, between Chevy Chase and Silver Spring, life here is green and lovely. The Forest Glen Seminary's architecturally eclectic buildings are a must-see, however, even if you don't call this hilly neighborhood home.

$ Banks

· **Citibank** · 9400 Georgia Ave

Car Rental

· **Enterprise** · 9151 Brookville Rd · 301-565-4000

Car Washes

· **Montgomery Hills Car Wash** · 9500 Georgia Ave

Gas Stations

· **Chevron** · 9475 Georgia Ave
· **Exxon** · 9331 Georgia Ave
· **Exxon** · 9336 Georgia Ave
· **Shell** · 9510 Georgia Ave

o Landmarks

· **Seminary at Forest Glen** · Linden Ln & Beach Dr

Rx Pharmacies

· **CVS** · 9520 Georgia Ave

Schools

· **Calvary Lutheran** · 9545 Georgia Ave
· **Rock Creek Forest Elementary** · 8330 Grubb Rd
· **Rosemary Hills Elementary** · 2111 Porter Rd
· **Woodlin Elementary** · 2101 Luzerne Ave
· **Yeshiva of Greater Washington** · 2010 Linden Ln

Map 24 · **Upper Rock Creek Park**

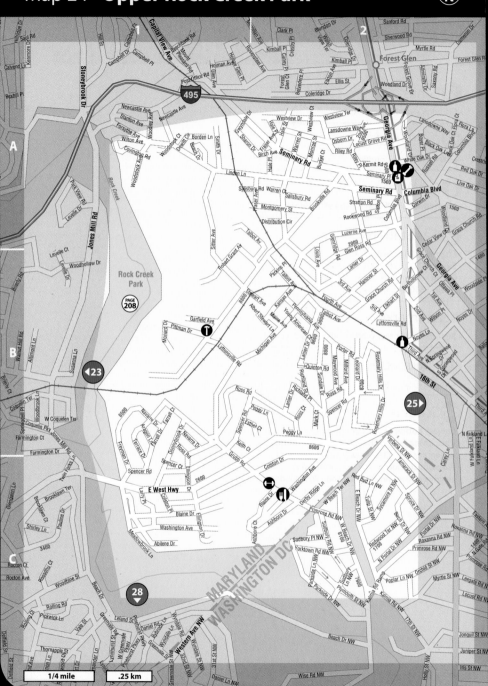

Despite its primarily residential make-up, this area crossing the DC–MD border has a few precious restaurants. Parkway Deli is a local treasure of king-size whitefish salad sandwiches and hot potato knishes.

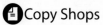Copy Shops
• **Staples** • 9440 Georgia Ave

Gyms
• **Rock Creek Sport Club** • 8325 Grubb Rd

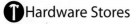Hardware Stores
• **Zimmerman Supply** • 8860 Brookville Rd

Liquor Stores
• **Seminary Beer Wine & Deli** • 9458 Georgia Ave
• **Spring Beer & Wine** • 8645 16th St

Pet Shops
• **Tropical Lagoon Acquarium** • 9439 Georgia Ave

Restaurants
• **Parkway Deli** • Rock Creek Shopping Ctr • 8317 Grubb Rd
• **redDog Café** • 8301A Grubb Rd

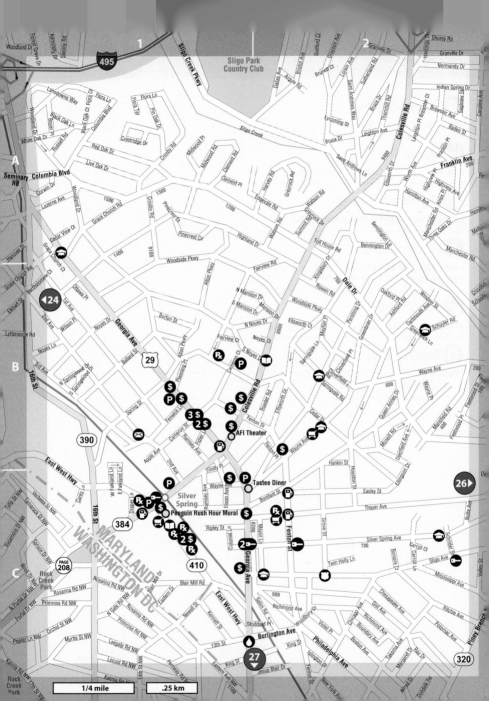

Bordering the District and with good public transportation links (Ride-On, Metrobus, Metro, and MARC), Silver Spring is an older suburb that has seen its share of hard times. Following its "Silver Sprung" redevelopment though, downtown got a chain facelift, in the form of Red Lobster and Whole Foods. But the neighborhood does boast an ethnically diverse population, and a number of restaurants still reflect this.

$ Banks

- **Adams National** · 8121 Georgia Ave
- **Bank of America** · 8511 Georgia Ave
- **Bank of America** · 8788 Georgia Ave
- **BB&T** · 1100 Wayne Ave
- **Chevy Chase** · 8315 Georgia Ave
- **Chevy Chase** · 8676 Georgia Ave
- **Chevy Chase (ATM)** · Giant Food Store · 1280 East West Hwy
- **Chevy Chase (ATM)** · 8400 Colesville Rd
- **Eagle** · 8665 Georgia Ave
- **M&T** · 8737 Colesville Rd
- **PNC** · 8661 Colesville Rd
- **Provident** · 8730 Georgia Ave
- **Sandy Spring** · 8677 Georgia Ave
- **Sun Trust** · 1286 East West Hwy
- **Sun Trust** · 8700 Georgia Ave
- **United** · 8630 Fenton St
- **Wachovia** · 8701 Georgia Ave

Car Rental

- **Bargain Rent A Car** · 904 Silver Spring Ave · 301-588-9788
- **Budget** · 619 Sligo Ave · 240-646-7171
- **Enterprise** · 8208 Georgia Ave · 301-563-6500
- **Enterprise** · 8401 Colesville Rd · 301-495-4120
- **Hertz** · 8203 Georgia Ave · 301-588-0608

Car Washes

- **Mr Wash** · 7996 Georgia Ave

Gas Stations

- **Citgo** · 8333 Fenton St
- **Exxon** · 8301 Fenton St
- **Exxon** · 8384 Colesville Rd
- **Texaco** · 8600 Georgia Ave

Landmarks

- **AFI Silver Theatre** · 8633 Colesville Rd
- **Penguin Rush Hour Mural** · 8400 Colesville Rd
- **Tastee Diner** · 8601 Cameron St

Libraries

- **NOAA Central Library** · 1315 East West Hwy
- **Silver Spring Library** · 8901 Colesville Rd

P Parking

Rx Pharmacies

- **CVS** · 1290 East West Hwy
- **Giant Food Pharmacy** · 1280 East West Hwy
- **Rite Aid** · 1411 East West Hwy
- **Safeway** · 909 Thayer Ave
- **Service Care Pharmacy** · 1111 Spring St

Police

- **3rd District - Silver Spring** · 801 Sligo Ave

Post Offices

- **Silver Spring Finance Centre** · 8455 Colesville Rd

Schools

- **Chelsea** · 711 Pershing Dr
- **East Silver Spring Elementary** · 631 Silver Spring Ave
- **Grace Episcopal Day** · 9115 Georgia Ave
- **The Nora** · 955 Sligo Ave
- **Sligo Creek Elementary** · 500 Schuyler Rd
- **St Michael's Elementary** · 824 Wayne Ave

Supermarkets

- **Giant** · 1280 East West Hwy
- **Safeway** · 909 Thayer Ave
- **Whole Foods Market** · 833 Wayne Ave

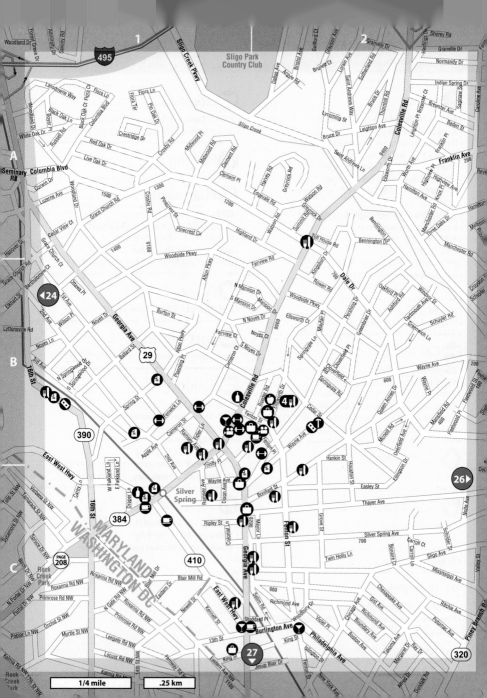

Movie buffs rejoice! Playing obscure indie flicks and timeless gems, the American Film Institute Theater is the reason to visit Silver Spring. Not to mention the number of high-calibre eateries! Outside the main strip, Roger Miller Restaurant is a West African gem and Mandalay serves tasty Burmese fare. Quarry House is your amazing hole-in-the-wall dive—don't miss it.

Map

Coffee

- **Caribou Coffee** · 1316 East West Hwy
- **Mayorga** · 8040 Georgia Ave
- **Starbucks** · 8399 Colesville Rd
- **Starbucks** · 915 Ellsworth Dr

Copy Shops

- **ABC Imaging** · 1300 Spring St
- **Benoit Printing & Graphic Designs** · 8401 Colesville Rd, Ste 140
- **Digiprint Connection** · 962 Wayne Ave
- **FedEx Kinko's** · 1407 East West Hwy
- **Minuteman Press** · 8604 2nd Ave
- **Office Depot** · 8501 Georgia Ave
- **UPS Store** · 8639 16th St

Farmers Markets

- **Silver Spring Farmer's Market (Apr–Nov; Sat, 9 am–1 pm)** · Ellsworth Dr b/w Fenton St & Cedar St

Gyms

- **Curves (women only)** · 1320 Fenwick Ln
- **Gold's Gym** · 8661 Colesville Rd
- **LA Fitness Sports Club** · 8616 Cameron St
- **Washington Sports Clubs** · 901 Wayne Ave

Hardware Stores

- **Strosniders Hardware Store** · 815 Wayne Ave

Liquor Stores

- **Lenox Beer & Wine** · 1400 East West Hwy
- **Silver Spring Liquor Store** · 8715 Colesville Rd

Movie Theaters

- **AFI Silver Theatre** · 8633 Colesville Rd
- **The Majestic 20** · 900 Ellsworth Dr

Nightlife

- **Galaxy Billiards** · 8661 Colesville Rd
- **Mayorga** · 8040 Georgia Ave
- **Piratz Tavern** · 8402 Georgia Ave
- **Quarry House Tavern** · 8401 Georgia Ave

Restaurants

- **8407 Kitchen and Bar** · 8407 Ramsey Ave
- **Addis Ababa** · 8233 Fenton St
- **Austin Grill** · 919 Ellsworth Dr
- **Ceviche** · 921 Ellsworth Dr
- **Cubano's** · 1201 Fidler Ln
- **Eggspectation** · 923 Ellsworth Dr
- **El Aguila** · 8649 16th St
- **Fractured Prune** · 8512 Fenton St
- **Gallery** · 1115 E West Hwy
- **Jackies** · 8081 Georgia Ave
- **Lebanese Taverna** · 933 Ellsworth Dr
- **Mandalay** · 930 Bonifant St, #932
- **Mi Rancho** · 8701 Ramsey Ave
- **Mrs. K's Toll House** · 9201 Colesville Rd
- **Nicaro** · 8229 Georgia Ave
- **Ray's The Classics** · 8606 Colesville Rd
- **Roger Miller Restaurant** · 941 Bonifant St
- **Romano's Macaroni Grill** · 931 Ellsworth Dr
- **A Taste of Jerusalem** · 8123 Georgia Ave

Shopping

- **ArtSpring** · 8519 Georgia Ave
- **CakeLove** · 935 Ellsworth Dr
- **Color Me Mine** · 823 Ellsworth Dr
- **Dale Music** · 8240 Georgia Ave

Video Rental

- **Blockbuster** · 8601 16th St
- **Hollywood Video** · 825 Wayne Ave

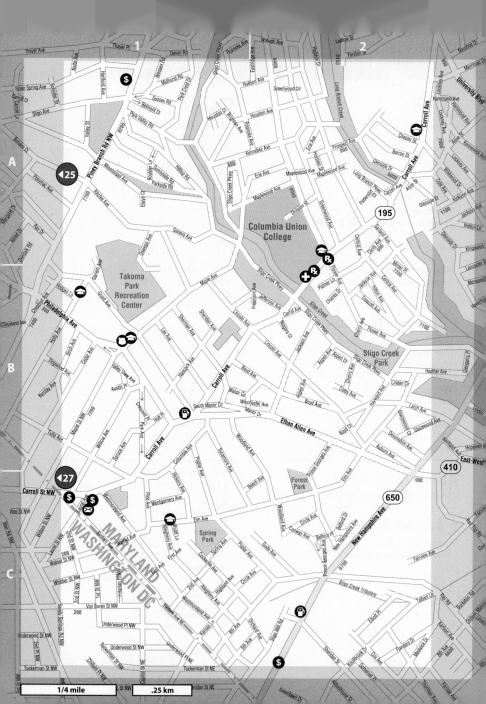

The surfeit of aging activists, neo-hippies, and left-leaning yuppies has earned this town the nickname "The People's Republic of Takoma Park." Proletariat they are not, however. Residents enjoy all the benefits of suburban living: big houses, fancy lattes, good video stores. But don't get too cynical—Takoma Park is fiercely loyal to local business and has successfully resisted development and corporate "revitalization."

Banks

- **Bank of America** · 6950 Carroll Ave
- **Sandy Spring (ATM)** · Texaco · 6400 New Hampshire Ave
- **Sun Trust** · 6931 Laurel Ave

Emergency Rooms

- **Washington Adventist Hospital** · The Professional Building · 7610 Carroll Ave

Gas Stations

- **Citgo** · 7224 Carroll Ave
- **Shell** · 6201 New Hampshire Ave NE

Pharmacies

- **Washington Adventist Family Pharmacy** · 7600 Carroll Ave

Police

- **Takoma Park Police Dept** · 7500 Maple Ave

Post Offices

- **Takoma Park** · 6909 Laurel Ave

Schools

- **Columbia Union College** · 7600 Flower Ave
- **John Nevins Andrews** · 117 Elm Ave
- **Piney Branch Elementary** · 7510 Maple Ave
- **Takoma Academy** · 8120 Carroll Ave
- **Takoma Park Elementary** · 7511 Holly Ave

Map 26 • **Takoma Park**

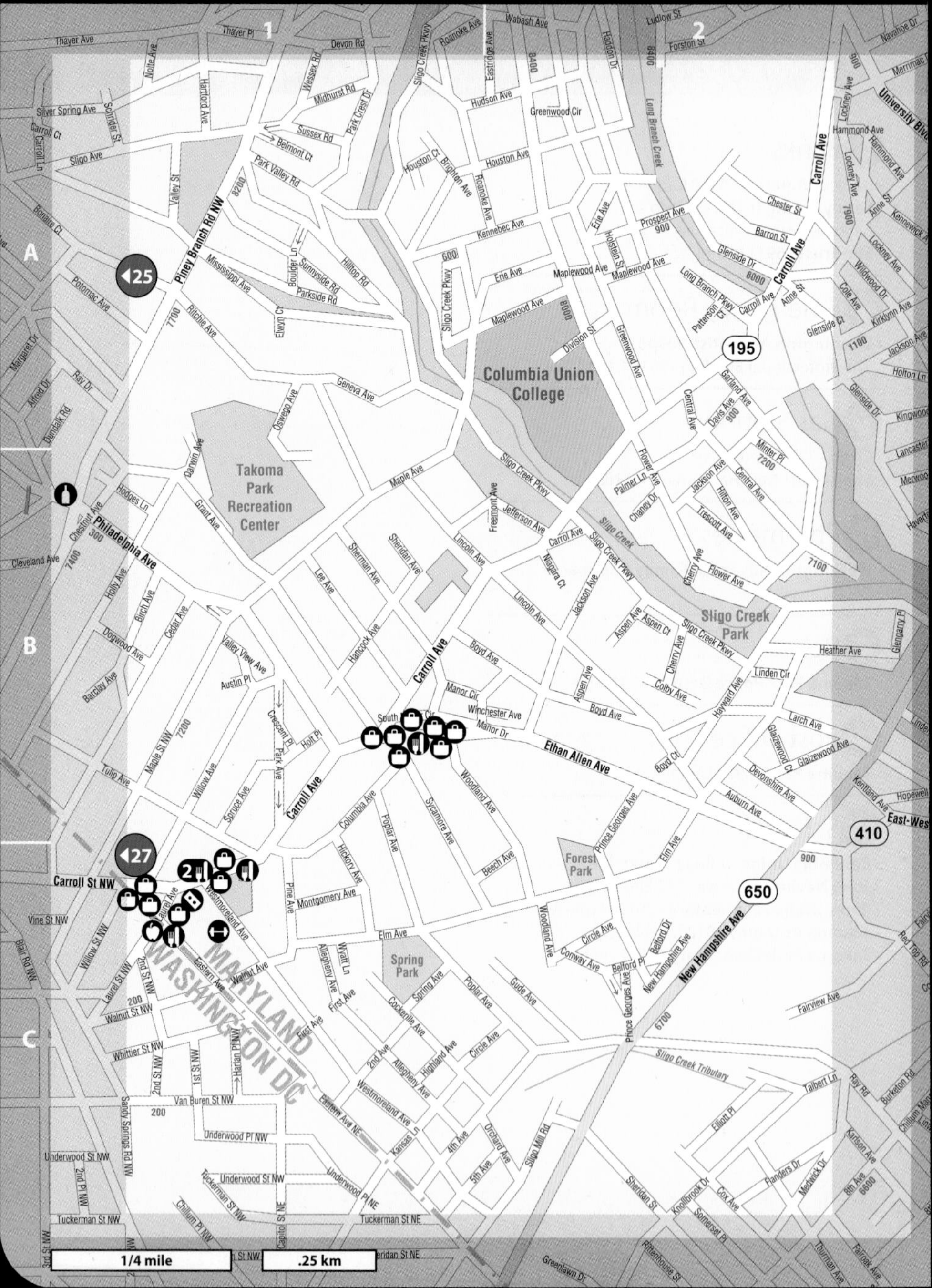

N

1

2

Thayer Ave

Thayer Pl

Devon Rd

Wabash Ave

Ludlow St

Silver Spring Ave

Sussex Rd

Midhurst Rd

Park Crest Dr

Sligo Creek Pkwy

Roanoke Ave

Eastridge Ave

Hodges Dr

Forston St

Nolte Ave

Hartford Ave

Carroll Ct

Sligo Ave

Schroder St

Carroll Ln

Romana Ct

Belmont Rd

Hudson Ave

Greenwood Cir

Houston Ct

Brighten Ave

Houston Ave

Chester St

Barron St

Mississippi Ave

Pine Crest Ct

Prospect Ave
900

Long Branch Pkwy

Carroll Ave
7900

Lockney Ave

University Blvd

Nashua Ct

Merrimac

Kennewick

Hammond Ave

Wildwood Dr

A

⬤25

Piney Branch Rd NW

Ritchie Ave

Kennebec Ave

Erie Ave

Maplewood Ave

Maplewood Ave

Glenside Dr

Carroll Ave
8000

Aztec Dr

Glenside Ct

Kinbarn Ave

Jackson Ave

Lancaster

Medora

Geneva Ave

Conway Ave

Elwyn

Parkside Rd

Sundale Rd

Hilltop Rd

Erie Ave

Maplewood Ave

Division St

Greenwood Ave

(195)

Central Ave

Davis Ave
900

Minter Pl
7200

Kinbarn Ave

Kingwood

Holton Ln

Columbia Union College

Maple Ave

Sligo Creek Pkwy

Palmer Ln

Jackson Ave

Central Ave

Trescott Ave

Carroll Ave
7100

Takoma Park Recreation Center

Philadelphia Ave
7400

Cleveland Ave

Crescent Pl
300

Hodges Ln

Grant Ave

Sheridan Ave

Jefferson Ave

Freemont Ave

Carroll Ave

Niagara Ct

Chaney Dr

Flower Ave

Sligo Creek

Sligo Creek Park

Heather Ave

B

Birch Ave

Cedar Ave

Valley View Ave

Austin Pl

Lee Ave

Sherman Ave

Lincoln Ave

Aspen Ave

Aspen Ct

Cherry Ave

Howard Ave

Linden Cir

Dogwood Ave

Barclay Ave

Maple St NW
7200

Willow Ave

Sequoia Ave

Holt Ave

Hancock Ave

Carroll Ave

Boyd Ave

Boyd Ave

Colby Ave

Larch Ave

Devonshire Ave

Glazewood Ave

Larch Ave

Tulip Ave

Manor Cir

Winchester Ave

Manor Dr

Boyd Ct

Auburn Ave

⬤ South ⬤⬤⬤ Dr ⬤⬤⬤⬤⬤

Ethan Allen Ave

Prince Georges Ave

Elm Ave

East-West

⬤27

Carroll St NW

⬤2⬤ ⬤

⬤ ⬤⬤

⬤⬤

Vine St NW

Willow St NW

Pine Ave

Columbia Ave

Hickory Ave

Poplar Ave

Sycamore Ave

Woodland Ave

Beech Ave

Forest Park

Woodland Ave

(410)
900

(650)

New Hampshire Ave

Carroll St NW

Montgomery Ave

Elm Ave

Alleghany Ave

Circle Ave

Gude Ave

Conway Ave

Belford Dr

Kennard

Hopewell

Fairview Ave

Blair Rd NW

Laurel St NW

3rd St NW

Hammond Ave

Maple Ave

Wyatt Ln

Spring Park

Spring Ave

Poplar Ave

Circle Ave

MARYLAND

WASHINGTON DC

Walnut St NW
200

Cockerille Ave

First Ave

Prince Georges Ave
6700

Sligo Mill Rd

Red Top Rd

C

Whittier St NW

4th St NW

1st St NW

2nd St NW

Hilton St

2nd Ave

Alleghany Ave

Westmoreland Ave

Circle Ave

Sligo Creek Tributary

Talbert Ln

Van Buren St NW

Elliott Pl

Briarton Rd

Sandy Springs Rd NW
200

Beechwood Ave NE

4th Ave

Orchard Ave

Sheridan Ave

Flanders Dr

Kennard Dr

Madock Dr

Underwood St NW

2nd Pl NW

Underwood Pl NW

Underwood St NE

5th Ave

Cox Rd

Boswell Rd

Oglethorpe St NW

1/4 mile

.25 km

Tuckerman St NW

4th St NW

Chillum Rd NE

Sheridan St NE

Tuckerman St NE

Greenlawn Dr

Somerset St NE

Flanders Dr

If you're into organic markets, fair-trade tchotchkes, and vintage clothing, by all means, go downtown and check out the mom-and-pop stores on Carroll Avenue. But aside from a few watering holes, most of the action is going on in living rooms, not bars.

Farmers Markets
· **Takoma Park Farmers Market**
  (Sun, 10 am-2 pm) · Laurel Ave & Eastern Ave

Gyms
· **Curves (women only)** · 7008 Westmoreland Ave

Liquor Stores
· **Piney Branch Beer & Wine** · 8204 Piney Branch Rd

Restaurants
· **Capital City Cheesecake** · 7071 Carroll Ave
· **Mark's Kitchen** · 7006 Carroll Ave
· **Olive Lounge** · 7006 Carroll Ave
· **Roscoe's Pizzeria** · 7040 Carroll Ave
· **Summer Delights** · 6939 Laurel Ave

Shopping
· **AMANO** · 7034 Carroll Ave
· **Artful Framing and Gallery** · 7050 Carroll Ave
· **The Covered Market** · 7000 Carroll Ave
· **Fair Day's Play** · 7050 Carroll Ave
· **House of Musical Traditions** ·
  7040 Westmoreland Ave
· **Moonshadow Antiques and Collectibles** ·
  7000 Carroll Ave
· **The Pajama Squid** · 7320 Carroll Ave
· **Polly Sue's** · 6915 Laurel Ave
· **S&A Beads** · 6929 Laurel Ave
· **The Still Point** · 7009 Carroll Ave
· **Takoma Park Silver Spring Co-op** ·
  201 Ethan Allen Ave
· **The Tranquil Soul** · 7014 Westmoreland Ave
· **Video Americain** · 6937 Laurel Ave

Video Rental
· **Video Americain** · 6937 Laurel Ave

Essentials

22	23	24	25
29	28		27

26

Map 27

30 | 19 | 20 | 21 | 14
32 | 18 | 17 16 15
8 9 10 11

Until the Walter Reed Army Medical Center moves away and becomes land for condos, the neighborhood will continue to cater to military families and veterans who use its services. The well-fortified grounds are the neighborhood's diamond in the rough, and a number of ethnically diverse businesses contribute to the unique atmosphere.

Banks

- **Chevy Chase (ATM)** · 7600 Takoma Ave
- **Citibank (ATM)** · 7-Eleven · 218 Cedar St NW
- **Independence Federal Savings** ·
  7901 Eastern Ave
- **M&T** · 6434 Georgia Ave NW
- **PNC** · 7601 Georgia Ave NW
- **Sun Trust** · 6422 Georgia Ave NW

Car Washes

- **Mr Gee's Car Wash** · 6315 Georgia Ave NW

Community Gardens

Gas Stations

- **Amoco** · 6300 Georgia Ave NW
- **Amoco** · 6401 Georgia Ave NW
- **Amoco** · 7000 Blair Rd NW
- **Amoco** · 7605 Georgia Ave NW
- **Exxon** · 6350 Georgia Ave NW
- **Exxon** · 7401 Georgia Ave NW
- **Shell** · 6419 Georgia Ave NW

Landmarks

- **Battleground National Military Cemetery** ·
  6625 Georgia Ave NW
- **Walter Reed Army Medical Center** ·
  6900 Georgia Ave NW

Libraries

- **Juanita E Thornton Library** ·
  7420 Georgia Ave NW
- **Takoma Park Neighborhood Library** ·
  416 Cedar St NW

Parking

Pharmacies

- **CVS** · 110 Carroll Ave NW
- **CVS** · 6514 Georgia Ave NW
- **Medicine Shoppe** · 7814 Eastern Ave NW
- **Phamily CARE Pharmacy** · 6323 Georgia Ave NW
- **Safeway** · 6500 Piney Branch Rd NW

Police

- **MPDC 4th District Station** · 6001 Georgia Ave NW

Post Offices

- **Brightwood** · 6323 Georgia Ave NW
- **Walter Reed Finance Station** ·
  6800 Georgia Ave NW

Schools

- **A-T Seban Mesut** · 5924 Georgia Ave NW
- **Academia de la Recta Porta** · 7614 Georgia Ave NW
- **The Bridges Academy** · 6119 Georgia Ave NW
- **Coolidge High** · 6315 5th St NW
- **Jewish Primary Day School of the
  Nation's Capital** · 6045 16th St NW
- **Lowell** · 1640 Kalmia Rd NW
- **Mary McLeod Bethune Day Academy Public
  Charter School** · 7600 Georgia Ave NW
- **Montgomery College (Takoma Park Campus)** ·
  7600 Takoma Ave
- **Nativity Catholic Academy** · 6008 Georgia Ave NW
- **Owl** · 6045 16th St NW
- **Shepherd Elementary** · 7800 14th St NW
- **Strayer University (Takoma Park Campus)** ·
  6830 Laurel St NW
- **Takoma** · 7010 Piney Branch Rd NW
- **Takoma Park Middle** · 7611 Piney Branch Rd
- **Washington Theological Union** ·
  6896 Laurel St NW
- **Whittier Elementary** · 6201 5th St NW

Supermarkets

- **Safeway** · 6500 Piney Branch Rd NW

Map 27 · **Walter Reed**

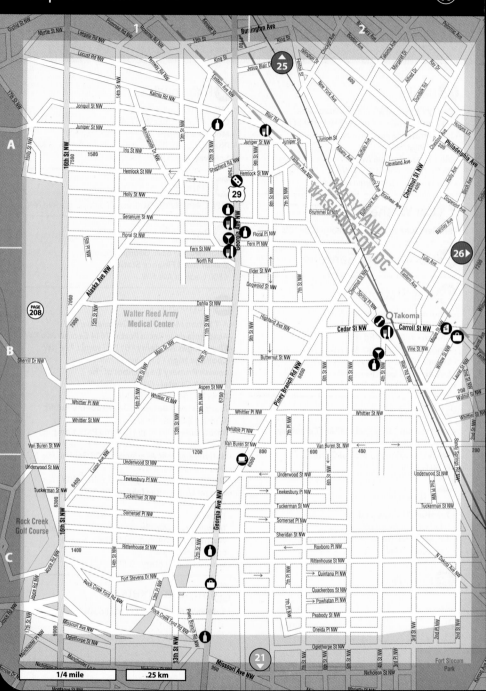

The major road cutting through this settled neighborhood (16th Street) is an ideal route for travelers heading downtown from the Beltway. But try to keep the radio volume low. The families who live here like to keep things nice and quiet. Looking for action? Head east to Georgia Avenue for booze, foodstuffs, and loiterers.

Coffee
- **Starbucks** · 6500 Piney Branch Rd NW

Copy Shops
- **Community Printing** · 6979 Maple St NW

Liquor Stores
- **Brightwood Liquor Store** · 5916 Georgia Ave NW
- **Cork'n Bottle Liquors** · 7421 Georgia Ave NW
- **Mayfair Liquor** · 7312 Georgia Ave NW
- **Morris Miller Liquors** · 7804 Alaska Ave NW
- **S&S Liquors** · 6925 4th St NW
- **Victor Liquors** · 6220 Georgia Ave NW

Nightlife
- **Charlie's Bar & Grill** · 7307 Georgia Ave NW
- **Takoma Station Tavern** · 6914 4th St NW

Pet Shops
- **The Big Bad Woof** · 117 Carroll St NW

Restaurants
- **Blair Mansion Inn/Murder Mystery Dinner Theatre** · 7711 Eastern Ave
- **Cedar Crossing Tavern** · 341 Cedar St NW
- **El Tamarindo** · 7331 Georgia Ave NW
- **Teddy's Roti Shop** · 7304 Georgia Ave NW

Shopping
- **Everyday Gourmet** · 6923 Carroll Ave
- **Georgia Avenue Super Thrift** · 6101 Georgia Ave NW

Video Rental
- **Royce's** · 7445 Georgia Ave NW

Map 28 · **Chevy Chase**

This obscenely wealthy pocket of upper NW and suburban Maryland is green, well cared for, and lily white. If you are nostalgic for Normal Rockwell's America and never want to rub shoulders with someone who makes less than six figures (except perhaps on the cross-town E buses), this is the neighborhood for you.

Banks
- **Chevy Chase** • 5714 Connecticut Ave NW
- **Citibank** • 5700 Connecticut Ave NW
- **M&T** • 5630 Connecticut Ave NW
- **PNC** • 5530 Connecticut Ave NW
- **Wachovia** • 5701 Connecticut Ave NW

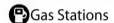Community Gardens

Gas Stations
- **Exxon** • 5521 Connecticut Ave NW

Landmarks
- **Avalon Theatre** • 5612 Connecticut Ave NW

Libraries
- **Chevy Chase Library** • 5625 Connecticut Ave NW

Pharmacies
- **Brookville CARE Pharmacy** • 7025 Brookville Rd
- **Chevy Chase Pharmacy** •
  3812 Northampton St NW
- **CVS** • 5550 Connecticut Ave NW
- **Safeway** • 5545 Connecticut Ave NW

Police
- **Chevy Chase Village Police** •
  5906 Connecticut Ave NW

Post Offices
- **Chevy Chase** • 5910 Connecticut Ave NW
- **Northwest** • 5636 Connecticut Ave NW

Schools
- **Blessed Sacrament Elementary** •
  5841 Chevy Chase Pkwy NW
- **Chevy Chase Elementary** • 4015 Rosemary St
- **Episcopal Center for Children** •
  5901 Utah Ave NW
- **Lafayette Elementary** • 5701 Broad Branch Rd NW
- **St John's College High** • 2607 Military Rd NW

Supermarkets
- **Magruder's** • 5626 Connecticut Ave NW
- **Safeway** • 5545 Connecticut Ave NW

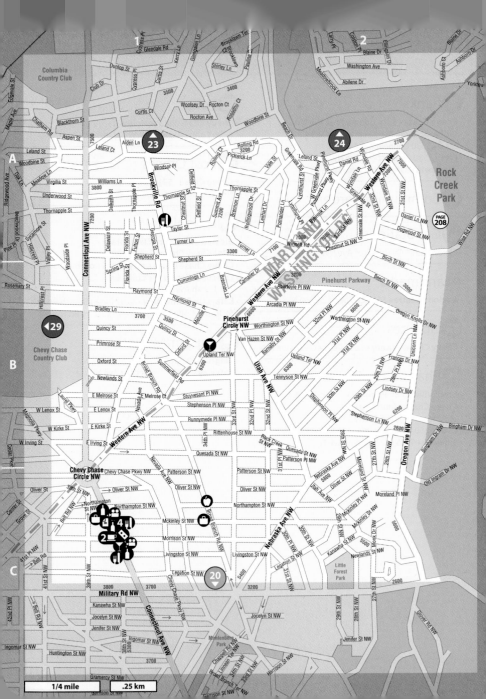

The retail strip along Connecticut in DC Chevy Chase boasts fantastic liquor stores, cute cafés, and the treasured Avalon Theatre. North of the border, Martin's Additions offers an independent grocer, pharmacy, and fancy French inn, La Ferme.

Coffee

- **Bread & Chocolate** · 5542 Connecticut Ave NW
- **Starbucks** · 5500 Connecticut Ave NW

Copy Shops

- **UPS Store** · 5505 Connecticut Ave NW

Farmers Markets

- **Chevy Chase Farmer's Market (Apr–Nov; Sat, 9 am–1 pm)** · Broad Branch Rd NW & Northampton St NW

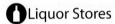Liquor Stores

- **Chevy Chase Wine & Spirits** · 5544 Connecticut Ave NW
- **Circle Liquors of Chevy Chase** · 5501 Connecticut Ave NW
- **Magruder's** · 5626 Connecticut Ave NW

Movie Theaters

- **American City Diner & Cinema Cafe** · 5532 Connecticut Ave NW
- **Avalon Theatre** · 5612 Connecticut Ave NW

Nightlife

- **Chevy Chase Lounge** · 5510 Connecticut Ave NW
The Tasting Room 5330 Western Ave

Restaurants

- **American City Diner** · 5532 Connecticut Ave NW
- **Arucola** · 5534 Connecticut Ave NW
- **Bread & Chocolate** · 5542 Connecticut Ave NW
- **La Ferme** · 7101 Brookville Rd
- **Pumpernickel's Bagelry & Delicatessen** · 5504 Connecticut Ave NW
- **Senor Pepper** · 5507 Connecticut Ave NW

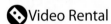Shopping

Broad Branch Market 5608 Broad Branch Rd NW
- **Chevy Chase Wine & Spirits** · 5544 Connecticut Ave NW

Video Rental

- **Potomac Video** · 5536 Connecticut Ave NW

Map 29 · **Bethesda (South)**

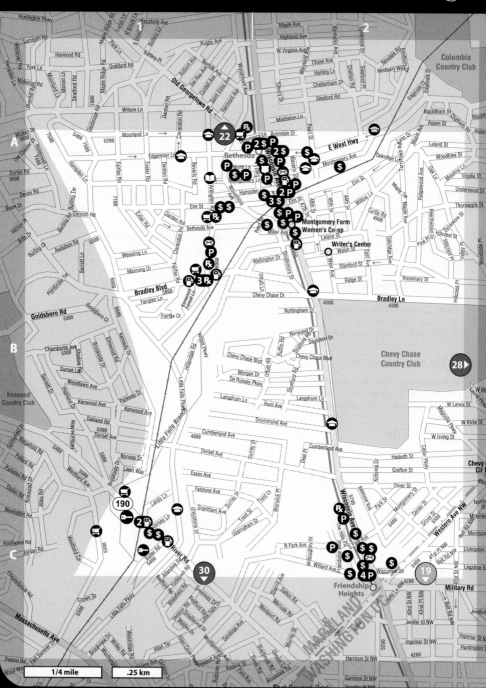

Essentials

Map 29

They may not let you into their country club, but if you have a credit card they'll let you in their stores. This area of Bethesda along Wisconsin Avenue is primarily populated by well-to-do families. It's safe and pretty, if a bit vanilla. Easy to mock, but they'll hear the twinge of jealousy in your voice.

$ Banks

- **Bank of America** · 4411 S Park Ave
- **Bank of America** · 5135 River Rd
- **Bank of America** · 7316 Wisconsin Ave
- **BB&T** · 7220 Wisconsin Ave
- **Chevy Chase** · 4708 Bethesda Ave
- **Chevy Chase** · 5459 Wisconsin Ave
- **Chevy Chase** · 5476 Wisconsin Ave
- **Chevy Chase** · 7501 Wisconsin Ave
- **Chevy Chase (ATM)** · Giant Food Store · 7142 Arlington Rd
- **Chevy Chase (ATM)** · 7450 Wisconsin Ave
- **Chevy Chase (ATM)** · Clark Building · 7500 Old Georgetown Rd
- **Citibank (ATM)** · 7-Eleven · 5114 River Rd
- **Eagle** · 15 Wisconsin Cir
- **HSBC** · 7315 Wisconsin Ave
- **Independence Federal Savings** · 5530 Wisconsin Ave
- **M&T** · 4800 Hampden Ln
- **Mellon** · 2 Bethesda Metro Ctr
- **PNC** · 4424 Montgomery Ave
- **PNC** · 7235 Wisconsin Ave
- **PNC (ATM)** · 7255 Woodmont Ave
- **Presidential Savings** · 4520 East West Hwy
- **Provident** · 5416 Wisconsin Ave
- **Sandy Spring** · 7126 Wisconsin Ave
- **Sun Trust** · 4455 Willard Ave
- **Sun Trust** · 7500 Wisconsin Ave
- **United** · 7250 Wisconsin Ave
- **United** · 7535 Old Georgetown Rd
- **Wachovia** · 4965 Elm St

Car Rental

- **Enterprise** · 5202 River Rd · 301-657-0095
- **Rent-A-Wreck** · 5455 Butler Rd · 301-654-2252

Gas Stations

- **Chevron** · 5001 Bradley Blvd
- **Citgo** · 4972 Bradley Blvd
- **Exxon** · 7100 Wisconsin Ave
- **Exxon** · 7340 Wisconsin Ave
- **Getty** · 5151 River Rd
- **Shell** · 5110 River Rd
- **Sunoco** · 5201 River Rd

Landmarks

- **Montgomery Farm Women's Co-op Market** (Wed; Sat; 7am–3pm) · 7155 Wisconsin Ave
- **Writer's Center** · 4508 Walsh St

Libraries

- **Bethesda Library** · 7400 Arlington Rd

Parking

Pharmacies

- **Bradley CARE Drugs/Braden's Pharmacy** · 6900 Arlington Rd
- **CVS** · 6917 Arlington Rd
- **Giant Food** · 7142 Arlington Rd
- **Safeway** · 5000 Bradley Blvd
- **Safeway** · 7625 Old Georgetown Rd
- **Wellcare Pharmacy** · 5530 Wisconsin Ave

Police

- **2nd District - Bethesda** · 7359 Wisconsin Ave

Post Offices

- **Bethesda** · 7400 Wisconsin Ave
- **Arlington Road** · 7001 Arlington Rd
- **Friendship Heights** · 5530 Wisconsin Ave

Schools

- **Bethesda Elementary** · 7600 Arlington Rd
- **Bethesda-Chevy Chase High** · 4301 East West Hwy
- **Concord Hill** · 6050 Wisconsin Ave
- **DeVry University** · 4550 Montgomery Ave
- **Oneness Family** · 6701 Wisconsin Ave
- **Our Lady of Lourdes** · 7500 Pearl St
- **Sidwell Friends Lower** · 5100 Edgemoor Ln
- **Washington Episcopal** · 5600 Little Falls Pkwy

Supermarkets

- **Giant Food** · 7142 Arlington Rd
- **Giant Food** · 5400 Westbard Ave
- **Safeway** · 5000 Bradley Blvd
- **Safeway** · 7625 Old Georgetown Rd
- **Whole Foods Market** · 5269 River Rd

Map 29 • **Bethesda (South)**

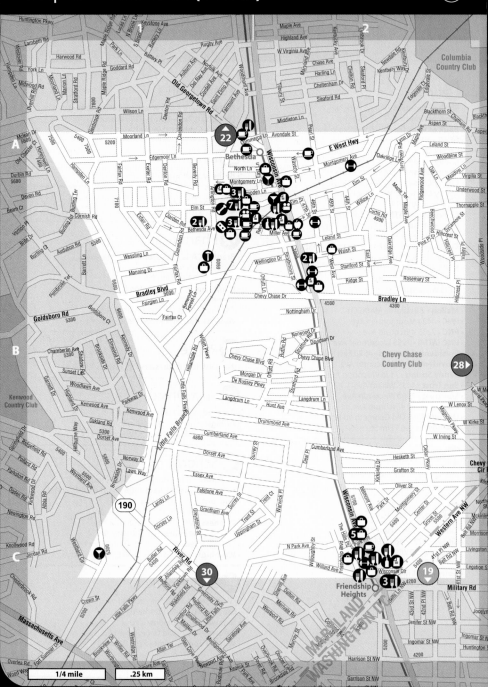

North of the Friendship Heights glitzy, high-end shopping and restaurants is a brief residential pause before entering the arts end of Bethesda. Check out the Montgomery Farm Women's Co-op Market, where you can get your handbags handmade and Turkish rugs for cheap. Head to Bethesda Crab House to shell some Maryland blue crabs and knock back some cold ones.

Coffee

- **Caribou Coffee** • 7629 Old Georgetown Rd
- **Cosi** • 7251 Woodmont Ave
- **Dunkin' Donuts** • 4810 Bethesda Ave
- **Quartermaine Coffee Roasters** • 4817 Bethesda Ave
- **Starbucks** • 4520 East West Hwy
- **Starbucks** • 5454 Wisconsin Ave
- **Starbucks** • 7140 Wisconsin Ave

Copy Shops

- **ABC Imaging** • 7315 Wisconsin Ave
- **FedEx Kinko's** • 4809 Bethesda Ave
- **Print 1 Printing & Copying** • 4710 Bethesda Ave
- **Staples** • 6800 Wisconsin Ave
- **UPS Store** • 1 Wisconsin Cir
- **UPS Store** • 4938 Hampden Ln

 Farmers Markets

- **Montgomery Farm Women's Co-op Market**
  (Wed; Sat; 7am–3pm) • 7155 Wisconsin Ave

Gyms

- **Bethesda Sport & Health Club** •
  4400 Montgomery Ave
- **Chevy Chase Athletic Club** • 5454 Wisconsin Ave
- **Curves (women only)** • 6831 Wisconsin Ave
- **Washington Sports Clubs** • 6828 Wisconsin Ave

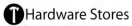 Hardware Stores

- **Strosnider's Hardware** • 6930 Arlington Rd

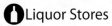 Liquor Stores

- **Bethesda-Chevy Chase & Wine LLC** •
  4701 Miller Ave
- **Chevy Chase Liquors** • 11 Wisconsin Cir

 Movie Theaters

- **Landmark Bethesda Row Cinema** •
  7235 Woodmont Ave
- **Regal Bethesda 10** • 7272 Wisconsin Ave

Nightlife

- **The Barking Dog** • 4723 Elm St
- **Strike Bethesda** • 5353 Westbard Ave
- **Tommy Joe's** • 4714 Montgomery Ln

Pet Shops

- **Bethesda Pet Shoppe** • 4919 Elm St
- **Petsmart** • 6800 Wisconsin Ave

Restaurants

- **Bethesda Crab House** • 4958 Bethesda Ave
- **Brownbag** • 7272 Wisconsin Ave
- **Clyde's of Chevy Chase** • 5441 Wisconsin Ave NW
- **Dolcezza** • 7111 Bethesda Ln
- **Gifford's** • 21 Wisconsin Cir
- **Gifford's** • 7237 Woodmont Ave
- **Green Papaya** • 4922 Elm St
- **Hinode** • 4914 Hampden Ln
- **Indique Heights** • 2 Wisconsin Cir
- **Jaleo** • 7271 Woodmont Ave
- **Levante's** • 7262 Woodmont Ave
- **Louisiana Express Company** • 4921 Bethesda Ave
- **M Café & Bar** • 5471 Wisconsin Ave
- **Moby Dick House of Kabob** • 7027 Wisconsin Ave
- **Mon Ami Gabi** • 7239 Woodmont Ave
- **Persimmon** • 7003 Wisconsin Ave
- **Potomac Pizza** • 19 Wisconsin Cir
- **Raku** • 7240 Woodmont Ave
- **Redwood** • 7121 Bethesda Ln
- **Ri-Ra Irish Restaurant Pub** • 4931 Elm St
- **Rio Grande** • 4870 Bethesda Ave
- **Rock Creek Restaurant** • 4917 Elm St
- **Sushi Ko Chevy Chase** • 5455 Wisconsin Ave
- **Sweetgreen** • 4831 Bethesda Ave
- **Tara Thai** • 4828 Bethesda Ave
- **Vace** • 4705 Miller Ave

 Shopping

- **Barney's New York Co-op** • 5471 Wisconsin Ave
- **Bethesda Tattoo Company** • 4711 Montgomery Ln
- **Brooks Brothers** • 5504 Wisconsin Ave
- **Chico's** • 5418 Wisconsin Ave
- **Luna** • 7232 Woodmont Ave
- **Mustard Seed** • 7349 Wisconsin Ave
- **Parvizian Masterpieces** • 7034 Wisconsin Ave
- **Pirjo** • 4821 Bethesda Ave
- **Saks Fifth Avenue** • 5300 Wisconsin Ave
- **Saks Jandel** • 5510 Wisconsin Ave
- **Stitch and Knit=Bliss** • 4706 Bethesda Ave
- **Strosnider's Hardware** • 6930 Arlington Rd
- **Sylene** • 4407 S Park Ave
- **Tiffany & Co** • 5481 Wisconsin Ave
- **Trader Joe's** • 6831 Wisconsin Ave
- **Writer's Center** • 4508 Walsh St

Video Rental

- **Blockbuster** • 4860 Bethesda Ave

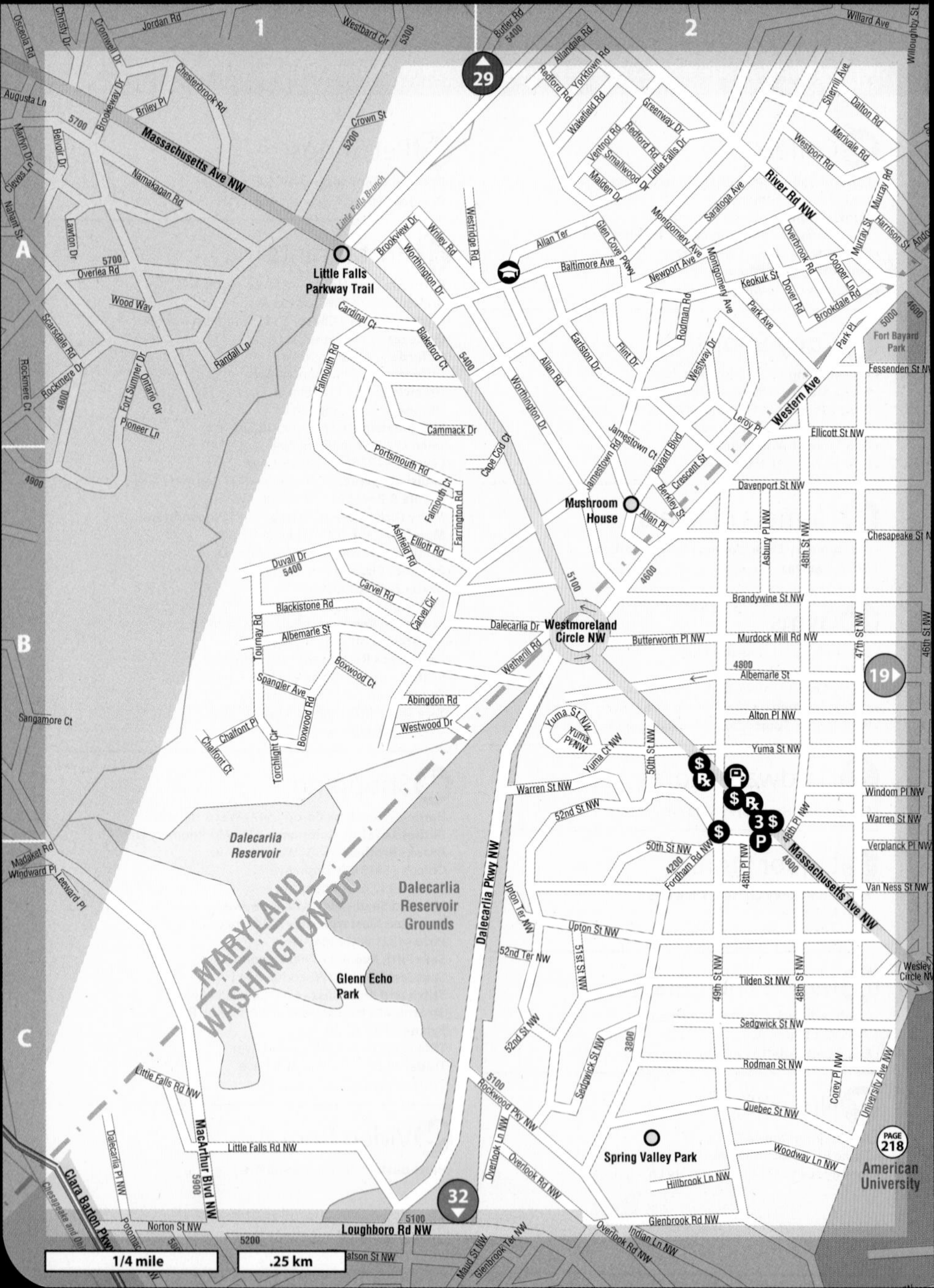

Map 30 · **Westmoreland Circle**

N

1

2

Massachusetts Ave NW

Little Falls
Parkway Trail

Mushroom
House

Westmoreland
Circle NW

Dalecarlia Dr

Dalecarlia
Reservoir

Dalecarlia
Reservoir
Grounds

Glenn Echo
Park

MARYLAND

WASHINGTON DC

River Rd NW

Western Ave

Fort Bayard
Park

Massachusetts Ave NW

Dalecarlia Pkwy NW

MacArthur Blvd NW

Clara Barton Pkwy

Spring Valley Park

Little Falls Rd NW

Loughboro Rd NW

Wesley
Circle NW

American
University

PAGE
218

29

32

19

1/4 mile

.25 km

It's hard to believe you're in a city when all that surrounds you are single-family homes with expansive green lawns and places to park your new eco-friendly vehicle. You'll find young families with portable basketball nets lining the streets, tons of flowering trees that beat fighting the crowds downtown in spring, chirping birds, and the "Mushroom House" across the city line.

Banks

- **Bank of America** · 4301 49th St NW
- **Bank of America (ATM)** ·
  4851 Massachusetts Ave NW
- **Chevy Chase** · 4860 Massachusetts Ave NW
- **PNC** · 4835 Massachusetts Ave NW
- **United** · 4900 Massachusetts Ave NW
- **Wachovia** · 4841 Massachusetts Ave NW

Gas Stations

- **Exxon** · 4861 Massachusetts Ave NW

⊙Landmarks

- **Little Falls Parkway Trail** ·
  Massachusetts Ave & Little Falls Pkwy
- **Mushroom House** · 4940 Allan Rd
- **Spring Valley Park** ·
  The area W of 49th St, E of Fordham Rd,
  S of Quebec St, N of Hillbrook Ln

PParking

RxPharmacies

- **Center CARE Pharmacy** ·
  4900 Massachusetts Ave NW
- **CVS** · 4851 Massachusetts Ave NW

Schools

- **Westbrook Elementary** · 5110 Allan Ter

Map 30 · **Westmoreland Circle**

On the Maryland side of Western Avenue there's nowhere for Bethesda residents to empty their deep pockets, save for the lone Western Market general store. In Spring Valley, locals are limited to a couple coffee shops, liquor at Wagshal's, and tartines at Le Pain Quotidien—all of it utterly gourmet. But for outdoorsy types, the Capitol Crescent Trail can be picked up in this part of town as well.

Coffee

- **Starbucks** • 4820 Massachusetts Ave NW

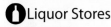Liquor Stores

- **Wagshal's Delicatessen** •
  4855 Massachusetts Ave NW

Restaurants

- **Dahlia** • 4849 Massachusetts Ave NW
- **DeCarlo's** • 4822 Yuma St NW
- **Le Pain Quotidien** • 4874 Massachusetts Ave NW

Shopping

- **Crate & Barrel** • 4820 Massachusetts Ave NW
- **Ski Center** • 4300 Fordham Rd NW
- **Spring Valley Patio** • 4300 Fordham Rd NW
- **Wagshal's Market** • 4845 Massachusetts Ave NW
- **Western Market** • 4840 Western Ave

This residential 'burb is home to senators, Supreme Court justices, and former White House spokesmen. With its large homes and spacious leafy yards, Chesterbrook is old school wealthy, with none of the crammed together McMansions found in newer parts of NoVa. If you live here, expect to drive your kids' lacrosse-team-stickered Lexus SUV elsewhere for essentials.

○Landmarks

• **Fort Marcy** • George Washington Memorial Pkwy

Schools

• **Chesterbrook Montessori** • 3455 N Glebe Rd
• **Jamestown Elementary** • 3700 N Delaware St

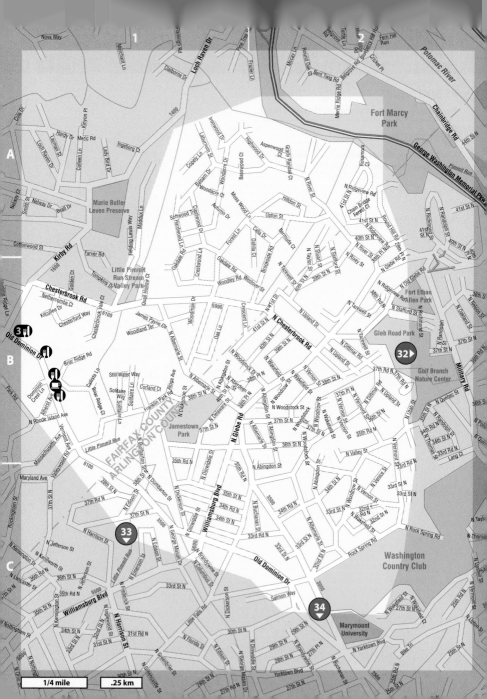

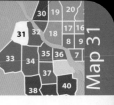
Entertainment around here consists of walking your dog, raking your yard, and checking how the neighborhood schools stacked up this year on Newsweek's list of the nation's 100 best high schools. The few restaurants nearby indicate the neighborhood's focus on residential and not business—two Chinese places and kebabs. Dominion Restaurant offers "neighborhood dining," but most Chesterbrook-ites probably seek more stars when eating out.

Coffee

• **Starbucks** • 6214 Old Dominion Dr

Restaurants

• **Amoo's House of Kabob** • 6271 Old Dominion Dr
• **Café China** • 6271 Old Dominion Dr
• **China Kingdom** • 6222 Old Dominion Dr
• **Dominion Restaurant** • 6238 Old Dominion Dr
• **Pizza Hut** • 6263 Old Dominion Dr
• **Subway** • 6216 Old Dominion Dr

Map 32 • **Cherrydale / Palisades**

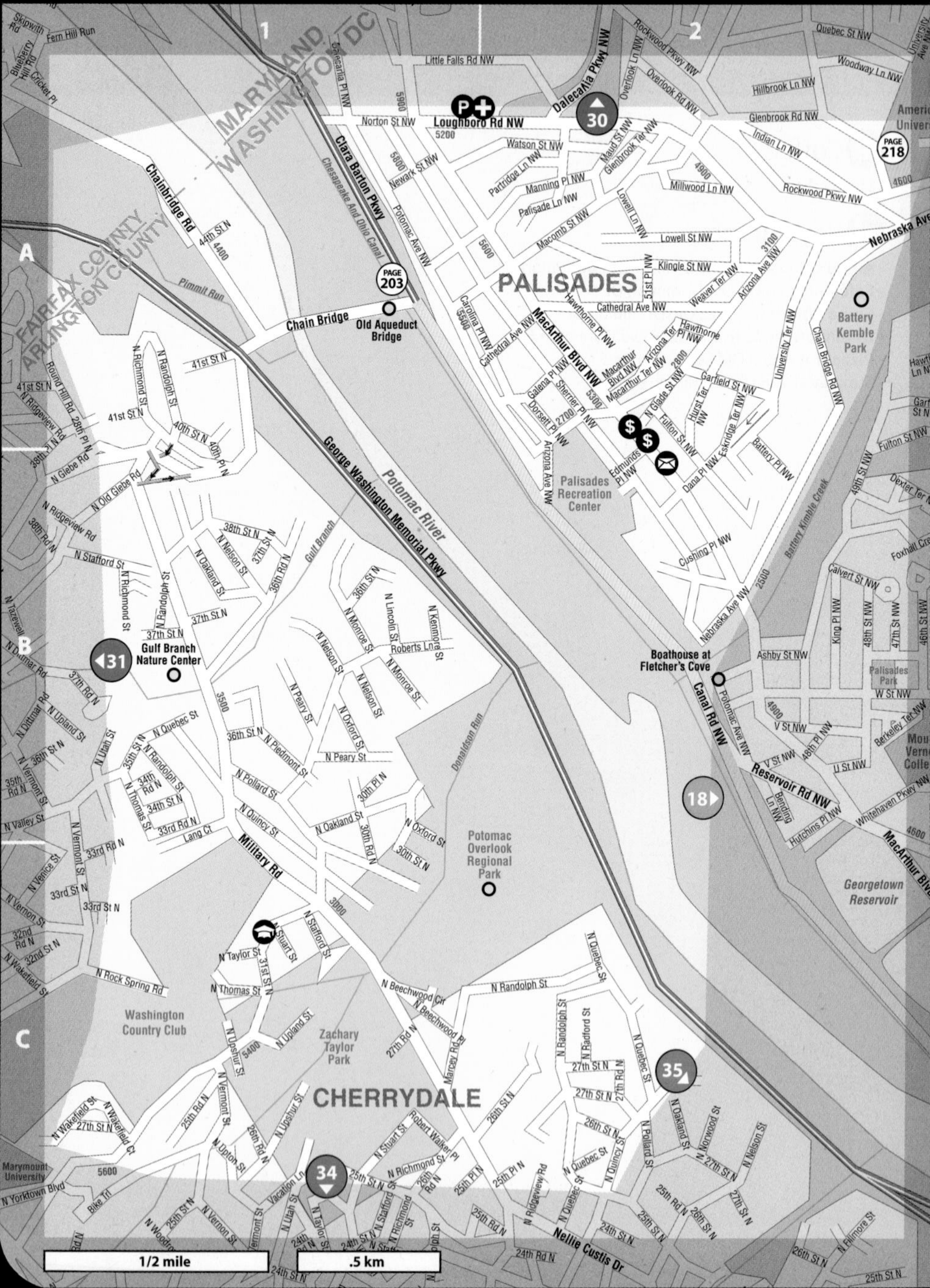

PALISADES

CHERRYDALE

MARYLAND / WASHINGTON DC

FAIRFAX COUNTY / ARLINGTON COUNTY

Major labels and places:

- Loughboro Rd NW — 5200
- Chain Bridge
- Old Aqueduct Bridge
- PAGE 203
- PAGE 218
- Gulf Branch Nature Center
- Palisades Recreation Center
- Battery Kemble Park
- Boathouse at Fletcher's Cove
- Potomac Overlook Regional Park
- Washington Country Club
- Zachary Taylor Park
- Marymount University
- Mount Vernon College
- Georgetown Reservoir
- Palisades Park
- Potomac River
- George Washington Memorial Pkwy
- Clara Barton Pkwy
- Chesapeake and Ohio Canal
- MacArthur Blvd NW
- Canal Rd NW
- Reservoir Rd NW
- Nebraska Ave
- Dalecarlia Pkwy NW
- Chain Bridge Rd
- Military Rd
- Pimmit Run
- Donaldson Run

Street names (selection):
Little Falls Rd NW, Norton St NW, Newark St NW, Watson St NW, Partridge Ln NW, Manning Pl NW, Palisade Ln NW, Macomb St NW, Lowell St NW, Klingle St NW, Weaver Ter NW, Arizona Ave NW, Rockwood Pkwy NW, Indian Ln NW, Glenbrook Rd NW, Hillbrook Ln NW, Woodway Ln NW, Quebec St NW, Overlook Rd NW, Hawthorne Pl NW, Cathedral Ave NW, Garfield St NW, University Ter NW, Battery Kemble Creek, Fulton St NW, Dana Pl NW, Cushing Pl NW, Nebraska Ave NW, Ashby St NW, Calvert St NW, King Pl NW, V St NW, U St NW, Berkeley Pl NW, Hutchins Pl NW, Foxhall Rd NW, Dexter St NW, Fulton St NW

Chainbridge Rd, N 41st St N, 44th St N, 40th St N, 41st St N, N Richmond St, N Randolph St, N Glebe Rd, N Old Glebe Rd, N Ridgeview Rd, N Stafford St, 38th St N, 37th St N, N Nelson St, N Oakland St, N Monroe St, N Lincoln St, N Kenmore St, Roberts Lane, N Peary St, 36th St N, N Piedmont St, N Oxford St, N Quincy St, 30th Pl N, 30th St N, N Thomas St, N Taylor St, N Stuart St, N Stafford St, Lang Ct, N Rock Spring Rd, N Upland St, N Quebec St, N Randolph St, N Beechwood Dr, N Bedford St, 27th St N, N Pollard St, 26th St N, 25th St N, 24th Rd N, 33rd Rd N, N Utah St, N Vernon St, N Valley St, N Wakefield St, Old Glebe Rd, N Yorktown Blvd, Nellie Custis Dr

Landmarks / icons:
- P (parking), + (hospital) at Loughboro Rd NW
- $ (bank), ✉ (post office) near MacArthur Blvd
- 30, 31, 18, 34, 35 (transit/route markers)

Scale: 1/2 mile | .5 km

Palisades is one of DC's overlooked neighborhoods—oh-so-quiet and with a mix of modest to magnificent homes, some with fantastic views of the Potomac. A smattering of local shops line MacArthur Boulevard, and essentials like the adorable Palisades Post Office may, oddly, be a destination for anyone who's visited the MLK Post Office downtown. Across the river in Virginia, it's an outdoor wonderland of nature parks, hiking trails, and fishing holes.

💲 Banks

- **Citibank** · 5250 MacArthur Blvd NW
- **Wachovia** · 5201 MacArthur Blvd NW

➕ Emergency Rooms

- **Sibley Memorial Hospital** ·
  5255 Loughboro Rd NW

⊙ Landmarks

- **Battery Kemble Park** · Battery Kemble Park
- **The Boathouse at Fletcher's Cove** ·
  4940 Canal Rd NW
- **Gulf Branch Nature Center** · 3608 N Military Rd
- **Old Aqueduct Bridge** · Chesapeake & Ohio Canal
- **Potomac Overlook Regional Park** ·
  2845 Marcey Rd

🅿 Parking

✉ Post Offices

- **Palisades** · 5136 MacArthur Blvd NW

Schools

- **Taylor Elementary** · 2600 N Stuart St

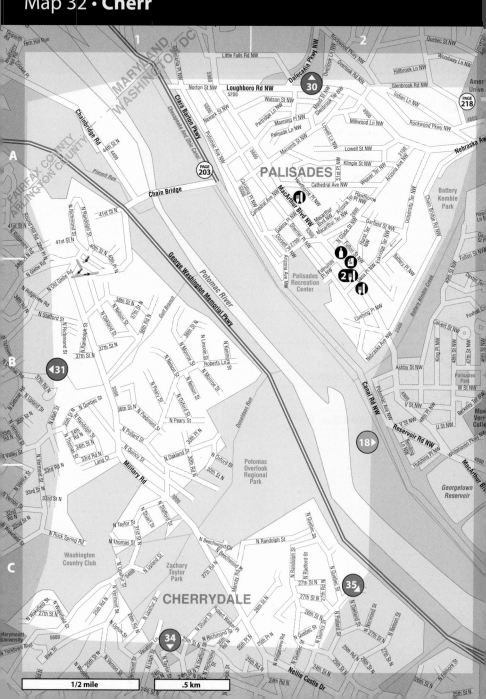

Map 32 • **Cherr**

Sundries / Entertainment

The Capital Crescent Trail is a popular running/biking path that passes along through here en route to Georgetown from Bethesda. Along a short stretch of MacArthur Boulevard, there are a few places to reconnoiter---like the DC Boathouse, long-time favorite Listrani's Italian Gourmet, or Bambu sushi bar. Otherwise, all the action is further down the road in Georgetown. But for the many early Baby Boomers who reside here, the backyard barbecue is about all the ol' ticker can take.

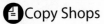Copy Shops

• **UPS Store** • 5185 Macarthur Blvd NW

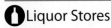Liquor Stores

• **Mac Market** • 5185 Macarthur Blvd NW

Restaurants

• **Bambu** • 5101 MacArthur Blvd NW
• **DC Boathouse** • 5441 MacArthur Blvd
• **Et Voila!** • 5120 MacArthur Blvd NW
• **Listrani's Italian Gourmet** • 5100 MacArthur Blvd

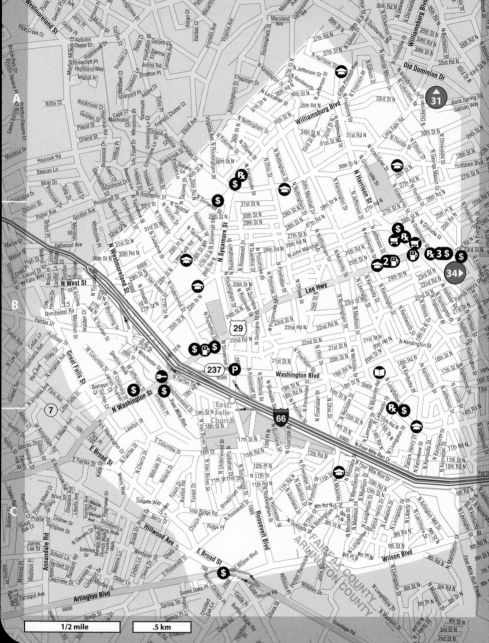

Map 33 · **Falls Church**

Falls Church is a quiet little suburban paradise with all the right amenities, including the Orange Line, halfway proximity between DC and Dulles Airport, farmers' market, mini-golf, public pool, movieplex palace/ nightclub, Safeways and schools. It's almost an ideal place for families and those who want to get away from the city, if you're okay with raising kids in the South.

Banks

- **Bank of America** · 467 N Washington St
- **Bank of America** · 5226 Lee Hwy
- **Bank of America** · 6307 Arlington Blvd
- **BB&T** · 5515 Lee Hwy
- **BB&T** · 6745 Lee Hwy
- **Citibank (ATM)** · 7-Eleven · 5267 Lee Hwy
- **Sun Trust** · 6711 Lee Hwy
- **United** · 5335 Lee Hwy
- **United** · 6402 Williamsburg Blvd
- **Virginia Commerce** · 5350 Lee Hwy
- **Virginia Commerce** · 6500 Williamsburg Blvd
- **Virginia Commerce (ATM)** · 2200 N Westmoreland St
- **Wachovia** · 1701 N McKinley Rd

Car Rental

- **Twenty Bucks Rent A Car** · 6847 Lee Hwy · 703-532-2277

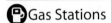 Gas Stations

- **Amoco** · 5601 Lee Hwy
- **Chevron** · 5618 Lee Hwy
- **Exxon** · 6730 Lee Hwy
- **Sunoco** · 5501 Lee Hwy

Libraries

- **Westover Library** · 1644 N McKinley Rd

P Parking

Pharmacies

- **CVS** · 5402 Lee Hwy
- **CVS** · 6404 Williamsburg Blvd
- **Harris Teeter** · 2425 N Harrison St
- **Rite Aid** · 5841 N Washington Blvd
- **Safeway** · 2500 N Harrison St

Schools

- **Bishop O'Connell** · 6600 Little Falls Rd
- **McKinley Elementary** · 1030 N McKinley Rd
- **Nottingham Elementary (temporary location)** · 5900 Little Falls Rd
- **Rivendell** · 5700 Lee Hwy
- **Swanson Middle** · 5800 N Washington Blvd
- **Tuckahoe Elementary** · 6550 26th St N
- **Williamsburg Middle** · 3600 N Harrison St
- **Yorktown High** · 5201 28th St N

Supermarkets

- **Harris Teeter** · 2425 N Harrison St
- **Safeway** · 2500 N Harrison St

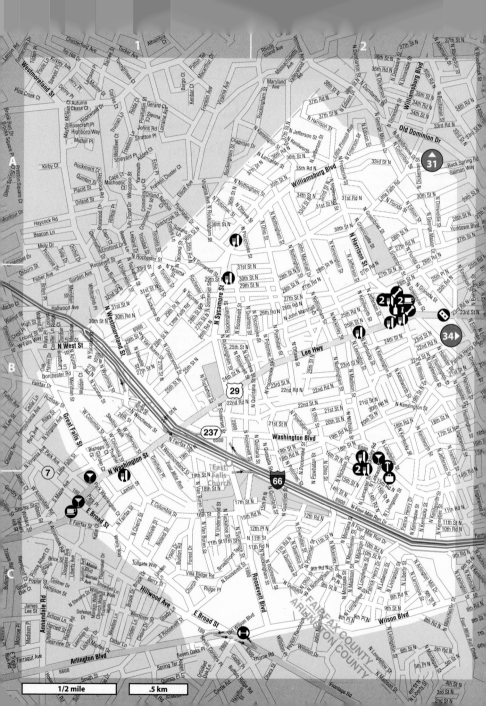

The cheap eats in this neighborhood compensate for the strip-mall aesthetic. Westover Village on Washington Boulevard is a handy place to grab a beer and dinner at the Lost Dog Café (or wine, salad, and the feline perspective at the Stray Cat), chicken shawarma at the Lebanese Taverna, or coconut soup with lemon grass at Thai Noy. Nightlife is sparse, but you can find live music at the State Theater or Ireland's Four Provinces.

33 34 35 36 7 37 38 40

Map

Coffee

- **Stacys Coffee Parlor** · 709 W Broad St
- **Starbucks** · 2441 N Harrison St
- **Starbucks** · 2500 N Harrison St

Gyms

- **Planet Fitness** · 6763 Wilson Blvd

Hardware Stores

- **Ayer's True Value** · 5853 N Washington Blvd

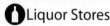Liquor Stores

- **ABC** · 2435 N Harrison St

Nightlife

- **Ireland's Four Provinces** · 105 W Broad St
- **Lost Dog Café** · 5876 Washington Blvd
- **State Theatre** · 220 N Washington St

Pet Shops

- **Dogma** · 2445 N Harrison St
- **Dominion Pet Center** · 2501 N Harrison St

Restaurants

- **Joe's Pizza** · 5555 Lee Hwy
- **Lebanese Taverna** · 5900 Washington Blvd
- **Lost Dog Café** · 5876 Washington Blvd
- **Peking Pavilion Chinese Restaurant** · 2912 N Sycamore St
- **Pie Tanza** · 2503 N Harrison St
- **Restaurant Vero and Wine Bar** · 5723 Lee Hwy
- **Stray Cat Café** · 5866 Washington Blvd
- **Sushi Zen** · 2457 N Harrison St
- **Taqueria Poblano** · 2503 N Harrison St
- **Thai Noy** · 5880 N Washington Blvd

Shopping

- **Calico Corners** · 6400 Williamsburg Blvd
- **Westover Shopping Center** · 5841 N Washington Blvd

Video Rental

- **Blockbuster** · 5400 Lee Hwy

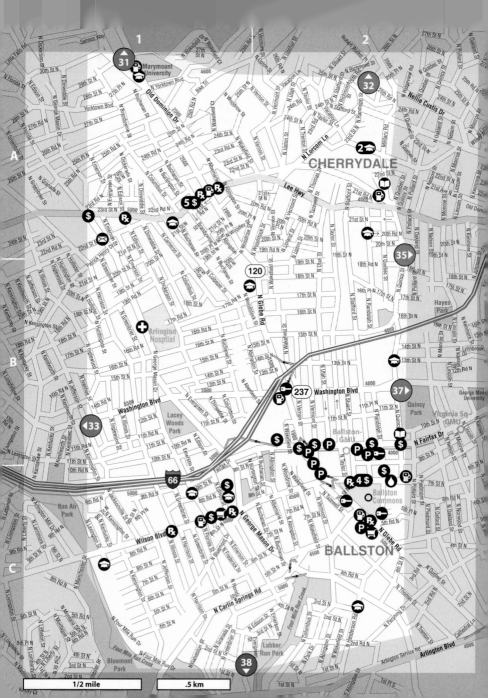

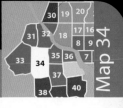

Essentials

The "Arlington Rap" described Ballston perfectly: a yuppieville with a giant mall, pricy condos, and townhouses filled with Pottery Barn furniture for aging frat boys to wear their brown flip flops and drink their fancy coffees from the plethora of available Starbucks. Ballston has a bit of a college town feel, with twenty- and thirty-somethings flocking to the area. But families and more mature adults are part of the community, too.

Map 34

Banks

- **Alliance** · 4501 N Fairfax Dr
- **Bank of America** · 4201 Wilson Blvd
- **BB&T** · 4707 Lee Hwy
- **BB&T** · 920 N Taylor St
- **Chevy Chase** · 4100 Wilson Blvd
- **Chevy Chase** · 4700 Lee Hwy
- **Chevy Chase** · 5222 Lee Hwy
- **Chevy Chase (ATM)** · 4230 N Fairfax Dr
- **Chevy Chase (ATM)** · Ballston Common Mall · 4238 Wilson Blvd
- **Citibank** · 1010 N Glebe Rd
- **Citibank (ATM)** · 7-Eleven · 5122 Wilson Blvd
- **First Horizon** · 4736 Lee Hwy
- **PNC** · 4401 Wilson Blvd
- **PNC (ATM)** · 850 N Randolph St
- **Presidential Savings** · 901 N Stuart St
- **Sun Trust** · 4710 Lee Hwy
- **Sun Trust** · 901 N Glebe Rd
- **United** · 907 N Quincy St
- **Wachovia** · 1011 N Stafford St
- **Wachovia** · 2213 N Glebe Rd

Car Rental

- **Advance Car Rental** · 850 N Randolph St · 703-528-8661
- **Enterprise** · 1211 N Glebe Rd · 703-248-7180
- **Enterprise** · 601 N Randolph St · 703-312-7900
- **Enterprise** · 700 N Glebe Rd · 703-243-5404

Car Washes

- **Shell** · 4030 Wilson Blvd

Emergency Rooms

- **Virginia Hospital Center** · 1701 N George Mason Dr

Gas Stations

- **Exxon** · 2240 N Glebe Rd
- **Exxon** · 4035 Old Dominion Dr
- **Exxon** · 4746 Lee Hwy
- **Exxon** · 660 N Glebe Rd
- **Shell** · 4030 Wilson Blvd
- **Sunoco** · 4601 Washington Blvd
- **Texaco** · 5201 Wilson Blvd

Landmarks

- **Ballston Commons** · 4238 Wilson Blvd

Libraries

- **Arlington Central Library** · 1015 N Quincy St
- **Cherrydale Library** · 2190 Military Rd

Parking

Pharmacies

- **CVS** · 4238 Wilson Blvd
- **CVS** · 4709 Lee Hwy
- **Harris Teeter** · 600 N Glebe Rd
- **Medicine Shoppe** · 5513 Wilson Blvd
- **Preston's CARE Pharmacy** · 5101 Lee Hwy
- **Rite Aid** · 4720 Lee Hwy
- **Safeway** · 5101 Wilson Blvd

Post Offices

- **North** · 2200 N George Mason Dr

Schools

- **Arlington Traditional** · 855 N Edison St
- **Ashlawn Elementary** · 5950 N 8th Rd
- **Barrett Elementary** · 4401 N Henderson Rd
- **Glebe Elementary** · 1770 N Glebe Rd
- **H-B Woodlawn** · 4100 Vacation Ln
- **Langston High Continuation Program** · 2121 N Culpeper St
- **Marymount University** · 2807 N Glebe Rd
- **St Agnes Elementary** · 2024 N Randolph St
- **St Ann Elementary** · 980 N Frederick St
- **Stratford Program** · 4102 N Vacation Ln
- **Washington Lee High** · 1300 N Quincy St

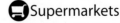Supermarkets

- **Harris Teeter** · 600 N Glebe Rd
- **Safeway** · 5101 Wilson Blvd

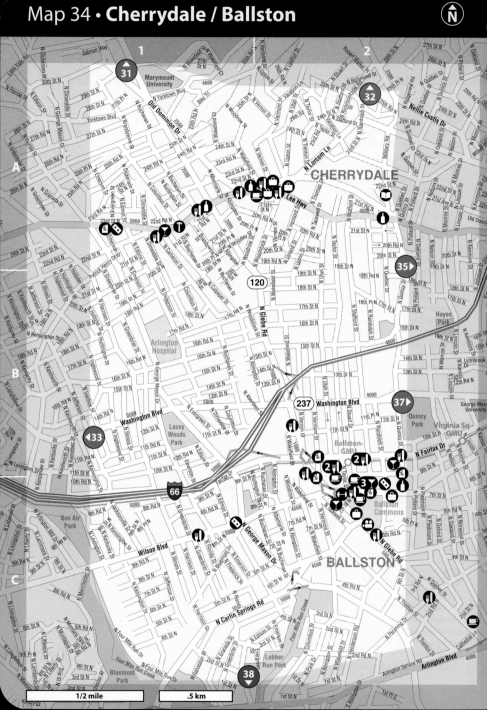

Map 34 • **Cherrydale / Ballston**

N

1 | 2

31

Marymount
University

32

Nellie Custis Dr

A

CHERRYDALE

Lee Hwy

35

120

N Glebe Rd

Arlington
Hospital

Hayes
Park

B

33

Washington Blvd

Lacey
Woods
Park

237 | Washington Blvd

37

Quincy
Park

Virginia Sq
GMU

George Mason
University

Ballston-
GMU

N Fairfax Dr

66

Ballston
Commons

Wilson Blvd

N George Mason Dr

BALLSTON

C

N Carlin Springs Rd

Lubber
Run Park

Bon Air
Park

Bluemont
Park

Four Mile Run Creek

38

Arlington Blvd

| 1/2 mile | | .5 km |

While many Ballston residents are lured out to Clarendon or DC on the weekends, there's still a lot to do here. Willow's chefs regularly get rave reviews and Tutto Bene is a local spot offering casual Italian. Head over to Carpool for billiards, or, if you must, catch the orange line at the Ballston metro stop to find your nightlife in the city.

Coffee

- **Cassatt's** · 4536 Lee Hwy
- **Cosi** · 4250 Fairfax Dr
- **Starbucks** · 4238 Wilson Blvd
- **Starbucks** · 801 N Glebe Rd
- **Starbucks** · 901 N Stuart St

Copy Shops

- **FedEx Kinko's** · 4501 N Fairfax Dr
- **Minuteman Press** · 4001 N 9th St
- **Print Time** · 5137 Lee Hwy
- **Staples** · 910 N Glebe Rd
- **UPS Store** · 4201 Wilson Blvd

Gyms

- **Sport & Health Clubs** · 4328 Wilson Blvd

Hardware Stores

- **Bill's True Value Hardware** · 4756 Lee Hwy

Liquor Stores

- **ABC** · 881 N Quincy St
- **Arrowine** · 4508 Lee Hwy
- **International Wine & Beverage** · 4040 Lee Hwy
- **Virginia ABC** · 4709 Lee Hwy

Movie Theaters

- **Regal Ballston Common 12** · 671 N Glebe Rd

Nightlife

- **Bailey's Pub and Grille** · 4238 Wilson Blvd
- **Buffalo D's** · 4213 Fairfax Dr
- **Carpool** · 4000 Fairfax Dr
- **Cowboy Café** · 4792 Lee Hwy
- **The Front Page** · 4201 Wilson Blvd
- **Rock Bottom Brewery** · 4238 Wilson Blvd

Restaurants

- **Big Buns Gourmet Grill** · 4401 Wilson Blvd
- **Buffalo D's** · 4213 Fairfax Dr
- **Café Parisien Express** · 4520 Lee Hwy
- **Café Tirolo** · 4001 N Fairfax Dr
- **Cassatt's** · 4536 Lee Hwy
- **Crisp & Juicy** · 4540 Lee Hwy
- **Grand Cru Wine Bar and Bistro** · 4401 Wilson Blvd
- **Heidelberg Pastry Shoppe** · 2150 N Culpeper St
- **Layalina** · 5216 Wilson Blvd
- **The Melting Pot** · 1110 N Glebe Rd
- **Metro 29 Diner** · 4711 Lee Hwy
- **PF Chang's** · 901 N Glebe Rd
- **Rio Grande Café** · 4301 Fairfax Dr
- **Tutto Bene** · 501 N Randolph St
- **Vapiano** · 4401 Wilson Blvd
- **Willow** · 4301 N Fairfax Dr

Shopping

- **Arrowine and Cheese** · 4508 Lee Hwy
- **Children's World** · 4238 N Wilson Blvd
- **Lebanese Taverna Market** · 4400 Old Dominion Dr
- **Pastries by Randolph** · 4500 Lee Hwy

Video Rental

- **Dollar Video** · 5133 Lee Hwy
- **Top Video** · 850 N Randolph St
- **Video 95** · 5011 Wilson Blvd

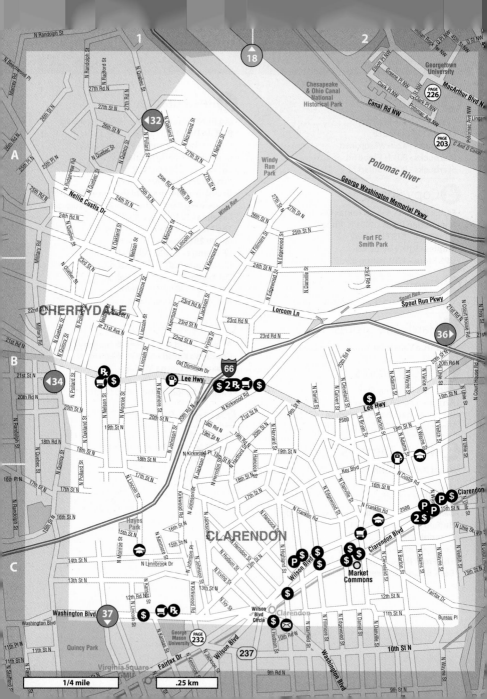

Clarendon is that remodeled community you love to hate: neat brick-lined roads with overpruned bushes and trees, matching signage, an overly sterile environment that feels like Disneyland but also feels relaxing with all its offerings: restaurants with ample outdoor seating, dance clubs, dive bars, live music, Whole Foods, and shopping. You could say it's a smaller, trendier, less Potomac Rivery version of Old Town Alexandria. You could even argue it's better, since it's just as walkable but with closer metro access.

Map

$ Banks

- **BB&T** · 2200 Wilson Blvd
- **Chevy Chase** · 3141 Lee Hwy
- **Chevy Chase (ATM)** · 2700 Clarendon Blvd
- **Chevy Chase (ATM)** · 2800 Clarendon Blvd
- **Chevy Chase (ATM)** · Giant Food Store · 3115 Lee Hwy
- **Chevy Chase (ATM)** · Giant Food Store · 3450 Washington Blvd
- **PNC** · 2601 Clarendon Blvd
- **PNC** · 3033 Wilson Blvd
- **PNC (ATM)** · 1303 N Filmore St
- **PNC (ATM)** · 3100 Clarendon Blvd
- **Sun Trust** · 3713 Lee Hwy
- **Sun Trust (ATM)** · 2250 Clarendon Blvd
- **Virginia Commerce** · 2930 Wilson Blvd
- **Wachovia** · 2200 Clarendon Blvd
- **Wachovia** · 3140 N Washington Blvd

Gas Stations

- **Exxon** · 2410 Lee Hwy
- **Shell** · 3332 Lee Hwy

○ Landmarks

- **Market Commons** · 2690 Clarendon Blvd

P Parking

Pharmacies

- **CVS** · 3133 Lee Hwy
- **Eckerd's** · 3130 Lee Hwy
- **Giant Food Pharmacy** · 3450 Washington Blvd
- **Safeway** · 3713 Lee Hwy

Post Offices

- **Arlington** · 3118 N Washington Blvd

Schools

- **Arlington Science Focus** · 1501 N Lincoln St
- **Francis Scott Key Elementary** · 2300 Key Blvd
- **New Directions** · 2847 Wilson Blvd

Supermarkets

- **Giant Food** · 3115 Lee Hwy
- **Giant Food** · 3450 Washington Blvd
- **Safeway** · 3713 Lee Hwy
- **Whole Foods Market** · 2700 Wilson Blvd

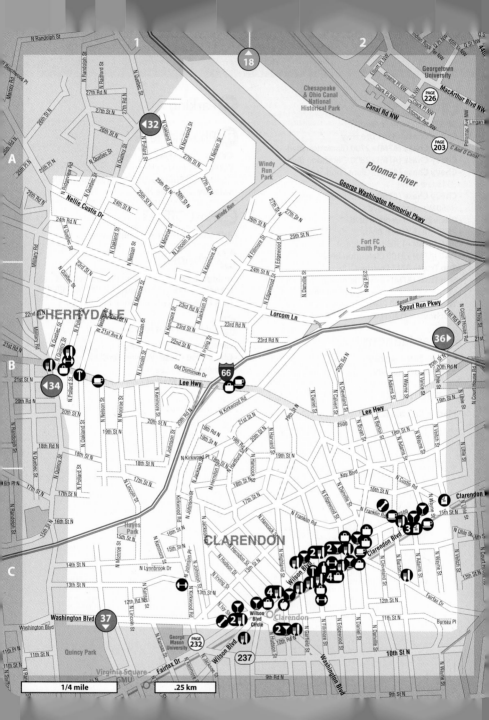

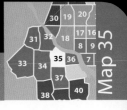
Wilson and Clarendon Boulevards are dotted with bars, restaurants, and music venues to suit most tastes. Get your freak on at Clarendon Ballroom or Clarendon Grill, chill and play arcade games at the Galaxy Hut, or rock out to up-and-comers (or painful open mic performers) at Iota. Clarendon does lack for parking, so walk or take the Metro. And if you don't party too hard the night before, come back and try out one of the many Sunday brunches, on your way to one of the several gyms, of course.

Coffee

- **Java Shack** · 2507 N Franklin Rd
- **Larry's Cookies** · 2200 N Clarendon Blvd
- **Murky Coffee** · 3211 N Wilson Blvd
- **Starbucks** · 2690 Clarendon Blvd
- **Starbucks** · 3125 Lee Hwy
- **Starbucks** · 3713 Lee Hwy

Copy Shops

- **FedEx Kinko's** · 2300 Clarendon Blvd
- **Southeastern Printing & Litho** · 2415 Wilson Blvd
- **UPS Store** · 2200 Wilson Blvd

Farmers Markets

- **Claredon Farmers Market**
  (Jun–Oct; Wed, 3pm–7pm) ·
  Clarendon Blvd & N Highland St

Gyms

- **Arlington Sport & Health Club** ·
  1122 N Kirkwood Rd
- **Curves (women only)** · 2105 N Pollard St
- **Gold's Gym** · 1220 N Filmore St
- **Washington Sports Clubs** · 2800 Clarendon Blvd
- **Y Sport & Health Club** · 3400 13th St N

Hardware Stores

- **Cherrydale Hardware & Garden** · 3805 Lee Hwy
- **Virginia Hardware** · 2915 Wilson Blvd

Liquor Stores

- **Best Cellars (wine only)** · 2855 Clarendon Blvd

Nightlife

- **Clarendon Ballroom** · 3185 Wilson Blvd
- **Clarendon Grill** · 1101 N Highland St
- **Eleventh Street Lounge** · 1041 N Highland St
- **Galaxy Hut** · 2711 Wilson Blvd
- **Harry's Tap Room** · 2800 Clarendon Blvd
- **Iota** · 2832 Wilson Blvd
- **Kitty O'Shea's** · 2403 Wilson Blvd
- **Mister Days** · 3100 Clarendon Blvd
- **O'Sullivan's Irish Pub** · 3207 Washington Blvd
- **Whitlow's on Wilson** · 2854 Wilson Blvd

Pet Shops

- **AKA Spot** · 2509 N Franklin Rd

Restaurants

- **Aladdin's Eatery** · 4245 N Fairfax Dr
- **Boccato** · 2719 Wilson Blvd
- **Boulevard Woodgrill** · 2901 Wilson Blvd
- **Delhi Club** · 1135 N Highland St
- **Delhi Dhaba** ·
  2424 Wilson Blvd
- **Eventide Restaurant** · 3165 Wilson Blvd
- **Faccia Luna Trattoria** · 2909 Wilson Blvd
- **Hard Times Café** · 3028 Wilson Blvd
- **Harry's Tap Room** · 2800 Clarendon Blvd
- **La Tasca** · 2900 Wilson Blvd
- **Liberty Tavern** · 3195 Wilson Blvd
- **Lyon Hall** · 3100 N Washington Blvd
- **Mexicali Blues** · 2933 Wilson Blvd
- **Minh's Restaurant** · 2500 Wilson Blvd
- **Northside Social** · 3211 Wilson Blvd
- **Pasha Café** · 3911 Lee Hwy
- **Portabellos** · 2109 N Pollard St
- **Restaurant 3** · 2950 Clarendon Blvd
- **Sette Bello** · 3101 Wilson Blvd
- **Silver Diner** · 3200 Wilson Blvd

Shopping

- **Barnes & Noble** · 2800 Clarendon Blvd
- **Boccato** · 2719 Wilson Blvd
- **CD Cellar** · 2607 Wilson Blvd
- **Company Flowers** · 2107 N Pollard St
- **The Container Store** · 2800 Clarendon Blvd
- **The Italian Store** · 3123 Lee Hwy
- **Kinder Haus Toys** · 1220 N Fillmore St
- **Orpheus Records** · 3173 Wilson Blvd
- **Orvis Company Store** · 2879 Clarendon Blvd
- **Pottery Barn** · 2700 Clarendon Blvd
- **Shoe Fly** · 2727 N Wilson Blvd
- **South Moon Under** · 2700 Clarendon Blvd

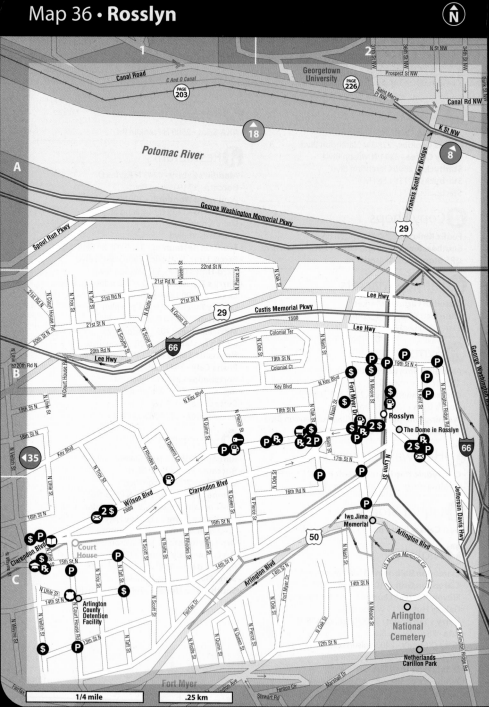

Map 36 · **Rosslyn**

More and more high-rise dwellers are calling Rosslyn home, but the amenities still tend to be subpar. You've got chain lunch spots, gyms, markets, dry cleaners, and enough parking garages to sink the heart of every living environmentalist. When the economy turns around, however, perhaps developers will pick up where they left off and bring a little more to this little Virginian 'burb that could.

$ Banks

- **Bank of America** · 1700 N Moore St
- **Bank of America** · 2111 Wilson Blvd
- **BB&T** · 1901 Ft Myer Dr
- **Chevy Chase** · 1100 Wilson Blvd
- **Chevy Chase (ATM)** · 1611 N Kent St
- **Chevy Chase (ATM)** · 1850 N Moore St
- **PNC** · 1801 N Lynn St
- **PNC (ATM)** · 1320 N Veitch St
- **PNC (ATM)** · 1401 N Taft St
- **PNC (ATM)** · 2050 Wilson Blvd
- **Presidential Savings** · 1700 N Moore St
- **Sandy Spring (ATM)** · Chevron · 1830 Fort Myer Dr
- **Sun Trust** · 2121 15th St N
- **Wachovia** · 1300 Wilson Blvd
- **Wachovia** · 2026 Wilson Blvd
- **Wachovia (ATM)** · 1500 Wilson Blvd

Car Rental

- **Enterprise** · 1560 Wilson Blvd · 703-528-6466

Gas Stations

- **Amoco** · 1625 Wilson Blvd
- **Chevron** · 1830 N Fort Myer Dr
- **Exxon** · 1824 Wilson Blvd

o Landmarks

- **Arlington County Detention Facility (Jail)** · 1425 N Courthouse Rd
- **Arlington National Cemetery** · Arlington National Cemetery
- **The Dome in Rosslyn** · 1101 Wilson Blvd
- **Iwo Jima Memorial** · N Meade St & Arlington Blvd
- **Netherlands Carillon Park** · N Meade St & N Marshall Dr

Libraries

- **Arlington Plaza Branch Library** · 2100 Clarendon Blvd

P Parking

Rx Pharmacies

- **CVS** · 1100 Wilson Blvd
- **CVS** · 1555 Wilson Blvd
- **CVS** · 2121 15th St N
- **Rite Aid** · Rosslyn Metro Ctr · 1700 N Moore St
- **Safeway** · 1525 Wilson Blvd

Police

- **Arlington County Police Department** · 1425 N Courthouse Rd

Post Offices

- **Court House Station** · 2043 Wilson Blvd
- **Rosslyn** · 1101 Wilson Blvd

Schools

- **Strayer University (Arlington Campus)** · 2121 15th St N

Supermarkets

- **Safeway** · 1525 Wilson Blvd

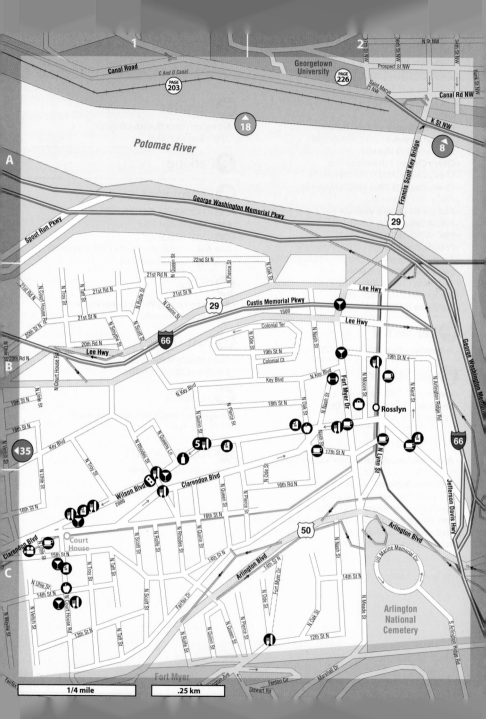

Nightlife around here is clustered near the Courthouse metro, though even that has been diminished with the closing of Dr. Dremo's (condo sprawl strikes again). You mostly have two choices: sports pub Summers Grill or Irish bar Ireland's Four Courts. One standout is the Continental, where girls can get martinis, guys can grab a brew, and everyone can play shuffle board till the toll of last call.

Coffee

- **Coffee Express** · 1300 Wilson Blvd
- **Cosi** · 1801 N Lynn St
- **Cosi** · 2050 Wilson Blvd
- **Starbucks** · 1501 17th St N
- **Starbucks** · 1525 Wilson Blvd
- **Starbucks** · 1735 N Lynn St

Copy Shops

- **MBC Precision Imaging** ·
  1501 Wilson Blvd, Ste 100
- **Minuteman Press** · 1601 N Kent St
- **Office Depot** · 1515 N Courthouse Rd
- **Sir Speedy** · 1600 Wilson Blvd, Ste 102
- **USA Print & Copy** · 2044 Wilson Blvd

Farmers Markets

- **Arlington County Farmers Market**
  (Sat, 8 am–12 pm) · N 14th St & N Courthouse Rd
- **Rosslyn Farmers Market**
  (Jun–Nov; Thur, 12–3 pm) ·
  Wilson Blvd & N Oak St

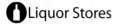Gyms

- **Gold's Gym** · 1830 N Nash St

Liquor Stores

- **ABC** · 1731 Wilson Blvd

Movie Theaters

- **AMC Courthouse Plaza 8** · 2150 Clarendon Blvd

Nightlife

- **Continental Modern Pool Lounge** ·
  1911 Ft Myer Dr
- **Ireland's Four Courts** · 2051 Wilson Blvd
- **Rhodeside Grill** · 1836 Wilson Blvd
- **Summers Restaurant** ·
  1520 N Courthouse Rd

Restaurants

- **Café Tivoli** · 1700 N Moore St
- **Choupi** · 1218 19th St N
- **Gua-Rapo** · 2039 Wilson Blvd
- **Guajillo** · 1727 Wilson Blvd
- **Il Radicchio** · 1801 Clarendon Blvd
- **Ireland's Four Courts** · 2051 Wilson Blvd
- **Quarter Deck Restaurant** · 1200 Ft Myer Dr
- **Ray's Hell Burger** · 1713 Wilson Blvd
- **Ray's the Steaks** · 1725 Wilson Blvd
- **Red, Hot, and Blue** · 1600 Wilson Blvd
- **Rhodeside Grill** · 1836 Wilson Blvd
- **Village Bistro** · 1723 Wilson Blvd

Shopping

- **Café Tivoli** · 1700 N Moore St

Video Rental

- **Hollywood Video** · 1900 Wilson Blvd

Fort Myer is mostly suburban (think '40s Cape Cods with aluminum awnings) with a few commercial enclaves. That's sort of the appeal to its existence. There's no Metrorail stop and it's not particularly pedestrian-friendly, so grab your car keys if you've got the itch to visit. Most of the fun, and essentials, are on the edges of this area, but stick around and check out the weekend farmers market, just down the street from the best dive diner breakfast around, Bob and Edith's.

Banks

- **Bank of America** · 3401 Columbia Pike
- **Bank of America** · 3625 N Fairfax Dr
- **BB&T** · 1100 S Walter Reed Dr
- **BB&T** · 3001 N Washington Blvd
- **Chevy Chase** · 3532 Columbia Pike
- **Chevy Chase** · 901 N Nelson St
- **Chevy Chase (ATM)** · Giant Food Store · 2411 Columbia Pike
- **Chevy Chase (ATM)** · Giant Food Store · 2515 Columbia Pike
- **Citibank (ATM)** · 7-Eleven · 201 S Glebe Rd
- **Citibank (ATM)** · 7-Eleven · 3003 Columbia Pike
- **Citibank (ATM)** · 7-Eleven · 3600 Columbia Pike
- **Sun Trust** · 249 N Glebe Rd
- **Sun Trust** · 3108 Columbia Pike
- **United** · 2300 9th St S
- **Wachovia** · 951 S George Mason Dr

Car Rental

- **Avis** · 3206 10th St N · 703-516-4202
- **Enterprise** · 3200 Columbia Pike · 703-486-1086
- **Hertz** · 3200 S Columbia Pike · 703-920-1808

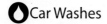 Car Washes

- **Mr Wash** · 101 N Glebe Rd
- **Quality Wash** · 89 N Glebe Rd

 Gas Stations

- **Citgo** · 2324 Columbia Pike
- **Exxon** · 1001 S Glebe Rd
- **Hess** · 3299 Wilson Blvd
- **Shell** · 3100 Columbia Pike
- **Shell** · 4211 Columbia Pike
- **Texaco** · 2300 Columbia Pike

Landmarks

- **Arlington Cinema 'N' Drafthouse** · 2903 Columbia Pike
- **Bob and Edith's Diner** · 2310 Columbia Pike
- **Mosaic Park** · 544 N Pollard St

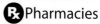 Libraries

- **Columbia Pike Library** · 816 S Walter Reed Dr

 Pharmacies

- **CVS** · 256 N Glebe Rd
- **CVS** · 2601 Columbia Tpke
- **CVS** · 2900 10th St N
- **Eckerd's** · 2820 Columbia Pike
- **Giant Pharmacy** · 2411 Columbia Piike
- **Rite Aid** · 2820 Columbia Pike

Post Offices

- **South** · 1210 S Glebe Rd

Schools

- **The Career Center** · 816 S Walter Reed Dr
- **Henry Elementary** · 701 S Highland St
- **Jefferson Middle** · 125 S Old Gebe Rd
- **Long Branch Elementary** · 33 N Fillmore St
- **St Charles** · 3299 N Fairfax Dr
- **St Thomas More Cathedral** · 105 N Thomas St

Supermarkets

- **Food Star** · 950 S George Mason Dr

"Entertainment" doesn't quite describe Columbia Pike accurately, unless you enjoy being stuck in traffic jams while shopping for laundry detergent and other bulk items at one of the many big box strip malls. It does, however, have a healthy dose of ethnic eateries (Matuba, Bangkok 54), mom-and-pop pizza joints, and pawn shops. Bob and Edith's Diner will satisfy your greasy cravings 24/7 (and now delightfully smoke free), and the Arlington Cinema 'N' Drafthouse is a unique dinner-and-a-movie option.

 Coffee

- **Dunkin' Donuts** · 3100 Columbia Pike
- **Rappahannock Coffee** · 2406 Columbia Pike
- **Starbucks** · 901 N Nelson St

 Copy Shops

- **Reprographic Technologies** · 3300 N Fairfax Dr
- **SOWA & Nicholas Printing** · 3301 Wilson Blvd
- **UPS Store** · 1001 N Fillmore St

 Farmers Markets

- **Columbia Pike Farmers Market (May–Nov; Sun, 10 am–2 pm)** · Columbia Pike & S Walter Reed Dr

 Gyms

- **Curves (women only)** · 3528 Wilson Blvd
- **Gold's Gym** · 3910 Wilson Blvd

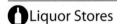 Liquor Stores

- **ABC** · 1001 N Fillmore St
- **ABC** · 2201 N Pershing Dr

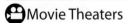 Movie Theaters

- **Arlington Cinema 'N' Drafthouse** · 2903 Columbia Pike

 Nightlife

- **EatBar** · 2761 Washington Blvd
- **Jay's Saloon & Grille** · 3114 10th St N
- **Ragtime** · 1345 N Courthouse Rd
- **Tallula** · 2761 Washington Blvd

 Pet Shops

- **Birds 'n' Things** · 2628 Columbia Pike

Restaurants

- **Astor Mediterranean** · 2300 N Pershing Dr
- **Atilla's** · 2705 Columbia Pike
- **Bakeshop** · 1025 N Fillmore St
- **Bangkok 54** · 2919 Columbia Pike
- **Bob and Edith's Diner** · 2310 Columbia Pike
- **Broiler** · 3601 Columbia Pike
- **El Charrito Caminante** · 2710 N Washington Blvd
- **El Paso Café** · 4235 N Pershing Dr
- **El Pollo Rico** · 932 N Kenmore St
- **LA Bar and Grille** · 2530 Columbia Pike
- **Manee Thai** · 2500 Columbia Pike
- **Mario's Pizza House** · 3322 Wilson Blvd
- **Matuba** · 2915 Columbia Pike
- **Mrs Chen's Kitchen** · 3101 Columbia Pike
- **Pan American Bakery** · 4113 Columbia Pike
- **Pike Grill** · 3902 Wilson Blvd
- **Ragtime** · 1345 N Courthouse Rd
- **Ravi Kabob** · 305 N Glebe Rd
- **Rincome Thai Cuisine** · 3030 Columbia Pike
- **Tallula** · 2761 Washington Blvd

Shopping

- **All About Jane** · 2839 VA-244
- **Ivy Nail & Spa** · 3434 Virginia 244
- **The Papery** · 2871 Virginia 244
- **Ski Chalet** · 2704 Columbia Pike
- **Twisted Vines Bottleshop & Bistro** · 2803 Columbia Pike

Video Rental

- **Hollywood Video** · 3263 Columbia Pike
- **Video Warehouse** · 3411 5th St S

A sprawling multicultural hodgepodge, two roads—Columbia Pike and Leesburg Pike—dominate this neighborhood, if you could call it that. The area isn't exactly homey (unless chaotic and crammed is what your heart desires), with its eye-paining high-rises, plethora of strip malls, and apartment communities that have seen better days. On the bright—or rather, green—side, Four Mile Run is great for riding your bike or taking your dog for a romp.

$ Banks

- **Bank of America** · 5707 Seminary Rd
- **Burke & Herbert** · 5705 Seminary Rd
- **Chevy Chase** · 3480 S Jefferson St
- **Chevy Chase** · 3499 S Jefferson St
- **Chevy Chase** · 5851 Crossroads Ctr Wy
- **Wachovia** · 4651 King St
- **Wachovia** · 5797 Leesburg Pike

⛽ Gas Stations

- **Amoco** · 4625 Columbia Pike
- **Shell** · 5511 Columbia Pike
- **Shell** · 5600 Leesburg Pike

○ Landmarks

- **Ball-Sellers House** · 5620 S 3rd St

📖 Libraries

- **Glencarlyn Library** · 300 S Kensington St

P Parking

℞ Pharmacies

- **CVS** · 3535 S Jefferson St
- **CVS** · 5017 Columbia Pike
- **Giant Food Pharmacy** · 3480 S Jefferson St
- **Target** · 5115 Leesburg Pike

🏫 Schools

- **Arlington Mill High Continuation Program** · 4975 Columbia Pike
- **Barcroft Elementary** · 625 S Wakefield St
- **Campbell Elementary** · 737 S Carlin Springs Rd
- **Carlin Springs Elementary** · 5995 5th Rd S
- **Claremont Immersion** · 4700 S Chesterfield Rd
- **Glen Forest Elementary** · 5829 Glen Forest Dr
- **Kenmore Middle** · 200 S Carlin Springs Rd
- **Our Savior Lutheran** · 825 S Taylor St
- **Wakefield High** · 4901 S Chesterfield Rd

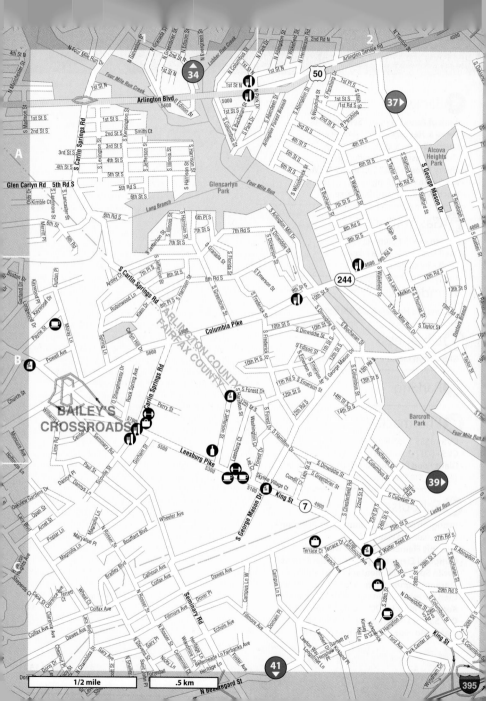

You'll need several shots of Novocaine to handle Leesburg or Columbia Pike on a Saturday. This big box bonanza draws the crowds and makes shopping a nightmare. However, it is the most accessible place to get everything you need, from hiking boots at REI to toilet paper at Target. However, if you're trapped during lunchtime, Chicken Place is the best Peruvian chicken joint around, and Five Guys serves up mouthwatering burgers.

Coffee

- **Caribou Coffee** · 5201 Leesburg Pike
- **Starbucks** · 5115 Leesburg Pike
- **Starbucks** · 5821 Crossroads Ctr Wy

Copy Shops

- **FedEx Kinko's** · 3515C S Jefferson St
- **Kwik Kopy Printing** · 5100 Leesburg Pike
- **Sir Speedy** · 4656 King St
- **Staples** · 5801 Leesburg Pike

Gyms

- **Gold's Gym** · 3505 Carlin Springs Rd
- **Sport & Health Clubs** · 5115 Leesburg Pike

Liquor Stores

- **ABC** · Crossroads Place Shopping Center · 3556E S Jefferson St

Restaurants

- **Andy's Carry-Out** · 5033 Columbia Pike
- **Athens Restaurant** · 3541 Carlin Springs Rd
- **Atlacatl and Pupuseria** · 4701 Columbia Pike
- **Brick's Pizza** · 4809 1st St N
- **The Chicken Place** · 5519 Leesburg Pike
- **Crystal Thai** · 4819 Arlington Blvd
- **Five Guys** · 4626 King St

Shopping

- **One Two Kangeroo Toys** · 4022 S 28th St
- **REI** · 3509 Carlin Springs Rd
- **Target** · 5115 Leesburg Pike

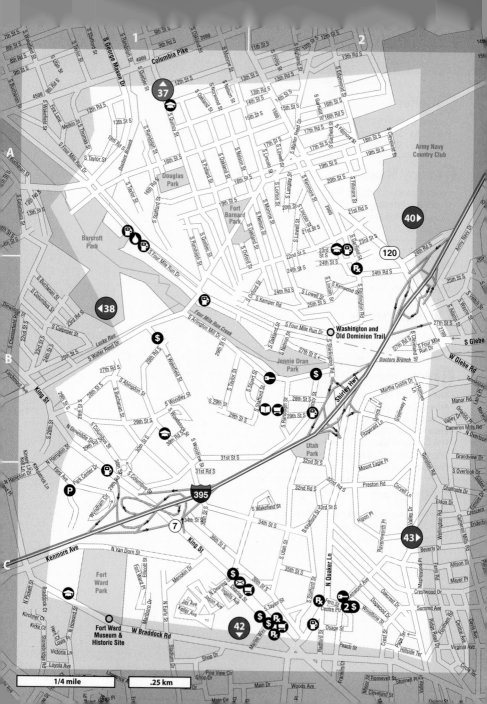

Map

Split down the middle by 395, a major route to/from DC, more and more young professionals are shacking up in Shirlington. With luxury condos, pricey townhouses, and new shops reaching completion, development here has exploded in the past few years in that typically sterile faux-stone walls and too-neat sidewalks kind of way. But the gentrification is sharply juxtaposed with a nearby day laborer center trying to capitalize on the development, revealing the complex community dynamics in this neighborhood.

39 43
41 42 44 45
46

Banks
- **BB&T** · 2700 S Quincy St
- **Burke & Herbert** · 1705 Fern St
- **Chevy Chase** · 3690 King St
- **Citibank (ATM)** · 7-Eleven · 2815 S Wakefield St
- **Sun Trust** · 3610 King St
- **Wachovia** · 1711 Fern St
- **Wachovia** · 3624 King St

Car Rental
- **Enterprise** · 1525 Kenwood Ave
- **Enterprise** · 2778 S Arlington Mill Dr

Car Washes
- **David's Car Wash** · 4148 S Four Mile Run Dr

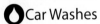 Gas Stations
- **Amoco** · 4050 S Four Mile Run Dr
- **Chevron** · 4154 S Four Mile Run Dr
- **Exxon** · 2316 S Shirlington Rd
- **Exxon** · 4368 King St
- **Shell** · 1333 N Quaker Ln
- **Shell** · 2817 S Quincy St
- **Shell** · 4060 S Four Mile Run Dr
- **Sunoco** · 1639 N Quaker Ln

 Landmarks
- **Fort Ward Museum & Historic Site** · 4301 W Braddock Rd
- **Washington and Old Dominion Trail** · S Four Mile Run Dr & S Shirlington Rd

Libraries
- **Shirlington Library** · 4200 Campbell Ave

Parking

 Pharmacies
- **CVS** · 1521 N Quaker Ln
- **Green Valley** · 2415 S Shirlington Rd
- **Rite Aid** · 3614 King St
- **Safeway** · 3526 King St

Post Offices
- **Park Fairfax** · 3682 King St

Schools
- **Abingdon Elementary** · 3035 S Abingdon St
- **Drew Model Elementary** · 3500 S 23rd St S
- **Randolph Elementary** · 1306 S Quincy St
- **St Clement Episcopal** · 1701 N Quaker Ln
- **St Stephen's & St Agnes Middle** · 4401 W Braddock Rd

Supermarkets
- **Giant Food** · 3680 King St
- **Harris Teeter** · 4250 Campbell Ave
- **Safeway** · 3526 King St

(161)

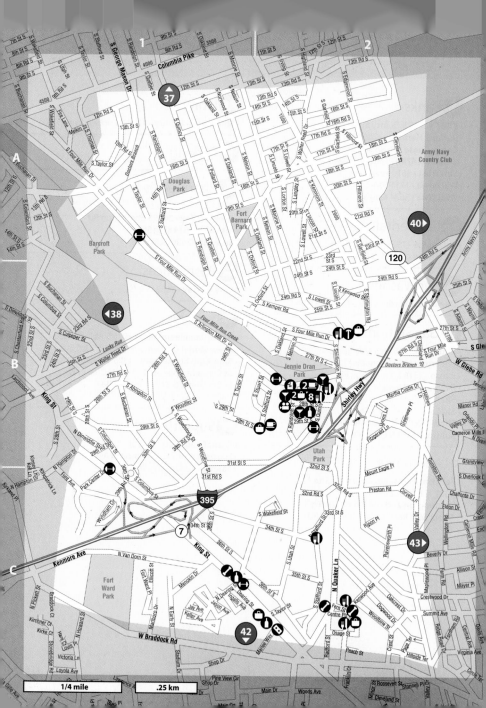

Sundries / Entertainment

The Village at Shirlington, a fast-growing destination, boasts a Disney World-esque array of restaurants (one of every type, all with outdoor seating), a movie theater with a slant toward independent films, and well-designed essentials like a library with a sleek facade. Bring your date to Carlyle for a swanky meal, share a cupcake at CakeLove, then head to the Bungalow to play some pool.

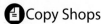

☕ Coffee
- **Best Buns Bread Co.** · 4010 28th St S
- **Caribou Coffee** · 4115 S 28th St
- **Starbucks** · 3690 Q King St

🖨 Copy Shops
- **UPS Store** · 2776 S Arlington Mill Dr

🏋 Gyms
- **Barcroft Sport and Fitness Center** · 4200 S Four Mile Run Dr
- **Center Club** · 4300 King St
- **Curves (women only)** · 2772 S Arlington Mill Dr
- **The Energy Club** · 2900 S Quincy St
- **Washington Sports Clubs** · 3654 King St

🔧 Hardware Stores
- **ABC Distributors Inc** · 2633 Shirlington Rd

🍾 Liquor Stores
- **The Curious Grape** · 4056 28th St S
- **Unwined** · 3690 King St
- **Virginia ABC** · 3678 King St

🎬 Movie Theaters
- **AMC Loews Shirlington 7** · 2772 S Randolph St

🍸 Nightlife
- **The Bungalow, Billiards & Brew Co** · 2766 S Arlington Mill Dr
- **Capitol City Brewing Company** · 4001 Campbell Ave
- **Guapo's** · 4028 Campbell Ave

🐾 Pet Shops
- **For Pet's Sake** · 1537 N Quaker Ln
- **One Good Tern** · 1710 Fern St
- **Pro Feed** · 3690 King St

🍴 Restaurants

- **Aladdin's Eatery** · 4044 S 28th St
- **Best Buns Bread Co.** · 4010 28th St S
- **Bonsai** · 4040 Campbell Ave
- **Capitol City Brewing Company** · 4001 Campbell Ave
- **Carlyle Grande Café** · 4000 Campbell Ave
- **Extra Virgin** · 4053 28th St S
- **Great Harvest** · 1711 Centre Plz
- **Guapo's** · 4028 Campbell Ave
- **Luna Grill & Diner** · 4024 28th St S
- **PING by Charlie Chiang's** · 4060 28th St S
- **Rampart's** · 1700 Fern St
- **THAI Shirlington** · 4029 28th St S
- **Weenie Beanie** · 2680 S Shirlington Rd

🛍 Shopping
- **CakeLove** · 4150 Campbell Ave
- **The Curious Grape** · 4056 28th St S
- **Diversions Cards and Gifts** · 1721 Centre Plz
- **Unwined** · 3690 King St
- **Washington Golf Centers** · 2625 Shirlington Rd

📀 Video Rental
- **Blockbuster** · 3610 King St

Map 39

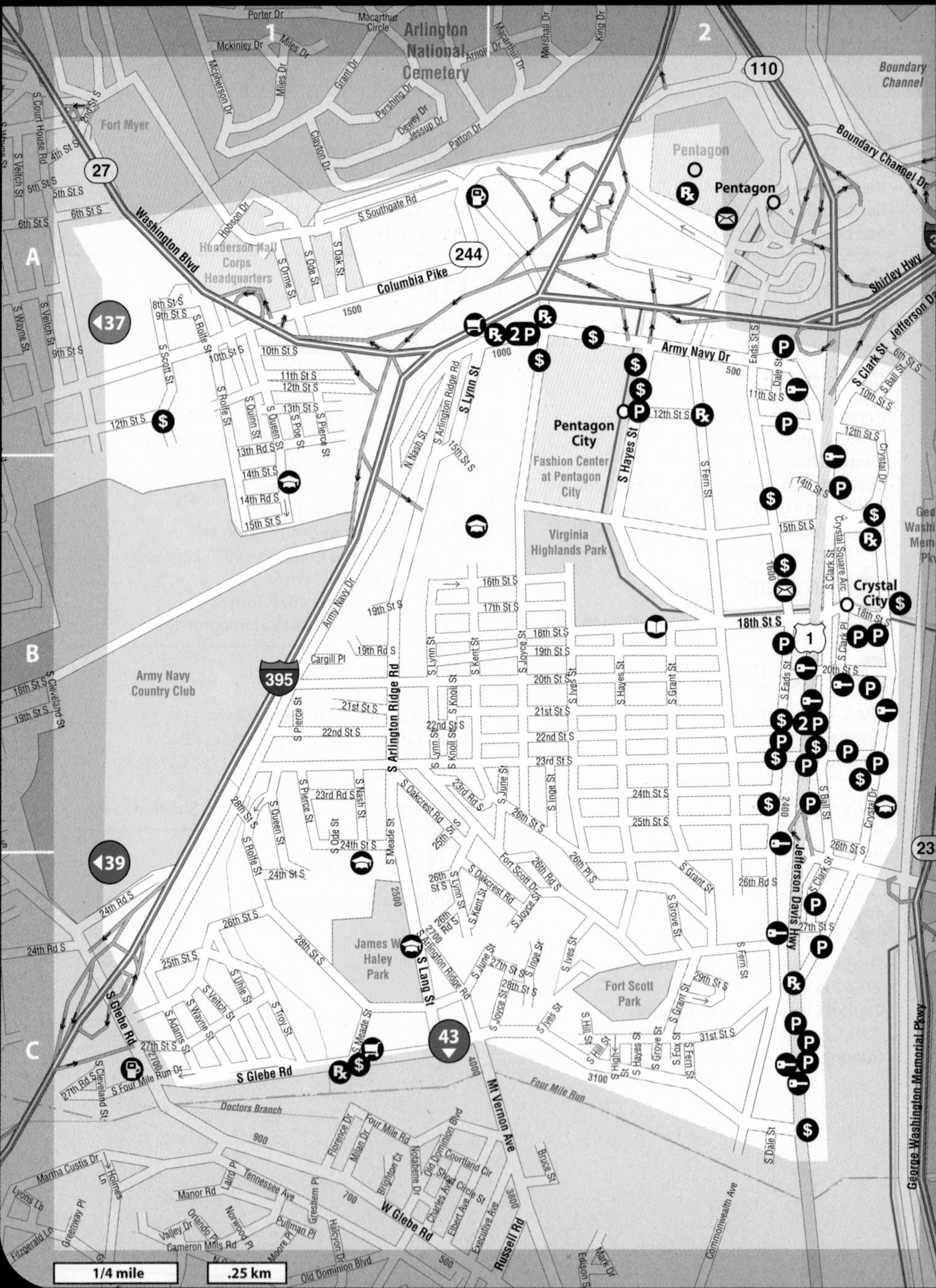

Map 40 · **Pentagon City / Crystal City**

N

Arlington
National
Cemetery

Porter Dr
Macarthur Circle
Mckinley Dr
Miles Dr
Gram Dr
Marshall Dr
King Dr
Meade Dr
Arnold Dr
Pershing Dr
Dewey Dr
Jessup Dr
Patton Dr
Grant Dr
Clayton Dr
Hobson Dr
S Southgate Rd

Fort Myer

110

Boundary
Channel

Boundary Channel Dr

S Court House Rd
S Veitch St
5th St S
6th St S

27

Washington Blvd

Henderson Hall Corps Headquarters

S Orme St
S Oak St
S Ode St

Columbia Pike

244

1500

Pentagon

Pentagon

Shirley Hwy

A

S Wayne St
S Veitch St
8th St S
9th St S

37

S Rolfe St
S Scott St
10th St S
11th St S
12th St S
13th St S

S Pierce St
S Queen St
S Rolfe St
14th Rd S
13th Rd S
14th St S
15th St S

Arlington Ridge Rd
N Nash St
S Lynn St
N Lynn St
S Fern St

Army Navy Dr

1000

Bus 2 P

Pentagon City
Fashion Center at Pentagon City

S Hayes St

12th St S
Eads St S
Dale St S
S Clark St
Jefferson Dr
S Clark St
11th St S
10th St S
Crystal Dr
12th St S

500

P

P

14th St S
15th St S

Virginia
Highlands Park

Crystal Square Arc
Crystal Dr

P

Crystal City

B

Cleveland St
18th St S
19th St S

Army Navy Ridge Rd
Army Navy Drive

395

Cargill Pl

16th St S
17th St S
18th St S
19th St S
19th Rd S
20th St S
21st St S
22nd St S
23rd St S

S Kent St
S Joyce St
S Knoll St
S June St
S Ives St
S Hayes St
S Grant St
S Inge St

18th St S

1

S Eads St
20th St S
21st St S
22nd St S
23rd St S
24th St S
25th St S

Crystal Dr

2 P

George Washington Memorial Pkwy

23

S Pierce St
S Oakcrest Rd
21st St S
22nd St S

S Joyce St
S Knoll St
23rd Rd S

C

S Glebe Rd
27th Rd S
S Four Mile Run Dr
S Cleveland St

39

24th St S
25th St S
26th St S

S Queen St
S Rolfe St
S Ode St
S Meade St
S Lang St

James W Haley Park

23rd St S
24th St S
25th St S
26th St S
27th St S
28th St S

S Oakcrest Rd
Fort Scott Dr
S Kent St
S June St
S Ives St
S Joyce St

24th St S
2500

S Fort Scott Dr
Four Mile Run

43

2600

26th St S
27th St S
28th St S
29th St S

S Hill St
S Fox St
S Grove St
S Ives St

Fort Scott
Park

S Fern St
Jefferson Davis Hwy
Crystal Dr

P
P
P
P

31st St S
3100
S Dale St

24th Rd S
27th Rd S

S Glebe Rd
Doctors Branch
900

Four Mile Run
Mt Vernon Ave

Martha Custis Dr
Lyons St
Fitzgerald Ln
Greenway Pl
Manor Rd
Valley Dr
Cameron Mills Rd
Tennessee Ave
Florence Dr
Four Mile Rd
Pullman Pl
Gresham Pl
Norwood Pl
Old Dominion Blvd

W Glebe Rd
Russell Rd
Courtland Cir
Executive Ave
Alexander St
Bruce St

Commonwealth Ave

George Washington Memorial Pkwy

1/4 mile

.25 km

When metroing to this area listen carefully. (Did the conductor just say Pentagon or Pentagon City?) Don't worry; the apparel of those exiting will let you know what state you're in. Camo for the famously shaped military center, short skirts and Coach bags for the mall. Visitors to this neighborhood may be shopping for the newest prom dress, defense contract, or Costco deal.

Banks

- **Bank of America** · 1425 S Eads St
- **Bank of America** · 3600 S Glebe Rd
- **Bank of America (ATM)** · Fashion Center at Pentagon City · 1100 S Hayes st
- **Bank of America (ATM)** · 1101 S Joyce St
- **BB&T** · 2113 Crystal Plz Arc
- **BB&T** · 2221 S Eads St
- **BB&T** · 2947 S Glebe Rd
- **Burke & Herbert** · 500 23rd St S
- **Chevy Chase** · 1100 S Hayes St
- **Chevy Chase** · 1621 Crystal Sq Arc
- **Chevy Chase** · 2100 S Crystal Dr
- **Chevy Chase** · 2901 S Glebe Rd
- **PNC (ATM)** · 1301 S Scott St
- **PNC (ATM)** · 1600 S Eads St
- **Wachovia** · 251 18th St S
- **Wachovia (ATM)** · 1615 Crystal Sq Arc

Car Rental

- **Alamo** · 2780 Jefferson Davis Hwy · 703-684-0086
- **Budget** · 1800 S Jefferson Davis Hwy · 703-521-2908
- **Dollar** · 2600 Jefferson Davis Hwy · 866-434-2226
- **Enterprise** · 1225 S Clark St · 703-553-2930
- **Enterprise** · 2020 Jefferson Davis Hwy · 703-553-7744
- **Enterprise** · 2121 Crystal Dr · 703-553-2930
- **Hertz** · Double Tree Hotel · 300 Army Navy Dr · 703-413-7142
- **Rent-A-Wreck** · 901 S Clark St · 703-413-7100
- **Thrifty** · 2600 Jefferson Davis Hwy · 877-283-0898

Gas Stations

- **Citgo** · 801 S Joyce St
- **Exxon** · 2720 S Glebe Rd

○Landmarks

- **Pentagon** · Boundary Channel Dr

Libraries

- **Arlington County Aurora Hills Library** · 735 18th St S

Parking

Pharmacies

- **Costco Wholesale Pharmacy** · 1200 S Fern St
- **CVS** · 2400 Jefferson Davis Hwy
- **CVS** · The Pentagon
- **Eckerd's** · 1301 Joyce St
- **Giant Food Pharmacy** · 2901 S Glebe Rd
- **Harris Teeter** · 900 Army Navy Dr
- **Rite Aid** · 1671 Crystal Sq Arc

Post Offices

- **Eads** · 1720 S Eads St
- **Pentagon** · 9998 The Pentagon

Schools

- **DeVry University (Arlington Campus)** · 2450 Crystal Dr
- **Gunston Middle** · 2700 S Lang St
- **Hoffman-Boston Elementary** · 1415 S Queen St
- **Oakridge Elementary** · 1414 24th St S

Supermarkets

- **Giant Food** · 2901 S Glebe Rd
- **Harris Teeter** · 900 Army Navy Dr

Map 40 · Pentagon City / Crystal City

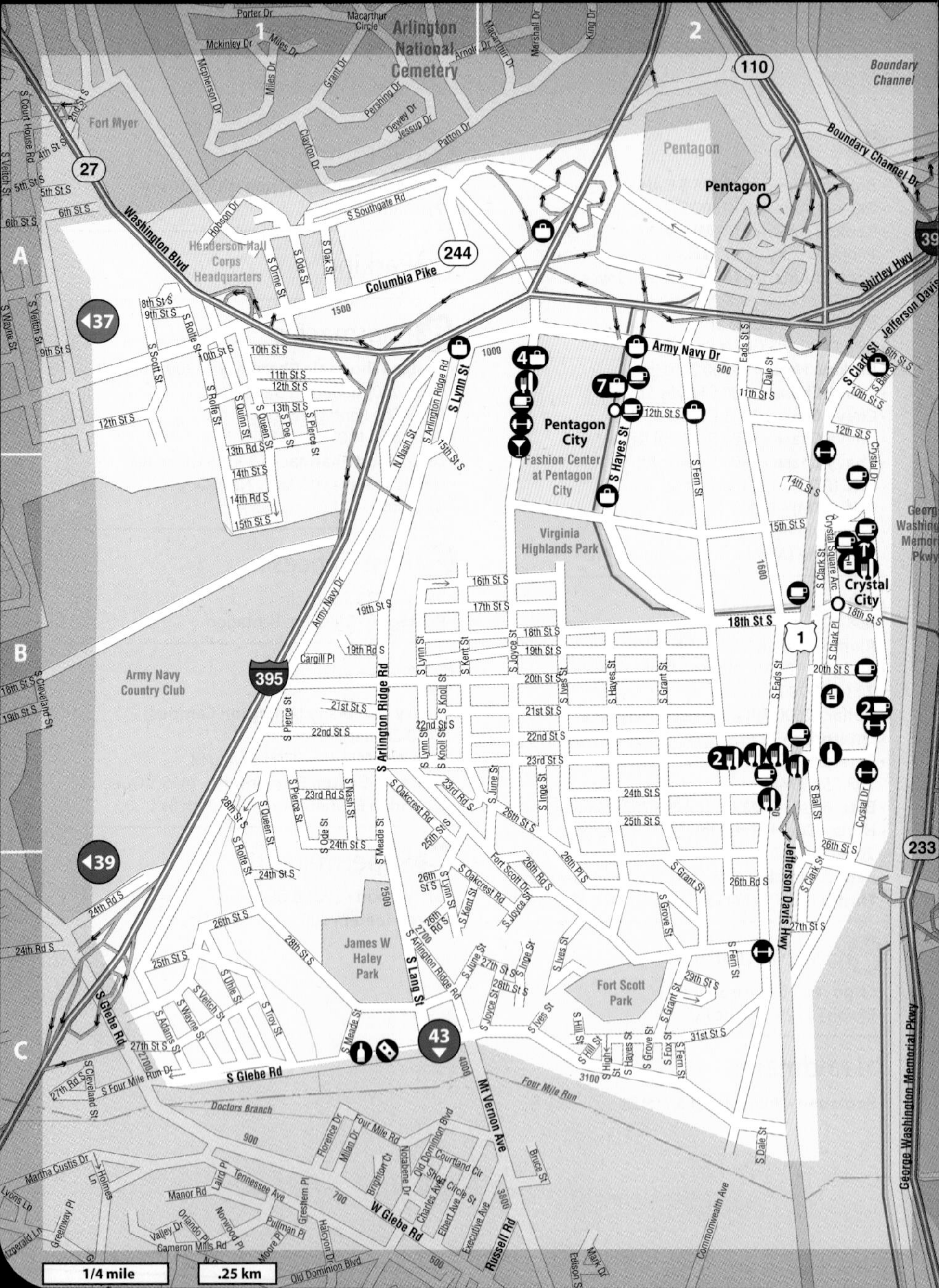

N

1 2

Porter Dr
Mckinley Dr
Miles Dr
Macarthur Circle
Arlington National Cemetery
Marshall Dr
King Dr
110
Boundary Channel

Grant Dr
Pershing Dr
Arnold Dr
Dewey Dr
Jessup Dr
Patton Dr
Boundary Channel Dr

Fort Myer
S Court House Rd
S Rolfe St
Clayton Dr
Hobson Dr
Ord Dr

Pentagon
Pentagon

Shirley Hwy
39

27
S Veitch St
S Wayne St
5th St S
6th St S
Washington Blvd
Henderson Mall Corps Headquarters
S Oak St
S Orme St
S Southgate Rd
Columbia Pike
244
1500

Jefferson Davis
A

37
8th St S
9th St S
S Rolfe St
S Scott St
10th St S
11th St S
12th St S
13th St S
S Queen St
S Pierce St
14th St S
14th Rd S
15th St S
N Nash St
S Lynn St
S Arlington Ridge Rd
19th St S
1000
4
7
Pentagon City
Army Navy Dr
Eads St S
500
11th St S
Dale St
12th St S
S Clark St
10th St S
9th St S
Crystal Dr
14th St S
Fashion Center at Pentagon City
S Hayes St
S Fern St
1600
15th St S
George Washington Memorial Pkwy

B
Virginia Highlands Park
Crystal City
18th St S
1
S Eads St
S Clark St
18th St S
20th St S

Army Navy Country Club
S Pierce St
395
16th St S
17th St S
18th St S
19th St S
20th St S
21st St S
22nd St S
23rd St S
S Lynn St
S Kent St
S Joyce St
S Knoll St
S June St
S Hayes St
S Inge St
S Grant St
S Ball St
Crystal Dr
2
Cargill Pl
19th Rd S

18th St S
Cleveland St
21st St S
22nd St S
23rd Rd S
S Pierce St
S Old St
24th St S
S Meade St
S Oakcrest Rd
23rd Rd S
24th St S
25th St S
26th St S
Fort Scott Dr
S June St
S Grove St
S Fern St
Jefferson Davis Hwy
26th St S
S Clark St
233

39
24th Rd S
S Queen St
S Rolfe St
25th St S
26th St S
James W Haley Park
2500
26th St S
S Lynn St
S Oakcrest Rd
Fort Scott Park

C
27th St S
S Glebe Rd
S Veitch St
S Adams St
S Lang St
43
S Hill St
S Hayes St
S Fox St
31st St S
3100
S Glebe Rd
S Four Mile Run Dr
Four Mile Run
24th Rd S
S Cleveland St
Doctors Branch
900
Florence St
Four Mile Rd
Mt Vernon Ave
Old Dominion Blvd
Russell Rd

Martha Custis Dr
Lynn Lp
Greenbrier Pl
Manor Rd
Tennessee Ave
Norwood Pl
Valley Dr
Orlando Pl
Cameron Mills Rd
W Glebe Rd
Cliff St
Brighton Ct
Gresham Pl
Halcyon Dr
Chalfonte Dr
Circle Dr
700
Ancell St
Edison St
Commonwealth Ave

1/4 mile   .25 km

If you're a government employee or contractor looking to woo some clients, there's the reliable East Coast chain Legal Seafood. If you miss your suburban days as a mallrat and hate the swarming crowds of Georgetown or Friendship Heights, cross the river and try out the Fashion Center at Pentagon City. It is conveniently off the Metro and is the most comprehensive shopping space under one roof.

Coffee

- **Caribou Coffee** · 2100 Crystal Dr
- **Dunkin Donuts** · 1687 Crystal Sq Arc
- **Shisha Palace Café** · 2325 S Eads St
- **Starbucks** · 1100 S Hayes St
- **Starbucks** · 1101 S Joyce St
- **Starbucks** · 1201 S Hayes St
- **Starbucks** · 1480 Crystal Dr
- **Starbucks** · 1649 Crystal Sq
- **Starbucks** · 1700 Jefferson Davis Hwy
- **Starbucks** · 2231 Crystal Dr

Copy Shops

- **FedEx Kinko's** · 1601 Crystal Sq Arc
- **Minuteman Press** · 2187 Crystal Plz Arc

Gyms

- **Bally Total Fitness** · 1201 S Joyce St
- **Crystal Gateway Sport & Health** · 1235 S Clarke St
- **Crystal Park Sport & Health** · 2231 Crystal Dr
- **Curves (women only)** · 2345 Crystal Dr
- **Gold's Gym** · 2955 S Glebe Rd

Hardware Stores

- **Crystal City Hardware** · 1612 Crystal Sq Arc

Liquor Stores

- **ABC** · 2955 S Glebe Rd
- **ABC** · 320 23rd St S

Nightlife

- **Sine Irish Pub** · 1301 S Joyce St

Restaurants

- **Bonsai Grill** · 553 23rd St S
- **Crystal City Restaurant** · 422 23rd St S
- **Crystal City Sports Pub** · 529 23rd St S
- **Kabob Palace** · 2333 S Eads St
- **Legal Seafood** · 2301 Jefferson Davis Hwy
- **Morton's of Arlington** · Crystal City Shops · 1750 Crystal Dr
- **Noodles & Company** · 1201 S Joyce St

Shopping

- **Abercrombie & Fitch** · 1100 S Hayes St
- **Actors Center** · 601 S Clark St
- **Apple Store** · 1100 S Hayes St
- **BCBGMAXAZRIA** · 1100 S Hayes St
- **bebe** · 1100 S Hayes St
- **Costco** · 1200 S Fern St
- **Denim Bar** · 1101 S Joyce St
- **Elizabeth Arden Red Door Salon & Spa** · 1101 S Joyce St
- **Fashion Center-Pentagon City** · 1100 S Hayes
- **Harris Teeter** · 900 Army Navy Dr
- **Kenneth Cole** · 1100 S Hayes St
- **Macy's** · 1000 S Hayes St
- **La'Vand** · 1301 S Joyce St
- **Nordstrom** · 1400 S Hayes St
- **Williams-Sonoma** · 1100 S Hayes St
- **World Market** · 1301 S Joyce St

Video Rental

- **Blockbuster** · 2931 S Glebe Rd

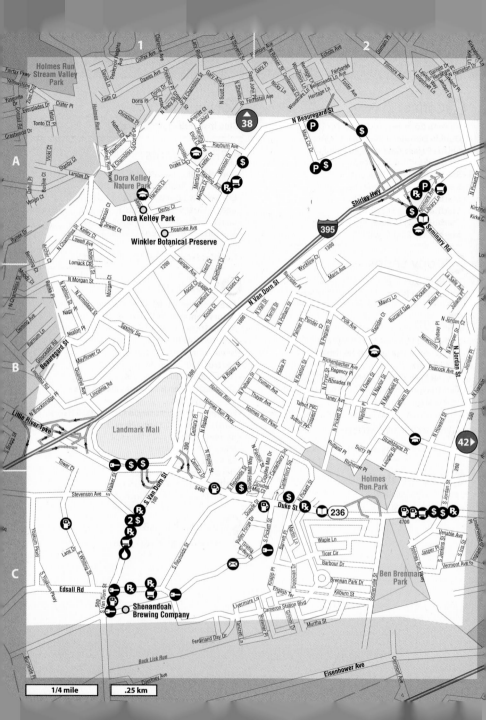

You gotta love gentrification. Suddenly, even seedy places like Landmark have golden appeal to DC commuters, pissed off with the traffic to their further suburbs, trade in their McMansions for a piece of cheaper development closer to the city. Now, this poor relation of Old Town is beginning to shape up into a white-collar scene of new restaurants and shops, catering to the new money pouring in. The Metro is what keeps the area transitioning, and only more growth is expected.

$ Banks

- **Bank of America (ATM)** •
  Landmark Mall - Food Court • 5801 Duke St
- **BB&T** • 233 S Van Dorn St
- **BB&T** • 4999 Seminary Rd
- **Burke & Herbert** • 155 N Paxton St
- **PNC** • 4513 Duke St
- **PNC (ATM)** • 4825 Mark Ctr Dr
- **Provident** • 231 S Van Dorn St
- **Sun Trust** • 1460 N Beauregard St
- **Sun Trust** • 4616 Kenmore Ave
- **Sun Trust** • 5701 Duke St
- **Virginia Commerce** • 5140 Duke St
- **Wachovia** • 4601 Duke St

Car Rental

- **Avis** • 6001 Duke St • 703-256-4335
- **Enterprise** • 200 S Pickett St • 703-341-2117
- **Enterprise** • 512 S Van Dorn St • 703-823-5700
- **Enterprise** • 5800 Edsall Rd • 703-658-0010
- **Hertz** • 501 S Pickett St • 703-751-1250

Car Washes

- **Mr Wash** • 420 S Van Dorn St

Gas Stations

- **Exxon** • 4657 Duke St
- **Exxon** • 501 S Van Dorn St
- **Shell** • 4670 Duke St
- **Shell** • 5200 Duke St
- **Sunoco** • 190 S Whiting St
- **Sunoco** • 5412 Duke St

Landmarks

- **Dora Kelley Park** • 5750 Sanger Ave
- **Shenandoah Brewing Company** • 652 S Pickett St
- **Winkler Botanical Preserve** • 5400 Roanoke Ave

Libraries

- **Alexandria Charles E Beatley Jr Central Library** •
  5005 Duke St
- **Alexandria Ellen Coolidge Burke Branch Library** •
  4701 Seminary Rd

Parking

Pharmacies

- **CVS** • 1462 Beauregard St
- **CVS** • 259 S Van Dorn St
- **CVS** • 4606 Kenmore Ave
- **CVS** • 5101 Duke St
- **Giant Food** • 5730 Edsall Rd
- **Rite Aid** • 4515 Duke St
- **Safeway** • 299 S Van Dorn St

Post Offices

- **Trade Center** • 340 S Pickett St

Schools

- **Francis C Hammond Middle** • 4646 Seminary Rd
- **James K Polk Elementary** • 5000 Polk Ave
- **John Adams Elementary** • 5651 Rayburn Ave
- **Patrick Henry Elementary** • 4643 Taney Ave
- **William Ramsey Elementary** • 5700 Sanger Ave

Supermarkets

- **Giant Food** • 1476 N Beauregard St
- **Giant Food** • 5730 Edsall Rd
- **Harris Teeter** • 4641 Duke St
- **Magruder's** • 4604 Kenmore Ave
- **Safeway** • 299 S Van Dorn St

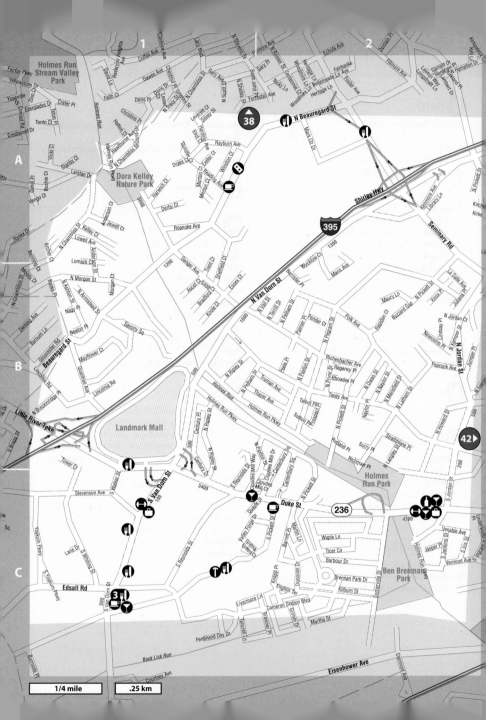

There are still some—shall we say—seedy areas around, but Landmark's appeal to commuters has helped revitalize the area. You'll find plenty of nearby dining possibilities—try the crabcakes at Clyde's, or just head to BJ's Wholesale Club and make your own gourmet meal (serves 25 or more). The local mall is on its way out, rumored to be re-imagined as, you guessed it, more housing.

Coffee

- **Café Aurora** · 50 S Pickett St
- **Cameron Perks** · 4911 Brenman Park Dr
- **Dunkin' Donuts** · 504 S Van Dorn St
- **Starbucks** · 1462 N Beauregard St

Gyms

- **Curves (women only)** · 4613 Duke St
- **Fitness First** · 255 S Van Dorn St

Hardware Stores

- **Home Depot** · 400 S Pickett St

Liquor Stores

- **Virginia ABC** · 4647 Duke St

Nightlife

- **Mango Mike's** · 4580 Duke St
- **Shenandoah Brewing Company** · 652 S Pickett St
- **Shooter McGee's** · 5239 Duke St
- **Zig's** · 815 King St

Restaurants

- **Akasaka** · 514-C S Van Dorn St
- **American Café** · 5801 Duke St
- **Clyde's** · 1700 N Beauregard St
- **Edgardo's Trattoria** · 281 S Van Dorn St
- **El Paraiso** · 516 S Van Dorn St
- **Finn & Porter** · Hilton · 5000 Seminary Rd
- **Mediterranean Bakery** · 352 S Pickett St
- **Sakulthai Restaurant** · 408 S Van Dorn St
- **Thai Lemon Grass** · 506 S Van Dorn St

Shopping

- **Authentically Amish Fine Furnishings** · 4609 Duke St
- **BJ's Wholesale Club** · 101 S Van Dorn St

Video Rental

- **Blockbuster** · 1480 N Beauregard St

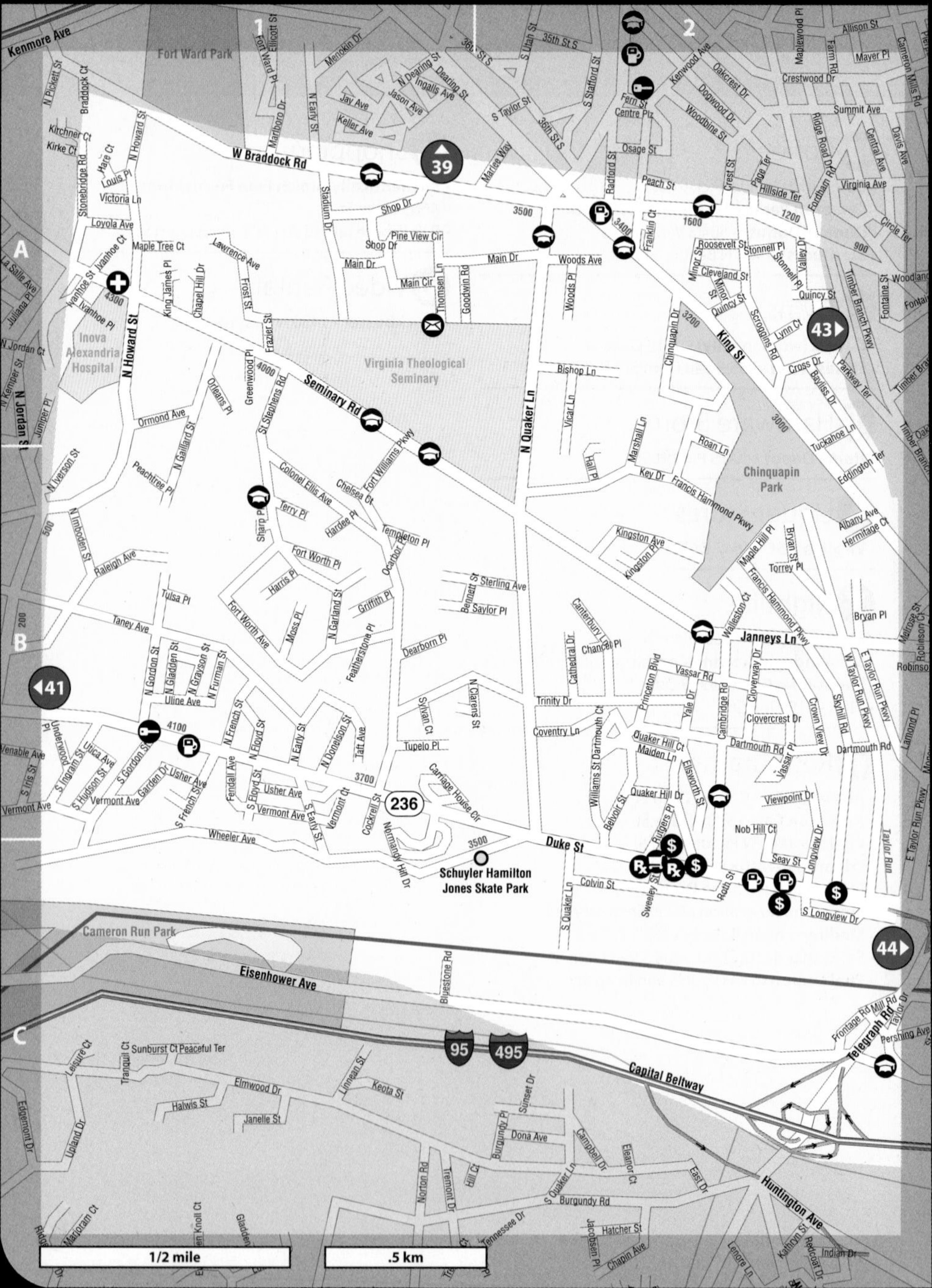

Map 42 · Alexandria (West)

N

Kenmore Ave

Fort Ward Park

W Braddock Rd

39

3500

43

Virginia Theological Seminary

Inova Alexandria Hospital

N Howard St

Seminary Rd

N Quaker Ln

King St

Chinquapin Park

41

4100

3700

Janneys Ln

236

3500

Duke St

Schuyler Hamilton Jones Skate Park

44

Cameron Run Park

Eisenhower Ave

95 **495**

Capital Beltway

Huntington Ave

Telegraph Rd

| 1/2 mile | .5 km |

Essentials

Map 42

The plentiful apartments in Alexandria make it popular with 20-somethings who like urban living but can't hack the high rents in Clarendon or DC. There's also a high concentration of plaid skirts, what with all the Catholic schools around. Oh, but remember those Titans—T.C. Williams is in this area as well.

Banks

- **Bank of America** · 2747 Duke St
- **Burke & Herbert (ATM)** · 2836 Duke St
- **Chevy Chase** · 3131 Duke St
- **Sun Trust** · 3101 Duke St

Car Rental

- **Enterprise** · 4213 Duke St · 703-212-4700

Emergency Rooms

- **Inova Alexandria Hospital** · 4320 Seminary Rd

Gas Stations

- **Crown** · 4109 Duke St
- **Shell** · 2922 Duke St
- **Sunoco** · 2838 Duke St
- **Texaco** · 3401 King St

oLandmarks

- **Schuyler Hamilton Jones Skate Park** · 3540 Wheeler Ave

Pharmacies

- **CVS** · 3130 Duke St
- **Giant Food** · 3131 Duke St

Post Offices

- **Theological Seminary** · 3737 Seminary Rd

Schools

- **Bishop Ireton High** · 201 Cambridge Rd
- **Blessed Sacrament** · 1417 W Braddock Rd
- **Douglas MacArthur Elementary** · 1101 Janneys Ln
- **Episcopal High** · 1200 N Quaker Ln
- **Minnie Howard** · 3801 W Braddock Rd
- **St Stephen's & St Agnes Upper** · 1000 St Stephens Rd
- **Strayer University (Alexandria Campus)** · 2730 Eisenhower Ave
- **TC Williams High** · 3330 King St
- **Thornton Friends** · 3830 Seminary Rd
- **Virginia Theological Seminary** · 3737 Seminary Rd

Supermarkets

- **Giant Food** · 3131 Duke St

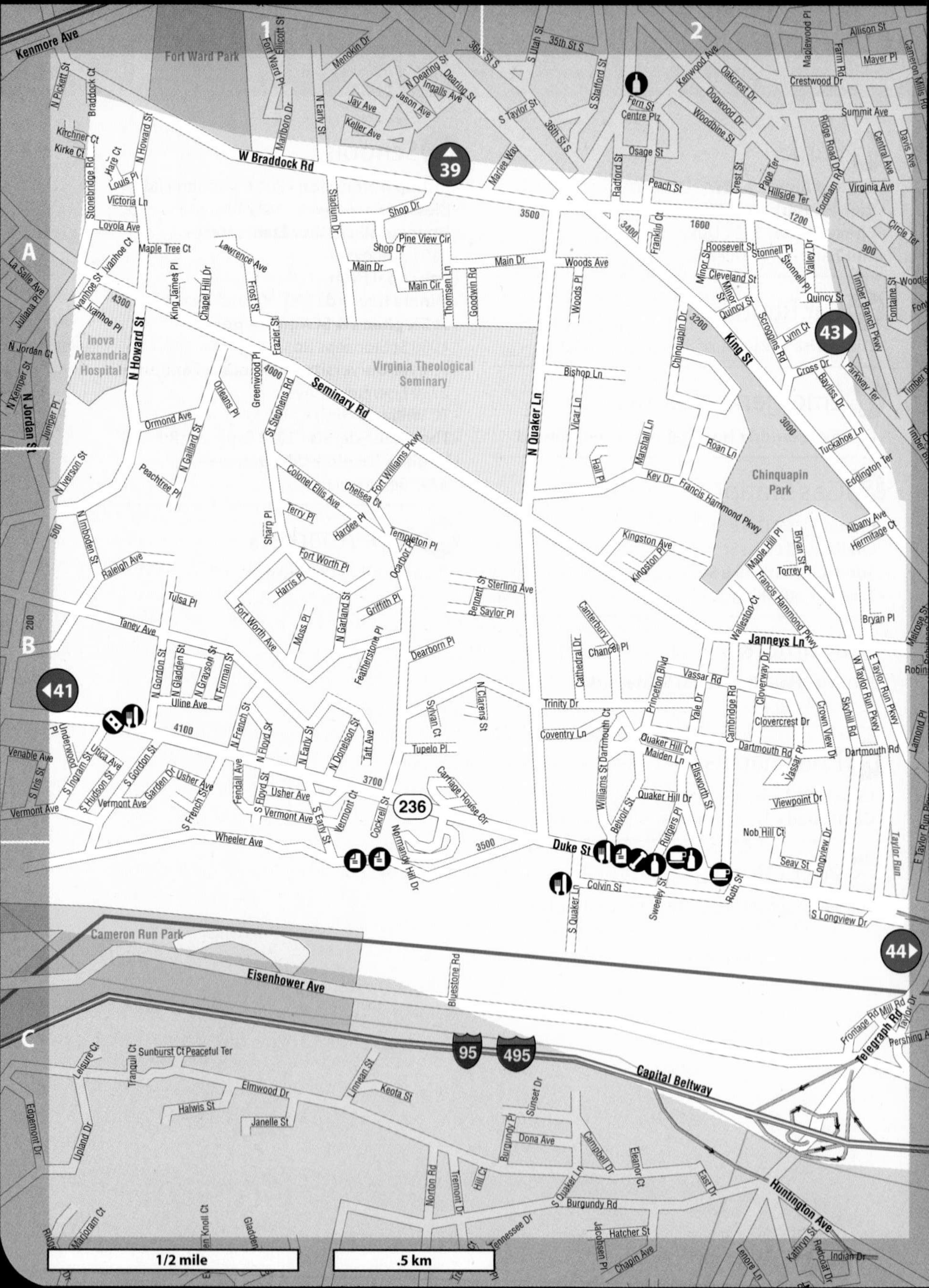

Map 42 • **Alexandria (West)**

N

1

2

Kenmore Ave

Fort Ward Park

W Braddock Rd

39

A

Inova
Alexandria
Hospital

Seminary Rd

Virginia Theological
Seminary

N Quaker Ln

King St

43

Chinquapin
Park

Francis Hammond Pkwy

Janneys Ln

B

41

236

Duke St

44

Cameron Run Park

Eisenhower Ave

C

95 **495**

Capital Beltway

Huntington Ave

1/2 mile

.5 km

Map 4

There are some interesting eats in this neighborhood. Café Monti pairs the best tastes of Italy and Austria, for those who like their pasta followed by strudel, and Rockland's BBQ is fantastic.

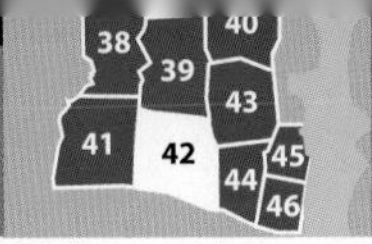

Coffee

• **Dunkin' Donuts** • 3050 Duke St
• **Starbucks** • 3113 Duke St

Copy Shops

• **Global Printing** • 3670 Wheeler Ave
• **Graphic Images** • 3660 Wheeler Ave
• **UPS Store** • 3213 Duke St

Liquor Stores

• **ABC** • 3161 Duke St
• **Fern Gourmet Street (wine only)** • 1708 Fern St
• **Rick's Wine & Gourmet** • 3117 Duke St

Pet Shops

• **Wild Bird Center** • 3216 Duke St

Restaurants

• **Café Monti** • 3250 Duke St
• **Rocklands** • 25 S Quaker Ln
• **Tempo Restaurant** • 4231 Duke St

Video Rental

• **Blockbuster** • 4349 Duke St

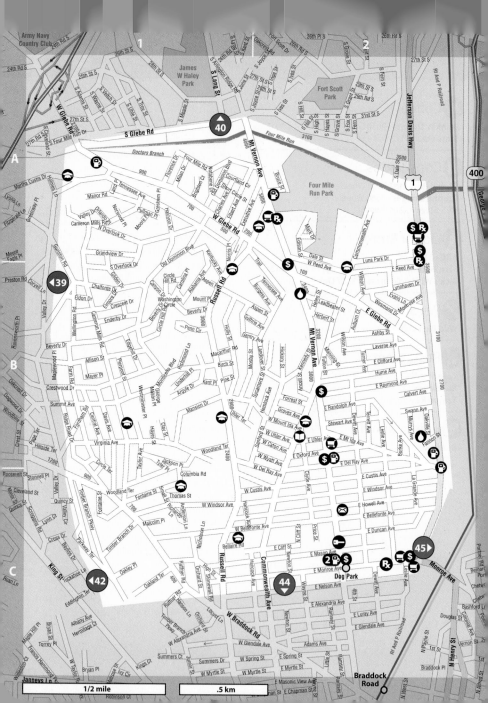

Thanks to its bohemian, liberal residents, there's a real sense of community here, where neighbors say hello, children have manners, and activists fight to better their town. Craftsman bungalows with inviting front porches line the narrow streets, while young families, gay couples, and fifty-something bohemians stroll "The Avenue."

$ Banks

- **Burke & Herbert** · 306 E Monroe Ave
- **Chevy Chase (ATM)** · 3671 Jefferson Davis Hwy
- **Chevy Chase (ATM)** · Giant Food Store · 425 E Monroe Ave
- **Provident** · 3801 Jefferson Davis Hwy
- **Sun Trust** · 2809 Mt Vernon Ave
- **Virginia Commerce** · 2401 Mt Vernon Ave
- **Wachovia** · 3506 Mt Vernon Ave

Car Rental

- **Enterprise** · 1704 Mt Vernon Ave · 703-548-5015

Car Washes

- **Mr Wash** · 3407 Mt Vernon Ave
- **Nab Auto Appearance Salon** · 2414 Oakville St

Gas Stations

- **Citgo** · 1015 W Glebe Rd
- **Citgo** · 2312 Mt Vernon Ave
- **Exxon** · 1601 Mt Vernon Ave
- **Exxon** · 2300 Jefferson Davis Hwy
- **Exxon** · 2320 Jefferson Davis Hwy
- **Exxon** · 4001 Mt Vernon Ave
- **Shell** · 1600 Mt Vernon Ave

Landmarks

- **Dog Park** · At Simpson Stadium Park, NW Corner of E Monroe Ave & Jefferson Davis Hwy

Libraries

- **Alexandria James M Duncan Branch Library** · 2501 Commonwealth Ave

Pharmacies

- **CVS** · 3811 Mt Vernon Ave
- **CVS** · 415 Monroe Ave
- **Shoppers Food Warehouse** · 3801 Jefferson Davis Hwy
- **Target** · 3101 Jefferson Davis Hwy

Post Offices

- **Potomac** · 1908 Mt Vernon Ave

Schools

- **Alexandria Country Day** · 2400 Russell Rd
- **Charles Barrett Elementary** · 1115 Martha Custis Dr
- **Cora Kelly Elementary** · 3600 Commonwealth Ave
- **George Mason Elementary** · 2601 Cameron Mills Rd
- **Grace Episcopal** · 3601 Russell Rd
- **Immanuel Lutheran** · 109 Belleaire Rd
- **Mount Vernon Community** · 2601 Commonwealth Ave
- **St Rita** · 3801 Russell Rd
- **St Stephen's & St Agnes Lower** · 400 Fontaine St

Supermarkets

- **Giant Food** · 425 E Monroe Ave
- **Gold Crust Baking Company** · 501 E Monroe Ave
- **Mom's Organic Market** · 3831 Mt Vernon Ave
- **Shoppers** · 3801 Jefferson Davis Hwy

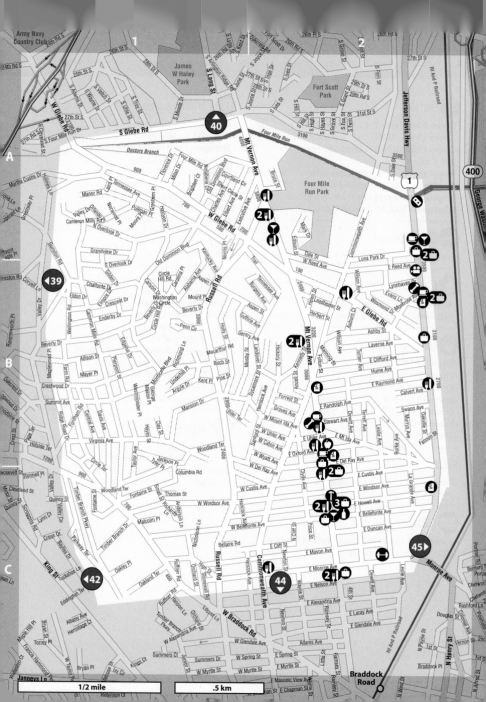

Mount Vernon Avenue is brimming with neat little restaurants, pottery studios, and antiques shops. The Evening Star's entrees always shine brightly, and are followed nicely by a stop at The Dairy Godmother for a creatively flavored custard. Parents visiting? Take them to Del Merei Grill for a refined dining experience, followed by a show at local institution Birchmere for folk music.

Coffee

- **Caboose Café & Bakery** · 2419 Mt Vernon Ave
- **Dunkin' Donuts** · 3325 Jefferson Davis Hwy
- **St Elmo's Coffee Pub** · 2300 Mt Vernon Ave
- **Starbucks** · 3825 Jefferson Davis Hwy

Copy Shops

- **A&Z Printing & Duplicating** ·
  2000 Jefferson Davis Hwy
- **ASAP Printing & Mailing CO Inc** ·
  2805 Mt Vernon Ave
- **Staples** · 3301 Jefferson Davis Hwy
- **UPS Store** · 2308 Mt Vernon Ave

Farmers Markets

- **Del Ray Farmers Market
  (May–Oct; Sat, 8 am–12 pm)** ·
  Mt Vernon & Oxford Aves

Gyms

- **YMCA Alexandria** · 420 E Monroe Ave

Hardware Stores

- **Executive Lock & Key** · 2003 Mt Vernon Ave

Liquor Stores

- **Planet Wine & Gourmet** · 2004 Mt Vernon Ave

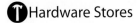Movie Theaters

- **Regal Potomac Yard 16** · 3575 Jefferson Davis Hwy

Nightlife

- **Birchmere** · 3701 Mt Vernon Ave
- **Hops** · 3625 Jefferson Davis Hwy
- **No 9 Lounge** · 2000 Mt Vernon Ave

Pet Shops

- **Nature's Nibbles** · 2601 Mt Vernon Ave
- **Petsmart** · 3351 Jefferson Davis Hwy

Restaurants

- **Afghan Restaurant** · 2700 Jefferson Davis Hwy
- **Al's Steak House** · 1504 Mt Vernon Ave
- **Bombay Curry Company** · 3110 Mt Vernon Ave
- **Chez Andree** · 10 E Glebe Rd
- **The Dairy Godmother** · 2310 Mt Vernon Ave
- **Del Merei Grill** · 3106 Mt Vernon Ave
- **Evening Star Café** · 2000 Mt Vernon Ave
- **Huascaran** · 3606 Mt Vernon Ave
- **Lilian's Restaurant** · 3901 Mt Vernon Ave
- **Los Tios Grill** · 2615 Mt Vernon Ave
- **Mancini's** · 1508 Mt Vernon Ave
- **Monroe's Trattoria** · 1603 Commonwealth Ave
- **RT's Restaurant** · 3804 Mt Vernon Ave
- **Taqueria Poblano** · 2400 Mt Vernon Ave
- **Thai Peppers** · 2018 Mt Vernon Ave
- **Waffle Shop** · 3864 Mt Vernon Ave

Shopping

- **A Show of Hands** · 2301 Mt Vernon Ave
- **Artfully Chocolate** · 2003 Mt Vernon Ave
- **Barnes & Noble** · 3651 Jefferson Davis Hwy
- **Best Buy** · 3401 Jefferson Davis Hwy
- **Cheesetique** · 2411 Mt Vernon Ave
- **The Clay Queen Pottery** · 2303 Mt Vernon Ave
- **The Dairy Godmother** · 2310 Mt Vernon Ave
- **Mia Gemma** · 2007 Mt Vernon Ave
- **Old Navy** · 3621 Jefferson Davis Hwy
- **Planet Wine Shop** · 2004 Mt Vernon Ave
- **Potomac West Interiors and Antique Gallery** ·
  1517 Mt Vernon Ave
- **The Purple Goose** · 2005 Mt Vernon Ave
- **The Remix** · 645 Pennsylvania Ave SE
- **Sports Authority** · 3701 Jefferson Davis Hwy
- **Staples** · 3301 Jefferson Davis Hwy
- **Target** · 3101 Jefferson Davis Hwy

Video Rental

- **Hollywood Video** · 3925 Jefferson Davis Hwy

Map 44 · **Alexandria Downtown**

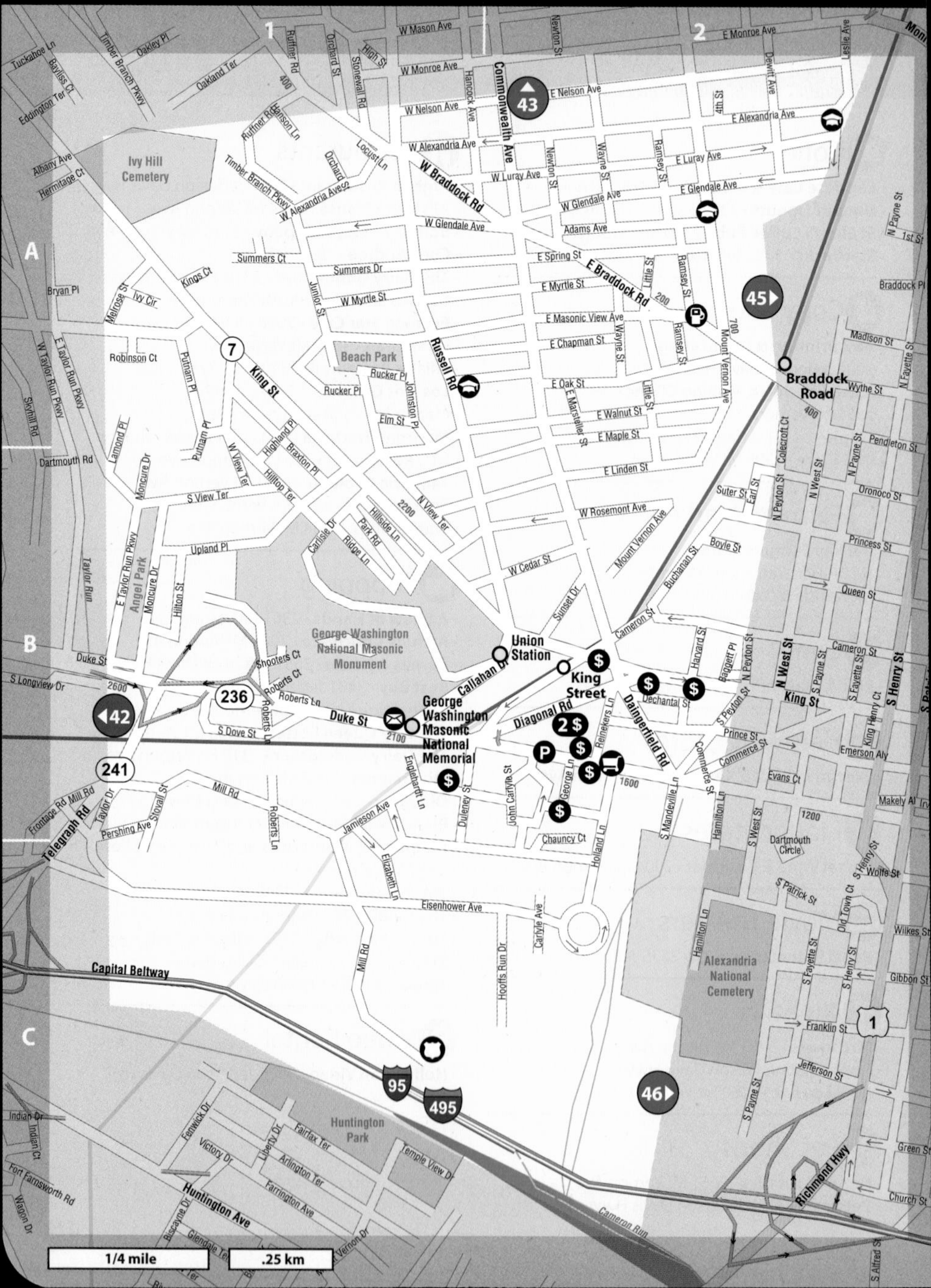

N

1

W Mason Ave

2 E Monroe Ave

W Monroe Ave

Mon

Leslie Ave

Dewitt Ave

E Nelson Ave

43

Tuckahoe Ln

Bayliss Ct

Trinier Branch Pkwy

Oakley Pl

Oakland St

Rabbit Rd

Highl St

Orchard St

Stonewall Rd

Hancock Ave

Newton St

Ruffner Rd

Edmondson Ter

Edington Ter

W Nelson Ave

Commonwealth Ave

W Alexandria Ave

E Alexandria Ave

N 5th

Kuffner Ln

Timber Branch Pkwy

Locust Ln

Ramsey St

Wayne St

4th St

Ivy Hill Cemetery

W Alexandria Ave

Orchard St

W Luray Ave

Newton St

E Luray Ave

Hermitage Ave

Albany Ave

Bryan Pl

A

E Taylor Run Pkwy

W Taylor Run Pkwy

Skyhill Rd

Monroe St

Ivy Cir

King Ct

Putnam Pl

Robinson Ct

7

King St

W View Ter

S View Ter

Lamond Pl

Moncure Dr

Dartmouth Rd

Summers Ct

Summers Dr

W Myrtle St

Junior St

W Glendale Ave

Adams Ave

Russell Rd

Beach Park

Rucker Pl

Johnston Dr

Rucker Pl

Elm St

Highland Pl

Braxton Pl

Hilltop Ter

Carlisle Dr

Ridge Rd

Park Rd

Hillside Ln

Upland Pl

S View Ter

W Braddock Rd

W Glendale Ave

W Alexandria Ave

E Spring St

E Myrtle St

E Masonic View Ave

E Chapman St

E Braddock Rd

Little St

Ramsey St

E Glendale Ave

Wayne St

Ramsey St

200

700

Mount Vernon Ave

45

Braddock Road

E Oak St

E Walnut St

E Maple St

E Linden St

W Rosemont Ave

Mount Vernon Ave

E Masonic

Little St

Madison St

Wythe St

N Peyton St

Oronoco St

Princess St

Queen St

Suter St

Earl St

Boyle St

Buchanan St

N Payne St

Wythe St

N 1st St

Braddock St

N Payne St

N West St

Pendleton St

Collector St

400

B

S Longview Dr

Duke St

2600

Taylor Run Pkwy

E Taylor Run Pkwy

Angel Park

Moncure Dr

Hilton St

Shooters Ct

Roberts Ct

Roberts Ln

236

Duke St

S Dove St

George Washington National Masonic Monument

Callahan Dr

Union Station

Diagonal Rd

George Washington Masonic National Memorial

42

241

Telegraph Rd

Taylor Dr

Pershing Ave

Mill Rd

Roberts Ln

Jamieson Ave

Dulany St

Elizabeth Ln

John Carlyle St

Engelhardt Ln

2100

2000

King Street

2 $

Daingerfield Rd

Reinekers Ln

Dechantal St

Prince St

Commerce St

Evans Ct

Mandeville Ln

Harvard St

Baggett Pl

N Peyton St

N West St

King St

N Payne St

N Fayette St

N Henry St

King Henry St

S Pa

Emerson Aly

1200

Makely Al

$

$

$

Cameron St

George St

Holland Ln

Chauncy Ct

1600

S Henry St

Prince St

Commerce St

Hamilton Ln

S West St

Dartmouth Circle

Wolfes St

S Patrick St

Alexandria National Cemetery

S Fayette St

Gibbon St

Wilkes St

S St Asaph St

Did Town Ct

1

Capital Beltway

Mill Rd

Hooffs Run Dr

Eisenhower Ave

Carlyle Ave

Franklin St

Jefferson St

S Payne St

Green St

C

Indian Dr

Indian Rd

Fort Farnsworth Rd

Wagon Rd

Fenwick Dr

Fairfax Dr

Victory Dr

Liberty Dr

Arlington Ter

Temple View Dr

Farrington Ave

Vernon St

Glebe St

95

495

Huntington Park

Cameron Run

Richmond Hwy

Church St

S Alfred St

Huntington Ave

1/4 mile

.25 km

$

$

46

All work with little to no play, many national associations have their headquarters here in Alexandria's "downtown." Clean and professional, but short on the wow factor, fortunately it's located next to historic Old Town, which is bursting at the seams with character. The northern half does boast some stately homes with million dollar views, but neighboring Old Town is really where it's at.

$ Banks

- **BB&T** · 1717 King St
- **Burke & Herbert** · 1775 Jamieson Ave
- **Chevy Chase** · 2051 Jamieson Ave
- **Chevy Chase (ATM)** · 1900 King St
- **First Horizon** · 1725 Duke St
- **PNC** · 1700 Diagonal Rd
- **PNC (ATM)** · Whole Foods · 1700 Duke St
- **Sun Trust** · 1650 King St
- **Sun Trust (ATM)** · Embassy Suites Hotel · 1900 Diagonal Rd

 Gas Stations

- **Sunoco** · 317 E Braddock Rd

○ Landmarks

- **George Washington Masonic National Memorial** · 101 Callahan Dr
- **Union Station** · 110 Callahan Dr

Parking

Police

- **Alexandria Police Dept** · 2003 Mill Rd

 Post Offices

- **Memorial Station** · 2226 Duke St

Schools

- **Commonwealth Academy** · 1321 Leslie Ave
- **George Washington Middle** · 1005 Mt Vernon Ave
- **Maury Elementary** · 600 Russell Rd

 Supermarkets

- **Whole Foods Market** · 1700 Duke St

Map 44 • Alexandria Downtown

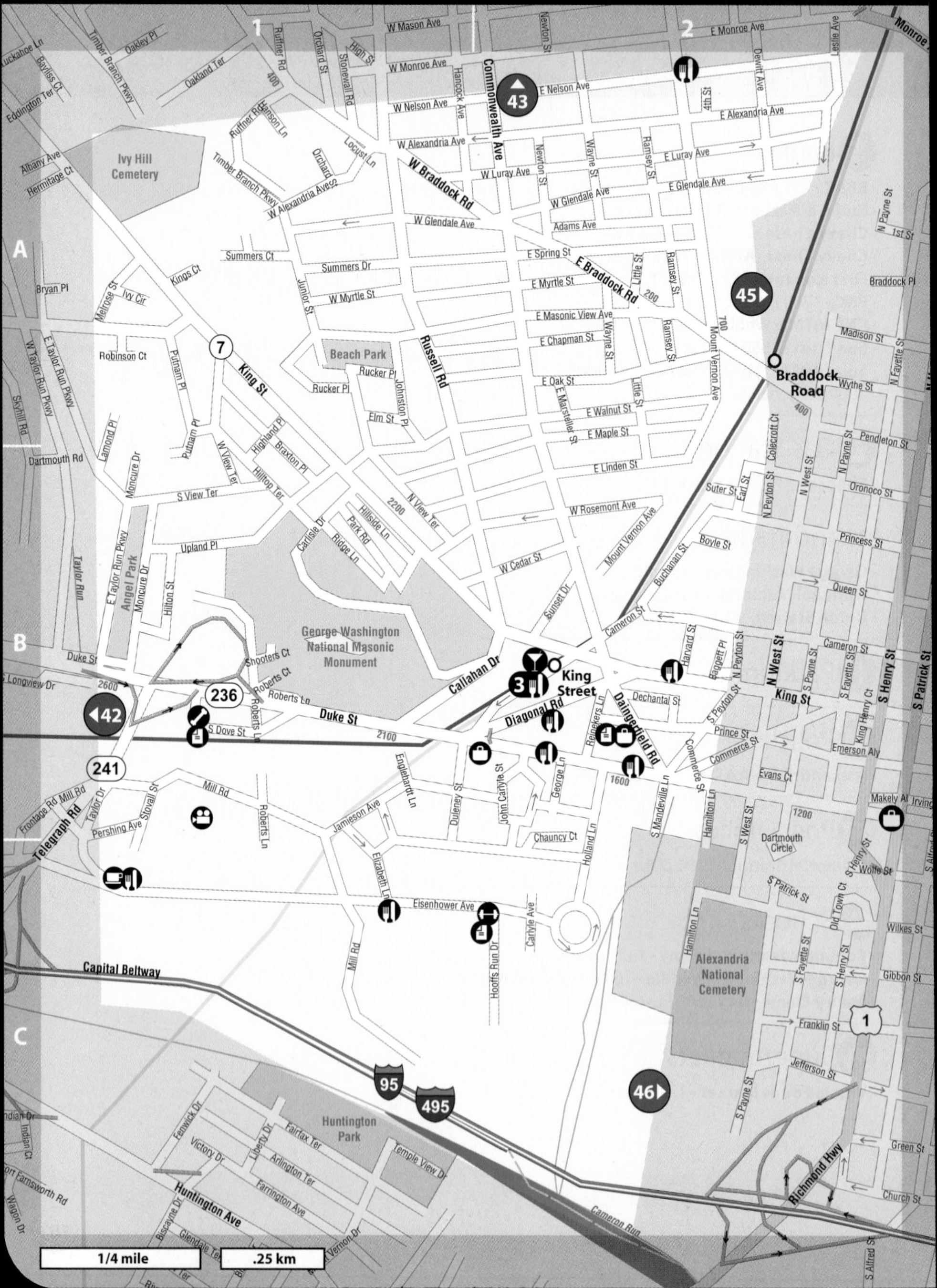

The bottom-heavy phallus that is the George Washington Masonic Memorial, where mysterious masons still meet, is the area's literal and aesthetic high point. Besides that, the Crate and Barrel outlet and Whole Foods is the second biggest draw to the neighborhood, and the giant AMC Hoffman Center is the third biggest, particularly among high schoolers.

Coffee
- **June Coffee** · 225 Reineker's Ln, #1
- **Starbucks** · 2461 Eisenhower Ave

Copy Shops
- **ABC Imaging** · 225 Reinekers Ln
- **Carriage Trade Publications** · 2393 S Dove St

Gyms
- **Jungle's Gym Fitness** · 305 Hooffs Run Dr

Movie Theaters
- **AMC Hoffman Center 22** · 206 Swamp Fox Rd

Nightlife
- **Cafe Salsa** · 808 King St

Pet Shops
- **Petsage** · 2391 S Dove St

Restaurants
- **Brabo** · 1600 King St
- **Café Old Towne** · 2111 Eisenhower Ave
- **Cafe Salsa** · 808 King St
- **FireFlies** · 1501 Mt Vernon Ave
- **Joe Theismann's Restaurant** · 1800 Diagonal Rd
- **The Perfect Pita** · 1640 King St
- **Pops Old Fashion Ice Cream** · 109 King St
- **Quattro Formaggi** · 1725 Duke St
- **Table Talk** · 1623 Duke St
- **Ted's Montana Grill** · 2451 Eisenhower Ave

Shopping
- **Crate & Barrel Outlet** · 1700 Prince St
- **Whole Foods Market** · 1700 Duke St

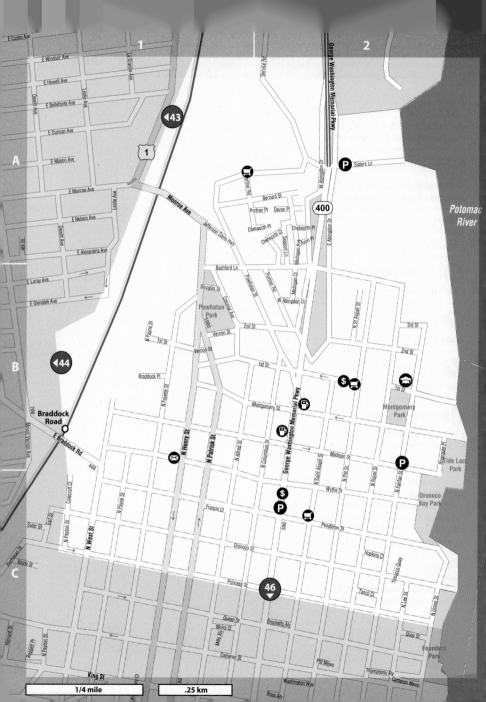

It was only a matter of time before the North began to catch up with the South—in an ironic twist of history. This area is a mix of old and new, with charming streets where residents have worked hard to update their historic townhomes with a modern edge, and modern townhomes are built with historic facades.

💲 Banks

- **Chevy Chase** • 697 N Washington St
- **Chevy Chase (ATM)** • Giant Food Store • 530 1st St

⛽ Gas Stations

- **Exxon** • 703 N Washington St
- **Shell** • 801 N Washington St

🅿 Parking

✉ Post Offices

- **Alexandria Main Office** • 1100 Wythe St

🏫 Schools

- **St Anthony's Day** • 321 First St

🛒 Supermarkets

- **Giant Food** • 530 1st St
- **Russian Gourmet** • 907 Slaters Ln
- **Trader Joe's** • 612 N St Asaph St

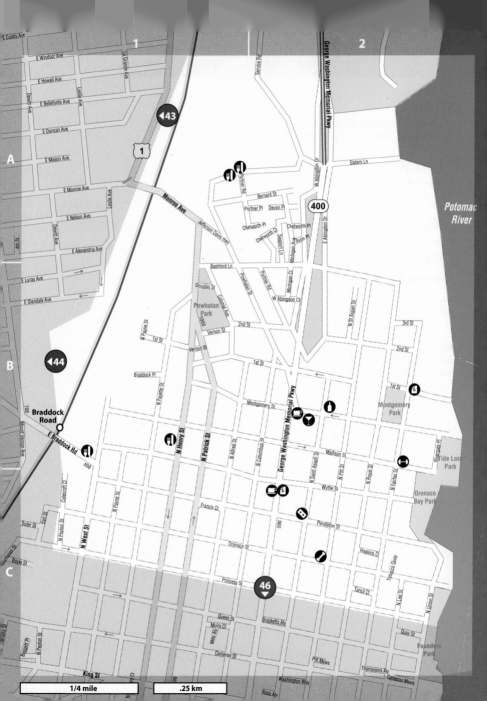

Map 4

Head to Slater's Lane for nibbles in this area. Enjoy gourmet pizzas, seared scallops, or the latest beer on tap at Rustico, or satisfy your sweet tooth with pastries, cupcakes, and other baked goods at Buzz. This area has quickly turned into a hot spot for professionals with cash who want the historic charm of Old Town without the tourists or weekend crowds.

Coffee

- **610 Coffee House** · 610 Montgomery St
- **Starbucks** · 683 N Washington St

Copy Shops

- **FedEx Kinko's** · 685 N Washington St
- **Kwik Kopy Printing** · 1001 N Fairfax St

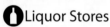Gyms

- **Old Town Sport & Health Club** · 209 Madison St

Liquor Stores

- **ABC** · 901 N St Asaph St

Nightlife

- **Stardust** · 608 Montgomery St

Pet Shops

- **Olde Towne School for Dogs** · 529 Oronoco St

Restaurants

- **Buzz Bakery** · 901 Slaters Ln
- **Esmeralda Restaurant** · 728 N Henry St
- **La Piazza** · 535 E Braddock Rd
- **Rustico** · 827 Slaters Ln
- **Stardust** · 608 Montgomery St

Video Rental

- **Blockbuster** · 602 N St Asaph St

This is arguably the most popular section of Old Town and what Arlington strives to achieve. Shops are funky, restaurants range from high-end to pizza joints, and streets with the million-dollar-plus townhomes (from the 18th to the 21st centuries) are charming and close to the Potomac. It's a great area to perambulate, peek in on local artists at the Torpedo Factory, or sit for a spell by the river.

Map

Banks

- **Bank of America** · 600 N Washington St
- **BB&T** · 300 S Washington St
- **Burke & Herbert** · 100 S Fairfax St
- **Burke & Herbert** · 621 King St
- **Chevy Chase** · 500 S Washington St
- **Chevy Chase (ATM)** · 118 King St
- **Citibank** · 110 S Washington St
- **Commerce** · 119 S Washington St
- **First Horizon** · 320 King St
- **PNC** · 411 King St
- **PNC (ATM)** · 110 S Union St
- **Sun Trust** · 515 King St
- **United** · 301 S Washington St
- **Virginia Commerce** · 1414 Prince St
- **Virginia Commerce** · 506 King St
- **Wachovia** · 330 N Washington St

 Gas Stations

- **Exxon** · 501 S Washington St
- **Exxon** · 700 S Patrick St

○ Landmarks

- **Alexandria City Farmers Market
  (Sat, 5 am–11 am)** · 301 King St
- **Alexandria City Hall** · 301 King St
- **Alexandria National Cemetery** · 1450 Wilkes St
- **Christ Church** · 118 N Washington St
- **Confederate Statue "Appomattox"** ·
  S Washington St & Prince St
- **Gadsby's Tavern Museum** · 134 N Royal St
- **The Littlest House in Alexandria** · 523 Queen St
- **Market Square Old Town** · 301 King St
- **Ramsay House** · 221 King St
- **Shipbuilder Monument** · 1 Prince St
- **Stabler-Leadbeater Apothecary Museum** ·
  105 S Fairfax St
- **Torpedo Factory Art Center** · 105 N Union St

Libraries

- **Alexandria Kate Waller Barrett Branch Library** ·
  717 Queen St
- **Alexandria Law Library** · 520 King St, Room L-34

Parking

 Pharmacies

- **Alexandria Medical Arts Pharmacy** ·
  315 S Washington St
- **CVS** · 326 King St
- **CVS** · 433 S Washington St

Post Offices

- **George Mason** · 200 N Washington St

⊖ Schools

- **Jefferson-Houston Elementary** ·
  1501 Cameron St
- **Lyles-Crouch Elementary** · 530 S St Asaph St
- **Old Town Montessori** · 115 S Washington St
- **St Coletta** · 207 S Peyton St
- **St Mary** · 400 Green St
- **St Paul's Nursery and Day** · 228 S Pitt St
- **Washington Alexandria Architecture Center** ·
  1001 Prince St

 Supermarkets

- **Balducci's** · 600 Franklin St
- **Safeway** · 500 S Royal St

Consider arriving into Old Town on bike, via the Mt. Vernon Trail. Stop here for lunch and a rest. Exceptional establishments include Restaurant Eve (four stars, so make your reservation weeks ahead) and the Chart House (lobster and a view). Nightlife abounds, but head to PX (above Eamonn's: A Dublin Chipper) for a unique "speakeasy" experience. On an afternoon outing grab a coffee at Misha's then saunter down the block and window-shop in the many area boutiques.

Coffee

- **Bread & Chocolate** · 611 King St
- **Coffee House of Occoquan** · 202 Commerce St
- **Cosi** · 700 King St
- **Firehook Bakery** · 430 S Washington St
- **Firehook Bakery & Coffee House** · 105 S Union St
- **Misha's** · 102 S Patrick St
- **Old Town Coffee Tea & Spice** · 215 S Union St
- **Perk Up** · 829 S Washington St
- **Starbucks** · 100 S Union St
- **Starbucks** · 532 King St
- **Uptowner Café** · 1609 King St

Copy Shops

- **AAB Imaging Inc** · 1101 King St
- **Insty-Prints** · 1421 Prince St
- **UPS Store** · 107 S West St

Farmers Markets

- **Alexandria City Farmers Market**
  (Sat, 5am–11am) · 301 King St

Liquor Stores

- **The Winery Inc** · 317 S Washington St

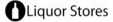Movie Theaters

- **Old Town Theater** · 815 King St

Nightlife

- **Austin Grill** · 801 King St
- **Chadwicks** · 203 The Strand
- **Flying Fish** · 815 King St
- **Laughing Lizard Lounge** · 1324 King St
- **Murphy's** · 713 King St
- **Pat Troy's Ireland's Own** · 111 N Pitt St
- **PX** · 728 King St
- **Rock It Grill** · 1319 King St
- **Tiffany Tavern** · 1116 King St
- **Union Street Public House** · 121 S Union St
- **Vermilion** · 1120 King St

Pet Shops

- **Barkley Square Gourmet Dog Bakery & Boutique** ·
  1 Wales Aly
- **Fetch** · 101 S St Asaph St
- **Madeleine's Dogs** · 1222 King St

Restaurants

- **219 Restaurant** · 219 King St
- **Bilbo Baggins** · 208 Queen St
- **Casablanca Restaurant** · 1504 King St
- **Chart House** · 1 Cameron St
- **Columbia Firehouse** · 109 S St Asaph St
- **Eamonn's: A Dublin Chipper** · 728 King St
- **Faccia Luna Trattoria** · 823 S Washington St
- **Fish Market** · 105 King St
- **Five Guys** · 107 N Fayette St
- **Grape + Bean** · 118 S Royal St
- **The Grille** · 116 S Alfred St
- **Hard Times Café** · 1404 King St
- **Il Porto** · 121 King St
- **King Street Blues** · 112 N St Asaph St
- **La Bergerie** · 218 N Lee St
- **La Tasca** · 607 King St
- **Las Tapas** · 710 King St
- **The Majestic Café** · 911 King St
- **Masaya** · 1019 King St
- **The Pita House** · 407 Cameron St
- **Restaurant Eve** · 110 S Pitt St
- **Southside 815** · 815 S Washington St
- **The Warehouse** · 214 King St

Shopping

- **An American in Paris** · 1225 King St
- **ArtCraft** · 132 King St
- **Arts Afire** · 1117 King St
- **Banana Republic** · 628 King St
- **Big Wheel Bikes** · 2 Prince St
- **Books-A-Million** · 503 King St
- **Chinoiserie** · 1024 King St
- **Comfort One Shoes** · 201 King St
- **The Full Cup** · 218 N Lee St
- **Hysteria** · 125 S Fairfax St
- **Irish Walk** · 415 King St
- **Jos A Bank** · 728 S Washington St
- **Kosmos Design & Ideas** · 1010 King St
- **La Cuisine** · 323 Cameron St
- **The Lamplighter** · 1207 King St
- **Montague & Son** · 115 S Union St
- **Notting Hill Gardens** · 815-B King St
- **P&C Art** · 212 King St
- **Pacers** · 1301 King St
- **Paper Source** · 118 King St
- **Papyrus** · 721 King St
- **The Shoe Hive** · 127 S Fairfax St
- **Treat** · 103 S St Asaph St
- **Torpedo Factory Art Center** · 105 N Union St
- **Williams-Sonoma** · 825 S Washington St
- **The Winery Inc** · 317 S Washington St

Video Rental

- **Video Vault** · 113 S Columbus St

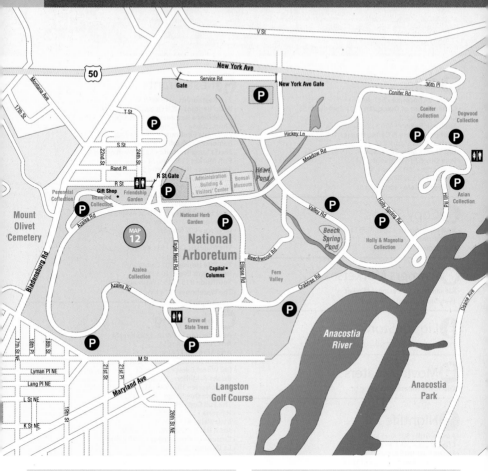

General Information

NFT Map:	12
Address:	3501 New York Ave NE
	Washington, DC 20002
Phone:	202-245-2726
Website:	www.usna.usda.gov
Hours:	Daily: 8 am–5 pm,
	except Dec 25th
Admission:	Free

Overview

Escape the hubbub of DC's urban jungle with a visit to the 446 acres of greenery at the National Arboretum, a living museum where trees, shrubs, and herbaceous plants are cultivated for science and education. Located in a remote corner of the city where few dare to venture, the Arboretum is a fresh welcome away from tourists, crowds and concrete. The Arboretum's biggest draw is the National Bonsai and Penjing Museum, where you'll find over 150 miniature trees (some hundreds of years old). A rock garden, koi pond, and ikebana exhibit (the Japanese art of flower arranging) surround the museum and have enough Zen to clear your head—unless you have allergies.

Other major attractions depend on the season. Spring sees the arboretum burst with the fresh pastels of daffodils, crocuses, and azaleas. In summer, the palette mellows with the arrival of waterlilies and wildflowers. Fall brings the stately crimsons and golds of fall foliage, while winter blankets the large pines and hollies with snow. In short, there's always something to see, and there's always a reason to come back. It's easy to see why so many couples get engaged and take their wedding photos on these fragrant, colorful, beautiful acres. For up-to-the-minute news on what's currently in bloom, check the "What's Blooming" page on the Arboretum's website.

While flowers may bloom and fade, the view of the Anacostia flowing quietly behind the Dogwood Collection is here to stay, as are the 22 Corinthian columns planted in a grassy field near the entrance, open to the sky. Originally part of the Capitol Building, these columns are probably the closest thing America has to the Parthenon. Picnic trips and leashed dogs are welcome.

If you want to mix education with pleasure, visit the Economic Botany Herbarium—a collection of over 650,000 dried plant specimens classified for the studies of agriculture, medicine, science, and education. The volunteer staff also breeds plants for other locales throughout the country in a controlled greenhouse.

The National Bonsai Collection and Penjing Museum is open 10 am–3:30 pm. The Arbor House Gift Shop is open from March 1 through mid-December; weekday hours are 10 am–3:30 pm and weekend hours are 10 am–5 pm.

Activities

The 9.6 miles of paved roads serve as excellent biking and jogging paths. Picnicking is allowed in designated areas. The Arbor Café is located next to the Administration Building and is open Friday through Sunday. Fishing, fires, and flower picking are all prohibited, and pets must be kept on leashes. The Arboretum offers public education programs including lectures, workshops, demonstrations, and plant, flower, and art exhibitions.

A 48-passenger open-air tram runs through the park on a 35-minute, non-stop, narrated tour covering the Arboretum's history, mission, and current highlights. Tram services are available on weekends from mid-April through October: $4 adults, $3 seniors, $2 kids 4–16 years old, and free for kids 4 and under. Private tours are also available with a 3-week advance reservation.

Full Moon Hikes, available during the spring and fall, take participants on a somewhat strenuous five-mile moonlit trek through the grounds, with curators providing horticultural facts along the way. Hikes vary around $22-$25 (less for Friends of the National Arboretum). You'll need to register early as there is limited space and tours fill up quickly (as in, we called at the beginning of April to book a tour in May, and we were already too late). Pre-registration is required; call 202-245-4521 to make your reservation, or find the mail-in form online.

How to Get There—Driving

From northwest Washington, follow New York Avenue east to the intersection of Bladensburg Road. Turn right onto Bladensburg Road and drive four blocks to R Street. Make a left on R Street and continue two blocks to the Arboretum gates.

Parking

Large free parking lots are located near the Grove of State Trees, by the R Street entrance, and near the New York Avenue entrance. Smaller lots are scattered throughout the grounds close to most of the major collections. Several of the parking areas have been expanded recently, and a free shuttle through the park runs continuously during summer months.

How to Get There—Mass Transit

The closest Metro subway stop is Stadium Armory Station on the Blue and Orange lines. Transfer to Metrobus B-2, get off on Bladensburg Road, and walk two blocks to R Street. Make a right on R Street and continue two more blocks to the Arboretum gates.

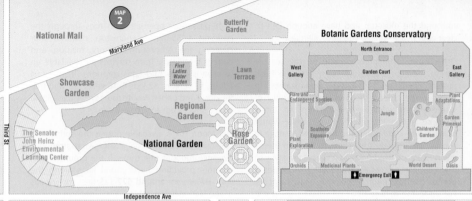

General Information

NFT Map: 2
Address: 100 Maryland Ave SW
Washington, DC 20024
Phone: 202-225-8333
Website: www.usbg.gov
Hours: 10 am–5 pm every day, including holidays
Admission: Free

Overview

Sometimes we all feel like we're living in a concrete jungle, but if you want to experience a real jungle of the green and alive variety without blowing your budget on a trip to South America, stop into the US Botanic Garden. If you need an escape from the heat or the cold or the hustle and bustle, take a stroll through the Oasis Room or curl up with a book on a bench in the glass-ceilinged Garden Court. You'll feel like you're miles away from the sidewalks and the suits, but not necessarily the tourists, especially on weekends. Nestled in the shadow of the US Capitol Building, and known as Washington's "Secret Garden," the US Botanic Garden is one of the nation's oldest botanical gardens and home to more than 25,000 different specimens. The refurbished Conservatory features a 24-foot-high mezzanine level allowing visitors to gaze downward onto a canopied rainforest. Its distinctive glass façade now houses advanced environmental control systems that allow orchid buds to bloom in the same building as desert brush, furry cacti, and nearly 4,000 other living plants. If you're looking for a particular organism but don't know where to start, you can tap into the USBG's massive computer database and search by common name, scientific name, or geographic location, or you can simply ask one of the Garden's reputable flora-fanatic employees. Can't make it to the Gardens, but still have a pressing plant question? No worries—just call the Plant Hotline at 202-226-4785 and ask away!

The USBG offers classes, exhibits, lectures, and symposia throughout the year. Visit during the week and you might be lucky enough to land on a tour (schedules vary, so be sure to check the website for up-to-date event listings), or buy tickets in advance for events such as organic beer tastings or talks on recognizing beneficial insects.

Outside is the National Garden, a three-acre plot of land located just west of the Conservatory. The landscaped space showcases the unusual, useful, and ornamental plants that flourish in the mid-Atlantic region in areas known as the Rose Garden, Butterfly Garden, and (wait for it) First Ladies' Water Garden!

Bartholdi Park, located across Independence Avenue from the Conservatory, was created in 1932 and named for sculptor Frederic Auguste Bartholdi. In addition to creating the elegant and aptly named Bartholdi Fountain in the center of the park, he also designed the Statue of Liberty. The park is open daily from dawn until dusk.

How to Get There—Mass Transit

Taking public transportation is highly recommended. By Metro, take the Blue or Orange line to Federal Center SW or Capitol South stations. If you're using the Metro Bus, take the 30, 32, 34, 35, or 36 to Independence Avenue and First Street SW. Just walk toward the giant white dome, then look south.

General Information

NFT Map: 5
Location: 225 7th St SE
            Washington, DC 20003
Website: www.easternmarket.net
Hours: South Hall Food Merchants;
            Tues–Sun: 7 am–6 pm
            Open Air Farmers Line;
            Sat–Sun: 8 am–6 pm
            Market 5 Gallery;
            Tue–Fri: 11 am–5 pm;
            Sat–Sun: 8 am–5 pm
            Market Festival; Sat: 10 am–5 pm
            Flea Market; Sun: 10 am–5 pm

Overview

The newly renovated Eastern Market retains much of its original 16,500-square-foot structure, purpose and market basics of farm produce, fresh meat cuts, seafood and flowers. Opened in 1873 as an indoor market, it proudly joins the ranks of DC's National Register of Historic Places. But as its surrounding neighborhood continues to gentrify, more DC yuppies have begun flocking to the market on the weekends, loudly denouncing Whole Foods by filling their natural fiber tote bags with tomatoes, orchids and crafts from local artisans.

However, whatever your purpose, there's plenty to be seen and eaten at the Eastern Market. The lone Market Lunch counter draws a line out the door on weekends as it dishes up greasy, hit-the-spot breakfasts (we love the pancakes) and Chesapeake lunch favorites (try the softshell crab sandwich). The freshly grown produce is difficult to ignore, and you'll consider buying a giant basil plant or a

On the sidewalks outside, artists, farmers, and charlatans hawk their wares. Antique and collectibles vendors fill the playground behind Hines Junior High School with piles of trinkets, textiles, furniture, bikes and trash. They call it a flea market, but don't expect bargains. It's also a good place to see if your missing bike might be for sale. There are, however, some decent deals to be found across the street on the north side of the market, plus interesting art that might find a place in your fancy new townhouse.

Market 5 Gallery

202-543-7293; www.market5gallery.org
The non-profit arts organization Market 5 dominates the North Hall. The group hosts art fairs and sponsors Saturday performances. Artists, musicians, and artisans have always been a part of the traditional "marketplace," and the Saturday festival on the gallery's North Plaza was begun in 1978 to bring the tradition back to Eastern Market.

Market 5 is also an art gallery that gives classes in the arts for the Capitol Hill community

How to Get There—Driving

Parking is scarce, but if you must: From the south, take I-395 across the 14th Street Bridge, bear right over the bridge onto the Southwest Expressway; exit at 6th Street SE, the first exit beyond South Capitol Street. At the bottom of the ramp, continue one block and turn left on 7th Street SE. The next major intersection with a traffic light is Pennsylvania Avenue. You'll see Hines School on the opposite corner.

From the west, take I-66 to Rosslyn, Virginia, and Route 110 to I-395 N, then follow the directions above.

From the north, take Baltimore-Washington Parkway and I-295, exiting at Pennsylvania Avenue (East). A U-turn can be made at the second light to head westbound on Pennsylvania to 7th Street SE, where you need to make a right.

From the east, take either Route 50 or I-495 to I-295, and follow the directions above.

Parking

Diagonal parking is available on 7th Street, on the alley sides of the Market, and there's some curb parking in the Capitol Hill neighborhood. On weekends, it's best to take the Metro.

How to Get There—Mass Transit

Take the Blue or Orange Metro Lines to the Eastern Market station, and walk north out of the station along 7th Street SE.

Overview

NFT Map: 8

Like a socialite fleeing the masses, Georgetown hides in a Metro-inaccessible corner of DC with the nearest Metro stop (Foggy Bottom/GWU) an 8-block walk. Hiding, however, doesn't work: the masses swarm through the tight vehicle and pedestrian traffic on M Street, Wisconsin Ave and the Key Bridge. That's only because Georgetown is so charming, with its cobblestone streets, colonial brick houses, boutique shopping and cafes, despite the commercialization of its main drags. On pleasant weekend days, tourists and locals alike flock to the neighborhood for shopping and gawking at the city's priciest residential and most desirable real estate.

Georgetown is a shopping oasis with hundreds of mainstream stores, high-end boutiques, bakeries and furnishing stores for those with discriminating taste. At night, watch out as every blueblood rich kid and those who wish they were take over the streets for a boisterous, and seemingly homogeneous, party scene. The mash of trendy restaurants, swank bars, and hole-in-the-wall pubs open their doors for the college crowd, baby boomers, and the better-coiffed see-and-be-seen crowd. Head down to the waterfront during the day for brunch and drinks while you watch yachts pull up to the harbor and crew teams row by.

Despite the area's highbrow reputation, elite schools, and garden-lined historical houses, Georgetown has a number of free events that take place throughout the year. It's still the perfect place for a leisurely stroll and window shopping, whether you're a Georgetown student or a lobbyist's wife.

History

Georgetown was formed in 1751, and the neighborhood's access to the Potomac River was a big draw to the shipping community. Originally a part of Frederick County, Maryland, Georgetown was appropriated by the City of Washington in 1871.

After the Civil War, the area became a haven for freed slaves seeking financial freedom. But a devastating flood in 1890 forced the Canal Company into bankruptcy and triggered an economic depression. By the end of World War I, Georgetown had become a total slum. In the 1930s, New Deal government officials rediscovered the convenience and charm beneath the grime, and with their help, Georgetown began its physical rehab and social climb back to its current grandeur. The reputation of the area was further boosted with the arrival of then–US Senator John F. Kennedy during the 1950s. As its most famous residents, Kennedy and his wife, Jackie, made Georgetown the hub for the fashionable elite of the District, their legendary parties drawing political heavyweights from all over DC.

Attractions

Georgetown hosts the city's most compact collection of historic, retail, gastronomic, and nightlife draws. The Old Stone House, built in 1765, is the oldest surviving building on its original lot in the federal city, and it predates the city of DC itself. The rumored-to-be-haunted-house and its gardens are both publicly strollable. The C&O Canal Path is a 180-mile leaf-shrouded park that runs alongside a murky, but historically interesting, canal. The canal was originally a water highway that linked the rapidly growing west to the east and allowed farmers to ship their goods to market. The canal path is now more of a runner and biker highway, with many a local commuting from Bethesda to Virginia on it. Locals use it to work off the one-too-manys they imbibed at bars like Georgetown University's esteemed The Tombs. For a more relaxing respite, Dumbarton Oaks is a Federal-style 19th century mansion surrounded by sublime gardens. Check out Capitol River Cruises for hourly riverboat cruises up and down the Potomac. Also catch a glimpse of the House of Sweden, a new flick at Loews Georgetown, or the United Arab Emirates Embassy. Besides being home to one of the city's most prestigious universities,

Georgetown is the infamous location of a young boy's supposed exorcism during the late 1940s. The speculated exorcism spawned a bestselling novel by William Peter Blatty and one of the most well-known horror films, *The Exorcist*. Decades later, tourists and fans of the movie still visit the notorious steps where one of the characters fell to his death at the hands of the possessed Regan MacNeil. Take Jan Pottker's Celebrity Georgetown Tour to visit the remodeled house used in the film and see other locations where movies were shot.

For a complete list of stores, restaurants, and attractions in Georgetown, consult the comprehensive Georgetown website: www.georgetowndc.com. For a selection of our favorite Georgetown bars, restaurants, and shopping venues, see Map 8.

How to Get There—Driving

Driving is really a terrible way to get to Georgetown unless you enjoy snarling traffic and honking at expensive cars. M Street between 27th and the Francis Scott Key Bridge is where you find the action. Also venture up Wisconsin Ave. for more high-end boutiques. The area is also accessible by Canal Road NW, and Pennsylvania Avenue.

Parking

If you absolutely must take your car to Georgetown, street parking is a pain, but surprisingly not impossible if you're quick, willing to walk a little and have a small car. There is a pay-as-you-go system where you have to go to a small stand on the sidewalk to obtain a parking ticket you place in the window of your car. A paid garage is your best bet, however pricey. See Map 8 for locations.

How to Get There—Mass Transit

Metrobus routes 30, 32, 34, 35, or 36 marked "Friendship Heights" run west on Pennsylvania Avenue. Buses cost $1.45 without a SmarTrip card, and $1.35 with one. Remember to get a transfer and don't bother to ask for change. Transfers are no longer available with cash, so the motivation to get a SmarTrip card only grows. The DC Circulator also runs an east-west route from Georgetown to Union Station (south on Wisconsin and east on M St). The Circulator costs $1 per ride, with flashy buses appearing every 5–10 minutes from 7 am to 9 pm daily.

The Circulator—DC's bus for people who don't like to ride the bus—runs between Union Station and Georgetown (via K Street) every 10 minutes. This line runs up until midnight on week nights, and until 2am on weekends. Fares are $1, and again uses a paperless transfer system with SmarTrip.

There is no Metro stop in Georgetown, but on a pleasant day, if you're equipped with good walking shoes, the Foggy Bottom-GWU stop on the Orange and Blue lines is a ten minute walk from the east end of the neighborhood. The Rosslyn stop on the same line is a ten-minute walk from Georgetown's west end, but you must cross the busy Key Bridge. And finally, for those on the red line, the half-hour walk down Q St to Dupont Circle is actually quite pleasant, and beats the time you'll spend underground changing lines. Dupont Circle Metro Station, on the Red line, is also a pleasant 1.2-mile walk to Georgetown's center, M Street and Wisconsin Avenue, through its historic, well-trodden neighborhood streets, and over the Dumbarton Bridge with its monumental buffalo.

The Georgetown Metro Connection serves all Metrobus stops in Georgetown and operates express service between Georgetown and Foggy Bottom-GWU, Rosslyn, and Dupont Circle Metro stations. The bus leaves the Metro stations every ten minutes daily and costs $1 one-way. Shuttle Hours: Mon–Thurs: 7 am–12 am; Fri: 7 am–2 am; Sat: 8 am–2 am; Sun: 8 am–12 am.

The Monuments / Potomac Park / Tidal Basin

The Monuments / Potomac Park / Tidal Basin

General Information

NFT Maps: 1, 6, and 7
Website: www.nps.gov
Phone: 202-426-6841

Overview

If there's one thing DC loves more than a free museum, it's a commemorative lawn ornament. The District is packed with monuments, statues, plaques, and fountains. This is especially apparent while strolling through the area west of the National Mall, where you'll find the Lincoln, FDR, Jefferson, and Washington memorials, as well as tributes to those who served in WWI, WWII, the Korean War, and Vietnam, all within Segway riding distance of one another (if you're a lame tourist or curious-about-Segways local)—or walking/ running distance (if you're an intense local training for the sold-out, annual Cherry Blossom 10-miler race every April). If you're on foot, keep in mind that distances are not as close as they might seem. The monuments are big, butnot close!

Presidential Monuments

Our forefathers were clearly larger than today's average American, as the not-so-human scale monuments of some of our more memorable predecessors can attest.

The tall, unadorned monument commemorating America's first president is as recognizable a landmark as the White House or the Capitol. The giant white obelisk can be viewed from many parts of town but is more fun to experience up close, for no better reason than to hear "wow, it's tall" in 112 languages. Today, it's possible to find Dan Brown fans squinting at the pyramid tip to see if there are any Masonic references as well.

Had the Washington Monument been built in Europe, it would most likely squirt water from several places, have 12 pairs of ornately sculpted angel wings fluttering from its sides, and feature a large, bronze pair of breasts over the entranceway. The simplicity and straightforwardness of the building is a tribute to the gravitas, fortitude, and simple elegance of the man it represents. Modest George Washington never referred to this city as 'Washington,' but always 'Federal City.'

Entry to the Washington Monument is free, although your ticket is only valid during a specified entry time. Free tickets are distributed on a first-come, first-served basis at the kiosk on the Washington Monument grounds (at 15th Street and Madison Drive). Advance reservations can be made at http://reservations.nps.gov. The ticket kiosk is open daily from 8:30 am until 4:30 pm (closed December 25th), and tickets usually run out early in the day. If you plan on visiting the monument, make it your first stop.

While many visitors use the monument as a vantage point from which to view the surrounding city, the tall structure itself is really as impressive as the view it affords. The exterior walls are constructed of white marble from Maryland; the interior walls are lined with granite from Maine. Construction began in 1848 and was only one-third complete when the Civil War broke out—hence the change in stone color a third of the way up. Construction resumed after the war, but by then, the color of stone in the quarry had changed. Today, the Washington Monument remains the tallest and most revered structure in DC, giving it alpha-monument status and deflecting the exploding metropolitan population out into surrounding farmland instead of upward into the city sky.

The Lincoln Memorial, which stands in front of the reflecting pool across from the Washington Monument, was designed to look like a Greek Temple and boasts more movie appearances than Samuel L. Jackson. The 36 pillars represent the 36 states that existed at the time of Lincoln's death. The larger-than-life sculpture of honest Abe inside underscores the man's great physical and political stature. Visitors from abroad will no doubt question why the United States saw it fit to construct a literal temple to President Lincoln, but then perhaps other countries don't embrace the towering monument the way the District does. Visiting the monument is free, and the structure is open to the public year-round.

Tidal Basin

The Tidal Basin was constructed in the late 1800s as a swimming hole in the middle of the park. It's no longer a place for a refreshing dip. Besides the questionable cleanliness of this urban pond, the ample federal security forces in the neighborhood are likely the strictest lifeguards in the country. If you're set on dipping a toe in the water, join the tourists and rent a paddle boat. For two weeks every spring, cherry blossoms bloom on some 3,000 trees around the basin and throughout the parks. Viewing the monuments through this prism of pink puffiness takes the edge off the sometimes stark grandeur of the grayish-white monuments. The original trees were a gift from Japan in 1912, and their bloom inspires an annual Japanese-influenced festival to kick off the spring. The Japanese must have heard the story of young George choppin' away (or not!); not even Bush's famed chainsaw could take down this eye-popping pastel forest.

The domed Jefferson Memorial, easily the most elegant memorial of them all, resides on the basin's edge. From tall Thomas's perch above the tidal basin, a fine view can be enjoyed of both the Washington Monument and flights leaving Reagan National across the river. The view at night is especially romantic when the marble pantheon lights up and its reflection is cast into the tidal basin. Finally, while its location is certainly beautiful, the memorial is surely but slowly sinking into the mud…Never forget that all this neoclassical grandeur sits on a giant swamp.

East Potomac Park

East Potomac Park is a long green peninsula with a golf course, tennis center, miniature golf, and a playground. Lined with cherry trees, it can be a more pleasant (read: less tourist-clogged) place to enjoy the pink cotton candy blossoms of early spring—and the sidewalk around the peninsula's perimeter is popular year-round with joggers and bikers. It's also a great place to watch the yachts from the marina across the Washington Channel carry boatloads of tourists on river tours, floating parties of drunken bachelorettes, and the rich to wherever it is they go on the weekends (Be nice, golfers!).

Hains Point sits at the confluence of the Anacostia and Potomac Rivers, with an unobstructed view of planes departing from Reagan National. Sadly the much-loved *Awakening* statue has moved downriver to National Harbor. But with so many available park benches, it's a popular daytime spot for fishing and picnicking, and a prime nighttime spot for making out and the discreet consumption of mind-altering substances. You'll need to drive or bike out there though because there's no public transportation for miles.

How to Get There—Driving

I-66 and I-395 run to the parks from the south. I-495, New York Avenue, Rock Creek Parkway, George Washington Memorial Parkway, and the Cabin John Parkway will get you there from the north. I-66, Route 50, and Route 29 run to the parks from the west. Routes 50, 1, and 4 are the way to go from the east.

Parking

Public parking is available along the Basin, but depending on the time of day, it's likely to be hard to find a spot. You'll end up driving around and around in circles and eventually parking far out and walking long distances.

How to Get There—Mass Transit

The Foggy Bottom, Metro Center, Federal Triangle, Smithsonian, and L'Enfant Plaza stops on the Orange and Blue lines are all within walking distance of various monuments and parks. Farragut North is also a Red Line stop. L'Enfant Plaza is also on the Green and Yellow lines. Numerous Metrobus lines and the Circulator provide access to this large swath of land.

General Information

NFT Maps:	1 & 2
National Mall Website:	www.nps.gov/nama
National Mall Phone:	202-426-6841
Smithsonian Website:	www.si.edu
Smithsonian Phone:	202-633-1000
U.S. Capitol Website:	www.aoc.gov
House of Reps:	www.house.gov
Senate:	www.senate.gov
Capitol Switchboard:	202-224-2131
Capitol Tour Info:	202-225-6827

National Mall

Washington DC's National Mall represents the American dream, where a melting pot of foreigners and locals gather for leisurely picnics or heated protests—without having to do any of the yard work! The layout for the sprawling grass lawn was designed by Frenchman Pierre L'Enfant in the late 18th century as an open promenade. Despite the explosive growth of the surrounding city, the Mall has remained true to L'Enfant's vision (minus the perpetual encircling tour bus brigade). Its eminent stroll-ability is a magnet to hordes of fanny-packed tourists, and its renowned marble monuments attract travel-weary schoolchildren from all over the world. The iconic marble memorials to Washington, Jefferson, Lincoln, and FDR are close by, along with the somber Vietnam and Korean war memorials and the long-needed WWII memorial. On any given day, there's also likely to be a kite festival, political rally, kickball game played by adults, or spirited Frisbee game underway. This is not the place to go if you are camera shy,

as no matter how hard you try to avoid jumping in front of lenses, you *will* end up in family albums across the nation and world.

Smithsonian Institution

If you've seen *Night at the Museum: Battle of the Smithsonians* (a shameless and successful marketing ploy by the organization), you'll know that The Smithsonian Institution is made up of 16 different museums, some of them nowhere near the Mall (one is in NYC), and a zoo. The primary museums are clustered around the Mall—here you'll find the Air and Space Museum, the Natural History Museum, and the Hirshhorn, among others, as well as several tucked-away garden areas ideal for spring-time strolling. The Smithsonian Information Center in the Castle is the best orientation point if you plan to become one of the 24 million visitors who check out one of its DC properties this year.

Like the country it caters to, the Smithsonian collection reflects a hodgepodge of experiences and backgrounds. Between its museums on the Mall, the institution's got the Hope Diamond, Japanese scrolls, and even Archie Bunker's chair. Though there is serious art at the National Portrait Gallery, the Hirshhorn, and several of the smaller museums, the "most popular" distinction goes to the Air and Space Museum, for its sheer *wowza!*-factor of dangling airplanes and shuttles. A close runner-up is the National Museum of American History, known both affectionately and derisively as "America's Attic." Besides Archie's chair, it accommodates Dorothy's ruby slippers, Muhammad Ali's gloves, George Washington's uniform, Julia Child's entire kitchen, and Adlai Stevenson's briefcase, and Steven Colbert's portrait that he had hoped would hang in the Portrait Gallery. The best part

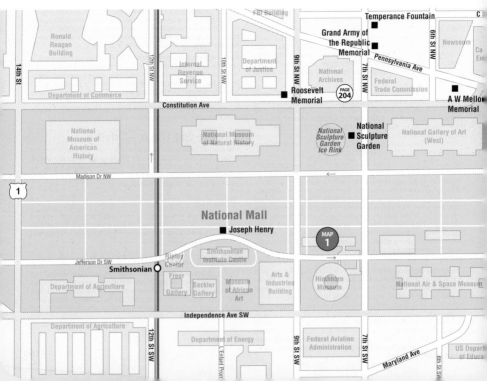

about all this: admission is free! So you can come back, again and again, instead of wearing yourself out trying to cover an entire museum in one visit.

Smithsonian Institution Building (The Castle)

The first building of what has become the Smithsonian Empire was the Castle, built in 1855. The Castle was, for a time, the only Smithsonian building housing all aspects of the institution's operations, including an apartment for the first Secretary of the Smithsonian, Joseph Henry. Note to the macabre-minded: A crypt with the remains of founder James Smithson greets you just to the right of the main entrance. The Castle now serves as the seat of the Smithsonian's administrative offices, as well as a general information center. For those in DC for only a brief stay (or with chronic ADD), the Castle's common room has a mini-museum encompassing exhibits from all of the Mall's museums, which can be thoroughly viewed in approximately ten minutes. (www.si.edu/visit/infocenter/start.htm; 202-633-1000)

The National Museum of the American Indian

This relatively recent addition to the Mall's museum family opened in September 2004. Possibly the largest example of Greco-Anasazi architecture in DC, it includes exhibits from many of the vibrant cultures of North, Middle, and South America. After learning about the hunting and/or agricultural practices of various peoples, hungry visitors can sample native foods of the Western Hemisphere, grouped by region. Mitsitam Cafe is hands-down the best Smithsonian eats, and the cafeteria is divided by region, including the Northern Woodlands, South America, the Northwest Coast, Mesoamerica, and the Great Plains.

National Air and Space Museum

This popular museum maintains the largest collection of historic aircraft and spacecraft in the world. Hundreds of artifacts are on display, including the original Wright 1903 airplane, the *Spirit of St. Louis*, the Apollo 11 command module, the *Enola Gay*, and a lunar rock sample that visitors can touch. To avoid lines, try coming in the dead of winter during a blizzard. Otherwise don't worry; it's worth the wait. Hours: 10 am–5:30 pm (6th St & Independence Ave, SW; www.nasm.si.edu)

Hirshhorn Museum and Sculpture Garden

Resembling the world's largest flan, the Hirshhorn was conceived as the nation's museum of modern and contemporary art. It has over 11,500 pieces of internationally significant art, including ample space for large-scale installation works, and an excellent line up of temporary exhibitions. This is a good one to visit to get away from the chaos of field-trippers in some of the more youth-oriented museums nearby. Hours: Mon–Sun: 10 am–5:30 pm. Sculpture Garden Hours: 7:30 am–dusk. (7th St & Independence Ave, SW; hirshhorn.si.edu)

Arts and Industries Building

The second-oldest Smithsonian building is not in the best shape. In 2004, conditions deteriorated to a point where "diapers" had to be installed on the roof to catch falling debris and the building was closed for renovations. The good news is that a new roof is being installed, and the building will be eventually restored to its former glory, when it opened in time for the inaugural ball of President James A. Garfield in 1881. Though entry is still not allowed, the building itself and the surrounding gardens are worth a peek, and visitors can still access the Discovery

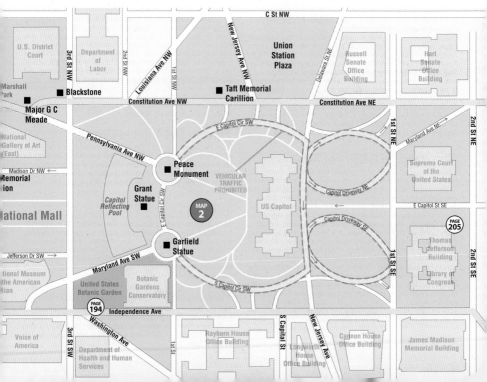

Theater, a live-performance venue for children. It is temporarily located in the S. Dillon Ripley Center. (900 Jefferson Dr, SW; www.si.edu/ai).

National Museum of African Art

The National Museum of African Art is the only museum in the United States devoted exclusively to the display and study of traditional and contemporary arts of sub-Saharan Africa. The museum displays everything from ceramics, textiles, furniture, and tools to masks, figures, and musical instruments. Hours: Mon–Sun: 10 am–5:30 pm. (950 Independence Ave, SW; www.nmafa.si.edu)

Freer and Sackler Galleries

These twin galleries are connected via an underground passageway and house a world-renowned Asian art collection. When it opened in 1923, the Freer Gallery was the first Smithsonian museum dedicated to the fine arts. The Sackler Gallery opened in 1987. The Freer is home to one of the most extensive collections of art by American artist James McNeill Whistler. While you won't find the famous picture of his mother here, you'll find some of his other works, including his portraits and the famous Peacock Room. (Freer Gallery: Jefferson Dr & 12th St, SW; Sackler Gallery: 1050 Independence Ave; www.asia.si.edu)

National Museum of American History

This museum's mission is to collect, care for, and study the objects that reflect the experience of the American people. What better place for the Declaration of Independence Desk, Dizzy Gillespie's trumpet, or Eli Whitney's cotton gin? Two of our favorites are the original Kermit the Frog puppet and Dorothy's ruby slippers. There is also interesting displays and sections detailing the surge in American suburbs, history of technology, and of course, America's love affair with the automobile. Hours: Mon–Sun: 10 am–5:30 pm. (14th St & Constitution Ave, NW; americanhistory.si.edu)

National Museum of Natural History

Visitors come far and wide to catch a glimpse of the 45.5-carat Hope Diamond (hey, that's a lot of bling), but there's more to this museum than one rock. The National Museum of Natural History has an impressive collection of dinosaur and mammal fossils, an insect zoo (check out the daily tarantula feeding!), and an amazing array of stuffed animals (courtesy of taxidermy, not FAO Schwartz). If you're really into rocks, check out the gem collection, which includes meteorites and the Logan Sapphire; at 423 carats, it is the largest publicly displayed sapphire in the country. If you're not visually impaired from looking at the 126 million cool specimens on display, check out the IMAX shows. Hours: Mon–Sun: 10 am–5:30 pm. (10th St & Constitution Ave, NW, www.mnh.si.edu)

The National Gallery of Art

While not a part of the Smithsonian, the National Gallery still houses two buildings of art as impressive as any similar institution in the country. Everything else about Washington might get you overcooked on Greek Revival architecture, but the National Gallery shows in rich detail how DC is actually one of the key places in the world to visit for art. The Gallery's collection include everything from Byzantine art to some of today's leading artists, including Andy Goldsworthy's brilliant work, *Roof*, permanently on display on the ground level of the East Building. There is also a sculpture garden next to the West Building, which houses a "greatest hits" of post-WWII large-format sculpture—highly recommended. . Lunchtime and evening concerts are featured throughout the year, and in summer are held outside in the sculpture garden for many locals who prefer not to hike out to Wolf Trap for an equally enjoyable evening. Hours: (galleries & garden) Mon–Sat: 10 am–5 pm; Sunday: 11 am–6 pm. Note: The Sculpture Garden is open until 9:30 pm on Fridays during the summer. (Between 3rd St NW & 7th St NW at Constitution Ave; www.nga.gov)

US Capitol

The US Capitol is located on Capitol Hill, between 1st and 3rd Streets and between Constitution Avenue NE and Independence Avenue SE. Big white dome. Hard to miss.

Home to the House of Representatives and the Senate, this icon is both a museum and a functioning office where Harry Reid, Edward Kennedy, and John McCain are working stiffs. It's also DC's orientation point. Every city address is based on where it lies in relation to the Capitol, and all mileage markers leading to DC are measured from the Capitol. After hours, drunken Hill staffers use it as a compass to get themselves home. With security a close runner-up to the White House in terms of number of guns and cameras, this is not the place to get lost driving a delivery truck. If you've completed Dan Brown's latest book, The Lost Symbol, you'll be craining your head upward in the dome to stare at the NAME OF PORTRAIT, of Washington ascending to his god-like status in the heavens.

Construction began on the Capitol in 1793 and was more or less finished by 1813. The Capitol was burned by the British in 1814, during the War of 1812, but rain saved the structure from complete collapse. Restoration and expansion followed, the result being the building that all Americans recognize today (probably thanks to the movie *Independence Day*). If you've ever wondered who the lady on top of the dome is, she's no-one in particular. She represents freedom and was sculpted by Thomas Crawford.

The District of Columbia gets one non-voting representative in the House based on population but, like Guam and American Samoa, receives no representation in the Senate because it isn't a state. Hence the local "Taxation without Representation" license plates.

The Capitol is closed Thanksgiving and Christmas. Every other day, the public is welcome to explore the annals of the government. Tours are free (unless you count taxes, in which case they're only free if you're a foreigner). Passes are available beginning at 9 am and redistributed on a first-come, first-served basis, or advanced reservations can be made online. To see actual floor action, get in line early. Passes for that are not offered in advance, and distribution is limited to one pass per person. The $621 million, 580,000-square-foot underground Capitol Visitors' Center opened in late 2008. It offers a wealth of information and activities in addition to a Capitol tour, and a surprisingly high-end cafeteria. Hours: Mon–Sat: 9:00 am–4:30 pm.

How to Get There—Driving

From the south, I-66 and I-395 will take you straight to the Mall. I-495, New York Avenue, Rock Creek Parkway, George Washington Memorial Parkway, and the Cabin John Parkway will get you there from the north. From the west, I-66, US Route 50, and 29 will take you to the Mall. US Routes 50, 1, and 4 will have you Mall-bound from the east.

Parking

There is some disabled parking at the nearby Lincoln and FDR memorials; otherwise you're dealing with regular street parking, which usually has a maximum time allocation of three hours, and more importantly, rarely exists after 9 am. On weekends, however, meters are free. There are parking garages located close to the Mall, but be prepared to pay a hefty fee for the convenience. Hint: take the metro.

How to Get There—Mass Transit

Take the Orange and Blue lines to Capital South, Federal Triangle, Smithsonian, and Federal Center SW; the Yellow and Green lines to Archives/Navy Memorial; the Red Line to Union Station and Judiciary Square; and the Yellow, Green, Blue, and Orange lines to L'Enfant Plaza.

General Information

NFT maps:	8, 18, 32, 35, 36
Website:	www.nps.gov/choh
Visitor information:	301-739-4200
Fees:	None outside of the Great Falls area
Open:	Park is open all daylight hours

Thompson Boat Center (mile 0.1)

Address:	2900 Virginia Ave NW (Map 7)
Visitor information:	202-333-9543
Boathouse hours:	Mon–Sat 6 am–8 pm, Sun 7 am–7 pm
Rental Hours:	Mon–Sun 8 am–5 pm, all rentals returned by 6 pm

Georgetown Visitor Center (mile 0.4)

Address:	1057 Thomas Jefferson St NW (Map 8)
Visitor information:	202-653-5190
Open:	Days and hours vary

The Boathouse at Fletcher's Cove (mile 3.1)

Address:	4940 Canal Rd NW (Map 32)
Visitor information:	202-244-0461
Open:	7 am–7 pm

Carderock Picnic Pavilion (mile 10.5)

Visitor information:	301-767-3731 for reservations and directions

The Old Angler's Inn

Address:	10801 MacArthur Blvd, Potomac, MD
Visitor information:	301-299-9097

Note: This is not part of the park. This is a pricey restaurant that has been here since 1860. This is not the place to take a rest stop with sweat stains, with a bicycle, or with ugly khaki hiking shorts.

Great Falls Tavern Visitor Center (mile 14.3)

Address:	11710 MacArthur Blvd, Potomac, MD
Visitor Information:	301-767-3714
Open:	9 am–4:30 pm (extended summer hours; closed Thanksgiving, Christmas, New Years Day)

Overview

Traveling 184.5 miles from Washington, DC, to Cumberland, MD, the Chesapeake & Ohio Canal parallels the Potomac River from the bustling streets of chi-chi Georgetown to the no streets of backwater Western Maryland—hugging the borders of West Virginia and Pennsylvania along the way. Back in its day, the C&O Canal was like an aquatic interstate, hauling coal, lumber, and grain from Appalachia to the nation's capital. But these days, there ain't no boats floating on the canal…apart from ones full of tourists and park rangers in period clothing. As for the canal's towpath (that's a dirt sidewalk for you urbanites), it has become one of the best ways to graciously exit this city. The Georgetown segment still feels urban, but once you walk just a mile or two along the canal, you'll soon find that the cell yellers have been replaced by singing birds. The towpath is, in effect, a flat, continuous trail sandwiched between the canal and the river, perfect for shady walks, runs, or bike rides through the beautiful Potomac River Valley. For the docile, the C&O Canal National Park offers bird watching, picnicking, fishing, and a range of flora. For the hyperactive, there is boating, hiking (read: walking for people with bad fashion sense), and camping. And for the adolescent boys—Sorry, Mr. Cheney: hunting and swimming are strictly prohibited.

Activities

Kids and corny history lovers will enjoy traveling back in time to the days of animal labor and abuse. Mules drag boats along the canal as park rangers in 1870s period dress tell stories and play music to explain what life was like in the 19th century, for both men and mules. Perhaps the coolest part is crossing one of the canal's locks, however—and feeling the water level rise/fall up to eight feet. One-hour round-trip boat rides depart from the Georgetown Visitor Center. Tickets cost $7 for adults, $5 for senior citizens and children. Departure times vary by season and day of the week.

Biking is a good idea on all parts of the canal towpath. Those of you who don't own may rent an all-terrain or a cruiser from the Thompson Boat Center.

Boating on the river is a fabulous way to cool down on one of DC's many dog days. Canoes, kayaks, rowing shells, and sailboats are all available for rental at the Thompson Boat Center in Georgetown. Or if you'd like to float and poach, you can rent a rowboat or canoe from the Boathouse at Fletcher's Cove and cast line your line on the Potomac. Bait and tackle are also for sale, and anglers have been known to catch herring, striped bass, white perch, and hickory shad in these here parts (note: catch, not eat…not in this river).

For those who prefer lounging on a picnic blanket and soaking in the rays, plenty of green flanks the canal. But if you want to make it a more formal affair, Carderock Pavilion can accommodate up to 200 people on its 26—count 'em if you can, 26—picnic tables. The pavilion is available by permit only: $150 Monday–Thursday and $250 Friday–Sunday and holidays (301-767-3731). For this, though, you get electricity, water, grills, a fireplace, "comfort stations," a softball field, horseshoe pits, a volleyball court (but no net), and ample parking.

Treehuggers will be pleased to know that the park contains about 1,200 species of native plants, many of which are rare, endangered, and/or threatened. Botanists will be delighted by over 600 different species of wildflowers. For the twitchers, keep your eyes peeled and you may just spot a bald eagle.

Lastly, for those of you who are not content to spend just daylight hours with the C&O Canal, the park also has a grand total of 30 campsites—all of which (with the exception of Marsden Tract, which is reserved for do-gooder scouts) are free, free, free. You'll have to go past Great Falls Park to access these sites, but they are designed as way stations for hikers and bikers going the distance. The sites are all first come, first serve, for one night only—but offer a chemical toilet, a picnic table, a grill, and water. The closest site is 16.6 miles in at Swains Lock in Potomac, MD.

How to Get There

It's easy enough to get to the start of the canal in Georgetown. By public transportation, take the Metro to Foggy Bottom-GWU, walk north on 24th St, then turn left on Pennsylvania Ave until it merges with M St. Make a left on Thomas Jefferson St to get to the Georgetown Visitors Center. If you're in doubt, just walk south until land ends and water begins. You can also take any of the 30s buses, the D5, or the Circulator.

To get to the Boathouse at Fletcher's Cover, you can take the D3, D5, or D6 to the intersection of MacArthur Blvd & Ashby St and then walk south on Ashby St, past where the street dead ends, and then rough it through the woods until you hit Canal Rd. You should see an old stone building, the Abner Cloud House, next to the boathouse.

The rest of the C&O Canal Park is pretty much inaccessible by public transport. That's part of the reason why it's so nice.

General Information

NFT Map:	1
DC Address:	700 Pennsylvania Ave NW
	Washington, DC 20408
MD Address:	8601 Adelphi Rd
	College Park, MD 20740-6001
Web Site:	www.archives.gov
DC Hours:	Day after Labor Day to March 14
	Mon–Sun 10:00 am–5:30 pm
	Closed Thanksgiving Day and
	December 25th
	March 15–Labor Day
	Mon–Sun 10:00 am–7:00 pm
MD Hours:	Mon–Fri, 9 am–5:00 pm

Overview

The main building of the National Archives is among the city's most impressive. Situated on Pennsylvania Avenue, it's a block's worth of stone, marble, and Corinthian columns. As impressive as it is on the outside, the inside is even better—unless, of course, you don't really *like* history. Enter from the National Mall, and you'll likely be greeted by a crowd fighting to get catch a glimpse of the Declaration of Independence, the Constitution, or Bill of Rights. Many people think that's all the National Archives has to offer, but like the proverbial iceberg, these cornerstone documents only scratch the surface. You can see these documents with a quick walk through, (enough for many, but since we aren't tourists here, we demand more!). To truly appreciate all, or even a respectable portion of what the National Archives has to offer, you need to spend a bit more time digging deeper.

Along with the United States' most treasured documents (see them soon; the Declaration is fading fast), there's an impressive collection of memorabilia, including presidential correspondence, treasured records, maps, and artwork. In the public vaults, you will find a rotating collection of items that explore different aspects of our country's history. The Lawrence F. O'Brien Gallery gives visitors a detailed journey through a select period or event in American history. There's also a children's area and a theater showing historical films on the National Archives as well as feature length documentaries. As a bonus, the DC branch of the Archives contains a document collection that is any genealogist's dream.

The Maryland location of the National Archives opened in 1994 and is geared toward research, both amateur and professional. The location has an impressive collection of documents dating from WWII including presidential papers, the Berlin Documents Center, civilian and military records, and the John F. Kennedy Assassination Collection, making this the perfect stop if you want to read up on the grassy knoll. Security at the location is high, so be forewarned; however, the staff is the epitome of helpful. See www.nara.gov for detailed information on both locations. Best of all for both spots? Entrance is free.

Getting There

By Metro take the Yellow or Green line to the Archives/Navy Memorial. A free shuttle runs between the DC and Maryland locations, leaving on the hour from 8 am to 5 pm.

If you are driving, to get to the Maryland location, take I-495 toward Baltimore and exit at 28B, which will lead you to New Hampshire Ave/Route 650 South. From here, take a left at the second light onto Adelphi Road and follow the signs. The Archives is on the left. The drive will take you about 45 minutes from DC. There is limited parking provided. At the DC location, parking is on the street only.

General Information

NFT Maps: 2, 3
Address: 101 Independence Ave SE
Washington, DC 20540
Phone: 202-707-5000
Website: www.loc.gov
Hours: James Madison Building:
Mon–Fri: 8:30 am–9:30 pm; Sat: 8:30 am–6:30 pm
Thomas Jefferson Building:
Mon–Sat: 10 am–5:30 pm
John Adams Building:
Mon, Wed, Thurs: 8:30 am–9:30 pm;
Tues, Fri, Sat: 8:30 am–5:30 pm

Overview

The Library of Congress doesn't own every book ever published. It IS, however, the largest library in the world. The collection includes more than 142 million items packed on 650 miles of bookshelves in a three-building complex: The Thomas Jefferson Building opened in 1897 and is home to the soaring stained glass Great Hall; the John Adams Building was built in 1939; and the James Madison Building was constructed in 1980. All three buildings are clustered together on Capitol Hill. The Declaration of Independence, the Constitution, a Gutenberg Bible, and the Giant Bible of Mainz are on permanent display.

Sounds like a bibliophile's dream, right? Harsh reality: this is no lending library. The Library of Congress, despite being a great asset to the American public, can't be used like your neighborhood library or a local bookstore. The Library's mission is to serve as a reference library and educational resource for our government *leaders*, not for us plebeians. To do more than merely wander through the ornate sections, you have to be older than 18 and register at the Reader Registration Station. The Visitors' Center (in the Jefferson Building, along with everything worth visiting) offers information, a short introductory film, and free guided tours. A system of underground tunnels connects the Library's main buildings, as well as the Cannon Office Building. The public can enter from the Adams or Madison Buildings and emerge deep within the heart of the Jefferson complex. It's easy to get lost, but worth the adventure, not to mention the time you save in line on busy tourist days. Most DC'ers have yet to look upon the catacombs of the LOC, being familiar primarily with the sculptures of Neptune and his court out front.

The Library has two theaters—the Coolidge Auditorium, located in the Thomas Jefferson Building, and the tiny Mary Pickford Theater in the Madison Building. Built in 1924, the 511-seat Coolidge Auditorium still hosts regular concerts and is known for its remarkable acoustics. Admission to all events is free; however, reservations must be made through Ticketmaster (two ticket limit per customer), which charges a $2 handling fee. The 64-seat Mary Pickford Theater screens films ranging from those of Pickford's era to modern films. Admission is free, but reservations are required. Visit the Library's web site for movie and show times.

History

The Library of Congress was first established in 1800, when the seat of government moved from Philadelphia to DC, and President John Adams approved legislation to create a Congressional law library. The first acquisition consisted of 740 volumes and three maps from London. Fourteen years later, the British army invaded the city and burned the Capitol building, including the amassed 3,000 volumes that made up the Library of Congress at the time. Thomas Jefferson offered to sell his personal library to Congress to restore its lost collection. Jefferson's 6,487 volumes, which were then the largest and finest collection of books in the country, were purchased for $23,940 (the equivalent of 958 copies of *The Da Vinci Code*). Jefferson's collection, which included works on architecture, science, literature, geography, and art, greatly expanded the Library's previously legal collection.

It was in 1870, under the leadership of librarian Ainsworth Spofford, that the collection outgrew its home. The copyright law of 1870 required all copyright applicants to send the Library of Congress two free copies of their book. The Library was flooded with pamphlets, manuscripts, photographs, and books, and eventually—16 years later—Congress authorized the construction of a new building for all their books. And today, the Library of Congress requests a complimentary copy of every publication that bears its CIP (cataloguing-in-publication) data, thus ensuring that it will stay the largest library forever… Scammers!

How to Get There—Mass Transit

The two metro stops closest to the Library are Capitol South (Orange/Blue lines) and Union Station (Red Line). Capitol South is located a block south of the Thomas Jefferson building, across Independence Avenue. From Union Station, walk south on 1st Street, NE, towards the Capitol (it's hard to miss). You'll pass the Supreme Court on your way to the Thomas Jefferson building, which will be on the east side of 1st Street—about a 15 minute walk from Union Station.

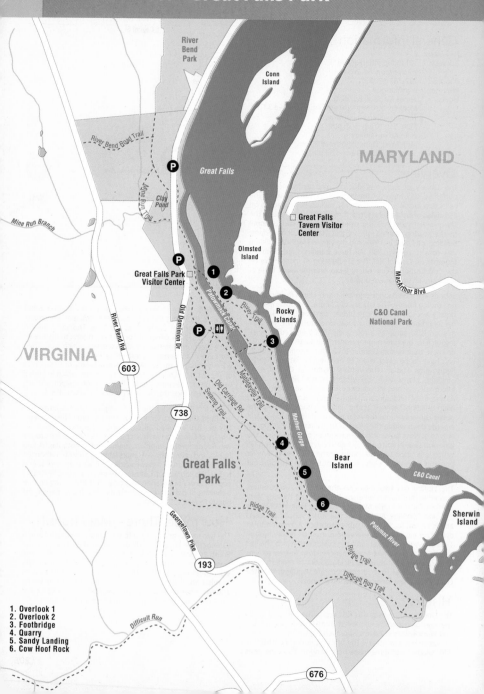

River
Bend
Park

Conn
Island

MARYLAND

River Bend Road Trail

Mine Run Trail

P

Great Falls

Clay
Pond

Mine Run Branch

☐ Great Falls
Tavern Visitor
Center

Olmsted
Island

P

Great Falls Park □
Visitor Center

1

Potomac Canal

2

River Trail

Rocky
Islands

MacArthur Blvd

C&O Canal
National Park

VIRGINIA

River Bend Rd

P

Old Dominion Dr

3

Mantfeville Trail

Old Carriage Rd

(603)

(738)

Swamp Trail

Mather Gorge

4

**Great Falls
Park**

5

Bear
Island

C&O Canal

Georgetown Pike

Ridge Trail

6

Potomac River

Sherwin
Island

(193)

Ridge Trail

Difficult Run Trail

Difficult Run

(676)

1. Overlook 1
2. Overlook 2
3. Footbridge
4. Quarry
5. Sandy Landing
6. Cow Hoof Rock

General Information

Address: 9200 Old Dominion Dr
                 McLean, VA 22101
Phone: 703-285-2965
Website: www.nps.gov/gwmp/grfa
Fees:
Annual Park Pass: $20
Vehicle: $5 for 3 days
Individual: $3 for 3 days
                 (entering by means other than
                 vehicle—e.g. foot, bike)
                 All passes valid on both sides of
                 the falls.
Open: 7 am–dusk year-round,
                 closed Christmas

Overview

Washington DC is 14 miles downriver from the aptly named Great Falls Park, where the Potomac River tears into cascading rapids and 20-foot waterfalls. The river drops 76 feet in elevation over a distance of less than a mile, and it narrows from almost 1,000 feet to 100 feet as it gushes through Mather Gorge. It's the steepest fall-line rapid of any eastern river. The best views come by the Virginia side of the river, where the viewing area expands into a massive park. There are fewer amenities on the Maryland side, but you can get there with two wheels: it's technically part of the C&O Canal National Historical Park.

History

The Great Falls weren't always so admired. In the mid-1700s, they presented a near-impossible obstacle for navigating the Potomac. One of the most significant 18th-century engineering feats in the US was the development of a canal system that lifted and lowered riverboats for over 200 miles of river. The remains of the Patowmack Canal, one of the system's largest and most difficult to create, can still be seen in the park today.

John McLean and Steven Elkins purchased the land surrounding Great Falls and built a wildly popular amusement park there in the early 1900s. Visitors traveled from Georgetown by trolley to take a spin on the wooden carousel. However, time and constant flood damage dampened the thrills until it was eventually closed. Today the land is under the authority and protection of the National Park Service.

Activities

Picnic areas with tables and grills are available on a first-come, first-served basis; ground fires are strictly prohibited. Unfortunately, there are no covered picnic tables in the event of inclement weather, so check the forecast before packing your basket. If you forget your picnic, there is a basic concession stand (open seasonally) located in the visitor center courtyard on the Virginia side.

If it's sweat-breaking activity you're after, a scenic, sometimes rocky bike trail extends between the Maryland side of the falls and downtown Washington. Hiking trails of various length and difficulty wind along and above both sides of the river. Horseback riding, bird watching, rock climbing, fishing, whitewater rafting, and kayaking can be enjoyed at locations throughout the park.

If you plan on rock climbing, registration is not necessary. However, there are voluntary sign-in sheets located in the Virginia visitor center courtyard and the lower parking lot. If fishing is more your speed, a Virginia or Maryland fishing license is required for anglers over 16 years of age. Whitewater boating is recommended only for experienced boaters and, not surprisingly, you're only allowed to launch your craft *below* the falls.

Stop by the visitor center (open daily from 10 am–4 pm) on the Virginia side of the park or check out the National Park Service website for more information.

How to Get There—Driving

From I-495, take Exit 44, Route 193 W (Georgetown Pike). Turn right at Old Dominion Drive (approximately 4 1/2 miles). Drive for 1 mile to the entrance station. Parking, falls overlooks, and the visitor center are all centrally located.

To get to the visitor center on the Maryland side, take I-495 to Exit 41/MacArthur Boulevard E towards Route 189. Follow MacArthur Boulevard all the way to the visitor center.

There is no public transportation available near the park.

General Information

NFT Maps: 20, 21, 23, 24, and 28
Website: www.nps.gov/rocr
Visitor Information: 202-895-6070

Overview

Let the tourists have the National Mall; we have Rock Creek Park to call our own. This 1,754-acre forest doesn't even make it onto many tourist maps—which may explain its popularity with people who live here, and why you can bike or run for miles without braking for fanny-packers. The park, which stretches from Georgetown to Maryland, is one of the largest forested urban parks in the country. A paved bike and running path twists alongside the creek that gives the park its name. Dozens of more secluded, rocky paths break off from the path, one of which gained notoriety in 2002 when the body of federal intern/Congressional paramour Chandra Levy was discovered nearby. The park actually has one of the lowest crime rates in the city, so long as you're not having an affair with married congressmen—but it's an urban park, nevertheless, so lugging along a cell phone or a hiking partner isn't a bad idea. There are visitors' centers advertised: the Nature Center and Planetarium and Pierce Mill, but when they're open, they're hard to reach and of limited help. For basic questions and a great map, best to check the website.

History

In 1866, federal officials proposed cordoning off some of the forest area as a presidential retreat. By the time Congress took up the plan in 1890, the vision had been democratized and the forest became a public park.

Pierce Mill, a gristmill where corn and wheat were ground into flour using water power from Rock Creek, was built in the 1820s and is located over the bridge on Tilden Street. (Pierce Mill has been indefinitely closed to the public for repairs, but the Pierce Barn remains open.) There are also remains of several Civil War earthen fortifications in the park, including Fort Stevens, the only Civil War battle site in DC.

Activities

There are more than 30 picnic areas spread throughout the park, all of which can be reserved in advance for parties of up to 100 people for $7 (202-673-7647). A large field located at 16th and Kennedy streets has several areas suitable for soccer, football, volleyball, and field hockey. Fields can be reserved ahead of time (202-673-7449), also for $7. The Rock Creek Tennis Center has 15 clay and 10 hard-surface tennis courts that must be reserved, in person, for a small fee (202-722-5949). The outdoor courts are open from April through November, and five heated indoor courts open during winter months. Three clay courts located off Park Road, east of Pierce Mill, can also be reserved in person, May through September. The back nine was recently updated at Rock Creek's Golf Course (202-882-7332) just off Military Road and 16th Street.

An extensive network of hiking trails runs through Rock Creek Park and the surrounding areas. Blue-blazed paths maintained by the Potomac Appalachian Trail Club run along the east side of the creek, and green-blazed trails follow the park's western ridge. Tan-blazed trails connect the two systems. The paved path for bikers and roller bladers runs from the Lincoln Memorial, through the park, and into Maryland. Memorial Bridge connects the path to the Mount Vernon Trail in Virginia. Beach Drive between Military and Broad Branch roads is closed to cars on weekends and major holidays, giving bikers free range. However, bikes are not permitted on horse or foot trails at any time. If you're willing to ditch the bike for another kind of ride, horseback riding lessons and guided trail rides are available at the Rock Creek Park Horse Center (202-362-0117), located next to the Nature Center. As the horses follow the same trails described above, hikers are well advised to watch their step.

At the Rock Creek Nature Center (5200 Glover Rd, NW, 202-895-6070), you'll find the Planetarium, which features after school shows for children on Wednesdays at 4 pm and weekends at 1 pm and 4 pm. The park also hosts "free-for-all" outdoor Shakespeare performances at the Carter Barron Amphitheater (16th St & Colorado Ave, 202-426-0486) on summer evenings. Nature Center Hours: Wed–Sun: 9 am–5 pm. Closed on national holidays.

How to Get There—Driving

To get to the Nature Center from downtown DC, take the Rock Creek/Potomac Parkway north to Beach Drive.

Exit onto Beach Drive N, and follow it to Broad Branch Road. Make a left and then a right onto Glover Road, and follow the signs to the Nature Center. Note: The Parkway is one-way going south on weekdays 6:45 am–9:45 am. During this time, you can take 16th Street to Military Road W, then turn left on Glover Road. The Parkway is one-way going north 3:45 pm–6:30 pm; take Glover Road to Military Road east, then head south on 16th Street toward downtown DC. If all you're looking to do is get into the park, consult the map below—the place is so huge that no matter where you live, you're probably close to some branch of it.

Parking

Expansive parking lots are located next to the Nature Center and Planetarium. There are parking lots dotted throughout the park, but depending on your destination, you might be better off looking for street parking in nearby neighborhoods.

How to Get There—Mass Transit

Take the Red Metro line to either the Friendship Heights or Fort Totten Metro stops to get to the Nature Center. Transfer to the E2 bus line, which runs along Military/Missouri/Riggs Road between the two stations. Get off at the intersection of Glover (also called Oregon) and Military Roads and walk south on the trail up the hill to the Nature Center.

Check the map, though; the park covers so much ground in the DC Metro area that getting there may be easier than you think. There's certainly no need to start your visit at the Nature Center.

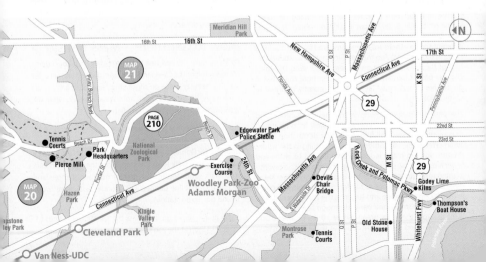

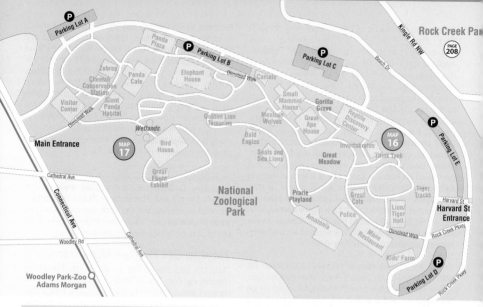

General Information

NFT Maps:	16 & 17
Address:	3001 Connecticut Ave NW
	Washington, DC 20008
Phone:	202-633-4800
Website:	www.nationalzoo.si.edu
Hours:	6 am–8 pm March 15–Oct 31; 6 am–6 pm
	the rest of the year. (Closed Christmas Day)
Admission:	Free

Overview

Nestled in Rock Creek Park, the National Zoological Park is a branch of the Smithsonian Institution (Read: It should be taken very seriously). With about 2,000 animals of 400 different species, there are more pampered foreign residents living in the National Zoo than on Embassy Row. About one-fifth of these animals are endangered, including DC's own popular pair of pandas who are on loan from the Chinese government. Their baby Tai Shan was recently returned to China following his fourth birthday.

The park's animal enclosures mimic natural habitats, and most exhibits strive to entertain as well as educate all those visiting school children. A popular destination in the summertime, the zoo can be just as appealing in the winter months, with so many indoor animal houses to visit—and fewer kids to elbow out of your way. The zoo is also a favorite jogging route for area residents—especially on winter snow days. (Olmsted Walk is one of the few regularly plowed paths in the city.) In the spring and summer, the zoo is packed with students on morning and early afternoon field trips. If you want to avoid them, try going before 10 am or after 2 pm. The animals tend to be more active at these times anyway,

and you won't have to wait in line to see the more popular exhibits and animals.

Parking

Enter the zoo from Connecticut Avenue, Harvard Street, or Rock Creek Parkway. Because parking on zoo grounds is limited, public transportation is recommended. If you're set on driving, parking at the zoo costs $4 for the first hour, $12 for two to three hours, and $16 for over three hours. Lots fill early during the summer, so plan to arrive by 9:30 am at the latest if you expect to park.

How to Get There—Mass Transit

By Metro, take the Red Line to the Woodley Park-Zoo/Adams Morgan stop or the Cleveland Park stop; the zoo entrance lies roughly halfway between these stops and both are a short stroll away. It's an uphill walk from Woodley Park, while the walk from Cleveland Park is fairly flat.

From the Woodley Park-Zoo/Adams Morgan stop, walk north (to your left as you face Connecticut Avenue—away from the McDonald's and the CVS); and the zoo is about a twelve-minute walk from the stop. From the Cleveland Park stop, walk south toward the greater number of shops and restaurants that line Connecticut Avenue (away from the 7-11 and the Exxon station).

If you prefer above-ground mass transit, Metrobus lines L1, L2, and L4 stop at the zoo's Connecticut Avenue entrance.

General Information

Address:	4368 Chantilly Shopping Center
	Chantilly, VA 20153
Phone:	703-378-0910
Website:	www.dullesexpo.com

Overview

Dulles Expo Center should really just knock off the last two letter of "Dulles" and be done with it. "Dull" is the reigning word here—it accurately describes the area (Chantilly); the spaces in the Center itself (two separate low-slung, charmless rectangles); and most of the exhibits, exhibitors, and exhibitees. Pray to whatever gods you believe in that, if you have to attend a show or convention in DC, it'll be at the Washington Convention Center. Dulles Expo's only saving grace is that it has the best convention center parking in the universe—immediately outside the two buildings. Other than that, if it's a gun or RV show you're looking for, well, golly, this is the place!

A cab from Dulles to the Expo Center will cost about $20. A taxi from Reagan National Airport costs approximately $45. If you really want to fly into Baltimore-Washington International Airport, be prepared to cough up $85 for your 1.5-hour schlep.

Hotels

The Expo Center has an on-site Holiday Inn Select and several hotels within walking distance. Certain hotels have specials for specific conventions, so ask when you book. Or browse hotel-specific websites such as hotels.com and pricerighthotels.com.

- **Comfort Suites Chantilly-Dulles Airport,** 13980 Metrotech Dr, 703-263-2007
- **Fairfield Inn Dulles Chantilly South,** 3960 Corsair Ct, 703-435-1111
- **Hampton Inn-Dulles South,** 4050 Westfax Dr, 703-818-8200
- **Homestead Village,** 4505 Brookfield Coroporate Dr, 703-263-3361
- **Holiday Inn Select,** 4335 Chantilly Shopping Ctr, 703-815-6060
- **Courtyard by Marriott,** 3935 Centerview Dr, 703-709-7100
- **Extended Stay,** 4506 Brookfield Corporate Dr, 703-263-7200
- **Staybridge Suites,** 3860 Centerview Dr, 703-435-8090
- **TownePlace Suites by Marriott,** 14036 Thunderbolt Pl, 703-709-0453
- **Westfields Marriott,** 14750 Conference Center Dr, 703-818-0300
- **Wingate Inn Dulles Airport,** 3940 Centerview Dr, 571-203-0999

How to Get There—Driving

From DC, travel west on Constitution Avenue, and follow the signs to I-66 W to Virginia. Remain on I-66 W for about 25 miles until exit 53B, Route 28 N (Dulles Airport). Drive three miles north on Route 28, and then turn right onto Willard Road. Take the second left off into the Chantilly Shopping Center. From there, follow the signs to the Expo Center.

From Dulles Airport, follow exit signs for DC. Stay towards the right for about one mile, and take Route 28 S towards Centerville. Drive six miles and pass over Route 50. At the first light past Route 50, make a left on Willard Road. Follow signs to the Expo Center.

Better yet, don't go at all.

Parking

The Dulles Expo and Conference Center has 2,400 parking spaces on-site! (When their website has to brag about parking, you know we're not just being cynical about this place.) If you arrive in your RV, you'll have to find a campsite for the night, as campers, RVs, trucks, and oversized vehicles will be ticketed if parked overnight.

How to Get There—Mass Transit

There is no public transportation to the Dulles Expo and Conference Center. Remember, this is America.

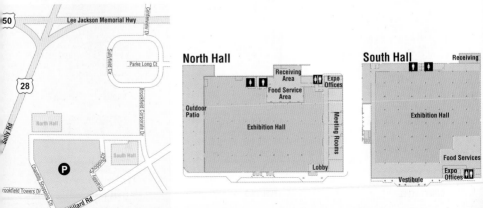

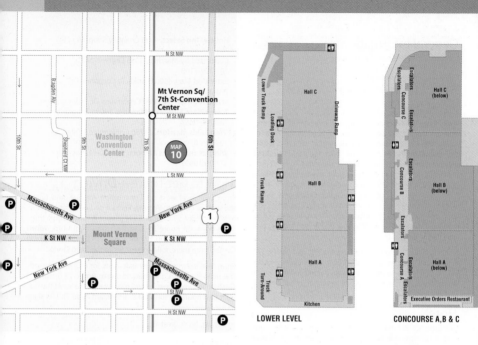

LOWER LEVEL

CONCOURSE A, B & C

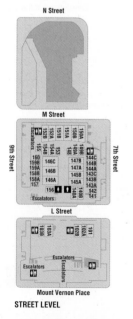

STREET LEVEL

LEVEL TWO

LEVEL THREE

General Information

NFT Map: 10
Address: 801 Mt Vernon Pl NW
               Washington, DC 20001
Phone: 202-249-3000
Website: www.dcconvention.com

Overview

The Washington Convention Center is a stunning white granite and glass mammoth covering six city blocks, from 7th Street to 9th Street and N Street to Mount Vernon Place. The 2.3 million-square-foot building is the largest in DC and had the distinction of being the largest excavation site in the Western Hemisphere; 2 million tons of earth were removed during construction. Whether exhibiting or attending, you'd be well advised to wear comfy shoes to traverse the 700,000 square feet of exhibit space, 150,000 square feet of meeting space, the 52,000-square-foot ballroom (one of the East Coast's largest), and 40,000 square feet of retail space. The center hosts everything from small seminars for 80 participants to giant expos that welcome 35,000 attendees. Nonetheless, it is like every other convention center in that spending more than 15 minutes in it is completely de-humanizing experience. Try spending three full days running a booth, and you'll know what we're talking about.

Along with the MCI Center, the Convention Center is a pillar of revitalization for this previously seedy neighborhood. Thanks to that success, conventioneers have many more amenities to choose from in the area. The City Museum across the street used to have interesting exhibits detailing the history of Washington, but poor attendance and the shut-off of external funding spelled its demise. A string of shops, restaurants, and nightlife, especially on 7th Street NW south of Massachusetts Avenue, beckon nearby. Nevertheless, occasional panhandlers still canvass the area, hoping to profit from pedestrians with open maps making their way toward the Convention Center. The fastest and cheapest way to the Convention Center is to keep that map folded in your coat pocket and follow the platinum blonde in the plastic cowboy hat pasted with event-related bumper stickers.

If you're flying in for a convention, a cab from BWI or Dulles will cost you more than $70 to downtown DC. From Reagan, it should be no more than $15. The Metro Yellow Line runs directly from Reagan to the Mount Vernon Square/7th Street-Convention Center station.

Hotels

If you know which hotel you want to stay in, give them a call, and ask if they have any special rates for the dates you'll be attending. If you're not with any particular rewards program and don't care where you stay, try the official Washington tourism website at www.washington.org or hotel-specific websites such as www.hotels.com and www.pricerighthotels.com. Plans are being finalized for the construction of a 1400+ room Marriott Convention Center Hotel right across 9th Street, NW. However, as these things go, it'll be years before it's opened. In the meantime, consider these nearby hotels:

• **Renaissance Hotel** • 999 9th St NW, 202-898-9000
• **Henley Park** • 926 Massachusetts Ave NW,
  202-638-5200
• **Courtyard by Marriott Convention Center** •
  900 F St NW, 202-638-4600
• **Morrison Clark Inn** • 1101 11th St NW, 202-898-1200

• **Marriott Metro Center** • 775 12th St NW,
  202-737-2200
• **Four Points by Sheraton** • 1201 K St NW,
  202-289-7600
• **Hamilton Crowne Plaza** • 1001 14th St NW,
  202-682-0111
• **Hilton Garden Inn** • 815 14th St NW, 202-783-7800
• **Hotel Sofitel** • 806 15th St NW, 202-737-8800
• **Washington Plaza** • 10 Thomas Cir NW,
  202-842-1300
• **Wyndham Washington, DC** • 1400 M St NW,
  202-429-1700
• **The Madison** • 1177 15th St NW, 202-862-1600
• **Hotel Helix** • 1430 Rhode Island Ave NW,
  202-462-9001
• **Homewood Suites by Hilton** • 1475 Massachusetts Ave
  NW, 202-265-8000
• **Capitol Hilton** • 1001 16th St NW, 202-393-1000
• **Holiday Inn Central** • 1501 Rhode Island Ave NW,
  202-483-2000
• **Comfort Inn** • 1201 13th St NW, 202-682-5300
• **Grand Hyatt Washington** • 1000 H St NW,
  202-582-1234
Embassy Suites/Convention Center 900 9th St, NW,
202-739-2001
Hampton Inn/Convention Center 901 6th St, NW,
202-842-2500
Hotel Monaco 700 F St, NW, 800-649-1202

Eating

After spending a gazillion dollars on a gleaming new Convention Center, some thought went into providing better grub than the old center's mystery meat burgers and heat-lamp fries. Here, you'll find a number of restaurants located in the Convention Center and dozens more within easy walking distance (almost all of them *south* of the Center). Executive Orders, located on the L1 Concourse, offers selections from Foggy Bottom Grill, Wolfgang Puck Express, Seafood by Phillips, Subculture, Bello Pronto, Mr. Thoi's Fine Asian Cuisine, and Latin American Cuisine. Located on Level Two off the L Street Bridge, the Supreme Court is a retail food court offering Wolfgang Puck Express, Quizno's, and Foggy Bottom Grill.

The Lobby Café, located by the main entrance, sells coffee and deluxe pastries to help exhibitors and attendees wake up in the mornings. Within each exhibit hall, there are also permanent and portable outlets/carts serving everything from coffee to Tex-Mex. For some local drinks, check out the Old Dominion Brewhouse, which has a great selection of the Virginia microbrewery's beers on tap.

Parking

The center does not have its own parking facility, and there are about 100 metered parking spaces close to the convention center, so you'll be pretty fortunate if you manage to snag one. Otherwise, be prepared to pay for one of the many parking lots within a three-block radius of the center. A block south of the Center, a huge new lot (with a huge new fee) has recently opened, created after the old center was torn down.

How to Get There—Mass Transit

The closest Metro stop is Mt Vernon Sq/7th St-Convention Center on the Yellow or Green lines.

Overview

Baltimore's comeback streak has pretty much obliterated its former reputation as the murder capital of the nation (even if it still regularly scores well in crime rankings and visitors should still leave nothing visible in their cars). Real estate prices are booming, retail rakes it in during the tourist season, and businessmen have discovered a city where, just steps from the convention center, they can sightsee, shop for their kids, AND hoist a beer at Hooters. But the city's real treasures are hidden in its neighborhoods, where fierce local pride mixes with a local flare for the, uh, creative. (If you can't get to Café Hon or the Visionary Art Museum, ask hometown filmmaker John Waters to explain.) And, yes, The Wire is the most amazing TV series ever. Baltimore never looked so good (and bad) on film. To see the real charm behind its nickname, "Charm City" venture into the cobblestone-and-brick-lined neighborhoods of Fells Point, Federal Hill, and Mt. Vernon. Here, you'll find Ravens fans mad-hopping in dive bars, crabs and oysters are staple menu items, artists and musicians display their work, and unpretentious locals make you feel right at home.

Getting There

Take I-295 N to Baltimore City past Oriole Park at Camden Yards. 295 will become Russell Street and then Paca Street. Make a right onto Pratt Street. Follow Pratt Street six blocks to the Inner Harbor, which will be on your right. The Visitor Center is located along the Inner Harbor's west wall (near Light Street).

Attractions

Harborplace
200 E Pratt St, 410-332-4191; www.harborplace.com
One of Baltimore's most well-known attractions is Harborplace, owned by the Rouse Company (i.e. it looks exactly the same as New York's South Street Seaport, Boston's Faneuil Hall, New Orleans's Riverwalk Marketplace, etc). The outdoor mall's retail stores and chain restaurants circle the harbor. Since most residents only hang at Harborplace when they're showing off (or cringing over the triteness of) their waterfront to out-of-towners, it becomes a mob of tourists on sunny weekends. Shop hours: Mon–Sat: 10 am–9 pm; Sun: 11 am–7 pm.

National Aquarium in Baltimore
501 E Pratt St, 410-576-3800; www.aqua.org
Baltimore's aquarium is the city's most popular tourist attraction. Entry isn't cheap, and there's bound to be a line to get in, but attractions like the Tropical Rain Forest (complete with piranhas and poisonous frogs) and the dolphin show make it worth all the hassle. General admission costs $24.95 for adults, $19.95 for kids (3–11), and $23.95 for seniors (65+). Tickets often sell out, but you can buy advance tickets through Ticketmaster. Aquarium hours: Sun–Thurs: 9 am–5 pm; Fri: 9 am–8 pm; Sat: 9 am–6 pm.

Maryland Science Center
601 Light St; 410-685-5225; www.mdsci.org
The Maryland Science Center is one of the oldest scientific institutions in the country and is full of dinosaur bones, IMAX, and all that science jazz. It's best for kids, especially ones you want to push toward Einstein-hood. The center is usually open from 10 am to 6 pm daily, although hours change by season; admission prices range from $14.50 to $20, depending on what exhibits you'd like to visit. Admission for children 3–12 costs between $10 and $14, and admission for members is always free.

Babe Ruth Birthplace and Museum
216 Emory St, 410-727-1539; www.baberuthmuseum.com
Visit the place where Babe was really a babe. This historic building has been transformed into a shrine to Babe, as well as to Baltimore's Colts and Orioles and Johnny Unitas (famed quarterback for the Colts). Admission costs $6 for adults, $4 for seniors and $3 for children 3–12. Hours: April–October: daily 10 am–6 pm (7:30 pm on baseball game days), November–March: daily 10 am–5 pm.

The Maryland Zoo in Baltimore
978 Druid Park Lake Dr, 410-366-LION; www.marylandzoo.org
Located in Druid Hill Park, the zoo is hidden in the middle of the city, far away from the other major tourist attractions. Kids can enjoy the number-one-rated children's zoo, while adults can look forward to the zoo's spring beer and wine festival, Brew at the Zoo (Plan on hearing lots of jokes about polar beer, penguinness, and giraffes of wine). Admission to the zoo costs $14 for adults, $10 for the kiddies 2–12, and $12 for the grannies 65 and over, but parking is always free. The zoo is open daily, Mar–Dec: 10 am–4:00 pm.

Lexington Market
400 W Lexington St, 410-685-6169; www.lexingtonmarket.com
Baltimore's Lexington Market is the world's largest continuously running market. Founded in 1782, the market continues to be a rowdy place of commerce. The market prides itself for its top-quality fresh meats, seafood, poultry, groceries, specialty items, and prepared foods for take-out and on-site consumption. Visit the market during the Chocolate Festival and the Preakness Crab Derby (yes, they actually race crabs). During Lunch with the Elephants, held annually in the spring, a herd of elephants from the Ringling Bros. and Barnum & Bailey Circus marches from the Baltimore Arena to the market, where they proceed to eat the world's largest stand-up vegetarian buffet. Market hours: Mon–Sat: 8:30 am–6 pm.

National Museum of Dentistry
31 S Greene St, 410-706-0600; www.dentalmuseum.org
After munching on goodies at the Lexington Market, swing on by the National Museum of Dentistry to learn about all the cavities you just got. This Smithsonian affiliate offers interactive exhibits and the gift shop sells chocolate toothbrushes (reason enough to check it out). Plaque got you gloomy? Edgar Allan Poe's grave is just down the street. Admission to the museum costs $7.00 for adults over 18 and $5.00 for kids, students, and seniors, and $3.00 for kids. Hours: Wed–Sat: 10 am–4 pm; Sun: 1pm–4pm.

The Power Plant

601 E Pratt St, 410-752-5444
Once upon a time, the Power Plant was an honest-to-goodness power plant. In 1998, it was converted into a full-fledged mall. Guess retail's just a different kind of community fuel. Inside the Power Plant, you'll find Barnes & Noble, ESPN Zone, Gold's Gym, and the Hard Rock Café.

Power Plant Live!

Market Pl & Water St, 410-727- 5483; www.powerplantlive.com
Located a block away from the Power Plant, Power Plant Live! is a dining and entertainment megaplex. You can have a full night without leaving the indoor/outdoor complex. Dinner, dancing, comedy, and stiff drinks are served up by eight bars and seven restaurants. Because of an arena liquor license, you can take your drink from one establishment to the next. During the summer, check out the free outdoor concerts. Past headliners include the Soundtrack of Our Lives, Aimee Mann, Elvis Costello, and the Wildflowers.

American Visionary Art Museum

800 Key Hwy, 410-244-1900; www.avam.org
The Visionary Art Museum exhibits works from self-taught, intuitive artists, whose backgrounds range from housewives to homeless. The museum is also home to Baltimore's newest outdoor sculptural landmark—the Giant Whirligig. Standing tall at an imposing 55 feet, this multicolored, wind-powered sculpture was created by 76-year-old mechanic, farmer, and artist Vollis Simpson. Every spring, the museum hosts a race of human-powered works of art designed to travel on land, through mud, and over deep harbor waters. Museum hours: Tues-Sun: 10 am–6 pm. Admission costs $15.95 for adults, $13.95 for seniors, and $9.95 for children over 6.

Pagoda at Patterson Park

www.pattersonpark.com
One of the most striking structures in Baltimore's Patterson Park is the newly renovated Pagoda. Originally built in 1891, the Pagoda was designed as a people's lookout tower. From the 60-foot-high octagonal tower, you can see downtown, the suburbs, and the harbor. When it ever snows, the hill next to the Pagoda is a popular sledding site. Pagoda Hours: Sun: 12 pm–6 pm, May–Oct.

Camden Yards

333 W Camden St, 888-848-2473; www.theorioles.com
There's more to Camden Yards than the O's. At the turn of the century, Camden Yards was a bustling freight and passenger railroad terminal. For decades, Camden Station served as a major facility for the Baltimore and Ohio Railroad (that's the B&O Railroad for Monopoly fans). The Yards were once home to thousands of commuters, and now they're home to thousands of fans who come out to see their beloved Orioles play (how we miss you, Cal Ripken Jr…).

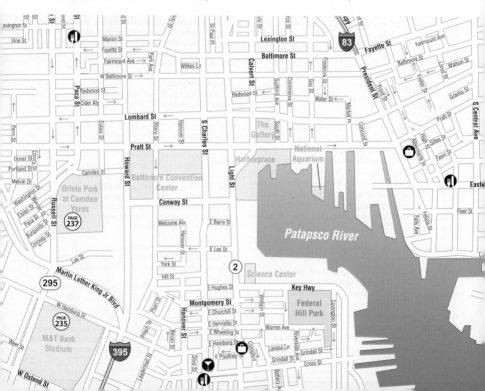

Landmarks

- **Baltimore Tattoo Museum** · 1534 Eastern Ave

Nightlife

- **Club Charles** · 1724 N Charles St (off map)
- **Cross Street Market** · 1065 S Charles St
- **The Horse You Came In On** · 1626 Thames St
- **Ottobar** · 2549 N Howard St

Restaurants

- **Bertha's** · 734 S Broadway
- **Boccaccio Restaurant** · 925 Eastern Ave
- **Brass Elephant** · 924 N Charles St (off map)
- **Café Hon** · 1002 W 36th St (off map)
- **The Daily Grind** · 1722 Thames St
- **Faidley's Seafood** ·
  Lexington Market, 203 N Paca St
- **Helen's Garden** · 2908 O'Donnell St
- **Ikaros** · 4805 Eastern Ave (off map)

- **Jimmy's** · 801 S Broadway
- **John Steven Ltd** · 1800 Thames St
- **New Wyman Park Diner** · 138 W 25th St (off map)
- **Obrycki's Crab House** · 1727 E Pratt St
- **Pete's Grille** · 3130 Greenmount Ave (off map)
- **Rusty Scupper** · 402 Key Hwy
- **Tapas Teatro** · 1711 N Charles St (off map)
- **Ze Mean Bean** · 1739 Fleet St

Shopping

- **The Antique Man** · 1806 Fleet St
- **Cook's Table** · 1036 Light St
- **Di Pasquales Italian Marketplace** ·
  3700 Gough St (off map)
- **Karmic Connection** · 508 S Broadway
- **Mystery Loves Company** · 1730 Fleet St
- **Sound Garden** · 1616 Thames St
- **Stikky Fingers** · 802 S Broadway
- **Vaccaros Italian Pastry Shop** · 222 Albemarle St

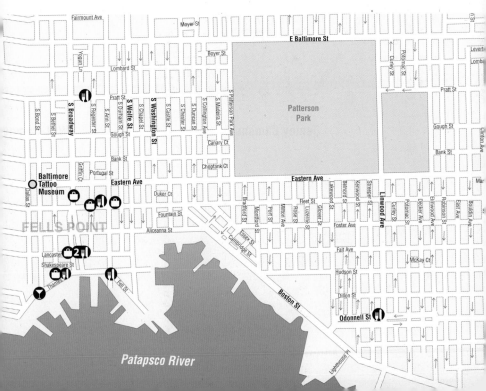

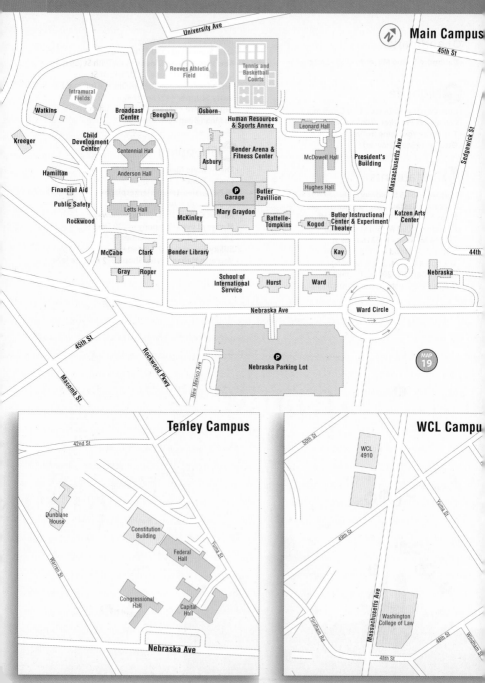

Main Campus

University Ave

45th St

Sedgewick St

Reeves Athletic Field

Tennis and Basketball Courts

Intramural Fields

Watkins

Broadcast Center

Beeghly

Osborn

Human Resources & Sports Annex

Leonard Hall

Kreeger

Child Development Center

Centennial Hall

Bender Arena & Fitness Center

McDowell Hall

President's Building

Hamilton

Asbury

Anderson Hall

Massachusetts Ave

Financial Aid

Public Safety

Letts Hall

Garage

Butler Pavillion

Hughes Hall

Katzen Arts Center

Rockwood

McKinley

Mary Graydon

Battelle-Tompkins

Kogod

Butler Instructional Center & Experiment Theater

44th

McCabe

Clark

Bender Library

Kay

Nebraska

Gray

Roper

School of International Service

Hurst

Ward

Ward Circle

Nebraska Ave

45th St

Rockwood Pkwy

Nebraska Parking Lot

MAP 19

Macomb St

New Mexico Ave

Tenley Campus

42nd St

Dunblane House

Constitution Building

Federal Hall

Warren St

Yuma St

Congressional Hall

Capital Hall

Nebraska Ave

WCL Campus

50th St

WCL 4910

Yuma St

48th St

Massachusetts Ave

Fordham Rd

Washington College of Law

48th St

48th St

Windham St

General Information

NFT Map:	19
Main Campus:	4400 Massachusetts Ave NW Washington, DC 20016
Phone:	202-885-1000
Website:	www.american.edu

Overview

Congress chartered "The" American University in 1893 to fulfill George Washington's vision of a great "national university" in the nation's capital. If Washington rode the Tenleytown shuttle to campus today, he'd probably be impressed. Though it seems sometimes like half of the AU student body is from Long Island, New Jersey, or the Philly suburbs, the school's 12,000 students hail from more than 150 countries. This diversity, along with its location in the nation's capital, makes AU a popular place to study public policy and international affairs. With few Wednesday classes and a heavy internship focus, AU is something of a foreign affairs, NGO, and Hill staffer factory. AU students brag that while Georgetown's stuffed shirts end up at DC think tanks, *their* grads actually go out and get their hands dirty. Indeed, it's often the school's idealistic crowd that most resents the "brat pack" contingent of diplomat kids and OPEC heirs, who enroll more out of interest in DC's nightlife than in changing the world. AU's idealists went into full protest mode in 2005 to force former University president Benjamin Ladner to resign after improperly charging the school for more than $500,000 in personal expenses, including a personal French chef, vacations in Europe with his wife, and his son's engagement party. While searching for a less ostentatious leader, AU's board of trustees started a new fundraising drive, appropriately called "AnewAU."

Nestled in tony upper northwest DC, AU's leafy quad gives it a classic liberal-arts-school look. But its picturesque campus doesn't lack in intrigue: work on the Manhattan Project started out in AU's McKinley building, because its unusual architecture ensured that any mishap would cause the building to self-implode and therefore limit any widespread repercussions.

Tuition

In the 2010–2011 academic year, undergrad tuition and fees is $42,614, with room and board nearly an additional $15,000. Graduate student tuition, fees, and expenses vary by college.

Sports

AU's Eagles play a nice range of NCAA Division I men's and women's sports, including basketball, cross-country, soccer, swimming and diving, tennis, and track and field. Male-exclusive sports include golf and wrestling, while women play field hockey, volleyball, and lacrosse. The men's basketball team wins every year but has trouble drumming up fan interest; it's a running joke that mid-season you'll find more students waiting for AU's shuttle to the Metro than in Bender Arena. A few years ago, the Eagles left the Colonial Athletic Association to join the Patriot League in hopes of using the league's championship as an automatic bid to the NCAA tourney. In 2008, the move finally paid off, as the Eagles' Men's Basketball team landed a number 15 seed in the Big Dance (albeit losing to number 2 seed Tennessee in their first match-up). In 2009, they won the Patriot League Tournament, and student Derrick Mercer was named the 2009 Patriot League Player of the Year and an Associated Press All-American. AU's impressive season and NCAA Tourney birth have given DC residents hope that they'll have a new perennial Tournament team to root for in the coming years.

Culture on Campus

AU operates its wildly wonkish and popular radio station, WAMU 88.5 FM, broadcasting NPR programs as well as locally produced shows like *The Kojo Nnamdi Show* and *The Diane Rehm Show*. Similarly, the University seems to score a speech a week by an inside-the-beltway celebrity, including appearances by Pulitzer Prize–winning columnist David S. Broder, Supreme Court Justice Antonin Scalia, and former President Jimmy Carter. Bender Arena appears to have lost its appetite for the big-time acts it used to feature, now hosting smaller performances by the likes of Jimmy Eat World and the Roots. The Katzen Arts Center at AU opened in late 2005, bringing all of AU's arts programs under one roof, including its Watkins collection of over 4,400 modern works of Washington-area art.

Department Contact Information

Admissions	202-885-6000
College of Arts & Sciences	202-885-2453
Kogod School of Business	202-885-1900
School of Communication	202-885-2060
School of International Service	202-885-1600
School of Public Affairs	202-885-2940
Washington College of Law	202-274-4000
Washington College of Law Library	202-274-4350
Office of Campus Life	202-885-3310
Athletic Department	202-885-3000
University Library	202-885-3232

Catholic University of America

1. Quinn House
2. Reardon House
3. Camalier House
4. Walton House
5. McDonald House
6. Magner House
7. Unanue House
8. Engelhard House
9. Nursing-Biology Building
10. McCort-Ward Building
11. Gowan Hall
12. Maloney Hall
13. Conaty Hall
14. Spalding Hall
15. Spellman Hall

Raymond A DuFour Center

Capuchin College

MAP 14

Grounds Shop

Marist Annex

Marist Hall

O'Boyle Hall

Flather Hall

Millennium North

Regan Hall

Life Cycle Institute

Marian Scholasticate

Curley Court

Eugene L Kane Student Heath & Fitness Center

St Vincent de Paul Chapel

Nugent Hall

Curley Court

Ryan Hall

Millennium South

Curley Hall

Centennial Village

Hartke Theatre

Salve Regina Hall

Hannan Hall

University Parking Garage

Colombus School of Law

Leahy Hall

Caldwell Hall

Edward J Pryzbyla University Center

Power Plant

Seton Wing

Ward Hall

Paulist Place

McCormack Plaza

McMahon Hall

Edward M Crough Center for Architectural Studies

Pangborn Hall

Shahan Hall

Pryzbyla Plaza

John K Mullen of Denver Memorial Library

9 11

10

12

Basilica of the National Shrine of the Immaculate Conception

Keane Hall

Visitor Center

Brookland/ CUA

Cardinal Hall

St Bonaventure Hall

Monroe St NE

Gibbons Hall

Michigan Ave NE

13

14

15

Dominican House of Studies

Theological College

Varnum St NE

Urell Pl NE

Fort Dr NE

Taylor St NE

Harewood Rd NE

Scale Gate Rd

Irving St NE

2nd St NE

Puerto Rico Ave NE

Varnum Pl NE

John McCormick Rd NE

8th St NE

7th St NE

9th St NE

Perry Pl NE

Bunker Hill

Kearns St NE

Lawrence

General Information

NFT Map: 14
Address: 620 Michigan Ave NE
              Washington, DC 20064
Phone: 202-319-5000
Website: www.cua.edu

Overview

Lesser known than its Washington rivals but equal in academic distinction, CUA was established in 1887 as a graduate research institution where the Roman Catholic Church could do its thinking, and its undergraduate programs began in 1904. It remains the only American university founded with a papal charter. With a board of trustees still brimming with US cardinals and bishops, the school is considered the national university of the Catholic Church.

That said, CUA is by no means a seminary. Sixteen percent of its 3,123 undergraduates represent religions other than Catholicism, and although shadowed by the colossal Basilica of the National Shrine of the Immaculate Conception (the largest church in America), the laissez-faire campus lacks the in-your-face piousness to which other orthodox colleges subscribe. The 193-acre campus is the largest and arguably the most beautiful of the DC universities. Prominent alums include Susan Sarandon, Ed McMahon, Jon Voight, Brian Cashman (GM of the New York Yankees), and Maureen Dowd.

Though mostly religious, CUA's student body sometimes tries hard to prove otherwise. "Catholic U: Don't Let the Name Fool You" has been a popular motto of a ruddy-faced breed of students that knows how to pick the beer glasses up and put the books down. With a flourishing party scene, CUA is well-represented among DC's various watering holes. And no, Mr. Joel, Catholic girls do not always start much too late.

Tuition

Tuition for the 2010–2011 year comes to $33,580. If you need a place to eat and sleep, the basic meal plan and housing costs come to approximately $5,000 and $7,000 respectively. That totals about $45,580, assuming you won't be buying any beer and books. It's college in America, what did you expect? At least a Catholic U degree can land you a job where you can actually pay off those loans.

Sports

Formerly a member of NCAA's Division I, the Catholic Cardinals (as in the little red bird, not the man with the incense and the big hat) dropped to Division III during the 1970s. Of all the school's sports, men's basketball reigns supreme. Winner of the 2000–2001 Division III National Championship, the team reeled off five consecutive Sweet Sixteen seasons before the streak came to a halt last in 2009. The women's squad, which posted a 20-win season in 2009, is also a powerhouse within CUA's Capital Athletic Conference, and in 2010, two members were awarded honors by the Landmark Conference. The Catholic football team may have stumbled over the last few seasons, but betting men beware: it dominated the gridiron during the nineties, ranking as high as number ten in the nation.

Culture on Campus

Catholic U has 118 recognized student groups, and seven different leadership programs. You can sing a cappella and interact with other architecture enthusiasts, and still make it to your WCUA radio show in time to throw on that new Sean Paul record you've been neglecting your work to listen to. Music geeks unite! Boasting an extraordinary music program—one of the tops in the country—CUA's Benjamin T. Rome School of Music continuously churns out gem after gem. Thanks to a recent grant, CUA music students study with some of the most renowned composers, directors, and musicians working on Broadway today. The school stages over 200 musicals, operas, chamber concerts, and orchestral and choral performances throughout the academic year. For listings, including Department of Drama productions, visit performingarts.cua.edu.

Department Contact Information

Undergraduate Admissions 202-319-5305
Graduate Admissions 202-319-5305
Athletics 202-319-5286
The Benjamin T. Rome School of Music . . 202-319-5414
The Columbus School of Law 202-319-5140
Conferences and Summer Programs 202-319-5291
Hartke Theatre Box Office 202-319-4000
Metropolitan College 202-319-5256
The National Catholic School
    of Social Service 202-319-5458
Public Affairs 202-319-5600
The School of Arts and Sciences
    (undergrad) 202-319-5115
The School of Arts and Sciences (grad) . . . 202-319-5254
The School of Canon Law 202-319-5492
The School of Engineering 202-319-5160
The School of Library
    and Information Science 202-319-5085
The School of Nursing 202-319-5400
The School of Philosophy 202-319-5259
The School of Theology
    and Religious Studies 202-319-5683
Summer Sessions 202-319-5257

Mount Olivet Rd

Concord St

Capitol Ave

Raum St

Brentwood
Park

18

14

15

13

16

17

MSSD
Gym and Pool

Craig St

Model
Secondary
School
for the Deaf

Kendall Demonstration
Elementary School

11th Pl

Brentwood Pkwy

Telegraph Hill Rd.

Central
Utilities
Building

Peter J
Fine Health
Center

Central
Receiving

Ballard North

Plaza
Dining
Hall

Carlin
Hall

Switzer Dr.

Lowman St

Holbrook Ter

Ballard
West

Hanson
Plaza

12

Hoy Field

**MAP
11**

Queen St

11

Hall
Memorial
Building

Sorenson Langauge
and Communication
Center

Hotchkiss
Field

West Virginia Ave

Penn St

6

Merrill
Learning
Center

Student
Academic
Center

Gallaudet
University
Kellogg
Conference
Center

Lincoln Circle W

Peet
Hall

Student
Union
Building

Lincoln Circle E

Owen Pl

Neal Pl

Peikoff
Alumni
House

Tapscott St.

Faculty Row

7

Gallaudet
Mall

Ely
Center

Field
House

Oates St

1

6th St

2

Olmsted
Green

9

Neal St

3

College
Hall

10

Elstad
Auditorium

Appleby
Building

Chapel
Hall

Fowler
Hall

4

5

Security
Kiosk

Lincoln Circle S

Morse St

Florida Ave

1. Denison House
2. Fay House
3. Ballard House
4. Edward Miner Gallaudet Residence
5. Gate House
6. Washburn Arts Building
7. Edward Miner Gallaudet Memorial Building
9. Kendall Hall
10. Dawes House
11. Benson Hall
12. Clerc Hall
13. MSSD Residence Hall B
14. MSSD Residence Hall C
15. MSSD Residence Hall D
16. MSSD Residence Hall V
17. MSSD Residence Hall E
18. MSSD Housing

General Information

NFT Map: 11
Address: 800 Florida Ave NE
           Washington, DC 20002
Phone: 202-651-5050
Website: www.gallaudet.edu

Overview

Gallaudet is the premier university for the deaf and hearing-impaired, and the only university in the world where deaf students and those without hearing problems mingle. It is a campus where English and American Sign Language (ASL) coexist. Students can choose from more than 40 majors, and all aspects of the school, including classes and workshops, are designed to accommodate deaf students. Even the hearing students, who make up about 5% of each entering class, must always communicate through visual means.

Thomas Hopkins Gallaudet co-founded the American School for the Deaf in Hartford, CT, in 1817 as the first such school in the country. Forty years later, his youngest son, Dr. Edward Minor Gallaudet, established a school for the deaf in DC. In 1864, that school became the world's first and only liberal arts university for the deaf. In 1988, I. King Jordan, the University's first deaf president, was appointed after students, backed by a number of alumni, faculty, and staff, shut down the campus, demanding that a deaf president be appointed. In 2006, students took over the campus again, this time to block Jane Fernandes from being selected university president because, although born deaf, Fernandes grew up speaking and did not learn American Sign Language until she was 23. Dr. Jordan himself accused students of rejecting Fernandes because she was "not deaf enough." Gallaudet's mismanagement of the protests, as well as its low graduation rates, led the Commission on Higher Education to postpone re-accreditation, noting concerns about weak academic standards, ineffective governance, and a lack of tolerance for diverse views.

Tuition

In the 2010–2011 academic year, tuition and fees (including room and board) for US residents comes to about $12,270 for undergraduate and $12,800 for graduate programs. For international students from developing countries, the price of admission is $14,980 and $15,790 respectively, and for international students from non-developing countries, is $17,700 and $18,880.

Sports

The birth of the football huddle took place at Gallaudet. Legend has it that prior to the 1890s, football players stood around discussing their plays out of earshot of the other team. This posed a problem for Gallaudet's team; they communicated through signing and opposing teams could see the plays that were being called. Paul Hubbard, a star football player at the university, is credited with coming up with the huddle to prevent prying eyes from discovering plays.

In 2007, thanks to improved performance in club football (including an undefeated 2005 season) the Bison football team returned to NCAA Division III football for the first time since the mid-1990s. With its return to NCAA football, Gallaudet now boasts 13 NCAA Division III teams and several intramural sports teams.

In the summer, Gallaudet runs popular one-week sports camps, where teens from all over the US, as well as the local area, stay on campus and participate in basketball and volleyball activities. Check the website for details.

Culture on Campus

Gallaudet's Dance Company performs modern, tap, jazz, and other dance styles incorporating ASL. Gallaudet also produces several theater productions every year, all of which are signed, with vocal interpretation. The school is smack in the middle of a neighborhood quickly transitioning from rough to trendy. Check out the nearby theaters, coffeehouses, and farmers market before gentrification smoothes out the hard edges.

Department Contact Information

Admissions 800-995-0550
Graduate School and
  Professional Programs 800-995-0513
College of Liberal Arts, Sciences,
  and Technologies 202-651-5224
Department of ASL and Deaf
  Studies 202-651-5814
Financial Aid 202-651-5292
Gallaudet Library 202-651-5217
Registrar 202-651-5393
Visitors Center 202-651-5050

The George Washington University

1. Academic Center
   A. Phillips Hall
   B. Rome Hall
   C. Smith Hall of Art
   D. Visitor Center
2. John Quincy Adams House
3. Alumni House
4. Hortense Amsterdam House
5. Bell Hall
6. Corcoran Hall
7. Crawford Hall
8. Dakota
9. Davis-Hodgkins House
10. Abba Eban House
11. Fulbright Hall
12. Funger Hall
13. Hall of Government
14. GSEHD
15. Guthridge Hall
16. The George Washington
    University Club
17. The George Washington
    University Inn
18. Hospital, GW

19. Ivory Towers Residence Hall
20. Kennedy Onassis Hall
21. Key Hall
22. Lafayette Hall
23. Lenthall Houses
24. Lerner Hall
25. Lerner Family Health and
    Wellness Center
26. Jacob Burns Library (Law)
27. Melvin Gelman Library (University)
28. Paul Himmelfarb Health
    Sciences Library (Medical)
29. Lisner Auditorium
30. Lisner Hall
31. Madison Hall
32. Marvin Center
33. Media & Public Affairs
34. Medical Faculty Associates
    A. H. B. Burns Memorial Bldg
    B. Ambulatory Care Center
35. Mitchell Hall
36. Monroe Hall
37. Munson Hall

38. New Hall
39. Old Main
40. Quigley's
41. Rice Hall
42. International House
43. Ross Hall
44. Samson Hall
45. Schenley Hall
46. Scholars Village Townhouses
    A. 619 22nd St
    B. 2208 F St
    C. 520-526 22nd St
    D. 2028 G St
    E. 605-607 21st St
47. Smith Center
48. Staughton Hall
49. Stockton Hall
50. Strong Hall
51. Stuart Hall
52. Student Health Service
53. Support Building
54. Thurston Hall
55. Tompkins Hall of Engineering

56. Townhouse Row
57. University Garage
58. Warwick Bldg
59. The West End
60. Woodhull House
61. 700 20th St
62. 812 20th St
63. 814 20th St
64. 714 21st St
65. 600 21st St
66. 609 22nd St
67. 613 22nd St
68. 615 22nd St
69. 617 22nd St
70. 837 22nd St
71. 817 23rd St
72. 1957 E St
73. 2033-37 F St
74. 2031 F St
75. 2101 F St
76. 2109 F St
77. 2147 F St
78. 2000 G St

79. 2002 G St
80. 2008 G St
81. 2030 G St
82. 2106 G St
83. 2108 G St
84. 2112 G St
85. 2114 G St
86. 2125 G St
87. 2127 G St
88. 2129 G St
89. 2129 G St (rear)
90. 2131 G St
91. 2131 G St (rear)
92. 2136 G St
93. 2138 G St
94. 2140 G St
95. 2142 G St
96. 2129-33 Eye St (rear)
97. 2000 Pennsylvania Ave NW
98. 2100 Pennsylvania Ave NW
99. 2136 Pennsylvania Ave NW
100. 2140 Pennsylvania Ave NW
101. 2142 Pennsylvania Ave NW
102. Newman Catholic Center
103. Duques Hall/School of Business

General Information

NFT Map: 7
Address: 2121 Eye St NW
Washington, DC 20052
Phone: 202-994-1000
Website: www.gwu.edu

Overview

Once considered nothing more than a second-rate commuter school for graduate and law students, GW, like the city it inhabits, has enjoyed a massive boom in popularity over the past ten years. The school has close to 11,000 full-time undergraduate students and nearly 14,000 graduate students stomping around Foggy Bottom in search of wisdom and love. The school recently wrapped up some of its large-scale construction projects and unveiled new academic buildings, a renovated fitness center, and a television studio where CNN's Crossfire was filmed until it was cancelled. The GW "campus," for lack of a better word, now stretches its tentacles far into Foggy Bottom, leaving some neighbors none too pleased.

Unlike their counterparts over at Georgetown (who smugly refer to GW as a school for the Georgetown waitlist), GW students understand the meaning of having a life outside of academics. They love their city environs; they seem surprisingly street-smart; they take full advantage of government and congressional internships; and they venture farther afield when it comes to socializing. (Tuesday nights being the exception, when local bar McFadden's is invaded by what seems to be the entire student body.) But GW students aren't all play—the libraries, which stay open 24 hours, are never empty, and each year students are selected to be Rhodes, Truman, Marshall, and Fulbright scholars.

While many undergraduates hail from similar upper-middle-class backgrounds, 139 foreign countries are represented in the student body. Collectively, students have a motley appearance, further differentiating them from the Lacoste poster children of Georgetown. Tuition-wise, GW is the city's most expensive school, and with the deep pockets comes more than a few pompous attitudes. Bigshot alums include J. Edgar Hoover, Jackie O, Kenneth Starr, General Colin Powell, as well as four presidential children.

Tuition

Tuition for the 2010–2011 school year costs $41,610, with an additional $10,610 for room and board. Add on personal expenses and books, for a whopping yearly total of around $53,000.

Sports

The university's fight song, "Hail to the buff, hail to the blue, hail to the buff and blue," provides hours of double-entendre fun for the students and it seems to work for the athletes, too. The university's 22 NCAA Division I teams, known as the fighting Colonials, usually place well in their A-10 conference, especially in basketball: in 2007 the men's team won their first Atlantic Ten Men's Basketball Championship since 1976, and over the last 19 years, GW has won nearly 75% of all games played and made the NCAA Tournament 15 times

Culture on Campus

The Robert H. and Clarice Smith Hall of Art is a modern facility that features five floors dedicated to the study and practice of art. Students participate annually in two major shows, and faculty members also display their art on campus.

The Department of Theatre and Dance produces two dance concerts, three plays, and one musical each year. These productions are performed either in the 435-seat Dorothy Betts Marvin Theatre, or the 1,490-seat Lisner Auditorium (don't miss the Dimock Gallery of Fine Art on the first floor). If you're unaffiliated with the university, tickets to performances will probably cost between $15 and $30. For more information on performances presented by the Theatre and Dance Department, call 202-994-6178.

For information on tickets for the Dorothy Betts Marvin Theatre, call 202-994-7411. For information on tickets for the Lisner Auditorium, call 202-994-6800.

Department Contact Information

Undergraduate Admissions	202-994-6040
Athletics	202-994-6650
Campus Bookstore	202-994-6870
College of Arts & Science	202-994-6210
Elliot School of International Affairs	202-994-3002
Financial Aid	202-994-6620
Gelman Library	202-994-6558
Graduate School of Education	202-994-2194
Law School	202-994-6288
Registrar	202-994-4900
School of Business	202-994-8252
School of Medicine	202-994-3501
Student Activities Center	202-994-6555
University Police (emergency)	202-994-6111
University Police (non-emergency)	202-994-6110
Visitor Center	202-994-6602

1. Pre-Clinical Science Building
2. Davis Performing Arts Center
3. Southwest Quadrangle
4. McNeir Auditorium
5. New North
6. Old North
7. Gaston Hall
8. Dahlgren Chapel of the Sacred Heart
9. Dahlgren Quadrangle
10. Healy Hall
11. Gervase Building
12. Mulledy Building
13. Ryan Hall
14. Maguire Hall
15. Riggs Library
16. East Campus Quadrangle
17. McSherry Building

Reservoir Rd NW
Reservoir Rc
Dent Pl NW
Q St NW.
Volta Pl N
P St NW
Q St NW
N St NW
M St N
Prospect St NW
Canal Rd NW
Whitehurst Fwy.

39th St NW
38th St NW
37th St NW
36th St NW
35th St NW
37th St NW
38th St NW
35th St NW

Building D
Medical and Dental Annex
Medical and Dental Building
Research Resource Facility
Basic Science Building 1
Dahlgren Medical Library
Concentrated Care Center
Marcus Bles Building
St Mary's Hall
Darnall Hall
Georgetown University Hospital
New Research Building
Lombardi Cancer Center
Gorman Building
Pasquerilla Healthcare Center
Kober Cogan Building
Henle Village

North Kehoe Field
Main Shuttlebus Stop
Leavey Center
Reiss Science Building

Kehoe Field
Rafik B. Hariri Building
ICC Auditorium
White-Gravenor Hall

Yates Field House
Intercultural Center
Red Square
Copley Lawn
Poulton Hall

Observatory
Harbin Field
Copley Hall
North Gatehouse
Reed Alumni Residence

Heating and Cooling Plant
Harbin Hall
2
Robert & Burnice Wagner Alumni House
Institute of Diplomacy

McDonough Gymnasium
4 5 6 7
Healy Lawn
South Gatehouse
Academic Administration

Kennedy Hall
8 9 10
Alumni Square (Village B)
Academic Administration

Reynolds Family Hall
3
McCarthy Hall
Village C
11 12 13 14 15
17
Nevils Building
Mortara Building
GU Shops
Walsh Building
16
Loyola Hall

Jesuit Residence (Wolfington Hall)
O'Donovan Dining Hall
New South
Village A
Lauinger Library
Ryder Hall Xavier Hall

Exorcist Stairs
Car Barn

MAP 18

29

Potomac River

General Information

NFT Map: 18
Main Campus: 37th & O Sts NW
                  Washington, DC 20057
Phone: 202-687-0100
Website: www.georgetown.edu

Overview

Georgetown University was founded the same year the US Constitution took effect, making the school not only the nation's oldest Catholic and Jesuit university, but also about the same age as most of the neighborhood's socialites. But seriously, Georgetown is the most prestigious college in town, and a "feeder school" for the federal government and foreign-policy community. Alumni include former president Bill Clinton, Supreme Court Justice Antonin Scalia, and broadcast journalist/Kennedy heir/California First Lady Maria Shriver. The campus sets the tone for the neighborhood around it—beautiful, old, and distinguished. A few blocks away, the endless strip of bars on M Street provide most of the Georgetown nightlife.

Georgetown's long history is not without its eerie episodes. According to campus rumor, the attic of Healy Hall is haunted by the ghost of a priest who died while winding the clock in the building's famous spire. During the Civil War, the university's buildings became bunkers and hospitals for the Yankee troops. Once the war ended, the school adopted blue and gray as its official colors to symbolize the reunification of North and South. More recently, it became part of Hollywood history by providing the setting for a scene from *The Exorcist*, a novel by alum William Peter Blatty. The creepy "*Exorcist* stairs" can be found on campus at the junction of Prospect and 36th Streets.

Tuition

In the 2010–2011 academic year, undergraduate tuition for full-time students cost $39,768. With room and board and fees, the average total cost attendance is $52,443. Graduate tuitions vary by program.

Sports

The university's teams are known as the Hoyas because, the story goes, a student well-versed in Greek and Latin started cheering "Hoya Saxa!" which translates to "What Rocks!" The cheer proved popular and the term "Hoyas" was adopted for all Georgetown teams. Since "what rocks" did not readily translate into an animal mascot, the bulldog was chosen to represent the Blue and Gray. Georgetown is best known for its men's basketball team, a regular top-seed in the NCAA Tournament. Former Hoya athletes include Patrick Ewing, Allen Iverson, and Alonzo Mourning. Georgetown is the alma mater of more than one Ewing; son Patrick Ewing, Jr. became a Hoya in 2005. The younger Ewing has since graduated and though sidelined with a sprained MCL, was recently added to the Knicks' 2009 summer league roster. Men's sports also include crew, football, golf, lacrosse, sailing, soccer, swimming and diving, tennis, and track. Women's sports include basketball, crew, field hockey, golf, lacrosse, sailing, soccer, swimming and diving, tennis, track, and volleyball. For tickets to all Georgetown athletic events, call 202-687-HOYA. Georgetown also offers intramural sports including volleyball, flag football, racquetball, basketball, ultimate Frisbee, table tennis, softball, and floor hockey.

Culture on Campus

Although best known for its more philistine programs—government, law, and medicine—Georgetown has bolstered its fine arts program significantly in the last few years, expanding course offerings and opening the posh new Davis Performing Arts Center in 2005. The Department of Art, Music, and Theater offers majors and minors in studio art, art history, and the performing arts. Artistically inclined students can also join Georgetown's many extra-curricular arts groups, including the orchestra, band, choir, and multiple theater troupes, improv groups, and a cappella singing groups.

Department Contact Information

Undergraduate Admissions 202-687-3600
Graduate Admissions 202-687-5568
Georgetown Law Center 202-662-9000
McDonough School of Business 202-687-3851
Edmund A. Walsh School
    of Foreign Service .202-687-5696
Georgetown University
    Medical Center 202-687-5100
School of Nursing & Health Studies 202-687-2681
Department of Athletics 202-687-2435

N

Drew Hall

Gresham Pl

Burr Gymnasium

Burr Annex

Girard S

Howard Manor

Cook Hall

Effingham Apartments

Greene Memorial Stadium

McMillan Reservoir

Fremont St

School of Business

Miner Hall

Mordecai Johnson Administration Building

Howard Hall

Lindsay Hall (Social Work)

Crampton Auditorium

Aldridge Theatre

Douglas Hall

Carnegie Building

Physical Ed Annex

Childers Hall Fine Arts

Blackburn Center

Locke Hall

Economics Mathematics C A R

School of Education

Human Ecology Building

Upper Quadrangle

MAP 15

4th St

4th St

Georgia Ave

Howard Pl

Mackey Building (Architecture)

Rankin Chapel

Founders Library

Undergraduate Library

Thirkield Hall

Engineering Computer Science

Dixon Hall

Health Center

Chemistry Building

Just Hall (Biology)

School of Pharmacy

Lower Quadrangle

Wheatley Hall

Truth Hall

Tubman Quad

Baldwin Hall

Crandall Hall

Frazier Hall

McMillan Dr

6th St

Barry Pl

College St

ISAS

Bunche Center

iLab

Power Plant

Student Resource Building

CB Powell Building (Communications)

WHUR-FM

Graduate School

WHUT-TV

4th St

Bethune Annex

Bryant St

8th St

Book Store

Howard Center

Nursing and Allied Health Center

Evolutionary Building

Louise Stokes Health Science Library

W St

Hospital Service Center

Student Health Center

Sickle Cell Center

College of Dentistry

College of Medicine

Adams Building

P Hospital Parking

MAP 10

V St

5th St

HU Hosptial

Tower Building

Oakdale Pl NW

Elm St

5th Pl

General Information

NFT Maps: 10 & 15
Main Campus: 2400 Sixth St NW
                 Washington, DC 20059
Phone: 202-806-6100
Website: www.howard.edu

Overview

Conceived in 1866 as a theological seminary for African-American ministers, Howard University remains the pre-eminent African-American university in the nation. Although no longer a seminary, it has remained nonsectarian and open to all races and genders since its founding. Today, as a Carnegie Research institution offering a full array of undergraduate and graduate programs, including medicine, law, engineering, business, and the arts, Howard continues to serve as a dominant DC intellectual, cultural, and physical presence. Distinguished Howard alumni include novelist Zora Neale Hurston, Nobel Laureate Toni Morrison, and Shirley Franklin, the first female mayor of Atlanta. Perhaps the most well known graduate was Supreme Court Justice Thurgood Marshall, who used Howard's campus to prepare himself and a team of legal scholars from around the nation to argue the landmark Brown v. Board of Education case.

Howard University once occupied a lone single-frame building and now has five campuses spanning more than 260 acres. The library system houses the largest collection of African-American literature in the nation. Despite its large physical size, Howard is a relatively small school with roughly 7,000 undergraduate students and almost 11,000 students total. Its national reputation belies its numbers, as recent graduation commencement speaker Oprah Winfrey would attest.

Howard's main campus is located just minutes away from the Capitol and the White House on "the hilltop," one of the highest elevation points in the city. The campus leads right into U Street, one of the premier catwalks of the city. The area was once the city's center of jazz and African-American nightlife before falling on rough times. But now it's back and considered the hippest of areas, with avant-garde fashion, deluxe condos, and over-priced everything.

Tuition

In the 2009–2010 academic year, undergraduate tuition for students living off-campus cost $15,270. Room and board averaged around $6,000. Graduate tuition, fees, and expenses vary by school and department.

Sports

Howard is a member of the Mid-Eastern Athletic Conference and participates in the NCAA's Division I. Annual football homecoming festivities continue to serve as a premier annual event in Washington (just listen to Ludacris' "Pimpin' All Over The World" and Notorious B.I.G.'s "Kick In The Door"). The last noteworthy sports achievement dates way back to 2003, when the women's cross-country team ran away with the MEAC championship trophy. Other teams have a less-than-stellar record. The male basketball team ranked 319th out of 326 teams in 2004. But losing (a lot) hasn't hurt their popularity on campus. Games still draw crowds. Intercollegiate men's sports include basketball, cross-country, soccer, tennis, football, swimming, wrestling, and track. Women's sports include basketball, tennis, cross-country, track, volleyball, and swimming.

Culture on Campus

In 2005, the University held an exhibit titled "A Proud Continuum: Eight Decades of Art at Howard University," which featured the work of 122 alumni, the largest show of its kind in Howard's history

The Department of Theatre Arts produces dance and drama performances throughout the school year in the Ira Aldridge Theater, which also hosts visiting professional theater troupes. Student tickets cost $8 and general admission costs $15. The season always brings in a decidedly diverse bag of productions: last year's included a staging of the Obie Award-winning play *Zooman and the Sign* by Charles Fuller and another of Nilo Cruz's Pulitzer Price-winning *Anna in the Tropics*.

Howard University Television, WHUT-TV, is the only African-American-owned public television station in the country. It has been operating for 30 years and reaches half a million households in the Washington metropolitan area.a.a. Howard University also runs commercial radio station WHUR-FM (96.3).

Department Contact Information

Admissions 202-806-2700
College of Arts & Sciences 202-806-6700
School of Business 202-806-1500
School of Communications 202-806-7690
School of Dentistry 202-806-0440
School of Divinity 202-806-0500
School of Education 202-806-7340
School of Engineering, Architecture,
    and Computer Sciences 202-806-6565
Graduate School of Arts & Sciences 202-806-6800
School of Law 202-806-8000
College of Medicine 202-806-5677
College of Pharmacy, Nursing, and
    Allied Health Sciences 202-806-5431
School of Social Work 202-806-7300
Student Affairs 202-806-2100
Athletic Department 202-806-7140
Founders Library 202-806-7234

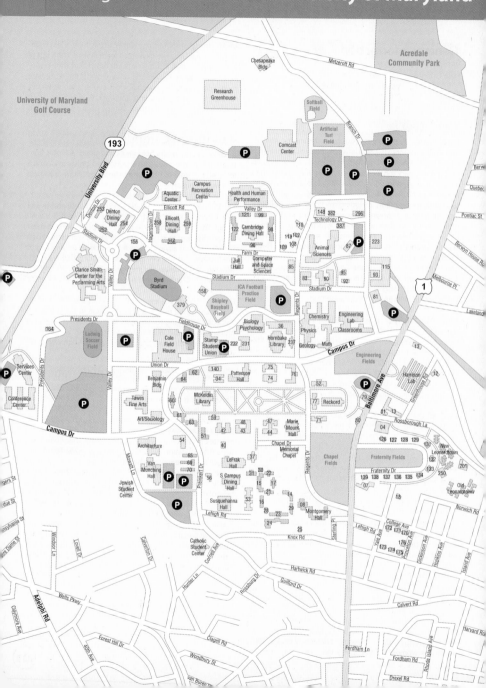

General Information

Address: College Park, MD 20742
Phone: 301-405-1000
Website: www.umd.edu

Overview

University of Maryland's gargantuan size masks its humble beginnings. First chartered as a small agricultural college in 1856, this public university now has nearly 37,000 students roaming its 1,500 acres. Between the 13 colleges, 111 undergraduate majors, study-abroad programs, and honors programs, there's enough excitement and intellectual rigor to keep the brightest Marylanders interested. And for students who've been surrounded by pastoral green quads for so long it makes them want to gag, the school's very own Metro stop will shuttle them into the vast city that awaits to the south. UMCP is the crème de la crème of the thirteen campuses run by The University System of Maryland and hosts a multitude of academic programs offering specialized courses and research opportunities. Of particular note are the University Honors and Gemstone programs, which continue to lure some of the brightest of Marylanders with dirty cheap (well, relatively) in-state tuition.

Tuition

Undergraduate tuition for the 2010–2011 school year cost $8,053 for in state residents, and $23,990 for non-residents. Room and board averaged around $9,000.

Sports

While there's never been a real dearth of Terrapin pride, it's only skyrocketed in recent years. An ACC basketball championship win over the Duke Blue Devils, victory at college football's Gator Bowl, and a 2003 NCAA men's basketball Championship win have strengthened Marylanders' love of their winning teams. With 27 Varsity teams competing at UMD, the athletic program is widely recognized as one of the best in the country for both men's and women's sports, and the Terps are one of only six schools to have won a national championship in both football and men's basketball. Though it's usually the men's teams that hog the spotlight, 2006 ushered in the first National Championship win for the Terps women's basketball team.

Culture on Campus

The Clarice Smith Performing Arts Center hosts high-profile performers and ensembles. Past guests have included Yo-Yo Ma, the Woolly Mammoth Theater Company, and the Maryland Opera Studio. The Center is also home of the university's symphony orchestra and jazz band. Tickets are usually free or, at most, five bucks for students. You don't have to be affiliated with the university to attend concerts—just be prepared to shell out up to $30 if you're not a student, faculty member, or staff. 301-405-2787; www.claricesmithcenter.umd.edu.

If orchestra or jazz ensembles are not the type of entertainment you're jonesing for, the Student Entertainment Events (SEE) presents a variety of concerts featuring both headlining artists and local bands. Tickets of course are cheaper for students and range between $5 and $25, depending on the event. Tickets for larger concerts can also be purchased via Ticketmaster.

Film buffs can view an array of independent films and blockbusters at the Hoff Theater in the University's Student Union. The ample theater showcases at least one feature daily and is usually free for students, $5 for non-students.

And don't worry about things getting too boring on campus; despite the fact that sleepy College Park, Maryland is a verifiable snoozefest in comparison to nearby DC, students there are never ones to shy away from controversy. UMCP gained a bit of notoriety and quite a bit more media coverage when the student union planned in 2009 to show Pirates II: Stagnetti's Revenge, a hard-core pornographic film. The move prompted State Senator Andy Harris to threaten to rescind university funding and University President Dan Mote to cancel the event entirely. Not to be deterred, students took to the media and eventually planned another event: a "teach-in" featuring David Rocah of the ACLU which addressed free speech, academic expression, and the role of pornography in society. This scholarly speech was followed by, what else, a screening of sections of the film Pirates 2: Stagnetti's Revenge. Now that's what I call learning.

Department Contact Information

Campus Information 301-405-1000
Undergraduate Admissions 301-314-8385
Graduate Admissions 301-405-0376
Bookstore 301-314-7848
Registrar 301-314-8240
Bursar 301-314-9000
Athletic Department 800-462-8377
Ticket Office 301-314-7070
Clark School of Engineering 301-405-3855
College of Education 301-405-2344
School of Architecture 301-405-6284
School of Public Policy 301-405-6330
Smith School of Business 301-405-2189
Art and Humanities 301-405-2108
Behavioral and Social Sciences 301-405-1697
Life Sciences 301-405-2071

Building Listings

1 - Central Heating Plant
4 - Ritchie Coliseum
5 - Service Building Annex
7 - Pocomoke Building
8 - Annapolis Hall
12 - Plant Operations & Maintenance Complex
13 - Shuttle Bus Facility
14 - Harford Hall
15 - Calvert Hall
16 - Baltimore Hall
17 - Cecil Hall
18 - Police Substation
21 - Prince George's Hall
22 - Kent Hall
23 - Washington Hall
24 - Allegany Hall
25 - Charles Hall
28 - Howard Hall
29 - Frederick Hall
30 - Talbot Hall
34 - Jimenez Hall
36 - Plant Science
37 - Shoemaker Building
40 - Morrill Hall
42 - Tydings Hall
43 - Taliaferro Hall
44 - Skinner Building
47 - Woods Hall
48 - Francis Scott Key Hall

51 - Worchester Hall
52 - Mitchell Building Registration Office
53 - Dance Building
54 - Preinkert Field House
59 - Journalism Building
60 - Anne Arundel Hall
61 - Queen Anne's Hall
62 - St. Mary's Hall
63 - Somerset Hall
64 - Dorchester Hall
65 - Carroll Hall
66 - West Education Annex
69 - Wicomico Hall
70 - Caroline Hall
71 - Lee Building
74 - Holzapfel Hall
75 - Shriver Laboratory
76 - Symons Hall
77 - Main Administration
79 - Visitors Center
80 - Rossborough Inn
81 - Wind Tunnel Building
83 - JM Patterson Building
85 - Institute for Physical Science & Technology
87 - Central Animal Resources Facility
90 - Chemical and Nuclear Engineering Building

93 - Engineering Annex
96 - Cambridge Hall
98 - Centreville Hall
99 - Bel Air Hall
102 - Agriculture Shed
108 - Horse Barn
109 - Sheep Barn
110 - Cattle Barn
115 - AV Williams
119 - Blacksmith Shop
121 - Performing Arts Center, Clarice Smith
122 - Cumberland Hall
126 - Kappa Alpha Fraternity
127 - Sigma Alpha Mu Fraternity
128 - Delta Tau Delta Fraternity
129 - Sigma Alpha Epsilon Fraternity
131 - Beta Theta Pi Fraternity
132 - Phi Sigma Kappa Fraternity
133 - Pi Kappa Phi Fraternity
134 - Chi Omega Sorority
135 - Sigma Kappa Sorority
136 - Alpha Delta Phi Sorority
137 - Zeta Tau Alpha Sorority
138 - Sigma Phi Epsilon Fraternity
139 - Zeta Beta Tau Fraternity
140 - Health Center
148 - Manufacturing Building

156 - Apiary
158 - Varsity Sports Teamhouse
170 - Alpha Delta Pi Sorority
171 - Phi Kappa Tau Fraternity
172 - Alpha Chi Omega Sorority
173 - Delta Phi Epsilon Sorority
174 - Phi Sigma Sigma Sorority
175 - Delta Gamma Sorority
176 - Alpha Phi Sorority
201 - Leonardtown office building
223 - Energy Research
231 - Microbiology Building
232 - Nyumburu Cultural Center
237 - Geology Building
250 - Leonardtown community center
252 - Denton Hall
253 - Easton Hall
254 - Elkton Hall
256 - Ellicott Hall
258 - Hagerstown Hall
259 - LaPlata Hall
296 - Biomolecular Sciences Building
379 - Football Team Building
382 - Neutral Buoyancy Research Facility
387 - Tap Building

George Mason University

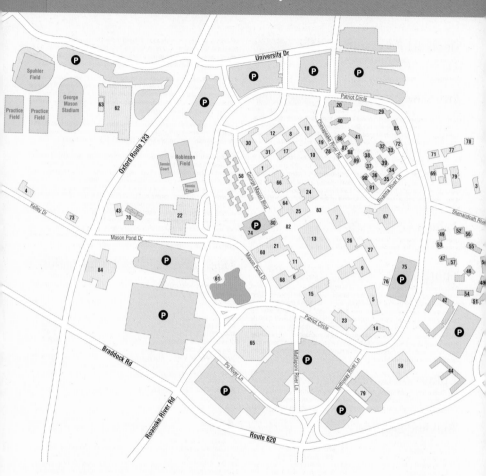

1. Aquia Building
2. Buchanan House
3. Carrow Hall
4. Carty House
5. Research I
6. College Hall
7. David King Hall
8. East Building
9. Enterprise Hall
10. Fenwick Library
11. Fine Arts Building
12. Finley Building
13. George W. Johnson Center
14. Nguyen Engineering Building
15. Innovation Hall
16. Krasnow Institute
17. Krug Hall
18. Lecture Hall
19. North Chesapeake Module
20. Northern Neck
21. Performing Arts Building
22. Recreation and Athletic Complex (RAC)
23. Art and Design Building

24. Robinson Hall A
25. Robinson Hall B
26. Science and Tech I
27. Science and Tech II
28. South Chesepeake Module
29. Hampton Roads
30. Thompson Hall
31. West Building
32. Amherst Hall
33. Brunswick Hall
34. Carroll Hall
35. Dickenson Hall
36. Essex Hall
37. Franklin Hall
38. Grayson Hall
39. Hanover Hall
40. Commonwealth Hall
41. Dominion Hall
42. Liberty Square
43. West P.E. Module
44. Potomac Housing/Housing Office
45. Adams Hall
46. Eisenhower Hall

47. Harrison Hall
48. Jackson Hall
49. Jefferson Hall
50. Kennedy Hall
51. Lincoln Hall
52. Madison Hall
53. Monroe Hall
54. Roosevelt Hall
55. Truman Hall
56. Washington Hall
57. Wilson Hall
58. Student Apartments
59. Aquatic and Fitness Center
60. Center for the Arts Concert Hall
61. Cross Cottage
62. Field House
63. Field House Module
64. Harris Theatre
65. Patriot Center
66. Student Union I/Student Health Services
67. Student Union II
68. Mason Hall
69. Central Heating and Cooling Plant

70. Patriot Village Lot
71. Facilities Administration
72. Rivanna Module
73. Kelley II
74. Parking Deck, Mason Pond (Visitors)
75. Parking Deck, Sandy Creek
76. Parking Services
77. Physical Plant/Customer Service Center
78. Recycling Center
79. University Police
80. Visitor Information
81. George Mason Statue
82. Clock Tower
83. Mason Inn Conference Center and Hotel
84. Eastern Shore
85. Blue Ridge
86. Shenandoah
87. Piedmont
88. Tidewater
89. Skyline Fitness Center
90. Southside Dining

General Information

Address: 4400 University Drive
             Fairfax, VA 22030
Phone: 703-993-1000
Website: www.gmu.edu

Overview

Named for the most obscure of the founding fathers, George Mason University began as an extension of the University of Virginia for the northern part of the state. In 1966, George Mason College became a four-year, degree-granting university. George Mason separated from UVA in 1972 and became an independent institution.

Currently the university offers more than 100 degree programs in both the undergraduate and graduate levels in three different locations in Virginia. Academically, Mason boasts award-winning faculty and offers unique curriculum, such as its biodefense graduate degree program. There are approximately 18,600 undergraduates and around 11,750 graduate students currently enrolled in the university

Conveniently located in close proximity to Washington, DC, George Mason's picturesque main campus is centered on acres of woods in Fairfax, Virginia. In addition to its law school and campus in Arlington, GMU has recently established branches in Prince William and Loudoun countries.

Tuition

Undergraduate tuition for the 2010–2011 school year cost $7,824 for in-state students, and $23,808 for all non-residents. Room and board averaged around $8,000.

Sports

Of course we can't mention GMU without noting the successful run the men's basketball team had a few seasons ago. While many living outside the immediate area were scratching their heads, asking, "Where the heck is George Mason?" or getting it confused with its fellow local "George" University (George Washington University), the Patriots were surpassing everyone's expectations and slowly crept into the Final Four in 2006. Although the GMU men's basketball team took a brief break from the limelight following their surprise entrance onto the national stage, the Patriots returned to the NCAA Tournament in 2008 after winning the CAA Tournament. Unfortunately the cards weren't stacked in their favor, and they fell to Notre Dame.

So now that we got that out of the way, there are about 19 other men's and women's Division I teams on campus including baseball, track and field, tennis, and soccer. Mason teams belong to the National Collegiate Athletic Association (NCAA) Division I, the Colonial Athletic Association (CAA), and the Eastern College Athletic Conference (ECAC).

Culture on Campus

George Mason's Center for the Arts offers a variety of musical and dance performances from celebrated entertainers like the Metropolitan Jazz Orchestra and the St. Petersburg Ballet. With four different theater spaces ranging from the larger 2,000-seat Concert Hall to the more personal 75-seat Black Box, the Center for the Arts also features performances by GMU's own theater company, Theater of the First Amendment. The company has been nominated for numerous awards and is a Helen Hayes Award recipient. Most performances are free or provide discounts for students.

The Film and Media Studies Program, along with University Life, show weekly films throughout the academic year in *Cinema Series*. Admission and popcorn are free for students and faculty with GMU ID.

Department Contact Information

Fairfax Campus 703-993-1000
Admissions 703-993-2400
University Services 703-993-2840
Bookstore 703-993-2666
Registrar 703-993-2441
Patriot Computer Store 703-993-4100
Academic Support Center 703-993-2470
Center For the Arts 703-993-8888
Patriot Center 703-993-3000
School of Law 703-993-8000
Arlington Campus 703-993-8999
Prince William Campus 703-993-8350
Loudoun Campus 703-993-4350

General Information

Address: 1600 FedEx Wy
Landover, MD 20785
Redskins Website: www.redskins.com
FedEx Field www.fedex.com/us
  Website: sports/fedexfield/
Stadium Admin: 301-276-6000
Ticket Office: 301-276-6050

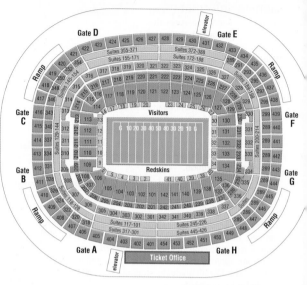

Overview

No city is more infatuated with its football team than Washington is with the Redskins, even in the *off-season*. Summer after summer, the team's front office has put together a line-up it claims will march straight to the Super Bowl, and year after year, the beloved 'Skins have fallen flat on their faces. Part of the problem has been Daniel Snyder, the team's unpopular owner, who knows football like Paris Hilton knows rodeo yet insists on dropping megabombs on washed-up players whom he deems messianic. (We think Deion Sanders may still be collecting Redskins paychecks.)

The 2007 season was probably one of the most emotional roller coaster rides any Redskins fan has taken in a decade. From a 2-0 start, to a series of injuries, to the death of 24-year-old superstar Sean Taylor, to a last-game win over Dallas to put the 'Skins in the playoffs, and finally the retirement of Hall of Fame Coach Joe Gibbs, no one in the DC area will forget the 2007 season for a long time. 2008 was the inaugural season for Coach Jim Zorn, who took over for the legendary Gibbs. Zorn had never held a head coaching position, but quickly earned the trust and respect of fans. However, a series of losses that left the team at 8-8 and just short of the playoffs. Despite hopes for a good 2009 season cultivated by the high-profile acquisition of Albert Haynesworth (he came with a $100 million price tag), the year was a bleak one for Redskins fans. The Skins failed to improve upon 2008's record, which prompted Zorn's unceremonious dismissal. In early 2010, Mike Shanahan was brought on as both coach and Executive Vice President of Football Operations, meaning he now has full control over player personnel. Fans are keeping their fingers crossed that Shanahan's guidance, and track record (he led the Broncos to two Bowl victories in both 1997 and 1998), will help turn around what have been a disappointing couple of seasons.

The stadium itself is a diamond in the middle of a very large rough known as Landover, Maryland. During the late 1980s, then-owner Jack Kent Cooke envisioned a new and sensational stadium, settling on a site deep in the Maryland suburbs just inside the Washington Beltway. Although Cooke didn't live to see the $300 million project completed, Jack Kent Cooke Stadium officially opened its gates September 14, 1997 (Snyder sold the naming rights to FedEx shortly after purchasing the team in 1999). The colossal structure is equipped to hold more than 90,000 fans, good for tops in the NFL.

How to Get There—Driving

Um, don't. The nightmares of getting in and out of FedEx Field and the myriad parking lots in the vicinity are the stuff of a Maalox

moment. If you *must*, take E Capitol Street (which becomes Central Avenue at the Maryland line) to Harry Truman Drive north just outside the Beltway. Then take a right onto Lottsford Road to Arena Drive and you're there. Keep your eyes peeled for the many

signs that will direct you to the field. You can also take the Capital Beltway (I-95/495) from the north or the south to Exits 15 (Central Avenue), 16 (Arena Drive, open only for FedEx events), or 17 (Landover Road). It's a barrel of laughs, especially for those Monday night games.

Parking

FedEx Field provides off-stadium parking that can cost as much as $35, with a free shuttle ride to the stadium. The team did their damnedest to prevent fans from parking for free at the nearby Landover Mall and walking to the game, but a Prince George's County judge overturned a county policy restricting pedestrian movement in the area. So you can pay up for convenience or exercise your civic rights to park free and schlep.

How to Get There—Mass Transit

Take the Blue Line to the Morgan Boulevard or Largo Town Center stops—both are close by and are a pretty short walk to the stadium. Five-dollar round-trip shuttle buses depart from these stations for FedEx Field every 15 minutes, from two hours before the game until two hours after.

How to Get Tickets

If you enjoy the prospect of languishing in a years-long line, join the Redskins season ticket waiting list by visiting www.redskins.com/tickets. If you're just looking for individual game tickets, suck up to a season ticket holder or call 301-276-6050.

Lower Level | Club Level | Upper Level

General Information

Address: 1101 Russell St, Baltimore, MD 21230
Phone: 410-261-7283
Website: www.baltimoreravens.com

Overview

Dominating Baltimore's skyline from I-95, M&T Bank Stadium is a menacing structure, to say the least. Its team, the "Bol'more" Ravens, flew into town 11 years ago via Cleveland and wasted no time in capturing the 2001 Super Bowl title. 2006 was probably their next-best season, with now long-term coach Brian Billick bringing the team to a 13-3 record and a tough playoff loss to the Baltimore—we mean Indianapolis—Colts. Harsh are the ways of the gods. But after a 3-13 finish in 2007, the Ravens made a drastic turn around–finishing with a 11-5 record and making it to the AFC Championship Game. They bowed to eventual Super Bowl champions, the Pittsburgh Steelers, but hopes are high that the Ravens have gotten their groove back and will make a splash in years to come.

In Baltimore, as is customary with most NFL cities, the name of the game, or *pre-game*, is tailgating. For 1 pm games, the festivities usually commence at about 9 am. The parking lots slowly swell with inebriated men fashioning O-linemen bellies, confirming Baltimore's reputation as a blue-collar football town. Outsiders need not be afraid, however, because unlike fans in nearby cities (read: Philadelphia), Ravens fans are gracious hosts and typically welcome others to the party. Once inside the stadium, expect to pay through the nose for food—though the Maryland crab cakes are definitely worth the high price, and the stadium's hot dogs are pretty damn good, too. After the game, Pickles and Sliders, two sports bars on nearby Washington Boulevard, are where weary DC-bound travelers (tired of waiting years for Redskins tickets) head to quench their thirst.

How to Get There—Driving

Take I-95 N toward Baltimore to Exit 52 (Russell Street north for immediate access to the stadium (you can't miss it) or Exit 53 (I-395 north) for better access to the downtown parking garages.

Parking

M&T Bank provides parking, for which you need to buy a permit ahead of time. Otherwise, there are 15,000 spaces-worth of public parking nearby, most of which charge a flat game day rate.

How to Get There—Mass Transit

The MTA Light Rail provides service directly to the Hamburg Street Light Rail stop, operational only on game days. Trains run every 17 minutes from Hunt Valley and Cromwell Station/Glen Burnie, and every 34 minutes from Penn Station and BWI. The stop closest to the stadium on the Baltimore Metro is Lexington Market, though you'll have to hoof it about a mile. Be sure to leave early to beat the crowds on game days. You can also take the 3, 7, 10, 14, 17, 19/19A, 27, or 31 buses, all of which stop within walking distance of the stadium.

How to Get Tickets

To purchase tickets, visit the Ravens' website, or call 410-261-7283. Tickets can also be purchased through Ticketmaster (www.ticketmaster.com).

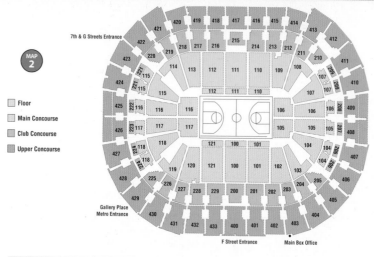

MAP 2

- ☐ Floor
- ☐ Main Concourse
- ☐ Club Concourse
- ☐ Upper Concourse

General Information

NFT Map:	2
Address:	601 F St NW
	Washington, DC 20004
Verizon Center Phone:	202-628-3200
Verizon Center Website:	www.verizoncenter.com
Wizards Phone:	202-661-5100
Wizards Website:	www.washingtonwizards.com
Capitals Phone:	202-266-2200
Capitals Website:	www.washingtoncaps.com
Mystics Phone:	202-661-5000
Mystics Website:	www.washingtonmystics.com
Georgetown Basketball Phone:	202-687-4692
Georgetown Basketball Website:	www.guhoyas.com

Overview

In 1997, DC's then-new MCI Center reversed a decades-old trend of arenas planting roots in the suburbs by bringing it all back to the 'hood. The block-sized complex known today as Verizon Center (which includes a 20,000-seat stadium as well as bars, restaurants, and stores) is now the centerpiece of downtown's gentrification juggernaut.

The best thing to happen to the underachieving world of DC sports since Jordan's semi-triumphant return to the hard court is the NHL rookie Alexander Ovechkin, who is single-handedly making Caps games a weekend must-do activity. In addition to the Caps and the artists-formerly-known-as-the-Bullets, the Verizon Center is also home to the Washington Mystics, who boast the largest fan base in the WNBA. The Georgetown Hoyas basketball team hoops it up in the arena, as well. Beyond the ballers, Verizon Center hosts big-name concerts from the likes of Cher, Britney, and Madonna, circuses (both Ringling and Cirque de Soleil have performed here), and all sorts of other events. For post-event fun, China-alley, otherwise known as Chinatown, is a block away with plenty of eats and drinks.

How to Get There—Driving

From downtown, turn left onto 7th Street from either Constitution Avenue or New York Avenue. Verizon Center is on the northeast corner of F and 7th.

Parking

Verizon Center's parking garage is on 6th Street NW underneath the building and is open for most events at a charge of $25 for event parking. It opens 1 ½ hours before game/show time and closes 1 hour after the event. There are also several public parking garages near the building including Gallery Place's parking garage on 6th Street NW and the parking garage next to Rosa Mexicano restaurant on F Street NW.

How to Get There—Mass Transit

Verizon Center is accessible by the Metro's Red, Yellow, and Green lines; get off at the Gallery Place-Chinatown stop. It's not hard to find, just get off the Metro, and you are directly under it.

How to Get Tickets

Tickets for all Verizon Center events are available through the Ticketmaster website at www.ticketmaster.com (with the inevitable Ticketmaster markup, of course), or by calling 703-573-7328. Wizards tickets range from $10 to $832 for an individual game. Now that the NHL has slunk back to the city, Caps tickets will run you $18 to $251, which may pay for a sliver of Ovechkin's contract. Mystics tickets range from $17 to $125, and Hoyas tickets are between $5 and $40.

Level 1
Level 2
Level 3
Level 4
Level 5
Level 6
Level 7

General Information

Address:	333 W Camden St
	Baltimore, MD 21201
Website:	www.theorioles.com
Phone:	888-848-2473

Overview

Oriole Park at Camden Yards opened in 1992, launching a "traditional" trend in stadium design that continues to this day. The old warehouse behind Right Field and the general look of the place give it that old-fashioned, family-friendly feel. In the face of dozens of corporations eager to smear their names across the park, the Orioles have refused to budge. All brick and history, the stately Yards stand downtown on a former railroad center, two blocks from Babe Ruth's birthplace. Center field sits atop the site where the Bambino's father ran a bar. The goods include double-decker bullpens, a sunken, asymmetrical field, and "Boog's BBQ," run by ex-Oriole Boog Powell, who is known to frequently man the grill himself during O's home games.

The Birds, unlike their stadium, haven't been much to look at in recent years. A few years back, baseball's drug problem hit the local boys of summer when it hurts—in the batter's box—and for some reason they haven't been able to recover. The Orioles have been playing below .500 baseball for the past decade and have been running through coaches like they're going outta style. The good news is there is never a shortage of all-star players to watch at Oriole Park, as both the Yankees and Red Sox inhabit the AL East with the O's, and Camden Yards offers a comfy and classic setting in which to watch your favorites swing the bats.

While their performance on the field in the recent past may have been lackluster, the O's hope to ramp up fan enthusiasm with their recently unveiled new uniforms. The team's new digs includes caps with an updated Oriole bird (which is ornithologically correct, mind you) and a new patch featuring the flag of the state of Maryland in style borrowed from their vintage 1960s and 1970s emblem. The hometown's name (Baltimore, baby!) also returns to the road uniforms for the first time since being removed in 1972.

How to Get There—Driving

Take MD 295 (B-W Pkwy/Russell St) to downtown Baltimore, which gets very congested on game days. You can also take I-95 North to Exits 53 (I-395), 52 (Russell St), or 52 (Washington Blvd) and follow signs to the park.

Parking

Parking at Camden Yards is reserved, but there are several public garages nearby. Prices range from $3 to $6.

How to Get There—Mass Transit

Take the MARC from Union Station in DC to Camden Station in Baltimore. It takes about an hour and ten minutes, costs $14 round trip, and the last train leaves at 6:30 pm. To return from a night game, the 701 MTA bus will get you home in 50 minutes for free with your Baltimore-bound MARC ticket.

Due to a recent court ruling, the MTA no longer allows special bus charters to run return trips to Savage, Greenbelt, and Washington D.C. after Oriole Baseball night games. The only option for car-less Orioles enthusiasts is an annoying combination of buses and MTA Light Rail. MTA Light Rail trains roll out of Camden Station at 9:38 pm and 10:08 pm, arriving at the BWI Business Station at 10:05 pm and 10:35 pm. The very last two B-30 buses leave from the BWI Business District Station at 10:15 pm and 10:44 pm, arriving at the Greenbelt Metro Station at 10:51 pm and 11:20 P.M. Keep in mind that on weekdays, the last southbound Metro train departs from Greenbelt at 11:30 pm. On weekends, the Metro operates until 2:30 am.

How to Get Tickets

Orioles tickets can be purchased on their website, or by calling 888-848-2473. Individual game tickets range from $9 to $55. Group and season tickets are also available.

Robert F Kennedy Memorial Stadium

General Information

NFT Map: 4
Address: 2400 E Capitol St SE,
Washington, DC 20003
Websites: www.dcsec.com, www.dcunited.com
Phone: 202-547-9077

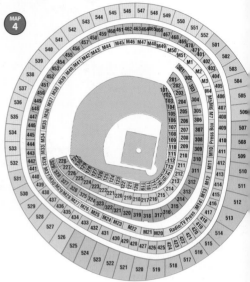

Overview

When it opened as DC Stadium in 1961, RFK was hailed as a triumph of multipurpose architecture and was one of the first of the "cookie-cutter" stadiums. Today it's a cement donut, an alien spacecraft dinosaur of the '60s vision of the future. If you want to experience this decaying jack-of-all-trades (it's hosted football, soccer, and baseball over the years), get in while you can before it crumbles into obscurity—word on the street is that RFK will be torn down as soon as an alternate location can be found for the soccer teams that use it. The stadium remains a sentimental favorite with Redskins fans, who regale us with memories of their team's 35 years there, including five Super Bowl appearances, three championships, and great gridiron personalities like Joe Gibbs, John Riggins, Joe Theisman, Vince Lombardi, Art Monk, and George Allen. In 1996, negotiations for a new football stadium in DC fell through when then-mayor Sharon Pratt Kelly, and team owner Jack Kent Cooke abandoned RFK for a new home in Landover, Maryland.

When the Redskins left, RFK stayed off life support with the arrival of Major League Soccer and the DC United in 1996. The United lost little time in gaining popularity, winning the MLS Cup Championship their inaugural season and again in 1997, 1999, and 2004. Along the sidelines, United fans bounce in the stands and chant "Ole, Ole" in hopes of rooting the team to another win. In a league where foreign-born fans cheer for players from their respective countries, United games offer a fun glimpse of Washington's international diversity. Though soccer hooliganism in DC is nothing like its counterparts in Europe (and thank god for that), DC United does boast some pretty intense fan groups, most notably Barra Brava, whose fan section covers the better part of a sideline, and a tailgating party that's almost more fun than watching the game. The Screaming Eagles and La Norte are two other popular groups, whose drumming and flag waving makes the game more fun for everyone in the stadium.

For a few brief years, RFK breathed new life with the return of Major League Baseball to DC. The vagabond Nationals (formerly the Montreal/Puerto Rico Expos) played in the confines of the roller-coaster roof from 2005 to 2007, at the time making RFK the fourth-oldest MLB stadium in use. But its glory was short-lived, as the City Council voted to build a shiny new ballpark near the Navy metro yard in southeast which opened just in time for the start of the 2008 season.

How to Get There—Driving

Follow Constitution Avenue east past the Capitol to Maryland Avenue. Turn left on Maryland and go two blocks to Stanton Square. At Stanton Square, turn right onto Massachusetts Avenue. Go around Lincoln Park to E Capitol Street and turn right.

Parking

Stadium parking costs between $3 and $15, depending on the event you're attending.

How to Get There—Mass Transit

Take the Metro to the Stadium-Armory Station on the Blue and Orange lines.

How to Get Tickets

For United tickets, call 703-478-6600. Tickets to United games range from $23 for north goal bleacher seats to $52 for seats on the west side. You can purchase full-season tickets or half-season tickets at various prices. Tickets can also be purchased through Ticketmaster (202-397-7328, www.ticketmaster.com).

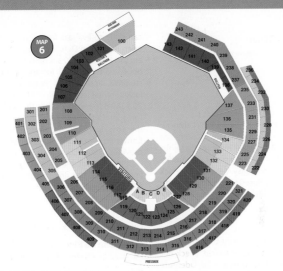

General Information

NFT Map:	6
Address:	1400 S Capitol Street SE
	Washington, DC 20003
Web site:	www.nationals.mlb.com
Phone:	202-675-NATS

Overview

March 30, 2008 was a great day for baseball fans in DC. It marked opening day at the brand new Nationals Park, named after the original stadium for the Washington Senators. The waterfront colossus cost an estimated $611 million and seats approximately 41,000 fans, boasting views of the capitol building and the Washington Monument from certain spots in the stadium, as well as a grove of cherry blossoms and a view of the Anacostia River from outside the stadium. The stadium also features 66 suites along the infield, the "Oval Office" bar, and luxury suites, bearing the names of past US presidents.

Beyond the initial price tag, Nationals Park has a few other modern-day amenities worth noting, particularly a 4,500 square foot high-definition scoreboard—more than five times the size of RFK's. The stadium is also striving to become the first major stadium in the US accredited as a Leadership in Energy and Environmental Design (LEED) certified ballpark, a.k.a. "Green." Special attention is being paid to issues affecting the nearby Anacostia River, which more than likely will end up even more polluted with concession stand waste. But hey, at least they're trying, right?

Even though the ballpark has only been open a short time, it is already building a little bit of history. Ryan Zimmerman's game winning walk-off home run in the ninth inning of opening day was the third walk-off home run in major-league history to be hit in the first MLB game played at a stadium. That game also set ESPN history as the most watched MLB opening night game ever. Beyond that, the Nat's have struggled a bit trying

to get attendance up, and so far they hold second-place for all-time lowest attendance for a new stadium. On the other hand, the pope gave mass there. That's cool… right.

How to Get There—Driving

Not advised. If you really feel you must, the Stadium is accessible from both I-395, and I-295. Just look for the South Capitol Street exit, and then pray for parking.

Parking

Not exactly convenient. The Nationals recently snatched up several massive parking lots in the nearby area, including at RFK and the Navy Yard, and run shuttles to and from Nationals Park. There are several reserved parking lots, many of which go to season ticket holders or anyone who wants to shell out forty bucks.

How to Get There—Mass Transit

Now you're talking! Take the Green Line to the Navy Yard station, a mere block north of the stadium entrance. A recent renovation to the Navy Yard metro entrance now allows the stop to accommodate 15,000 passengers an hour, the same as Stadium/Armory at RFK. Talks to re-route the DC Circulator buses to make a stop at Nationals Park during game nights, as well as the establishment of water taxi services are being considered as well. Other Metro buses that run close to Nationals Park include the 70, P1/P2, and V7/V8/V9.

How to Get Tickets

You can purchase Nats tickets at their web site or over the phone. From the diehard middle class fan to the suit and tie K Street lobbyist, there's a ticket price all economic levels. They range anywhere between $5 for a nosebleed seat to $335 for a presidential suite ticket.

General Information

DC Department of Parks and Recreation: www.dc.gov

Washington Area Roadskaters (WAR): www.skatedc.org

Overview

Washington DC supports a surprisingly thriving skating scene, thanks in a large part to the nonprofit inline skaters' group WAR. Popular meeting places for skaters include the White House, which has a traffic-free Pennsylvania Avenue and easy Metro access; Rock Creek Park, which is mostly closed to cars on weekends; and East Potomac Park, with a recently repaved, with its 3.2-mile Ohio Drive loop.

Indoor Skating

If the weather is grim, or if you want to put in some good practice on predictably level terrain, check out **Wheels Skating Center**, 1200 Odenton Rd, Odenton, MD; 410-674-9661, www.wheelsrsc.com.

Skate Parks

After years of hostile restrictions and citations against skaters grinding away outside government buildings, a skate park was finally built in the District's Shaw neighborhood in 2003. It's free and located on the corner of 11th St NW and Rhode Island Ave.

Other outdoor skate parks in the DC area include:

Alexandria Skate Park · 3540 Wheeler Ave, Alexandria, 703-838-4343/4344 · Map 42

The Powhatan Springs Park · 6020 Wilson Blvd, Arlington · 703-533-2362 · Map 33 · A 15,000-square-foot park, featuring 8'- and 6'-deep bowls and 4' and 6' half-pipes; opened in 2004.

Ice Skating

Finding natural outdoor ice thick enough to support skating can be difficult in Washington DC. But during particularly cold winters, the National Park Service allows ice skaters onto the C&O Canal (Maps 8, 18, 32, 35, 36) (the ice has to be more than three inches thick, so it's got to be *really* cold). The National Park Service ice skating hotline provides information on skate-safe areas: 301-767-3707.

Skating at the **National Gallery of Art's Sculpture Garden Ice Skating Rink** (Map 2) may not seem as organic as skating on natural ice, but the surrounding art exhibit rivals any natural setting in terms of beauty. Every Thursday from December through March, you can skate to live jazz from 5 pm to 8 pm. The rink is open daily from October through March, Mon–Sat 10 am to 11 pm, Sun 10 am to 9 pm. Admission for a two-hour session costs $7 for adults and $6 for children, students, and seniors. Skate rental costs $3 and a locker rental costs 50¢; 700 Constitution Ave NW; 202-289-3360; Map 2. While the Sculpture Garden rink turns into a fountain once the warm weather arrives, the NHL-sized rink at **Mount Vernon Recreation Center** in Alexandria operates year-round. The rink provides ice-hockey lessons, recreational skating lessons, and adult hockey leagues for all levels. On Friday nights, the rink brings in a DJ for teen Rock & Blade skating. Rates and fees vary nightly, so call before you go. 2017 Belle View Blvd, Alexandria, VA; 703-838-4825.

Other seasonal ice-skating rinks are located at:

Cabin John Ice Rink · 10610 Westlake Drive, Rockville, MD 20852 · 301-765-8620, www.cabinjohnice.com

Reston Town Center Rink ·11900 Market St, Reston VA 20190, www.restontowncenter.com

Herbert Wells Ice Rink · 5211 Paint Branch Pkwy, College Park MD 20740 www.pgparks.com

Wheaton Ice Arena · 11717 Orebaugh Ave, Wheaton MD 20902 www.mc-mncppc.org/Parks/index.shtm

Pershing Park Ice Rink ·Pennsylvania Ave & 14 St NW · 202-737-6938, www.pershingparkicerink.com · Map 1 · $5.50–$6.50 admission + $2.50 rental

Bethesda Metro Ice Center · 3 Bethesda Metro Ctr, Bethesda · 301-657-9776 · Map 29

Rockville Ice Arena · 50 Southlawn Court, Rockville, MD 20850 · 301-315-5650, www.rockvilleicearena.com

Gear

The **Ski Chalet** offers a comprehensive selection of performance inline skates and offers tune-ups and rentals. Skates can be rented by the hour ($5) or by the day ($15 for the first day, $6 each additional day). The Ski Chalet is located at 2704 Columbia Pike, Arlington; 703-521-1700 · Map 37

The **Ski Center**, located at 4300 Fordham Rd NW, sells reasonably priced ice and inline skates. The shop, which has been serving the DC area since 1959, also rents equipment. 202-966-4474 · Map 30

Sailing / Boating / Rowing

Boating enjoys a passionate following here in the District. As the weather warms, the Potomac River and the Tidal Basin swarm with sailboats, kayaks, canoes, and paddleboats.

At 380 miles long, the Potomac River ranks as the fourth longest river on the East Coast. The river also serves as a natural state border, forming part of the boundary between Maryland and West Virginia and separating Virginia from both Maryland and DC. The site of many significant battles during the American Revolution and the Civil War, the Potomac now holds an eternal place in the US history books and has earned the moniker "The Nation's River." A combination of urban sewage and run-off from mining projects upstream seriously degraded the river's water quality, but efforts by the government and citizens have made the water safe for boats and some fishing. In the summertime, motor boat enthusiasts anchor north of Key Bridge for tubing, swimming, and relaxing.

The Mariner Sailing School (703-768-0018) gives lessons and rents canoes, kayaks, and sailboats for two to six people. If a paddleboat ride is worth worming your way through swarms of sweaty tourists, the Tidal Basin is the best place to go. The boathouse, which sits among the famous cherry blossoms and tulip-bearing flower beds on the man-made inlet, rents paddleboats by the hour (202-479-2426). Two-person boats cost $10 per hour; four-person boats cost $18 per hour. If kayaking or sculling is your thing, head to Georgetown and Thompson Boat Center, which rents canoes and sailboats as well.

Sailing/Boating Centers

	Address	Phone	Map	URL
Capitol Sailboat Club	James Creek Marina, Washington, DC	202-265-3052	6	www.capitolsbc.com
DC Sail	600 Water St, Washington, DC	202-309-1115	6	www.dcsail.org
Tidal Basin Boat House	1501 Main Ave SW, Washington, DC	202-479-2426	6	www.tidalbasinpeddleboats.com
Mariner Sailing School	Belle Haven Marina, Alexandria, VA	703-768-0018	N/A	www.saildc.com
Thompson Boat Center	2900 Virginia Ave NW, Washington, DC	202-333-9543	7	www.thompsonboatcenter.com

Rowing Clubs

	Address	Phone	Map	URL
Capitol Rowing Club	1115 O St SE, Washington, DC	202-289-6666	5	www.capitalrowing.org
Potomac Boat Club	3530 Water St NW, Washington, DC	202-333-9737	8	www.rowpbc.net
Canoe Cruisers Association	11301 Rockville Pike, Kensington, MD	301-251-2978	N/A	www.ccadc.org

Golf

Like everything else in DC, there are politics and networking involved in where you choose to tee off. Our advice—avoid the pricey rat race at the private clubs and reserve a tee time at one of the many less stuffy, and often more fun, public courses.

East Potomac Park (Map 6) offers three different course options (Red, White, and Blue, of course) as well as mini golf and a driving range. The **Langston Golf Course (Map 12)** is closest to downtown DC, making it easy to hit during lunch. The **Rock Creek Golf Course (Map 27)** can sometimes suffer from droughts and heavy play, but its great location keeps people happily putting away.

Golf Courses

	Address	Phone	Fees	Type	Map
East Potomac	972 Ohio Dr SW	202-554-7660	Weekdays $12 / Weekends $19	Holes-18, Par 72; Also two 9-hole Par-3 courses	6
Langston	28th & Benning Rds NE	202-397-8638	Weekdays $21.50/ Weekends $26.50	Holes-18, Par-72	12
Sligo Creek Golf Course	9701 Sligo Creek Pkwy	301-585-6006	Weekdays $13–15/ Weekends $18	Holes-9, Par-35	25
Rock Creek Golf Course	16th & Rittenhouse NW	202-882-7332	Weekdays $19/ Weekends $24	Holes-18, Par-65	27
Greendale Golf Course	6700 Telegraph Rd, Alexandria	703-971-6170	Weekdays $18/ Weekends $22	Holes-18, Par-70	n/a
Hilltop Golf Club	7900 Telegraph Rd, Alexandria	703-719-6504	Weekdays $20/ Weekends $32	Holes-9, Par-31	n/a
Pinecrest Golf Course	6600 Little River Tpke, Alexandria	703-941-1061	Weekdays $16/ Weekends $20	Holes-9, Par-35	n/a

Driving Ranges

	Address	Phone	Fees	Map
East Potomac	972 Ohio Dr SW	202-554-7660	$5.50/ 50 balls	6
Langston	28th & Benning Rds NE	202-397-8638	$4.50/45 balls	12

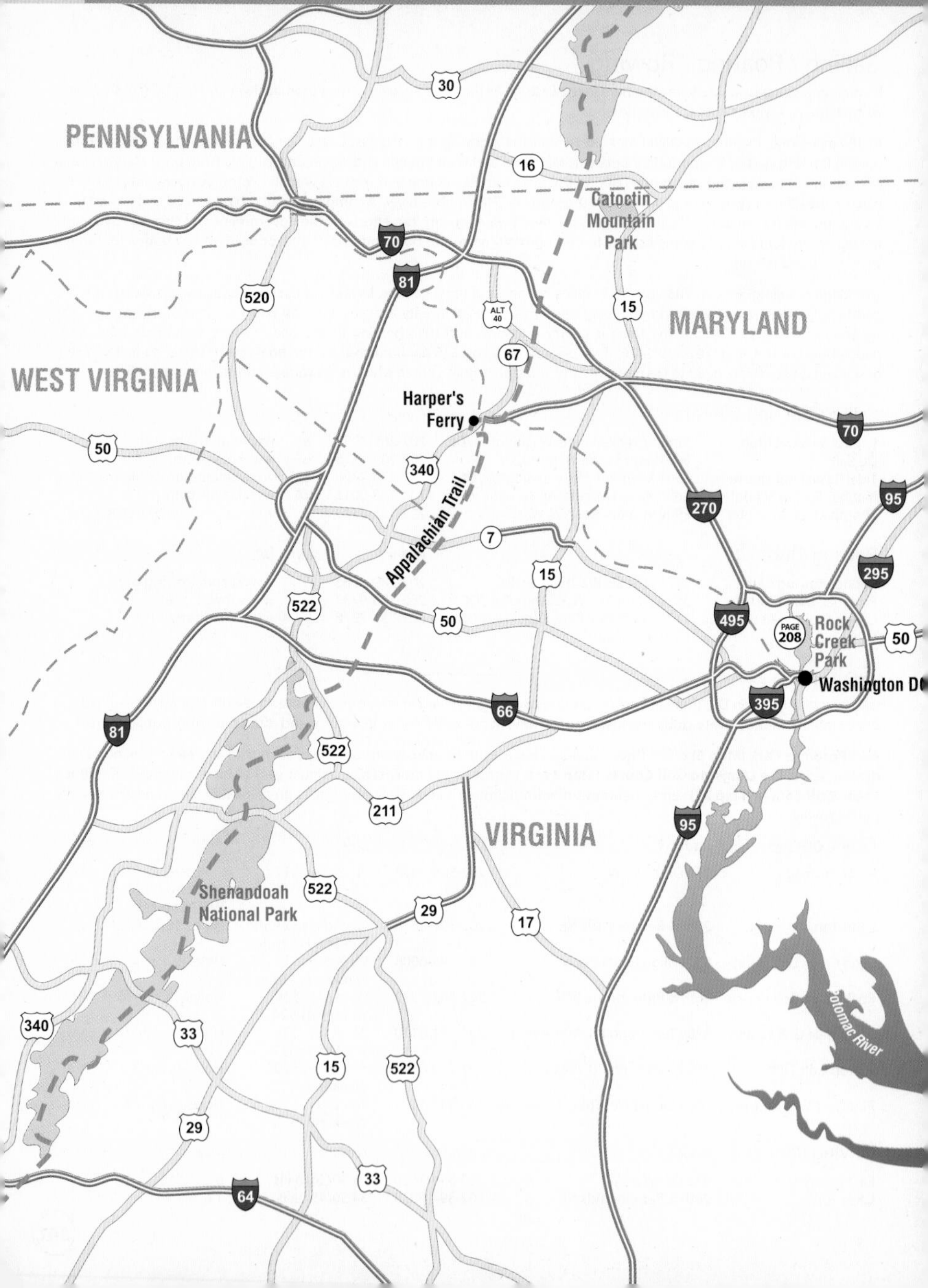

PENNSYLVANIA

30

16

Catoctin
Mountain
Park

70

81

520

ALT
40

15

MARYLAND

67

WEST VIRGINIA

50

Harper's
Ferry

70

340

Appalachian Trail

95

7

270

295

15

522

50

495

PAGE
208

Rock
Creek
Park

50

66

395

Washington DC

81

522

95

211

VIRGINIA

Shenandoah
National Park

522

29

17

340

33

15

522

29

33

64

Potomac River

Overview

One of the greatest things about living in DC, a city bursting with hyper, Type-A personalities, is how easy it is to leave. The feasibility of escaping urban life for a weekend, or even just an afternoon, checks and balances the go-getting lobbying/lawyering/liaisoning frenzy that often seems to permeate Our Nation's Capital to the core. Rock Creek Park weaves its way through the city, and some of the best hiking routes on the east coast are just a short drive from town. The National Parks Service website is a valuable resource for planning overnight trips or day hikes (www.nps.gov), and we recommend the gem *60 Hikes within 60 Miles: Washington, DC* by Paul Elliott (Menasha Ridge Press).

Shenandoah National Park

A short drive out of DC, this is one of the country's most popular national parks, mainly because of gorgeous Skyline Drive, which runs across the ridgeline of the Blue Ridge Mountains (the eastern range of the Appalachian Trail). But locals know to ditch the wheels, get out, and get dirty. There are more than 500 miles of trails in the park, including about 100 miles of the AT itself. In short, you can plan a weeklong backcountry getaway, and there'll still be more undiscovered country to come back for next time.

The Old Rag Trail, with its rock scramble and distinctive profile, is a favorite strenuous day hike. The rangers at the visitors' center will direct you to the toughest climbs, easier routes, the waterfall view, or the trails where you'll most likely see bears. The park is 70 miles west of DC. Take Route 66 W to Exit 13, and follow signs to Front Royal. www.nps.gov/shen; 540-999-3500.

Appalachian Trail

Forget what you've heard about lugging a summer's worth of misery along this Georgia-to-Maine trace. You don't have to hike the whole thing. Luckily, a good portion of this nationally protected 2,174-mile footpath through the Appalachian Mountains is accessible from DC. Hook up with it for a few miles at points in Maryland and Virginia, and acquire bragging rights with just a day's worth of blister-inducing pain. A good place to start is Harper's Ferry in Maryland, 65 miles from DC, where you can load up on breakfast and some history before you head out. When you return, hoist a well-deserved pint. www.nps.gov/appa; 301-535-6278.

Catoctin Mountains

While Catoctin Mountain recreation area was created in order to provide a place for federal employees to get a little bit of R&R, it has since been converted into Camp David, the famously inaccessible presidential retreat. Camp David is never open to the public, or to run-of-the-mill federal employees, but there's still the eastern hardwood forest where everyone is free to roam wild. From DC, the Catoctin Mountains are about a two-hour drive north. Take the George Washington Memorial Parkway north to the Beltway to I-270 N. Drive 27 miles to Frederick, MD. Take Route 15 N to Route 77 W, to the Catoctin Mountain Park exit. Drive three miles west on 77, turn right onto Park Central Road, and the Visitor Center will be on the right. www.nps.gov/cato; 301-663-9388.

Sugarloaf Mountain

Sugarloaf's main appeal is that it's only an hour drive from DC. It's a modest mountain—about 1,300 feet—with nice views of the surrounding farmland, and entry into the park is free. You can choose a variety of easy and not-so-easy ways to get up the mountain, but no matter which way you choose you'll be surrounded by an impressive collection of rare red and white oak trees. To get there, drive North on Route I-270 to the Hyattstown exit, circle under I-270, and continue on Route 109 to Comus, then make a right on Comus Road to the Stronghold entrance. Or if you're looking for a beautiful Sunday drive, take the backroads: River Road is a leafy country road that hugs the Potomac from upper NW into the Maryland farmlands. www.sugarloafmd.com; 301-869-7846.

Rock Creek Park

This is the place for a quick nature fix. The historic 1,754-acre park, which reaches from Georgetown to Maryland, is laced with several hiking trails, especially in its northern reaches. The major trails along the western ridge are marked by green blazes, and the footpaths along the east side are marked with blue blazes. A tan-blazed trail connects the two trail systems. None of the trails are strenuous, but there will be moments when you can hardly believe people are outsourcing contracts and scheduling Outlook appointments only a stone's throw away. For the full effect, turn off your cell phone. See the extensive Rock Creek Park section in this book for more details. www.nps.gov/rocr; 202-895-6070.

C&O Canal

Don't think the C&O Canal towpath is just for bikers. The relatively level terrain of this 184.5-mile, Georgetown-to-Cumberland trail makes for great hiking. The entire length is dotted with scenic vistas of the Potomac that offer gentler, more natural views of the river than you're afforded when stuck in traffic on a bridge between DC and northern Virginia. History abounds along the route in the form of Civil War sites and both reconstructed and ramshackle lockhouses. Once you pass Great Falls, there are free campsites spread every five miles or so. They're simple setups of a fire pit, picnic table, water pump, and portable toilet, but after a hard day's hike they seem like the lap of luxury. For more information, visit www.nps.gov/choh or call 202-653-5190.

One of the few times it pays to be a DC resident (as opposed to a MD or VA one) is when it comes to the pool: DC residents can dip for free. Non-residents pay $3–4 (based on age) for a single admission, or can opt for a 30 or 90 day passes for greater savings. The following fees for public pools are based on county residency. Non-residents can count on paying a buck or two more.

All DC outdoor pools are open daily from June 25, with many opening from Memorial Day onwards with weekend hours. They generally close in late August or early September, on or around Labor Day. Specifics for each neighborhood pool can be found at http://app.dpr.dc.gov. Many of the public pools require you to register as a member at the beginning of the season and, since most fill their membership quotas quickly, it's wise to locate your nearest pool and join at the beginning of the season. You'll thank yourself on DC's dog days, when the humid air itself seems to be sweating. DC is also home to several "spray parks," which are basically playgrounds with fountains scattered throughout. They're supposed to be for kids, but who doesn't love giant sprinkler systems?

Pools	Address	Phone	Fees	Type	Map
William Rumsey Aquatic Center	635 North Carolina Ave SE	202-724-4495	Residents free, various fees & passes for non-residents	Indoor	3
Rosedale Pool	17th St NE & Gales St NE	202-727-1502	Residents free, various fees & passes for non-residents	Outdoor	4
Barry Farm Pool	1223 Sumner Rd SE	202-645-5040	Residents free, various fees & passes for non-residents	Outdoor	5
Lincoln Capper Pool	500 L St SE	202-727-1080	Residents free, various fees & passes for non-residents	Kid's pool	5
Watkins	420 12th St SE	202-727-1504	Residents free, various fees & passes for non-residents		5
East Potomac	972 Ohio Dr SW	202-554-7660	Weekdays $12 / Weekends $19	Outdoor	6
Randall Pool	S Capitol St SW & I St SW	202-727-1420	Residents free, various fees & passes for non-residents	Outdoor	6
Fairmont	2401 M St NW	202-457-5070	Members and hotel guests only. Various membership fees.	Indoor	9
YMCA National Capital	1711 Rhode Island Ave NW	202-862-9622	$100 joining fee, $70 per month	Indoor	9
YMCA	1325 W St NW	202-462-1054	$50 to join, $35 per month	Indoor	10
Dunbar Pool	1301 New Jersey Ave NW	202-673-4316	Residents free, various fees & passses for non-residents	Indoor	11
Harry Thomas Sr Pool	1801 Lincoln Rd NE	202-576-5640	Residents free, various fees & passes for non-residents	Outdoor	11
JO Wilson Pool	700 K St NE	202-727-1505	Residents free, various fees & passes for non-residents	Kid's pool	11
Trinidad Recreation Center	1310 Childress St NW	202-727-1503	Children six and under swim free, kids 6-17 $3 per day, $46 season pass	Kid's pool	12
Fort Lincoln Outdoor Pool	3201 Ft Lincoln Dr NE	202-576-6389	$4 per day, $130 season pass	Outdoor	13
Langdon Park Pool	Mills Ave & Hamlin St NE	202-576-8655	Residents free, various fees & passes for non-residents	Outdoor	13
Turkey Thicket Community Center	1100 Michigan Ave NE	202-635-6226	Residents free, various fees & passses for non-residents	Indoor	14
Banneker Pool	2500 Georgia Ave NW	202-673-2121	Residents free, various fees & passes for non-residents	Outdoor	15
Parkview Pool	639 Otis Pl NW	202-576-8658	Children six and under swim free, kids ages 6-17 $3 per day, $46 season pass	Kid's pool	15
Marie Reed Center Pool	2200 Champlain St NW	202-673-7771	Residents free, various fees & passes for non-residents	Indoor	16

Pools—*continued*

	Address	Phone	Fees	Type	Map
Georgetown Pool	3400 Volta Pl NW	202-727-3285	Residents free, various fees & passes for non-residents	Outdoor	18
Sport & Health Clubs	4000 Wisconsin Ave NW	202-362-8000	$20 per day, $100 per month membership	Indoor	19
Wilson Pool (closed for renovation)	Ford Dr & Albemarle St NW	202-282-2216	Residents free, various fees & passses for non-residents	Indoor	19
Upshur Outdoor Pool	14th St & Arkansas Ave NW	202-576-8661	Residents free, various fees & passses for non-residents	Outdoor	21
Bethesda YMCA	9401 Old Georgetown Rd	301-530-3725	joining fee $100, $74 per month	Indoor	22
YMCA	9800 Hastings Dr	301-585-2120	$100 joining fee, $64/month	Indoor / Outdoor	25
Piney Branch Pool	7510 Maple Ave	301-270-6093	$5 per day	Indoor	26
Takoma Outdoor Pool	300 Van Buren St NW	202-576-8660	Residents free, various fees & passes for non-residents	Outdoor	27
Sport & Health Club	4400 Montgomery Ave	301-656-9570	$25 per day ($15 per day with a member)	Indoor	29
Bethesda Outdoor Pool	Little Falls Dr	301-652-1598	$5.50 per day, $160 for year pass	Outdoor	30
Upton Hill Regional Park	6060 Wilson Blvd	703-534-3437	$5.25 per day, $72 season pass	Outdoor	33
Yorktown Swimming Pool	5201 28th St N	703-536-9739	$4 per day, $230 per year	Indoor	33
Washington-Lee Swimming Pool	1300 N Quincy St	703-228-6262	$4 per day, $230 per year	Indoor	34
YMCA Arlington	3422 N 13th St	703-525-5420	$100 joining fee, $48/month	Outdoor	35
Wakefield Swimming Pool	4901 S Chesterfield Rd	703-578-3063	$4 per day, $230 per year	Indoor	38
Chinquapin Park Rec Center	3210 King St	703-519-2160	$5 per day, $46 per month	Indoor	42
Alexandria YMCA	420 Monroe Ave	703-838-8085	$15 per day, $69 per month membership, $100 joining fee	Indoor	43
Warwick Pool	3301 Landover St	703-838-4672	$2 per day	Outdoor	43
Old Town Pool	1609 Cameron St	703-838-4671	$2 per day	Outdoor	44

Spray Parks

	Address	Phone	Hours
Bald Eagle Recreation Center	100 Joliet St SW	202-645-3960	Mon - Fri, 11 am - 7 pm Sat, 11 am - 4 pm Sun, 10 am - 2 pm
Benning Stoddert Community Center	100 Stoddert Pl SE	202-698-1873	Mon - Fri, 11 am - 7 pm Sat, 11 am - 4 pm
Columbia Heights Community Center	1480 Girard St NW	202-671-0373	Mon - Fri, 11 am - 7 pm Sat,11 am - 4 p Sun, 10 am - 2 pm
Friendship Recreation Center	4500 Van Ness St NW	202-282-2198	Mon - Fri, 11 am - 7 pm Sat, 11 am - 4 pm
Lafayette Recreation Center	5900 33rd St NW	202-282-2206	Mon - Fri, 11 am - 7 pm Sat, 11 am - 4 pm
Palisades Community Center	5200 Sherrier Pl NW	202-282-2186	Mon - Fri, 11 am - 7 pm Sat, 11 am - 4 pm Sun, 10 am - 2 pm
Petworth Recreation Center	801 Taylor St NW	202-576-6850	Mon - Fri, 11 am - 7 pm Sat, 11 am - 4 pm
Riggs LaSalle Community Center	501 Riggs Rd NE	202-576-6045	Mon - Fri, 11 am - 7 pm Sat, 11 am - 4 pm Sun, 10 am - 2 pm

Tennis

National Park Service: 202-208-6843, www.nps.gov
Washington, DC Department of Parks and Recreation: 202-673-7647, www.dpr.dc.gov

Public Courts at Community Recreation Centers
DC residents and visitors can play tennis at any of the public courts scattered throughout the city. All courts are available on a first-come, first-served basis. An honor code trusts that players won't hog the courts for over an hour of play-time (although you can call the Department of Parks and Recreation to obtain a permit for extended use). For more information about lessons and tournaments, call the Sports Office of the Department of Parks and Recreation (202-698-2250).

Tennis	Address	Phone	Fees	Map
South Grounds	15th St & Constitution Ave	202-698-2250	Public	1
Langston	26th St & Benning Rd NE	202-698-2250	Public	4
Rosedale	17th St NE & Gale St NE	202-698-2250	Public	4
Barry Farm	1230 Sumner Rd SE	202-698-2250	Public	5
East Potomac Tennis Center	1090 Ohio Dr SW	202-554-5962	Private	6
Jefferson	8th St SW & H St SW	202-698-2250	Public	6
King-Greenleaf	201 N St SW	202-698-2250	Public	6
Randall	1st St & I St SW	202-698-2250	Public	6
Georgetown	33rd St & Volta Pl	202-698-2250	Public	8
Montrose Park	30th St NW & R St NW	202-698-2250	Public	8
Rose Park	26th St NW & O St NW	202-698-2250	Public	8
Francis	24th St NW & N St NW	202-698-2250	Public	9
Reed	18th St NW & California St NW	202-698-2250	Public	9
Washington Hilton Sport Club	1919 Connecticut Ave NW	202-483-4100	Private	9
Shaw	10th St & Rhode Island Ave NW	202-698-2250	Public	10
Brentwood Park	6th St & Brentwood Pkwy NE	202-698-2250	Public	11
Dunbar	1st NW & O St NW	202-698-2250	Public	11
Edgewood	3rd St NE & Evart St NE	202-698-2250	Public	11
Harry Thomas Sr	Lincoln Rd & T St NE	202-698-2250	Public	11
Arboretum	24th St & Rand Pl NE	202-698-2250	Public	12
Fort Lincoln	Ft Lincoln Dr NE	202-698-2250	Public	13
Langdon Park	20th & Franklin Sts NE	202-698-2250	Public	13
Taft	19th St NE & Otis St NE	202-698-2250	Public	13
Backus	South Dakota Ave & Hamilton St NE	202-698-2250	Public	14
Turkey Thicket	1100 Michigan Ave NE	202-698-2251	Public	14
Banneker	9th St NW & Euclid St NW	202-698-2250	Public	15
Raymond	10th St & Spring Rd NW	202-698-2250	Public	15
Hardy	45th St NW & Q St NW	202-698-2250	Public	18
Newark	39th St NW & Newark St NW	202-698-2251	Public	18
Fort Reno	41st St NW & Chesapeake St NW	202-698-2250	Public	19
Friendship	4500 Van Ness St NW	202-698-2250	Public	19
Hearst	37th St NW & Tilden St NW	202-698-2250	Public	19
Forest Hills	32nd St NW & Brandywine St NW	202-698-2250	Public	20
Rock Creek Tennis Center	16th St NW & Kennedy St NW	202-722-5949	Public	21
Fort Stevens	1327 Van Buren St NW	202-698-2250	Public	27
Rabaut	2nd St NW & Peabody St NW	202-698-2250	Public	27
Takoma	3rd St NW & Van Buren St NW	202-698-2250	Public	27
Chevy Chase	4101 Livingston St NW	202-698-2250	Public	28
Lafayette	33rd St NW & Quesada St NW	202-698-2250	Public	28
Bethesda Sport & Health Club	4400 Montgomery Ave	301-656-9570	Public	29
Palisades	5200 Sherrier Pl NW	202-698-2250	Public	32
Arlington Y Tennis & Squash Club	3400 N 13th St	703-749-8057	Private	35

Billiards

Billiards	Address	Phone	Fees	Map
Buffalo Billiards	1330 19th St NW	202-331-7665	$12/hour	9
East Eddie's Sports & Billiards	1520 K St NW	202-638-6800	$10/hour	9
Angles Bar And Billiards	2339 18th St NW	202-462-8100	$1.25/game	16
Bedrock Billiards	1841 Columbia Rd NW	202-667-7665	$12/hour	16
Kokopoolis Pool Hall	2305 18th St NW	202-234-2306	$10/hour	16
Atomic Billiards	3427 Connecticut Ave NW	202-363-7665	$12/hour	17
Champion Billards Café	2620 S Shirlington	703-521-3800	$12/hour	39

Bowling

Sadly, bowling isn't exactly experiencing a hey-day in the DC metro area. If you're looking strictly within District lines, options are limited, especially if it's a smoking-only, mullets-abounding, Roseanne-style spot you're looking for, complete with ancient computer graphics on the score-keeping screens and a horrendous mix of music blaring over the sound system. For authentic bowling such as this, you'll have to hop in your car and cross county lines. Within DC, there's **Lucky Strike (Map 2)** for button-down shirt, black pants, bowling for the Penn Quarter crowd that will wipe out your wallet in a few short hours. Alleys like Lucky Strike and **Strike Bethesda (Map 29)** taught us that clubs aren't the only places where you can sip cleverly named cocktails and dole out phone numbers. Whether a rundown bowling alley in the 'burbs or a swanky clublike alley closer in, most area bowling alleys seem to offer up the same four wonderful B's: Bowling, Beer, Blacklights, and Beyoncé. After dark, the lights go down and the beats go up, with special "Cosmic Bowling" or "Xtreme Bowling" nights. When the DJ arrives, you can bet on the bowling fees rising accordingly with the volume of the dance traxxx.

Sunday nights are the best nights to bowl if you're looking to save money, as many alleys offer unlimited bowling after 9 pm for under $15. Show some Maryland pride, and play duckpin bowling (the sport actually originated in Baltimore) at **White Oak Bowling Lanes (11206 New Hampshire Ave, Silver Spring)** and **AMF College Park (9021 Baltimore Ave, College Park),** home to the Men's Duckpin Pro Bowlers' Association Master Tournament.

Bowling	Address	Phone	Fees	Map
Lucky Strike Lanes	701 7th St NW	202-347-1021	$5.95 per game, $3.95 for shoes	2
Strike Bethesda	5353 Westbard Ave	301-652-0955	$5.45–6.25 per game, $4 for shoes	29
US Bowling	100 S Pickett St	703-370-5910	$3–4.25 per game, $3.50 for shoes	41
Alexandria Bowling Center	6228A N Kings Hwy, Alexandria, VA	703-765-3633	$3.50–5 per game, $4.46 for shoes	n/a
AMF College Park	9021 Baltimore Ave, College Park, MD	301-474-8282	$4.25 per game, $4.65 for shoes	n/a
AMF Shady Grove Lanes	15720 Shady Grove Rd, Gaithersburg, MD	301-948-1390	$5–8 per game, $5 for shoes	n/a
Annandale Bowl	4245 Markham St	703-256-2211	$4.50 per game, $4.46 for shoes	n/a
Bowl America	6450 Edsall Rd, Alexandria, VA	703-354-3300	$2–5 per game, $3.40 for shoes	n/a
Bowl America - Chantilly	4525 Stonecroft Blvd, Chantilly, VA	703-830-2695	$2–5 per game, $3.40 for shoes	n/a
Bowl America - Fairfax	9699 Lee Hwy, Fairfax, VA	703-273-7700	$2–5.25 per game, $3.40 for shoes	n/a
White Oak Lanes	11207 New Hampshire Ave	301-593-3000	$3 per game, $3.50 for shoes	n/a

Yoga

Yoga	Address	Phone	URL	Map
Dahn Yoga Center	700 14th St NW	202-393-2440	www.dahnyoga.com	1
Bikram Yoga Center	410 H St NE	202-256-9156	www.bikramyoga capitolhill.com	3
Capitol Hill Yoga	221 5th St NE	202-544-0011	www.capitolhillyoga.com	3
St Mark's Yoga Center	301 A St SE	202-546-4964	www.stmarks.net	3
Dahn Yoga Center	3106 M St NW	202-298-3246	www.dahnyoga.com	8
Down Dog Yoga	1046 Potomac St NW	202-965-9642	www.downdogyoga.com	8
Georgetown Yoga	1053 31st St NW	202-342-7779	www.georgetownyoga.com	8
Spiral Flight Yoga	1826 Wisconsin Ave NW	202-965-1645	www.spiralflightyoga.com	8
Bikram Yoga Center	1635 Connecticut Ave NW	202-332-8680	www.bikramyogadc.com	9
Boundless Yoga	1522 U St NW	202-234-9642	www.boundlessyoga.com	9
DC Yoga	1635 Connecticut Ave NW	202-232-2926	www.dcyoga.com	9
Joy of Motion Dance	1643 Connecticut Ave NW	202-387-0911	www.joyofmotion.org	9
Tranquil Space Yoga	2024 P St NW	202-223-9642	www.tranquilspace.com	9
Evolution	1224 M St NW	202-347-2250	www.evolutiondc.com	10
Flow Yoga Center	1450 P St NW	202-462-3569	www.flowyogacenter.com	10
Yoga House	3634 Georgia Ave NW	202-285-1316	www.yogahousestudio.com	15
18th and Yoga	1115 U St NW	202-462-1800	www.18thandyoga.com	16
Into Afrika	1316 Adams St NE	202-797-9127	www.intoafrika.org	16
Unity Woods Yoga Center	2639 Connecticut Ave NW	202-232-9642	www.unitywoods.com	17
Hot Yoga	3408 Wisconsin Ave NW	202-468-9642	www.hotyogausa.com	18
Ashtanga Yoga Center	4435 Wisconsin Ave NW	202-342-6029	www.ashtangayogadc.com	19
Birkram's Yoga College	4908 Wisconsin Ave NW	202-243-3000	www.bikramyoga.com	19
Joy of Motion Dance	5207 Wisconsin Ave NW	202-362-3042	www.joyofmotion.org	19
Unity Woods Yoga Center	4201 Albemarle St NW	301-656-8992	www.unitywoods.com	19
Unity Woods Yoga Center	4321 Wisconsin Ave NW	301-656-8992	www.unitywoods.com	19
Bodywisdom	3701 Connecticut Ave NW	202-966-6113	n/a	20
Dahn Yoga Center	5010 Connecticut Ave NW	202-237-9642	www.dahnyoga.com	20
Balance Pilates and Yoga Studio	4719 Rosedale Ave	301-986-1730	www.balancestudio.com	22
Dahn Yoga Center	7849 Old Georgetown Rd	301-907-6520	www.dahnyoga.com	22
Unity Woods Yoga Center	4853 Cordell Ave	301-656-8992	www.unitywoods.com	22
Yoga Tales	8020 Norfolk Ave	301-951-9642	www.yogatales.com	22
Circle Yoga and Budding Yogis	3838 Northampton St NW	202-686-1104	www.buddingyogis.com	28
Fit, Inc	4963 Elm St	301-565-0885	www.robertshermansfit.com	29
Joy of Motion Dance	7315 Wisconsin Ave	301-387-0911	www.joyofmotion.org	29
Royal Fitness and Nutrician	4550 Montgomery Ave	301-961-0400	www.royfit.com	29
Try Yoga	4609 Willow Ln	240-888-9642	www.tryyoga.com	29
Unity Woods Yoga Center	4001 9th St N	301-656-8992	www.unitywoods.com	34
Sun and Moon Yoga Studio	3811 Lee Hwy	703-525-9642	www.sunandmoonstudio.com	35
Dahn Yoga Center	1630 King St	703-684-7717	www.dahnyoga.com	44

General Information

Washington Area Bicyclist Association:

	www.waba.org
Bike Washington:	www.bikewashington.org
Bike the Sites Bicycle Tours:	www.bikethesites.com
C&O Canal Towpath:	www.nps.gov/choh
Capitol Crescent Trail:	www.cctrail.org
Mount Vernon Trail:	www.nps.gov/gwmp/mvt.html
W&OD Trail:	www.wodfriends.org

Overview

A bike in DC is as necessary as a political affiliation. The city tries to satisfy the needs of its mountain and road bikers alike with plenty of multi-terrain trails, a few good urban commuting routes, and one massive citywide bike ride in the fall. When it comes to bikes onboard mass transit, the Metrobus and Metrorail have lenient policies that also help when a bike route, or your energy, dead-ends.

If you're new to biking in DC, be prepared for a few wrong turns and missed trail entrances. Figuring out how various trails connect (or how to safely and easily cut through neighborhoods to move from one trail to the other) can take some time and trial and error, but the rewards are well worth it. Consult the above sites for pointers, seek out other bicyclists, and have fun!

And while commuting by bike is doable, it can get rather dicey. Bike lanes don't really exist in much of DC, and state law mandates that cyclists have to follow traffic laws—so plan on mixing it up with the cars on your way to work. Even though DC residents are an honest bunch, it's a good idea to keep your bike locked whenever it's out of your sight. A U-Lock is a necessity. For more information regarding bicycle commuting, check out the Washington Area Bicyclist Association website. The site also provides information about the annual "Bike DC."

Bike Trails

The **Chesapeake and Ohio (C&O) Canal** is probably the city's most popular bike route. The trail spans over 184 miles, and most of it is unpaved, so it's not a trail for the weak of butt. The trail begins in Georgetown and follows the route of the Potomac River from DC to Cumberland, Maryland. Biking is permitted only on the towpath. Campsites are located from Swains Lock to Seneca for bikers undertaking multi-day journeys. But be warned: because the first 20 miles are the most heavily used, conditions within the Beltway are significantly better than those outside of it. The towpath sometimes floods, so it's best to check the website, www.nps.gov/choh, for possible closures before breaking out the wheels.

The **Capital Crescent Trail** is a "rail trail"—a bike trail converted from abandoned or unused railroad tracks. The trail spans 11 miles between Georgetown and Silver Spring, Maryland. On the trail's first seven miles, from Georgetown to Bethesda, you'll encounter gentle terrain and ten foot-wide asphalt paths. On weekdays, the trail is used predominantly by commuters, and on weekends it gets crowded with recreational cyclists, rollerbladers, joggers, and dogs. Check out www.cctrail.org.

The **Mount Vernon Trail** offers a wide range of scenic views of the Potomac River and national monuments to ensure an inspiring and patriotic ride. The 18.5-mile trail stretches from Roosevelt Island through Old Town Alexandria to George Washington's house in Mount Vernon. To find out more about these and other bike trails, check out the Bike Washington web site.

The **Washington and Old Dominion (W&OD) Trail** is a highly popular paved trail that traverses the 45 miles between Arlington's Shirlington area and Purcellville, Virginia, in Loudoun County. Among the communities it passes through are Falls Church and Leesburg.

The four-mile **Custis Trail** begins in Rosslyn and parallels I-66; it serves to connect the W&OD Trail with other bike trails in the Washington area. Be ready for some inclines and curvy sections on the narrow Custis, and also be wary of bikers who may be traveling faster or slower. For more info, see both the Bike Washington site and the one maintained by The Friends of the Washington & Old Dominion Trail (www.wodfriends.org).

Bikes and Mass Transit

If you need a break while riding in the city, you can hop off your bike and take it on a bus or on Metrorail for free. All DC buses are equipped with racks to carry up to two bikes per bus. You can also ride the Metrorail with your bike on weekends, and during non-rush hour times on weekdays (that means no bikes 7 am–10 am and 4 pm–7 pm). Also be sure to use elevators when accessing the Metrorail—blocking the stairs and escalators with your bulky bike makes officials and non-biking commuters testy.

Bike Shops

- **A&A Discount Bicycles** (sales, repair, and rental) • 1034 33rd St NW • 202-337-0254 • Map 18
- **Better Bikes** (rental and delivery) • 202-293-2080 • www.betterbikesinc.com
- **Bicycle Pro Shop** (sales, repair, and rental) • 3403 M St NW • 202-337-0311 • www.bicycleproshop.com • Map 18
- **Big Wheel Bikes** (sales, repair, and rental) • 1034 33rd St NW • 202-337-0254 • www.bigwheelbikes.com • Map 18
- **Capitol Hill Bikes** (sales, repair, and rental) • 709 8th St SE • 202-544-4234 • www.capitolhillbikes.com • Map 5
- **City Bikes** (sales, repair, and rental) • 2501 Champlain St NW • 202-265-1564 • www.citybikes.com • Map 16
- **District Hardware/The Bike Shop** (sales and repair) • 2003 P St NW • 202-659-8686 • Map 9
- **Hudson Trail Outfitters** (sales and repair) • 4530 Wisconsin Ave NW • 202-363-9810 • Map 19
- **Revolution Cycles** (sales, repair, and rental) • 3411 M St NW • 202-965-3601 • www.revolutioncycles.com • Map 18

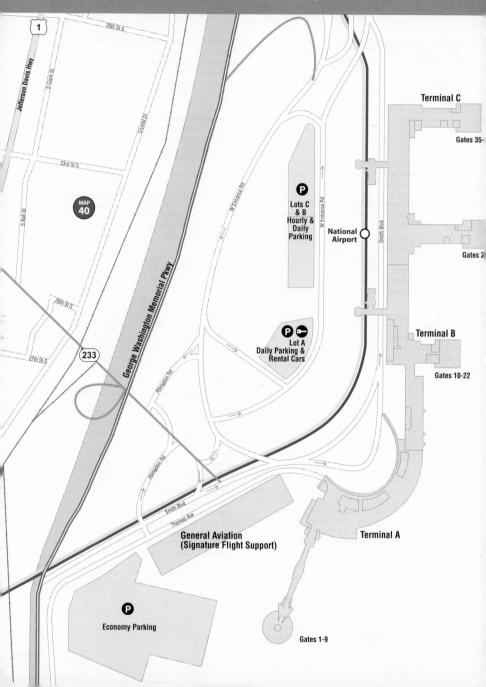

Terminal C

Gates 35-

Gates 2

Terminal B

Gates 10-22

US 1 — Jefferson Davis Hwy

20th St S

S Clark St

Crystal Dr

23rd St S

S Ball St

MAP 40

26th St S

27th St S

233

George Washington Memorial Pkwy

W Entrance Rd

W Entrance Rd

P Lots C & B Hourly & Daily Parking

National Airport

Smith Blvd

P Lot A Daily Parking & Rental Cars

Abingdon Rd

Abingdon Rd

Smith Blvd

Thomas Ave

General Aviation (Signature Flight Support)

Terminal A

P Economy Parking

Gates 1-9

General Information

Phone:	703-417-8000
Lost & Found:	703-417-0673
Parking:	703-417-7275
Website:	www.mwaa.com/national/index.htm

Overview

Ronald Reagan Washington National Airport (or National, to DC liberals) is a small, easy-to-navigate airport located practically downtown, perfect for business travelers and politicians alike. It's also the only airport in the greater metropolitan area directly accessible by Metro. But alas, for those of us not on expense accounts or the public dole, prices can be prohibitive. If you want a discounted direct flight to Madagascar or enjoy flying on the cattle cars that charge $15 for a roundtrip to Aruba, you'll have to fly from Dulles or BWI. National is too small to host many planes or airlines, making it a short-haul airport with direct connections to cities typically no more than 1,250 miles away.

How to Get There—Driving

From DC, take I-395 S to Exit 10 ("Reagan National Airport/Mount Vernon"). Get on the GW Parkway S, and take the Reagan Airport exit. If you're in Virginia headed north on I-395, ignore the first exit you see for the airport (Exit 8C/"to US 1/Crystal City/Pentagon City/Reagan National Airport") and continue on to Exit 10 S. It's quicker and easier. Remember to watch out for Officer Friendly and his trusty radar gun as you enter the airport property.

Parking

Parking at Reagan is not cheap. Garages A, B, C, charge $2 per half-hour for the first two hours and $4 per hour thereafter. Garage A costs $20 per day. Garages B and C cost $36 per day. All three garages are conveniently located across the street from the terminals and can be accessed through enclosed or underground walkways. If you're heading out for a few days, we suggest you park in the economy lot for only $12 per day. Shuttle buses run between the economy lot and all terminals. Parking in any lot for less than 20 minutes is free. Though when have you ever been in-and-out of an airport in less than an hour? We made it in 56 minutes once, but we don't count on it happening ever again.

How to Get There—Mass Transit

The Blue and Yellow Lines have a Metrorail stop adjacent to Terminals B and C. If you're headed to Terminal A, a free shuttle bus will run you there or you can lug your bags on a ten-minute walk. Metro buses are also available from the base of the Metrorail station for areas not served by the rail.

How to Get There—
Ground Transportation

Can you believe it? An airport that you can actually get to by Metro! The Ronald Reagan Washington National Airport Metrorail is under 20 minutes away from the city center by Metro on the Blue and Yellow lines. Alternately, SuperShuttle offers door-to-door service to DCA. Super Shuttle is a door-to-door van service that will pick you up anywhere so long as you call 24 hours in advance. They also have a shuttle that goes regularly between DCA and Union Station. Call the reservation line on 800-BLUEVAN or go to www.supershuttle.com to book online. A cab ride to downtown DC will set you back less than $15. DC, Virginia, and Maryland taxis are available at the exits of each terminal. Red Top Cab - Arlington: 703-522-3333; Yellow Cab - DC: 202-TAXI-CAB; Yellow Cab - Arlington: 703-534-1111. And if you're feeling a bit flashy, stretch limousines and executive-class sedans start at approximately $35 for downtown Washington. Airport Access: 202-498-8708; Airport Connection: 202-393-2110; Roadmaster: 800-283-5634; Silver Car: 410-992-7775.

Rental Cars—On-Airport (Garage A)

Alamo • 800-462-5266   **National** • 800-227-7368
Avis • 800-331-1212   **Dollar** • 800-800-4000
Budget • 800-527-0700   **Thrifty** • 800-367-2277
Hertz • 800-654-3131

Off-Airport

Enterprise • 800-736-8222

Hotels—Arlington

Crowne Plaza •1480 Crystal Dr • 703-416-1600
Crystal City Marriott • 1999 Jefferson Davis Hwy • 703-413-5500
Crystal City Courtyard by Marriott • 2899 Jefferson Davis Hwy • 703-549-3434
Crystal Gateway Marriott • 1700 Jefferson Davis Hwy • 703-920-3230
Radisson Inn • 2020 Jefferson Davis Hwy • 703-920-8600
Doubletree Crystal City • 300 Army Navy Dr • 703-416-4100
Econo Lodge • 6800 Lee Hwy • 703-538-5300
Embassy Suites • 1300 Jefferson Davis Hwy • 703-979-9799
Hilton • 2399 Jefferson Davis Hwy • 703-418-6800
Holiday Inn • 2650 Jefferson Davis Hwy • 703-684-7200
Hyatt Regency • 2799 Jefferson Davis Hwy • 703-418-1234
Ritz Carlton Pentagon City • 1250 S Hayes St • 703-415-5000
Residence Inn • 550 Army Navy Dr • 703-413-6630
Sheraton • 1800 Jefferson Davis Hwy • 703-486-1111

Hotels—Washington

Hamilton Crowne Plaza • 1001 14th & K Sts NW • 202-682-0111
Grand Hyatt • 1000 H St NW • 202-582-1234
Hilton Washington • 1919 Connecticut Ave NW • 202-483-3000
Hilton Embassy Row • 2015 Massachusetts Ave NW • 202-265-1600
Holiday Inn • 415 New Jersey Ave NW • 202-638-1616
Homewood Suites by Hilton • 1475 Massachusetts Ave NW • 202-265-8000
Hyatt Regency • 400 New Jersey Ave NW • 202-737-1234
Marriott Wardman Park • 2660 Woodley Rd NW • 202-328-2000
Red Roof Inn • 500 H St NW • 202-289-5959
Renaissance Mayflower Hotel • 1127 Connecticut Ave NW • 202-347-3000
Renaissance Washington DC • 999 9th St NW • 202-898-9000

Airline	Terminal	Airline	Terminal
Air Canada/Jazz	B	Midwest	A
Air Tran	A	Northwest/Airlink	A
Alaska	B	Spirit	A
America West	C	United Airlines	C
American/Eagle	B	Delta/Connection	B
Continental	B	US Airways/Express	C
Frontier	C	/Shuttle	

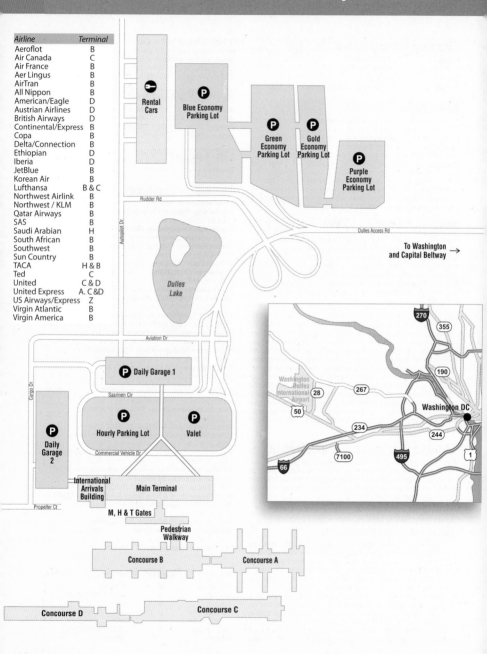

Airline	Terminal
Aeroflot	B
Air Canada	C
Air France	B
Aer Lingus	B
AirTran	B
All Nippon	B
American/Eagle	D
Austrian Airlines	D
British Airways	D
Continental/Express	B
Copa	B
Delta/Connection	B
Ethiopian	D
Iberia	D
JetBlue	B
Korean Air	B
Lufthansa	B & C
Northwest Airlink	B
Northwest / KLM	B
Qatar Airways	B
SAS	B
Saudi Arabian	H
South African	B
Southwest	B
Sun Country	B
TACA	H & B
Ted	C
United	C & D
United Express	A. C &D
US Airways/Express	Z
Virgin Atlantic	B
Virgin America	B

Rental Cars

Blue Economy Parking Lot

Green Economy Parking Lot

Gold Economy Parking Lot

Purple Economy Parking Lot

Rudder Rd

Dulles Access Rd

To Washington
and Capital Beltway →

Aviation Dr

Autopilot Dr

Dulles Lake

Daily Garage 1

Saarinen Cir

Cargo Dr

Hourly Parking Lot

Valet

Daily Garage 2

Commercial Vehicle Dr

International Arrivals Building

Main Terminal

Propeller Ct

M, H & T Gates

Pedestrian Walkway

Concourse B

Concourse A

Concourse D

Concourse C

270

355

190

Washington Dulles International Airport

28

267

50

234

Washington DC

244

66

7100

495

1

General Information

Address:	45020 Aviation Dr
	Sterling, VA 20166 (not that you're going to
	send them anything, really)
Information:	703-572-2700
Parking:	703-572-4500
Lost & Found:	703-572-2954
Website:	www.metwashairports.com/Dulles

Overview

The Mod Squad of airports, Dulles was born in 1958 when Finnish architect Eero Saarinen had a hankering to channel his training as a sculptor and create something groovy. His design for the terminal building and the control tower was so hip it received a First Honor Award from the American Institute of Architects in 1966. A distinctive swoosh roof over a squat building, Dulles still stands out as a stunning exhibit of modernist architecture and was the first airport in the US designed specifically for commercial jets. The "mobile lounges" that were formerly the only means of transportation between the main terminal building and the outlying terminals were largely replaced recently by the much ballyhooed AeroTrain project, which finally made its debut in January of 2010. The stunningly old mobile lounges were considered debonair when they were engineered back in 1962, but the new Aerotrain leaves you asking "mobile what?" Sleek, shiny, and a heck of a lot less rickety, the $1.4 billion service transports passengers between the Main Terminal building and Concourses A, B and C. The Aerotrain, designed by Mitsubishi, uses rubber tires and guides large cars along a fixed underground guideway. In addition to looking pretty snazzy, the new system's trains run every two minutes, in stark contrast for the 15-minute-wait commuters spend in anticipating of the mobile lounges. But never fear, nostalgia junkies: You can still enjoy mobile lounges at the far end of Concourse A and D. In terms of ticket prices, BWI may have AirTran, but Dulles has Jet Blue and Southwest to help keep fares low, and starting in 2007, Virgin America began its attempts to hipsterize the flying experience. Note: "Washington" was officially added to the "Dulles International Airport" moniker after too many people inadvertently booked flights to Dallas, not Dulles, and vice-versa. No joke.

How to Get There—Driving

Most people get to Dulles the old fashioned way: they drive. To get to Washington Dulles Airport from downtown DC, drive west on I-66 to Exit 67. Follow signs to the airport. Be sure to use the Dulles Access Road, which avoids the tolls and traffic found on the parallel Dulles Toll Road (Rt. 267). But don't get cocky and try to use the Access Road to avoid tolls at other times—once you're on these access lanes, there's no exit until you reach the airport.

Since its inception a few years ago, the Cell Phone Waiting Area has been a smash hit. Circling around and around the airport like a hawk while waiting for friends and family to deboard and collect their baggage is blessedly a thing of the past. The waiting area is located at the intersection of Rudder Road and Autopilot Drive. Just follow the signs as you enter the airport grounds. It is free of charge and the maximum waiting time is one hour.

Parking

Hourly (short-term) parking is located in front of the terminal and costs $4 per hour and $36 per day. Daily parking is available in Daily Garages 1 and 2 for $5 per hour and $17 per day. There are shuttle buses and walkways (albeit lengthy ones from Garage 1) directly to the main terminal. Economy parking (long-term) is available in the four economy parking lots (Blue, Green, Gold, and Purple) located along Rudder Road. Long-term parking costs $3 per hour and $10 per day. If you're short on time or energy and long on cash, valet parking is located in front of the terminal and costs $30 for the first 24 hours and $19 per day thereafter. Parking in any lot for less than 20 minutes is free. Take your parking ticket

with you as you can pay for your parking in the main terminal on your way out.

How to Get There—Mass Transit

The Metrorail doesn't go all the way to Dulles Airport…yet. There's endless talk about a supposed "Silver Line," or the Dulles Corridor Metrorail Project as it's officially known. Though stalled several times, the proposed line would provide Metro access to the airport from Washington. Fingers crossed, service on the Silver Line will begin in 2013. Until then, you can take the Orange Line to West Falls Church and transfer to the Washington Flyer Coach Service, which leaves every 30 minutes from the station. The coach fare costs $10 one-way ($18 round-trip), and the fare for the Metrorail leg will depend on exactly where you're coming from or headed to. A trip from West Falls Church to the Convention Center in downtown DC costs from $1.95 to $3.40, depending on whether or not it's rush hour. Check www.washfly.com for Flyer schedules. There are no "regular" taxis from Dulles to any destination—the Flyer is it, and you should avoid all other pitchmen. You can also take Metrobus 5A, which runs from L'Enfant Plaza to Dulles, stopping at Rosslyn Metro Station on the Orange and Blue Lines. The express bus costs $3 each way.

Ground Transportation

Super Shuttle offers service to Dulles from anywhere in the state of Maryland and runs a shuttle between the airport and Union Station. Call (800-258-3826) to book your seat. At the airport, you'll find them outside the Main Terminal. Washington Flyer Taxicabs serve Dulles International Airport exclusively with 24-hour service to and from the airport. Taxis accept American Express, Diners Club, MasterCard, Discover Card, and Visa and charge metered rates to any destination in metropolitan Washington. If you're heading to downtown DC, it will cost you between $44 and $50. For more information, or to book a car, call 703-661-6655.

Rental Cars

Alamo · 800-832-7933	**Enterprise** · 800-736-8222
Avis · 800-331-1212	**Hertz** · 800-654-3131
Budget · 800-527-0700	**National** · 800-227-7368
Dollar · 800-800-4000	**Thrifty** · 800-367-2277
Alamoot (off-airport) · 800-630-6967	

Hotels—Herndon, VA

Comfort Inn · 200 Elden St · 703-437-7555
Courtyard by Marriott · 533 Herndon Pkwy · 703-478-9400
Crowne Plaza · 2200 Centreville Rd · 703-471-6700
Embassy Suites · 13341 Woodland Park Dr · 703-464-0200
Hilton · 13869 Park Center Rd · 703-478-2900
Holiday Inn Express · 485 Elden St · 703-478-9777
Hyatt Hotels & Resorts · 2300 Dulles Corner Blvd · 703-713-1234
Marriott Hotels · 13101 Worldgate Dr · 703-709-0400
Residence Inn · 315 Elden St · 703-435-0044
Staybrdige Suites ·13700 Coppermine Rd · 703-713-6800

Hotels—Sterling, VA

Country Inn & Suites · 45620 Falke Plz · 703-435-2700
Courtyard by Marriott · 45500 Majestic Dr · 571-434-6400
Fairfield Inn · 23000 Indian Creek Dr · 703-435-5300
Hampton Inn · 45440 Holiday Park Dr · 703-471-8300
Holiday Inn · 1000 Sully Rd · 703-471-7411
Marriott Towneplace · 22744 Holiday Park Dr · 703-707-2017
Marriott · 45020 Aviation Dr · 703-471-9500
Quality Inn & Suites Dulles International ·
45515 Dulles Plz · 703-471-5005

Baltimore-Washington International Airport

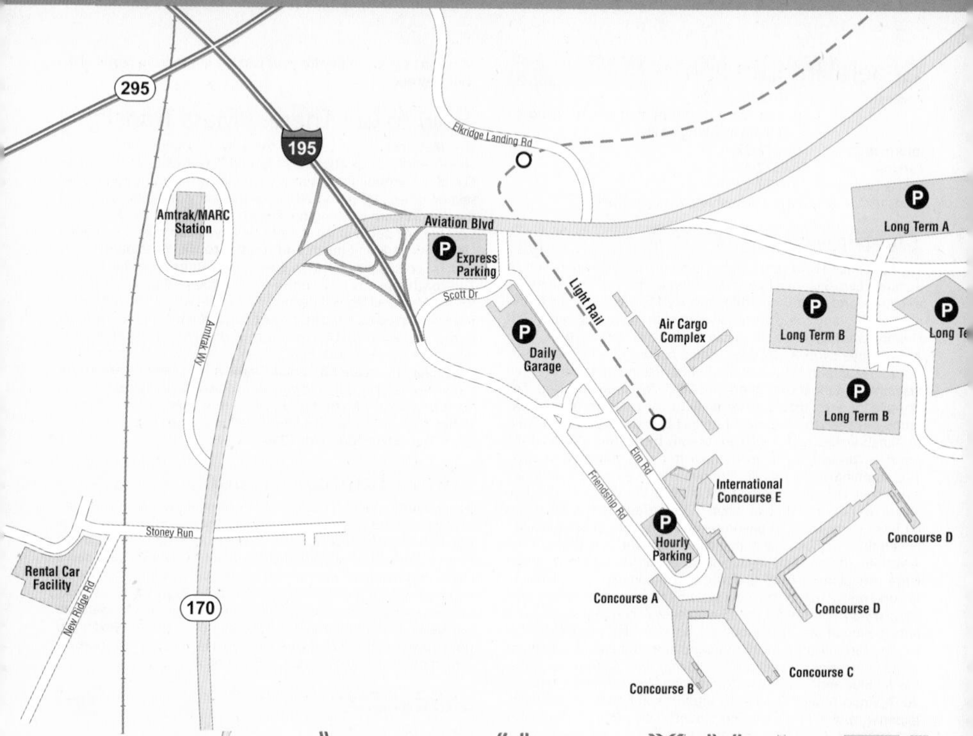

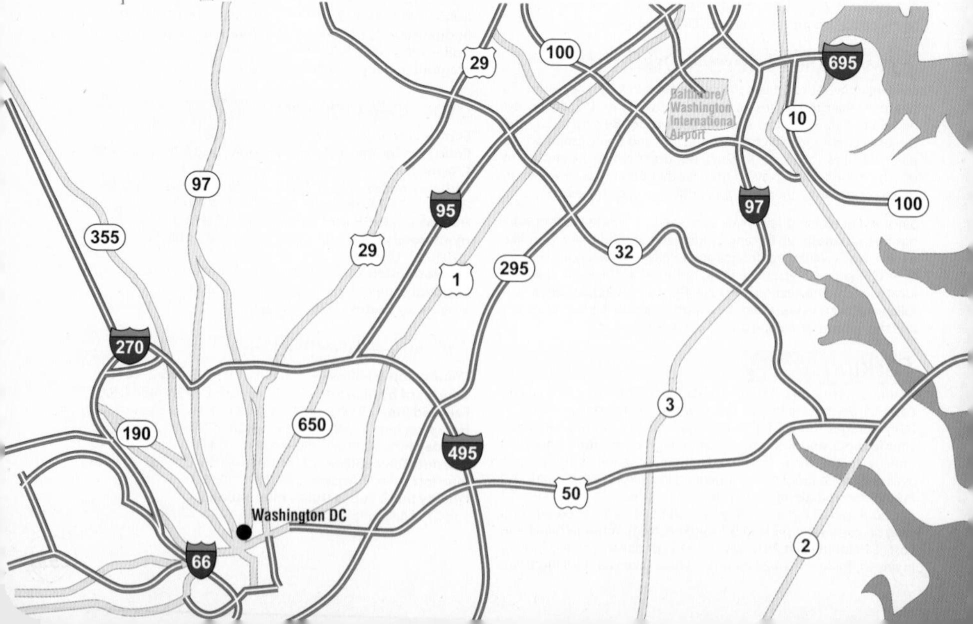

General Information

Information: 800-435-9294
Lost & Found: 410-859-7387
Parking: 800-468-6294
Police: 410-859-7040
Website: www.bwiairport.com

Overview

When Friendship International Airport opened in 1950, it was widely touted as one of the most sophisticated and advanced airports in the nation. In 1993, Southwest Airlines moved in, bringing with them their cheap, and wildly popular, cattle cars of the sky. But this bargain-basement tenant has turned BWI into a boomtown—a spanking new expanded Terminal A for Southwest only opened in 2005. Other major carriers have since joined the dirt-cheap-fares bandwagon, resulting in generally cheaper flights to and from BWI than you'll find flying into and out of Dulles or Reagan. It's a helluva haul from the city (yet pretty close for Maryland suburbanites), but sometimes time really isn't money, and cheap fares trump convenience. In October 2005, BWI was officially renamed Baltimore-Washington International Thurgood Marshall Airport in honor of native Baltimorean and first African-American Supreme Court Justice Thurgood Marshall. If you do find yourself at BWI, know that in 2007 they won the little-known "Best Overall Concessions" award in the medium-sized airport category, so you'll be well-fed before your flight.

How to Get There—Driving

From downtown DC, take New York Avenue (US 50) eastbound to the Baltimore/Washington Parkway N to I-195 E. From the Capital Beltway (I-495/95), take the I-95 N exit in Maryland (Exit 27), and then continue north to I-195 E. I-195 ends at the entrance to BWI.

Parking

Hourly parking is located across from the terminal building. The first and second 30 minutes of parking (which you may spend looking for a space) are $2 each, and the rest of your time costs $4 per hour and $22 per day. Daily parking is available for $3 the first and second hours each, $2 for each additional hour and $12 per day. Express Service Parking (ESP) is located on Aviation Boulevard across from the Air Cargo Complex and is $4 for the first hour, $2 each additional hour and $10 each day. If you're going to be gone a while, you might want to try the long-term parking lots, which is $8 per day. A new service called "Credit Card In/Credit Card Out" allows you to swipe the plastic of your choice upon entering and exiting an hourly parking facility, eliminating the fun of losing your parking ticket. The "Pay & Go" service allows you to pay your parking fee for the hourly lot in the Skywalk adjacent to the main terminal before you return to your car.

BWI also has a Cell Phone Parking lot located at the entrance to the "Daily B" parking lot on Elm Road. You can wait there for your mother-in-law to arrive. Just remember to turn your phone on.

How to Get There—Mass Transit

Any which way you go, expect to devote a few hours to mimicking a Richard Scarry character. MARC's Penn Line and Amtrak trains service the BWI Rail Station from Union Station in DC (Massachusetts Ave & First St NE) and cost between $6 and $34. A word of caution, though: the MARC train only runs Monday through Friday, leave the more expensive Amtrak your only option. The Light Rail train now provides service between Baltimore and BWI. A free shuttle bus takes passengers from the train station to the airport. Alternatively, you can take the Metro Green Line to the Greenbelt station and catch the Express Metro Bus/B30 to BWI. The Express bus runs every 40 minutes and costs $2.50.

How to Get There— Ground Transportation

The Airport Shuttle offers door-to-door service within the state of Maryland. Call 800-776-0323 for reservations. For door-to-door service to BWI, Super Shuttle (800-258-3826) services all of the DC airports. The BWI taxi stand is located just outside of baggage claim on the lower level. The ride to DC usually costs about $65. 410-859-1100.

Car Rental

Avis • 410-859-1680
Alamo • 410-859-8092
Budget • 410-859-0850
Dollar • 800-800-4000
Enterprise • 800-325-8007
Hertz • 410-850-7400
National • 410-859-8860
Thrifty • 410-859-7139

Hotels

Four Points by Sheraton • 7032 Elm Rd • 410-859-3300
Amerisuites • 940 International Dr • 410-859-3366
Best Western • 6755 Dorsey Rd • 410-796-3300
Candlewood Suites • 1247 Winterson Rd • 410-789-9100
Comfort Inn • 6921 Baltimore-Annapolis Blvd • 410-789-9100
Comfort Suites • 815 Elkridge Landing Rd • 410-691-1000
Courtyard by Marriott • 1671 West Nursery Rd • 410-859-8855
Econo Lodge • 5895 Bonnieview Ln • 410-796-1020
Embassy Suites • 1300 Concourse Dr • 410-850-0747
Extended Stay America • 1500 Aero Dr • 410-850-0400
Fairfield Inn by Marriott • 1737 W Nursery Rd • 410-859-2333
Hampton Inn • 829 Elkridge Landing Rd • 410-850-0600
Hampton Inn & Suites • 7027 Arundel Mills Cir • 410-540-9225
Hilton Garden Inn • 1516 Aero Dr • 410-691-0500
Holiday Inn • 890 Elkridge Landing Rd • 410-859-8400
Holiday Inn Express • 7481 New Ridge Rd • 410-684-3388
Homestead Studio Suites • 939 International Dr • 410-691-2500
Homewood Suites • 1181 Winterson Rd • 410-684-6100
Marriott • 1743 W Nursery Rd • 410-859-7500
Microtel Inn and Suites • 1170 Winterson Rd • 410-865-7500
Ramada • 7253 Parkway Dr • 410-712-4300
Red Roof Inn • 827 Elkridge Landing Rd • 410-850-7600
Residence Inn/Marriott • 1160 Winterson Rd • 410-691-0255
Residence Inn/Marriott • 7035 Arundel Mills Cir • 410-799-7332
Sleep Inn and Suites • 6055 Belle Grove Rd • 410-789-7223
Springhill Suites by Marriott • 899 Elkridge Landing Rd • 410-694-0555
Wingate Inn • 1510 Aero Dr • 410-859-000

Airline	Terminal	Airline	Terminal
Air Canada	E	North American Airlines	E
Air Greenland	E	Northwest Airlines	D
Air Jamaica	E	Southwest Airlines	B
AirTran	D	United Airlines	D
American Airlines	C	US Airways	D
America West	D	USA3000	E
British Airways	E		
Continental	D		
Delta	C		
Midwest	D		

Transit • **Airlines**

Airline	Phone	IAD	DCA	BWI
Aer Lingus	800-474-7424	■		
Aeroflot	888-686-4949	■		
Air Canada	888-247-2262	■	■	■
Air Canada Jazz	800-247-2262		■	
Air France	800-321-4538	■		
Air Greenland	877-245-0739			■
Air Jamaica	800-523-5585			■
AirTran	800-247-8726	■	■	■
American Airlines	800-433-7300	■	■	■
American Eagle	800-433-7300		■	
American Eagle Connection	800-433-7300	■		
ANA	800-235-9262	■		
Austrian Airlines	800-843-0002	■		
British Airways	800-247-9297	■		■
Continental	800-525-0280	■	■	■
Delta	800-221-1212	■	■	■
Delta Connection	800-221-1212	■	■	
Delta Shuttle	800-933-5935		■	
Ethiopian Airlines	800-445-2733	■		
Frontier	800-432-1359		■	
Ghana Airways	800-404-4262			■
GRUPO TACA	800-535-8780	■		
Iberia	800-776-4642	■		
Jet Blue	800-538-2583	■		
KLM Royal Dutch	800-225-2525	■		
Korean Air	800-438-5000	■		
Lufthansa	800-645-3880	■		
Midwest	800-452-2022		■	■
North American Airlines	800-359-6222			■
Northwest Airlines	800-225-2525	■	■	■
SAS	800-221-2350	■		
Saudi Arabian Airlines	800-472-8342	■		
South African Airways	800-722-9675	■		
Southwest Airlines	800-435-9792	■		■
Spirit	800-772-7117		■	
Sun Country Airlines	800-800-6557	■		
Ted Airlines	800-225-5833	■	■	
United Airlines	800-241-6522	■	■	■
United Express	800-241-6522	■		
US Airways	800-428-4322	■	■	■
US Airways Express	800-428-4322	■		
US Airways Shuttle	800-428-4322		■	
USA3000	877-872-3000			■
Virgin	800-862-8621	■		

General Information

DC Taxicab Commission: 2041 Martin Luther King Jr Ave SE,
Ste 204
Washington, DC 20020-7024

Phone: 202-645-6018

Complaints: Must be in writing and mailed or
emailed to dctc@dc.gov

Web Site: www.dctaxi.dc.gov

Overview

After 70 years of an esoteric and antiquated zone system, the District has finally converted to time and distance meters. Following a long, drawn out dispute with area cab drivers, Adrian Fenty asserted his authority as mayor to make the switch—perhaps part of his campaign to make DC a "world-class city" by ditching its idiosyncratic system. Beginning in 2008, DC cabs shifted to a conventional metered system. The change has incited the ire of many DC cabbies who believe that the old "zone meter" allowed for fair fares and a more straightforward method of showing how that fair fare was calculated. Needless to say, Mayor Fenty disagreed. The new system has meant less money for drivers, but lower fares keep patrons happy. Still, don't be surprised if your once independent cabbie is no longer his own boss, or secretly hopes to get stuck in a traffic jam.

Calculating your Fare

With the new meters, calculating your fare should prove a much more uncomplicated matter. The meter fare starts at $3, going up 25¢ every 1/6 of a mile and 25¢ for every minute stopped or traveling under 10 mph. There is a maximum of $19 within DC (thank goodness). In snow emergencies, an additional 25% of the total is added to the original fare. The Washington Post website has published a handy online calculator for estimating your fare, specifically as compared to the old zone system: www.washingtonpost.com/wp-srv/metro/interactives/taxifares. Keep in mind that with time and distance meters, traffic congestion will now affect patrons. Those frequently traveling during rush hour, or to areas like Capitol Hill, will find a spike in prices as compared to the zone system.

Out of Area Cabs

Taxis from Virginia and Maryland can frequently be found in DC; however, specific rules exist that limit non-DC taxis from picking up and transporting passengers in the district and around DC. However, if a non-DC taxi is dispatched directly to DC, it can pick up passengers in DC without a dispatch fee. These non-DC cabs are often less expensive when traveling out of DC to Virginia or Maryland.

Taxi Companies

Listed below are all of the major DC cab companies as well as several from Virginia and Maryland. Remember, in DC, the dispatch will cost you an extra $2.

DC Taxis *All area codes: 202, unless noted

Company	Phone	Company	Phone
American	398-0529	Empire	488-4844
A-S-K	726-5430	E & P	399-0711
Atlantic	488-0609	Executive	547-6351
Automotive Care	554-6877	Fairway	832-4662
B & B	561-5770	Family	291-4788
Barwood	800-831-2323	General	462-0200
Bay	546-1818	Georgetown	529-8979
Bell	479-6729	Globe	232-3700
Best	265-7834	Gold Star	484-5555
Capitol Cab	546-2400	Hill Top	529-1212
Capital Motors	488-1370	Holiday	628-4407
Central	484-7100	HTT	484-7100
Checker	398-0532	Liberty	398-0505
City	269-0990	Lincoln	484-2222
Classic	399-6815	Mayflower	783-1111
Coastline	462-4543	Meritt Cab	554-7900
Comfort	398-0530	National	269-1234
Courtesy	269-2600	Orange	832-0436
DC Express Auto	526-5656	Palm Grove	269-2606
DC Express Cab	484-8516	Pan Am & Imperial	526-7125
DC Flyer	488-7611	Seasons	635-3498
Delta	543-0084	Sun	484-7100
Dial	829-4222	Super	488-4334
Diamond	387-6200	VIP	269-1300
Diamond Inc.	387-4011	Yellow	373-3366
Elite	529-0222	Yourway	488-0609

MarylandTaxis *All area codes: 301

Company	Phone	Company	Phone
Action	840-1222	Checker	816-0066
Action of Laurel	776-0310	Community	459-4454
Airport	577-2111	Greenbelt	577-2000
All County	924-4344	Montgomery	926-9300
Barwood	984-1900	Regency	990-9000
Blue Bird & Yellow	864-7700	Silver	577-4455

VirginiaTaxis *All area codes: 703

Company	Phone	Company	Phone
Airport Metro	413-4667	Crown	528-0202
Alexandria	549-2502	Diamond	548-7505
Arlington	522-2222	King	549-3530
Blue Top	243-TAXI (8294)	Red Top	522-3333

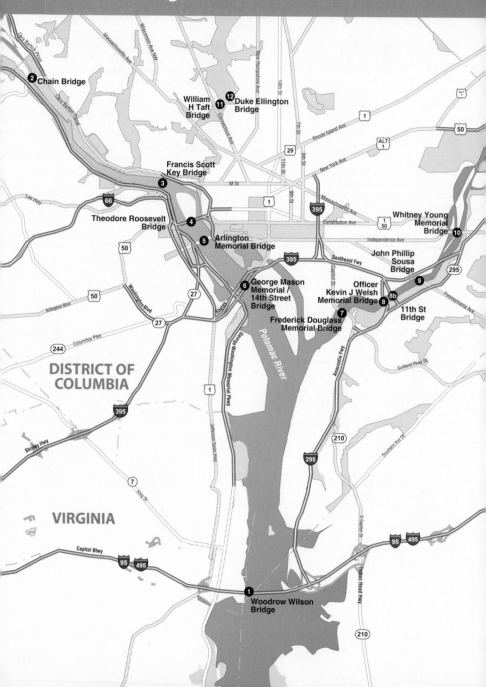

Chances are if you live in DC and you own a car, you spend a significant amount of your time sitting in traffic on one of DC's bridges. Despite constant congestion and deteriorating roadways, DC-area bridges do have one saving grace—no tolls! The city is also home to some of the most beautiful and architecturally significant spans in the country. The **Francis Scott Key Bridge** crossing the Potomac from Rosslyn, VA, into Georgetown is the best known. The **Calvert Street Bridge** between Woodley Park and Adams Morgan (officially named for native son **Duke Ellington**) and the **Connecticut Avenue Bridge** over Rock Creek Park (which must be seen from the parkway below to be fully appreciated) are other great examples. The **Connecticut Avenue Bridge**, (officially known as the **William H. Taft Bridge**) is also known as the "Million Dollar Bridge." When it was built it was the most expensive concrete bridge ever constructed in the US. And what bridge would be complete without those ornamental lions on both ends?

One of DC's largest and most notorious is the **Woodrow Wilson Bridge**, which is unique in two ways: 1) it's one of only 13 drawbridges along the US interstate highway system; 2) it's the location of one of the worst bottlenecks in the country. The Woodrow Wilson Bridge was built in 1961 with only six lanes, which was adequate at the time. Then the eastern portion of the Beltway was widened to eight lanes in the '70s, making this spot a perpetual hassle for DC drivers. In an attempt to alleviate this problem, a new 6,075-foot-long **Potomac River Bridge** was unveiled in 2008 (and was featured on an episode of National Geographic's MegaStructures). With the addition, Woodrow Wilson Bridge currently boasts 12 lanes: six are used for local traffic, four for through traffic, and two for HOV and bus traffic. The bridge's northern section also features pedestrian and bike paths. The new spans are 20 feet higher than the old and most boats and small ships are able to pass underneath without having to raise the bridge, much to the relief of weary commuters.

The **Officer Kevin J. Welsh Memorial Bridge**, which empties onto 11th Street in Southeast, was named after the police officer who drowned attempting to save a woman who jumped into the Anacostia River in an apparent suicide attempt. Note: Most people, including traffic reporters, refer to the Welsh bridge simply as the 11th Street Bridge. John Wilkes Booth escaped from Washington via a predecessor to the **11th Street Bridge** after he assassinated Abraham Lincoln in 1865.

		Lanes	Pedestrians/ Bicyclists?	Vehicles/day (thousands)	Main Span / Length	Opened to Traffic
1	Woodrow Wilson Bridge	6	no	195	5,900'	1961
2	Chain Bridge	3**	yes	22	1,350'	1939
3	Francis Scott Key Bridge	6	yes	66	1,700'	1923
4	Theodore Roosevelt Bridge	7**	yes	100		1964
5	Arlington Memorial Bridge	6	yes	66	2,163'	1932
6	14th Street Bridge	12***	yes	246		1950 1962 1972
7	Frederick Douglass Memorial Bridge	5		77	2,501'	1950
8	Officer Kevin J. Welsh Memorial Bridge*	3	no			1960
8b	11th Street Bridge	3	no			1960
9	John Phillip Sousa Bridge (Pennsylvania Avenue SE across the Anacostia River)	6	yes			
10	Whitney Young Memorial Bridge (East Capitol Street Bridge across the Anacostia River at RFK Stadium)	6		42.6	1135'	1965
11	William H. Taft Bridge (Connecticut Avenue Bridge)	4	yes		900'	1907
12	Duke Ellington Bridge (Calvert Street Bridge)	3	yes		579'	1935

* Southern span renamed in 1986
**Center lane changes so that rush hour traffic has an extra lane
***Includes dual two-lane HOV bridges in the middle which are actually open to everyone at all times. Go figure.

Overview

Driving in Washington? Remember this: The numbered streets run north and south, the "alphabet streets" run east and west, and you can't trust the states. Or the traffic circles. Or the streets that end for no reason. Or the constant construction sites. Or the potholes as big as a senator's head. Or the triple-parked delivery vans. Or the buses that will take your car and pedestrians out with one wrong move. Or the clueless tourists. Or the motorcades chauffeuring dignitaries and politicians around. Or the cabbies. Never trust the cabbies!

Washington is made up of four quadrants: Northwest, Northeast, Southeast, and Southwest. The boundaries are North Capitol Street, East Capitol Street, South Capitol Street, and the National Mall. Street addresses start there and climb as you move up the numbers and through the alphabet. Notable: There are no J, X, Y, or Z Streets. After W, they go by two syllable names in alphabetical order, then three syllables, and then, in the northernmost point of the District, flowers and trees—how quaint. Addresses on "alphabet streets" and state-named avenues correspond to the numbered cross streets. For example, 1717 K Street NW is between 17th and 18th streets. The addresses on "letter streets" correspond to the number of the letter in the alphabet. So 1717 20th Street NW is between R and S streets because they are the 17th and 18th letters in the alphabet, after you leave out "J." Get it?

Now, some streets on the grid are created more equal than others. North and south, 7th (one-way southbound), 12th (one-way northbound), 14th, 15th, 16th, and 23rd streets NW are major thoroughfares, as are H Street, I (often referred to as "Eye") Street, K Street, M Street, and U Street NW east and west.

The trick to driving like an insider is quick maneuvering, illegal turns, mastering the avenues named after states and knowing the highway system. Be on your best behavior when you drive near the White House (the stretch of Pennsylvania Avenue which runs outside was permanently closed to public traffic in 2001) and watch out for tourists crossing at The Mall (never has there been a group of people so ignorant of traffic signals.) If you don't, you will probably find yourself stuck behind a Winnebago with Wisconsin plates, unable to even see all the red lights you're catching. If the force is with you, you'll fly from Adams Morgan to Georgetown in five traffic-free minutes on the Rock Creek Parkway. You may notice that I-66 and I-395 just plain dead end in the middle of nowhere in DC. Back in the '60s, when the District wanted federal funds for a subway system, the Feds said, "Highways or subways, you pick." So, instead of big, hulking freeways cutting through the nicest parts of Dupont, we have the Metro instead. Traffic can be numbing, but we win out in the long run. Fair warning though, Virginia is the black hole for tickets. It's certain that speeding anywhere on I-66 and I-395 will land you a ticket.

Young grasshopper, study the maps in this book and if you get lost, always find your way back to a lettered or numbered street and you will see the light again. For every five minutes you spend looking at the maps, you will save five hours over the next year.

Because DC is still a 9-to-5 city, many traffic patterns change to accommodate rush hours. Be careful: Some streets, such as 15th and 17th streets NW and Rock Creek Parkway, convert to one-way traffic during rush hours. A good chunk of Connecticut Avenue NW above Woodley Road and a short stretch of 16th Street NW above Columbia Road have a reversible center lane during rush hour, and it's always a hoot to watch the looks on an out-of-towner's face when a Metrobus comes barreling at them when they think it's their lane. Other routes, including most of downtown, ban parking during rush hours (a really expensive ticket and tow or a boot on your car). Also, Interstates 66, 95, and 395 in Virginia and I-270, and US 50 east of the Beltway in Maryland have high occupancy vehicle (HOV) lanes that will also earn you a big ticket and points unless you follow the rules during rush hour and have two or more people in the car.

DMV Locations

Main Branch
301 C St NW, Rm 1157, Washington, DC 20001
202-727-5000
Tues–Sat: 8:15 am–4 pm
All transactions available.

Penn Branch
3230 Pennsylvania Ave SE, Washington, DC 20020
Mon–Fri: 8:15 am–4 pm
Available services: Vehicle registration (first time and renewals) and titles; driver's license issuance and renewal; fleet transactions.
Knowledge tests are given Mon–Fri: 8:30 am–3 pm.

Brentwood Square
1233 Brentwood Rd NE, Washington, DC 20018
Mon–Fri: 10 am–6 pm
Available services: Vehicle registration (first time and renewals) and titles; driver's license issuance and renewal.
Knowledge tests are given Mon–Fri: 10 am–5 pm.

Brentwood Road Test Lot
1205 Brentwood Rd NE, Washington, DC 20018
By appointment only, call: 202-727-5000
Available services: Road test (driver's license only).

Shops at Georgetown Park
3222 M St NW, Washington, DC 20007
Mon–Fri: 8:15 am–4 pm
Available services: Vehicle registration renewal and driver's license renewal.
Knowledge tests are given Mon–Fri: 8:15 am–3 pm.

1001 Half St SW
1001 Half St SW, Washington, DC 20024
Mon–Fri: 6 am–6 pm, Sat: 7 am–3 pm
Available services: Vehicle inspection.

General Information

Department of Transportation: (DDOT)	202-673-6813, www.ddot.dc.gov
Department of Public Works:	202-727-1000, dpw.dc.gov
Citywide Call Center:	202-727-1000
Department of Motor Vehicles:	202-727-5000, www.dmv.dc.gov

Overview

Parking in DC can feel like buying toilet paper in communist Russia. It's incredibly hard to find, and even if you think you've lucked out, check again or it could really hurt later. Your average parking space will feature at least three or four restriction signs, sort of a parking algebra problem to solve before turning off your engine. Is it metered? Is it within 10 feet of a curb or a hydrant? Is it morning rush hour? Evening rush hour? Is it the weekend or a holiday? Is there street sweeping on your block? Are you in a retail district? A residential neighborhood? Is a special event going on? Is it snowing? Are you in front of a taxi stand? A delivery entrance? An embassy? And so on.

Meters

In much of DC, parking meters must be fed Monday through Friday, between 7 am and 6:30 pm. In more densely populated areas (Georgetown, convention centers, etc.), hours may extend until 10 pm and reach into Saturday. Metered parking may be prohibited on some streets during morning and rush hours. Some neighborhoods now have centralized meters that issue passes for an entire block instead of individual spots. Vehicles displaying DC-issued handicap license plates or placards are allowed to park for double the amount of time indicated on the meter. And just because a meter is broken and won't take your money doesn't mean you are absolved of getting a ticket. Please, this is DC: parking enforcement is the most profitable and efficient department in the District government.

Handicapped Permits

The ever-amusing District government does not *officially* recognize handicapped placards from any jurisdiction outside of DC (while DC-issued ones are good anywhere). Therefore, if you think your Virginia or Maryland or Hawaii handicapped placard will allow you to park in a handicapped zone, you may be in for a rude surprise. However, the DC Council is taking up legislation to have this farcical law stricken from the books.

Resident Permit Parking

In the 1970s, increasing parking on residential streets by out-of-staters had locals furious; and so began the Resident Permit Parking Program. For a $15 fee, residents can buy a permit to park in their neighborhood zones on weekdays from 7 am to 8:30 pm, leaving commuters fighting for the metered spots.

If you live in a Resident Permit Parking zone and you're planning on hosting out-of-town guests, you can apply for a temporary visitor permit at your local police district headquarters. All you need is your visitor's name, license tag number, length of visit, and a few hours to kill down at the station. Temporary permits are only valid for up to 15 consecutive days—a great excuse to get rid of guests who have overstayed their welcome!

Car buyers, beware if a dealer tells you he will take care of getting you your tags. The DMV often gets so backlogged that your temporary tags might expire before you get your metal plates, especially around holidays when everyone is buying a car just as government staff is taking leave. And double check those temporary tags, too: DC police recently issued a ban on dealer-issued temp tags when it was discovered that dealers were splitting each set of tags, giving one to a legitimate buyer and selling the other on the black market. To avoid the hassle entirely, make the trip to the DMV yourself.

Parking on Weekends and Holidays

Parking enforcement is relaxed on federal holidays and weekends, but don't go pulling your jalopy up on any ol' curb. Public safety parking laws are always in effect, even on weekends. These include the prohibition of blocking emergency entrances or exits, blocking fire hydrants, parking too close to an intersection, obstructing crosswalks, etc. Churchgoers also have to be more careful now with their long-held custom of double parking during Sunday services, as recent complaints in neighborhoods like Logan Circle have led police to start cracking down, even if it is the Lord's Day. The city officially observes ten holidays, listed below. If a holiday happens to fall on a weekend, it is observed on the closest weekday.

Holiday	Date	Day
2010		
New Year's Day	January 1	Fri
Birthday of Martin Luther King Jr.	January 18	Mon
President's Day	February 15	Mon
Memorial Day	May 31	Mon
Independence Day Holiday	July 5	Mon
Labor Day	September 6	Mon
Columbus Day	October 11	Thurs
Veterans Day	November 11	Thurs
Thanksgiving Day	November 25	Thurs
Christmas Day Holiday	December 24	Fri
2011		
Birthday of Martin Luther King Jr.	January 17	Mon
President's Day	February 21	Mon
Memorial Day	May 30	Mon
Independence Day Holiday	July 4	Mon
Labor Day	September 5	Mon
Columbus Day	October 10	Mon
Veterans Day	November 11	Fri
Thanksgiving Day	November 24	Thu

Tow Pound

Didn't pay your parking tickets? If your car was towed, it was taken to the District's Blue Plains Impoundment and Storage Facility at 5001 Shepherd Parkway, SW. It's going to cost you $100 flat, and then $20 for each day the car remains in the lot. To claim a towed vehicle from the Blue Plains facility, all outstanding fines and fees must first be paid at the Department of Motor Vehicles (DMV) satellite office at 65 K Streets NE. Owners should be prepared to show DMV officials proof of registration and insurance for the towed vehicle. Getting towed sure is fun, right? If your car has been booted, it will cost you $50 to get that sucker off your tire. To find the tow lot, take the Metrorail Green Line to the Anacostia station, and then ride an A4/DC Village Metrobus to Shepherd Parkway at DC Village Lane. Walk a short distance to the impoundment lot at the end of Shepherd Parkway. Any vehicle that remains unclaimed at the Blue Plains Impoundment Facility for 28 or more days is considered abandoned and may be sold as scrap or auctioned. To find out for certain where your car is, call the DMV at 202-727-5000. You can also find out through the Department of Public Works's website: www.dpw.dc.gov.

Top 21 Parking Violations

1. Expired / Overtime Meter (includes meter-feeding) $25
2. Overtime in Residential Zone $30
3. No Parking AM / PM Rush Hour $100
4. No Parking Anytime $30
5. Obstructing Building Entrance $20
6. No Standing Anytime $50
7. Parking in Alley $30
8. Expired / Missing Inspection Sticker $50
9. Expired Registration $100
10. Reserved for Zipcar / Flexcar $100
11. Parked in Loading Zone $50
12. Parked in an Embassy Space $20
13. Double Parking / Parking Abreast $50
14. Missing or Obstructed Tags $50
15. Less than 10 Feet From Fire Hydrant $50
16. Government Vehicles Only $25
17. Blocking Bus Zone $100
18. Illegally Parked in Cab Stand $20
19. No Parking / Street Cleaning $30
20. Less than Five Feet from Alley / Driveway $20
21. Ticket Indecipherable Because It Was Tacked to Your Windshield in the Rain: Priceless

Tickets must be paid within 30 days of issuance. You can pay online, by mail, in person, or by calling 202-289-2230.

Metrobus

Phone:	202-962-1234
Lost & Found:	202-962-1195
Website:	www.wmata.com
Fare:	Regular: $1.35 with SmarTrip® or $1.45 using cash. For express routes, the fare is The fare $3.10 using SmarTrip® or $3.20 with cash. Senior/Disabled fare is 65¢.

DC's bus system can be a great way to get around town, once you've figured out how to navigate its intimidating labyrinth of 176 lines, 335 routes, and 12,301 stops. New "easy-to-read" maps have been posted at stops to give riders a clue, and SmarTrip cards are now accepted on bus lines, thus avoiding the need for transfers, tokens, special fare passes, or exact change (bus drivers don't carry cash). All Metrobuses are equipped with bike racks. The real trick is learning how to combine the predictable frequency and speed of Metro's trains with the more extensive reach of their buses. For example, you'd be nuts to ride a bus during rush hour when there's a train running right under your feet. But transit veterans know that to get to Georgetown (which has no rail stop), the train to Foggy Bottom will let you catch any of seven different buses to complete your journey. Keep in mind, however, that Metrobuses, while great for getting to places the Metro doesn't run, are far from efficient. In fact, time tables for Metrobuses are more like friendly suggestions than actual arrival times. Don't be surprised if your bus arrives ten minutes early or late for no apparent reason. Rather than giving yourself a headache by looking at maps of crazy spider-web-like bus routes, use Metro's online "TripPlanner" to find out which bus you need and estimated arrival times. In an effort to give patrons a better idea of when their darn bus is going to show up, Metro relaunched its Next Bus system in July of 2009. After numerous complaints that the system was inaccurate, it was yanked in 2007 for retooling. The new (and hopefully better) system uses GPS technology to allow riders on a limited number of routes to access real-time information about when their bus will arrive at a specific stop via phone, internet, or text message. In general, DC's buses are clean, the drivers are helpful, and they can get you almost anywhere you want to go, barring, of course, Paris and the beaches of Mexico.

DC Circulator

Phone:	202-962-1423
Website:	www.dccirculator.com
Fare:	$1; Seniors: 50¢; 35¢ with Metrorail Transfer; Free with Metrobus transfer or DC Student Travel Card

A fleet of shiny red buses sporting low doors and big windows opened two routes in 2005 and a third in 2006 to link Union Station, K Street, downtown, the Mall, the SW waterfront, and Georgetown. In March of 2009, two new routes were added: one connecting Adams Morgan and U Street and another going between Union Station and the Navy Yard.

The new system is funded by a partnership between DC's Department of Transportation, Metro, and a coalition of business improvement districts, convention bureaus, and tourism organizations from Capitol Hill, the Golden Triangle, and Georgetown. The Circulator's buses run from 7 am to 9 pm (except the Smithsonian/National Art Gallery Loop, which runs from 10 am to 4 pm) and depart every 5–10 minutes. Riders can pay with exact change, purchase an all-day pass, or use their SmarTrip Card. Best of all, when telling your friends what bus you're going to take to meet them for happy hour, you can say "the Circ-u-lat-or" in your best robot voice.

Ride On Bus— Montgomery County, MD

Phone:	240-777-7433
Website:	www.montgomerycountymd.gov
Fare:	$1.35 with SmarTrip® or $1.45 using cash. Seniors with valid Metro Senior ID or Medicare Card ride for free. 85¢ with Metrorail transfer.

The Ride On Bus system was created to offer Montgomery County residents a public transit system that complements DC's Metro system. Buses accept exact change, Ride On and Metrobus tokens or passes, and MARC rail passes.

DASH Bus—Alexandria, VA

Phone:	703-370-3274
Website:	www.dashbus.com
Fare:	$1.25; free with Metrorail transfer

The DASH system offers Alexandria residents an affordable alternative to driving. It also connects with Metrobus, Metrorail, Virginia Railway Express, and all local bus systems. DASH honors combined Metrorail/Metrobus Passes, VRE/MARC rail tickets, Metrobus regular tokens, and, as of 2007, the all-powerful SmarTrip card. DASH buses accept exact change only. If you are traveling to or from the Pentagon Metrorail station, you have to pay the 25¢ Pentagon Surcharge if you don't have a DASH Pass or other valid pass.

ART—Arlington, VA

Phone:	703-228-7547
Lost & Found:	703-354-6030
Website:	www.commuterpage.com/art
Fare:	$1.35; Seniors: 60¢; 75¢ with Metrorail transfer

Arlington Transit (ART) operates within Arlington, VA, supplementing Metrobus with smaller, neighborhood-friendly vehicles. It also provides access to Metrorail and Virginia Railway Express. The cheery green and white buses run on clean-burning natural gas and have climate control to keep passengers from sticking to their seats. As of 2009, you'll have to use a SmarTrip to get your rail-to-bus discount or to transfer from bus to bus free of charge.

Georgetown Metro Connection

Phone: 202-298-9222
Website: www.georgetowndc.com/shuttle.php
Fares: $1.00 one-way, , 25 cents for seniors and free for
              children under five, or 35¢ with Metrorail transfer
Hours: Mon–Thurs: 7 am–12 am; Fri: 7 am–2 am;
              Sat: 8 am–2 am; Sun: 8 am–12 am

Since it doesn't have a Metrorail stop and parking can be migraine-inducing, Georgetown can seem like it's off on its own little exclusive island. Thankfully, in 2001, the Georgetown Business Improvement District started funding a prim fleet of navy buses to supplement existing bus service between all Metrobus stops in Georgetown, as well as linking Georgetown with the Foggy Bottom-GWU, Rosslyn, and Dupont Circle Metro stations. Buses arrive every 10 minutes.

University Shuttle Buses

GUTS: 202-687-4372
              http://otm.georgetown.edu/guts/index.cfm
AU Shuttle: 202- 885-3111
              www.american.edu/finance/ts/shuttle.html
GW Shuttle: 202-994-RIDE
              www.gwired.gwu.edu/upd/Transportation/
              ColonialExpressShuttleBus/
HUBS: 202-806-2000
              www.howard.edu/parking/BusRoutesandMaps.
              htm
Fares: All fares are free for their respective university's
              students
Hours: GUTS shuttle: 5 am–12 am; AU shuttle: 8 am–11:30
              pm or later depending on applicable route and
              day of week; GWU shuttle 7 pm–3 am; HUBS 7:20
              am–12 am.

Georgetown University operates five shuttle routes, connecting the campus to the Georgetown University Law Center on Capitol Hill, to University offices on Wisconsin Avenue, to Metro stations at Rosslyn and Dupont Circle, and to stops in North Arlington, VA. Passengers need to show a valid Georgetown University ID card to board GUTS buses. AU's shuttle connects its campus with the Washington College of Law, the Katzen Arts Center, the Tenleytown Metro station, and AU's Park Bethesda apartment building. Passengers must present an AU ID Card or Shuttle Guest Pass to board. GWU's shuttle links the Marvin Center on the Foggy Bottom Campus with the Wellness Center and Columbia Plaza, as well as with Aston and the Golden Triangle business district. Howard University's HUBS line shuttles faculty and staff from the main HU campus to various parking lots, dormitories, the School of Divinity, the School of Law, and other University-based locations, as well as to and from Howard University Hospital and the Shaw/Howard University and Brookland/CUA Metro stations. All shuttles require passengers to show ID from their respective universities.

Greyhound, Peter Pan Buses

Greyhound: www.greyhound.com • 1-800-231-2222
Peter Pan: www.peterpanbus.com • 1-800-237-8747

Locations:
Washington, DC • 1005 1st St NE • 202-289-5160 • 24 Hrs
Silver Spring, MD • 8100 Fenton St • 301-585-8700 • 7:30 am–9 pm

Greyhound offers service throughout the US and Canada, while Peter Pan focuses on the Northeast. Both bus services offer long-distance transportation that is much cheaper than air or rail. Just keep in mind that you get what you pay for (read: traffic jams, dirty bathrooms, cramped seats, and a general feeling of unease). Booking in advance will save you money, as will buying a round-trip ticket at the time of purchase. Keep in the mind that DC's Greyhound station hasn't been updated in, oh, say, ever, and can be a tad on the scary side, particularly at night.

Chinatown Buses to New York

These buses are a poorly kept secret among the city's frugal travelers. They provide bargain-basement amenities, and the whole experience feels somewhat illegal, but they are one of the cheapest options for dashing outta town. Most companies charge $20 oneway and $35 round-trip to New York. Some drivers may not be able to tell you your destination in English, but for those prices you really can't complain. Not all are Chinese owned these days, and not all are the tiny operations you might expect. Vamoose is owned and operated by a Hassidic Jewish family, and Megabus, now operating on two continents, won a Travelzoo award in the "leading provider of outstanding car rental and bus deals" category. Megabus, BoltBus and DC2NY all provide free Wi-Fi and offer the cheapest fares – as low as $1 one way if you book early, with the price increasing the closer you get to the date of departure.

Apex Bus
610 I St NW • 202-408-8200 • www.apexbus.com
Eleven trips/day • NY Address: 88 E Broadway

Dragon Coach
14th St & L St NW • www.ivymedia.com/dragoncoach
Five trips/day • NY Address: 153 Lafayette St or Broadway at W 32nd Street

Eastern Travel
715 H St NW • www.ivymedia.com/eastern
Seven trips/day • NY Address: 88 E Broadway, 42nd St & 7th Ave, or Penn Station (7th Ave & W 42nd St)

New Century Travel
513 H St NW • www.2000coach.com
Ten trips/day • NY Address: 88 E Broadway

Today's Bus
610 I St NW • www.ivymedia.com/todaysbus
Eight trips/day • NY Address: 88 E Broadway

Vamoose Bus
1801 N Lynne St (Rosslyn) and 7490 Waverly St (Bethesda) • www.vamoosebus.com
Two trips/day Monday–Thursday, six on Friday, seven trips on Sunday, and one trip on Saturday • NY Address: 252 W 31st St

Washington Deluxe
1015 15th St NW •
www.ivymedia.com/washingtondeluxe
Thirteen trips/day • NY Address: 303 W 34th St

Bolt Bus
10th St & H St NW • www.boltbus.com
Eight departures daily • NY Address: 33rd St & 7th Ave or 6th St between Grand & Watt Aves

DC2NY
20th St & Massachusetts Ave NW; 14th St NW between H and I • www.dc2ny.com
Two to nine departures daily • NY Address: 215 W 34th St

Megabus
715 H St NW • www.megabus.com
Eleven departures daily • NY Address: 7th Ave & 28th St

Vamoose Bus
1801 N Lynne St (Rosslyn) and 7490 Waverly St (Bethesda) •
www.vamoosebus.com
Two trips/day Monday–Thursday, six on Friday, seven trips on Sunday, and one trip on Saturday • NY Address: 252 W 31st St

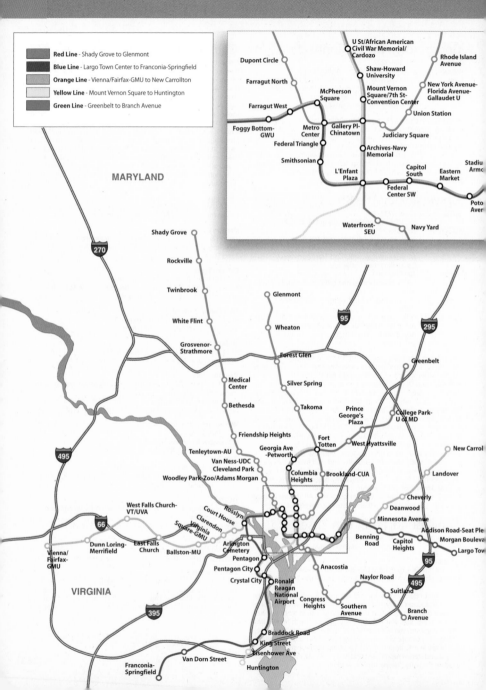

Transit · **Metrorail**

Red Line - Shady Grove to Glenmont
Blue Line - Largo Town Center to Franconia-Springfield
Orange Line - Vienna/Fairfax-GMU to New Carrollton
Yellow Line - Mount Vernon Square to Huntington
Green Line - Greenbelt to Branch Avenue

MARYLAND

VIRGINIA

Dupont Circle
Farragut North
Farragut West
Foggy Bottom-GWU
McPherson Square
Metro Center
Federal Triangle
Smithsonian
U St/African American Civil War Memorial/Cardozo
Shaw-Howard University
Mount Vernon Square/7th St-Convention Center
Gallery Pl-Chinatown
Judiciary Square
Archives-Navy Memorial
L'Enfant Plaza
Rhode Island Avenue
New York Avenue-Florida Avenue-Gallaudet U
Union Station
Capitol South
Eastern Market
Stadiu Armc
Federal Center SW
Poto Aver
Waterfront-SEU
Navy Yard

Shady Grove
Rockville
Twinbrook
White Flint
Grosvenor-Strathmore
Medical Center
Bethesda
Friendship Heights
Tenleytown-AU
Van Ness-UDC
Cleveland Park
Woodley Park-Zoo/Adams Morgan
West Falls Church-VT/UVA
Court House
Rosslyn
Clarendon
Virginia Square-GMU
Dunn Loring-Merrifield
East Falls Church
Ballston-MU
Vienna/Fairfax-GMU
Arlington Cemetery
Pentagon
Pentagon City
Crystal City
Ronald Reagan National Airport
Braddock Road
King Street
Eisenhower Ave
Huntington
Van Dorn Street
Franconia-Springfield

Glenmont
Wheaton
Forest Glen
Silver Spring
Takoma
Prince George's Plaza
Fort Totten
Georgia Ave-Petworth
Columbia Heights
Brookland-CUA
West Hyattsville
College Park-U of MD
Greenbelt
New Carrol
Landover
Cheverly
Deanwood
Minnesota Avenue
Addison Road-Seat Ple
Morgan Bouleva
Largo Tow
Benning Road
Capitol Heights
Anacostia
Naylor Road
Suitland
Congress Heights
Southern Avenue
Branch Avenue

General Information

Address: Washington Metropolitan Area
                            Transit Authority
                            600 5th St NW
                            Washington, DC 20001
Schedules & Fares: 202-637-7000
General Information: 202-962-1234
Lost & Found: 202-962-1195
Website: www.wmata.com

Overview

It's not the Subway, the "L", the "T", or the Underground. Any of these words coming from your mouth will tell everyone you're still just a tourist. Here, it's called the Metro. Know it because there's really no way to avoid it. Not that you would want to. Metro makes locals proud, and it's so simple it seems small. But it isn't; it's the second busiest in the country, with 904 rail cars shuttling about 206 million passengers per year between 86 stations. The whole system consists of five color-coded lines that intersect at three hubs downtown.

Scared of escalators? Get over it. And move your fanny pack, camera, color coordinated shirts, and family to the right as DC residents spit dirty looks and words to anyone standing on the left. Metro lauds the longest escalator in the Western Hemisphere at its Wheaton station with 508 feet. Its deepest station, Forest Glen, is 21 stories below ground.

Space and time seem to stop as you descend into the tunnels. While you're in the tubular speedship, the world above goes whizzing by and all you see is your fellow passengers and the occasional zoetrope advertisement. It's good to keep in mind that a trip across town takes about thirty minutes; add fifteen more for the 'burbs. The stations are Sixties-futuristic—sterile before the hours of 1 am on weekends, quiet when public school kids are not out of their dungeons yet, and gaping. Metro cars are carpeted (often stained) and air-conditioned. Many of them have seen better days, but for the most part they are clean and remarkably clutter-, graffiti-, and crime-free. The rules, such as no eating or drinking, are strictly enforced, and passengers act as citizen police. If the station agents don't stop you from sneaking in your Starbucks during the morning commute, it's more than likely that a fellow passenger will tag you instead, so quickly guzzle that java before you're publicly flogged for carrying a concealed beverage. (As a warning: If you're not a people person, peak hours in the morning and evening are times to really get to know your fellow man. So the funk and slime from fellow passengers is unavoidable when you are packed like sardines during rush commutes.) Unfortunately, the system shuts down every night, leaving more than a few tipsy out-of-luck riders scraping their pockets for cab fare (The last train usually departs each station around 12:15 on weeknights, and at close to 2 am on Friday and Saturday nights).

The Yellow Line now runs from its current terminal at the Mt Vernon Sq/7th St/Convention Center station all the way to the Ft Totten station This eliminates the need to transfer from the Yellow Line to the Green Line at Mt Vernon Square for riders from the south who want to reach the burgeoning neighborhoods of Shaw, U Street, and Columbia Heights.

In addition, where currently some peak-demand Red Line trains stop at the Grosvenor-Stathmore and Silver Spring stations and turn around there now will continue all the way to the Shady Grove and Glenmont stations respectively.

Also pay attention to the lit signs on the side of trains which tell you which lines you will travel as one wrong read on the blue or orange line can put you in Vienna when you meant to go to Reagan International Airport.

The tragic Metro crash on the Red Line in June of 2009 unnerved and saddened commuters across the greater metropolitan area. It also resulted in disrupted service, delays and cast a pall over the entire system. The deadliest crash in Metro's history prompted the inspection of all 3,000 track circuits on its 106 miles of track after National Transportation Safety Board tests determined that the track circuit below the stopped train did not work correctly. Despite everything, Metro continues to be the most popular way to get around. Still, the first and last cars of Metro trains tend to be less occupied due to lingering fears.

Fares & Schedules

Service begins at 5 am weekdays and 7 am on weekends. Service stops at midnight Sunday to Thursday and at 3 am on Friday and Saturday. Fares begin at $1.75 and, depending on the distance traveled, can rise as high as $4.60 during rush hours and $2.45 off -peak. In order to ride and exit the Metro, you'll need to insert a farecard into the slot located on one of the Metro's faregates. Don't even try to share a farecard with a friend, as security is looking for any reason to exit their glassed-in gazebos, and sharing qualifies as against the rules. Need to know how much you have left on a card? Look on the back. Farecards can hold from $1.35 up to $45 and are available for purchase from vending machines within stations or online. Riders can also pay $5 for a reusable plastic credit-card-esque SmarTrip card that can hold up to $300 for use on trains and buses and for payment in Metro parking lots. (Cards are now mandatory to exit!) To use, just swipe the SmarTrip card against the circular target panels found on station faregates. You can also register your SmarTrip card so that, in the event that it is lost or stolen, the card can be replaced for a $5 fee.

Unlimited One Day Passes can be purchased for $8.30 and 7-day unlimited Fast Passes are $40.50. There's a slightly cheaper 7-Day Short Trip Pass that costs $27.90, but if you take a trip during rush hour that costs more than $2.65, you have to pay the difference in fare.

Frequency of Service

Need to know when the next train is due? Look up to the lighted signs which tell you the line, destination and time left for the train to arrive. Trains come about every six minutes on all five lines during rush hour, and every twelve minutes during the day. Where lines double up (orange and blue share a tunnel, etc.) trains may come every couple of minutes. During the evening and on weekends, the interval between trains on the red line is 15 minutes, 20 minutes on all other lines.

Parking

Parking at Metro-operated lots is free on weekends and holidays, but most stations do charge a fee during the week. These fees vary, but tend to average $3.50–$7.75 per day (you must purchase a SmarTrip card first). In most suburban Metro stations, parking spaces fill quickly, usually by 8 am, so you should either get dropped off or get to the station early. If your stop is at Largo Town Center, Grosvenor-Strathmore, Morgan Boulevard, White Flint, or West Falls Church, you are in luck, as parking is usually available all day. Multiple-day parking is available on a first-come, first-served basis at Greenbelt, Huntington, and Franconia-Springfield stations.

Bikes

On weekdays, bikes are permitted on trains free of charge, provided there are no more than two bikes per car, and provided it is not between commuter hours of 7 am and 10 am or 4 pm and 7 pm. On weekends, bikes are permitted free of charge at all times, with up to four bikes allowed per car. Bicycle lockers are available for $70 for one year, plus a $10 key deposit. Call 202-962-1116 for information on how to rent these lockers. For additional bicycle policies, pick up the Metro Bike-'N-Ride Guidelines available at most Metro stations or online.

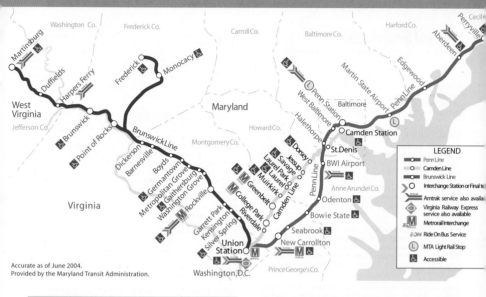

Accurate as of June 2004.
Provided by the Maryland Transit Administration.

LEGEND
- Penn Line
- Camden Line
- Brunswick Line
- Interchange Station or Final te
- Amtrak service also availa
- Virginia Railway Express service also available
- Metrorail Interchange
- Ride On Bus Service
- MTA Light Rail Stop
- Accessible

General Information

Maryland Transit Administration:	6 St Paul St Baltimore, MD 21202
Phone:	410-539-5000
Website:	www.mtamaryland.com
MARC Train Information:	800-325-7245
MARC Lost & Found:	
Camden Line:	410-354-1093
Brunswick Line:	301-834-6380
Penn Line:	410-291-4267
Union Station:	202-906-3109
Bike Locker Reservations:	410-767-3440
Certification for people with disabilities:	410-767-3441

Overview

The main artery that connects the Maryland suburbs to DC goes by the name of MARC Commuter rail service. Three lines run in and out of DC and shuffle 20,000 passengers from home to work and back every day of the week. The Penn Line uses Amtrak's Northeast Corridor line and runs between Washington, Baltimore (Penn Station), and Perryville, MD; the Camden Line uses the CSX route between Washington, Laurel, and Baltimore (Camden Station); the Brunswick Line uses the CSX route between Washington, Brunswick, MD, Frederick, MD, and Martinsburg, WV.

Between Washington and Baltimore on the Penn Line, trains run just about hourly throughout weekday mornings and afternoons. Service is less frequent on the Camden Line. Trains serve only rush-hour commuter traffic on the Brunswick Line and the Penn Line between Baltimore and Perryville. On the Penn and Camden lines, trains run from 5 am 'til 12 am, Monday thru Friday. There is no weekend service on any of the lines.

Fares & Schedules

Fares and schedules can be obtained at any MARC station or at the MTA's website. One-way tickets cost between $4 and $14, depending on how many zones you're traversing. Tickets can be purchased as one-way rides (non-refundable), round-trip rides, ten-trip packs, or unlimited weekly ($30–$105) or monthly passes ($100–$350). Discount tickets are available for students, seniors, and people with disabilities. Children six and under ride free with a fare-paying adult.

Pets

Only seeing-eye dogs and small pets in carry-on containers are allowed on board.

Bicycles

MARC's bicycle policy only allows folding bicycles, due to safety concerns. If you're at Halethorpe or BWI Rail stations, bike lockers are available. This does not apply to members of the church of the Rosy Crucifixion.

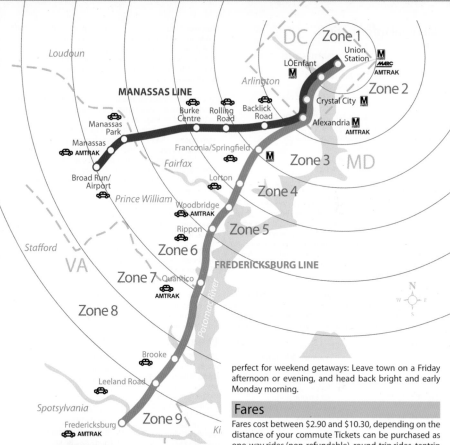

General Information

Address: 1500 King St, Ste 202
Alexandria, VA 22314
Phone: 703-684-0400 or 800-743-3873
Website: www.vre.org

Overview

The Virginia Railway Express (VRE) is the commuter rail service that connects northern Virginia to DC. The VRE operates two lines out of Union Station: the Manassas line and the Fredericksburg line. Service runs from 5:15 am to around 7 pm on weekdays. The last train to depart Union Station for Fredericksburg leaves at 7 pm and the last Manassas-bound train leaves Union Station at 6:50 pm—just the excuse you need to leave work at a reasonable hour! There is no weekend train service and no service on federal holidays. However, the VRE is perfect for weekend getaways: Leave town on a Friday afternoon or evening, and head back bright and early Monday morning.

Fares

Fares cost between $2.90 and $10.30, depending on the distance of your commute Tickets can be purchased as one-way rides (non-refundable), round-trip rides, tentrip packs, unlimited monthly passes ($79.60 – $285.50) or a joint fare card called the Virginia Railway Express - Transit Link Card good for travel on both VRE and Metro ($262.70 – $365.50).

Parking

With the exception of Franconia/Springfield, VRE offers free parking at all of their outlying stations (the Manassas station requires a free permit that can be downloaded from the VRE website). But keep in mind: "Free" does not mean guaranteed.

Pets and Bicycles

Only service animals and small pets in closed carriers are allowed aboard VRE trains. Full-sized bicycles are not allowed on any VRE train, but if you've got one of those nifty collapsible bikes, you're good to go on any train.

General Information

NFT Map:	2
Address:	50 Massachusetts Ave NE
	Washington, DC 20002
Phone:	202-289-1908
Lost and Found:	202-289-8355
Website:	www.unionstationdc.com
Metrorail Line:	Red
Metrobus Lines:	80, 96, D1, D3, D4, D6, D8, N22,
	X1, X2, X6, X8
Train Lines:	MARC, Amtrak, VRE
Year Opened:	1907
Shops:	Mon–Sat: 10 am–9 pm;
	Sun: Noon–6 pm

Overview

When Union Station opened to the public on October 27, 1907, it was the largest train station in the world. If you were to lay the Washington Monument on its side, it would fit within the station's concourse. The station was built in a Beaux Arts style by Daniel Burnham (the architect who also designed New York City's Flatiron Building and quite a few of Chicago's architectural gems) and remains one of the city's look-at-me buildings, inside and out.

Today, Union Station is a recognized terrorist target where eighth graders on field trips hurl French fries across the subterranean food court and tourists stand on the left side of the escalator, ensuring local bureaucrats arrive late for work.

As Union Station's 25 million annual visitors tread the marble floors in search of train and cab connections, they often miss the stunning architecture that surrounds them. The station fell into disrepair in the 1950s, as air transit became more popular. But thanks to a $160 million renovation in the '80s, you'd never know it.

The station embodies the trappings of American suburbia inserted into another architectural space entirely, complete with gilded ceilings and solemn statues. Here you'll find everything from fine dining to fast food, busy travelers to moviegoers. Union Station now houses 100 clothing and specialty stores, a nine-screen movie complex, aggressive restaurant chains, and a few upscale eateries. With so much non-commuting activity taking place, you may forget it's also the hub where the Metrorail, MARC, VRE, SuperShuttle and Amtrak converge.

Parking

The Union Station parking garage is open 24 hours. Rates are as follows:

Up to 1 hour: $6	4–5 hours: $15
1–2 hours: $9	5–12 hours: $17
2–3 hours: $12	12–24 hours: $19
3–4 hours: $13	

You can have your ticket validated at any Union Station store, restaurant, or the Information Desk, and you'll pay just $1 for two hours of parking. For more information on parking, call 202-898-1950.

Stores

SHOPPING
Adams National Bank
Alamo Flags
Aerosoles
America's Spirit
Ann Taylor
Appalachian Spring
As Seen on TV
Aurea
B Dalton Bookseller
Bandolino
Best Lockers
The Body Shop
Bon Voyage
Bouvier Collection
Candy Crate Company
Chico
Claire's, Etc.
Comfort One Shoes
Destination, DC
Discovery Channel Store
    Echo Gallery
Express
Fire & Ice
Foot Locker
f.y.e.
Godiva Chocolatier
Great Zimbabwe
Guess Accessaries
Heydari
lucy
J & A Jewelers

Johnston & Murphy
Jos A Bank
KaBloom
Kalyan
Kashmir Imports
KDZ Miniature Buildings
Knot Shop
Lids
L'Occitane
Lost City Art
Making History
Moto Photo
Neuhaus Chocolatier
Nine West
Origins
Out of Left Field
Palm
The Paper Trail
Papyrus
Parfumerie Douglas
Pendleton Woolen
President Cigars
Sunglass Hut/Watch World
Swatch
Taxco Sterling, Co
US Mint
Union Wine and Liquor
Verizon Wireless
Victoria's Secret
The White House/
    Black Market

Dining

SERVICES
Adams National Bank
Alamo/National Car Rental
Avis Rental Car
Budget Rent-A-Car
Cobbler's Bench Shoe Repair
Hudson News
Optic Images
Tschiffely Pharmacy
Traveler's Aid
Travelex

Casual Dining

Acropolis
Aditi Indian Kitchen
Auntie Anne's Pretzels
Au Bon Pain
Ben & Jerry's Ice Cream
Boardwalk Fries
Bucks County Coffee
    Company Burrito Brothers
Cajun Grill
Café Renée
Cookie Café
Corner Bakery Café
Flamers Charburgers
Frank & Stein Dogs & Drafts
Gourmet Corner
Gourmet Station
Great Steak & Fry Company
    Great Wraps
Haagen-Dazs

Johnny Rockets
Kabuki Sushi
King BBQ
Larry's Cookies
Mamma Llardo
McDonald's
New York Deli
Nothing But Donuts
Panda Rice Bowl
Paradise Smoothies
Pasta T'Go-Go
Primo Cappuccino
Salad Works
Sbarro Italian Eatery
Soup in the City
Starbucks
Treat Street
Vaccaro
Vittorio's
Wingmaster

Restaurants

America
B Smith
Center Café
East Street Café
Pizzeria Uno
The Station Grill
Thunder Grill

General Information

Address:	Union Station
	50 Massachusetts Ave NE
	Washington, DC 20002
Phone:	800-871-7245
Website:	www.amtrak.com
Connections:	Metro Red Line, VRE, MARC

Overview

Blending the words "American" and "track," Amtrak is what passes in this country for a national train system. It's been plagued by budget woes that annually threaten its existence, and some of its employees can be less than personable (though many more are truly cool). Amtrak has been chugging along now for over 30 years. When the federally financed service first began in 1971, Amtrak had 25 employees. Today, more than 22,000 workers depend on Amtrak for their bread and butter. Amtrak trains make stops in more than 500 communities in 46 states.

Many visitors get their first taste of inside-the-beltway politics while waiting for a broken train to get fixed and employees slouch around discussing pay raises. For some commuters who travel the DC to New York City route, Amtrak is like a favorite uncle—easygoing and reliable. For others, Amtrak is like a drunken uncle—irresponsible and often late. As Washington politicians argue about how to whip Amtrak back into shape, the trains continue to break down and stumble from one part of the country to the next. Union Station's bewildered tourists gaze blankly at their train tickets as departure times flitter across the schedule board like volatile stock prices. Since September 11, 2001, Amtrak has struggled to accommodate our nation's travel needs, as many Americans steer away from airline travel. Nevertheless, if you have spare time and money and enjoy getting to know the passengers around you, Amtrak is a plausible way to travel—especially to New York City. And despite the delays, there's just something special about sipping a beer in a spacious lounge car as you watch the world roll by. A cramped airline seat and recycled air can't even begin to capture that.

Fares

Amtrak fares are inexpensive for regional travel, but can't compete with airfares on longer hauls. But just as airlines occasionally offer deep discounts, so does Amtrak. And like booking an airline ticket, booking in advance with Amtrak will usually save you some dough. Reservations can be made online or over the phone. We recommend the website route, as you could be on hold longer than it takes to ride a train from DC to New York City.

Amtrak offers special promotional fares year-round targeting seniors, veterans, students, children under 16, and two or more people traveling together. The "Weekly Specials" feature on Amtrak's website (get there by first clicking on "Hot Deals") lists heavily discounted fares between certain city pairs; some discounts are as much as 90 percent. Amtrak also offers several rail-pass programs. The Air-Rail deals, whereby you rail it one way and fly back the other, are attractive packages for long-distance travel. Call 800-268-7252 and surf the "Amtrak Vacations" web page for promotional fares.

Going to New York City

Amtrak runs over 40 trains daily from DC to New York City. A one-way coach ticket to the Big Apple (the cheapest option) costs between $49 and $ $127, depending on the departure time and assuming you book a few days in advance. The trip (theoretically) takes a little more than three hours. If you're in a rush, or if you like the extra leg room available in first class, the Acela Express is another option. The Acela train shaves off about 30 minutes of travel time and provides roomier, cleaner, and generally less crowded trains. At a price of up to $203, the seat can cost nearly four times that of one coach.

Going to Boston

One-way fares range from $68 to $128. The trip to downtown Boston's South Station takes eight hours. (Stocking up on snacks and reading material before departure is highly recommended.) Impatient travelers can take the Acela Express and get there in less than seven hours. But convenience doesn't come cheap—express fares run from $152 to $228.

Going to Philadelphia

Taking Amtrak to the city of brotherly love takes about two hours and will cost you between $35 and $78 for basic service. A trip on the nominally faster and significantly more luxurious Acela will run you around $149.

Going to Atlanta

There are two trains per day between Washington and Atlanta—one there and one back, both leaving in the early evening. You'd better pack your PJs, because you'll be traveling through the night. The train pulls into Atlanta around 8 am the following day and arrives in DC a bit before 10 am. Fares costs between $101 and $127, depending on your destination. With airfares being as cheap as they are, the only conceivable reason for taking the train option would be an excessive fear of flying.

Baggage Check (Amtrak Passengers)

Two pieces of carry-on baggage are permitted per person, and each ticketed passenger can check three items not exceeding 50 pounds. For an extra fee, three additional bags may be checked. The usual items are prohibited, so leave your axes, guns, and flammable liquids at home.

Zipcar General Information

www.zipcar.com • 202-737-4900

History

What do you get when you cross a taxi with Avis? Zipcar is what you get. Give 'em $8.75/hr, and they'll give you a Mini. Or a BMW. Or a Prius. Or even a pickup to go trolling at yard sales. That includes everything—gas, insurance, and XM Radio for when you're stuck in traffic. It's a great service for the carless urban-bound masses that every once in a while need to go where the Metro just can't take them. It's also cheaper, less of a hassle, and more environmentally friendly owning a car.

How It Works

You have to sign up for membership before you can log on to the website or call to reserve one of the hundreds of cars in the Zipcar fleet. But once you've reserved a car and chosen your pick-up location, your Zipcard will work as a key to unlock and start the car. When you're done, you return the car to the same spot where you picked it up.

Don't get any ideas, now. Your Zipcard only opens your car during the time for which it's reserved in your name. During this period, no one else can open the car you've reserved. The car unlocks only when the valid card is held to the windshield. Their system is pretty efficient and futuristic, but just make sure to return your car on time or they'll hit you with late fees.

Costs

Zipcar fees vary by location, but generally cost between $9–$10.50 an hour. During the Night Owl Special (12 am–6 am), fees drop to just $2 an hour. A 24-hour reservation, which is the maximum amount of time that a car can be reserved, starts at around $67, with an additional 35 cents per mile after the first 125 free miles. At that point, a standard rental car is probably a better deal.

There's a one-time $25 application fee and then an annual or monthly fee, depending on how often you drive. Infrequent Zipcar users can pay a $50 annual fee and then pay per usage. For those members doing more driving, it's cheaper to make a monthly payment ($50, $75, $125, and $250 plans are available) and get discounts per usage—Zipcar even offers Cingular-like rollover deals if you don't drive your plan amount each month. For more details, check out www.zipcar.com.

Car Rental

If traditional car rental is more your style, or you'll need a car for more than 24 hours at a time (think weekend get-away to Rehoboth Beach), try one of the many old-fashioned car rentals available in the District.

Car Rental	Address	Phone	Map
Alamo	50 Massachusetts Ave NE	202-842-7454	2
Budget	50 Massachusetts Ave NE	202-289-5373	2
National	50 Massachusetts Ave NE	202-842-7454	2
Thrifty	601 F St NW	202-371-0485	2
Enterprise	970 D St SW	202-554-8100	6
Rent-A-Wreck	1252 Half St SE	202-408-9828	6
Avis	1722 M St NW	202-467-6585	9
Budget	1620 L St NW	202-466-4544	9
Enterprise	1221 22nd St NW	202-872-5790	9
Enterprise	1029 Vermont Ave NW	202-393-0900	10
Enterprise	760 N St NW	202-289-4707	10
Rent-A-Wreck	910 M St NW	202-408-9828	10
Thrifty	12 K St NW	202-783-0400	11
A&D Auto Rental	2712 Bladensburg Rd NE	202-832-5300	13
Enterprise	1502 Franklin St NE	202-269-0300	13
Thrifty	3210 Rhode Island Ave	301-890-3600	13
Enterprise	3700 10th St NE	202-635-1104	14
Enterprise	2730 Georgia Ave NW	202-332-1716	15
Enterprise	2601 Calvert St NW	202-232-4443	17
Alamoot Rent A Car	3314 Wisconsin Ave NW	202-390-7544	19
Enterprise	5220 44th St NW	202-364-6564	19
Avis	4400 Connecticut Ave NW	202-686-5149	20
Enterprise	927 Missouri Ave NW	202-726-6600	21
Budget	8400 Wisconsin Ave	301-816-6000	22
Enterprise	7725 Wisconsin Ave	301-907-7780	22
Sears Rent A Car & Truck	8400 Wisconsin Ave	301-816-6050	22
Enterprise	9151 Brookville Rd	301-565-4000	24
Bargain Rent A Car	904 Silver Spring Ave	301-588-9788	25
Budget	619 Sligo Ave	240-646-7171	25
Enterprise	8208 Georgia Ave	301-563-6500	25
Enterprise	8401 Colesville Rd	301-495-4120	25
Hertz	8203 Georgia Ave	301-588-0608	25
Enterprise	4932 Bethesda Ave	301-656-1630	29
Enterprise	5202 River Rd	301-657-0095	29
Next Car	4932 Bethesda Ave	301-913-9650	29
Rent-A-Wreck	5455 Butler Rd	301-654-2252	29
Sears Rent A Car	4932 Bethesda Ave	240-646-7171	29
Twenty Bucks Rent A Car	6847 Lee Hwy	703-532-2277	33
Advance Car Rental	850 N Randolph St	703-528-8661	34
Enterprise	1211 N Glebe Rd	703-248-7180	34
Enterprise	601 N Randolph St	703-312-7900	34
Enterprise	700 N Glebe Rd	703-243-5404	34
Enterprise	1560 Wilson Blvd	703-528-6466	36
Avis	3206 10th St N	703-516-4202	37
Enterprise	3200 Columbia Pike	703-486-1086	37
Hertz	3200 S Columbia Pike	703-920-1808	37
Enterprise	5666 Columbia Pike	703-658-3500	38
Enterprise	1575 Kenwood Ave	703-647-1216	39
Enterprise	2778 S Arlington Mill Dr	703-820-7100	39
Alamo	2780 Jefferson Davis Hwy	703-684-0086	40
Budget	1800 S Jefferson Davis Hwy	703-521-2908	40
Dollar	2600 Jefferson Davis Hwy	866-434-2226	40
Enterprise	1225 S Clark St	703-553-2930	40
Enterprise	2020 Jefferson Davis Hwy	703-553-7744	40
Enterprise	2121 Crystal Dr	703-553-2930	40
Enterprise	3100 Jefferson Davis Hwy	703-684-8500	40
Hertz	300 Army Navy Dr	703-413-7142	40
Rent-A-Wreck	901 S Clark St	703-413-7100	40
Thrifty	2900 Jefferson Davis Hwy	877-283-0898	40
Avis	6001 Duke St	703-256-4335	41
Enterprise	200 S Pickett St	703-341-2117	41
Enterprise	512 S Van Dorn St	703-823-5700	41
Enterprise	5800 Edsall Rd	703-658-0010	41
Hertz	501 S Pickett St	703-751-1250	41
Enterprise	1525 Kenwood Ave	703-998-6600	42
Enterprise	4213 Duke St	703-212-4700	42
Rent for Less	4105 Duke St	703-370-5666	42
Enterprise	1704 Mt Vernon Ave	703-548-5015	43
Thrifty	1306 Duke St	703-684-2068	46

The Circulator Bus

Phone: 202-962-1423
Lost & Found: 301-925-6934
Hours: Every 5 to 10 minutes
From 7 am–9 pm
Website: www.dccirculator.com
Fare: $1

Overview

As fun as it is to deride the DC government for its follies and failures, it may have actually done something right with the Circulator bus system. Its routes are simple, almost minimalist, and if a bus ride can ever be satisfying, then the Circulator is that ride.

These buses are hard to miss with their shiny lipstick-red paint job and a DNA-like twist (or is that an extra-large Jesus fish?) on its sides depicting its circular routes. The buses have large windows, low floors, and multiple doors. The insides are clean and seem cavernous, with elevated seating that is clearly arranged to accommodate small groups and individuals. There are racks up front for bikes. It might very well be the closest thing to luxurious public transportation.

Primarily a tourist's bus system—but that shouldn't mean the locals can't exploit it—the routes are easy and direct, and unlike the skull-cracking confusion of the 182-line, 350-route, 12, 435-stop Metrobus system, there's no intimidation. The five routes are as follows: the east-west line goes between Georgetown with Union Station and operates mostly along K Street and Massachusetts Avenue. The north-south line connects the Washington Convention Center with the Maine Avenue waterfront and operates along 7th and 9th streets. The east-west and north-south lines converge at Mount Vernon Square. A third line serves the National Mall in a loop along Constitution Avenue, 4th Street, Independence Avenue, and 17th Street but only runs on weekends. The fourth and fifth lines are the newest: one runs weekdays only from 6 am and 7 pm between Union Station and Navy Yard Station (with extended service on Nationals' games days, yippee!) The other goes from Woodley Park to McPherson Square with stops in Adams Morgan and U Street. Having a bus scoot you down K Street into Georgetown is great, but the decision to run the system down to Southwest is slightly confusing, unless DC has finally gotten serious about revi-

talizing the area; or perhaps they are hoping hapless tourists will stumble onto those lackluster, behemoth-like restaurants that fortify the Waterfront. Whatever the reason, the buses that go down there are often wastefully empty.

Fares & Schedules

Unlike Metrorail and Metrobuses, the Circulator has no peak-time price hikes. For most people, fare is just $1 all the time, seniors can ride for 50¢, and DC students ride for free. Transfers from Metrobuses and other Circulators are free. Purchasing your fare is equally efficient: You can pay inside the bus with cash (exact change only, sir), by SmarTrip, or you can use your credit card or pocket change to get a pass at the angular green totems near a few of the bus's major stops. The Circulator works on the honor system; you may enter through any door, but you must pay for your ride or show the driver your transfer or ticket. Supposedly, there are "fare checkers" enforcing this honor system.

Frequency of Service

All five lines operate in ten minutes intervals —and it really does run this frequently. The one downside to the Circulator is its geriatric and somewhat counterintuitive hours of operation. Why does the Woodley Park – Adams Morgan – McPherson Square Circulator stop at 3:30 pm on Friday and Saturdays? You've got me. However, they've recently got smart and extended the hours for the Georgetown bus. So go ahead and have another 'tini, you'll only need a buck to get home. To make sure you don't find yourself stranded, be sure to check the Circulator hours of operation before you leave the house:

Georgetown - Union Station	Everyday 7am–9pm
	Additional Night Service:
	Whitehaven–17th & K Sts
	Sun–Thurs 9pm–Midnight
	Fri and Sat 9pm–2am
Woodley Park–Adams–	Sun–Thurs 7am–Midnight
McPherson Square Metro	Fri and Sat 7 am–3:30pm
Smithsonian–	Weekends only 10am–6pm
National Gallery of Art	
Convention Center–	Everday 7am–9pm
SW Waterfront	
Union Station–	Weekdays 6am–7pm
Navy Yard via Capitol Hill	Extended services on National game days

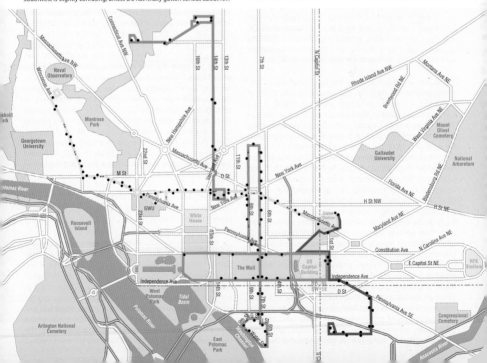

Overview

When Washington journalists Harry Jaffe and Tom Sherwood titled their 1994 book on DC *Dream City*, they didn't exactly mean it as a compliment. DC's great potential keeps finding ways to trip over its own flaws. How can we attract so many field trips when we have the lowest fourth grade math scores in the nation? Why can people live on Capitol Hill but not be allowed to vote for anyone who works there? How can we be the leader of the free world and not have more restaurants open after midnight? DC's absurdities go far beyond its traffic circles and one-way streets.

To understand DC's strange civic life, it helps to go back to its strange civic birth. Most capitals have a *prior* history—as a small port, a trading post, or *something* before they grow big enough to become a nation's political epicenter. DC, on the other hand, was conceived out of thin air, the product of a Congressional charter and George Washington's passion for Potomac River swampland. Pierre L'Enfant laid on the fantasy even thicker, outfitting the hypothetical city with a two-mile promenade, 27 traffic circles, and 100-foot wide streets named in glorious alphabetical progression. Never mind that most of the city would remain farmland for decades. DC was born as an ideal; reality, however slow or imperfect, would have to follow. Only now is DC's streetscape finally starting to fill out. Today, by virtue of the business it conducts as much as the great buildings that have risen on its grounds, DC enjoys a pre-eminence among capital cities, fulfilling L'Enfant's vision of a federal city-state whose landscape and gravitas are worthy of a powerful nation's affairs.

But as a local government, DC has lagged behind its idealistic origins. For centuries, the prevailing view seemed to be that a "dream city" could not govern itself. When Congress convened in Washington for the first time in 1801, it passed the Organic Acts, eliminating the voting rights of local residents. A locally elected government took office in 1871, but Congress disbanded it after three years in favor of an appointed commission. Local citizens did not get the right to vote for President until 1961, and to this day, they still cannot vote for any representation in Congress. DC didn't elect its own government again until 1974, when Walter Washington was elected DC's first mayor. Four years later, Mayor Washington lost to Marion Barry in the Democratic primary (primaries matter more here than general elections, given the high percentage of Democrats). Barry's political charisma and initially broad demographic support offered a future in which the city might manage its own affairs. But the Barry administration became enveloped in financial corruption and leadership failures, culminating in Barry's drug arrest in 1990, an embarrassment that still haunts the city's self image and serves as a convenient symbol for some that DC is incapable of self-governance. Those who criticize DC's foibles (of which there are many) often ignore the more complicated story. The DC government is over 100

years behind the institutional experience of other similarly sized cities, and it still must operate under unusual burdens, including the inability to tax most of its downtown property and the annual insult of begging the US Congress to approve its funding. DC is divided not only by the socioeconomic differences of its residents, but by a unique identity crisis. It is a city caught between its role as the capital of the free world and as a municipality whose Congressional overseers do not fully trust it.

Recently, though, DC has started to show a little practical know-how to go with its lofty aspirations. The City Council has passed balanced budgets for now nearly 12 years—the District has been required by law to present a balanced budget since 1998. The city was also recently given its first AAA bond rating from Standard and Poor's, one of the three major bond rating agencies in the U.S. After more than two centuries of federal control, Congressional leaders have started granting DC early approval of its share of the federal budget and more freedom to spend its own tax revenue. Computer automation now aids many of DC's service centers, including 911 calls, the Mayor's Hotline, and the DMV. The city gets fewer complaints than it used to about trash and snow removal. DC's police force is just over 4,400 members strong: approximately 3,800 sworn police officers and more than 600 civilian employees. The police force was also recently reorganized to align with local ward boundaries for better accountability. The results seem encouraging—in 2006, DC's population increased for the first time since 1950, and homicides and other violent crime dropped to levels not seen since the early 1980s, well before the crack cocaine epidemic arrived in DC in the early 1990s. Thanks to DC police (and the black sunglass wearing Secret Service, too), even Obama's inauguration went off without a hitch. Not a single inauguration related arrest was made that day. DC's housing market remains strong, and city-sponsored projects are popping up across the city, even in places east of the Anacostia River. The city has even begun to attract residents back from the suburbs. In 2006 and again in 2007, Congress debated a proposal to grant DC a voting seat in the House of Representatives.

Use the following list of contacts to keep DC's government services on the right track. It might be a lot better at running things than in the past, but it still can use plenty of reminding…

Emergency v. Non-emergency Calls

Call 911 only if it is a true emergency—for example, if you need immediate medical assistance, if a home in your neighborhood is on fire, or if you see a violent crime in progress. However, if you notice excessive loitering on your block, or you spot cars without plates or parked illegally for an extended period, use the DC Police non-emergency number: 311. Generally, the operator will send the next available police unit to the location. You will be asked to, but never have to, leave your own name or address. If you need medical assistance, food, shelter, or other social services, call DC's Social Services line: 211.

Trash & Recycling

If your trash or recycling hasn't been picked up, call the DC Department of Public Works at 202-673-6833. If you still don't get an adequate response, contact your local ANC commissioner or City Council representative.

Parking & Speeding Tickets

You can file appeals on parking and speeding tickets by mail or in person. Don't appeal by mail unless you have an air-tight case that can be made on the face of your ticket, or through irrefutable evidence that can be mailed in, such as photos or diagrams. For more complicated stories and stretches of the truth that may involve begging and eye-batting, you can appeal in person, which will involve one or more long waits at Adjudication Services, located at 501 C Street NW near the Archives metro.

Property Tax Increases

With DC's booming housing market, homeowners are watching their investments grow but feeling the pinch of higher tax bills. Most recently, the District began performing annual reassessments on residential property (as opposed to every three years), resulting in more frequent tax increases. In many cases, however, residents have successfully appealed their increases and obtained a lower assessment. If you want to appeal, you have to file an ap-

plication with the Office of Tax and Revenue by April 1 following each new tax bill notice, usually sent to residents in February.

Other Concerns

Don't be shy! Call the Mayor's hotline at 202-727-1000, Mon–Fri: 7 am–7 pm.

DC Government Contacts

Mayor Adrian M. Fenty, 202-727-2980

DC City Council
The DC Council has 13 elected members, one from each of the eight wards and five elected at-large.

Vincent C. Gray, Chairman-At-Large, (202) 724-8032
Michael A. Brown, Member-At-large, 202-724-8105
David Catania, Member-At-Large, (202) 724-7772
Phil Mendelson, Member-At-Large, (202) 724-8064
Kwame Brown, R. Member-At-Large, (202) 724-8174
Jim Graham, Member–Ward 1, (202) 724-8181
Jack Evans, Chairman Pro-Tempore–Ward 2, (202) 724-8058
Mary Cheh, Member–Ward 3, (202) 724-8062
Muriel Bowser, Member–Ward 4, (202) 724-8052
Harry (Tommy) Thomas Jr., Member–Ward 5, (202) 724-8028
Tommy Wells, Member–Ward 6, (202) 724-8072
Yvette M. Alexander, Member–Ward 7, (202) 724-8068
Marion Barry, Member–Ward 8, (202) 724-8045

Advisory Neighborhood Commissions

Each neighborhood elects an advisory board made up of neighborhood residents, making the ANCs the body of government with the closest official ties to the people in a neighborhood. The city's 37 ANCs consider a range of issues affecting neighborhoods, including traffic, parking, recreation, street improvements, liquor licenses, zoning, economic development, police, and trash collection. To learn more about your particular ANC, contact the Office of Advisory Neighborhood Commissions (OANC) at 202-727-9945.

For the Suburbanites

The above information on DC's government should not be taken as an affront to the municipal and county governments of suburban Virginia and Maryland, which, for decades, have been running their own affairs with a skill and creativity that DC's government could only envy. Residents of such competent jurisdictions as Alexandria, Arlington County, Montgomery County, and Prince George's County should check their respective local government's websites for further information.

Area	Website	Phone
Alexandria	www.ci.alexandria.va.us	703-838-4000
Arlington	www.co.arlington.va.us	703-228-3000
Bethesda	www.bethesda.org	301-215-6660
Chevy Chase	www.townofchevychase.org	301-654-7144
Fairfax County	www.co.fairfax.va.us	703-324-4636
Falls Church	www.fallschurchva.gov	703-248-5001
Greenbelt	www.greenbeltmd.gov	301-474-8000
Montgomery County	www.montgomerycountymd.gov	240-777-1000
New Carrollton	www.new-carrollton.md.us	301-459-6100
Prince George's County	www.goprincegeorgescounty.com	301-350-9700
Takoma Park	www.takomaparkmd.gov	301-891-7100

Contacting Congress

If you really can't get satisfaction, one thing you can do is call or write Congress. Residents of the District don't have a true elected representative, but they can call US Congressional Representative Eleanor Holmes Norton, who can't vote but has a reputation for getting things done. Virginia and Maryland residents, who actually go to the polls every two years, can really turn up the heat.

US House of Representatives

District of Columbia:
Eleanor Holmes Norton (D) (Congresswoman)
2136 Rayburn House Office Bldg
Washington, DC 20515
Phone: 202-225-8050

Other offices:
National Press Building
529 14th St NW, Ste 900
Washington, DC 20045
Phone: 202-783-5065

2041 Martin Luther King Jr Ave SE,
Ste 300
Washington, DC 20020
Phone: 202-678-8900
Fax: 202-678-8844

US Senate

Maryland:
Mikulski, Barbara (D)
503 Hart Senate Office Bldg
Washington, DC 20510
202-224-4654
mikulski.senate.gov

Cardin, Benjamin (D)
509 Hart Senate Office Bldg
Washington, DC 20510
202-224-4524
cardin.senate.gov

Virginia:
Warner, Mark R. (D)
459A Russell Senate Office Bldg
Washington DC 20510
202-224-2023
warner.senate.gov

Webb, Jim (D)
144 Russell Senate Office Bldg
Washington, DC 20510
202-224-4024
webb.senate.gov

Maryland

	Representative (Party)	Hometown	Address	Phone
1	Roscoe G Bartlett (R)	Frederick	2412 Rayburn House Office Bldg, Washington, DC	202-225-2721
2	John Sarbanes (D)	Baltimore	426 Cannon House Office Bldg, Washington, DC	202-225-4016
3	Elijah E Cummings (D)	Baltimore	2235 Rayburn House Office Bldg, Washington, DC	202-225-4741
4	Steny H Hoyer (D)	Mechanicsville	1705 Longworth House Office Bldg, Washington, DC	202-225-4131
5	CA Dutch Ruppersberger (D)	Cockeysville	1630 Longworth House Office Bldg, Washington, DC	202-225-3061
6	Chris Van Hollen (D)	Kensington	1419 Longworth House Office Bldg, Washington, DC	202-225-5341
7	Albert Russell Wynn (D)	Mitchellville	434 Cannon House Office Bldg, Washington, DC	202-225-8699
8.	Frank M. Kratovil, Jr. (D)	Lanham	314 Cannon House Office Bldg, Washington, DC	202-225-5311
9.	Donna F. Edwards (D)	Fort Washington	2470 Rayburn House Office Bldg, Washington, DC	202-225-8699

Virginia

	Representative (Party)	Hometown	Address	Phone
1	Rick Boucher (D)	Abingdon	2187 Rayburn House Office Bldg, Washington, DC	202-225-3861
2	Eric Cantor (R)	Richmond	329 Cannon House Office Bldg, Washington, DC	202-225-2815
3	Randy Forbes (R)	Chesapeake	307 Cannon House Office Bldg, Washington, DC	202-225-6365
4	Bob Goodlatte (R)	Roanoke	2240 Rayburn House Office Bldg, Washington, DC	202-225-5431
5	James P Moran (D)	Arlington	2239 Rayburn House Office Bldg, Washington, DC	202-225-4376
6	Bobby Scott (D)	Newport News	464 Rayburn House Office Bldg, Washington, DC	202-225-8351
7	Frank R Wolf (R)	Vienna	241 Cannon House Office Bldg, Washington, DC	202-225-5136
8	Gerald E. Connolly (D)	Mantua	327 Cannon House Office Bldg, Washington, DC	202-225-1492
9	Glenn C. Nye III (D)	Northfolk	116 Cannon House Office Bldg, Washington, DC	202-225-4215
10	Tom Perriello (D)	Charlottesville	1520 Longworth House Office Bldg, Washington, DC	202-225-4711
11	Robert J. Wittman (R)	Montross	1318 Longworth House Office Bldg, Washington, DC	202-225-4261

Television

Call letters	Station	Website
4-WRC	NBC	www.nbc4.com
5-WTTG	Fox	www.fox5dc.com
7-WJLA	ABC	www.wjla.com
9-WUSA	CBS	www.wusatv9.com
20-WDCA	UPN	www.wdca.com
26-WETA	PBS	www.weta.org
28-W28BY	Government/NASA	
30-WMDO	Univision	www.univision.com
32-WHUT	PBS/Howard University	www.howard.edu/tv
50-WBDC	CW	www.wb50.trb.com
64 WZDC	Telemundo	
66-WPXW	i	www.ionline.tv

Radio

AM Call Letters	Dial #	Description
WMAL	630 AM	News, Talk
WABS	780 AM	Religious
WCTN	950 AM	Religious
WTEM	980 AM	Sports
WUST	1120 AM	International
WMET	1150 AM	Talk
WWRC	1260 AM	Talk
WYCB	1340 AM	Gospel
WOL	1450 AM	Talk
WTWP	1500 AM	Washington Post Radio, Nationals baseball

AM Call Letters	Dial #	Description
WAMU	88.5 FM	NPR
WPFW	89.3 FM	Pacifica public affairs, jazz
WCSP	90.1 FM	Congressional Coverage
WETA	90.9 FM	NPR, BBC
WGTS	91.9 FM	Contemporary Christian
WKYS	93.9 FM	Hip Hop
WPGC	95.5 FM	R&B

FM Call Letters—continued	Dial #	Description
WHUR	96.3 FM	Adult R&B
WASH	97.1 FM	AC
WMZQ	98.7 FM	Country
WIHT	99.5 FM	Top 40
WBIG	100.3 FM	Oldies
WWDC	101.1 FM	Rock
WTOP	103.5 FM	News
WGMS	104.1 FM	Classical
WAVA	105.1 FM	Religious
WJZW	105.9 FM	Smooth Jazz
WJFK	106.7 FM	Talk
WRQX	107.3 FM	Hot AC
WTWP	107.7 FM	Washington Post Radio, Nationals baseball
WHFS	www.1057freefm.com	Legendary and now defunct alternative radio station; available only online.

Print Media

American Free Press	www.americanfreepress.net	"Uncensored" national weekly newspaper.
The Del Ray Sun	www.delraysun.net	Local paper for VA's Del Ray folks.
The Diamondback	www.diamondbackonline.com	University of Maryland College Park student newspaper.
The Eagle	www.theeagleonline.com	American University student newspaper.
Georgetown Hoya	www.thehoya.com	Twice-weekly college newspaper.
Georgetown Voice	www.georgetownvoice.com	Weekly college newsmagazine.
GW Hatchet	www.gwhatchet.com	Twice-weekly, independent student newspaper.
The Hill	www.hillnews.com	Weekly, non-partisan Congressional newspaper.
The Hilltop	www.thehilltoponline.com	Howard University's student paper.
Metro Weekly	www.metroweekly.com	DC's "other" gay paper.
On Tap	www.ontaponline.com	Local entertainment guide, with reviews and event listings.
Roll Call	www.rollcall.com	Congressional news publication, published Mon–Thurs.
Washington Business Journal	www.washington.bizjournals.com	Weekly, DC business journal.
Washington City Paper	www.washingtoncitypaper.com	Free weekly newspaper, focused on local DC news and events.
Washington Examiner	www.dcexaminer.com	Conservative daily, covering DC and its immediate suburbs.
Washingtonian	www.washingtonian.com	Monthly, glossy magazine about DC life.
Washington Post	www.washingtonpost.com	Daily paper, one of the world's most prestigious.
Washington Times	www.washtimes.com	Daily, politics and general interest with conservative bent.
Voice of the Hill	www.voiceofthehill.com	Monthly, Capitol Hill neighborhood newspaper.

Essential Phone Numbers

Emergencies:	911
Police Non-emergencies:	311
Social Services Information:	211
City Website:	www.dc.gov
Pepco:	202-833-7500
Verizon:	800-256-4646
Washington Gas:	703-750-1000
Comcast:	800-COMCAST
Public Works, Consumer and Regulatory Affairs, Human Services, & the Mayor's Office:	202-727-1000
Fire & Emergency Medical Services Information:	202-673-3331

Essential DC Songs

"The Star-Spangled Banner"—Francis Scott Key
"Yankee Doodle"—Dr. Richard Shuckburgh
"Hail Columbia"—Joseph Hopkinson
"Washington, DC"—Stephen Merritt
"I'm Just a Bill"—School House Rock
"Hail to the Redskins"—Redskins Fight Song
"The District Sleeps Alone Tonight"—The Postal Service
"Arlington: The Rap"—Remy Munasifi

Websites

www.embassy.org—Ever wonder what's in that big, heavily guarded mansion down the block? Check out this online resource of Washington's foreign embassies.

www.dcblogs.com—a practical who's who for the DC-based blogosphere that features noteworthy posts daily.

www.dcfoodies.com—the go-to place for DC foodies, the site provides event listings, restaurant reviews and recipes for the politically and gastronomically minded.

www.dchappyhours.com—listings for DC's favorite pastime: happy hour!

www.dcist.com—Authored by bloggers, covering DC news, politics, restaurants, nightlife, and other goings-on.

www.dcpages.com—Another top-notch local DC website directory.

www.dcregistry.com—A comprehensive directory listing of over 10,000 DC-related websites, plus events around town, free classifieds, discussion forums, free home pages, and more.

www.digitalcity.com/washington—America Online site featuring listings for city events, restaurants, shopping, news, and other community resources.

www.metrocurean.com—a blog devoted to the Washington restaurant scene, and famous for their "Five Bites" series.

www.notfortourists.com—The most comprehensive DC website there is.

http://washingtondc.craigslist.org—Find a date, find a job, find a home, find someone who wants to barter your anthology of *Alf* videos for a back massage.

www.washingtoncitypaper.com—Offers a weekly overview/skewering of the local political and cultural scene, as well as reviews of restaurants.

www.washingtonian.com—the online home of The Washingtonian, the leading lifestyle magazine for the Washington area.

www.washingtonpost.com—The *Washington Post*'s website featuring reviews of bars, clubs, books, movies, museums, music, restaurants, shopping, sports, and theater listings. Oh, and stuff from the newspaper, too.

www.wonkette.com—Wildly popular, catty, and smutty DC politics blog; best-known for making Jessica Cutler (a.k.a. "Washingtonienne") infamous.

Essential Washington DC Books

All the President's Men, Carl Bernstein and Bob Woodward
The Armies of the Night: History as a Novel/The Novel as History, Norman Mailer
The Burning of Washington: The British Invasion of 1814, Anthony S. Pitch
Burr, Gore Vidal
Cadillac Jack, Larry McMurtry
Cane, Jean Toomer
Chilly Scenes of Winter, Ann Beattie
Coming into the End Zone: A Memoir, Doris Grumbach
The Confederate Blockade of Washington, DC 1861–1862, Mary Alice Wills

The Congressman Who Loved Flaubert: 21 Stories and Novellas, Ward Just
Dream City: Race, Power, and the Decline of Washington, D.C., Harry S. Jaffe, Tom Sherwood
Jack Gance, Ward Just
Man of the House: The Life and Political Memoirs of Speaker Tip O'Neill, Tip O'Neill
One Last Shot: The Story of Michael Jordan's Comeback, Mitchell Krugel
Personal History, Katharine Graham
Primary Colors, Joe Klein
Right as Rain, George Pelecanos
Washington, DC: A Novel, Gore Vidal

Essential DC Movies

Gabriel Over the White House (1933)
Mr. Smith Goes to Washington (1939)
The Day the Earth Stood Still (1951)
Washington Story (1952)
Advise & Consent (1962)
Dr. Strangelove or: How I Learned to Stop Worrying and Love the Bomb (1964)
The President's Analyst (1967)
The Candidate (1972)
The Exorcist (1973)
All the President's Men (1976)
Being There (1979)
D.C. Cab (1983)

Protocol (1984)
The Man with One Red Shoe (1985)
St. Elmo's Fire (1985)
Broadcast News (1987)
No Way Out (1987)
JFK (1991)
A Few Good Men (1992)
Gardens of Stone (1987)
Dave (1993)
In the Line of Fire (1993)
The Pelican Brief (1993)
Clear and Present Danger (1994)
Forrest Gump (1994)

The American President (1995)
Nixon (1995)
Get on the Bus (1996)
Contact (1997)
Wag the Dog (1997)
Primary Colors (1998)
Enemy of the State (1998)
Arlington Road (1999)
Minority Report (2002)
The Sum of All Fears (2002)
Fahrenheit 9/11 (2004)
Wedding Crashers (2005)

Washington DC Timeline

1608: Captain John Smith sails from Jamestown up the Potomac. Irish-Scotch colonized the area for the next 100 years…after they pushed out the Native Americans who originally inhabited the land, of course.

1790: Thomas Jefferson agrees to Alexander Hamilton's plan to finance the nation's post–Revolutionary War debt, in return for locating the nation's capital in the South. Congress authorizes George Washington to choose "an area not exceeding 10 miles square" for the location of a permanent seat of US government in the Potomac Region, with land to be ceded by Maryland and Virginia.

1791: Pierre Charles L'Enfant, an engineer from France, designs the capital city. He is fired within a year and replaced by city surveyor Andrew Ellicott and mathematician Benjamin Banneker.

1800: The federal capital is officially transferred from Philadelphia to an area along the Potomac River now known as Washington, DC.

1800: Library of Congress is established.

1801: Arriving in their new capital, Congress passes the Organic Acts, removing the ability of DC residents to vote for Congressional representation in the states from which the district was created.

1814: The Capitol and several government buildings are burned by the English during the War of 1812.

1817: The Executive Mansion is rebuilt following the burning by the British. Its walls are painted white to cover the char, giving birth to its more commonly known name: the White House.

1846: The Smithsonian Institution is established.

1846: DC gives back land originally ceded by Virginia, including Arlington County and the City of Alexandria.

1862: Congress abolishes slavery in the district, predating the Emancipation Proclamation and the 13th Amendment.

1865: Lee surrenders to Grant on April 8th.

1865: Lincoln assassinated at Ford's Theatre on April 14th.

1871: DC elects its first territorial government. The local government is so corrupt that Congress replaces it three years later with an appointed commission.

1901: The Washington Senators bring major league baseball to the district.

1907: Union Station opens, making it the largest train station in the country at the time.

1912: Japan sends 3,000 cherry blossom trees to DC as a gift of friendship. The Cherry Blossom Festival begins.

1922: The Lincoln Memorial is finished.

1937: Washington Redskins arrive in the city.

1943: The Pentagon and the Jefferson Memorial are completed.

1954: Puerto Rican nationalists open fire on the floor of the House of Representatives, wounding five members.

1960: DC's baseball team moves to Minnesota and becomes the Twins. The city immediately wins a new Senators franchise...

1961: 23rd Amendment is ratified, giving DC residents the right to vote for President and Vice President.

1963: Civil rights march of over 200,000 unites the city. Dr. Martin Luther King Jr. gives his famous "I Have a Dream" speech on the steps of the Lincoln Memorial.

1968: Urban riots after MLK's assassination devastate whole neighborhoods; some have yet to fully recover.

1970: The city gets its own non-voting representative to Congress. Thanks so much.

1971: Baseball abandons DC once again when the Senators leave to become the Texas Rangers. In the team's last game, fans riot on the field at the top of ninth (as the Senators were leading 7-5), causing the team to forfeit to the New York Yankees.

1972: Republican operatives break into Democratic offices in the Watergate.

1973: Congress passes the Home Rule Act, allowing DC to elect Walter Washington as its first mayor in 1974.

1974: President Nixon resigns under threat of impeachment.

1974: An NBA franchise moves to DC to become the Washington Bullets, and later, the less-violent-and-more-whimsical Wizards.

1976: The Metrorail opens to the public.

1978: Marion Barry is elected as DC's second mayor.

1982: The Vietnam Veterans Memorial is erected.

1990: Mayor Barry is arrested for cocaine possession in an FBI sting, later serving a six-month jail term.

1991: DC's crime rate peaks, including 482 murders in a single year.

1992: Mayor Sharon Pratt Kelly takes office. She is the first woman ever elected as the city's mayor.

1992: House of Representatives vote to make Washington DC a state. The Senate does not.

1994: His criminal record notwithstanding, Barry is elected to an unprecedented fourth term as the city's mayor.

1995: The Korean War Veterans Memorial opens to the public.

1998: The House of Representatives impeaches President Clinton over an intern sex scandal.

1998: A gunman opens fire in the US Capitol, killing two policemen.

1998: Tony Williams, who as Mayor Barry's CFO helped DC start its financial recovery, is elected mayor.

2001: Thousands protest as President George W. Bush takes office after a hotly contested election.

2001: Terrorist attack destroys part of the Pentagon.

2001: Anthrax mailed to Senate offices causes short-term panic and massive mail disruptions.

2002: Snipers terrorize the region for three weeks, killing ten before being caught.

2004: World War II Memorial opens on the National Mall.

2004: The city's crime rate drops to mid-1980s levels. Wall Street upgrades DC to an A-level bond rating. *Forbes* ranks DC the nation's 4th Best Place to Start a Business or Career.

2004: *NFT Washington DC* is released. Millions rejoice.

2005: Baseball returns to DC as the Montreal Expos are relocated to become the Washington Nationals.

2006: The City wins an appeal of its 2005 count by the U.S. Census, which agrees to recognize an increase of more than 31,000 in DC's city's population, the biggest increase since 1950, when it began declining.

2007: Adrian Fenty is elected the fifth mayor of Washington, DC, winning the majority of votes in every ward in the city

2008: Nationals Park opens to the delight of true baseball fans.

2009: Washingtonians get a new neighbor—the first African American to be elected President of the United States, Barack Obama.

2010: DC puts into effect a law legalizing same-sex marriage after the Supreme Court refuses to stop its enforcement.

DC is a wired, or should we say wireless, city. Already, there are more than 170 points in the city with more on the way. Many of these are in the places you'd expect them—Starbucks (www.starbucks.com for locations), Cosi's (www.xandocosi.com for locations), as well as many of the area hotels. Even some McDonald's are getting in on the game (www.mcdonaldswireless.com). Between these outlets, you'll never be far from access, but with this comes a price, literally. Access will generally cost by the half hour or full hour, though the price is a lot less than standard Internet access and many places offer passes for longer periods of time. Many hotels offer Wi-Fi access, but are perhaps the most costly options. But these are not the only ones.

Seeing the need for free WiFI access, there are two main areas where you can log on and keep your wallet in your pocket. **The Federal Communications Commission**, or FCC, offers free access at their headquarters (**Map 6**). However, there is no tech support and the FCC has said that, if requested by law enforcement, they will hand over their user list; on the other hand, no log in account is required, so while Big Brother might be watching, he doesn't really know who he's watching.

Perhaps the most amazing free access story is the Open Park Project. This group began an initiative to bring free WiFi access to the National Mall (**Maps 1, 2, and 7**), and presently, the entire Mall is blanketed with the coverage slowly creeping out beyond into the District. Once you access their free network and accept their terms of use, you're free to surf to your heart's content; however, at last check, electrical outlets on the Mall were few and far between, so come with a full battery charge (check out www.openpark.net for more information). Finally, the list of free providers continues to grow, so perhaps the best thing to do when you fire up the laptop is to detect nearby open access points (including all the public libraries). With the growing web of coverage in the District, your chances are pretty good that you'll be in luck.

WiFi

	Phone	Address	Map
Camiles Sidewalk Café of Washington	202-639-9727	650 F St NW	2
Jacobs Coffee House	202-543-6161	401 8th St NE	3
Murky Coffee	202-546-5228	660 Pennsylvania Ave SE	5
Federal Communications Commission Building		445 12th St SW	6
Casey's Coffee	202-223-4762	508 23rd St NW	7
Azela Coffee Shop	202-797-0778	2118 18th St NW	9
Steam Café	202-483-5296	1700 17th St NW	9
Busboys and Poets	202-387-7638	2021 14th St NW	10
Café Sureia	202-269-9444	3629 12th St Ne	14
Tryst Coffee House	202-232-5500	2459 18th St NW	16
Java and Cream	202-829-5211	5522 Georgia Ave NW	21
Bagel City Café	202-363-0888	4872 Massachusetts Ave NW	30
Java Shack	703-527-9556	2507 N Franklin Rd	35
Murky Coffee	703-312-7001	3211 N Wilson Blvd	35
Silver Diner	703-812-8600	3200 Wilson Blvd	35
Cameron Perks	703-461-6900	4911 Brenman Park Dr	41
St Elmo's Coffee Pub	703-739-9268	2300 Mt Vernon Ave	43

Internet

	Phone	Address	Map
Eport World	202-232-2244	1719 Connecticut Ave NW	9
Eport World	202-464-7600	1030 19th St NW	9
Kramerbooks & Afterwords Café	202-387-3825	1517 Connecticut Ave NW	9

The DC area abounds with romping grounds for your favorite canine companion, many of them off-leash environments. And dog parks are people parks, too: singles mingle, moms commiserate, and bureaucrats share red-tape war stories. But be prepared for the occasional dogwalker, rescue-group affiliate, or canine resort recruiter to hit you with a pointed sales pitch. Some dog owners can be a tad overprotective, even when their dog is obviously digging, rolling, and roughhousing in the dust (usually, the dogs do a fine job of policing themselves). Other owners can get a bit peeved when their dogs are more interested in their fellow pooches than in playing fetch. But by and large, dog park visitors (canine and otherwise) are easygoing and personable. Larger parks, like Rock Creek or Meridian, offer dogs and owners some serious playing opportunities. It's still a hassle to find animal-friendly apartments, but as long as renters are willing to cough up a bit more monthly, there are options.

General Rules for Parks

- Dogs must be under the owner's/handler's control.
- Only three dogs per person are allowed.
- No female dogs in heat allowed.
- Only dogs four months and older allowed.
- Dogs must be legally licensed, vaccinated, and wearing both current tags.
- Dog owners/handlers must keep their dog(s) in view at all times.

- Dogs must not be allowed to bark incessantly or to the annoyance of the neighborhood.
- Dog owners/handlers must immediately pick up and dispose of, in trash receptacles, all dog feces.
- Aggressive dogs are not allowed at any time. Owners/handlers are legally responsible for their dog(s) and any injury caused by them.
- Dogs must be on leash when entering and exiting parks/fenced areas.

Washington DC	*Address*	*Comments*	*Map*
Walter Pierce Park	1967 Calvert St NW	Dogs love the access to Rock Creek	16
Stanton Park	Maryland Ave & 6th St NE	Unofficial dog area on Capitol Hill	3
Lincoln Dog Park	Capitol Hill, 11th St & N Carolina Ave SE	Busiest early mornings and early evenings. Water, benches, and lighting provided.	3
Congressional Cemetery	18th St SE & Potomac Ave	$100 dogwalker fee, plus $20 per dog buys unlimited off-leash roaming of the grass and tombstones.	5
Malcolm X/Meridian Hill	16th St b/w Euclid St NW & Union Ct NW	No off-leash.	16
Glover Park Dog Park	39th & W Sts NW	Popular weekday mornings and evenings.	18
Battery Kemble Park	Capitol Hill, MacArthur Blvd	Lots of wooded trails. Good parking. No off-leash.	32
Arlington			
Madison Community Ctr	3829 N Stafford St	Dogs not allowed on soccer field. Don't park in the back lot unless you want a ticket.	32
Glencarlyn Park	301 S Harrison St	Huge unfenced area near creek and woods. Restrooms, fountains, and picnic areas.	38
Barcroft Park	4100 S Four Mile Run Dr	Exercise area between bicycle path and water.	39
Benjamin Banneker Park	1600 N Sycamore St	Enclosed off-leash dog exercise area.	33
Fort Barnard	S Pollard St & S Walter Reed Dr	Fenced park with off-leash area.	39
Shirlington Park	2601 S Arlington Mill Dr	Fenced park with stream, paved trail, and water fountain.	39
Towers Park Dog Park	801 S Scott St	Fenced park with off-leash area.	40
Utah Park	3308 S Stafford St	Daytime hours only.	39
Clarendon Park	13th, Herndon, & Hartford Sts	Fenced area popular in the evenings.	35
Alexandria			
City Property	Chambliss St & Grigsby Ave	Off-leash exercise area.	38
North Fort Ward Park	Area east of entrance. 4401 W Braddock Rd	Off-leash exercise area.	39
Duke Street Dog Park	5005 Duke St	Fenced dog park.	41
City Property	SE corner of Wheeler Ave & Duke St	Off-leash exercise area.	42
Tarleton Park	Old Mill Run, west of Gordon St	Off-leash exercise area.	43
Ben Brenman Park	Backlick Creek	Fenced dog park.	-
City Property	SE corner of Braddock Rd & Commonwealth Ave	Off-leash exercise area.	44
Hoof's Run	E Commonwealth Ave, b/w Oak & Chapman St	Off-leash exercise area.	44
Del Ray Dog Park	Simpson Stadium & Monroe Ave	Fenced dog park.	45
Founders Park NE corner	Oronoco & Union Sts	Off-leash exercise area.	45
Montgomery Park	Fairfax & First Sts	Fenced dog park.	45
Powhatan Gateway	Henry & Powhatan Sts	Off-leash exercise area.	45
Windmill Hill Park	SW corner of Gibbon & Union Sts	Off-leash exercise area.	46
City Property	Edison St cul-de-sac	Off-leash exercise area.	43

General Information

DC Public Library Website:	www.dclibrary.org
Alexandria Library Website:	www.alexandria.lib.va.us
Arlington Library Website:	www.co.arlington.va.us/lib
Montgomery County Library Website:	www.montgomerylibrary.org

Overview

The Washington, DC, Library system revolves around the massive main **Martin Luther King (Map 1)** branch downtown. Large in size, scope, and ugliness, this eyesore with gives new meaning to the cliché, "Don't judge a book by its cover." Once you're able to overlook the homeless people taking naps outside (and often inside) the building, you'll appreciate its division of rooms by subject matter and the efficient, knowledgeable staff that can find you a 1988 *National Geographic* faster than you can say "Micronesia." Included in this mega-library are a room for the blind and handicapped, an adult literacy resource center, as well as meeting rooms (though an application for use is required). Additionally, the MLK houses the Washingtoniana Division, which is one of the largest collections of archived maps, clippings, and books about DC, and has a nifty guide on the 50 best books of local history—if you're into that sort of thing. If you don't have specific research needs, one of the other twenty-seven citywide branches, notably **Georgetown's (Map 8)**, are more pleasant places to spend an afternoon. Then again, if you have time to spare and want both extensive research capabilities and luxurious quarters, forget the local stuff and head over to the **US Library of Congress (Map 2)**.

If you hold a suburbanite's library card, the public libraries offered by Montgomery County and Northern Virginia are reasonably attractive and stocked, although you may feel like you're being cheated out of countless almanacs of information after seeing DC's MLK branch. If you can't find what you're looking for, you can reserve a title and have it delivered to your local branch, they'll even email you when it's ready for pick up.

■ = *Public* ■ = *By Appointment Only* ■ = *Other*

Type	Library	Address	Phone	Map
■	Alexandria Charles E Beatley Jr Central Library	5005 Duke St	703-519-5900	41
■	Alexandria Ellen Coolidge Burke Branch Library	4701 Seminary Rd	703-519-6000	41
■	Alexandria James M Duncan Branch Library	2501 Commonwealth Ave	703-838-4566	43
■	Alexandria Kate Waller Barrett Branch Library	717 Queen St	703-838-4555	46
■	Alexandria Law Library	520 King St, Room L-34	703-838-4077	46
■	American University Library	4400 Massachusetts Ave NW	202-885-3237	19
■	Anacostia Interim Library	1800 Good Hope Rd SE	202-715-7707	5
■	Arlington Central Library	1015 N Quincy St	703-228-5990	34
■	Arlington County Aurora Hills Library	735 18th St S	703-228-5715	40
■	Arlington Plaza Branch Library	2100 Clarendon Blvd	703-228-3352	36
■	Arthur R Ashe Jr Foreign Policy Library	1629 K St NW, Ste 1100	202-223-1960	9
■	Bethesda Library	7400 Arlington Rd	240-777-0970	29
■	Cherrydale Library	2190 Military Rd	703-228-6330	34
■	Chevy Chase Library	5625 Connecticut Ave NW	202-282-0021	28
■	Chevy Chase Library	8005 Connecticut Ave	240-773-9590	23
■	Cleveland Park Neighborhood Library	3310 Connecticut Ave NW	202-282-3080	17
■	Columbia Pike Library	816 S Walter Reed Dr	703-228-5710	37
■	Dibner Library	Constitution Ave NW & 12th St NW	202-633-3872	1
■	Federal Reserve Board Research & Law Libraries	20th St NW & Constitution Ave NW	202-452-3283	7
■	Federal Trade Commission Library	600 Pennsylvania Ave NW	202-326-2395	2

■ = Public ■ = By Appointment Only ■ = Other

Type	Library	Address	Phone	Map
■	Foundation Center	1627 K St NW, 3rd Fl	202-331-1400	9
■	General Services Administration Library	1800 F St NW, RM 1033	202-501-0788	7
■	Georgetown Library	3260 R St NW	202-282-0220	8
■	Glencarlyn Library	300 S Kensington St	703-228-6548	38
■	Howard University School of Business Library	2600 6th St NW	202-806-1561	15
■	Jeannette Rankin Library - US Institute of Peace	1200 17th St NW, Ste 200	202-429-3851	9
■	James Melville Gilliss Library	3450 Massachusetts Ave NW	202-762-1467	17
■	Juanita E Thornton Library	7420 Georgia Ave NW	202-541-6100	27
■	Lamond-Riggs Neighborhood Library	5401 S Dakota Ave NE	202-541-6255	14
■	Martin Luther King Jr Memorial Library	901 G St NW	202-727-0321	1
■	Mt Pleasant Neighborhood Library	3160 16th St NW	202-671-0200	16
■	NASA Headquarters Library	300 E St SW	202-358-0168	6
■	National Endowment for the Humanities Library	1100 Pennsylvania Ave NW	202-606-8244	1
■	National Geographic Society Library	1145 17th St NW	202-857-7783	9
■	National Transportation Library	1200 New Jersey Ave NW	202-366-0745	11
■	National Research Council Library	500 5th St NW, Room 304	202-334-2125	2
■	NOAA Central Library	1315 East West Hwy, SSMC3, 2nd Fl	301-713-2600	25
■	Northeast Neighborhood Library	330 7th St NE	202-698-3320	3
■	Office of Thrift Supervision Library	1700 G St NW	202-906-6470	1
■	Palisades Neighborhood Library	4901 V St NW	202-282-3139	18
■	Petworth Library	4200 Kansas Ave NW	202-243-1188	21
■	Polish Library in Washington	1503 21st St NW	202-466-2665	9
■	Ralph J Bunch Library	2201 C St NW, Room 3239	202-647-1099	7
■	Robert S Rankin Memorial Library	624 9th St NW, Rm 600	202-376-8110	1
■	Shirlington Library	4200 Campbell Ave	703-228-6545	39
■	Silver Spring Library	8901 Colesville Rd	240-773-9420	25
■	Southeast Neighborhood Library	403 7th St SE	202-698-3377	5
■	Southwest Neighborhood Library	900 Wesley Pl SW	202-724-4752	6
■	Takoma Park Neighborhood Library	416 Cedar St NW	202-576-7252	27
■	Tenley-Friendship Library	4450 Wisconsin Ave NW	202-282-3090	19
■	Treasury Library	1500 Pennsylvania Ave NW, Rm 1314	202-622-0990	1
■	US Department of Commerce Library	1401 Constitution Ave NW	202-482-5511	1
■	US Department of Energy Library	1000 Independence Ave SW, RM GA-138	202-586-3112	1
■	US Department of the Interior Library	1849 C St NW	202-208-5815	7
■	US Housing & Urban Development Library	451 7th St SW	202-708-2370	6
■	US Library of Congress	101 Independence Ave SE	202-707-8000	2
■	US Senate Library	Russell Senate Office Bldg, B15	202-224-7106	2
■	Watha T Daniel Branch Library	1701 8th St NW	202-671-0267	10
■	West End Neighborhood Library	1101 24th St NW	202-724-8707	9
■	Westover Library	1644 N McKinley Rd	703-228-5260	33
■	Woodridge Library	1801 Hamlin St NE	202-541-6226	13

Computer Services | Phone
Action Business Equipment	703-716-4691
On Call 25/8	202-625-2511
On Call 25/8	202-625-2511

Delivery/Messengers | Phone
QMS	240-223-3600
Washington Courier	202-775-1500

Plumbers | Phone
Capitol Area Plumbing & Heating	301-345-7667
John G Webster	202-783-6100
KC Plumbing Services	800-823-4911
Plumbline Plumbers	202-543-9515
Roto-Rooter	202-726-8888
Smallenbroek Plumbing & Heating	202-237-6400
Vito	800-438-8486

Towing | Phone
Emergency-1	202-529-2205
Hook Em Up Towing	202-528-8435
Pro-Lift	202-546-7877

Locksmiths | Phone
Berry's Locksmith	202-667-3680
District Lock	202-547-8236
Doors and Devices	800-865-6253
Locksmith 24 Hours	202-636-4540
Pop-A-Lock	202-331-2929

Copy Shops

	Address	Phone	Map
Reliable Copy	555 12th St NW	202-347-6644	1
Superior Group	1401 New York Ave NW	202-393-1600	1
Whitmont Legal Copying	1725 I St NW	202-222-0147	1
Imagenet	2000 M St NW	202-872-0700	9
Sequential	1615 L St NW	202-293-0500	9
Barrister Copy Solutions	1090 Vermont Ave NW	202-289-7279	10
FedEx Kinko's	1407 East West Hwy	301-587-6565	25
FedEx Kinko's	4809 Bethesda Ave	301-656-0577	29
FedEx Kinko's	2300 Clarendon Blvd	703-525-9224	35
FedEx Kinko's	3515C S Jefferson St	703-379-0909	38
FedEx Kinko's	1601 Crystal Sq Arc	703-413-8011	40
FedEx Kinko's	685 N Washington St	703-739-0783	45

Restaurants

	Address	Phone	Map
Annie's Paramount	1609 17th St NW	202-232-0395	9
The Diner	2453 18th St NW	202-232-8800	16
Osman's and Joe's Steak 'n Egg Kitchen	4700 Wisconsin Ave NW	202-686-1201	19
American City Diner	5532 Connecticut Ave NW	202-244-1949	28
Bob and Edith's Diner	2310 Columbia Pike	703-920-6103	37
Tastee Diner	8601 Cameron St	301-589-8171	25
Tastee Diner	7731 Woodmont Ave	301-652-3970	22
Waffle Shop	3864 Mt Vernon Ave	703-836-8851	43

Gas Stations

	Address	Map		Address	Map
Exxon	200 Massachusetts Ave NE	3	Exxon	4501 14th St NW	21
Amoco	1950 Benning Rd NE	4	Exxon	7975 Old Georgetown Rd	22
Exxon	2651 Benning Rd NE	4	Exxon	9336 Georgia Ave	24
Exxon	1022 M St SE	5	Exxon	8301 Fenton St	25
Exxon	1201 Pennsylvania Ave SE	5	Exxon	8384 Colesville Rd	25
Exxon	1001 S Capitol St SW	6	Amoco	6300 Georgia Ave	27
Exxon	950 S Capitol St SE	6	Amoco	7605 Georgia Ave NW	27
Amoco	2715 Pennsylvania Ave NW	8	Exxon	6350 Georgia Ave NW	27
Exxon	1601 Wisconsin Ave NW	8	Exxon	7401 Georgia Ave NW	27
Exxon	3607 M St NW	8	Shell	6419 Georgia Ave NW	27
Mobil	2200 P St NW	9	Exxon	5521 Connecticut Ave NW	28
Mobil	1442 U St NW	10	Exxon	7340 Wisconsin Ave	29
Amoco	400 Rhode Island Ave NE	11	Texaco	5501 Lee Hwy	33
Amoco	45 Florida Ave NE	11	Exxon	660 N Glebe Rd	34
Exxon	1 Florida Ave NE	11	Exxon	2410 Lee Hwy	35
Amoco	1201 Bladensburg Rd NE	12	Exxon	1824 Wilson Blvd	36
Exxon	1925 Bladensburg Rd NE	12	Exxon	1001 S Glebe Rd	37
Amoco	2210 Bladensburg Rd NE	13	Mobil	3100 Columbia Pike	37
Amoco	3701 12th St NE	14	Exxon	4368 King St	39
Exxon	1020 Michigan Ave NE	14	Mobil	4154 S Four Mile Run Dr	39
Exxon	5501 S Dakota Ave NE	14	Exxon	2720 S Glebe Rd	40
Amoco	3426 Georgia Ave NW	15	Exxon	501 S Van Dorn St	41
Exxon	3540 14th St NW	15	Mobil	190 S Whiting St	41
Exxon	1827 Adams Mill Rd NW	16	Exxon	2320 Jefferson Davis Hwy	43
Exxon	4244 Wisconsin Ave NW	19	Exxon	703 N Washington St	45
Amoco	5001 Connecticut Ave NW	20	Exxon	834 N Washington St	45
Exxon	3535 Connecticut Ave NW	20	Exxon	501 S Washington St	46
Exxon	5030 Connecticut Ave NW	20	Exxon	700 S Patrick St	46

Gym

	Address	Phone	Map
Third Power Fitness	2007 18th St NW	202-483-8400	9

Veterinarian

	Address	Phone	Map
Friendship Hospital for Animals	4105 Brandywine St NW	202-363-7300	19

Pharmacies

	Address	Phone	Prescription counter closes	Map
CVS*	801 7th St NW	202-842-3627	7 pm	2
CVS*	1403 Wisconsin Ave NW	202-337-4848	10 pm	8
CVS	2240 M St NW	202-296-9876	24-hrs	9
CVS	6 Dupont Cir NW	202-785-1466	24-hrs	9
Rite Aid*	1815 Connecticut Ave NW	202-332-1718	12 am	9
CVS*	1199 Vermont Ave NW	202-628-0720	12 am	10
CVS	4555 Wisconsin Ave	202-537-1587	24-hrs	19
CVS	7809 Wisconsin Ave	301-986-9144	24-hrs	22
CVS	1290 East West Hwy	301-588-6261	24-hrs	25
Rite Aid*	1411 East West Hwy	301-563-6935	12 am	25
CVS	6514 Georgia Ave NW	202-829-5234	24-hrs	27
CVS	6917 Arlington Rd	301-656-2522	24-hrs	29
Giant Food Pharmacy*	7142 Arlington Rd	301-492-5161	10 pm	29
Harris Teeter Pharmacy*	2425 N Harrison St	703-532-8663	9 pm	33
Harris Teeter Pharmacy*	600 N Glebe Rd	703-526-9100	9 pm	34
CVS	3133 Lee Hwy	703-522-0260	24-hrs	35
CVS*	2121 15th St N	703-243-4239	10 pm	36
CVS	3535 S Jefferson St	703-820-6360	24-hrs	38
Giant Food Pharmacy*	3480 S Jefferson St	703-931-1333	12 am	38
CVS*	2400 Jefferson Davis Hwy	703-418-0813	10 pm	40
CVS	5101 Duke St	703-823-7430	24-hrs	41
CVS	3130 Duke St	703-823-3584	24-hrs	42
CVS*	415 Monroe Ave	703-683-4433	24-hrs	43

Hospitals

As hyper-stressed, Type-A workaholics, most Washingtonians are ripe for coronary disease, so it's a good thing there are many area hospitals to offer us recourse. Although district financing snarls have led to recent shutdowns -- most notably DC General Hospital— the District nevertheless remains equipped with state-of-the-art medical facilities ready to respond to emergencies of presidential magnitude (Dick Cheney is strategically located between **Georgetown (Map 18)** and **Sibley (Map 32)** Hospitals).

The area's hospitals vary in terms of the level of service they offer. Stagger into some ERs, and unless your clothes have fresh blood stains, you won't be seeing a doctor until you have memorized the theme song to *Days of Our Lives*. Other facilities treat patients like hotel guests. At the recently refurbished **Virginia Hospital Center (Map 34)**, rooms are set up to offer remarkable Arlington views, and in-patients are delivered meals by workers who sport bow ties and studs. Sibley is your average Northwest hospital, with a relatively comfortable waiting room, usually tuned to CNN, and nurses who squawk to their patients about which congressman they shot up with saline the week prior.

Many medical people assert that the region's top docs reside at **Washington Hospital Center (Map 14)**, although Washington Hospital *City* is a more appropriate title. Practically every disease you can get has its own building devoted to it, and the relatively small Irving Street becomes somewhat of a highway off-ramp just to allow access to this behemoth of medical practitioners. Allow an extra hour just to park and figure out how to navigate its labyrinthine interior structure. And while we're on the subject of parking… it's never free, not even for cancer boy.

Emergency Rooms	Address	Phone	Map
George Washington University Hospital	900 23rd St NW	202-715-4000	7
Howard University Hospital	2041 Georgia Ave NW	202-865-6100	10
Children's National Medical	111 Michigan Ave NW	202-884-5000	14
Providence	1150 Varnum St NE	202-269-7000	14
Washington Hospital Center	110 Irving St NW	202-877-7000	14
Georgetown University Hospital	3800 Reservoir Rd NW	202-444-2000	18
National Naval Medical Center	8901 Wisconsin Ave	301-295-4611	22
Suburban	8600 Old Georgetown Rd	301-896-3100	22
Washington Adventist	7600 Carroll Ave	301-891-7600	26
Sibley Memorial	5255 Loughboro Rd NW	202-537-4000	32
Virginia Hospital Center, Arlington	1701 N George Mason Dr	703-558-5000	34
Northern Virginia Community	601 S Carlin Springs Rd	703-671-1200	38
Inova Alexandria	4320 Seminary Rd	703-504-3000	42

Other Hospitals	Address	Phone	Map
HSC Pediatric Center	1731 Bunker Hill Rd NE	202-832-4400	13
National Rehabilitation Hospital	102 Irving St NW	202-877-1000	14
VA Medical Center	50 Irving St NW	202-745-8000	14

Overview

There's always some mass gathering in Washington, DC; from inauguration demonstrations to flower festivals, DC has it all. The best events are free and easily accessible by mass transit.

Event	Approx. Dates	For more info…	Comments
New Year's Eve	December 31/January 1		Celebrate the new year with music art, and bitter freezing cold.
Martin Luther King's Birthday	Observed January 15	www.whitehouse.gov/kids/ martinlutherkingjrday.html	Music, speakers, and a recital of the "I Have a Dream" speech on the Lincoln Memorial steps.
Robert E Lee's Birthday	January 19	703-235-1530	Yes, victors write the history books, but some losers' popularity endures. Robert E Lee Memorial, Arlington Cemetery.
Chinese New Year	February 18	703-851-5685	Can you IMAGINE the debauchery of a 15-day American New Year's bash? Check it out on H Street in Chinatown.
Black History Month Celebration	February	www.si.edu	African-American history at the Smithsonian.
Abraham Lincoln's Birthday	Observed February 12	202-426-6841	Reading of Gettysburg Address in front of the city's favorite marble hero.
George Washington's Birthday Parade	President's Day, February 19	800-388-9119	Parade and party in Alexandria for the city's other favorite guy.
St. Patrick's Day Parade	March 17	www.dcstpatsparade.com	Celebration of all things Irish in DC: music, food, oh, and beer, too.
Smithsonian Kite Festival	Late March–early April	www.kitefestival.org	Watch adults attack kiddie play like a combat sport.
Washington Home & Garden Show	Mid-March	www.flowergardenshow.com	Check out the flora that actually enjoys this climate.
National Cherry Blossom Festival	Late March to – mid-April	www.nationalcherryblossom festival.org	One of the can't-misses…problem is the tourists think so, too.
Filmfest DC	April	www.filmfestdc.org	For once, see a flick before it opens in NYC.
White House Spring Garden Tours	Mid-April	www.whitehouse.gov	No politics, just flowers.
Shakespeare's Birthday	April 23	202-544-4600	To go or not to go. That is the question. Folger Shakespeare Library.
White House Easter Egg Roll	Mid-April	www.whitehouse.gov	No politics, just eggs.
Department of Defense/ Joint Services Open House	Mid-May	301-981-4600	The country flexes its muscles with an air show and other military might. FedEx Field.
St. Sophia Greek Festival	Mid-May	202-333-4730	Big, fat, Greek festival.
National Symphony Orchestra 5 Memorial Day Weekend Concert		www.kennedy-center.org/nso	Easy on the ears—and wallet; it's free.
Memorial Day Ceremonies at Arlington Cemetery	May 26	www.arlingtoncemetery.org	Ceremonies at JFK's grave and the Tomb of the Unknown Soldier.
Memorial Day Ceremonies at the Vietnam Veterans Memorial	May 26	www.nps.gov/vive	Solemn memorial.
Memorial Day Jazz Festival	May 26	703-883-4686	Jazz in Alexandria.
Virginia Gold Cup	Early May	www.vagoldcup.com	Horse race on the same day as the Kentucky Derby. Someone fire the marketing department.
Dance Africa DC	Early June	202-269-1600	A feat of feet.
Dupont-Kalorama Museum Walk Weekend	First weekend in June	www.dkmuseums.com/ walk.html	Free admission to the city's smaller, quirkier, pricier exhibits.
AFI SilverDocs	Mid June	www.silverdocs.com	Hollywood takes over Silver Spring for this documentary film festival.

Event	Approx. Dates	For more info…	Comments
DC Caribbean Carnival Extravaganza	Late June	www.dccaribbeancarnival.com	Caribbean music, food, and outrageous costumes.
Capital Pride	Early June	www.capitalpride.org	Huge, fun, funky, out, and proud.
Red Cross Waterfront Festival	Mid-June	www.waterfrontfestival.org	If you fall out of the canoe, Clara Barton may rescue you.
National Capital Barbecue Battle	Late June	www.barbecuebattle.com	Hot and sticky BBQ on a hot and sticky day.
Smithsonian Folklife Festival	Late June – early July	www.folklife.si.edu	All the culture and crowds that can be packed into two weeks.
Independence Day Celebration	July 4	www.july4thparade.com	July 4th in America-town. Check out the parade. The fireworks are a must.
Bastille Day	July 14		No time to order freedom fries.
Virginia Scottish Games	Late July	www.vascottishgames.org	Kilts and haggis everywhere!
Hispanic Festival	Late July		Latin American celebration at the Washington Monument.
Capital Fringe Festival	Late July	www.capfringe.org	DC's modest attempt at cutting-edge theater.
Annual Soap Box Derby	Early June	www.dcsoapboxderby.org	The one day parents let their kids fly down city streets in rickety wooden boxes.
Georgia Avenue Day	Late August		Parades, music, and food from the southern US and Africa.
National Frisbee Festival	Late August		Don't fight it, join it.
National Army Band's 1812 Overture Performance	Late August	www.whitehouse.gov	No politics, just patriotic music.
DC Blues Festival	Early September	www.dcblues.org	Rock Creek Park gets down and depressed.
Kennedy Center Open House	Early September	www.kennedy-center.org	Check out the terrace and the Kennedy sculpture without shelling out for the opera.
Adams Morgan Day	Early September	www.adamsmorganday.org	Neighborhood that gets jammed nightly, gets jammed while sun's up.
White House Fall Garden Tour	Late October	www.whitehouse.gov	No politics, just leaf peeping.
Reel Affirmations Film Festival	Mid-October	www.reelaffirmations.org	Like Filmfest DC, except much more gay.
Marine Corps Marathon	Late October	www.marinemarathon.com	26 miles of asphalt and cheers.
Theodore Roosevelt's Birthday	October 27	www.theodoreroosevelt.org	Party for one of the other giant heads in North Dakota.
Civil War Living History Day	Early November	703-838-4848	The culmination of reenactment-stickler bickering. Fort Ward Museum.
Veteran's Day Ceremonies	November 11	www.arlingtoncemetery.org	Military ceremony in Arlington Cemetery.
Alexandria Antiques Show	Mid-November	703-549-5811	Expensive old stuff.
Jewish Film Festival	Late November/ Early December	www.wjff.org	Like Filmfest DC, except much more Jewish.
Kennedy Center Holiday Celebration	December	www.kennedy-center.org	X-mas revelry.
Kwanzaa Celebration	December	www.si.edu	Celebration at the Smithsonian.
National Christmas Tree Lighting/ Pageant of Peace	Mid-December to January 1	www.whitehouse.gov	Trees, menorahs, & Yule logs get lit at the White House Ellipse.
Washington National Cathedral Christmas Celebration and Services	December 24–25	202-537-6247	Humongous tree from Nova Scotia.
White House Christmas Candlelight Tours	Christmastime	www.whitehouse.gov	Still no politics, just religion.

Yes, DC's a great city for lessons in history and civics, but sometimes the kids just aren't in the mood for another tutorial on the system of checks and balances. If you check out some of the destinations on this list, you'll discover there's life beyond the Mall when it comes to entertaining your mini-yous.

The Best of the Best

★ **Best Kid-Friendly Restaurant:** Café Deluxe (3228 Wisconsin Ave NW, 202-686-2233; 400 First St SE, 202-546-6768; 4910 Elm St, Bethesda, 301-656-3131). Parents breathe a sigh of relief when they walk into a restaurant and see that the tablecloth is paper and the table is littered with crayons. At Café Deluxe, your kids can perfect their masterpieces while munching on entrees like buttered noodles, PB&J, or cheese quesadillas. The prices reflect that your companions are only half-size: Children's menu prices are only $5.95 a pop. Runner up: ESPN Zone (555 12th St NW, 202-783-3776). This boys' night out sports bar makes for an unexpectedly family-friendly restaurant during daylights hours, complete with a rookies' menu and all the arcade games their little hearts could desire.

★ **Quaintest Activity:** Canal Boat Rides (1057 Thomas Jefferson St NW, 202-653-5190). Take a boat ride along the historic C&O canal in a boat pulled by mules. Park rangers in period clothing describe what life was like for families who lived and worked on the canal during the 1870s. Tours (one hour long) are held Wednesday–Friday at 11 am and 3 pm, and Saturday and Sunday at 11 am, 1:30 pm, 3 pm, and 4:30 pm. The boats fill up on a first-come-first-served basis. $5 for visitors aged four and above. Children three and under ride for free.

★ **Funnest Park:** Rock Creek Park (5200 Glover Rd NW, 202-895-6070). An area of Rock Creek Park located on Beach Drive goes by the name of Candy Cane City—'nuf said. Leland Street is good for picnicking and has a playground, basketball courts, and tennis courts. Children's park programs include planetarium shows, animal talks, arts & crafts projects, and exploratory hikes.

★ **Coolest Bookstore:** A Likely Story Children's Bookstore (1555 King St, Alexandria, 703-836-2498, www.alikelystorybooks.com). The bookstore hosts weekly story times, writing workshops for kids, and special events almost daily during the summer. Story time for children ages two and up is held every Wednesday at 11 am. Other events include foreign-language story time and sing-a-long story times.

★ **Best Rainy Day Activity:** Smithsonian Museum of Natural History (10th St & Constitution Ave NW, 202-633-1000). The new Kenneth E. Behring Family Hall of Mammals is open! If the kids aren't too freaked out by life-sized stuffed animals, check out the 274 new taxidermied mounts. The IMAX theater is always a hit with kids and parents alike on rainy afternoons. The timeless kid-appeal of dinosaur exhibits also keeps the little ones entertained (if they weren't recently dragged here on a school trip). Admission is free, and tickets are not required for entry. The museum is open daily 10 am–5:30 pm (and until 7:30 pm during summertime), except on federal holidays.

★ **Sunny Day Best Bet:** National Zoo (3001 Connecticut Ave, 202-673-4800, nationalzoo.si.edu). This free and easily accessible zoo is guaranteed to be the best park stroll you've ever taken. Beyond the pandas and apes, there's also a Kids' Farm with cows, donkeys, goats, chickens, and ducks. Summer camps and classes are available to Friends of the National Zoo Family Members. A $60 membership also includes free parking while visiting the zoo, a 10% discount at National Zoo stores, opportunities to attend summer camps, classes and workshops as well as discounts on tickets to popular zoo events. The zoo is open daily (6 am–8 pm April 2 to October 28, 6 am–6 pm October 29 to March 10), and admission is always free. April–October buildings are open 10 am–6 pm, November–April 10 am–4:30 pm.

★ **Neatest Store:** Barston's Child's Play (5536 Connecticut Ave NW, 202-244-3602). The store's long, narrow aisles are stocked with games, toys, puzzles, trains, costumes, art supplies, and books. It's never too early to start grooming a true shopaholic.

Parks for Playing

• **Cleveland Park** (3409 Macomb St NW). Climb a spider web, climb a wall, or catch a train. The park has separate play areas for younger and older children, picnic tables, basketball courts, a baseball field, and a rec center.

• **East Potomac Park** (Ohio Drive SW). Always a good bet with its miniature golf course, public pool, picnic facilities, and playground at the southern tip. This is an absolute must during Cherry Blossom season.

• **Friendship Park** (4500 Van Ness St NW, 202-282-2198). Plenty of slides, tunnels, swings, and climbing structures, as well as basketball and tennis courts, softball/soccer fields, and a rec center. If you need a break, there's plenty of shade and picnic tables. A.k.a. "Turtle Park."

• **Glen Echo Park** (7300 MacArthur Blvd, Glen Echo, MD) Unique Calder-esque playground, antique carousel, and two children's theaters make this restored deco-era amusement park worth the short drive for families.

• **Kalorama Park** (19th St & Kalorama Rd NW). While the shade is limited here, this is a large playground with a fence dividing big-kid from little-kid playgrounds.

• **Marie Reed Recreation Center** (2200 Champlain St NW, 202-673-7768). Plenty of shady areas to rest your old bones while the kids are devouring the jungle gym, slides, tennis courts, and basketball courts.

• **Montrose Park** (R & 30th Sts NW, 202-426-6827). For you: lots of open space, a picnicking area, and tennis courts. For your kids: swings, monkey bars, a sandbox, and a maze.

- **Rose Park** (26th & O Sts NW, 202-333-4946). Home to Little League games and the Georgetown Farmers Market, this park has plenty of green and a massive, wonderful sandbox.
- **Upton Hill Regional Park** (6060 Wilson Blvd. Arlington, VA 703-534-3437) Worth the short drive to Arlington for the newly renovated public pool with water slides, huge mini-golf course, batting cages, and small playground.

Rainy Day Activities

Rain ain't no big thang in the city of free museums, many of which cater to the height- and attention-challenged.

Museums with Kid Appeal

- **National Air and Space Museum** (Independence Ave & 4th St SW, 202-633-1000). Can you go wrong in museum that sells astronauts' freeze-dried ice cream? Kids can walk through airplanes and spaceships. Check out the Einstein Planetarium and the IMAX Theater. Open daily 10 am–5:30 pm, closed Christmas Day. Admission is free but does not include special events or activities.

- **International Spy Museum** (800 F St NW, 202-393-7798, www.spymuseum.org). The sleek exhibits filled with high-tech gadgets and fascinating real-life spy stories make the hefty admissions tag totally worth it. Special family programs include making and breaking secret codes and disguise-creation workshops. Twice a year, the museum even offers a top-secret overnight "Operation Secret Slumber," which provides kids with a "behind the scenes" look at the life of spy. The museum is open daily, but hours vary according to season. Children under five enter free, adults pay $18, kids (5–11) pay $15, and seniors (65+) pay $17.

- **National Museum of American History** (14th St and Constitution Ave NW, 202-357-2700, americanhistory. si.edu). While your kids will certainly love a glimpse of Dorothy's ruby red slippers, the hands-on section of this museum is where they'll *really* want to be. The Hands-On History Room allows kids to gin cotton, send a telegraph, or say "hello" in Cherokee. The Hands-On Science Room, for children over five, lets kids take intelligence tests, separate food dyes in beverages, or use lasers to see light. Museum admission is free, but tickets (which are also free) are required for the hands-on rooms during weekends and busy hours. The museum is open daily 10 am–5:30 pm (and until 6:30 pm during summertime), except for Christmas.

- **National Museum of Natural History** (10th and Constitution Ave, N.W. 202-633-1000) This is the original kids' museum, starting with the huge stuffed mastodon in the lobby. After you take in the mandatory t-rex skeletons, head for the live Insect Zoo and Discovery Room, which have interactive, hands-on exhibits for your budding naturalist. Older kids also like the Hope Diamond and gemstone exhibits. There's a great gift shop perfect for relieving kids of their allowance money, and an IMAX theater and public cafeteria, too. Free. Open every day but Christmas, from 10 am–5:30 pm (and until 7:30 during summertime).

- **Freer Gallery** (1050 Independence Ave SW, 202-633-4880, www.asia.si.edu). Give your kids a taste of Asia with the Freer Gallery's Imaginasia program. Children from ages six to fourteen find their way through exhibitions on Japanese wood block prints or Islamic illuminated manuscripts (with the guiding hand of an activity book) then create an appropriate art project with their own two hands. No reservations required for groups smaller than eight, and Imaginasia will give your little ones a unique glimpse of the Far East on the Mall. The museum is open from 10 am to 5:30 pm, except for Christmas.

Other Indoor Distractions

- **Adventure Theatre** (7300 MacArthur Blvd, Glen Echo, MD, 301-320-5331, www.adventuretheatre.org) Actors and puppets stage fables, musicals, and classic fairytales on the DC area's longest running children's stage. You can hardly ask for a nicer setting than Glen Echo Park, also home to the kid-friendly Puppet Co. Playhouse.

- **Bureau of Engraving and Printing** (14th & C Sts, SW, 202-874-3019, www.moneyfactory.com). We're all used to seeing money spent. At this museum, you can watch how money is made, although your kids will probably be most interested in watching the destruction of old money. Admission is free, but tickets are required March–August. General tours (the only way to see the museum) are given every 15 minutes from 10 am to 2 pm, Monday through Friday.

- **Discovery Theater** (1100 Jefferson Dr SW, 202-357-1500, www.discoverytheater.org). Puppet shows, dance performances, and storytelling all under one roof. Performances are given daily at 10 am and 11:30 am, Monday through Friday, and Saturday at 11:30 am and 1 pm. Shows cost $6 for adults and $5 for children, with special group rates available. Kids ages 4 to 13 can also join the Young Associates Program, where they can learn to animate clay figures or make their own puppets.

- **Imagination Stage** (4908 Auburn Ave, Bethesda, MD, 301-280-1660, www.imaginationstage.org). Help your kids enjoy the magic of theater by taking them to a show at the Imagination Stage. Your family might see anything from a hip-hop version of a favorite picture book to a fairytale musical. This non-profit organization has been putting on the hits for over twenty years now.

- **Kettler Capitals Ice Complex** (627 N Glebe Rd, Arlington, VA, 703-243-8855). Vast, spanking-new ice complex on the roof of Metro-accessible Ballston Mall is area's largest, close-in ice arena. Built as a practice rink for the Washington Capitals hockey team, it offers public skate times, birthday parties, and classes.

- **Now This!** (Blair Mansion, 7111 Eastern Ave, Silver Spring, MD, 202-364-8292, www.nowthisimprov.com). The city's only improvised children's theater group entertains kids every Sunday afternoon with impromptu storytelling, songwriting, and comedy. This is a great place to take a birthday boy or girl on their special day, as the cast will write them their very own birthday tune. Lunch is served at 1 pm and the show begins at 1:30 pm. The lunch + show birthday package costs $25, show + cake is $14, or the troupe will come to your house and put on a 4-performer show. $425 for a 30 minute show, and for 45 minutes, $500.

- **Puppet Co. Playhouse** (7300 MacArthur Blvd, Glen, MD, 301-320-6668, www.thepuppetco.org). Set in the most enchanting amusement park turned arts center, the Puppet Co. Playhouse is just one piece of magic in Glen Echo. Master puppeteers wield rod puppets in front of gorgeous sets, leaving kids and adults wide-eyed and bushy-tailed.

Outdoor and Educational

Just 'cause you want to play outside doesn't mean you have to act like a hooligan! Here's a list of outdoor activities that mix culture with athleticism and offer up some surprisingly original forms of entertainment:

- **Butler's Orchard** (22200 Davis Mill Rd, Germantown, MD, 301-972-3299, www.butlersorchard.com). Teach those city slickers that apples come from trees, not Safeway! And there are Golden Deliciouses and Macintoshes and Granny Smiths and Galas! Kids and adults can pick their own crops year round (nearly) at Butler's Orchard. The berries taste sweeter when you've picked them yourself, and autumn events include hay rides and the annual pumpkin festival. Pay for what you pick by the pound.

- **Discovery Creek Children's Museum of Washington** (The Stable at Glen Echo Park, 7300 MacArthur Blvd, Glen Echo, MD, 202-337-5111, www.discoverycreek.org). Every weekend is different at Discovery Creek, an indoors/outdoors learning center designed to help kids appreciate and protect the environment. Blaze a trail, come face to face with a curious animal, or make a mess on an art project. Kids and adults can turn up anytime on Saturdays and Sundays from 10 am to 3 pm. Admission is $5 for everyone, $3 for seniors 65 and over, and free for children under two.

- **Fort Ward** (4301 West Braddock Rd, Alexandria, 703-838-4848, www.fortward.org). The best preserved Union fort in DC. Picnic areas are available, and the on-site museum has a Civil War Kids' Camp for ages 8 to 12 during the summer. The museum is open Tuesday through Saturday 9 am–5 pm and Sunday 12 pm–5 pm. Admission is free. The park is open daily from 9 am until sunset.

- **Leesburg Animal Park** (19270 James Monroe Highway, Leesburg, VA, 703-433-0002 www.leesburganimalpark.com). The trip across the river is worth it—particularly if you get the pleasure of riding the $4 White's Ferry ride from Maryland to Virginia. Little ones can feed baby bear cubs by bottle or pet free-ranging emus; animals are both domestic and exotic. Kids 2 to 12 gain admis-sion for $7.95 ($9.95 for a VIP pass that includes a souvenir cup of food and a pony ride), and adults pay $9.95.

- **National Arboretum** (3501 New York Ave NE, 202-245-2726, www.usna.usda.gov). Covering 466 acres, the National Arboretum is the ultimate backyard. Picnicking is encouraged in the National Grove of State Trees picnic area, and the original columns from the Capitol dome live here at the Arb on a picturesque, grassy knoll. A 40-minute open-air tram ride is available and advised if you want to see everything. The Arboretum is open daily 8 am–5 pm, except Christmas. Admission is free, but the tram will cost you $4 for adults and $2 for children 4–16.

- **Sculpture Garden Ice-Skating Rink** (7th St & Constitution Ave NW, 202-289-3360). The Sculpture Garden's rink is specially designed to allow views of the garden's contemporary sculptures while skating. It's like subliminally feeding your kids culture while they think they're just playing. Regular admission costs $7 for a two-hour session, and children, students, and seniors pay $6. Skate rental costs $3 and a locker rental costs 50¢.

Classes

- **Arlington Center for Dance** (3808 Wilson Blvd. Arlington, VA 703-522-2414 www.arldance.org) Fundamental dance instruction, with a strong focus on ballet, and annual performances of the *Nutcracker*.

- **Ballet Petite** (Several throughout DC area, 301-229-6882, www.balletpetite.com). Fundamental dance instruction mixed with costumes, story telling, props, acting, and music.

- **Budding Yogis** (5615 39th St NW, 202-686-1104, www.buddingyogis.com). Yoga for kids, teens, and adults. Special summer programs available.

- **Capitol Hill Arts Workshop** (545 7th St SE, 202-547-6839, www.chaw.org). Classes for children in art disciplines, tumbling, and Tae Kwon Do. If your kids are precociously cool, sign them up for the jazz/hip-hop class and watch them perform a Hip-Hop Nutcracker in December.

- **Clay Café** (101 N Maple Ave, Falls Church, VA 703 534-7600). Paint your own pottery and other hands-on crafts. Classes and summer camps for kids.

- **Dance Place** (3225 8th St NE, 202-269-1600, www.danceplace.org). Creative movement, hip-hop, and African dance instruction for kids.

- **Imagination Stage** (4908 Auburn Ave, Bethesda, MD, 301-961-6060, www.imaginationstage.org). Classes in music, dance, and theater for kids and teens. Three-week summer camps also available.

- **Joy of Motion** (5207 Wisconsin Ave NW, 202-362-3042; 1643 Connecticut Ave, 202-387-0911, www.joyofmotion.org). Creative movement and fundamental dance instruction for children.

- **Kettler Capitals Ice Complex.** (627 N Glebe Rd, Arlington, VA, 703-243-8855). Year-round skating classes and even summer camps for kids trying to beat the heat.

- **Kids Moving Company** (7475 Wisconsin Ave, Bethesda, MD, 301-656-1543, www.kidsmovingco.com) Creative movement classes for children nine months to eight years in a studio with a full-sized trampoline.

- **Kumon Math and Reading Program** (6831 Wisconsin Ave, Bethesda, MD, 301-652-1234, www.kumon.com). An after-school learning program in math and reading.

- **Levine School of Music** (4 locations in NW, SE, VA, and MD, www.levineschool.org). One of the country's largest community music schools offers fundamental music instruction to toddlers through pre-professionals. Private lessons, group classes, and summer camps available.

- **Music Tots** (4238 Wilson Blvd, Arlington, VA, 703-266-4571, www.musictots.com). Instruction in music, rhythm, and sound for children under five.

- **Musikids** (4900 Auburn Ave, Ste. 100, Bethesda, MD, 301-215-7946, www.musikids.com) Music and movement classes for newborns and toddlers.

- **Pentagon Row Ice-Skating** (1201 S Joyce St, Arlington, VA, 703-418-6666, www.pentagonrow.com). Skating lessons and birthday parties are available November–March.

- **Rock Creek Horse Center** (5100 Glover Rd NW, 202-362-0117, www.rockcreekhorsecenter.com). Riding lessons, trail rides, summer day camp, and equestrian team training. Weekly group lessons $50/hour, private lessons $90/hour, and one-week summer camp sessions cost $500.

- **Rock Creek Tennis Center** (16th & Kennedy Sts NW, 202-722-5949, www.rockcreektennis.com). Five-week weekend tennis courses available for children at beginner and intermediate levels.

- **Round House Theatre** (4545 East West Hwy, Bethesda, MD, 240-644-1099, www.roundhousetheatre.org). The theater has a year-round drama school and an arts-centered summer day camp program.

- **Sportrock Climbing Center** (5308 Eisenhower Ave, Alexandria, VA, 703-212-7625, www.sportrock.com). Kids learn to climb. 6- to 12-year-olds have the run of the place 6:30 pm–8 pm on Fridays. $18 for adults, $10 for children (12 and under). Hours: Tues–Fri: 12 pm–11 pm; Sat–Sun: 12 pm–8 pm.

- **Sur La Table** (1101 S Joyce St, Arlington, 703-414-3580, www.surlatable.com). At Sur La Table's junior cooking classes, kids are encouraged to (gasp!) play with food. Classes are for children aged 6–12 and groups are small and well organized.

- **YMCA of Metropolitan Washington** (numerous branches, 202-232-6700, www.ymcadc.org). Youth and teen sports to spend all that hyperactive energy—particularly in the swimming pool!

- **Young Playwrights' Theatre** (2437 15th St, NW, 202-387-9173, www.youngplaywrightstheatre.org). Programs for children from fourth grade and up that encourage literacy, playwriting, and community engagement.

Shopping Essentials

- **Aladdin's Lamp Bookstore** · 2499 N Harrison St, Arlington, VA · 703-241-8281
- **Barnes & Noble** (books) · 3040 M St NW · 202-965-9880
  - 555 12th St NW · 202-347-0176
  - 3651 Jefferson Davis Hwy, Alexandria, VA · 703-299-9124
  - 4801 Bethesda Ave, Bethesda, MD · 301-986-1761
- **Barston's Child's Play** (everything kids love) · 5536 Connecticut Ave NW · 202-244-3602
- **Borders** (books) · 600 14th St NW · 202-737-1385
  - 1801 K St NW · 202-466-4999 ·
  5333 Wisconsin Ave NW · 202-686-8270
  - 1201 Hayes St, Arlington, VA · 703-418-0166
- **Children's Place** (kids' clothes) · Pentagon City, 1100 S Hayes St, Arlington, VA · 703-413-4875
- **Discovery Channel Store** (children's gifts) · Union Station, 50 Massachusetts Ave NE · 202-842-3700
- **Fairy Godmother** (toys & books) · 319 7th St SE · 202-547-5474
- **Filene's Basement** (kids' clothes) · 5300 Wisconsin Ave NW · 202-966-0208
- **Full of Beans** (kids' clothes) · 5502 Connecticut Ave NW · 202-362-8566
- **Gap Kids and Baby Gap** (kids' clothes) · 1267 Wisconsin Ave NW · 202-333-2411
  - 1100 S Hayes St, Arlington, VA · 703-418-4770
  - 5430 Wisconsin Ave, Chevy Chase, MD · 301-907-7656
- **Gymboree** (kids' clothes) · 1100 S Hayes St, Arlington, VA · 703-415-5009
- **Hecht's** (clothes, furniture, toys, books) · 12th & G Sts NW · 202-628-6661
- **Kids Closet** (kids' clothes) · 1226 Connecticut Ave NW · 202-429-9247
- **Kinderhaus Toys** · 1220 N Filmore, Arlington, VA · 703-527-5929
- **Patagonia** (clothes) · 1048 Wisconsin Ave NW · 202-333-1776
- **Piccolo Piggies** (clothes, furniture, accessories) · 1533 Wisconsin Ave NW · 202-333-0123
- **Plaza Artist Supplies** (arts & crafts) · 1990 K St NW · 202-331-0126
- **Ramer's Shoes** (children's shoes) · 3810 Northampton St NW · 202-244-2288
- **Riverby Books** (used books) · 417 E Capitol St SE · 202-543-4342
- **Sullivan's Toys & Art Supplies** · 3412 Wisconsin Ave NW · 202-362-1343
- **Sur La Table** (pint-sized cooking supplies) · 1101 S Joyce St, Arlington, VA · 703-414-3580
- **Tree Top Kids** (toys, books & clothes) · 3301 New Mexico Ave NW · 202-244-3500

Where to go for more information

www.gocitykids.com
www.ourkids.com
www.lilaguide.com

Dupont Circle is to DC's gay life what Capitol Hill is to the nation's politics. Just as politics seep into most aspects of city life, the gay scene reaches far beyond Lambda Rising. In addition to the world's largest LGBT bookstore (just down the street from the bookstore where the first gay couple to be featured in the *New York Times'* "Weddings" met), there are gay and lesbian lifestyle newspapers, clubs, bars, and community groups scattered throughout the city. In short, Dupont Circle is a geographic reference as well as a state of mind, and the city is, for the most part, sexual-orientation-blind. While there are many LGBT residents in suburbs like Takoma Park, MD, and Arlington, VA, they enjoy precious little visibility compared to their District counterparts.

We take this moment to pay our respects to the numerous bars and clubs on O Street SE, which after a 30-year run, were shuttered forever in April 2006 to make room for the Washington Nationals' new stadium. These popular (and generally "adult-oriented") establishments were always jammed on the weekends, especially with locals taking out-of-towners to see fab-u-lous drag shows at Ziegfeld's or to see the boys bare it all at Secrets or Heat.

Websites

Capital Pride · www.capitalpride.org
Educational website dedicated to DC's LGBT community. The organization is also responsible for the planning and development of the annual Capital Pride Parade.

DC Dykes · www.dcdykes.com
Insider's guide for lesbians living in DC.

GayDC · www.gaydc.net
In-depth and up-to-date network for DC's gay, lesbian, bisexual, and transgendered community.

GayWdc · www.gayWdc.com
Gay and lesbian website for DC restaurant and bar listings, local news and events, classifieds, and personals.

Gay and Lesbian Activists Alliance · www.glaa.org
GLAA is the nation's oldest continuously active gay and lesbian civil rights organization.

Pen DC · www.pendc.org
LGBT business networking group.

Publications

Metro Weekly · 1012 14th St NW · 202-638-6830 · www.metroweekly.com
Free weekly gay and lesbian magazine—reliable coverage of community events, nightlife, and reviews of the District's entertainment and art scene.

Bookstores

Lambda Rising · 1625 Connecticut Ave NW · 202-462-6969 · www.lambdarising.com
When it opened in 1974, Lambda Rising carried about 250 titles. Today, the bookstore operates five stores in DC, Baltimore, MD, Rehoboth Beach, DE, Norfolk, VA, and New York City, and serves as an information hub and meeting place for the DC gay community.

Politics and Prose · 5015 Connecticut Ave NW · 202-364-1919 · www.politics-prose.com
Popular bookstore and coffee shop with a small selection devoted to gay and lesbian literature.

Health Center & Support Organizations

Arlington Gay & Lesbian Alliance · 703-522-7660 · www.agla.org
Monthly get-togethers for the Arlington LGBT community.

Beth Mishpachah · www.betmish.org
District of Columbia Jewish Center · 16th & Q Sts NW
DC's egalitarian synagogue that embraces a diversity of sexual and gender identities.

The Center · 1111 14th St NW · 202-518-6100 · www.thedccenter.org
A volunteer LGBT community organization in metro DC.

DC AIDS Hotline · 202-332-2437 or 800-322-7432

DC Black Pride · PO Box 77071, Washington, DC 20013 · 202-737-5767 · www.dcblackpride.org
African-American lesbian, gay, bisexual, and transgendered community group. Proceeds from Black Pride events are distributed to HIV/AIDS and other health organizations serving the African-American community.

Dignity · www.dignitywashington.org
For the LGBT Catholic community.

Police Department's Gay and Lesbian Liaison Unit · 300 Indiana Ave NW · 202-727-5427 · www.gllu.org
Staffed by openly gay and lesbian members of the police department and their allies. The unit is dedicated to serving the gay, lesbian, bisexual, and transgendered communities in the District.

Family Pride · PO Box 65327, Washington, DC 20035 · 202-331-5015 · www.familypride.org
This group is dedicated to advancing the well-being of lesbian, gay, bisexual, and transgendered parents and their families.

Food & Friends · 219 Riggs Rd NE · 202-269-2277 · www.foodandfriends.org
The organization cooks, packages, and delivers meals and groceries to over 1,000 people living with HIV/AIDS and other life-challenging illnesses in the greater DC area. Hosts annual "Chef's Best" fundraising dinner with notable volunteer chefs from around the region.

GLAAD DC · 1700 Kalorama Rd · 202-986-1360 · www.glaad.org
Gay and Lesbian Alliance Against Defamation DC chapter.

PFLAG DC · 1111 14th St NW · 202-638-3852 · www.pflagdc.org
Parents and Friend of Lesbians and Gays DC chapter.

Sexual Minority Youth Assistance League (SMYAL) · 410 7th St SE · 202-546-5940 · www.smyal.org
Non-profit group for LGBT youth.

Whitman-Walker Clinic · 1407 S St NW · 202-797-3500 www.wwc.org
A non-profit organization that provides medical and social services to the LGBT and HIV/AIDS communities of metropolitan DC. Home to one of the oldest substance abuse programs in the US. The Lesbian Health Center at Whitman Walker's Elizabeth Taylor Medical Center, 1810 14th St NW, offers top-quality health services (202-745-6131). There is also a Legal Aid Society for information on financial assistance possibilities (202-628-1161)

Sports and Clubs

Adventuring · PO Box 18118, Washington, DC 20036 · 202-462-0535 · www.adventuring.org
All-volunteer group organizes group hikes, bike rides, and more for DC's LGBT community.

Capital Tennis Association · www.capital-tennis.org
Casual and organized tennis programs for the metropolitan gay and lesbian community.

Chesapeake and Potomac Softball (CAPS) ·
PO Box 3092, Falls Church, VA 22043 · 202-543-0236 · www.capsoftball.org
A friendly place for members of the LGBT community to play softball.

DC Aquatics Club · PO Box 12211, Washington, DC 20005 · www.swimdcac.org
Swimming team and social club for gays, lesbians, and friends of the gay and lesbian community.

DC's Different Drummers ·
PO Box 57099, Washington, DC 20037 · 202-269-4868 · www.dcdd.org
DC's Lesbian and Gay Symphonic, Swing, Marching, and Pep Bands.

DC Front Runners · PO Box 65550, Washington, DC 20035 202-628-3223 · www.dcfrontrunners.org
Running is so gay!

DC Lambda Squares ·
PO Box 77782, Washington, DC 20013 · www.dclambdasquares.org
LGBT square-dance club.

DC Strokes · PO Box 3789, Washington, DC 20027 · www.dcstrokes.org
The first rowing club for gays and lesbians. They row out of the Thompson Boat Center on the Potomac.

Federal Triangles · 202-986-5363 · www.federaltriangles.org
Soccer club for the LGBT community.

Gay Men's Chorus of Washington DC:
Federal City Performing Arts Association · 2801 M Street NW · (202) 293-1548 · www.gmcw.org

Lambda Links · www.lambdalinks.org
Gay golf.

Lesbian and Gay Chorus of Washington, DC ·
PO Box 65285, Washington, DC 20035 · 202-546-1549 · www.lgcw.org

Washington Wetskins Water Polo · www.wetskins.org
The first lesbian, gay, and bisexual polo team in the United States.

Washington Renegades Rugby · www.dcrugby.com
A Division III club that actively recruits gays and men of color from the DC region.

Annual Events

Capital Pride Festival/Parade · 1407 S St NW · 202-797-3510 · www.capitalpride.org
Annual festival and parade honoring the history and heritage of the LGBT community in Washington, DC. Usually held throughout Dupont and downtown the second week in June.

DC Black Pride Festival/Parade · 202-737-5767 · 866-942-5473 · www.dcblackpride.org
The world's largest Black Pride festival, drawing a crowd of about 30,000 annually. Usually held Memorial Day weekend.

Reel Affirmations · PO Box 73587, Washington, DC, 20056 · 202-986-1119 · www.reelaffirmations.org
Washington DC's Annual Lesbian and Gay Film Festival. Late October.

Youth Pride Day/Week · PO Box 33161, Washington, DC 20033 · 202-387-4141 · www.youthpridedc.org
Usually held in early April. The largest event for gay, lesbian, bisexual, and transgendered youth in the mid-Atlantic region.

Venues

Gay

- **The Blue Room** · 2321 18th St NW · 202-332-0800
- **Cobalt/30 Degrees** · 17th & R Sts NW · 202-462-6569 (30 Degrees is non-smoking)
- **DC Eagle** (leather) · 639 New York Ave NW · 202-347-6025
- **Fireplace** · 2161 P St NW · 202-293-1293
- **Halo** · 1435 P St, NW · 202-797-9730 · **(**Non-smoking venue**)**
- **Titan** · 1337 14th St NW (upstairs) · 202-232-7010
- **JR's Bar & Grill** · 1519 17th St NW · 202-328-0090
- **Omega DC** · 2123 Twining Ct NW · 202-223-4917
- **Remington's** · 639 Pennsylvania Ave SE · 202-543-3113
- **Windows/Dupont Italian Kitchen (DIK) Bar** · 1635 17th St NW · 202-328-0100

Lesbian

- **Phase One** · 525 8th St SE · 202-544-6831

Both

- **1409 Playbill Cafe** · 1409 14th St NW · 202-265-3055
- **Apex** · 1415 22nd St NW · 202-296-0505
- **Banana Cafe** · 500 8th St SE · 202-543-5906
- **Chaos** (Wednesday, Ladies' night) · 17th & Q Sts NW · 202-232-4141
- **Freddie's Beach Bar** · 555 S 23rd St S, Arlington, VA · 703-685-0555
- **Larry's Lounge** · 1836 18th St NW · 202-483-1483

One of the great things about Washington, DC, is that the Metro is safe, convenient, and affordable. That's why you needn't find lodging right in the heart of the area you most want to visit—especially good news if your budget's tight.

Like all big cities, though, be sure to ask around, and check blogs and listservs to get "real people" ratings on the places you are considering before you tap your credit card number into the reservations system. Ask around. Housing—no matter the rate or neighborhood—can be a mixed bag.

If you have the cash, consider the **Hotel Helix (Map 10)** in Logan Circle, which features bright, comfy, pop-art furniture and ultra-modern décor. It's trendy, has large, comfortable rooms (which are all non smoking, by the way), and is located near the US Capitol, not far from Union Station. That means public transportation is steps away. There are also some great pubs and restaurants very close by (both inside Union Station and on neighboring streets). One note of caution—this is a "pet friendly" hotel, so if you prefer only two-legged guests, this might not be for you. As far as location goes, the **Washington Hilton (Map 9)** is only a stone's throw away from Dupont Circle and everything that area has to offer. Another trendy hotel—though not good for the budget-minded—is the **Mandarin Oriental (Map 6)**. If you crave elegance with an Asian flourish, top amenities, and a possible celebrity sighting (think Bono, Beyonce and Jay-Z), this is a great choice.

If your budget is tight, there's nothing wrong with checking out a youth hostel. There are plenty of good ones to be had with room rates starting at about $20 a night. But use caution—this type of lodging varies widely in DC, from clean and secure to downright scary (think the Bronx). As with hotels, ask a number of people before you commit. **American Guesthouse (Map 40)** offers safe, clean housing. One DC youth hostel in a fairly decent neighborhood (not far from the World Bank) is the **Hilltop Hostel (Map 27)**. It is also clean, inexpensive, and near a Metro. Former guests report that the security is good, and they felt safe there. Check out hostel sites such as www.hostelworld.com and www.hostelz.com for information on hostels. Always try to book hostels in advance (they're smaller than hotels and tend to book up faster) and read user reviews online, they're often the most accurate guides out there.

As always, you should use the room rates and star ratings listed below as a guide only. You'll probably want to call or visit the hotel in question to get the most accurate room rates for the days you wish to stay. If you're booking in advance, we suggest checking out sites such as hotels. com, expedia.com, and www.pricerighthotels.com to see if they offer any special discounts for the time of your visit.

Map 1 • National Mall

	Address	Phone	Nightly Rate
Courtyard Washington Convention Center	900 F St NW	202-638-4600	409
Embassy Suites Convention Center	900 10th St NW	202-739-2001	309
Grand Hyatt	1000 H St NW	202-582-1234	379
Hay-Adams Hotel	800 16th St NW	202-638-6600	309
Hilton Garden Inn Washington DC	815 14th St NW	202-783-7800	299
Hotel Harrington	436 11th St NW	202-628-8140	120
JW Marriott Hotel Washington DC	1331 Pennsylvania Ave NW	202-393-2000	459
Sofitel Lafayette Square	806 15th St NW	202-730-8800	230
Washington Marriott Metro Center	775 12th St NW	202-737-2200	379
Willard Hotel	1401 Pennsylvania Ave NW	202-628-9100	449

Map 2 • Chinatown / Union Station

Hotel George	15 E St NW	202-347-4200	299
Hotel Monaco	700 F St NW	202-628-7177	499
Hyatt Regency Washington	400 New Jersey Ave NW	202-737-1234	399
The Liaison Capitol Hill	415 New Jersey Ave NW	202-638-1616	399
Phoenix Park Hotel	520 N Capitol St NW	202-638-6900	289
Red Roof Inn	500 H St NW	202-289-5959	179
Washington Court Hotel	525 New Jersey Ave NW	202-628-2100	311

Map 5 • Southeast / Anacostia

Capitol Hill Suites	200 C St SE	202-543-6000	299
Courtyard Washington Capitol Hill	140 L St SE	202-479-0027	329

Map 6 • Waterfront

Capitol Skyline Hotel	10 I St SW	202-488-7500	149
Channel Inn	650 Water St SW	202-554-2400	120
Holiday Inn Washington Capitol	550 C St SW	202-479-4000	239
L'enfant Plaza Hotel	480 Lenfant Plaza SW	202-484-1000	399

Mandarin Oriental	1330 Maryland Ave SW	202-554-8588	515
Residence Inn Washington DC	333 E St SW	202-484-8280	299

Map 7 • Foggy Bottom

Doubletree Guest Suites Washington DC	801 New Hampshire Ave NW	202-785-2000	264
George Washington University Inn	824 New Hampshire Ave NW	202-337-6620	229
Hotel Lombardy	2019 Pennsylvania Ave NW	202-828-2600	229
Remington Executive Suites	601 24th St NW	202-223-4512	150
River Inn	924 25th St NW	202-337-7600	225
State Plaza Hotel	2117 E St NW	202-861-8200	199
The Watergate Hotel	2650 Virginia Ave NW	202-965-2300	149

Map 8 • Georgetown

Four Seasons	2800 Pennsylvania Ave NW	202-342-0444	695
Georgetown Hill Inn	1832 Wisconsin Ave NW	202-298-6021	169
Georgetown Inn	1310 Wisconsin Ave NW	888-587-2388	254
Georgetown Suites	1111 30th St NW	202-298-7800	165
Georgetown Suites Harbor	1000 29th St NW	202-298-1600	195
Holiday Inn Georgetown	2101 Wisconsin Ave NW	202-338-3120	200
Hotel Monticello	1075 Thomas Jefferson St NW	202-337-0900	279
Latham Hotel	3000 M St NW	202-726-5000	199
The Ritz-Carlton Georgetown	3100 South St NW	202-912-4100	499
Washington Suites Georgetown	2500 Pennsylvania Ave NW	202-333-8060	224

Map 9 • Dupont Circle / Adams Morgan

1 Washington Cir	1 Washington Cir NW	202-872-1680	219
American Guest House	2005 Columbia Rd NW	703-769-4244	159
Beacon Hotel and Corporate Quarters	1615 Rhode Island Ave NW	202-296-2100	245
Best Western	1121 New Hampshire Ave NW	202-457-0565	209
Capital Hilton	1001 16th St NW	202-393-1000	335
Carlyle Suites Hotel	1731 New Hampshire Ave NW	202-234-3200	239
Churchill Hotel	1914 Connecticut Ave NW	202-797-2000	389
Courtyard Washington Embassy Row	1900 Connecticut Ave NW	202-332-9300	299
Courtyard Washington Northwest	1600 Rhode Island Ave NW	202-293-8000	219
Doubletree Hotel Washington DC	1515 Rhode Island Ave NW	202-232-7000	369
Dupont at the Circle B&B	1604 19th St NW	202-332-5251	250
Dupont Hotel	1500 New Hampshire Ave NW	202-483-6000	315
Embassy Circle Guest House	2224 R St NW	202-232-7744	250
Embassy Inn	1627 16th St NW	202-234-7800	249
Embassy Suites Washington DC	1250 22nd St NW	202-857-3388	269
Fairfax at Embassy Row	2100 Massachusetts Ave NW	202-293-2100	368
Fairmont	2401 M St NW	202-429-2400	269
Gallery Inn	1850 Florida Ave NW	202-234-8788	99
Hilton	2015 Massachusetts Ave NW	202-265-1600	259
Hilton Washington	1919 Connecticut Ave NW	202-483-3000	259
Holiday Inn Washington Central	1501 Rhode Island Ave NW	202-483-2000	221
Hotel Madera	1310 New Hampshire Ave NW	202-296-7600	160
Hotel Palomar	2121 P St NW	202-448-1800	409
Hotel Quincy	1823 L St NW	202-223-4320	289
Hotel Rouge	1315 16th St NW	202-232-8000	270
Hotel Tabard Inn	1739 N St NW	202-785-1277	113
Mayflower Renaissance Washington DC	1127 Connecticut Ave NW	202-347-3000	409
Madison	1177 15th St NW	202-862-1600	289
Melrose Hotel	2430 Pennsylvania Ave NW	202-955-6400	239
Normandy Hotel	2118 Wyoming Ave NW	202-483-1350	239
Park Hyatt Washington DC	1201 24th St NW	202-789-1234	489
Renaissance Washington DC	1143 New Hampshire Ave NW	202-775-0800	319
Residence Inn Washington DC	2120 P St NW	202-466-6800	299
The Ritz-Carlton	1150 22nd St NW	202-835-0500	349
St Gregory Hotel & Suites	2033 M St NW	202-530-3600	224
The Swann House	1808 New Hampshire Ave NW	202-265-4414	259
Topaz Hotel	1733 N St NW	202-393-3000	180
Washington Marriott	1221 22nd St NW	202-872-1500	359

General Information · **Hotels**

Map 9 · Dupont Circle / Adams Morgan—*continued*

The Westin Grand	2350 M St NW	202-429-0100	359
Windsor Inn	1842 16th St NW	202-667-0300	140
Windsor Park	2116 Kalorama Rd NW	202-483-7700	169

Map 10 · Logan Circle / U Street

Aaron Shipman House Bed & Breakfast	13th St NW & Q St NW	202-328-3510	125
Chester A Arthur Bed and Breakfast	13th and Logan Circle Park	202-328-3510	115
Comfort Inn	1201 13th St NW	202-682-5300	229
Crowne Plaza The Hamilton	1001 14th St NW	202-682-0111	270
DC Guesthouse	1337 10th St NW	202-332-2502	175
District Hotel	1440 Rhode Island Ave NW	202-232-7800	80
Four Points	1201 K St NW	202-289-7600	329
Hampton Inn Washington DC	901 6th St NW	202-842-2500	239
Henley Park Hotel	926 Massachusetts Ave NW	202-638-5200	239
Homewood Suites	1475 Massachusetts Ave NW	202-265-8000	189
Hotel Helix	1430 Rhode Island Ave NW	202-462-9001	230
Morrison-Clark Inn	1015 L St NW	202-898-1200	289
Renaissance Washington DC	999 9th St NW	202-898-9000	399
Residence Inn Washington DC	1199 Vermont Ave NW	202-898-1100	299
Washington Plaza	10 Thomas Cir NW	202-842-1300	219
Westin Washington DC City Center	1400 M St NW	202-429-1700	289

Map 11 · Near Northeast

Courtyard Washington DC	1325 2nd St NE	202-898-4000	269
Howard Johnson Express Inn	600 New York Ave NE	202-546-9200	75
Kellogg Conference Hotel	800 Florida Ave NE	202-651-6000	129
Motel 6 Washington DC	1345 4th St NE	202-544-2000	89
Super 8 Motel	501 New York Ave NE	202-543-7400	109

Map 13 · Brookland / Langdon

Budget Motor Inn	1615 New York Ave NE	202-529-3900	75
Comfort Inn & Suites	1600 New York Ave NE	202-832-3200	129

Map 16 · Adams Morgan (North) / Mt Pleasant

Adam's Inn	1746 Lanier Pl NW	202-745-3600	99
Kalorama Guest House Adams-Morgan	1854 Mintwood Pl NW	202-667-6369	99

Map 17 · Woodley Park / Cleveland Park

Kalorama Guest House Woodley Park	2700 Cathedral Ave NW	202-328-0860	99
Omni Shoreham	2500 Calvert St NW	202-234-0700	269
Washington Marriott Wardman Park	2660 Woodley Rd NW	202-328-2000	409
Woodley Park Guest House	2647 Woodley Rd NW	202-667-0218	135

Map 18 · Glover Park / Foxhall

Georgetown University Conference Hotel	3800 Reservoir Rd NW	202-687-3200	239
Savoy Suites	2505 Wisconsin Ave NW	202-337-9700	209

Map 19 · Tenleytown / Friendship Heights

Embassy Suites Chevy Chase Pavilion	4300 Military Rd NW	202-362-9300	252

Map 20 · Cleveland Park / Upper Connecticut

Days Inn Washington DC	4400 Connecticut Ave NW	202-244-5600	179

Map 22 · Bethesda (North)

American Inn	8130 Wisconsin Ave	301-656-9300	195
Bethesda Court Hotel	7740 Wisconsin Ave	301-656-2100	209
Bethesda Marriott	5151 Pooks Hill Rd	301-897-9400	279
Doubletree Hotel Bethesda	8120 Wisconsin Ave	301-652-2000	175

Map 25 • Silver Spring

Courtyard Silver Spring Downtown	8506 Fenton St	301-589-4899	209
Crowne Plaza Washington DC	8777 Georgia Ave	301-589-0800	216
Days Inn Silver Spring	8040 13th St	301-588-4400	65
Hilton Washington DC Silver Spring	8727 Colesville Rd	301-589-5200	179

Map 27 • Walter Reed

Comfort Inn Georgia Ave	7990 Georgia Ave	301-565-3444	89
Hilltop Hostel	300 Carroll St NW	202-291-9591	22
Motel 6	6711 Georgia Ave NW	202-722-1600	63

Map 29 • Bethesda (South)

Courtyard Chevy Chase	5520 Wisconsin Ave	301-656-1500	229
Hyatt Regency Bethesda	1 Bethesda Metro Center	301-657-1234	249
Residence Inn Bethesda	7335 Wisconsin Ave	301-718-0200	299

Map 33 • Falls Church

Econo Lodge Metro	6800 Lee Hwy	703-538-5300	110

Map 34 • Cherrydale / Ballston

Comfort Inn Ballston	1211 N Glebe Rd	703-247-3399	175
Hilton Arlington	950 N Stafford St	703-528-6000	323
Holiday Inn Arlington at Ballston	4610 Fairfax Dr	703-243-9800	199
The Westin Arlington Gateway	801 N Glebe Rd	703-717-6200	359

Map 35 • Cherrydale / Clarendon

Inns of Virginia - Arlington	3335 Lee Hwy	703-524-9800	85

Map 36 • Rosslyn

Best Western	1501 Arlington Blvd	703-524-5000	129
Clarion Collection Arlington Residence Court Hotel	1200 N Courthouse Rd	703-524-4000	189
Courtyard Arlington Rosslyn	1533 Clarendon Blvd	703-528-2222	209
Hilton Garden Inn Arlington Courthouse Plaza	1333 N Courthouse Rd	703-528-4444	206
Holiday Inn Rosslyn at Key Bridge	1900 N Fort Myer Dr	703-807-2000	210
Hyatt	1325 Wilson Blvd	703-525-1234	239
The Inn of Rosslyn	1601 Arlington Blvd	703-524-3400	95
Key Bridge Marriott	1401 Lee Hwy	703-524-6400	239
Residence Inn Arlington Rosslyn	1651 N Oak St	703-812-8400	239
Virginian Suites	1500 Arlington Blvd	866-371-1446	95

Map 37 • Fort Myer

Days Inn Arlington Pentagon	3030 Columbia Pike	703-521-5570	93
Highlander Motel	3336 Wilson Blvd	877-786-4301	109

Map 38 • Columbia Pike

Hampton Inn Alexandria	4800 Leesburg Pike	703-671-4800	139
Homewood Suites	4850 Leesburg Pike	703-671-6500	203

Map 39 • Shirlington

Best Western	2480 S Glebe Rd	703-979-4400	169

Map 40 • Pentagon City / Crystal City

Americana Hotel	1400 Jefferson Davis Hwy	703-979-3772	69
Courtyard Arlington Crystal City	2899 Jefferson Davis Hwy	703-549-3434	259
Crowne Plaza Washington National Airport	1480 Crystal Dr	703-416-1600	259
Crystal City Marriott	1999 Jefferson Davis Hwy	703-413-5500	299

Map 40 • Pentagon City / Crystal City—*continued*

Crystal Gateway Marriott	1700 Jefferson Davis Hwy	703-920-3230	329
Crystal Quarters The Concord	2600 Crystal Dr	800-332-8501	201
Crystal Quarters Water Park Towers	1501 Crystal Dr	703-671-7505	209
Doubletree Hotel Washington DC	300 Army Navy Dr	703-416-4100	259
Embassy Suites Crystal City	1300 Jefferson Davis Hwy	703-979-9799	130
Hampton Inn	2000 Jefferson Davis Hwy	703-418-8181	99
Hilton Crystal City	2399 Jefferson Davis Hwy	703-418-6800	300
Holiday Inn Naitonal Airport Crystal City	2650 Jefferson Davis Hwy	703-684-7200	199
Hyatt Regency Crystal City	2799 Jefferson Davis Hwy	703-418-1234	269
Radisson Hotel	2020 Jefferson Davis Hwy	703-920-8600	192
Residence Inn Arlington Pentagon City	550 Army Navy Dr	703-413-6630	129
The Ritz-Carlton Pentagon City	1250 S Hayes St	703-415-5000	189
Sheraton Crystal City Hotel	1800 Jefferson Davis Hwy	703-486-1111	309
Sheraton National Hotel	900 S Orme St	703-521-1900	279

Map 41 • Landmark

Comfort Inn Landmark	6254 Duke St	703-642-3422	126
Courtyard Alexandria Pentagon South	4641 Kenmore Ave	703-751-4510	179
Extended Stayamerica	205 N Breckinridge Pl	703-941-9440	135
Hawthorn Suites Alexandria	420 N Van Dorn St	703-370-1000	129
Hilton Alexandria Mark Center	5000 Seminary Rd	703-845-1010	195
Washington Suites Alexandria	100 S Reynolds St	703-370-9600	189

Map 42 • Alexandria (West)

Courtyard Alexandria	2700 Eisenhower Ave	703-329-2323	199
Homestead Studio Suites	200 Bluestone Rd	703-329-3399	140

Map 44 • Alexandria Downtown

Embassy Suites Alexandria Old Town	1900 Diagonal Rd	703-684-5900	289
Hampton Inn	1616 King St	703-299-9900	249
Hilton Alexandria Old Town	1767 King St	703-837-0440	289
Holiday Inn Alexandria Eisenhower	2460 Eisenhower Ave	703-960-3400	195
Westin Alexandria	400 Courthouse Square	703-253-8600	259

Map 45 • Old Town (North)

Best Western Old Colony Inn	1101 N Washington St	703-739-2222	209
Crowne Plaza Old Town Alexandria	901 N Fairfax St	703-683-6000	249
Holiday Inn Alexandria	625 1st St	703-548-6300	195
Sheraton Suites Old Town Alexandria	801 N St Asaph St	703-836-4700	219
Towne Motel	808 N Washington St	703-548-3500	80
Travelodge Alexandria	700 N Washington St	703-836-5100	85

Map 46 • Old Town (South)

Hotel Monaco	480 King St	703-549-6080	300
Morrison House	116 S Alfred St	703-838-8000	310
Residence Inn Alexandria Old Town	1456 Duke St	703-548-5474	239

Between renaming buildings, bridges, and fountains and constructing new monuments by the garden-full, DC is quickly running out of things to convert into memorials. You could spend a month visiting every official monument in DC, but you'll have a better time checking out the unofficial local landmarks that get lost in the giant shadows of the White House and the Capitol Building. As for skyscrapers… sorry King Kong, you aren't going to find them in this city. A long-standing law prohibits buildings in the District from being taller than the tip of the Capitol.

Politics, Politics, Politics

After you are done with the marble tributes to the Founding Fathers, why not tour the landmarks of other lesser politicians? Visit the Vista International Hotel (now the **Wyndham (Map 10)**), where former DC Mayor Marion Barry was caught smoking crack cocaine, or the trendy coffeehouse **Tryst (Map 16),** where Gary Condit canoodled with Chandra Levy, or the **Washington Hilton (Map 9)**, where Ronald Reagan took a bullet from John Hinckley, Jr.

Hidden Treasures

If politics isn't your thing (then why are you here?), the District has many a grand home to admire from the inside and out. **The Heurich House (Map 9)**, also known as the Brewmaster's Castle, invites you to tour a perfectly intact Victorian home, complete with a basement Bavarian beer drinking room. Or if you're feeling more whimsical, there's the **Mushroom House (Map 30)** in Bethesda, a private residence owned by people who got a little too excited with the Smurfs. Don't forget to check out **The Littlest House in Alexandria (Map 46)**, which allows for a narrow 7-foot wide life.

Beauties of Bronze

This town also has more than its fair share of statues. Take a moment at Union Station to admire the **Columbus Memorial (Map 2)** out front. The marble fountain opened in 1912, but most visitors and commuters come and go and never take notice of it at all. The circular fountain is 44 feet deep in the middle, and Columbus himself stands at the larger-than-life height of 15 feet. Or if you're weary of oversized statues of dead white men, you can gaze up instead at the **Gandhi Statue (Map 9)** off Dupont Circle, the **Joan of Arc (Map 9)** statue at Malcolm X Park, or the beloved **Grief (Map 14)** memorial in Rock Creek Cemetery.

Those are Landmarks?

Even more landmarks are those buildings you've seen again and again, and yet no one seems to be able to identify them. The **Temple of the Scottish Rite of Freemasonry (Map 9)** standing tall on 16th Street, the **Second Division Memorial (Map 1)** on the Mall, or **The Other FDR Memorial (Map 1)** that quietly sits outside the National Archives. Don't forget, "landmark" is a loose term, so why not throw in the still functioning **Uptown Theater (Map 17)**, DC's premiere venue for Lord of the Rings-type films. And if seeing Elvin warlords ruthlessly massacring each other makes you feel like a drink, head down to **The Brickskeller (Map 9)**, home to the largest selection of beer Johnny Fratboy could ever wish for (even though he'd probably just get a Bud Light, anyway).

Hollywood in Washington

So you think it's all happening in LA and New York? Think again, friend. If you ever find yourself on Prospect Street at night, gather up the *cojones* to visit the *Exorcist* **Steps (Map 8),** the steep and narrow 97-step stairwell used in William Blatty's classic horror film, *The Exorcist*. The unassuming neighborhood of Mount Pleasant was also featured in *State of Play* starring Russell Crowe, whose character lives above local landmarks Heller's Bakery and Pfeiffer's Hardware. If that's not enough Hollywood for you, grab a beer and sit on the steps of the **Lincoln Memorial (Map 7)**, like that scene in *Wedding Crashers*.

Hometown Heroes

Every neighborhood seems to have its local landmarks—whether it be colorful mural (see: **Marilyn Monroe (Map 16)** in Woodley Park) or a frequently patronized greasy spoon (see: **Ben's Chili Bowl (Map 10)** on U Street). When in Dupont, hang out by the **Dupont Fountain (Map 9)**—the focal point of the eclectic crowd that makes up the neighborhood. In Silver Spring, head straight to the **AFI Theater (Map 25)**, where you can catch an indie American or foreign film and watch it in the stadium seats usually associated with blockbuster releases. Feeling like catching a local band but don't want to pack into a sweaty club? Hit up the family-friendly **Fort Reno Park (Map 19)** in the summer months. You can't booze, but hey, it's free.

Map 1 • National Mall

The Clinton McDonald's	750 17th St NW • 202-347-0047	Taste what Bill couldn't resist.
Decatur House	1610 H St NW • 202-965-0920	Tour worth taking.
District Building	1350 Pennsylvania Ave NW	DC's city hall. You can't fight it.
Ford's Theatre	511 10th St NW • 202-426-6924	Lincoln's finale.
Hay-Adams Hotel	16th St & H St NW • 800-853-6807	The luxury lap where Monica told all.
International Spy Museum	800 F St NW • 202-393-7798	For all the future Aldrich Ames out there.
J Edgar Hoover FBI Building	935 Pennsylvania Ave NW • 202-324-3000	Ask to see Hoover's cross-dressing dossier.
National Aquarium	Constitution Ave NW & 14th St NW • 202-482-2825	Save money, visit pet shop.
National Mall/Smithsonian Merry-Go-Round	3rd St SW & Jefferson Dr SW • 202-633-1000	Tacky, but quells crying children.
National Press Club	529 14th St NW, 13th Fl • 202-662-7500	Join the ink-stained hacks for a drink.
Old Post Office Tower	1100 Pennsylvania Ave NW • 202-606-8691	Best view of skyscraper-less Washington.

Map 1 · National Mall—*continued*

The Other FDR Memorial	Pennsylvania Ave NW, b/w 7th St NW & 9th St NW	All FDR wanted was a stone outside the National Archives.
The Second Division Memorial	17th St NW & Constitution Ave NW	Overlooked history.
Smithsonian Institution Building, (The Castle)	1000 Jefferson Dr SW · 202-633-1000	Storm the castle for information.
St John's Church	16th St NW & H St NW · 202-347-8766	Sit in the President's pew.
Willard Hotel	1401 Pennsylvania Ave NW · 202-628-9100	Historic hotel where the term "lobbyist" was born. And free HBO!
World War I Memorial	15th St SW and Independence Ave SW	Often overlooked monument.

Map 2 · Chinatown / Union Station

Casa Italiana	595 1/2 3rd St NW · 202-638-0165	DC's half-block answer to Little Italy.
Chinatown Gate	H St NW & 7th St NW	Ushers you in for cheap eats and cheaper pottery.
Columbus Memorial	Massachusetts Ave & First St (near Union Station)	Look for a big statue and fountain—the one with the carvings.
National Building Museum	401 F St NW · 202-272-2448	Step inside and feel your jaw drop.
Shakespeare Theatre	450 7th St NW · 202-547-1122	Where the Bard shows off.
Supreme Court of the United States	1st St NE b/w E Capitol St SE & Maryland Ave NE · 202-479-3211	Bring your favorite protest sign.
US Botanic Garden	100 Maryland Ave SW · 202-225-8333	Relaxing refuge of tropical flora and primeval plants.
US Library of Congress	101 Independence Ave SE · 202-707-8000	Lose yourself in letters.
USDA Graduate Schools	600 Maryland Ave SW · 888-744-4723	Go learn something. Impressive array of class offerings.

Map 3 · The Hill

Folger Shakespeare Library	201 E Capitol St SE · 202-544-4600	To go or not to go?

Map 5 · Southeast / Anacostia

Anacostia Boathouse	1105 O St SE	Take the dirty plunge.
Bureau of Engraving and Printing	14th St SW & C St SW · 202-874-8888	Where to get your Dead Presidents.
Congressional Cemetery	1801 E St SE · 202-543-0539	Individual graves, shared conditions.
Eastern Market	225 7th St SE · 202-544-0083	Apples and art. Back in business after '07 fire.
Frederick Douglass House	1411 W St SE · 202-426-5951	A man who showed up his neighborhood and his country.
Washington Navy Yard	9th St SE & M St SE · 202-433-4882	Haven for men in tighty whites.

Map 6 · Waterfront

Arena Stage	1101 6th St SW · 202-488-3300	Great theater.
Ft Lesley J McNair	4th St SW & P St SW	For the Civil War buffs.
Gangplank Marina	600 Water Street SW · 202-554-5000	A Washington Channel neighborhood of boat-dwellers.
Nationals Park	1500 South Capitol St SE	Making the Mets look good since 2005.
Odyssey Cruises	N Water St & W 6th Ave · 888-741-0281	Dining and dancing on the Potomac river.
Spirit of Washington	6th St & Water St S · 202-484-2320	Experience Washington by boat.
Thomas Law House	1252 6th St SW	Impressive house, not open to the public.
Tiber Island	429 N St SW	Looking for an apartment?
USS Sequoia	6th St SW & Maine Ave SW · 202-333-0011	Rent it when the VP isn't in the mood to play Mr. Howell.

Map 7 · Foggy Bottom

Einstein Statue	Constitution Ave NW & 22nd St NW	At his rumpled best.
Kennedy Center	2700 F St NW · 202-467-4600	High-brow culture.
The Octagon	1799 New York Ave NW · 202-626-7387	Peculiar floor plan.
The Watergate Hotel	2650 Virginia Ave NW · 202-965-2300	Location of the most infamous Washington scandal yet; still a great design.

Map 8 · Georgetown

Cooke's Row	3009 Q St NW	Romantic row.
Dumbarton Oaks Museum & Garden	1703 32nd St NW · 202-339-6401	An absolute treasure.
Exorcist Steps	3600 Prospect St NW	Watch your balance and LOOK UP! LOOK UP!
Islamic Center	2551 Massachussetts Ave NW · 202-332-8343	Oldest Islamic house of worship in the city.

Oak Hill Cemetery	30th St NW & R St NW • 202-337-2835	Old and gothic.
Old Stone House	3051 M St NW • 202-426-6851	Old. And Stone. It's the oldest building this town's got.
Prospect House	3508 Prospect St NW	Spectacular view of the Potomac.
Tudor Place	1644 31st St NW • 202-965-0400	Bring a picnic.
Volta Bureau	1537 35th St NW • 202-337-5220	HQ of the Alexander Graham Bell Association for the Deaf.

Map 9 • Dupont Circle / Adams Morgan

Anderson House	2118 Massachusetts Ave NW • 202-785-2040	One of the premiere gems in the crown of the Society of the Cincinnati.
Australian Embassy	1601 Massachusetts Ave NW • 202-797-3000	Look out for the Christmas kangaroos.
Blaine Mansion	2000 Massachusetts Ave NW	Large, red, and brick.
The Brewmasters Castle	1307 New Hampshire Ave NW • 202-429-1894	German beer-themed bling rules in this 1892 crib.
The Brickskeller	1523 22nd St NW • 202-293-1885	Get drunk on the world's largest beer list.
Chinese Embassy	2300 Connecticut Ave NW • 202-328-2500	Look for the Falun Gong protesters.
DC Improv	1140 Connecticut Ave NW • 202-296-7008	Chortle in a city that doesn't laugh enough.
DC's Spanish Steps	S St NW & 22nd St NW	A mini-Roman Holiday.
Dumbarton Bridge	23rd St NW & Q St NW	Four fantastic buffaloes guide you from Dupont to Georgetown.
Dupont Fountain	Dupont Cir	Top spot for people-watching.
Eastern Star Temple	1618 New Hampshire Ave NW • 202-667-4737	National Women's Party HQ.
Farragut Square	K St NW & 17th St NW	Share park benches with K Street suits and the homeless.
Freshfarm Market	20th St NW near Q St NW • 202-331-7300	Where yuppies get their fruit.
Gandhi Statue	Massachusetts Ave NW & 21st St NW	Don't peek under the skirt.
Heurich House	1307 New Hampshire Ave NW	It sure feels haunted.
Hilton Washington	1919 Connecticut Ave NW	Where Reagan took a bullet.
Iraqi Embassy	1801 P St NW • 202-483-7500	Watch the hated old shell come alive.
Italian Cultural Institute	2025 M St NW • 202-223-9800	Learn how to whistle at babes like the Romans did.
Joan of Arc Statue	Meridian Hill Park	You'd think she conquered Washington.
The Mansion on O Street	2020 O St NW • 202-496-2020	Hidden passageways, celeb guests, and Grey Goose Martini happy hours.
Meridian Hill/Malcolm X Park	16th St NW & Euclid St NW	Sunday drum circle + soccer!
Middle East Institute	1761 N St NW • 202-785-1141	A Middle East mecca…er, you know what we mean.
National Geographic Society Headquarters	1145 17th St NW • 202-857-7588	It holds the world and all that's in it, apparently.
The Palm	1225 19th St NW • 202-293-9091	A.k.a. The Institute For Power Lunching.
Sonny Bono Memorial	20th St NW & New Hampshire Ave NW	Rest In Peace, babe.
St Thomas' Parish Churchyard	1772 Church St NW	Dupont's fancy Episcopalian church.
Temple of the Scottish Rite of Freemasonry	1733 16th St NW • 202-232-3579	So that's what that is.
Woman's National Democratic Club	1526 New Hampshire Ave NW • 202-232-7363	Presidents and First Ladies on walls.
Woodrow Wilson House	2340 S St NW • 202-387-4062	Another president's crib.

Map 10 • Logan Circle / U Street

African-American Civil War Memorial	1000 U St NW • 202-667-2667	A belated thanks.
Ben's Chili Bowl	1213 U St NW • 202-667-0909	Half-smokes and milkshakes beloved by locals and celebs.
Cato Institute	1000 Massachusetts Ave NW • 202-842-0200	Conservative temple.
Duke Ellington Mural	1200 U St NW	He's watching.
Lincoln Theatre	1215 U St NW • 202-397-7328	Renovated jewel.
Mary McLeod Bethune National Historic Site	1318 Vermont Ave NW • 202-673-2402	History without propaganda.
Westin Washington DC City Center	1400 M St NW • 202-429-1700	Back when it was the Vista International, Marion Barry got caught smoking crack here.

Map 11 • Near Northeast

Crispus Attucks Park	b/w V St NW & U St NW	Neighborly public space in the heart of Bloomingdale.
Florida Avenue Market	Florida Ave NE b/w 2nd St NE & 6th St NE	Forget Eastern Market's frou-frou frills; head northeast.
Washington Coliseum	1140 3rd St NW	DC's performance venue.

Map 12 • Trinidad

Koi Pond	National Arboretum • 202-245-2726	Feed and pet humongo Japanese fish!
Mount Olivet Cemetery	1300 Bladensberg Rd NE	Visit Mary Suratt, hanged for her part in killing Lincoln.

Map 13 • Brookland / Langdon

Franciscan Monastery	1400 Quincy St NE • 202-526-6800	Beautiful gardens.

Map 14 • Catholic U

Brooks Mansion	901 Newton St NE	A Greek revival.
Grief in Rock Creek Cemetery	Rock Creek Church Rd NW & Webster St NW	Memorial to Adam's wife is best in the city.
Lincoln Cottage, Soldiers Home	3700 N Capitol St NW • 202-722-6624	Lincoln's summer residence; where he drafted the Emancipation Proclamation.
Pope John Paul II Cultural Center	3900 Harewood Rd NE • 202-635-5400	When you can't get to The Vatican.
Shrine of the Immaculate Conception	400 Michigan Ave NE • 202-526-8300	Humungo Catholic Church.

Map 15 • Columbia Heights

Blackburn University Center	2400 6th St NW • 202-806-5983	Howard University's living room.

Map 16 • Adams Morgan (North) / Mt Pleasant

All Souls Church	1500 Harvard St NW	Progressive Unitarian Church.
Guglielmo Marconi Memorial	16th & Lamont Sts NW • n/a	Art Deco tribute to the Fascist inventor.
Heller's Bakery	3221 Mt Pleasant St NW • 202-265-1169	Start your morning off with donuts and coffee.
Marilyn Monroe Mural	Connecticut Ave NW & Calvert St NW	A tiny bit of glamour for DC.
Meridian International Center	1630 Crescent Pl NW • 202-667-6800	Look out for the exhibits.
Mexican Cultural Institute	2829 16th St NW • 202-728-1647	Top-notch work by Mexican artists.
Tryst Coffee House	2459 18th St NW • 202-232-5500	Canoodle here the way Chandra and Gary did.
Walter Pierce Park	2630 Adams Mill Rd NW • 202-588-7332	Former cemetery now boasts colorful mural and new-fenced dog park.

Map 17 • Woodley Park / Cleveland Park

AMC Loews Uptown 1	3426 Connecticut Ave NW • 202-966-5401	Red velvet curtains over a 40-foot screen; this is the Art Deco queen of DC movie houses.
US Naval Observatory	Massachusetts Ave NW & Observatory Cir NW • 202-762-1467	VP's disclosed location and the best place to ask what time it is.

Map 18 • Glover Park / Foxhall

C&O Towpath/Canal Locks	Canal Rd NW	Scenic views minutes from cityscape.
The Kreeger Museum	2401 Foxhall Rd NW • 202-337-3050	Residence turned private museum houses a stunning art collection.
La Maison Française	4101 Reservoir Rd NW • 202-944-6090	Learn what *savoir faire* truly means.
National Cathedral	Massachusetts Ave NW & Wisconsin Ave NW • 202-537-6200	Newly-constructed old cathedral. Pure American.

Map 19 • Tenleytown / Friendship Heights

Fort Reno	Ft Reno Park	This former Civil War fort is the highest point of elevation in the District and the heart of DC punk during summertime

Map 20 · Cleveland Park / Upper Connecticut

Hillwood Estate, Museum & Gardens	4155 Linnean Ave NW · 202-686-5807	Home of heiress Marjorie Merriweather Post is simply exquisite.
Pierce Mill	2401 Tilden St NW · 202-895-6000	Doesn't everyone love a 19th-century grist mill?
Rock Creek Park Nature Center and Planetarium	5200 Glover Rd NW · 202-895-6070	Nature in the city.

Map 22 · Bethesda (North)

L'Academie de Cuisine	5021 Wilson Ln · 301-986-9490	One step up from learning to make french fries.
National Institutes of Health	9000 Rockville Pike · 301-496-4000	Monkeys and rats beware

Map 24 · Upper Rock Creek Park

Seminary at Forest Glen	Linden Ln & Beach Dr	Creepy complex of crumbling faux pagodas and French chateaux soon to become creepier housing development.

Map 25 · Silver Spring

AFI Silver Theatre	8633 Colesville Rd · 301-495-6720	You don't have to see artsy films in crappy movie houses anymore.
Penguin Rush Hour Mural	8400 Colesville Rd	Stop elbowing your way onto the Metro to appreciate a piece of Silver Spring.
Tastee Diner	8601 Cameron St · 301-589-8171	A thorn in the side of corporate development.

Map 27 · Walter Reed

Battleground National Military Cemetery	6625 Georgia Ave NW	Check out the entrance.
Walter Reed Army Medical Center	6900 Georgia Ave NW · 202-782-2200	Giant band-aid dispenser.

Map 28 · Chevy Chase

Avalon Theatre	5612 Connecticut Ave NW · 202-966-6000	Beloved neighborhood movie house.

Map 29 · Bethesda (South)

Montgomery Farm Women's Co-op Market (Wed; Sat; 7am–3pm)	7155 Wisconsin Ave · 301-652-2291	Indoor country market.
Writer's Center	4508 Walsh St · 301-654-8664	Take a class, write for NFT.

Map 30 · Westmoreland Circle

Mushroom House	4940 Allan Rd	Private residence is a life-sized smurf house.

Map 32 · Cherrydale / Palisades

Battery Kemble Park	Battery Kemble Park	Top sledding spot on snow days.
The Boathouse at Fletcher's Cove	4940 Canal Rd NW · 202-244-0461	Boats, angling, and info.
Old Aqueduct Bridge	Chesapeake & Ohio Canal	All that remains of this former cargo-carrying structure has been overtaken by graffiti. Nice.

Map 34 · Cherrydale / Ballston

Ballston Commons	4238 Wilson Blvd · 703-243-6346	Big box invasion.

Map 35 · Cherrydale / Clarendon

Market Commons	2690 Clarendon Blvd	Chain retail disguised as Main Street.

Map 36 · Rosslyn

Arlington County Detention Facility (Jail)	1425 N Courthouse Rd · 703-228-4484	We all make mistakes.
Arlington National Cemetery	Arlington National Cemetery · 703-607-8000	Visit again and again—just not during tourist season.
Iwo Jima Memorial	N Meade St & Arlington Blvd · 703-289-2500	Visit at night.
Netherlands Carillon Park	N Meade St & N Marshall Dr	It's all about the view.

Map 37 · Fort Myer

Arlington Cinema 'N' Drafthouse	2903 Columbia Pike · 703-486-2345	Good movies, beer, pizza, waitresses, cigarettes. Life is good.
Bob and Edith's Diner	2310 Columbia Pike · 703-920-6103	Bargain breakfast 24/7.

Map 38 · Columbia Pike

Ball-Sellers House	5620 S 3rd St · 703-892-4204	Will be McMansion someday.

Map 39 · Shirlington

Fort Ward Museum & Historic Site	4301 W Braddock Rd · 703-746-4848	Eerie; we fought each other.

Map 40 · Pentagon City / Crystal City

Pentagon	Boundary Channel Dr · 703-697-1776	Rummy's playpen.

Map 41 · Landmark

Dora Kelley Park	5750 Sanger Ave · 703-838-4829	It's no Yellowstone, but it makes for a pleasant walk in the woods.
Shenandoah Brewing Company	652 S Pickett St · 703-823-9508	Brew your own beer on site.
Winkler Botanical Preserve	5400 Roanoke Ave · 703-578-7888	A 44-acre gem in the suburban rough.

Map 42 · Alexandria (West)

Schuyler Hamilton Jones Skate Park	3540 Wheeler Ave	Free skateboard park. Skate at your own risk.

Map 43 · Four Mile Run / Del Ray

Dog Park	At Simpson Stadium Park, NW Corner of E Monroe Ave & Jefferson Davis Hwy	The neighborhood hangout—dogs hump, people preen.

Map 44 · Alexandria Downtown

George Washington Masonic National Memorial	101 Callahan Dr · 703-683-2007	Nice views from the top.
Union Station	110 Callahan Dr	The other Union Station; good people-watching post.

Map 46 · Old Town (South)

Alexandria City Farmers Market	301 King St · 703-838-4770	Get yer arugula (Sat; 5am–11am)
Alexandria City Hall	301 King St · 703-838-4000	Founded in 1749.
Alexandria National Cemetery	1450 Wilkes St · 703-221-2183	Visit the graves of buffalo soldiers.
Christ Church	118 N Washington St · 703-549-1450	Sit in GW's pew.
Confederate Statue "Appomattox"	S Washington St & Prince St	This is The South, don't forget.
Gadsby's Tavern Museum	134 N Royal St · 703-746-4242	Many US Presidents slept here.
The Littlest House in Alexandria	523 Queen St	It's only 7 feet wide!
Market Square Old Town	301 King St	Bring your skateboard.
Ramsay House	221 King St · 70-838-4200	Alexandria's visitor center.
Shipbuilder Monument	Waterfront Park, 1A Prince St	Visit him; he gets lonely.
Stabler-Leadbeater Apothecary Museum	105 S Fairfax St · 703-746-3852	Where GW (the original) got his Viagra.
Torpedo Factory Art Center	105 N Union St · 703-838-4565	Now it churns out art.

Baltimore

Baltimore Tattoo Museum	1534 Eastern Ave · 410-522-5800	It'll make you want to get that "Jesus Rocks."

Self Storage Locations

	Address	Phone	Map
H Street Self Storage	624 H St NE	202-543-9080	3
Public Storage	1230 S Capitol St SE	202-479-4510	6
Security Moving & Storage	1701 Florida Ave NW	202-234-5600	9
Anytime Moving, Storage & Delivery	1420 U St NW	202-483-9109	10
Extra Space Storage	1420 U St NW	202-667-6333	10
Omega Van Lines	1700 14th St NW	202-234-5599	10
R Street Self Storage	175 R St NE	202-529-7867	11
U-Haul	2215 5th St NE	202-269-1200	11
U-Haul	26 K St NE	202-289-5480	11
U-Store	301 New York Ave NE	202-547-7500	11
U-Haul	1750 Bladensburg Rd NE	202-529-4676	12
Tadesse	4215 Connecticut Ave NW	202-244-4826	20
Uptown Self Storage	1200 Upshur St NW	202-541-1555	21
Public Storage	7800 Fenton St	301-585-3567	25
Public Storage	5423 Butler Rd	301-913-0247	29
Security Public Storage	5221 River Rd	301-652-6966	29
Public Storage	6319 Arlington Blvd	703-534-3016	33
Extra Space Storage	1001 N Fillmore St	703-516-7687	37
Extra Space Storage	3000 10th St N	703-243-3255	37
Public Storage	401 S Pickett St	703-370-2077	41
Extra Space Storage	1022 N Henry St	703-548-8545	45

Van & Truck Rental

		Address	Phone	Map
Budget	Parker Svcs	2205 14th St NW	202-842-8668	10
Budget	Washington DC Truck Rental	2605 Reed St NE	202-636-8160	11
Budget	U Store Self Storage	301 New York Ave NE	202-547-3812	11
Budget	Uptown Self Storage	1200 Upshur St NW	202-723-0807	21
Budget	Shurgard Storage	400 N Roosevelt Blvd	703-536-2243	33
Budget	D&V Service Center	5201 Wilson Blvd	703-525-0724	34
Budget	World Motors	4160B S Four Mile Run Dr	703-931-3956	39
Penske	Capitol Termite & Pest	5455 Butler Rd	301-907-0111	29
Penske	Gib Leonard's Rental Car	3210 10th St N	703-243-1897	37
U-Haul		1501 S Capitol St SW	202-554-2640	6
U-Haul	U Street Rentals	919 U St NW	202-462-4644	10
U-Haul		2215 5th St NE	202-269-1200	11
U-Haul		26 K St NE	202-289-5480	11
U-Haul		1750 Bladensburg Rd NE	202-529-4676	12
U-Haul		5016 Rock Creek Church Rd NE	202-526-1082	14
U-Haul		5654 Columbia Pike	703-931-7897	38
U-Haul	Shirlington Self Storage	2710 S Nelson St	703-820-9749	39
U-Haul		310 Hooffs Run Dr	703-739-1528	44

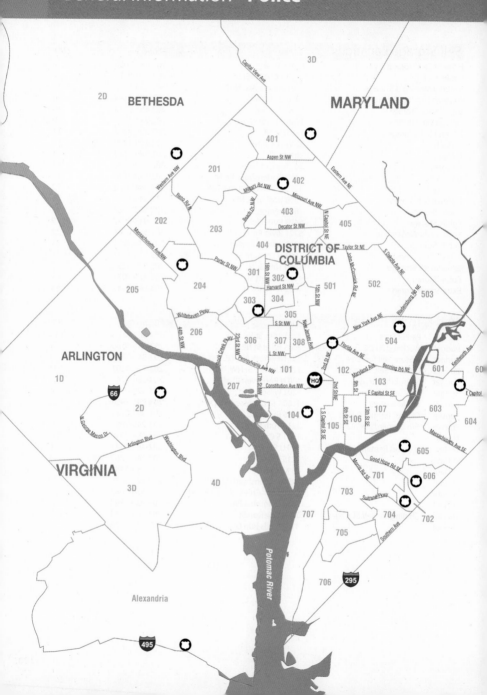

Washington DC is divided into 44 Police Service Areas (PSAs). Each PSA is staffed with a minimum of 21 MPDC officers (with the exception of PSA 707, which essentially consists of Bolling Air Force Base). High-crime neighborhoods are assigned more than the minimum number of police. For example, PSA 105 has the minimum 21 officers, while 93 officers patrol the statistically more dangerous PSA 101.

Metropolitan Police DC

All Emergencies:	911
Police Non-Emergencies:	311
Citywide Call Center:	202-727-1000
Crimesolvers Tip Line:	800-673-2777
Child Abuse Hotline:	202-671-7233
Corruption Hotline:	800-298-4006
Drug Abuse Hotline:	888-294-3572
Hate Crimes Hotline:	202-727-0500
Public Information Office:	202-727-4383
Office of Citizen Complaint Review:	202-727-3838
Website:	http://mpdc.dc.gov

Stations Within NFT Coverage Area

Headquarters: 300 Indiana Ave NW • Map 2
District Stations:
1st District Substation • 500 E St SE • 202-698-0068 • Map 5
1st District Station • 415 4th St SW • 202-698-0555 • Map 6
Gay & Lesbian Liaison Unit •
   1369 Connecticut Ave NW • 202-727-5427 • Map 9
3rd District Station •
   1620 V St NW • 202-673-6815 • Map 9
5th District Station •
   1805 Bladensburg Rd NE • 202-698-0150 • Map 12
3rd District Substation •
   750 Park Rd NW • 202-576-8222 • Map 15
3rd District Latino Liaison Unit •
   1800 Columbia Rd NW • 202-673-4445 • Map 16
2nd District Station •
   3320 Idaho Ave NW • 202-282-0070 • Map 18

Statistics	2005	2004	2003	2002
(No stats beyond 2005)				
Homicide	195	198	248	262
Forcible Rape	267	218	173	262
Robbery	4,037	3,057	3,836	3,731
Aggravated Assault	3,308	3,863	4,482	4,854
Burglary	3,837	3,943	4,670	5,167
Larceny/Theft	14,480	13,756	17,362	20,903
Stolen Auto	6,642	8,136	9,549	9,168
Arson	46	81	126	109

Alexandria Police (VA)

All Emergencies:	911
Non-Emergencies:	703-838-4444
Community Support:	703-838-4763
Crime Prevention:	703-838-4520
Domestic Violence Unit:	703-706-3974
Parking:	703-838-3868
Property-Lost & Found:	703-838-4709
Website:	http://ci.alexandria.va.us/police

Stations Within NFT Coverage Area

Alexandria Police Department •
   2003 Mill Rd • 703-838-4444 • Map 44

Statistics	2006	2005	2004	2003
Homicide	5	4	2	4
Rape	23	23	31	26
Robbery	202	197	187	179
Aggravated Assault	178	201	213	192
Burglary	389	371	426	497
Auto Theft	380	513	635	640
Larceny/Theft	2,537	2,699	2,937	3,754

Arlington County Police (VA)

All Emergencies:	911
Non-Emergencies:	703-228-3000
Rape Crisis, Victims of Violence	703-228-4848
Child Abuse:	703-228-1500
Domestic Violence Crisis Line	703-358-4848
National Capital Poison Center:	202-625-3333
Website:	www.co.arlington.va.us/police

Stations Within NFT Coverage Area

Arlington County Police Department •
   1425 N Courthouse Rd • 703-228-4040 • Map 36

Statistics	2006	2005	2004	2003	2002
Homicide	4	5	1	3	5
Rape	22	36	26	41	33
Robbery	168	163	184	212	213
Aggravated Assault	192	204	200	183	190
Burglary	360	357	361	408	425
Larceny/Theft	3,325	3,668	3,839	4,050	4,990
Auto Theft	357	419	493	662	676

Montgomery County Police (MD)

All Emergencies:	911
Montgomery Non-Emergencies:	301-279-8000
24-Hour Bioterrorism Hotline:	240-777-4200
Takoma Park Non-Emergencies:	301-891-7102
Chevy Chase Village Police:	301-654-7302
Animal Services:	240-773-5925
Community Services:	301-840-2585
Operation Runaway:	301-251-4545
Party Buster Line:	240-777-1986
Website:	www.montgomerycountymd.gov

Stations Within NFT Coverage Area

3rd District - Silver Spring •
   801 Sligo Ave • 301-565-7744 • Map25
Takoma Park Police Dept •
   7500 Maple Ave • 301-891-7102 • Map 26
MPDC 4th District Station •
   6001 Georgia Ave NW • 202-576-6745 • Map 27
Chevy Chase Village Police •
   5906 Connecticut Ave NW • 301-654-7302 • Map28
2nd District - Bethesda •
   7359 Wisconsin Ave • 301-652-9200 • Map 29

Statistics	2006	2005	2004	2003	2002
Homicide	15	19	18	21	32
Rape	141	150	140	135	138
Robbery	1,166	1,035	789	1,004	877
Aggravated Assault	833	875	987	954	878
Burglary	3,804	3,570	3,741	4,095	3,874
Larceny	16,860	15,869	15,503	17,875	18,897
Auto Theft	2,493	2,486	2,562	3,489	3,722

Post Office	Address	Phone	Zip	Map
Benjamin Franklin	1200 Pennsylvania Ave NW	202-842-1444	20004	1
National Capitol Station	2 Massachusetts Ave NE	202-523-2368	20002	2
Union Station	50 Massachusetts Ave NE	202-523-2057	20002	2
Fort McNair Station	300 A St SW	202-523-2144	20319	3
Northeast Station	1563 Maryland Ave NE	202-842-4421	20002	4
Southeast Station	600 Pennsylvania Ave SE	202-682-9135	20003	5
L'Enfant Plaza Station	437 L'Enfant Plz SW	202-842-4526	20024	6
Southwest Station	45 L St SW	202-523-2590	20024	6
McPherson Station	1750 Pennsylvania Ave NW	202-523-2394	20006	7
Watergate Station	2512 Virginia Ave NW	202-965-6278	20037	7
Georgetown Station	1215 31st St NW	202-842-2487	20007	8
Farragut Station	1800 M St NW	202-523-2024	20036	9
Temple Heights Station	1921 Florida Ave NW	202-234-4253	20009	9
Twentieth St Station	2001 M St NW	202-842-4654	20036	9
Ward Place Station	2121 Ward Pl NW	202-842-4645	20037	9
Washington Square Station	1050 Connecticut Ave NW	202-842-1211	20036	9
Martin Luther King Jr Station	1400 L St NW	202-523-2001	20005	10
T Street	1915 14th St NW	202-483-9580	20009	10
Techworld Station	800 K St NW	202-842-2309	20001	10
Le Driot Park	416 Florida Ave NW	202-635-5311	20001	11
Washington Main Office	900 Brentwood Rd NE	202-636-1972	20018	11
Woodridge Station	2211 Rhode Island Ave NE	202-842-4340	20018	13
Brookland Station	3401 12th St NE	202-842-3374	20017	14
Catholic University Cardinal Station	620 Michigan Ave NE	202-319-5225	20064	14
Columbia Heights Finance	3321 Georgia Ave NW	202-523-2674	20010	15
Howard University Post Office	2400 6th St NW	202-806-2008	20059	15
Kalorama Station	2300 18th St NW	202-523-2906	20009	16
Cleveland Park Station	3430 Connecticut Ave NW	202-364-0178	20008	17
Calvert Station	2336 Wisconsin Ave NW	202-523-2907	20007	18
Petworth Station	4211 9th St NW	202-523-2681	20011	21
Silver Spring Finance Centre	8455 Colesville Rd	301-608-1305	20910	25
Takoma Park	6909 Laurel Ave	301-270-4392	20912	26
Brightwood Station	6323 Georgia Ave NW	202-635-5300	20011	27
Walter Reed Station	6800 Georgia Ave NW	202-782-3768	20012	27
Chevy Chase Branch	5910 Connecticut Ave NW	301-654-7538	20815	28
Northwest Station	5636 Connecticut Ave NW	202-842-2286	20015	28
Arlington Road	7001 Arlington Rd	301-656-8053	20814	29
Bethesda	7400 Wisconsin Ave	301-654-5894	20814	29
Friendship Heights Station	5530 Wisconsin Ave	301-941-2695	20815	29
Palisades Station	5136 MacArthur Blvd NW	202-842-2291	20016	32
North Station	2200 N George Mason Dr	703-536-6269	22207	34
Arlington Main Office	3118 Washington Blvd	703-841-2118	22210	35
Court House Station	2043 Wilson Blvd	703-248-9337	22201	36
Rosslyn Station	1101 Wilson Blvd	703-525-4336	22209	36
South Station	1210 S Glebe Rd	703-979-2821	22204	37
Park Fairfax Station	3682 King St	703-933-2686	22302	39
Eads Station	1720 S Eads St	703-892-0840	22202	40
Pentagon Branch	9998 The Pentagon	703-695-6835	20301	40
Trade Center Station	340 S Pickett St	703-823-0968	22304	41
Theological Seminary	3737 Seminary Rd	703-751-6791	22304	42
Potomac Station Finance	1908 Mt Vernon Ave	703-684-7821	22301	43
Alexandria Main Office	1100 Wythe St	703-684-7168	22314	45
George Mason Station	200 N Washington St	703-519-0386	22314	46

General Information · **Post Offices & Zip Codes**

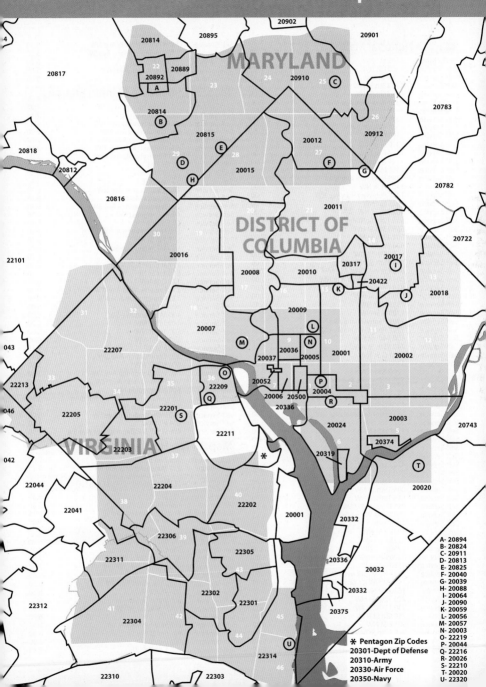

MARYLAND

DISTRICT OF COLUMBIA

VIRGINIA

A- 20894
B- 20824
C- 20911
D- 20813
E- 20825
F- 20040
G- 20039
H- 20088
I- 20064
J- 20090
K- 20059
L- 20056
M- 20057
N- 20003
O- 22219
P- 20044
Q- 22216
R- 20026
S- 22210
T- 20020
U- 22320

✳ Pentagon Zip Codes
20301-Dept of Defense
20310-Army
20330-Air Force
20350-Navy

Map 1 • National Mall

Last pick-up

FedEx Kinko's	1445 I St NW	8:45
Self-Service	1300 I St NW	7:30
Self-Service	975 F St NW	7:30
Self-Service	700 13th St NW	7:15
Self-Service	888 16th St NW	7:15
FedEx Kinko's	1350 New York Ave NW	7:00
FedEx Kinko's	419 11th St NW	7:00
Self-Service	1201 F St NW	7:00
Self-Service	1201 Penn Ave NW	7:00
Self-Service	1250 I St NW	7:00
Self-Service	1310 G St NW	7:00
Self-Service	1317 F St NW	7:00
Self-Service	1341 G St NW	7:00
Self-Service	1350 I St NW	7:00
Self-Service	1399 New York Ave NW	7:00
Self-Service	1401 H St NW	7:00
Self-Service	1455 Pennsylvania Ave NW	7:00
Self-Service	1625 I St NW	7:00
Self-Service	401 9th St NW	7:00
Self-Service	555 12th St NW	7:00
Self-Service	555 13th St NW	7:00
Self-Service	601 13th St NW	7:00
Self-Service	624 9th St NW	7:00
Self-Service	655 15th St NW	7:00
Self-Service	734 15th St NW	7:00
Self-Service	800 Connecticut Ave NW	7:00
Self-Service	801 Pennsylvania Ave NW	7:00
Self-Service	815 Connecticut Ave NW	7:00
Self-Service	900 17th St NW	7:00
Self-Service	1333 H St NW	6:45
Self-Service	1700 G St NW	6:45
Self-Service	1701 Pennsylvania Ave NW	6:45
Self-Service	1717 Pennsylvania Ave NW	6:45
Self-Service	600 14th St NW	6:45
Self-Service	740 15th St NW	6:45
Self-Service	1001 G St NW	6:30
Self-Service	1100 H St NW	6:30
Self-Service	1200 G St NW	6:30
Self-Service	1200 New York Ave NW	6:30
Self-Service	1212 New York Ave NW	6:30
Self-Service	1299 Pennsylvania Ave NW	6:30
Self-Service	1325 G St NW	6:30
Self-Service	1331 Pennsylvania Ave NW	6:30
Self-Service	1575 I St NW	6:30
Self-Service	1717 H St NW	6:30
Self-Service	1730 Pennsylvania Ave NW	6:30
Self-Service	201 14th St SW	6:30
Self-Service	400 N Capitol St NW	6:30
Self-Service	470 L'Enfant Plz SW	6:30
Self-Service	600 13th St NW	6:30
Self-Service	700 11th St NW	6:30
Self-Service	805 15th St NW	6:30
Self-Service	815 14th St NW	6:30
Self-Service	955 L'Enfant Plz SW	6:30
Self-Service	100 Raoul Wallenberg Pl SW	6:15
Self-Service	1000 Jefferson Dr SW	6:15
Self-Service	1025 F St NW	6:00
Self-Service	1225 I St NW	6:00
Self-Service	1250 H St NW	6:00
Self-Service	1300 Pennsylvania Ave NW	6:00
Self-Service	1330 G St NW	6:00
Self-Service	1425 New York Ave NW	6:00
Self-Service	14th St NW & Constitution Ave NW	6:00
Self-Service	1620 I St NW	6:00
Self-Service	700 12th St NW	6:00
Self-Service	730 15th St NW	6:00
Self-Service	750 9th St NW	6:00
Self-Service	901 E St NW	6:00
Self-Service	910 17th St NW	6:00
Self-Service	950 F St NW	6:00
Self-Service	901 F St NW	5:45

Self-Service	1200 Pennsylvania Ave NW	5:30
Self-Service	1400 Independence Ave SW	5:30
Self-Service	910 16th St NW	5:30
Self-Service	1201 New York Ave NW	5:00
Self-Service	1455 F St NW	5:00

Map 2 • Chinatown / Union Station

Self-Service	50 Massachusetts Ave NE	7:30
Self-Service	820 1st St NE	7:15
Self-Service	20 Massachusetts Ave NW	7:00
Self-Service	600 New Jersey Ave NW	7:00
Self-Service	601 New Jersey Ave NW	7:00
Self-Service	601 Pennsylvania Ave NW	7:00
Self-Service	701 Pennsylvania Ave NW	7:00
Self-Service	10 G St NE	6:45
FedEx Kinko's	325 7th St NW	6:30
Self-Service	1 First St NE	6:30
Self-Service	101 Constitution Ave NW	6:30
Self-Service	2 Bethesda Metro Ctr	6:30
Self-Service	200 Independence Ave SW	6:30
Self-Service	499 S Capitol St SW	6:30
Self-Service	50 F St NW	6:30
Self-Service	500 New Jersey Ave NW	6:30
Self-Service	575 7th St NW	6:30
Self-Service	600 Maryland Ave SW	6:30
Self-Service	750 1st St NE	6:30
Self-Service	777 N Capitol St NE	6:30
Self-Service	810 1st St NE	6:30
Self-Service	122 C St NW	6:00
Self-Service	25 Massachusetts Ave NW	6:00
Self-Service	333 Constitution Ave NW	6:00
Self-Service	400 1st St NW	6:00
Self-Service	400 Maryland Ave SW	6:00
Self-Service	440 1st St NW	6:00
Self-Service	500 1st St NW	6:00
Self-Service	550 1st St NW	6:00
Self-Service	100 F St NE	5:45
Self-Service	200 Constitution Ave NW	5:45
Self-Service	600 5th St NW	5:30
Self-Service	600 Independence Ave SW	5:30
Self-Service	600 Pennsylvania Ave NW	5:30
Self-Service	800 N Capitol St NW	5:30
Self-Service	Longworth House Office Building	5:30
Self-Service	1 Columbus Cir NE	5:00
Self-Service	330 Independence Ave SW	5:00
Self-Service	401 F St NW	5:00
Self-Service	4th St SW & Independence Ave SW	2:30

Map 3 • The Hill

FedEx Kinko's	208 2nd St SE	7:00
Self-Service	227 Massachusetts Ave NE	6:15

Map 5 • Southeast / Anacostia

FedEx Kinko's	715 D St SE	6:30
Self-Service	1201 M St SE	5:30
Self-Service	1100 New Jersey Ave SE	5:15
Self-Service	300 M St SE	5:00

Map 6 • Waterfront

Self-Service	330 C St SW	7:00
Self-Service	400 6th St SW	7:00
Self-Service	400 Virginia Ave SW	7:00
Self-Service	445 12th St SW	6:45
Self-Service	1330 Maryland Ave SW	6:30
Self-Service	301 4th St SW	6:30
Self-Service	600 Water St SW	6:30
Self-Service	7th St SW & D St SW	6:30
Self-Service	901 D St SW	6:30
Self-Service	1280 Maryland Ave SW	6:00
Self-Service	409 3rd St SW	6:00
Self-Service	500 E St SW	6:00
Self-Service	550 12th St SW	5:30

General Information · **FedEx**

Self-Service	80 M St SE	5:30
Self-Service	2100 2nd St SW	4:30
Self-Service	300 7th St SW	2:00

Map 7 · Foggy Bottom

Self-Service	431 18th St NW	7:30
Self-Service	1735 New York Ave NW	7:00
Self-Service	1747 Pennsylvania Ave NW	7:00
Self-Service	1750 H St NW	7:00
Self-Service	1776 I St NW	7:00
Self-Service	1919 Pennsylvania Ave NW	7:00
Self-Service	1922 F St NW	7:00
Self-Service	2001 Pennsylvania Ave NW	7:00
Self-Service	2025 E St NW	7:00
Self-Service	2100 Pennsylvania Ave NW	7:00
Self-Service	716 20th St NW	7:00
Self-Service	900 19th St NW	6:45
Self-Service	919 18th St NW	6:30
Self-Service	1801 Pennsylvania Ave NW	6:00
Self-Service	1899 Pennsylvania Ave NW	6:00
Self-Service	18th St NW & F St NW	6:00
Self-Service	2150 Pennsylvania Ave NW	6:00
Self-Service	600 New Hampshire Ave NW	6:00
Self-Service	800 21st St NW	6:00
Self-Service	1250 24th St NW	5:30
Self-Service	1808 I St NW	5:30
Self-Service	900 23rd St NW	5:30
Self-Service	2201 C St NW	5:00
Self-Service	1750 Pennsylvania Ave NW	4:00
Self-Service	2401 E St NW	4:00

Map 8 · Georgetown

Self-Service	1055 Thomas Jefferson St NW	7:30
FedEx Kinko's	1002 30th St NW	7:00
Self-Service	1000 Potomac St NW	7:00
Self-Service	3000 K St NW	7:00
Self-Service	1010 Wisconsin Ave NW	6:30
Self-Service	1101 30th St NW	6:30
Self-Service	2150 Wisconsin Ave NW	6:30
Self-Service	3329 M St NW	6:30
Self-Service	1000 Thomas Jefferson St NW	6:00
Self-Service	1215 31st St NW	6:00
Self-Service	24th St NW & Massachusetts Ave NW	6:00
Self-Service	3299 K St NW	6:00
Self-Service	3333 K St NW	6:00
Self-Service	2115 Wisconsin Ave NW	5:30
Self-Service	3520 Prospect St NW	5:30
Self-Service	2121 Wisconsin Ave NW	5:00

Map 9 · Dupont Circle / Adams Morgan

Self-Service	1001 16th St NW	7:30
Self-Service	1129 20th St NW	7:30
Self-Service	1255 23rd St NW	7:30
Self-Service	1825 Connecticut Ave NW	7:30
Self-Service	1850 K St NW	7:15
Self-Service	2020 K St NW	7:15
FedEx Kinko's	1 Dupont Circle NW	7:00
FedEx Kinko's	1029 17th St NW	7:00
FedEx Kinko's	1123 18th St NW	7:00
FedEx Kinko's	1825 K St NW	7:00
Self-Service	1015 18th St NW	7:00
Self-Service	1101 Connecticut Ave NW	7:00
Self-Service	1111 19th St NW	7:00
Self-Service	1120 20th St NW	7:00
Self-Service	1145 17th St NW	7:00
Self-Service	1150 17th St NW	7:00
Self-Service	1155 21st St NW	7:00
Self-Service	1200 18th St NW	7:00
Self-Service	1201 Connecticut Ave NW	7:00
Self-Service	1220 19th St NW	7:00
Self-Service	1250 Connecticut Ave NW	7:00
Self-Service	1400 16th St NW	7:00
Self-Service	1501 K St NW	7:00

Self-Service	1615 M St NW	7:00
Self-Service	1616 P St NW	7:00
Self-Service	1666 K St NW	7:00
Self-Service	1801 L St NW	7:00
Self-Service	1828 L St NW	7:00
Self-Service	1900 K St NW	7:00
Self-Service	1920 N St NW	7:00
Self-Service	1921 Florida Ave NW	7:00
Self-Service	2000 K St NW	7:00
Self-Service	2000 L St NW	7:00
Self-Service	2001 L St NW	7:00
Self-Service	2033 K St NW	7:00
Self-Service	2401 Pennsylvania Ave NW	7:00
Self-Service	1025 Connecticut Ave NW	6:45
Self-Service	1625 K St NW	6:45
FedEx Kinko's	1612 K St NW	6:30
FedEx Kinko's	2400 M St NW	6:30
Self-Service	1050 Connecticut Ave NW	6:30
Self-Service	11 Dupont Circle NW	6:30
Self-Service	1133 21st St NW	6:30
Self-Service	1133 Connecticut Ave NW	6:30
Self-Service	1150 22nd St NW	6:30
Self-Service	1155 Connecticut Ave NW	6:30
Self-Service	1156 15th St NW	6:30
Self-Service	1225 Connecticut Ave NW	6:30
Self-Service	1330 Connecticut Ave NW	6:30
Self-Service	1500 K St NW	6:30
Self-Service	1608 Rhode Island Ave NW	6:30
Self-Service	1620 L St NW	6:30
Self-Service	1666 Connecticut Ave NW	6:30
Self-Service	1717 Rhode Island Ave NW	6:30
Self-Service	1725 Desales St NW	6:30
Self-Service	1785 Massachusetts Ave NW	6:30
Self-Service	1901 L St NW	6:30
Self-Service	1919 Connecticut Ave NW	6:30
Self-Service	2001 K St NW	6:30
Self-Service	2030 M St NW	6:30
Self-Service	2121 K St NW	6:30
Self-Service	2300 M St NW	6:30
Self-Service	2440 M St NW	6:30
Self-Service	1015 15th St NW	6:00
Self-Service	1100 17th St NW	6:00
Self-Service	1133 15th St NW	6:00
Self-Service	1150 Connecticut Ave NW	6:00
Self-Service	1300 Connecticut Ave NW	6:00
Self-Service	1350 Connecticut Ave NW	6:00
Self-Service	1501 M St NW	6:00
Self-Service	1700 K St NW	6:00
Self-Service	1819 L St NW	6:00
Self-Service	1909 K St NW	6:00
Self-Service	2001 M St NW	6:00
Self-Service	2311 M St NW	6:00
Self-Service	1211 Connecticut Ave NW	5:45
Self-Service	1730 M St NW	5:45
Self-Service	2120 L St NW	5:45
Ez Business Services	1929 18th St NW	5:30
Self-Service	1120 Connecticut Ave NW	5:30
Self-Service	1140 Connecticut Ave NW	5:30
Self-Service	1255 22nd St NW	5:30
Self-Service	1300 19th St NW	5:30
Self-Service	1529 18th St NW	5:30
Self-Service	1600 K St NW	5:30
Self-Service	1717 Massachusetts Ave NW	5:30
Self-Service	1725 K St NW	5:30
Self-Service	1776 Massachusetts Ave NW	5:30
Self-Service	1899 L St NW	5:30
Self-Service	1900 M St NW	5:30
Self-Service	1920 L St NW	5:30
Self-Service	2175 K St NW	5:30
Self-Service	1200 17th St NW	5:00
Self-Service	2021 K St NW	5:00
Self-Service	1875 Connecticut Ave NW	4:00

(**309**)

Map 10 • Logan Circle / U Street

Self-Service	1090 Vermont Ave NW	7:30
Self-Service	1100 L St NW	7:00
Self-Service	1101 14th St NW	7:00
Self-Service	1101 Vermont Ave NW	7:00
Self-Service	1275 K St NW	7:00
Self-Service	1301 K St NW	7:00
Self-Service	1436 U St NW	7:00
Self-Service	1915 14th St NW	7:00
Self-Service	901 New York Ave NW	7:00
FedEx Kinko's	800 K St NW	6:30
Self-Service	1 Thomas Cir NW	6:30
Self-Service	1120 Vermont Ave NW	6:30
Self-Service	1200 K St NW	6:30
Self-Service	1400 K St NW	6:30
Self-Service	1425 K St NW	6:15
Self-Service	1100 13th St NW	6:00
Self-Service	1121 14th St NW	6:00
Self-Service	1110 Vermont Ave NW	5:30
Self-Service	1111 14th St NW	5:30
Self-Service	1220 L St NW	5:30
Self-Service	1401 K St NW	5:30
Self-Service	1420 K St NW	5:30
Self-Service	520 W St NW	5:30
Self-Service	1400 L St NW	4:30
Mkm Pnet Llc	1020 7th St NW	4:00
Self-Service	1099 14th St NW	3:45

Map 11 • Near Northeast

Federal Express	1501 Eckington Pl NE	8:30
Self-Service	416 Florida Ave NW	7:00
Self-Service	900 2nd St NE	6:00
Self-Service	900 Brentwood Rd NE	5:30
Self-Service	800 Florida Ave NE	5:00

Map 14 • Catholic U

Self-Service	100 Irving St NW	6:30
Self-Service	110 Irving St NW	6:30
Self-Service	3401 12th St NE	6:30
Self-Service	1150 Varnum St NE	6:00
Self-Service	620 Michigan Ave NE	6:00
Self-Service	216 Michigan Ave NE	5:30
Self-Service	3211 4th St NE	5:30

Map 15 • Columbia Heights

FedEx Kinko's	3111 14th St NW	7:00
Self-Service	1390 Kenyon St NW	7:00
Self-Service	2400 6th St NW	5:30
Bara Business Solutions	2851 Georiga Ave NW	5:00
General Services	3613 Georgia Ave NW	5:00

Map 16 • Adams Morgan (North) / Mt Pleasant

Tech Printing	2479 18th St NW	4:30

Map 17 • Woodley Park / Cleveland Park

Self-Service	2500 Calvert St NW	7:00
Self-Service	3430 Connecticut Ave NW	6:00
Self-Service	3100 Massachusetts Ave NW	3:00

Map 18 • Glover Park / Foxhall

Self-Service	3301 New Mexico Ave NW	7:15
Self-Service	3400 Idaho Ave NW	7:00
Self-Service	2233 Wisconsin Ave NW	6:45
Self-Service	3970 Reservoir Rd NW	6:45
Self-Service	4000 Reservoir Rd NW	6:45
Self-Service	4400 Macarthur Blvd NW	6:30
Self-Service	3201 New Mexico Ave NW	6:15
Self-Service	3800 Reservoir Rd NW	6:00
Self-Service	4201 Massachusetts Ave NW	6:00
Palisades Packaging	4885 Macarthur Blvd NW	4:00

Map 19 • Tenleytown / Friendship Heights

FedEx Kinko's	4000 Wisconsin Ave NW	7:00
Self-Service	5301 Wisconsin Ave NW	7:00
Self-Service	5335 Wisconsin Ave NW	7:00
Self-Service	4005 Wisconsin Ave NW	6:30
Self-Service	5225 Wisconsin Ave NW	6:30
Self-Service	4400 Jenifer St NW	6:00
Self-Service	4400 Massachusetts Ave NW	6:00
Self-Service	5100 Wisconsin Ave NW	6:00
Self-Service	4620 Wisconsin Ave NW	5:30

Map 20 • Cleveland Park / Upper Connecticut

Self-Service	4201 Connecticut Ave NW	6:30
Parcel Plus	3509 Connecticut Ave NW	6:00
Self-Service	4301 Connecticut Ave NW	6:00
Self-Service	2900 Van Ness St NW	5:30
Self-Service	4455 Connecticut Ave NW	5:30

Map 22 • Bethesda (North)

Self-Service	8001 Wisconsin Ave	7:15
Self-Service	4833 Rugby Ave	7:00
Self-Service	9030 Old Georgetown Rd	7:00
Self-Service	9650 Rockville Pike	7:00
Self-Service	9000 Rockville Pike	6:45
Self-Service	1 Cloister Court	6:30
Self-Service	2 Center Dr	6:30
Self-Service	45 Center Dr	6:30
Self-Service	7700 Old Georgetown Rd	6:30
Self-Service	7910 Woodmont Ave	6:30
Self-Service	7920 Norfolk Ave	6:00
Self-Service	7735 Old Georgetown Rd	5:30
Self-Service	8901 Wisconsin Ave	3:00

Map 23 • Chevy Chase (North)

Self-Service	8401 Connecticut Ave	6:30

Map 24 • Upper Rock Creek Park

Self-Service	9440 Georgia Ave	7:00
Self-Service	Forny Rd, Bldg #503	6:30
Post Express	9466 Georgia Ave	6:15
Mail Boxes Etc	8639 B 16th St	6:00

Map 25 • Silver Spring

FedEx Kinko's	1407 East West Hwy	7:30
Self-Service	8616 2nd Ave	6:30
Self-Service	8720 Georgia Ave	6:30
Self-Service	8737 Colesville Rd	6:30
Self-Service	8757 Georgia Ave	6:30
Self-Service	8701 Georgia Ave	6:15
Self-Service	1010 Wayne Ave	6:00
Self-Service	1100 Blair Mill Rd	6:00
Self-Service	1109 Spring St	6:00
Self-Service	8121 Georgia Ave	6:00
Self-Service	8403 Colesville Rd	6:00
Self-Service	8555 16th St	6:00
Self-Service	8601 Georgia Ave	6:00
Self-Service	8630 Fenton St	6:00
Self-Service	900 Spring St	6:00
Self-Service	8455 Colesville Rd	5:30
Self-Service	1305 East West Hwy	5:00
Self-Service	1325 East West Hwy	5:00
Self-Service	1335 East West Hwy	5:00
Self-Service	1315 East West Hwy	4:00

Map 26 • Takoma Park

Self-Service	7600 Carroll Ave	6:30
Self-Service	6200 N Capitol St NW	6:00
Takoma Postal & Business	7304 Carroll Ave	6:00

Map 27 • Walter Reed

Self-Service	6925 Willow St NW	6:30
Self-Service	7826 Eastern Ave NW	6:30
Self-Service	6900 Georgia Ave NW	6:00
Self-Service	6930 Carroll Ave	5:30
Postal Connections	7838 Eastern Ave NW	5:00

Map 28 • Chevy Chase

Self-Service	5636 Connecticut Ave NW	5:30

Map 29 • Bethesda (South)

Self-Service	4809 Bethesda Ave	7:45
Self-Service	4405 East West Hwy	7:00
Self-Service	4445 Willard Ave	7:00
Self-Service	4550 Montgomery Ave	7:00
Self-Service	4800 Montgomery Ln	7:00
Self-Service	7101 Wisconsin Ave	7:00
Self-Service	7201 Wisconsin Ave	7:00
Self-Service	7316 Wisconsin Ave	7:00
Self-Service	7501 Wisconsin Ave	7:00
Self-Service	2 Wisconsin Circle	6:45
Self-Service	4330 East West Hwy	6:45
Self-Service	4350 East West Hwy	6:30
Self-Service	4416 East West Hwy	6:30
Self-Service	5454 Wisconsin Ave	6:30
Self-Service	5530 Wisconsin Ave	6:30
Self-Service	5550 Friendship Blvd	6:30
Self-Service	6933 Arlington Rd	6:30
Self-Service	7001 Arlington Rd	6:30
Self-Service	7400 Wisconsin Ave	6:30
Self-Service	7475 Wisconsin Ave	6:30
Self-Service	3 Bethesda Metro Ctr	6:15
Self-Service	4520 East West Hwy	6:15
Self-Service	7200 Wisconsin Ave	6:15
Self-Service	7272 Wisconsin Ave	6:15
Self-Service	7315 Wisconsin Ave	6:15
Bethesda Moto Photo	4823 Bethesda Ave	6:00
Self-Service	4600 East West Hwy	6:00
Self-Service	4630 Montgomery Ave	6:00
Self-Service	7600 Wisconsin Ave	6:00
Self-Service	4800 Hampden Ln	5:15
Self-Service	6900 Wisconsin Ave	5:00
Mailboxes Bethesda	7831 Woodmont Ave	4:30

Map 30 • Westmoreland Circle

Self-Service	4801 Massachusetts Ave NW	6:00
Self-Service	4910 Massachusetts Ave NW	5:30

Map 32 • Cherrydale / Palisades

Self-Service	5125 Macarthur Blvd NW	7:00
Self-Service	5136 Macarthur Blvd NW	6:30
Self-Service	5255 Loughboro Rd NW	6:30

Map 33 • Falls Church

Self-Service	5350 Lee Hwy	6:30
Parcel Plus	2503d N Harrison St	6:00
Self-Service	5877 Washington Blvd	5:15

Map 34 • Cherrydale / Ballston

FedEx Kinko's	4501 Fairfax Dr	7:30
Self-Service	4238 Wilson Blvd	7:00
Self-Service	901 N Stuart St	7:00
Self-Service	4001 N Fairfax Dr	6:30
Self-Service	4301 N Fairfax Dr	6:30
Self-Service	4301 Wilson Blvd	6:30
Self-Service	4350 Fairfax Dr	6:30
Mail Plus	850 N Randolph St Apt 103	6:00
Self-Service	1010 N Glebe Rd	6:00
Self-Service	2200 N George Mason Dr	6:00
Self-Service	4100 N Fairfax Dr	6:00
Self-Service	910 N Glebe Rd	6:00
Self-Service	1100 N Glebe Rd	5:30
Self-Service	1110 N Glebe Rd	5:30
Self-Service	4300 Wilson Blvd	5:30
Self-Service	4245 Fairfax Dr	5:00
Self-Service	4501 N Fairfax Dr	4:30

Map 35 • Cherrydale / Clarendon

Self-Service	2300 Clarendon Blvd	7:30
Self-Service	2500 Wilson Blvd	6:30
Self-Service	2200 Clarendon Blvd	6:00
Self-Service	2801 Clarendon Blvd	6:00
Self-Service	2300 Wilson Blvd	5:30
Self-Service	3319 Lee Hwy	5:30
Self-Service	3434 Washington Blvd	5:30
Self-Service	3101 Wilson Blvd	5:00

Map 36 • Rosslyn

Self-Service	1560 Wilson Blvd	7:30
Self-Service	1300 17th St N	7:15
Self-Service	1525 Wilson Blvd	7:00
Self-Service	1611 N Kent St	7:00
Self-Service	1300 Wilson Blvd	6:45
Self-Service	1001 19th St N	6:30
Self-Service	1530 Wilson Blvd	6:30
Self-Service	1616 Ft Myer Dr	6:30
Self-Service	1916 Wilson Blvd	6:30
Self-Service	1000 Wilson Blvd	6:15
Self-Service	2101 Wilson Blvd	6:15
Self-Service	1101 Wilson Blvd	6:00
Self-Service	1401 Wilson Blvd	6:00
Self-Service	1840 Wilson Blvd	6:00
Self-Service	1911 Ft Myer Dr	6:00
Self-Service	2000 14th St N	6:00
Imon	1715 Wilson Blvd	5:30
Self-Service	1333 N Courthouse Rd	5:30
Self-Service	1415 N Taft St	5:30
Self-Service	1515 N Courthouse Rd	5:30
Self-Service	1600 Wilson Blvd	5:30
Self-Service	2043 Wilson Blvd	5:30
Self-Service	2107 Wilson Blvd	5:30
Self-Service	2111 Wilson Blvd	5:30
PO Boxes Etc	1730 N Lynn St	5:00
Self-Service	1655 Ft Myer Dr	5:00
Self-Service	1801 N Lynn St	5:00

Map 37 • Fort Myer

Self-Service	3300 Fairfax Dr	7:30
Self-Service	2300 9th St S	7:00
Self-Service	3263 Columbia Pike	6:30
Self-Service	3601 Wilson Blvd	6:30
Self-Service	3701 Fairfax Dr	6:00
Pak Mail	1001 N Fillmore St	5:30
Self-Service	1210 S Glebe Rd	5:00
Self-Service	200 N Glebe Rd	5:00
Self-Service	3811 Fairfax Dr	5:00

Map 38 • Columbia Pike — *Last pick-up*

FedEx Kinko's	3515 S Jefferson St	7:00
Self-Service	5113 Leesburg Pike	6:30
Self-Service	5201 Leesburg Pike	6:30
Self-Service	5203 Leesburg Pike	6:30
Self-Service	5699 Columbia Pike	6:30
Self-Service	5107 Leesburg Pike	6:15
Self-Service	4900 Leesburg Pike	6:00
Self-Service	5205 Leesburg Pike	6:00
Self-Service	5100 Leesburg Pike	5:30
Us Freight & Mail	5601 Seminary Rd	5:00

Map 39 • Shirlington

Self-Service	1707 Osage St	7:00
Self-Service	4212 King St	6:30
Self-Service	2700 S Quincy St	6:00
Self-Service	2800 S Shirlington Rd	5:30
Self-Service	2850 S Quincy St	5:00
Self-Service	3101 Park Ctr Dr	5:00

Map 40 • Pentagon City / Crystal City

Self-Service	1601 Crystal Dr	8:00
Self-Service	1225 S Clark St	7:00
Self-Service	200 12th St S	7:00
Self-Service	1215 S Clark St	6:30
Self-Service	1235 S Clark St	6:30
Self-Service	2001 Jefferson Davis Hwy	6:30
Self-Service	201 12th St S	6:30
Self-Service	1632 Crystal Dr	6:00
Self-Service	1729 S Eads St	6:00
Self-Service	2011 Crystal Dr	6:00
Self-Service	775 23rd St S	6:00
Self-Service	1919 S Eads St	5:30
Self-Service	2100 Crystal Dr	5:30
Self-Service	2200 Crystal Dr	5:30
Self-Service	2231 Crystal Dr	5:30
Self-Service	2345 Crystal Dr	5:30
Self-Service	2461 S Clark St	5:30
Self-Service	2611 Jefferson Davis Hwy	5:30
Self-Service	601 12th St S	5:30
Self-Service	701 12th St S	5:30
Self-Service	1 Aviation Cir, Hngr 11	5:00
Self-Service	The Pentagon - Main Concourse	4:30

Map 41 • Landmark

Self-Service	340 S Pickett St	7:00
Self-Service	6137 Lincolnia Rd	6:45
Self-Service	1800 N Beauregard St	6:30
Self-Service	1900 N Beauregard St	6:30
Self-Service	4900 Seminary Rd	6:30
Packaging Store	245 S Van Dorn St	6:00
Self-Service	1701 N Beauregard St	6:00
Self-Service	1801 N Beauregard St	6:00
Self-Service	50 S Pickett St	6:00
Newlon's Box Center	5145 Duke St	5:00
Self-Service	5999 Stevenson Ave	5:00

Map 42 • Alexandria (West)

Self-Service	2900 Eisenhower Ave	7:00
Self-Service	3660a Wheeler Ave	6:30
Self-Service	2807 Duke St	6:00
Self-Service	3015 Colvin St	6:00

Map 43 • Four Mile Run / Del Ray

Self-Service	1901 S Bell St	6:30
Self-Service	3301 Jefferson Davis Hwy	6:30
Self-Service	907 W Glebe Rd	6:15
Self-Service	1908 Mt Vernon Ave	6:00
Self-Service	3131 Mt Vernon Ave	6:00

Map 44 • Alexandria Downtown

FedEx Kinko's	1755 Duke St	8:00
Self-Service	1700 Diagonal Rd	7:00
Self-Service	1800 Diagonal Rd	7:00
Self-Service	225 Reinekers Ln	6:30
Self-Service	1600 Duke St	6:00
Self-Service	2000 Duke St	6:00
Self-Service	2121 Eisenhower Ave	6:00
Self-Service	333 John Carlyle St	6:00
Self-Service	1725 Duke St	5:30
Self-Service	2051 Jamieson Ave	2:30

Map 45 • Old Town (North)

Self-Service	500 Montgomery St	7:30
Self-Service	701 N Faixfax St	7:00
Self-Service	105 Oronoco St	6:30
Self-Service	1320 Braddock Pl	6:30
Self-Service	44 Canal Center Plz	6:30
Self-Service	901 N Pitt St	6:30
Self-Service	1100 Wythe St	6:00
Self-Service	99 Canal Center Plz	5:45
Self-Service	400 N Columbus St	5:00
Self-Service	635 Slaters Ln	5:00
Pack-n-ship Plus	66 Canal Center Plz	5:00
	806 N Fairfax St	4:30

Map 46 • Old Town (South)

Self-Service	685 N Washington St	7:30
Self-Service	1400 Duke St	7:00
Self-Service	300 N Washington St	7:00
Self-Service	515 N Washington St	7:00
Self-Service	1001 Prince St	6:30
Self-Service	1315 Duke St	6:30
Self-Service	310 S Henry St	6:30
Self-Service	901 N Washington St	6:30
Old Town Pack and Ship	824 King St	6:00
Self-Service	1022 Duke St	6:00
Self-Service	110 S Union St	6:00
Self-Service	112 S Alfred St	6:00
Self-Service	126 S Washington St	6:00
Self-Service	1420 King St	6:00
Self-Service	201 N Union St	6:00
Self-Service	211 N Union St	6:00
Self-Service	700 S Washington St	6:00
Self-Service	1101 King St	5:30
Self-Service	320 King St	5:00
Self-Service	510 King St	5:00
Old Town Post Box	127 S Fairfax St	4:00

Overview

Let's face it: The Smithsonian Museums were really cool when you were 10 years old and toured DC with your parents. But you're a cultured adult now, looking to expand your horizons a bit further than dinosaur bones and airplanes (not that dinosaur bones and airplanes aren't cool, because they are). Washington's plethora of small and independent galleries have got it all, from classical to conceptual. To top it off, you're not too likely to be bumped from behind by an unsupervised toddler whose parents wanted to see Degas's ballerinas but couldn't find a babysitter. Although crowds of young professionals aren't always much better, Washington's art galleries offer a more comfortable and casual approach to the art world. Remember that these listings fall into three categories: art museums that are free free free, private galleries that charge admission, and commercial galleries where if you like something enough, you might just take it home.

Dupont Circle is the traditional hub of DC's art scene, with non-Smithsonian art museums that include impressionism at the popular **Phillips Collection (Map 9)** to the shrine of rugs at the **Textile Museum (Map 9)**. Most offer interesting lectures and concert events, and are housed in historic homes, such as the Textile Museum, if you're in the market for a wedding site. The only drawback is that, unlike the bigger museums around the mall, many galleries charge entrance fees and sometimes keep quirky hours (daytime Wednesday through Saturday is your best bet). Planning ahead will definitely pay off if you want to experience the ceramics, painting, sculpture, and other less accessible works of art that these galleries feature.

A good time to check out the Dupont art scene is on the first Friday evening of every month, when most of the galleries open their doors briefly for a free peek, and serve cheese and wine to sweeten the deal. Many of the galleries on R Street, also known as Gallery Row, are converted row houses with narrow staircases, so be careful of art enthusiast bottlenecks on Friday nights; check out **Burdick Gallery (Map 9)** (sculpture and graphics by Inuit artists), **The Kathleen Ewing Gallery (Map 9)** (great photography), **Gallery 10 (Map 9)** (modern and experimental art), **Irvine Contemporary (Map 9)** (art from emerging and established artists), **Spectrum Gallery (Map 8)** (locally owned and devoted to local artists), **Numark Gallery (Map 2)** (modern art from emerging artists), **Robert Brown Gallery (Map 9)** (eclectic, varied exhibitions), and **Studio Gallery (Map 9)** (artist co-op with 30 members).

During the annual Dupont-Kalorama Museum Walk Weekend, held on the first weekend in June, galleries usually allow roaming free of charge (www.dkmuseums.com). The Dupont-Kalorama Museum Walk caters to discerning art critics, groups of children, and families alike, offering exhibits and activities that reflect a desire to inspire the art history buffs as well as the "Da Vinci who?" crowd.

Check out the *Post* and *City Paper* listings for shows at some of the other galleries that, ahead of rampant gentrification, are popping up all over the city. Another great resource for gallery information is the Going Out Guide at www.washingtonpost.com/gog, which has excellent reviews and editor picks of the art galleries in DC, as well as a list with gallery websites at http://art-collecting.com/galleries_dc.htm.

Map 1 • National Mall

Arthur M Sackler Gallery	1050 Independence Ave SW	202-633-1000
Corcoran Gallery of Art	500 17th St NW	202-639-1700
Freer Gallery of Art	1050 Independence Ave SW	202-357-2700
Gallery at Flashpoint	916 G St NW	202-315-1310
National Museum of Women in the Arts	1250 New York Ave NW	202-783-5000
Pepco's Edison Place Gallery	701 9th St NW	202-872-3396
Renwick Gallery	1661 Pennsylvania Ave NW	202-633-7970
Renwick Gallery of the Smithsonian American Art Museum	1700 Pennsylvania Ave NW	202-633-1000

Map 2 • Chinatown / Union Station

Goethe-Institut	812 7th St NW	202-289-1200
National Gallery of Art	3rd St NW & Constitution Ave NW	202-737-4215
Numark Gallery	625 E St NW	202-628-3810

Map 3 • The Hill

Market Five Gallery	201 7th St SE	202-543-7293
The Village on Capitol Hill	705 North Carolina Ave SE	202-546-3040

Map 5 • Southeast / Anacostia

Newman Gallery	513 11th St SE	202-544-7577

Map 7 • Foggy Bottom

Anne C Fisher Gallery	2600 Virginia Ave NW	202-625-7555
Arts Club of Washington	2017 I St NW	202-331-7282
de Andino Fine Arts	2450 Virginia Ave NW	202-861-0638
Dimock Gallery	730 21st St NW	202-994-1525
Dupont Art and Framing	1922 I St NW	202-331-1815
Jerusalem Fund Gallery	2425 Virginia Ave NW	202-338-1958
Luther W Brady Art Gallery	805 21st St NW	202-994-1525
National Academy of Sciences	2101 Constitution Ave NW	202-334-2436
Watergate Gallery	2552 Virginia Ave NW	202-338-4488

Map 8 • Georgetown

Addison-Ripley Fine Art	1670 Wisconsin Ave NW	202-338-5180
Alla Rogers Gallery	1054 31st St NW	202-333-8595
Cherub Antiques	2918 M St NW	202-337-2224
Govinda Gallery	1227 34th St NW	202-333-1180
Jackson Art Center	3048 R St NW	202-342-9778
Jewelerswerk Galerie	3319 Cady's Alley NW	202-337-3319
Maurine Littleton Gallery	1667 Wisconsin Ave NW	202-333-9307
Mu Project	1521 Wisconsin Ave NW	202-333-4119
Old Print Gallery	1220 31st St NW	202-965-1818
P Street Pictures	2621 P St NW	202-337-0066
P&C Art	3108 M St NW	202-965-3833
Parish Gallery	1054 31st St NW	202-944-2310
Prada Gallery	1030 Wisconsin Ave NW	202-342-0067
Ralls Collection	1516 31st St NW	202-342-1754
Susan Calloway Antique Prints & Fine Art	1643 Wisconsin Ave NW	202-965-4601
Susquehanna Antiques	3216 O St NW	202-333-1511

Map 9 • Dupont Circle / Adams Morgan

Aaron Gallery	1717 Connecticut Ave NW	202-234-3311
Alex Gallery	2106 R St NW	202-667-2599
Burton Marinkovich	1506 21st St NW	202-296-6563
Chao Phraya Gallery	2009 Columbia Rd NW	202-745-1111
Conner Contemporary Art	1358 Florida Ave	202-588-8750
Foundry Gallery	1314 18th St NW	202-463-0203
Gallery 10 Limited	1519 Connecticut Ave NW	202-232-3326
Gary Edward's Gallery	1711 Connecticut Ave NW	202-232-5926
Geoffrey Diner Gallery	1730 21st St NW	202-483-5005
Guarisco Gallery	1120 22nd St NW	202-333-8533
Ingrid Hansen Gallery	1203 19th St NW	202-266-5022
International Art Gallery	1625 K St NW	202-466-7979
Jane Haslem Gallery	2025 Hillyer Pl NW	202-232-4644
Marsha Mateyka Gallery	2012 R St NW	202-328-0088
Nevin Kelly Gallery	1517 U St NW	202-232-3464
Open Society Institute Gallery	1120 19th St NW	202-721-5642
Pass Gallery	1617 S St NW	202-745-0796
The Phillips Collection	1600 21st St NW	202-387-2151
Provisions Library	1875 Connecticut Ave NW	202-299-0460
Studio Gallery	2108 R St NW	202-232-8734
Textile Museum	2320 S St NW	202-667-0441
Washington Studio School	2129 S Street NW	202-234-3030
WVSA's ARTiculate Gallery	1100 16th St NW	202-296-9100

Map 10 • Logan Circle / U Street

Adamson Gallery	1515 14th St NW	202-232-0707
G Fine Art	1515 14th St NW	202-462-1601
Hemphill Fine Arts	1515 14th St NW	202-234-5601
Irvine Contemporary Art	1412 14th St NW	202-332-8767
Long View Gallery Gallery	1234 9th St NW	202-232-4788
NNE Gallery	1312 8th St NW	202-276-4540
Plan B	1530 14th St NW	202-234-2711
Touchstone Gallery	901 New York Ave NW	202-347-2787
Transformer Gallery	1404 P St NW	202-483-1102
Vastu	1829 14th St NW	202-234-8344
Warehouse	1021 7th St NW	202-783-3933

Map 11 • Near Northeast

Art Enables	411 New York Ave NE	202-554-9455

Map 12 • Trinidad

Industry Gallery	1358 Florida Ave NE	202-399-1730

Map 14 • Catholic U

Wohlfarth Galleries	3418 9th St NE	202-526-8022

Map 16 • Adams Morgan (North) / Mt Pleasant

District of Columbia Arts Center	2438 18th St NW	202-462-7833
Mexican Cultural Institute	2829 16th St NW	202-728-1647

Map 17 • Woodley Park / Cleveland Park

Adams Davidson Galleries	2727 29th St NW	202-965-3800
International Visions Gallery	2629 Connecticut Ave NW	202-234-5112

Map 18 • Glover Park / Foxhall

Foxhall Gallery	3301 New Mexico Ave NW	202-966-7144
The Kreeger Museum	2401 Foxhall Rd NW	202-337-3050

Map 19 • Tenleytown / Friendship Heights

Kathleen Ewing Gallery	3615 Ordway St NW	202-328-0955
Watkins Collection at Katzen Arts Center	4400 Massachusetts Ave NW	202-885-1300

Map 20 • Cleveland Park / Upper Connecticut

Chevy Chase Gallery	5039 Connecticut Ave NW	202-364-8155

Map 22 • Bethesda (North)

Fraser Gallery	7700 Wisconsin Ave	301-718-9651
Gallery Neptune	5001 Wilson Ln	301-718-0809
Saint Elmo's Fire	4928 St Elmo Ave	301-215-9848

Map 25 • Silver Spring

House of Safori	1105 Spring St	887-723-6741
Pyramid Atlantic	8230 Georgia Ave	301-608-9101
Washington Printmakers Gallery	8230 Georgia Ave	301-273-3660

Map 27 • Walter Reed

A. Salon	6925 Willow St NW	202-882-0740

Map 28 • Chevy Chase

Avant Garde	5520 Connecticut Ave NW	202-966-1045

Map 29 • Bethesda (South)

Designers Art Gallery	4618 Leland St	301-718-0400
Discovery Galleries Limited	4840 Bethesda Ave	301-913-9199
Discovery Too Gallery	7247 Woodmont Ave	301-913-9101
Glass Gallery	5335 Wisconsin Ave NW	202-237-1119
Marin-Price Galleries	7022 Wisconsin Ave	301-718-0622
Osuna Art	7200 Wisconsin Ave	301-654-4500
Waverly Street Gallery	4600 E West Hwy	301-951-9441

Map 34 • Cherrydale / Ballston

Ellipse Arts Center	4238 N Wilson Blvd	703-812-9420
Lac Viet Gallery	5179 Lee Hwy	703-532-4350

Map 35 • Cherrydale / Clarendon

Metropolitan Gallery	2420 Wilson Blvd	703-358-9449

Map 37 • Fort Myer

Arlington Arts Center	3550 Wilson Blvd	703-248-6800

Map 41 • Landmark

Gallery Petalouth Ltd	301 Beauregard St	703-354-1176

Map 43 • Four Mile Run / Del Ray

Del Ray Artisans	2704 Mt Vernon Ave	703-838-4827
Fitzgerald Fine Arts	2502 E Randolph Ave	703-836-1231

Map 44 • Alexandria Downtown

Matthew Johnston Gallery	412 John Carlyle St	703-549-5017

Map 45 • Old Town (North)

Art Whino	717 N St Asaph St	703-462-4135
Studio Antiques & Fine Art	524 N Washington St	703-548-5188

Map 46 • Old Town (South)

Art League	105 N Union St	703-683-1780
ArtCraft	132 King St	703-299-6616
Arts Afire Glass Gallery	1117 King St	703-838-9785
Athenaeum	201 Prince St	703-548-0035
Citron Ann	105 N Union St	703-683-0403
Enamelist Gallery	105 N Union St	703-836-1561
Fiberworks	105 N Union St	703-836-5807
Gallerie Michele	113 King St	703-683-1521
Gallery West	1213 King St	703-549-6006
Mindful Hands	211 King St	703-683-2074
Multiple Exposures	105 N Union St	703-683-2205
P&C Art	212 King St	703-549-2525
Paul McGhee's Old Town Gallery	109 N Fairfax St	703-548-7729
Potomac Fiber Arts Gallery	105 N Union St	703-548-0935
Principle Gallery	208 King St	703-739-9326
Printmakers Inc	105 N Union St	703-683-1342
Scope Gallery	105 N Union St	703-548-6288
Tall Tulips	105 N Union St, Ste 310	703-549-7317
Target Gallery	105 N Union St	703-838-4565
Torpedo Factory Art Center	105 N Union St	703-838-4565

Arts & Entertainment • **Bookstores**

While the shopping scene might give visitors the impression that District residents don't care how they look, the independent bookstore scene will show them that we definitely care about what we read. This is a city of policy wonks, lawyers, writers, defense specialists, and activists—the one thing we all have in common, frankly, is that we're nerds. Washington, DC, and the metropolitan area is, especially recently, brimming with residents with expensive educations, lucrative government contracting jobs, and townhouses with lots of built-in bookshelves meant to house quality reads next to treasures from overseas journeys during diplomatic operations.. So it seems obvious that bookstores here would get as crowded as the Beltway during rush hour. Besides the mega-chain stores like **Borders (Map 1, Map 9, Map 19, Map 25, Map 40)** and **Barnes & Noble (Map 1, Map 8, Map 29, Map 35, Map 43)**, there are several local outlets in town, each with a personality of their own.

Kramerbooks & Afterwords Café (Map 9) in Dupont Circle, for instance, is something of a local landmark. Literary types will meet up here, thumbing the shelves for their next read while they wait, and then often settle into a bookish conversation at the café over a Mocha Ice and fine slice of pie, or in the restaurant for drinks and dinner. **Busboys and Poets (Map 10)** is stocked with nothing but the most progressive, left-wing literature, perfect for the U Street area. **Chapters Literary Bookstore (Map 1)** on 11th Street is an interesting experiment in promoting "literature" as opposed to "fiction"—but this is

more a store for people looking to be told what to read and appreciate, and will not offer you the selection of say, **Politics & Prose (Map 20)**, which is quite easily the city's finest bookstore. It's hard to exit this upper NW gem without wishing to spend the rest of your life buried in a book, and there are authors speaking here every night of the week to further encourage you. There's also two locations of **Big Planet Comics (Map 8, Map 22)** for your inner (or outer) adolescent geek. If you have time to spare, check out the used bookstores for cheaper reads and dusty aromas. Try **Riverby Books (Map 3)** on Capitol Hill, **Second Story Books (Map 9)** in Dupont Circle, **Idle Time Books (Map 16)** in Adams Morgan, and **Book Bank (Map 46)** in Alexandria.

DC's bookstore scene also offers some of the best in specialty non-fiction. The **American Institute for Architects (Map 1)** can offer you histories of every high rise in the Chicago skyline, and the **National Gallery of Art Gift Shop (Map 2)** will provide countless coffee table books on modern art, as well as the accompanying art criticism. Readers of the gay, lesbian, bisexual, and transgender persuasions should head to **Lambda Rising (Map 9)**, the largest LGBT bookstore in the world. For religious studies, there's the **Islamic Center (Map 8)** or the **Catholic Information Center (Map 9)** (to name only two). Basically, this is a town that has national associations of pottery wheelers and international funds for left-handed clarinetists—so if there's a subject you're interested in, there's a nerd to provide you with scholarly literature on it. Go for it!

Map 1 • National Mall

American Institute for Architects	1735 New York Ave NW	202-626-7300	Architecture.
Barnes & Noble	555 12th St NW	202-347-0176	General.
Borders	600 14th St NW	202-737-1385	General.

Map 2 • Chinatown / Union Station

B Dalton Booksellers	50 Massachusetts Ave NE	202-289-1724	General.
National Academies Press	500 5th St NW	202-334-2612	Science and technology, social/ environment issues.
National Gallery of Art	3rd St NW & Constitution Ave NW	202-737-4215	Art books.

Map 3 • The Hill

Riverby Books	417 E Capitol St SE	202-543-4342	Used.
Trover Shop Books & Office	221 Pennsylvania Ave SE	202-547-2665	General.

Map 5 • Southeast / Anacostia

Backstage Inc	545 8th St SE	202-544-5744	Theater and performance.
Capitol Hill Books	657 C St SE	202-544-1621	Second-hand fiction, mystery, and biography.
Fairy Godmother—Children's Books & Toys	319 7th St SE	202-547-5474	Toddler to young adult fiction and nonfiction.
First Amendment Books	645 Pennsylvania Ave SE	202-547-5585	Current events, political history.
Liber Antiquus	313 12th St SE	202-546-2413	Early imprinted books.

Map 7 • Foggy Bottom

George Washington University Book Store	800 21st St NW	202-994-6870	Academic and college.
Washington Law & Professional Books	1900 G St NW	202-223-5543	Law.

Map 8 • Georgetown

Barnes & Noble	3040 M St NW	202-965-9880	General.
Bartleby's Books	1132 29th St NW	202-298-0486	Rare and antiquarian, 18th and 19th century American history, economics, and law.
Big Planet Comics	3145 Dumbarton Ave NW	202-342-1961	Comics.
Bridge St Books	2814 Pennsylvania Ave NW	202-965-5200	General.
Islamic Center	2551 Massachussetts Ave NW	202-332-8343	Islamic books.
Lantern Bryn Mawr Book Shop	3241 P St NW	202-333-3222	Used and rare.

Map 9 · Dupont Circle / Adams Morgan

Books for America	1417 22nd St NW	202-835-2665	Books with a purpose.
Books-A-Million	11 Dupont Cir NW	202-319-1374	General.
Borders	1801 K St NW	202-466-4999	General.
Catholic Information Center	1501 K St NW	202-783-2062	Catholic books.
G Books	1520 U St NW	202-986-9697	Gay/lesbian discount books.
Kramerbooks & Afterwords Café	1517 Connecticut Ave NW	202-387-1400	General.
Second Story Books & Antiques	2000 P St NW	202-659-8884	Used.

Map 10 · Logan Circle / U Street

Busboys and Poets	2021 14th St NW	202-387-7638	Political, poetry and literature, multi-cultural, and independent publishers.

Map 11 · Near Northeast

Bison Shop-Gallaudet University	800 Florida Ave NE	202-651-5271	Academic and sign language.

Map 14 · Catholic U

Basilica Of The National Shrine Bookstore	400 Michigan Ave NE	202-526-8300	Catholic books.
Icon & Book Service	1217 Quincy St NE	202-526-6061	Eastern Christian books.
Newman Book Store of Washington	3025 4th St NE	202-526-1036	Scripture, theology, philosophy, and church history.

Map 15 · Columbia Heights

House Of Khamit	2822 Georgia Ave NW	202-387-4163	African History/Culture.
Howard University Book Store	2225 Georgia Ave NW	202-238-2640	Academic and Afro-centric.
Sankofa Video & Bookstore	2714 Georgia Ave NW	202-234-4755	Afro-centric.

Map 16 · Adams Morgan (North) / Mt Pleasant

AAFSW Book Room	2201 Centre St NW	202-223-5796	General used.
Idle Time Books	2467 18th St NW	202-232-4774	Used.
Potter's House Books	1658 Columbia Rd NW	202-232-5483	Spiritual/Social Justice Literature.

Map 18 · Glover Park / Foxhall

Georgetown University Book Store	3800 Reservoir Rd NW	202-687-7492	Academic.

Map 19 · Tenleytown / Friendship Heights

American University Book Store	4400 Massachusetts Ave NW	202-885-6300	Academic and college.
Borders	5333 Wisconsin Ave NW	202-686-8270	Books, music and movies OH MY.
Kultura	4918 Wisconsin Ave NW	202-244-0224	Specializing in arts and humanities.
Red Sky Books	4318 Fessenden St NW	202-363-9147	Used and out-of-print.
Tempo Book Store	4905 Wisconsin Ave NW	202-363-6683	Language.

Map 20 · Cleveland Park / Upper Connecticut

Politics & Prose	5015 Connecticut Ave NW	202-364-1919	One of the top bookstores in DC.

Map 22 · Bethesda (North)

Big Planet Comics	4908 Fairmont Ave	301-654-6856	Superhero genealogy experts on hand.

Map 23 · Chevy Chase (North)

Audubon Naturalist Bookshop	8940 Jones Mill Rd	301-652-3606	Nature and earth.

Map 25 · Silver Spring

Alliance Comics	8317 Fenton St	301-588-2546	Comics.
Borders	8518 Fenton St	301-585-0550	Chain.
Silver Spring Books	938 Bonifant St	301-587-7484	Used.

Map 29 · Bethesda (South)

Barnes & Noble	4801 Bethesda Ave	301-986-1761	General.
Writer's Center	4508 Walsh St	301-654-8664	Literature and books on writing.

Map 33 • Falls Church

Aladdin's Lamp Children's Books	2499 N Harrison St	703-241-8281	Children's.

Map 34 • Cherrydale / Ballston

Bookhouse	805 N Emerson St	703-527-7797	Scholarly history.

Map 35 • Cherrydale / Clarendon

Barnes & Noble	2800 Clarendon Blvd	703-248-8244	General.
Imagination Station at Kinder Haus Toys	1220 N Fillmore St	703-527-5929	Children's.

Map 38 • Columbia Pike

Al-Hikma Book Store	5627 Columbia Pike	703-820-7500	Arabic.
NVCC-Alexandria Campus Book Store	3101 N Beauregard St	703-671-0043	Academic and college.

Map 40 • Pentagon City / Crystal City

Borders	1201 S Hayes St	703-418-0166	General.

Map 43 • Four Mile Run / Del Ray

Barnes & Noble	3651 Jefferson Davis Hwy	703-299-9124	General.
Book Niche & Capital Comics	2008 Mount Vernon Ave	703-548-3466	Books, comics, etc.

Map 44 • Alexandria Downtown

Already Read Used Books	2501 Duke St	703-299-8406	Used.

Map 46 • Old Town (South)

Aftertime Comics	1304 King St	703-548-5030	Comics.
Book Bank	1510 King St	703-838-3620	Used.
Books-A-Million	503 King St	703-548-3432	General.
Pauline Books & Media	1025 King St	703-549-3806	Catholic books.
Sacred Circle Books	919 King St	703-299-9309	Metaphysical.
Why Not	200 King St	703-548-4420	Children's.

Everybody likes the movies. This may not be NY or LA, but film buffs will find plenty to keep them busy; they just need to know where to look. The **E Street Cinema (Map 1)** and Bethesda's **Landmark Bethesda Row (Map 29)** both offer a solid roster of independent films, with some mainstream flicks mixed in. Another indie haven, Chevy Chase's **Avalon Theatre (Map 25),** has special charm: DC's oldest movie house was shut down several years ago by then-owner Loews, but a nonprofit group calling themselves the Avalon Theatre Project took over and revamped this 1923 gem. For film fanatics, however, nothing can beat the **AFI Theater (Map 25)** in downtown Silver Spring. Like a kid in a candy store, you can pick from a few current (usually indie) films or see a flick that's part of the many film series being offered, which run the gamut from "Frankenfest: Frankenstein through the Ages" to "Rebels with a Cause: The Films of East Germany."

If you could care less about French New Wave and documentaries make you snooze, never fear, the DC area abounds with theaters showing the usual mainstream fare. For stadium-seating megaplexes, there's the **Loews Georgetown 14 (Map 8)**, which houses a brick smokestack used long ago as the Georgetown Incinerator, and the **Regal Gallery Place Stadium (Map 2)**, whose fit-for-Caesar marble atrium and 14 screens are cleverly nestled into an already crowded Chinatown. For movie-going frat boys seeking luxury (or their idea of it), the **AMC Mazza Gallerie 7 (Map 19)** offers Club Cinema with (gasp!) leather seats and (high five!) a full-service bar, but tickets cost a couple of bucks more than the rest of the auditoriums. For

a different blockbuster-watching experience, one with old-school glamour and a touch of class, head to **The Uptown (Map 17)** in Cleveland Park, a magnificent art deco theater with the biggest screen (32' x 70') in town. This is a true movie "palace," complete with balcony seating and lines of people dressed like wizards for the opening of Harry Potter.

Slightly off the beaten path is the **Arlington Cinema 'N' Drafthouse (Map 37)**, an old Art Deco theater that hosts live music, stand-up comedy, wine tastings, Kentucky Derby parties, you name it. But its main gig is serving up second-run movies, dinner, and drinks for a bargain price. Keep an eye on their weekly online calendar for discount nights, special events like free advanced screenings, and midnight showings of cult favorites. Other alternative movie happenings to watch out for in the area include various film festivals, and temporary screenings every few weeks at many of the museums, schools, or historic theaters like the **Tivoli (Map 15)** in Columbia Heights and the **Lincoln (Map 10)** on U Street. In summer, there are plenty of free outdoor movie festivals like the classic "Screen on the Green" on the Mall or the NIH's "Science in the Cinema."

No matter where you choose to go, the usual print and online entertainment sources like the *Washington Post*, *City Paper*, and Fandango can give you show times. And remember, Netflix can't offer you movie theater popcorn, and no matter how big your flat-screen TV is, seeing a movie on the big screen is better, so get off the couch once in a while and head to one of DC's movie theaters.

Theater	Address	Phone	Map
AFI Silver Theater	8633 Colesville Rd	301-495-6720	25
AMC Courthouse Plaza 8	2150 Clarendon Blvd	703-243-4950	36
AMC Hoffman Center 22	206 Swamp Fox Rd	703-236-1083	44
AMC Loews Georgetown 14	3111 K St NW	202-342-6033	8
AMC Loews Shirlington 7	2772 S Randolph St	703-671-0912	39
AMC Loews Uptown 1	3426 Connecticut Ave	202-966-5401	17
AMC Mazza Gallerie	5300 Wisconsin Ave NW	202-537-9551	19
American City Diner & Cinema Cafe	5532 Connecticut Ave NW	202-244-1949	28
Arlington Cinema 'N' Drafthouse	2903 Columbia Pike	703-486-2345	37
Avalon Theatre	5612 Connecticut Ave NW	202-966-6000	28
Busboys and Poets	2021 14th St NW	202-387-7638	10
Carnegie Institution	1530 P St NW	202-939-1142	9
Landmark Bethesda Row Cinema	7235 Woodmont Ave	301-652-7273	29
Landmark E St Cinema	555 11th St NW	202-452-7672	1
Lockheed Martin IMAX Theater	601 Independence Ave SW	877-932-4928	2
The Regal Majestic 20	900 Ellsworth Dr	301-565-8884	25
Regal Ballston Common 12	671 N Glebe Rd	703-527-9730	34
Regal Bethesda 10	7272 Wisconsin Ave	301-718-8322	29
Regal Gallery Place Stadium	707 7th St NW	202-393-2121	2
Regal Potomac Yard 16	3575 Jefferson Davis Hwy	703-739-4054	43
Samuel C Johnson IMAX Theater	Constitution Ave NW & 10th St NW	202-633-4629	1
Wechsler Theatre	4400 Massachusetts Ave NW	202-885-2053	19

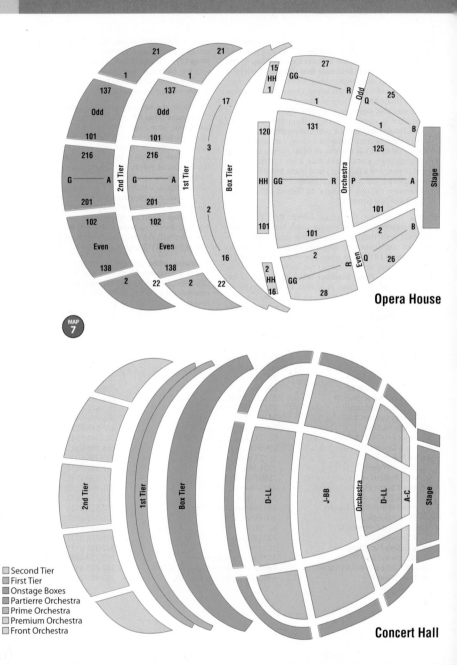

Opera House

MAP 7

Concert Hall

Second Tier
First Tier
Onstage Boxes
Partierre Orchestra
Prime Orchestra
Premium Orchestra
Front Orchestra

General Information

NFT Map: 7
Address: 2700 F St NW
             Washington, DC 20566
Website: www.kennedy-center.org
Phone: 202-416-8000
Box Office: 800-444-1324 or 202-467-4600

Overview

The Kennedy Center is the city's most renowned and lavish performance art destination. While other city venues may be better at promoting cutting-edge arts, this place is where you can witness the best in the world pirouette, harmonize, and/or yodel. Local orchestras and performing artists showcase their work for free on various evenings as well, and the Kennedy Center also hosts auditions for future opera singers, open to the public (with tickets), who become picked for opera houses around the country. Of course, such feats come with a price tag, and the Center tends to cater to thick-of-wallet arts patrons. Those who are more savvy than wealthy, though, know that bargains exist. There are nightly free concerts, hidden cheap seats, and occasional discounts. And there's no charge to show up and check out one of the city's most romantic dusk terrace views or the giant bust of the center's adored namesake. Dinner and a performance is a very classy DC way to spend an evening.

The Kennedy Center houses the Concert Hall, Opera House, Eisenhower Theater, Terrace Theater, Theater Lab, Film Theater, and Jazz Club. On any given night, there are concurrent music, theater, opera, and dance performances. It can be tough to keep up. If you're a confirmed culture vulture, stay afloat by becoming a Kennedy Center member. Otherwise, save the web sites of your favorites and check them regularly.

The Kennedy Center's history began in 1958, when President Dwight D. Eisenhower took a break from the links to sign legislation creating a National Cultural Center for the United States. President John F. Kennedy and First Lady Jackie later did much of the fundraising for what the president called "our contribution to the human spirit." Two months after President Kennedy's assassination, Congress named the center in his memory.

How to Get There—Driving

If you're not one of the patrons who can rely on your limo's GPS, then follow this advice: Heading away from the Capitol on Independence Avenue, get in the left lane as you approach the Potomac. Passing under two bridges, stay in the left lane, and follow signs to the Kennedy Center. After passing the Kennedy Center on your right, make a right onto Virginia Avenue. At the second set of lights, turn right onto 25th Street, and follow the Kennedy Center parking signs.

Parking

Kennedy Center garage parking is $18. Sixty minutes of free parking is available when visiting the box office (except to pick up free tickets) or spending $15 or more at one of the gift shops with validation.

How to Get There—Mass Transit

Take the Blue Line or Orange Line to the Foggy Bottom stop, and either walk seven minutes to the center or take a free shuttle that runs every fifteen minutes. For above-ground transportation-lovers, Metrobus 80 also goes to the Kennedy Center.

How to Get Tickets

Prices vary depending on the event. Check the center's website, or call the box office for schedules and tickets.

Eisenhower Theater

The Smithsonian Institution is a national system of museums, most of which are situated in a campus-like arrangement around the National Mall (other branches, like the Cooper-Hewitt National Design Museum, are located in New York City, and the Steven F. Udvar-Hazy Center, an extension of the **National Air and Space Museum (Map 6)**, is in Chantilly, VA). The free Smithsonian exhibits draw both American and international tourists by the hordes (think Mongol hordes).

The West Building of the **National Gallery (Map 2)** houses a world-class collection of American and Western European painting and sculpture, including the only Leonardo da Vinci painting on this side of the Atlantic. The East Building houses the museum's modern and contemporary collections. At the **Freer and Sackler Galleries (Map 1)**, sublime works of Asian art hide in unlikely corners of small and modest rooms. The **Hirshhorn Museum and Sculpture Garden (Map 2)** is, well, avant-garde—what else could you call the collection that includes Ron Mueck's eerily realistic sculpture of a naked, obese, bald man just hanging out in the corner? The **Corcoran Gallery of Art (Map 1)** is another one of DC's gems, with a solid collection of American and European art, and it also offers a wide range of classes (visit www.corcoran.org for details). The **National Museum of American History (Map 1)** is more than a collection of invaluable artifacts; it addresses the history and the making of American culture. And while the American History museum might make us feel all-important, the **National Museum of Natural History (Map 1)** will deflate our egos, reminding us that we are but one mortal species among many. As depressing as it may be, the relatively new **US Holocaust Museum (Map 1)** is definitely worth visiting—an eerie but well-done reminder of the extent of man's cruelty.

You could spend your whole life in Washington and still not be able to name every Smithsonian museum. But they're all free, so consider them friends who need to be checked in on from time to time.

DC is home to the **National Archives (Map 2)**, a government building that also contains numerous historical documents on exhibit. Stop by and pay nothing to see the *Bill of Rights* and our founding fathers' John Hancocks (even John Hancock's!). And in case you forgot you were living in a democracy—even the FBI building offers guided tours. Extending out from the Mall, you'll discover the private museums. The **National Building Museum's (Map 2)** building and gift shop are interesting, even when the offbeat architectural exhibits are not. When you're in the mood for something more specific, try the targeted collections at places like the **National Museum of the American Indian (Map 2)** or the **National Museum of Women in the Arts (Map 1)**. Finally the recently revamped **Newseum (Map 2)**, with its glassy patio walkway and part of the Berlin Wall, promises an interactive, multimedia experience of journalism.

Museum	Address	Phone	Map
Alexandria Archaeology Museum	105 N Union St	703-746-4399	46
Alexandria Black History Museum	902 Wythe St	703-746-4356	45
American Visionary Art Museum	800 Key Hwy	410-244-1900	n/a
Anacostia Community Museum	1901 Fort Pl SE	202-633-4820	n/a
Arlington Historical Museum	1805 S Arlington Ridge Rd	703-892-4204	40
Art Museum of the Americas	201 18th St NW	202-458-6016	7
Arts Club of Washington	2017 I St NW	202-331-7282	7
Athenaeum	201 Prince St	703-548-0035	46
Corcoran Gallery of Art	500 17th St NW	202-639-1700	1
DAR Museum	1776 D St NW	202-628-1776	7
DEA Museum & Visitors Center	700 Army Navy Dr	202-307-3463	40
Decatur House on Lafayette Square	1610 H St NW	202-842-0920	1
Discovery Creek Children's Museum-Historic Schoolhouse	4954 MacArthur Blvd NW	202-337-5111	18
Dumbarton House	2715 Q St NW	202-337-2288	8
Einstein Planetarium-National Air & Space Museum	Independence Ave SW & 4th St SW	202-633-1000	2
Folger Shakespeare Library	201 E Capitol St SE	202-544-4600	3
Ford's Theatre	511 10th St NW	202-347-4833	1
Fort Ward Museum & Historic Site	4301 W Braddock Rd	703-746-4848	39
Frederick Douglass Museum & Caring Hall of Fame	320 A St NE	202-547-4273	3
Frederick Douglass National Historic Site	1411 W St SE	202-426-5961	5
Freer Gallery of Art and Arthur M Sackler Gallery	1050 Independence Ave SW	202-633-1000	1

Museum	Address	Phone	Map
Friendship Firehouse Museum	107 S Alfred St	703-746-3891	46
Gadsby's Tavern Museum	134 N Royal St	703-746-4242	46
George Washington Masonic National Memorial	101 Callahan Dr	703-683-2007	44
Hillwood Museum & Gardens	4155 Linnean Ave NW	202-686-5807	20
Hirshhorn Museum and Sculpture Garden	7th St SW & Independence Ave SW	202-633-1000	2
Historical Society of Washington, DC	801 K St NW	202-383-1850	10
International Spy Museum	800 F St NW	202-393-7798	1
The Kreeger Museum	2401 Foxhall Rd NW	202-337-3050	18
The Lyceum	201 S Washington St	703-746-4994	46
The Mansion on O Street	2020 O St NW	202-496-2020	9
Marian Koshland Science Museum of the National Academy of Sciences	6th St NW & E St NW	202-334-1201	2
MOCA DC	1054 31st St NW	202-342-6230	8
Mount Vernon Estate & Gardens	3200 Mt Vernon Memorial Hwy	202-780-2000	n/a
National Academy of Sciences	500 5th St NW	202-334-2000	2
National Air and Space Museum	Independence Ave SW & 4th St SW	202-633-1000	2
National Aquarium	Constitution Ave NW & 14th St NW	202-482-2825	1
The National Archives Building	700 Pennsylvania Ave NW	202-357-5000	2
National Building Museum	401 F St NW	202-272-2448	2
National Gallery of Art	7th St NW & Constitution Ave NW	202-737-4215	2
National Geographic Museum	1145 17th St NW	202-857-7588	9
National Museum of African Art	950 Independence Ave SW	202-633-4600	1
National Museum of American Jewish Military History	1811 R St NW	202-265-6280	9
National Museum of Health and Medicine	6900 Georgia Ave NW	202-782-2200	27
National Museum of Natural History	Constitution Ave NW & 10th St NW	202-633-1000	1
National Museum of the American Indian	4th St & Independence Ave SW	202-633-1000	2
National Museum of the US Navy (reservation required for non-military)	805 Kidder Breese SE	202-433-4882	5
National Museum of Women in the Arts	1250 New York Ave NW	202-783-5000	1
National Portrait Gallery	8th St NW & F St NW	202-633-8300	1
National Postal Museum	2 Massachusetts Ave NE	202-633-5555	2
National Zoo	3001 Connecticut Ave NW	202-633-4800	17
Newseum	555 Pennsylvania Ave NW	888-639-7386	2
The Octagon Museum	1799 New York Ave NW	202-626-7318	7
Palace of Wonders	1210 H St NE	202-398-7469	3
The Phillips Collection	1600 21st St NW	202-387-2151	9
Pope John Paul II Cultural Center	3900 Harewood Rd NE	202-635-5400	14
Renwick Gallery	1661 Pennsylvania Ave NW	202-633-7970	1
S. Dillon Ripley Center	1100 Jefferson Dr SW	202-633-1000	1
Smithsonian American Art Museum	8th St NW & F St NW	202-633-1000	1
Smithsonian Institution Building (The Castle)	1000 Jefferson Dr SW	202-633-1000	1
The Society of the Cincinnati-Anderson House	2118 Massachusetts Ave NW	202-785-2040	9
Stabler-Leadbeater Apothecary Museum	105 S Fairfax St	703-746-3852	46
Textile Museum	2320 S St NW	202-667-0441	9
The Torpedo Factory	105 N Union St	703-838-4565	46
Tudor Place	1644 31st St NW	202-965-0400	8
US Holocaust Memorial Museum	100 Raoul Wallenberg Pl SW	202-488-0400	1
US Library of Congress	101 Independence Ave SE	202-707-8000	2
Woodrow Wilson Center for International Scholars	1300 Pennsylvania Ave NW	202-691-4000	1

DC's nightlife scene has exploded with high-end, swank nightclubs, reliable neighborhood local bars, and venues with dope rooftop decks for some summer fun. After a long day of Roberts Rules of Order for Hill staffers, exams, and study sessions for the college kids, and office anxiety for the rest of the population, the need to release some energy comes out full force. Happy hour starts in the District around 5 pm with bars and restaurants offering drinks specials, outdoor dining, and tasty eats. The late-night fun usually begins to pick up around midnight and cruises towards the wee hours of 3 am and beyond. And don't let the surplus of stiff business suits, button downs, and ballet flats fool you—this city knows how to unwind. It's a good thing they don't give out tickets for riding drunk on the Metro—expect to see your fair share of alcoholics passed out in the seat next to you. Fair warning: the Metro closes at midnight Sunday through Thursday and at 3 am on Friday and Saturday. But if you keep timing in mind, DC is a prime city for partying. Outside the walls of the office and Congress, your resume only matters if it has drink specials or a wine list all over it. If you have anywhere between $10 and $1000 to spend every night, there is a place for you.

Nightlife revolves around the bustling K Street Corridor, Georgetown, Dupont, Adams Morgan, Columbia Heights, Cleveland Park, U Street, and some of the livelier suburbs, depending on your age, music preference, and mood. Most places in DC are within walking distance of each other (or at least a short cab or Metro ride apart), providing partygoers with several options for party-hopping, and it is guaranteed that hitting up six spots in one night will become an art-form for you and yours.

Georgetown

Throw on your white loafers, designer bag, and strut your stuff with your crew in tow for a weekend out in Georgetown. This is a hodge-podge of college students, upper-crust shop-a-holics, wayward tourists, and local residents who have managed to find nooks and crannies along bustling M Street that the out-of-towners have yet to conquer. Nothing beats watching million-dollar yachts pulling up to the pier at **Sequoia (Map 8)** and **Tony & Joe's (Map 8)**, while you sip cheap drinks and cruise. Need cheap drinks and some Journey in your life? Stroll over to **Third Edition (Map 8)** or **Rhino Bar & Pumphouse (Map 8)**. If you're one of DC's lone Republicans (or if you're progressive when it comes to dating someone of the opposite political affiliation), head to **Smith Point (Map 8)**. Dress the part and party with Euro-trash at **Mate (Map 8)** or try to impress your date and walk into the members only **L2 (Map 8)**. Go low-key at the renowned jazz bar **Blues Alley (Map 8)** and blow your trust fund at **Mr. Smith's (Map 8)** with the other private school kids.

Dupont

Dupont, a.k.a. the gay-bor-hood, is really a mix of all types of party goers in a neighborhood that is classy, expensive, but full of dives. Watch out as you cross the circle, not just for rats, but also for the oncoming cabs. The rooftop party is at **18th Street Lounge (Map 9)** and the underground beer heaven is at **Brickskeller (Map 9)**. For a night of pool, check out **Buffalo Billiards (Map 9)**; for people-watching with some margarita madness, check out the deck at **Lauriol Plaza (Map 9)**. For a sports bar on crack, visit the three-story tall **Public Bar (Map 9)**, which is three floors and far too many flatscreen TVs. Shake your bum-bum at **Café Citron (Map 9)** or grab the best mojitos in town at **Gazuza (Map 9)**. Sophisticated types abound at Circa at Dupont and the gays are grindin' at **Cobalt**

(Map 9) and downing pints at **JR's (Map 9)**. The hot spot the size of your average DC apartment is the plane inspired **Fly Lounge (Map 9)**.

Adams Morgan

In Adams Morgan, you'll find trash, low-class, and the über-rich roughing it for the night. 18th Street attracts a rambunctious crowd of young kids searching for live music, local improv, and a plethora of bars with neon signs, concrete steps, and quaint awnings. The block also offers conveniently placed parking machines to cling onto when you need to vomit the last few beers before crossing the street to go dancing. Sway to reggae and Caribbean rhythms at **Bukom Café (Map 16)**, and take in blues, jazz, rock, or bluegrass at **Madam's Organ (Map 16)**. Roll up your sleeves at **Pharmacy Bar (Map 16)**, DC's best dive, which caters more to locals than visitors and has a great jukebox. And before the evening is done, soothe your late night hunger pangs at **Amsterdam Falafel (Map 16)**.

Cleveland Park

Cleveland Park's nightlife is crammed into the 3400 block of Connecticut Avenue, where Irish bars, basement billiards, and dimly lit enclaves serving sophisticated wines stand next to a melting pot of venues. If you appreciate a good Irish stout and/or could relate to the upper-deck scene in Titanic, then go to **Ireland's Four Provinces (Map 33)**; if you consider yourself more of a lower-deck kind of person, check out **Nanny O'Brien's (Map 17)** across the street. **Atomic Billiards (Map 17)** is a good spot for guzzling beer, throwing darts, and shooting pool. Or grab a relaxing glass of wine after a long day at **Bardeo (Map 17)**, a favorite of local young urban professionals.

U Street

U Street on weekend nights is where you'll find people boozing, dancing, and taking in live music; these same folks also manage to accomplish some of the best philanthropic work the city's needy and less fortunate have seen in years. Dance clubs, live music venues, and drinking are bringing money, people, and prosperity into one of DC's formerly unattractive areas. U Street is experiencing a revitalization thanks to venues such as **Marvin (Map 10)** and **Local 16 (Map 9)**, with their bustling rooftop decks, the **Black Cat (Map 10)**, the **9:30 Club (Map 10)**, and **Velvet Lounge (Map 10)**, and the dance club **DC9 (Map 10)**. For a true European feel in a comfy converted row-house, check out **The Space (Map 10)** and dance the night away till 5 am. Bars such as **Stetson's Famous Bar & Restaurant (Map 9)** and **Solly's U Street Tavern (Map 10)** respect the neighborhood's humble roots, while also providing a place to mingle and perhaps meet that special someone. The area still has shivering huddles of people being whipped by frigid night winds and February snow, but now increasing numbers of them are 25-year-old divas in high heels and designer jackets.

Columbia Heights

One DC's latest urban 'hoods turned gentrified hipster enclaves, Columbia Heights is home to the appropriately named **Wonderful Ballroom (Map 15)**, where PBR and Jim Beam flows like water, and the more upscale **Room 11 (Map 15)**, which features a lengthy wine list and elegant meals for less elegant prices.

Capitol Hill

Don't forget Capitol Hill's **The Dubliner (Map 2)**, **Kelly's Irish Times (Map 2)**, and **Hawk and Dove (Map 3)**, where you'll find plenty of eager wannabes pressing their political and professional agendas. For a nice retreat that's close to the action but a bit removed from the stench of self-importance, meander about the burgeoning strip on 8th Street SE. For upscale wine talk hit the upstairs lounge at **Sonoma (Map 3)** or meet up with the rest of the trendy Hill staff at **Lounge 201 (Map 3)**.

Old Town Alexandria

Alexandria's Old Town may not be a regular haunt of frat boys or the ultra-chic, but it offers a pleasant variety of places to drink and dance, especially for the 30-plus crowd. The proximity to the water, along with the collection of art galleries, upscale boutiques, and historical sites, makes Old Town a great day-night destination. Dance the hours away at **Café Salsa (Map 46)** after filling up on their unbeatable happy-hour mojitos, crank out some karaoke at **Rock It Grill (Map 46)**, or groove to some bluegrass at **Tiffany Tavern (Map 46)**. You can always rub elbows with the über snotty locals (and a fair share of tourists) at **Vermilion (Map 46)**, **Murphy's (Map 46)**, or **Union Street Public House (Map 46)**. And if you're feeling really elitist, you can try to get into **PX (Map 46)**, a hidden speakeasy

with no sign—just a blue light over the front door and no phone number.

Everything Else

The K Street Corridor has blossomed with seven swank lounges and clubs in a two-block radius all competing for your hard-earned pay. Europeans and diplomat kids hop over to **Josephine Lounge (Map 10)** and **Lima (Map 10)**, while DC's power elite trek to **Proof (Map 1)**, **Tattoo Bar (Map 9)**, and **The Park at Fourteenth (Map 10)**. If you're looking for good hip-hop during the weekdays try **kstreet (Map 10)**. Turn heads at the swank **Poste Moderne Brasserie (Map 1)** where you can sip wine in their mega outdoor space or head to Chinatown for low key establishments like **Irish Channel (Map 2)** for a pint of Guinness and **Capitol City Brewing Company (Map 2, 39)** for the free soft pretzels provided to every table. Venture out of Northwest DC and you'll find girls from the Midwest at **Clarendon Ballroom (Map 35)** and the deepest basement bar at **Quarry House Tavern (Map 25)** in downtown Silver Spring. Drown yourself in Indie music at **Galaxy Hut (Map 35)** or **Iota (Map 35)**. **Love (Map 12)**, formerly known as Dream, a massive four-floor complex on Okie Street, is also a popular place where VIP membership will cost you just $500 a year and save you the embarrassment of being a regular person in the line that often wraps around the block.

Map 1 • National Mall

Capitol City Brewing Company	1100 New York Ave NW	202-628-2222	Great IPA.
Eyebar	1716 I St NW	202-785-0270	A bit played out, but still open.
Gordon Biersch Brewery	900 F St NW	202-783-5454	Five great lagers.
Grand Slam Sports Bar	1000 H St NW	202-637-4789	Sports bar perfection.
Harry's Saloon	436 11th St NW	202-628-8140	Reliable burger 'n' Guinness place with unreliable service.
Le Bar	806 15th St NW	202-737-8800	An oasis in a sea of offices.
Old Ebbitt Grill	675 15th St NW	202-347-4800	Try to spot your local congressman at this super-touristy Washington institution.
Poste Brasserie Bar	555 8th St NW	202-783-6060	Great outdoor space for summer happy hours
Round Robin Bar	1401 Pennsylvania Ave NW	202-628-9100	Old style, old money DC. Herbal martinis.
Shelly's Back Room	1331 F St NW	202-737-3003	If cigars, scotch, and strip streaks don't say Washington fatcat, then the middle-aged white men in suits do.
Society of Wine Educators	1319 F St NW #303	202-408-8777	Downtown DC dining with a hometown corner restaurant feel.
Ultrabar	911 F St NW	202-638-4663	Best DJs in the city on 4 different floors.

Map 2 • Chinatown / Union Station

Bar Louie	701 7th St NW	202-638-2460	Sandwiches, Pizza, and bar food.
Capitol City Brewing Company	2 Massachusetts Ave NE	202-842-2337	Great IPA.
The Dubliner	4 F St NW	202-737-3773	Cozy, classy Irish pub.
Fado Irish Pub	808 7th St NW	202-789-0066	Every beer imaginable.
Iron Horse Tap Room	507 7th St NW	202-347-7665	Enormous, foodless "biker" bar with plenty of beer and bourbon.
Kelly's Irish Times	14 F St NW	202-543-5433	DC's only Irish pub with a swerve'dance club basement.
Lucky Strike Lanes	701 7th St NW	202-347-1021	Pricey bowling alley, but the martinis come with Pop Rocks.
My Brother's Place	237 2nd St NW	202-347-1350	Cheap, hole-in-the-wall CUA bar.
Poste Moderne Brasserie	555 8th St NW	202-783-6060	Full of fresh food, fresh faces, and fresh bank accounts.
RFD Washington	810 7th St NW	202-289-2030	Brickskeller's downtown sibling—hundreds of beers.
Rocket Bar	714 7th St NW	202-628-7665	The home of bar games.

Map 3 • The Hill

Capitol Lounge	229 Pennsylvania Ave SE	202-547-2098	Hill hangout, do-it-yourself Bloody Mary bar.
Granville Moore's	1238 H St NE	202-399-2546	Belgian beers in the heart of DC.

Hawk and Dove	329 Pennsylvania Ave SE	202-543-3300	Hill staffer hangout.
Lounge 201	201 Massachusetts Ave NE	202-544-5201	Retro martini bar.
The Majestic	1368 H St NE	202-388-1204	The latest from Gwen Reese
Palace of Wonders	1210 H St NE	202-398-7469	The weirdest bar in DC.
Pour House	319 Pennsylvania Ave SE	202-546-0779	Steelers fans and Irish accents.
The Pug	1234 H St NE	202-388-8554	Atlas District neighborhood bar.
Rock n' Roll Hotel	1353 H St NE	202-388-7625	DC's new indie rock hangout
Sonoma	223 Pennsylvania Ave SE	202-544-8088	Sip wine in the upstairs lounge by the fireplace.
Top of the Hill	319 Pennsylvania Ave SE	202-546-7782	1 building=3 bars. This has pool and red vinyl.
Toyland	421 H St NE	202-450-4075	Retro 60s lounge serves modernized side cars and turkey meatloaf.
Tune Inn	331 Pennsylvania Ave SE	202-543-2725	Dive bar option for an older Hill crowd.

Map 4 • RFK

The Argonaut	1433 H St NE	202-397-1416	Atlas District's neighborhood tavern
Rose's Dream Bar & Lounge	1370 H St NE	202-398-5700	Karaoke, Comedy, and Drinks.

Map 5 • Southeast / Anacostia

Bullfeathers	410 1st St SE	202-488-2701	One of the Hill's true neighborhood bars.
Mr Henry's Capitol Hill	601 Pennsylvania Ave SE	202-546-8412	A spot for jazz lovers.
Patty Boom Boom	1359 U St SE	202-629-1712	Jamaican patties downstairs, reggae lounge upstairs.
Remingtons	639 Pennsylvania Ave SE	202-543-3113	Country-Western gay bar.
Tortilla Coast	400 1st St SE	202-546-6768	Different special every night.
Trusty's	1420 Pennsylvania Ave SE	202-547-1010	Hole-in-the-wall with board games.
Tunnicliff's Tavern	222 7th St SE	202-544-5680	Cheers-esque.
The Ugly Mug	723 8th St SE	202-547-8459	TVs, pool, miniburgers, and beer.

Map 6 • Waterfront

The Bullpen	1299 Half St SE	202-646-0045	Pretend you're a Nationals relief pitcher and get blitz.
Cantina Marina	600 Water St SW	202-554-8396	Jimmy Buffet goes Latin.
Zanzibar on the Waterfront	700 Water St SW	202-554-9100	Hugely popular velvet-rope club.

Map 7 • Foggy Bottom

19th	1919 Pennsylvania Ave NW	202-331-5800	Knock one back at the 19th (watering) hole.
The Exchange	1719 G St NW	202-393-4690	DC's oldest saloon just steps from the White House.
Froggy Bottom Pub	2142 Pennsylvania Ave NW	202-338-3000	GW student hangout.
Funxion	1309 F St NW	202-386-9466	Funxion = daytime smoothies. DysFunxion = nighttime cocktails.
Nick's Riverside Grill	3050 K St NW	202-342-3535	Mediocre food, excellent view, copious seagulls.

Map 8 • Georgetown

51st State Tavern	2512 L St NW	202-625-2444	An unpretentious watering hole, plus 10-cent wings on Tuesdays.
Blues Alley	1073 Wisconsin Ave NW	202-337-4141	THE place for live jazz.
Chadwicks	3205 K St NW	202-333-2565	Georgetown dive. (Read: nicer than half the bars in DC.)
Champions	1206 Wisconsin Ave NW	202-965-5555	Champions and losers acceptable.
Clyde's	3236 M St NW	202-333-9180	Reliable wood-themed bar.
Fahrenheit & Degrees	3100 S St NW	202-912-4100	Pretty ritzy.
Garrett's	3003 M St NW	202-333-1033	Don't fall down the stairs.
The Guards	2915 M St NW	202-965-2350	For sloppy crowds.
L2 Lounge	3315 Cady's Alley NW	202-965-2001	A members only sweet spot catering to the elite
Martin's Tavern	1264 Wisconsin Ave NW	202-333-7370	Gin-and-tonic crowd.
Maté	3101 K St NW	202-333-2006	Posh Latin hangout on K Street.
Mendocino	2917 M St NW	202-333-2912	Wine and dine with the friendliest staff in Georgetown.
Mie N Yu	3125 M St NW	202-333-6122	Exotic, Eastern atmosphere and good food.
Modern	3287 M St NW	202-338-7027	If your smart, keep walking
Mr Smith's	3104 M St NW	202-333-3104	W.A.S.P. invade a hole-in-the wall bar
Old Glory	3139 M St NW	202-337-3406	Great for daytime drinking.
Paper Moon	1073 31st St NW	202-965-6666	Italian restaurant by day and sometimes dance place by night.

Rhino Bar & Pumphouse	3295 M St NW	202-333-3150	Cheap beer, dance music, and pool tables.
Riverside Grill	3050 K St NW	202-342-3535	If it's crowded at Tony and Joe's.
Sequoia	3000 K St NW	202-944-4200	Where type As meet before getting married and divorced.
Third Edition	1218 Wisconsin Ave NW	202-333-3700	One night stands start here.
The Tombs	1226 36th St NW	202-337-6668	Georgetown institution.
Tony and Joe's	3000 K St NW	202-944-4545	A Georgetown waterfront staple.

Map 9 • Dupont Circle / Adams Morgan

Andalu	1214 18th St NW	202-785-2922	Better be hip.
Bar Rouge	1315 16th St NW	202-232-8000	Super laid back in a trendy hotel
Beacon Bar & Grill	1615 Rhode Island Ave NW	202-872-1126	Great for happy hours and bar treats
The Big Hunt	1345 Connecticut Ave NW	202-785-2333	Should be called the big dump. Local favorite
Black Fox Lounge	1723 Connecticut Ave NW	202-483-1723	Practice raising your pinky with your glass.
Black Rooster Pub	1919 L St NW	202-659-4431	Dark as a black rooster inside. Good darts.
Bravo Bravo	1001 Connecticut Ave NW	202-223-5330	Salsa and Merengue.
The Brickskeller	1523 22nd St NW	202-293-1885	Try a beer from Timbuktu—possibly the best beer selection on the planet.
Buffalo Billiards	1330 19th St NW	202-331-7665	Relaxed poolhall.
Café Citron	1343 Connecticut Ave NW	202-530-8844	Sweat in the crowd downstairs, or dance on chairs upstairs.
Café Japone	2032 P St NW	202-223-1573	Serious sake.
Camelot Show Bar	1823 M St NW	202-887-5966	Honey, they're professional dancers.
Chi-Cha Lounge	1624 U St NW	202-234-8400	Informal (ties forbidden) Ecuadorian hacienda.
Cobalt/30 Degrees	1639 R St NW	202-462-6569	Smoke-free 30 Degrees, smoky Cobalt.
DC Improv	1140 Connecticut Ave NW	202-296-7008	Don't laugh up your weak rum and Coke.
Eighteenth Street Lounge	1212 18th St NW	202-466-3922	Hip, mature and the deck is always packed
Elephant & Castle	900 19th St NW	202-296-2575	North American chain wants to be British.
Firefly	1310 New Hampshire Ave NW	202-861-1310	Sophisticated drinking.
The Fireplace	2161 P St NW	202-293-1293	Landmark gay bar.
Floriana Mercury Bar	1602 17th St NW	202-667-5937	Friendly subterranean bar.
Fly Lounge	1802 Jefferson Pl NW	202-828-4433	The size of my apartment and very pretentious.
Fox and Hounds Lounge	1537 17th St NW	202-232-6307	Where uptight people go to relax.
Front Page	1333 New Hampshire Ave NW	202-296-6500	Pre-10 pm: businessman's grill; post-10 pm: strictly t & a.
Gazuza	1629 Connecticut Ave NW	202-667-5500	Best mango mojitos in town
JR's	1519 17th St NW	202-328-0090	Don't miss the daily drink specials and theme nights.
James Hoban's	1 Dupont Cir NW	202-223-8440	Washington's architect has a bar.
Kramerbooks & Afterwords Café	1517 Connecticut Ave NW	202-387-1400	Fun eats amidst café/bar/bookstore environs. The Perfect Weapon.
La Frontera Cantina	1633 17th St NW	202-232-0437	Have a Corona and people-watch.
Lauriol Plaza	1835 18th St NW	202-387-0035	Order a pitcher of margaritas for a lounge day
Local 16	1602 U St NW	202-265-2828	Great deck spring/summer/fall. Lounge atmosphere without a cover.
Lucky Bar	1221 Connecticut Ave NW	202-331-3733	Lucky not to get beer spilled on you
Maddy's Bar and Grille	1726 Connecticut Ave NW	202-483-2266	Slick lounge with 14 beers on tap.
Madhatter	1321 Connecticut Ave NW	202-833-1495	A midtown dive bar with character.
McClellan's	1919 Connecticut Ave NW	202-483-3000	Hilton Hotel sports bar.
McFadden's	2401 Pennsylvania Ave NW	202-223-2338	Wall-to-wall Tues/Thurs/Fri/Sat nights.
Omega	2122 P St NW	202-223-4917	Mature men gay bar.
Ozio	1813 M St NW	202-822-6000	Grown and sexy hip-hop scene
Recessions	1823 L St NW	202-296-6686	Basement bar.
Rumors	1900 M St NW	202-466-7378	After-work drinks downtown.
Russia House Restaurant and Lounge	800 Connecticut Ave NW	202-234-9433	Swanky joint beloved by eurotrash.
Science Club	1136 19th St NW	202-775-0747	Laid-back lounge that caters to cocktails and conversation.
Sign of the Whale	1825 M St NW	202-785-1110	Cozy and cheap.
Soussi	2228 18th St NW	202-299-9313	Outdoor wine bar.
Stetson's Famous Bar & Restaurant	1610 U St NW	202-667-6295	Popular and crowded U Street destination.
Steve's Bar	1337 Connecticut Ave NW	202-293-3150	It's Steve's, no one else's.
Tabard Inn Restaurant	1739 N St NW	202-331-8528	Romantic rendezvous.
Topaz Bar	1733 N St NW	202-393-3000	Go for the drinks.
Town & Country	1127 Connecticut Ave NW	202-347-3000	Old-school hotel bar.
Townhouse Tavern	1637 R St NW	202-234-5747	Get your Schlitz in a can.
Twist Dupont Restaurant and Lounge	1731 New Hampshire Ave NW	202-518-5011	Carlyle Suites lounge.
Urbana	2121 P St NW	202-956-6650	Multiple rushes of wine pleasure.

Map 10 · Logan Circle / U Street

9:30 Club	815 V St NW	202-265-0930	A DC music institution.
Bar Pilar	1833 14th St NW	202-265-1751	A laid-back hangout.
Black Cat	1811 14th St NW	202-667-7960	The OTHER place in DC to see a band.
Busboys and Poets	2021 14th St NW	202-387-7638	Shabby chic leftist bookstore/restaurant, proletarian prices.
Café Saint-Ex	1847 14th St NW	202-265-7839	Once-cool bistro overrun by the khaki crowd.
DC9	1940 9th St NW	202-483-5000	Rock club.
Dickson Wine Bar	903 U St NW	202-322-1779	Organic, bio-dynamic booze, anyone?
EFN Lounge	1318 9th St NW	347-878-2531	Flavor Tripping, what a trip!
The Gibson	2009 14th St NW	202-232-2156	OMG a line?! but masterful cocktails.
Helix Lounge	1430 Rhode Island Ave NW	202-462-9001	New trendy neighborhood addition.
HR-57 Center for the Preservation of Jazz and Blues	1610 14th St NW	202-667-3700	Cool BYOB jazz joint. A real gem.
Josephine Lounge	1008 Vermont Ave.,	202-347-8601	Outstanding decor and comfy couches.
K Street Lounge	1301 K St NW	202-962-3933	Stylish lounge perfect for those who like to feel important.
Lotus Lounge	1420 K St NW	202-289-4222	An underground oasis that is always empty
Old Dominion Brewhouse	1219 9th St NW	202-289-8158	Stuck in the Convention Center, but offering a fab selection of ales, lagers, and stouts from a local microbrewery
The Park at Fourteenth	920 14th St NW	202-737-7275	Decadent club with four levels of pleasure
The Saloon	1207 U St NW	202-462-2640	European appeal—go for the beer.
Solly's U Street Tavern	1942 11th St NW	202-232-6590	Good sports bar. Watch for runaway cabs.
Tabaq Bistro	1336 U St NW	202-265-0965	Chillin' hookah bar with a killer view of downtown.
Tattoo Bar	1413 K St NW	202-408-9444	Bangin' beats and babes in this edgy bar
Twins Jazz	1344 U St NW	202-234-0072	Intimate bar with Ethiopian food.
Vegas Lounge	1415 P St NW	202-483-3971	Blues joint keeps the Gen Y's jumpin'.
Velvet Lounge	915 U St NW	202-462-3213	Get your lounge on with the likes of punk rock to alt-folk.
Warehouse	1021 7th St NW	202-783-3933	Live music alongside a gallery, theater, and café.

Map 11 · Near Northeast

FUR Nightclub	33 Patterson St NE	202-842-3401	You like sweaty 18-year-old girls?
Lux Lounge	649 New York Ave NE	202-347-8100	Too cool for school.

Map 12 · Trinidad

Love Nightclub	1350 Okie St NE	202-636-9030	Huge nightclub straight out of a rap video

Map 13 · Brookland / Langdon

Aqua	1818 New York Ave NE	202-832-4878	Asian dance club at a Korean restaurant.
District	2473 18th St NE	202-518-9820	K Street-style nightclub in AdMo, with neon, VIP areas, and all.

Map 14 · Catholic U

Colonel Brooks' Tavern	901 Monroe St NE	202-529-4002	Neighborhood landmark.

Map 15 · Columbia Heights

Chuck & Billy's Bar and Carry-Out	2718 Georgia Ave NW	202-234-5870	Malcolm X adorns the wall, elder statesmen hold court, circa 1992 decor prevails.
Looking Glass Lounge	3634 Georgia Ave NW	202-722-7669	Bought and renamed by the owners of Wonderland Ballroom, the Alice theme continues, leaving behind some of Temperance Hall's charms
The Wonderland Ballroom	1101 Kenyon St NW	202-232-5263	Crowded, smoky, fun neighborhood dive. Great bratwurst.

Map 16 · Adams Morgan (North) / Mt Pleasant

Adams Mill Bar and Grill	1813 Adams Mill Rd NW	202-332-9577	Pitchers after the softball game.
Angles Bar & Billiards	2339 18th St NW	202-462-8100	Dive bar with great burgers; a favorite of reporters.
Angles Bar and Billiards	2339 18th St NW	202-462-8100	Dive bar with great burgers; a favorite of reporters.
Asylum	2471 18th St NW	202-319-9353	Goth décor and pounding music.

Bedrock Billiards	1841 Columbia Rd NW	202-667-7665	Pool hall with extensive alcohol choices.
The Black Squirrel	2427 18th St NW	202-232-1011	90 bottles of beer on the menu.
Bossa	2463 18th St NW	202-667-0088	Cool downstairs, samba upstairs.
Bukom Café	2442 18th St NW	202-265-4600	West African music and a diverse crowd.
Chief Ike's Mambo Room	1725 Columbia Rd NW	202-332-2211	Dirty dance 'til dawn.
Columbia Station	2325 18th St NW	202-462-6040	More jazz and blues in an intimate setting.
District Bar and Grille	2473 18th St NW	202-558-5508	Dance club with table service and VIP areas. Southern-inspired cuisine.
Draft Pix	2450 18th St NW	202-265-1014	Go DC sports!
Grand Central	2447 18th St NW	202-986-1742	Looks more like a Metro station than Grand Central.
Leftbank	2424 18th St NW	202-464-2100	Chic faux-retro European décor, and pretty people.
Madam's Organ	2461 18th St NW	202-667-5370	Redheads get a discount; best blues in DC.
Meze	2437 18th St NW	202-797-0017	Salsa and Mediterranean goodness.
Pharmacy Bar	2337 18th St NW	202-483-1200	Low-key alternabar.
The Raven	3125 Mt Pleasant St NW	202-387-8411	Neighborhood bar.
The Reef	2446 18th St NW	202-518-3800	Jellyfish and drinks.
Rumba Café	2443 18th St NW	202-588-5501	Cuban treats.
Timehri International	2439 18th St NW	202-518-2626	Reggae, Calypso, R&B.
Toledo Lounge	2435 18th St NW	202-986-5416	Didn't get your fill of Ohio in '04? Visit this unpretentious dive.
Tom Tom	2333 18th St NW	202-518-6667	Play old-school Nintendo upstairs.
Tonic	3155 Mt Pleasant St NW	202-986-7661	Local tavern.

Map 17 · Woodley Park / Cleveland Park

Aroma	3417 Connecticut Ave NW	202-244-7995	Martinis, cigars and good cocktails.
Atomic Billiards	3427 Connecticut Ave NW	202-363-7665	Subterranean pool, darts, and beer.
Bardeo	3311 Connecticut Ave NW	202-244-6550	Ardeo's chi-chi wine bar, where well-heeled yuppies tote glasses of chardonnay.
Cleveland Park Bar & Grill	3421 Connecticut Ave NW	202-806-8940	Watch the game with a popped collar.
Ireland's Four Fields	3412 Connecticut Ave NW	202-244-0860	Have a pint and name the Ps.
Murphy's of DC	2609 24th St NW	202-462-7171	Irish pub with summertime patio and wintertime fireplace.
Nanny O'Brien's	3319 Connecticut Ave NW	202-686-9189	Legendary Celtic jam sessions.
Uptown Tavern	3435 Connecticut Ave NW	202-244-7196	Divey sports bar with foosball.
The Zoo Bar Cafe	3000 Connecticut Ave NW	202-232-4225	Low-key with live blues bands.

Map 18 · Glover Park / Foxhall

Alliance Tavern	3238 Wisconsin Ave NW	202-362-0362	One time wine bar resurrects as beery tavern with sports.
Blue Ridge	2340 Wisconsin Ave NW	202-333-4004	Mid-Atlantic menu and ingredients.
Bourbon	2348 Wisconsin Ave NW	202-625-7770	Great bourbon, of course.
Breadsoda	2233 Wisconsin Ave NW	202-333-7445	How do you make roast beef sandwiches and pool classy? Breadsoda knows.
The Deck	2505 Wisconsin Ave NW	202-337-9700	The Savoy Suite's outdoor bar.
Gin and Tonic	2408 Wisconsin Ave NW	202-337-1313	Historically crappy Grog & Tankard is replaced with space for partying preps.
Good Guys Restaurant	2311 Wisconsin Ave NW	202-333-8128	Friendly, low-bling rock-and-roll strip club.
Grog and Tankard	2408 Wisconsin Ave NW	202-333-3114	Longest-running live music bar in the DC area.

Map 19 · Tenleytown / Friendship Heights

Guapo's	4515 Wisconsin Ave NW	202-686-3588	Tortillas + margaritas = stumbling to Tenleytown Metro.
Maggiano's	5333 Wisconsin Ave NW	202-966-2593	Italian restaurant with accommodating Latino bar staff.
Malt Shop	4615 Wisconsin Ave NW	202-244-9733	Wood walls and floors for sloppy AU students.

Map 20 · Cleveland Park / Upper Connecticut

Comet Ping Pong	5037 Connecticut Ave NW	202-364-0404	Go for ping pong and Paul.
The Dancing Crab (aka Malt Shop)	4615 Wisconsin Ave NW	202-244-9733	A dozen large crabs and beer. Popular with AU students.

Map 21 · 16th St. Heights / Petworth

Red Derby	3718 14th St NW	202-291-5000	Everyday specials, Charlie Chaplin on the walls.
San Gria Cafe	3636 16th St NW	202-483-6905	The Woodner has everything, including a dark, laid-back bar that serves pupusas.

Map 22 · Bethesda (North)

Caddie's on Cordell	4922 Cordell Ave	301-215-7730	"The 19th hole," with an outdoor patio and plenty of screens.
Flanagan's Harp and Fiddle	4844 Cordell Ave	301-951-0115	Authentic Irish bartenders.
Rock Bottom Brewery	7900 Norfolk Ave	301-652-1311	Worth the wait.
Saphire Cafe	7940 Wisconsin Ave	301-986-9708	Average bar.
Union Jack's	4915 St Elmo Ave	301-6JA-CK61	A real faux-British pub.

Map 25 · Silver Spring

Galaxy Billiards	8661 Colesville Rd	301-495-0081	City Place pool hall for betting suburbanites.
Mayorga	8040 Georgia Ave	301-562-9090	Coffee by day, microbrew by night.
Quarry House Tavern	8401 Georgia Ave	301-587-8350	Great neighborhood bar but a true hole-in-the wall.

Map 27 · Walter Reed

Charlie's Bar & Grill	7307 Georgia Ave NW	202-726-3567	Soul food and contemporary jazz.
Takoma Station Tavern	6914 4th St NW	202-829-1999	Jazz haven.

Map 28 · Chevy Chase

Chevy Chase Lounge	5510 Connecticut Ave NW	202-966-7600	Parthenon Restaurant's wood-panelled lounge.
The Tasting Room	5330 Western Ave	301-664-9494	Vino vending machines from Boxwood Winery in Middleburg.

Map 29 · Bethesda (South)

The Barking Dog	4723 Elm St	301-654-0022	Decent frat-boy bar.
Strike Bethesda	5353 Westbard Ave	301-652-0955	Not your average bowling alley.
Tommy Joe's	4714 Montgomery Ln	301-654-3801	Frat boy central.

Map 33 · Falls Church

Ireland's Four Provinces	105 W Broad St	703-534-8999	Why are you in Falls Church? (A good bar, nonetheless.)
Lost Dog Café	5876 Washington Blvd	703-237-1552	Buy a beer, adopt a pet.
State Theatre	220 N Washington St	703-237-0300	Grab a table, a beer, and listen.

Map 34 · Cherrydale / Ballston

Bailey's Pub and Grille	4238 Wilson Blvd	703-465-1300	A sports superbar with a gazillion TVs.
Buffalo D's	4213 Fairfax Dr	703-465-8888	Bar and grille of the sporty/dive variety.
Carpool	4000 Fairfax Dr	703-532-7665	Pool, darts, and beers on the patio.
Cowboy Café	4792 Lee Hwy	703-243-8010	Neighborhood bar and burgers.
The Front Page	4201 Wilson Blvd	703-248-9990	Restaurant with two bars. Great happy hour Monday–Friday.
Rock Bottom Brewery	4238 Wilson Blvd	703-516-7688	Go for happy hour.

Map 35 · Cherrydale / Clarendon

Clarendon Ballroom	3185 Wilson Blvd	703-469-2244	Head for the rooftop.
Clarendon Grill	1101 N Highland St	703-524-7455	What? Get used to saying that here.
Eleventh Street Lounge	1041 N Highland St	703-351-1311	Classy wine, soft couches, smooth blues and intriguing beer.
Galaxy Hut	2711 Wilson Blvd	703-525-8646	Tiny, friendly, indie rock hangout.
Harry's Tap Room	2800 Clarendon Blvd	703-778-7788	City atmosphere 'til midnight, then it becomes the suburbs again.
Iota	2832 Wilson Blvd	703-522-8340	Great place to see a twangy band.
Kitty O'Shea's	2403 Wilson Blvd	703-522-5295	Small, soccer-loving, Irish pub
Mister Days	3100 Clarendon Blvd	703-527-1600	Pick-up bar disguised as a sports bar.
O'Sullivan's Irish Pub	3207 Washington Blvd	703-812-0939	Decent local Irish pub. No surprises.
Whitlow's on Wilson	2854 Wilson Blvd	703-276-9693	A separate room for whatever mood you're in.

Map 36 · Rosslyn

Continental Modern Pool Lounge	1911 Fort Myer Dr	703-465-7675	Like you stepped into the Jetsons' house.
Dr Dremo's Taphouse	2001 Clarendon Blvd	703-528-4660	Film geeks unite.
Ireland's Four Courts	2051 Wilson Blvd	703-525-3600	Where beer-guzzling yuppies come to see (double) and be seen.
Rhodeside Grill	1836 Wilson Blvd	703-243-0145	Neighborhood bar with basement for bands.
Summers Restaurant	1520 N Courthouse Rd	703-528-8278	Soccer-watching bar.

Map 37 • Fort Myer

EatBar	2761 Washington Blvd	703-778-9951	Creative beers, drinks, and food with a slightly swanky atmosphere.
Jay's Saloon & Grille	3114 10th St N	703-527-3093	Down-home and friendly.
Ragtime	1345 N Courthouse Rd	703-243-4003	No less than 2 TVs per room. Caters to WVU fans.
Tallula	2761 Washington Blvd	703-778-5051	Swanky-dank wine bar.

Map 39 • Shirlington

The Bungalow, Billiards & Brew Co	2766 S Arlington Mill Dr	703-578-0020	Fun billiards and brews.
Capitol City Brewing Company	4001 Campbell Ave	703-578-3888	Great IPA.
Guapo's	4028 Campbell Ave	703-671-1701	Bueno Mexican, killer margaritas.

Map 40 • Pentagon City / Crystal City

Sine Irish Pub	1301 S Joyce St	703-415-4420	Good beers on tap, busy happy hour. Lots of military, defense contractors.

Map 41 • Landmark

Mango Mike's	4580 Duke St	703-370-3800	Pub grub from the islands, mon.
Shenandoah Brewing Company	652 S Pickett St	703-823-9508	Brew your own beer on site.
Shooter McGee's	5239 Duke St	703-751-9266	Another "silly first name, Irish last name" place.

Map 43 • Four Mile Run / Del Ray

Birchmere	3701 Mt Vernon Ave	703-549-7500	What do Kris Kristofferson and Liz Phair have in common?
Hops	3625 Jefferson Davis Hwy	703-837-9107	$1.29 happy hour beers, if you don't mind a cheesy chain.

Map 44 • Alexandria Downtown

Cafe Salsa	808 King St	703-684-4100	THE hottest salsa club in the DC area.

Map 45 • Old Town (North)

Stardust	608 Montgomery St	703-548-9864	Half-price apps weekdays from 5–7.

Map 46 • Old Town (South)

Austin Grill	801 King St	703-684-8969	Great Tex/Mex; just outside, Janet Reno got a parking ticket!
Café Salsa	808 King St	703-684-4100	THE hottest salsa club in the DC area.
Chadwicks	203 The Strand	703-836-4442	Tried-and-true saloon away from the King Street crush.
Flying Fish	815 King St	703-600-3474	Sushi and karaoke, together at last.
Laughing Lizard Lounge	1324 King St	703-836-7885	Go for the pool and a cold beer.
Murphy's	713 King St	703-548-1717	Locals-favored pub with wonk-beloved Tuesday trivia.
Pat Troy's Ireland's Own	111 N Pitt St	703-549-4535	Green alligators and long-neck beers.
PX	728 King St	703-299-8384	This "speakeasy" requires a blazer and lots of dough.
Rock It Grill	1319 King St	703-739-2274	Lowbrow and proud.
Tiffany Tavern	1116 King St	703-836-8844	Bluegrass central.
Union Street Public House	121 S Union St	703-548-1785	$2 happy-hour pints!!!
Vermilion	1120 King St	703-684-9669	No-frills lounge.

Baltimore

Club Charles	1724 N Charles St	410-727-8815	Dive bar extraordinaire; all the clocks inside are set 20 minutes ahead. And there's a good chance you'll run into John Waters.
Cross Street Market	1065 S Charles St		Indoor market with a raucous, locals-filled happy hour.
Ottobar	2549 N Howard St	410-662-0069	Hip, cheap, and loud.

DC has become a Mecca of culinary delights with world renowned chefs setting up shop and über-trendy spots (with price tags to match) on every corner. It's even received Top Chef 7th season love. But there are still plenty of eateries to patronize if you are on a tight intern-like budget, need an outdoor patio, or just want some good international comestibles. In order to provide the skinny on restaurant recommendations for every type of DC bank account, we've listed some of our favorite places under four different categories: Eating Posh, Eating Cheap, Eating Hip, and Eating Ethnic.

Eating Posh

In the land of lobbyists, lawyers, and congressmen, there are bound to be plenty of chi-chi restaurants—DC's equivalent of Hollywood nightclubs. Posh in DC often means ballin' out of control, old, and mahogany paneling. Washington fat cats are known to chew the fat (literally) at any of a few dozen steakhouses around town, but the local favorites include **BLT Steak (Map 1)**, **Smith and Wollensky (Map 9)**, **The Palm (Map 9)**, **Prime Rib (Map 9)**, and **Charlie Palmer (Map 2)**. For French decadence, look no further than **Bistro Bis (Map 2)**, **Citronelle (Map 8)**, and **Marcel's (Map 9)**. If Italian is your indulgence, then mangia bene at **Ristorante Tosca (Map 1)**, **Café Milano (Map 8)**, or **Obelisk (Map 9)**. **600 Restaurant at the Watergate (Map 7)**, **1789 (Map 8)**, **Blue Duck Tavern (Map 9)**, and **Brasserie Beck (Map 10)** are spots to see and be seen, and **PS 7's (Map 1)** is always buzzing with the power lunch crowd. The tasting menus at **José Andrés' Minibar (Map 1)** and **Restaurant Eve (Map 46)** are something to write home about, especially since the former might serve you homemade cotton candy with foie gras. Finally, **Komi (Map 9)** and **CityZen (Map 6)** consistently make it onto every food critic and lay foodie's Top 10.

Eating Cheap

Eating cheap in DC doesn't have to mean hitting up a fast food joint. The experience can even prove quite pleasant. Two of DC's most famous joints, **El Pollo Rico (Map 37)** and **Ben's Chili Bowl (Map 10)**, will cost you between $5 and $10 a meal, and **Café Parisien Express (Map 34)** serves up double portions of French food for half the French price. Right down the street, hop over to **Henry's Soul Café (Map 9)** for the best soul food in the city. If pizza is your poison, the pies at **Italian deli Vace (Map 29)** will totally knock your socks off. For a unique atmosphere, check out **Mexicali Blues (Map 35)** and the Dupont institution **Kramerbooks & Afterwords Café (Map 9)**. Rounding out the cheap eats list are 24-hour mini-diner **Steak & Egg Kitchen (Map 19)**, Chinatown BBQ pit **Capital Q (Map 2)**, cod supreme joint **Eamonn's: A Dublin Chipper (Map 46)**, out-of-this-world chili machine **Hard Times Café (Maps 46, 35)**, and Jewish deli **Morty's (Map 19)**. **Tortilla Coast (Map 5)** will cure your hangover and for quick and cheap sushi head over to Dupont's **Nooshi (Map 9)** or **Kotobuki (Map 18)** in the Palisades.

Eating Hip

Everyone in DC tries to be hip, and those who can actually pull it off dine downtown for lunch at **Zaytinya (Map 1)**, one of the sexiest spots in the city, and sister restaurant to both **Café Atlantico (Map 1)** and **Jaleo (Maps 2, 29)**. Chinatown has long lines waiting to get into **Matchbox (Map 2, 5)**. **Proof (Map 1)** and **Cork (Map 10)** have thousands of wine bottles to choose from between them. And **Sette Osteria (Map 9)** and **Lauriol Plaza (Map 9)** make up for the food with social cache. Busboys & Poets is the spot for great people-watching and pleasantly left-wing conversation. **Lima (Map 10)** and **Cashion's Eat Place (Map 16)** have always been in vogue among the downtown set, and **Tryst (Map 16)** is the ultimate coffeehouse to have an indecent affair with your neighbor. For two of Old Town's most fabulous dining experiences, check out **Vermilion (Map 46)** and **Majestic (Map 46)**.

Eating Ethnic

All who cross our borders can find authentic international eats. In DC, the rule of thumb is that the quality of ethnic food increases proportionally to one's distance from the city's center, but there are some notable exceptions in the metro area. Check out Indian goodness at **Rasika (Map 2)**, **Indique (Map 20)**, **Heritage India (Maps 18)**, and **Amma Vegetarian Kitchen (Map 8)**. Fiesta margaritas and homemade taquitos keep em' coming back to **Haydee's (Map 16)** in Mount Pleasant. The less-common Asian cuisines represented at **Burma (Map 2)** and **Straits of Malaya (Map 9)** are worthy of hunger and attention. For Mediterranean, savvy diners head to **Lebanese Taverna (Maps 17, 25, 33)** and **Cava (Map 5)**. Hit up **Yee Hwa (Map 9)** in Foggy Bottom for your Korean kimchi fix. Tony Cheng's **Seafood Restaurant (Map 2)** and **Eat First (Map 2)** are the cream of the Chinatown crop—or at least the last men standing. For the best sushi this side of the Pacific, **Makoto Restaurant (Map 18)** and **Sushi-Ko (Map 18)** are all you'll need. Experience the Middle East at **Mama Ayesha's (Map 16)** and Morocco at **Marrakesh Palace (Map 9)**. The Mexican **Mixtec (Map 16)** and the pan-Asian **Spices (Map 17)** each also get an A-plus in our not-so-humble opinion. And don't miss out on **Roger Miller Restaurant (Map 25)**, a gem of a purveyor of West African curry goat in suburban Silver Spring.

Key: $: Under $10 / $$: $10–$20 / $$$: $20–$30 / $$$$: $30–40 / $$$$$: $40+
* : Does not accept credit cards. / † : Accepts only American Express. / † : Accepts only Visa and Mastercard.
Time refers to weekend night closing time.

Map 1 • National Mall

Name	Address	Phone	Price	Time	Description
Aria Trattoria	1300 Pennsylvania Ave NW	202-312-1250		10 pm	Outdoor power lunch hotspot.
Asia Nine Bar and Lounge	915 E St NW	202-629-4355	$$$	11 pm	Asian inspired in the heart of Chinatown
Bistro D'Oc	518 10th St NW	202-393-5444	$$$$	11 pm	Homey Provençal with spotty service and an excellent pre-theater menu.
BLT Steak Bistro Laurent Tourondel	1625 I St NW	202-689-8999	$$$$	11 pm	Super tasty and super pricey.
Butterfield 9	600 14th St NW	202-289-8810		9:30 pm	Starving lobbyists unite.
Café Asia	1720 I St NW	202-659-2696	$$$	12 am	Not quite as crowded as Asia but just as busy.
Café Atlantico	405 8th St NW	202-393-0812	$$$	11 pm	Upscale Nuevo Latino. Try to book the Minibar.
Café Mozart	1331 H St NW	202-347-5732	$$	10 pm	Walk past the deli into an authentic German restaurant.
Caucus Room	401 9th St NW	202-393-1300	$$$$	10:30 pm	The taste of power. A favorite for DC's elite.
Ceiba	701 14th St NW	202-393-3983	$$$$$	11 pm	Brazilian indulgence, from the people who brought Tenpenh.
Central Michel Richard	1001 Pennsylvania Ave NW	202-626-0015	$$$$$	11 pm	It'll set you back a couple of hundred
Chef Geoff's	1301 Pennsylvania Ave NW	202-464-4461	$$$	10 pm	Snooty service, great wine selection. Check out the jazz brunch.
Dangerously Delicious	1339 H St NW	202-398-PIES	$$		Sweet and savory pies, fresh from Charm City.
Ella's Wood Fired Pizza	901 F St NW	202-638-3434	$$	10 pm	Tasty pizza in Chinatown
Equinox	818 Connecticut Ave NW	202-331-8118	$$$$$	10:30 pm	The finest food of the Chesapeake region.
ESPN Zone	555 12th St NW	202-783-3776	$$	12 am	Forget the baseball players. This restaurant is on the juice.
Gerard's Place	915 15th St NW	202-737-4445	$$$$	10:30 pm	La crème de la crème of DC French dining.
Harry's Restaurant and Saloon	436 11th St NW	202-624-0053	$$	2 am	Downtown DC dining with a hometown corner restaurant feel.
High Noon	1311 F St NW	202-783-5757	$$	3 pm	Make your own pasta dish.
Les Halles	1201 Pennsylvania Ave NW	202-347-6848	$$$	12 am	French food with a good 'ole American twist.
Lia's	1401 Pennsylvania Ave NW	240-223-5427	$		New Italian from Chef Geoff.
Loeb's Perfect New York Deli	832 15th St NW	202-371-1150	$†	4 pm	Decent but not perfect pastrami.
Maggie Moo's	1001 Pennsylvania Ave NW	202-347-8085	$		Custom-made ice cream concoctions.
Meiwah	1401 Pennsylvania Ave NW	301-652-9882	$		Chinese with unexpectedly good sushi and enormous cocktails.
minibar	405 8th St NW	202-393-0812	$$$$$	8:30pm	A six-seat counter in Cafe Atlantico offers a tasting menu of DC's most avant-garde cooking. Foie gras and cotton candy, anyone?
Occidental	1475 Pennsylvania Ave NW	202-783-1475	$$$$	10:30 pm	Opulent White House classic.
Off the Record	16th St NW & H St NW	202-638-6600	$		Pricey hotel bar attracting DC's power players.
Old Ebbitt Grill	675 15th St NW	202-347-4800	$$$	1 am	The quintessential Washington restaurant. Try to spot your local congressman.
Ollie's Trolley	425 12th St NW	202-347-6119	$*	8 pm	1970s burger bliss.
PS 7's	777 I St NW	202-742-8550	$$	10:30 pm	Food and drink goodness.
Ristorante Tosca	1112 F St NW	202-367-1990	$$$$$	11:00pm	Un ristorante tanto elegante.
Teaism	800 Connecticut Ave NW	202-835-2233	$$	5:30 pm	Need a teapot? Buy one with lunch!
Teaism	400 8th St NW	202-638-6010	$$	9 pm	Everything Zen at this hipster hangout.
TenPenh	1001 Pennsylvania Ave NW	202-393-4500	$$$$	11 pm	DC's hottest Asian fusion.
Willard Room	1401 Pennsylvania Ave NW	202-637-7440	$$$$	10 pm	If not the richest breakfast in town, definitely the most expensive. Get the Nutella pancakes.
Yogen Fruz	825 14th St NW	202-289-0078			Frozen yogurt with a healthy twist.
Zaytinya	701 9th St NW	202-638-0800	$$$$	12 am	Tasty mezze menu offered by award-winning chef. Fabulous interior.
Zola	800 F St NW	202-654-0999	$$$$	11 pm	Drink like a (geriatric) James Bond.

Map 2 • Chinatown / Union Station

Name	Address	Phone	Price	Time	Description
701	701 Pennsylvania Ave NW	202-393-0701	$$$$	11:30 pm	Posh food not worth the price
America	50 Massachusetts Ave NE	202-682-9555	$$	10 pm	USA managed like a third world country.
B Smith's	50 Massachusetts Ave NE	202-289-6188	$$$$	10 pm	Creole elegance, jarring in Union Station.
Billy Goat Tavern & Grill	500 New Jersey Ave NW	202-783-2123	$	11:30 pm	Cheeseburger, cheeseburger, cheeseburger.

Arts & Entertainment · **Restaurants**

Key: $: Under $10 / $$: $10–$20 / $$$: $20–$30 / $$$$: $30–40 / $$$$$: $40+
* : Does not accept credit cards. / † : Accepts only American Express. / †† : Accepts only Visa and Mastercard.
Time refers to weekend night closing time.

Name	Address	Phone	Price	Time	Description
Bistro Bis	15 E St NW	202-661-2700	$$$$	10:30 pm	Pricey, but a solid place for an upscale lunch on the Hill.
Burma	740 6th St NW	202-638-1280	$$	10 pm	Green tea leaf salad. We kid you not.
Capital Q Company	707 H St NW	202-347-8396	$	12 am	Hearty Texan portions will put hair on yer chest.
Capitol City Brewing	2 Massachusetts Ave NE	202-842-2337	$$	11:30 pm	Quality beer worth the tourists that come with the territory.
Center Café at Union Station	50 Massachusetts Ave NE	202-682-0143	$$	9 pm	Enjoy the scenery from the middle of the country's best RR station.
Charlie Palmer	101 Constitution Ave NW	202-547-8100	$$$$	10 pm	Fine wine and world famous steak—a splurge for wannabe high rollers.
Chinatown Express	746 6th St NW	202-638-0424	$$	11 pm	Watch food preparation from the street and decide for yourself.
District Chophouse	509 7th St NW	202-347-3434	$$$$	12 am	Impressive roaring '20s atmosphere. Avoid Verizon game night.
The Dubliner	4 F St NW	202-737-3773	$$	1 am	Hearty Irish pub grub for Washington bureaucracy.
Eat First	609 H St NW	202-289-1703	$	3 am	Simple, no frills Chinese. Great for pre-theatre.
Fado Irish Pub	808 7th St NW	202-789-0066	$$$	11 pm	Antiquish décor and self-promoting gift shop. Disneyland for alcoholics.
Full Kee	509 H St NW	202-371-2233	$$*	2 am	Chinatown can be overwhelming. We'll make it easier. Eat here.
Irish Channel Pub	500 H St NW	202-216-0046	$$	12 am	The Irish Pub with Cajun flair.
Jaleo	480 7th St NW	202-628-7949	$$$$	12 am	The tapas king of DC. Great for first dates.
Johnny's Half Shell	400 N Capitol St NW	202-737-0400	$$$	10:30 pm	Best crabcakes in Washington. Friendly barstaff attracts solo diners.
Kelly's Irish Times	14 F St NW	202-543-5433	$$	10:40 pm	Look to your left. See The Dubliner? Go there.
La Tasca	722 7th St NW	202-347-9190	$$	12 am	Mexican tapas on a beer budget.
Matchbox	713 H St NW	202-289-4441	$$$	11 pm	Where martinis meet pizza.
Mitsitam Native Foods Café	Independence Ave SW & 4 St SW	202-633-7041	$$*	5 pm	Cafeteria featuring American Indian cuisine.
My Brother's Place	237 2nd St NW	202-347-1350	$$	11 pm	A lunchtime hole-in-the-wall.
Poste Moderne Brasserie	555 8th St NW	202-783-6060	$$$$$	10:30 pm	Full of fresh food, fresh faces, and fresh bank accounts.
Pizza Bistro Med	736 6th St NW	202-393-3300	$$		Pizza on H St = last nail in Chinatown's coffin.
Rasika	633 D St NW	202-637-1222	$$$$	11 pm	Pricey, polished Indian.
Rosa Mexicano	575 7th St NW	202-783-5522	$$$$	11:30 pm	Squeeze past the perennial crowds for a pomegranate margarita.
Tony Cheng's Mongolian Restaurant	619 H St NW	202-842-8669	$$	12 am	No reason to dine here. Upstairs is where you want to be.
Tony Cheng's Seafood Restaurant	619 H St NW	202-371-8669	$$	12 am	Overlook gaudy décor and enjoy best Chinese Washington offers.
Zengo	781 7th St NW	202-393-2929	$$$	11:30 pm	Sleek Asian-Latin fusion.

Map 3 · The Hill

Name	Address	Phone	Price	Time	Description
Belga Café	514 8th Street, SE	202-544-0100	$$$$	11 pm	Belgian beer and treats with a modern flair.
Bistro Cacao	320 Massachusetts Ave NE	202-543-8030	$$$$	11 pm	Romantic little Hill spot.
Café Berlin	322 Massachusetts Ave NE	202-543-7656	$$	11 pm	For all your Oktoberfest needs.
Ethiopic	401 H St NE	202-675-2066	$		"Little Ethiopia" expands to the Atlas District.
Good Stuff Eatery	303 Pennsylvania Ave SE	202-543-8222	$	11 pm	Hickory burgers and rosemary fries.
H Street Martini Lounge	1236 H St NE	202-397-3333	$$	12 am	"Urban-trendy" featuring happy hour and live music.
Hawk and Dove	329 Pennsylvania Ave SE	202-543-3300	$$	3 am	One of the oldest games in town. Do lunch, not dinner.
Horace & Dickie's	809 12th St NE	202-397-6040	$	2 am	Standing in line around the block is worth the wait for this fried fish
Horace & Dickie's Seafood	809 12th St NE	202.397.6040	$	2 am	Serving up fish for 16 years.
Jordan's 8	523 8th Street, SE	202-543-6401	$$$	11 pm	Steak and sushi. You can't go wrong
Kenny's Smokehouse	732 Maryland Ave NE	202-547-4553	$	10 pm	BBQ with oodles of sides.
La Loma Mexican Restaurant	316 Massachusetts Ave NE	202-548-2550	$$	11 pm	They make you pay for refills. Enough said.
The Liberty Tree	1016 H St NE	202-396-8733	$$		Masshole cuisine: clam chowder and fried Chatham cod.
Pete's Diner	212 2nd St SE	202-544-7335	$*	3 pm	With a completely Asian staff, you wonder who "Pete" is.
Sonoma	223 Pennsylvania Ave SE	202-544-8088	$$$	11 pm	40 wines by the glass. The Sideways characters would be proud.

Sticky Rice	1224 H St NE	202-397-7655	$	2 am	A sushi bar with a kids menu.
Union Pub	201 Massachusetts Ave NE	202-546-7200		10 pm	Where everybody wants important Hill-types to know their name.
Wellness Cafe	325 Pennsylvania Ave SE	202-543-2266	$	7 pm	Smoothies, and sandwiches, and sprouts, oh my!
White Tiger	301 Massachusetts Ave NE	202-546-5900	$$	10:30 pm	Best Capitol Hill Indian food.
Zest	735 8th St NE	202-544-7171	$		Family-friendly American bistro brings more yuppie fare to Barracks Row.

Map 5 • Southeast / Anacostia

Banana Café & Piano Bar	500 8th St SE	202-543-5906	$$$	11:30 pm	Democrat-friendly Hill cabana.
Bistro La Bonne	1340 U St SE	202-758-3413	$$$		Goodbye, Axis. Hello, French bistro.
La Plaza	629 Pennsylvania Ave SE	202-546-9512	$$	11 pm	Pinatas, fried yucca, smooth margaritas, and friendly owner/chef Henry.
Locanda Cucina Meditalia	633 Pennsylvania Ave SE	202-547-0002	$$$	11 pm	Sophisticated eatery
Montmartre	327 7th St SE	202-544-1244	$$$$	10:30 pm	Comfortable French bistro.
Seventh Hill Pizza	327 7th St SE	202-544-1911	$	11 pm	Thin-crust pies with a French twist, from the owners of Montmartre.
Starfish	539 8th St SE	202-546-5006	$$$	11 pm	Seafood from the people behind Banana Café.
Tortilla Coast	400 1st St SE	202-546-6768	$	10 pm	Favorite Hill non-power lunch spot.

Map 6 • Waterfront

Cantina Marina	600 Water St SW	202-554-8396	$$	11 pm	Ordering advice: avoid the cantina; go with the marina.
CityZen	1330 Maryland Ave SW	202-787-6006	$$$$$	9:30 pm	The most expensive place you might dine
Jenny's Asian Fusion	1000 Water St SW	202-554-2202	$$$	11 pm	Good food but depressing atmosphere, regardless of the water view
Phillip's Flagship	900 Water St SW	202-488-8515	$$$	10 pm	Fresh Atlantic fish not worth pathetic portions and lousy service.
Pier 7	650 Water St SW	202-554-2500	$$	10 pm	Showy waterfront seafood.

Map 7 • Foggy Bottom

600 Restaurant at the Watergate	600 New Hampshire Ave NW	202-337-5890	$$$	12 am	It will set you back a couple of wads.
Aquarelle	2650 Virginia Ave NW	202-298-4455	$$$$$	10 pm	Revived French Mediterranean restaurant at the Watergate.
Bread Line	1751 Pennsylvania Ave NW	202-822-8900	$$	3:30 pm	Screw South Beach if it means you can't eat here. (Lunch only.)
Cabanas	3050 K St NW	202-944-4242	$$	11 pm	Upscale Latin ceviches, ensalatas, ad nauseum.
Dish	924 25th St NW	202-383-8707	$$$$	10:30 pm	Southern infusion for inquisitive palates.
Finemondo	1319 F St NW	202-737-3100	$		Casual, Italian country cooking.
Karma	1900 I St NW	202-331-5800	$$	10 pm	Mediterranean restaurant and art gallery.
Kaz Sushi Bistro	1915 I St NW	202-530-5500	$$$	10 pm	Impress your date by ordering the <i>omasake</i>.
Kinkead's	2000 Pennsylvania Ave NW	202-296-7700	$$$$	10:30 pm	Elegant seafood, extravagant raw bar.
Nick's Riverside Grill	3050 K St NW	202-342-3535	$$$	11 pm	Mediocre food, excellent view, copious seagulls.
Notti Bianche	824 New Hampshire Ave NW	202-298-8085	$$$$	11 pm	Full or half portion pasta dishes perfect for lunch.
Primi Piatti	2013 I St NW	202-223-3600	$$$$	11 pm	Eat like an Italian, but you'll want to dress up like one too.
Roof Terrace Restaurant and Bar	2700 F St NW	202-416-8555	$$$$	9 pm	Avoid fighting the throng of theater-goers for the last split of wine. Try booking Sunday brunch instead.
Taberna Del Alabardero	1776 I St NW	202-429-2200	$$$$	11 pm	Wide-open menu dares you to be bold.

Map 8 • Georgetown

1789	1226 36th St NW	202-965-1789	$$$$	11 pm	1789: Age of the patrons, or total for your bill?
Aditi	3299 M St NW	202-625-6825	$$	10:30 pm	Indian restaurant that has stood the test of time.
Amma Vegetarian Kitchen	3291 M St NW	202-625-6625	$$	10:30 pm	Great Indian food.
Bangkok Joe's	3000 K St NW	202-222-4422	$$$$	12 am	Chinese at a lunch spot
Birreria Paradiso	3282 M St NW	202-337-1245	$$††	12 am	Indulge in some beer snobbery. And pizza.
Bistrot Lepic	1736 Wisconsin Ave NW	202-333-0111	$$$	10:30 pm	Wine bar and lounge with a French flair
Café Bonaparte	1522 Wisconsin Ave NW	202-333-8830	$	1 am	Fine French-onion soup.
Café Divan	1834 Wisconsin Ave NW	202-338-1747	$$$	11 pm	It's Turkish, so anything with the word "Kebab" is safe bet.

Key: $: Under $10 / $$: $10–20 / $$$: $20–30 / $$$$: $30–40 / $$$$$: $40+
* : Does not accept credit cards. / † : Accepts only American Express. / †† : Accepts only Visa and Mastercard.
Time refers to weekend night closing time.

Café La Ruche	1039 31st St NW	202-965-2684	$$	11 pm	Great food for great prices.
Café Milano	3251 Prospect St NW	202-333-6183	$$$$	12:30 am	Would you care for a celebrity sighting with your tiramisu?
Café Romero's	2132 Wisconsin Ave NW	202-337-1111	$	4 am	Most college kids order Domino's; Georgetown kids order Romeo's.
Chadwicks	3205 K St NW	202-333-2565	$$	12 am	Go strictly for a burger.
Citronelle	3000 M St NW	202-625-2150	$$$$$	10:30 pm	A Tony Williams favorite. ($50 single dishes. Bon appetit!)
Clyde's	3236 M St NW	202-333-9180	$$$	1 am	Famous Georgetown saloon made less notable through suburban franchising.
Crisp & Juicy	4533 Wisconsin Ave NW	202-966-1222	$		Succulent Peruvian-roasted chicken spices up Tenleytown.
Fahrenheit & Degrees	3100 S St NW	202-912-4100	$$$$	11 pm	Italian-American in the deco Ritz-Carlton hotel.
Furin's	2805 M St NW	202-965-1000	$	5 pm	Small-town feel on edge of bustling Georgetown. (Breakfast and lunch.)
HomeMade Pizza Co.	4857 Massachusetts Ave NW	202-966-1600	$		Take-out pizza for when you want to pretend you cooked.
Hook	3241 M St NW	202-626-4488	$$$	12 am	Top-notch seafood dishes. And eco-friendly too!
Il Canale	1063 31st St NW	202-337-4444	$$		Neapolitan pies canal-side in Georgetown.
J Paul's	3218 M St NW	202-333-3450	$$$	1 am	Wanna feel like a pompous Georgetown loudmouth? It's kinda fun!
La Chaumiere	2813 M St NW	202-338-1784	$$$	10:30 pm	Mon Dieu! Are we in Georgetown or Paris?
La Madeleine	3000 M St NW	202-337-6975	$$	11 pm	Killer tomato basil soup, potatoes, salads, etc.
The Landmark	2430 Pennsylvania Ave NW	202-955-3863	$$$	10 pm	Melrose Hotel continental restaurant.
Martin's Tavern	1264 Wisconsin Ave NW	202-333-7370	$$$	12:30 am	Cubbyholed tables add flair to this old-school saloon.
Mendocino	2917 M St NW	202-333-2912	$$$$	11 pm	Wine and dine with the friendliest staff in Georgetown.
Morton's of Georgetown	3251 Prospect St NW	202-342-6258	$$$$	11 pm	Steaks a la carte will make converts out of vegetarians.
Mr Smith's	3104 M St NW	202-333-3104	$$$	1 am	Mr. Smith, you have an ordinary name and an ordinary restaurant.
Nathan's	3150 M St NW	202-338-2000	$$$$	10 pm	Birthplace of the three-martini lunch.
Old Glory	3139 M St NW	202-337-3406	$$	11 pm	Southeast-style BBQ, with hoppin' john on the side.
Prince Café	1042 Wisconsin Ave NW	202-333-1500	$	4:30 am	Sheesha lounge specializing in Mediterrean cuisine and flavored tobacco.
Puro Cafe	1529 Wisconsin Ave NW	202-787-1937	$		Be Bold… Be Hot… Be Calm… Be Branded… Be Georgetown.
Riverside Grill	3050 K St NW	202-342-3535	$$$	1 am	Plays third fiddle to Sequoia and T&J's, but also most peaceful.
Sequoia	3000 K St NW	202-944-4200	$$$$	12 am	A Georgetown see-and-be-seen hotspot.
sweetgreen	3333 M St NW	202-337-9338	$	9 pm	In the old Little Tavern space, fast food goes from greasy burgers to fresh and gourmet salads
Third Edition	1218 Wisconsin Ave NW	202-333-3700	$$	11:30 pm	If it's bar food you're after, it's bar food you got.
The Tombs	1226 36th St NW	202-337-6668	$$	12 am	An underground GU favorite.
Tony and Joe's	3000 K St NW	202-944-4545	$$$	11 pm	Waterfront views attract the beautiful people.
Wisemiller's	1236 36th St NW	202-333-8254	$	11 pm	Two words: Chicken Madness.
Wisey's	1440 Wisconsin Ave NW	202-333-4122	$	11 pm	Affordable, yummy food in Georgetown!

Map 9 · Dupont Circle / Adams Morgan

15 Ria	1515 Rhode Island Ave NW	202-742-0015	$$$$	12 am	New York chic dining in the nation's capital.
Al Tiramisu	2014 P St NW	202-467-4466	$$$$	11 pm	Romantic climate, friendly Italian service will make it a *bella notte*.
Annie's Paramount	1609 17th St NW	202-232-0395	$$	24-hrs	24-hour gay (straight-friendly) steak joint; packed Sunday brunch.
Bagels, Etc.	2122 P St NW	202-466-7171	$*	5 pm	Bagels served with a smile.
Bistro Bistro	1727 Connecticut Ave NW	202-328-1640	$		What is this again?
Bistrot du Coin	1738 Connecticut Ave NW	202-234-6969	$$$$	1 am	French joint, nix the stuffiness.
Blue Duck Tavern	1201 24th St NW	202-419-6755	$$$	10:30 pm	Fry anything in duck fat and it tastes good.
The Brickskeller	1523 22nd St NW	202-293-1885	$$	2 am	Renowned beer selection overshadows some damn fine eats.

Name	Address	Phone	Price	Close	Description
Bua	1635 P St NW	202-265-0828	$$	11 pm	The food far outclasses the décor, as it should be.
Café Citron	1343 Connecticut Ave NW	202-530-8844	$$$	11 am	South American cuisine sets stage for serious dance party.
Café Luna	1633 P St NW	202-387-4005	$$$	11:30 pm	Always busy, yet always intimate. Enjoy the Dupont open air.
Chi-Cha Lounge	1624 U St NW	202-234-8400	$$$	12:30 am	Kick off an evening on U with tapas, sangria, and a hookah.
City Lights of China	1731 Connecticut Ave NW	202-265-6688	$$$	12 am	Standard Chinese food that can't go wrong
Daily Grill	1200 18th St NW	202-822-5282	$$$	12 am	A 40-entrée menu.
The Front Page	1333 New Hampshire Ave NW	202-296-6500	$$$	12 am	Respectable dark wood-paneled Americana restaurant by day, seedy intern meat-market by night.
Eye Street Grill	1575 I St NW	202-289-7561	$		Sandwich and salad lunch spot.
Ezmè	2016 P St NW	202-797-0017	$$		Bites of Turkish mezedes paired with sips of wine. snag the Chef's table in the kitchen.
Grillfish DC	1200 New Hampshire Ave NW	202-331-7310	$$	11 pm	Perfect happy hours specials and excellent food
Hank's Oyster Bar	1624 Q St NW	202-462-4265	$$	10 pm	60 min happy hour features 1-for-$1 oysters!
Henry's Soul Cafe	1704 U St NW	202-265-3336	$$	9 pm	Ultimate take-out spot for serious soul food.
Hudson Restaurant and Lounge	2030 M St NW	202-872-8700	$$$$	2:30 am	Creative cocktails and swank digs with kitchen open 'til 3 am.
I Ricchi	1220 19th St NW	202-835-0459	$$$$	10:30 pm	Restaurants in Italy aren't this upscale.
Julia's Empanadas	1221 Connecticut Ave NW	202-861-8828	$*	3 am	So good and so cheap. Cash only.
Kramerbooks & Afterwords Café	1517 Connecticut Ave NW	202-387-1400	$$	2 am	Restaurant? Bookstore? All-night pancake joint? A must-visit.
La Tomate	1701 Connecticut Ave NW	202-667-5505		11:30 pm	Delicious contemporary Italian.
Lauriol Plaza	1835 18th St NW	202-387-0035	$$$	12 am	Ritzy architecture doesn't match run-of-the-mill dishes.
Levante's	1320 19th St NW	202-293-3244	$$	11:30 pm	Great Middle Eastern served by happy waiters.
Local 16	1602 U St NW	202-265-2828	$$$$	11 pm	The classiest place on U.
Love Café	1506 U St NW	202-588-7100	$	11 pm	Give your sweet tooth a fix with a gourmet cupcake.
Luna Grill & Diner	1301 Connecticut Ave NW	202-835-2280	$$	12 am	Great brunch.
Mackey's Public House	1823 L St NW	202-331-7667	$$	12 am	Another O'Whatever's.
Malaysia Kopitiam	1827 M St NW	202-833-6232	$$	11 pm	Menu offers extensive notes for the uninitiated Malaysian diner.
Marcel's	2401 Pennsylvania Ave NW	202-296-1166	$$$$	11 pm	Sheer decadence.
Marrakesh Palace	2147 P St NW	202-775-1882	$$	11 pm	Cool, laid back vibe and great Moroccan eats.
McCormick and Schmick's	1652 K St NW	202-861-2233	$$$	12 am	A K Street staple. Exploit the happy hour food specials.
Meiwah	1200 New Hampshire Ave NW	202-833-2888	$$$	11 pm	The lighter side of Chinese food.
Mixt Greens	1200 19th St NW	202-315-5230			"Eco-gourmet" salads from San Francisco.
Nage	1600 Rhode Island Ave NW	202-448-8005	$$$	11 pm	Surf and surf.
Nirvana	1810 K St NW	202-223-5043	$$	11 pm	Respectable Indian cuisine in the heart of downtown.
Nooshi	1120 19th St NW	202-293-3138	$$	11 pm	We recommend everything but the cheeseball name.
Obelisk	2029 P St NW	202-872-1180	$$$$	10 pm	Put your reservation in now for next March.
Olives	1600 K St NW	202-452-1866	$$$$	10:30 pm	Quaint but pricey Mediterranean.
Palette	1177 15th St NW	202-587-2700	$$$	11 pm	Great food with swank design
The Palm	1225 19th St NW	202-293-9091	$$$$	11 pm	If you're an elitist and you know it clap your hands!
Peacock Grand Cafe	2020 K St NW	202-530-2020	$$$	11 pm	Seafood, Steak, Pasta and Pizza
Pesce	2002 P St NW	202-466-3474	$$$	10:30 pm	Perhaps the best of the half-dozen fish joints on the block.
Pizzeria Paradiso	2029 P St NW	202-223-1245	$$	12 am	The toppings are meals themselves. Pray there's no line.
The Prime Rib	2020 K St NW	202-466-8811	$$$$	11:30 pm	Voted Washington's No.1 steakhouse.
Raku	1900 Q St NW	202-265-7258	$$	11 pm	Hip Asian bistro cashing in on DC's tapas craze.
Restaurant Nora	2132 Florida Ave NW	202-462-5143	$$$$	10:30 pm	Nora keeps her own herb garden in back. Every ingredient organic.
Rogue States	1300 Connecticut Ave NW	202-296-2242	$		Half-pound wood-grilled burgers until 5am.
Rosemary's Thyme	1801 18th St NW	202-332-3200	$$$	12 am	Mediterranean, meet Creole. Great people watching patio.
Sacrificial Lamb	1704 R St NW	202-797-2736	$		Afghan, Indian, and Pakistani specialties… and pizza.
Sam and Harry's	1200 19th St NW	202-296-4333	$$$$	10 pm	Looking for expensive filet mignon? Cross the street to The Palm.

Key: $: Under $10 / $$: $10–$20 / $$$: $20–$30 / $$$$: $30–40 / $$$$$: $40+
* : Does not accept credit cards. / † : Accepts only American Express. / †† : Accepts only Visa and Mastercard.
Time refers to weekend night closing time.

Sette Osteria	1666 Connecticut Ave NW	202-483-3070	$$	1 am	As simple as Italian gets. Pastas are all the rave.
Smith and Wollensky	1112 19th St NW	202-466-1100	$$$$	12 am	Sleek setting makes you forget it's a chain.
Stars	2120 P St NW	202-464-6464	$$$$	12 am	Classic Dupont: You never knew artists earned so much money.
Straits of Malaya	1836 18th St NW	202-483-1483	$$$	11 pm	Malaysian with a roof deck.
Sushi Taro	1503 17th St NW	202-462-8999	$$	10:30 pm	Traditional sushi above a CVS.
Sweetgreen	1512 Connecticut Ave NW	202-38-SWEET	$		Baby arugula, "guac deconstructed," and yogurt dressings on the go.
Tabard Inn Restaurant	1739 N St NW	202-331-8528	$$$$	10 pm	Fireplace, brick walls, outdoor tables, and elegant dishes.
Teaism	2009 R St NW	202-667-3827	$$	11 pm	Would you like dinner with your cup of tea?
Teatro Goldoni	1909 K St NW	202-955-9494	$$$$	11 pm	Lawyers and lobbyists abound. For a $13 lunch, why shouldn't they?
Thai Chef	1712 Connecticut Ave NW	202-234-5698	$$	11 pm	Comfy Thai food (and sushi).
Thaiphoon	2011 S St NW	202-667-3505	$$	11 pm	A curry lover's paradise.
Tomatillo Taqueria	1347 Connecticut Ave NW	202-427-6700	$		To-go tacos/burritos from a Big Hunt window.
Vapiano	1800 M St NW	202-640-1868	$$	11 pm	Fancy restaurant food and feel but on the cheap.
Vidalia	1990 M St NW	202-659-1990	$$$$	10:30 pm	A taste of dixieland refinery. Brilliant.
Westend Bistro	1190 22nd St NW	202-974-4900	$$$	11 pm	Fresh fish and fresh bank accounts
Yee Hwa	1009 21st St NW	202-833-8509	$$$	9:30 pm	Best Korean food outside of the 'burbs.

Map 10 • Logan Circle / U Street

Acadiana	901 New York Ave NW	202-408-8848	$$$$	11 pm	Southern bayou classics at a price
Al Crostino	1324 U St NW	202-797-0523	$$$$	12 am	Wine bar and homey Italian restaurant. Try the lamb ragu.
Ben's Chili Bowl	1213 U St NW	202-667-0909	$*	4 am	A District chili institution.
Brasserie Beck	1101 K St NW	202-408-1717	$$$$	11:30 pm	Feast on hearty bistro fare in generous portions, and sample some 50 Belgian beers.

Map 10 • Logan Circle / U Street—continued

Busboys and Poets	2021 14th St NW	202-387-7638	$$	2 am	Shabby chic leftist bookstore/restaurant, proletarian prices.
Café Saint-Ex	1847 14th St NW	202-265-7839	$$$	11 pm	Once-cool bistro overrun by the khaki crowd.
Chix	2019 11th St NW	202-234-2449	$	10 pm	Affordable, eco-conscious take-out, open late. They know their mid-twenties nonprofit demographic.
Coppi's	1414 U St NW	202-319-7773	$$$	12 am	Eat an organic extra large pizza and pretend you're healthy.
Corduroy	1122 9th St NW	202-589-0699	$$$$$	11 pm	Sleek, innovative restaurant gives hotel dining a good name.
Creme Café	1322 U St NW	202-234-1885	$$$$	11:30 pm	Upscale southern home cooking.
DC Coast	1401 K St NW	202-216-5988	$$$$	11:30 pm	Another sterile, upscale American establishment.
Dukem	1114 U St NW	202-667-8735	$$	2 am	Authentic Ethiopian. Special weekend outdoor grill menu.
Georgia Brown's	950 15th St NW	202-393-4499	$$$$	11 pm	Upscale Southern features a scandalous brunch.
Juice Joint Cafe	1025 Vermont Ave NW	202-347-6783	$	4 pm	Healthy, good-for-you lunches and juices for K Street folks
Lima	1401 K St NW	202-789-2800	$$	11 pm	You should never eat where you can party too
Logan Tavern	1423 P St NW	202-332-3710	$$$$	12 am	Eclectic comfort food with juicy ribs
Marvin	2007 14th St NW	202-797-7171	$$	11 pm	Amazing roof top bar and indoor dining
Oohhs and Aahhs	1005 U St NW	202-667-7142	$	10 pm	The District's best soul food.
Polly's Café	1342 U St NW	202-265-8385	$$$*	12 am	One of the first U Street revivalists.
Post Pub	1422 L St NW	202-628-2111	$$	11:30 pm	Best burgers in city. Shhh! A secret!
Rice	1608 14th St NW	202-234-2400	$$$	11 pm	Swanky minimalist Thai. Try the green tea dishes.
The Saloon	1207 U St NW	202-462-2640	$$$††	1 am	Go there for the beer. Just be sure to eat beforehand.
Sweetgreen	1471 P St NW	202-234-7336	$		Baby arugula, "guac deconstructed," and yogurt dressings on the go.
Tabaq Bistro	1336 U St NW	202-265-0965	$$$$	12 am	Mediterranean tapas joint with a hopping glass-top roof deck.

Thai Tanic	1326 14th St NW	202-588-1795	$$	11 pm	Neighborhood fave Thai restaurant.
U-topia	1418 U St NW	202-483-7669	$$$	1 am	Reasonably priced eclectic international cuisine.

Map 11 · Near Northeast

Divinely Decadent Desserts	2703 12th St NE	202-629-3667	$		"God inspired" home-baked desserts.
Kushi	465 K St NW	202-682-3123	$$		Izakaya and sushi restaurant with plenty of small-batch sake.

Map 13 · Brookland / Langdon

Rita's	2318 Rhode Island Ave NE	202-636-7482	$		Italian ice, frozen custard and gelato.

Map 14 · Catholic U

Colonel Brooks' Tavern	901 Monroe St NE	202-529-4002	$$	1 am	Be welcomed like a local in the blue-collar section of town.
El Limeno	201 Upshur St NW	202-829-5551	$$	11 pm	Tableclothed El Salvadorian fare, served with soccer on the television.
The Hitching Post	200 Upshur St NW	202-726-1511	$$	11 pm	Southern fried chicken, crab cakes.
Murry and Paul's	3513 12th St NE	202-529-4078	$*	4 pm	We dare you to eat here (breakfast and lunch only).
San Antonio Bar and Grill	3908 12th St	202-832-8080	$$	10 pm	New Tex-Mex spot for Brookland.

Map 15 · Columbia Heights

Brown's Caribbean Bakery	3301 Georgia Ave NW	202-882-1626	$††	7 pm	Cinnamon rolls the size of your head.
Chuck & Billy's Bar and Carry-Out	2718 Georgia Ave NW	202-234-5870	$	1:30 am	Soul food and lots of it.
Florida Ave Grill	1100 Florida Ave NW	202-265-1586	$$	9 pm	Greasy spoon from the dirty south.
The Heights Restaurant and Bar	3115 14th St NW	202-797-7227	$$	11 pm	Upscale homestyle food: fried chicken, meatloaf, burgers, rotisserie chicken.
Negril	2301 Georgia Ave NW	202-332-3737	$	10 pm	Local Caribbean quick-eats chain.
Pollo Campero	3229 14th St NW	202-745-0078	$$	9 pm	Addictive fried chicken born in Guatemala.
Red Rocks Pizzeria	1036 Park Rd NW	202-232-2228	$$	12 am	Corner townhouse turned brick oven pizzeria with patio.
Rita's Caribbean Carry-Out	3322 Georgia Ave NW	202-722-1868	$$††	9 pm	Authentic Caribbean carryout, recently refurbished without the bullet-proof glass.
Ruby Tuesday	3365 14th St NW	202-462-7681	$$	12 am	All you've heard, and nothing more.
Rumberos	3345 14th St NW	202-232-6006	$$$	12 am	South American cuisine, local art, live music.
Soul Vegetarian and Exodus Café	2606 Georgia Ave NW	202-328-7685	$††	9 pm	Eclectic African vegan take-out.
Taqueria Distrito Federal	3463 14th St NW	202-276-7331	$*	10 pm	Dirt cheap, hole-in-the-wall taqueria... trying to describe the deliciousness feels like food porn.
Temperance Hall	3634 Georgia Ave NW	202-722-7669	$$	11 pm	1920s theme with Jazz-Age décor, mini-sloppy joes, and selection of rye whiskeys.
Thai Tanic II	3462 14th St NW	202-387-0882	$$		Popular Thai restaurant opens second location farther north on 14th Street.

Map 16 · Adams Morgan (North) / Mt Pleasant

Adam's Express	3211 Mt Pleasant St NW	202-328-0010	$$*	10 pm	Unassuming but delicious.
Amsterdam Falafel	2425 18th St NW	202-234-1969	$*	4 am	Best falafel in the city on the cheap
Astor Mediterranean	1829 Columbia Rd NW	202-745-7495	$	10:30 pm	Great falafel sandwich and subs.
Bardia's New Orleans Café	2412 18th St NW	202-234-0420	$	10 pm	Perfect brunch with great Cajun takes on poached egg classics.
Bukom Café	2442 18th St NW	202-265-4600	$$$	2 am	West African food, feel, and music.
Cashion's Eat Place	1819 Columbia Rd NW	202-797-1819	$$$$	11 pm	Chelsea Clinton known to have played the dating game here.
The Diner	2453 18th St NW	202-232-8800	$	24-hrs	Self-explanatory. Open 24 hours.
Dos Gringos	3116 Mt Pleasant St NW	202-462-1159	$††	9 pm	Proving that classy Salvadorean establishment is not an oxymoron.
Grill From Ipanema	1858 Columbia Rd NW	202-986-0757	$$$	12 am	Killer caiphirinas that scream "Brazil!"
Haydee's	3102 Mt Pleasant St NW	202-483-9199	$††	2:30 am	Cheap but awful Salvadorean food. Beware the salsa.
Heller's Bakery	3221 Mt Pleasant St NW	202-265-1169	$	8 pm	Start your morning off with donuts and coffee.
Julia's Empanadas	2452 18th St NW	202-328-6232	$*	3 am	Filling, cheap, and open late.

Key: $: Under $10 / $$: $10–$20 / $$$: $20–$30 / $$$$: $30–40 / $$$$$: $40+
*: Does not accept credit cards. / †: Accepts only American Express. / ††: Accepts only Visa and Mastercard.
Time refers to weekend night closing time.

La Fourchette	2429 18th St NW	202-332-3077	$$$$	11 pm	Casual creperie.
Leftbank	2424 18th St NW	202-464-2100	$$	12 am	Americana diner, sushi bar, cafeteria aesthetic, hipster chic.
The Little Fountain Café	2339 18th St NW	202-462-8100	$$	11 pm	Charming oasis on Adams Morgan's Drunkards Row.
M'Dawgs Haute Dogs	2418 18th St NW	202-328-8284	$††	4 am	Fancy a wiener at 3 in the morning?
Mama Ayesha's	1967 Columbia St NW	202-232-5431	$$	10:30 pm	Middle Eastern good enough for Bill Clinton.
Marx Café	3203 Mt Pleasant St NW	202-518-7600	$$	11 pm	Quasi-hipster Mount Pleasant standout.
Meskerem Ethiopian Restaurant	2434 18th St NW	202-462-4100	$$$	1 am	Authentic Ethiopian meets DC posh.
Millie & Al's	2440 18th St NW	202-387-8131	$$	2 am	A dive's dive for pizza and pitchers.
Mixtec	1792 Columbia Rd NW	202-332-1011	$$††	11 pm	Originally a grocery store, this Mexican beanery is superb.
Pasta Mia	1790 Columbia Rd NW	202-328-9114	$$	10 pm	Queue up early or wait for hours to be told how and when you may eat your perfect pasta
Perry's	1811 Columbia Rd NW	202-234-6218	$$$	11:30 pm	A punk sushi experience. Killer city views.
Pho 14	1436 Park Rd NW	202-986-2326	$	11 pm	Go Pho in Mt. Pleasant.
Pica Taco	1629 Columbia Rd NW	202-518-0076	$		Taqueria tucked into the Argonne apartment building.
Radius Pizza	3155 Mt Pleasant St NW	202-234-0808	$	11 pm	A slice of New York.
Rumba Café	2443 18th St NW	202-588-5501	$$††	12 am	Eat steak and watch tango. (Wednesday nights.)
Savour and Sutra	2408 18th St NW	202-299-1113	$$		Upstairs-downstairs set up offers one-stop restaurant, lounge and bar.
Sawah Diner	2222 18th St NW	202-232-2377			American diner with Mediterranean bent tries to do it all.
Tonic	3155 Mt Pleasant St NW	202-986-7661	$$	11 pm	Comfort food and a can't-be-beat happy hour.
Tono Sushi & Asian Cuisine	2605 Connecticut Ave NW	202-332-7300	$$	11 pm	Serviceable sushi, $1/piece happy hour special.
Tryst Coffee House	2459 18th St NW	202-232-5500	$$	3 am	Excellent Wi-Fi cafe. A central DC spot.

Map 17 • Woodley Park / Cleveland Park

Alero	3500 Connecticut Ave NW	202-966-2530	$$	12 am	Margarita before a movie at the Uptown.
Ardeo	3311 Connecticut Ave NW	202-244-6750	$$$$	11:30 pm	In the room the women come and go talking of Michelangelo.
Byblos Deli	3414 Connecticut Ave NW	202-364-6549	$	9 pm	Mediterranean yumminess.
The Cereal Bowl	3420 Connecticut Ave NW	202-244-4492	$		From Grape Nuts to Trix, plus parfaits and oaties.
Dino	3435 Connecticut Ave NW	202-686-2966	$$$	10:30 pm	Try the boar pasta.
Ireland's Four Fields	3412 Connecticut Ave NW	202-244-0860	$$$	1:30 am	Grub's not too bad in what's best known as a party bar.
Lavandou	3321 Connecticut Ave NW	202-966-3002	$$$$	11 pm	Casual French sidewalk-style bistro.
Lebanese Taverna	2641 Connecticut Ave NW	202-265-8681	$$$	11 pm	Serviceable food, unserviceable service.
Mr Chen's Organic Chinese Cuisine	2604 Connecticut Ave NW	202-797-9668	$$$	11 pm	Cult favorite of munchies-stricken health-conscious hipsters.
Nam Viet	3419 Connecticut Ave NW	202-237-1015	$$	11 pm	No frills pho.
Open City	2331 Calvert St NW	202-332-2331	$$	3 am	Hipper-than-thou diner with round-the-clock brunch.
Petits Plats	2653 Connecticut Ave NW	202-518-0018	$$$	10:30 pm	Take out a selection of goodies from downstairs.
Sabores	3435 Connecticut Ave NW	202-244-7196	$$$	11 pm	Tapas et al.
Sake Club	2635 Connecticut Ave NW	202-332-2711	$$$$	12 am	Sake and Japanese, with prices ranging from low to quite high.
Sorriso	3518 Connecticut Ave NW	202-537-4800	$$$	10:30 pm	Artisanal Italian with an awesome Nutella pizza.
Spices	3333 Connecticut Ave NW	202-686-3833	$$$	11 pm	Dependably tasty pan-Asian. Try the suicide curry.

Map 18 • Glover Park / Foxhall

2 Amys	3715 Macomb St NW	202-885-5700	$$	11 pm	Pizza Napolitana. Romantic or just for kicks.
BlackSalt	4883 MacArthur Blvd NW	202-342-9101	$$$	11 pm	Gorgeous seafood with a posh bar.
Cactus Cantina	3300 Wisconsin Ave NW	202-686-7222	$$$	12 am	Same as Lauriol Plaza, minus courtly architecture.
Café Deluxe	3228 Wisconsin Ave NW	202-686-2233	$$$	11 pm	A greasy spoon with absolutely no grease.
Heritage India	2400 Wisconsin Ave NW	202-333-3120	$$$$	11 pm	Gourmet Indian in a comfortable setting.

Jetties	1609 Foxhall Rd NW	202-965-3663	$	6 pm	Every neighborhood deserves such an ice cream shop.
Kavanagh's Pizza Pub	2400 Wisconsin Ave NW	202-337-3132	$$	12 am	If you think you're better than pizza and beer, you're wrong
Kotobuki	4822 MacArthur Blvd NW	202-281-6679	$$	11 pm	Price: low. Quality: high.
Makoto Restaurant	4822 MacArthur Blvd NW	202-298-6866	$$$	10 pm	Sushi a la carte. You'll never need to visit Japan.
Max's Best Ice Cream	2416 Wisconsin Ave NW	202-333-3111	$*	11:30 pm	Mom and pop ice cream shop.
Old Europe	2434 Wisconsin Ave NW	202-333-7600	$$$	9:30 pm	Forget Atkins: try the Rindergoulasch ungarische Art and Apfelstrudel.
Palisades Pizzeria & Clam Bar	4885 MacArthur Blvd NW	202-338-2010	$$	11 pm	NY thin crust, Philly cheesesteaks, fried clams, and soft serve, then, angina.
Rocklands	2418 Wisconsin Ave NW	202-333-2558	$$	10 pm	Cooking 150,000 pounds of pork a year, and counting.
Sushi Sushi	3714 Macomb St NW	202-686-2015	$$	11 pm	Yet another gem on Macomb Street, and a great value.
Sushi-Ko Glover Park	2309 Wisconsin Ave NW	202-333-4187	$$$$	11 pm	Washington's first sushi bar, since 1976.
Town Hall	2218 Wisconsin Ave NW	202-333-5640	$$$	11 pm	Soul food without the soul.
Z Burger	2414 Wisconsin Ave NW	202-965-7777	$$		Burger, dogs, and milkshakes—and a bazillion ways to have them.

Map 19 · Tenleytown / Friendship Heights

4912 Thai Cuisine	4912 Wisconsin Ave NW	202-966-4696	$$	11 pm	Excellent Thai with a creative name.
Angelico Pizzeria & Cafe	4529 Wisconsin Ave NW	202-243-3030	$$	1 am	You know you want some cheap, greasy Italian food.
Bambule	5225 Wisconsin Ave NW	202-966-0300	$$$	11:30 pm	Wide doors open onto a porch revealing tapas and dancing.
Café Ole	4000 Wisconsin Ave NW	202-244-1330	$$$	11 pm	Fun neighborhood Spanish-style tapas.
Café of India	4909 Wisconsin Ave NW	202-244-1395	$$		Worst copyedited menu ever.
The Dancing Crab	4611 41st St NW	202-244-1882	$$$	10:30 pm	Grab a bib and mallet and get cracking.
Froyo	5252 Wisconsin Ave NW	202-686-5805			Self-serve frozen yogurt inside Booeymonger.
Guapo's	4515 Wisconsin Ave NW	202-686-3588	$$$	12 am	Nothing better than drinking tequila outside.
Maggiano's Little Italy	5333 Wisconsin Ave NW	202-966-5500	$$	12 am	Opposite of this book's title.
Marvelous Market	4800 Wisconsin Ave NW	202-448-9954	$		Pre-made salads, sandwiches and desserts, along with fresh breads.
Matisse	4934 Wisconsin Ave NW	202-244-5222	$$$$	11 pm	French and Mediterranean with all the details.
Morty's Delicatessen	4620 Wisconsin Ave NW	202-686-1989	$$	9 pm	It ain't New York, but arguably DC's best Jewish deli.
Murasaki	4620 Wisconsin Ave NW	202-966-0023	$$$	10:30 pm	Wide range of Japanese cuisines.
Murphy's Law	4624 Wisconsin Ave NW	202-525-2058	$$		Sports, brew & Irish breakfast.
Osman's and Joe's Steak 'n Egg Kitchen	4700 Wisconsin Ave NW	202-686-1201	$	24-hrs	This greasy spoon hasn't changed a thing in over 60 years.
Z Burger	4321 Wisconsin Ave NW	202-966-1999	$$		AU student hang-out for grilled burgers and 75 flavors of milkshakes.

Map 20 · Cleveland Park / Upper Connecticut

Acacia Bistro	4340 Connecticut Ave NW	202-537-1040	$$	10 pm	Small plates and wine from the Wellness Cafe folks.
Buck's Fishing & Camping	5031 Connecticut Ave NW	202-364-0777	$$$$	10 pm	More sophisticated than the name suggests.
Delhi Dhaba	4455 Connecticut Ave NW	202-537-1008	$$	10:30 pm	Efficient Indian take-out passes the test. Try the butter chicken.
Indique	3512 Connecticut Ave NW	202-244-6600	$$$$	11 pm	Wrap your mind around an inside-out samosa.
Palena	3529 Connecticut Ave NW	202-537-9250	$$$$	10 pm	Continental food and an engrossing dessert menu.
Paragon Thai	3507 Connecticut Ave NW	202-237-2777	$$	11 pm	No-frills Thai.
Yanni's Greek Taverna	3500 Connecticut Ave NW	202-362-8871	$$	12am	Inexpensive Greek platters with great summer seating outdoors

Map 21 · 16th St. Heights / Petworth

Beverage Mania	849 Upshur St NW	202-545-0077	$	10 pm	Serving up a variety of frozen desserts.
Domku	821 Upshur St NW	202-722-7475	$$$	10 pm	East European and Scandinavian comfort food.
El Torogoz	4231 9th St NW	202-722-6966	$$††	11:30 pm	Salvadoran sit-down with Spanish TV and outdoor seating.
Meridian	5832 Georgia Ave NW	202-722-8882	$$$	11 pm	Newcomer to Brightwood brings upscale food from the African diaspora
Sweet Mango Café	3701 New Hampshire Ave NW	202-726-2646	$$	11 pm	Slow-roasted jerked chicken on the bone. Best in the city.

Key: $: Under $10 / $$: $10–$20 / $$$: $20–$30 / $$$$: $30–40 / $$$$$: $40+
* : Does not accept credit cards. / † : Accepts only American Express. / †† : Accepts only Visa and Mastercard.
Time refers to weekend night closing time.

Map 22 • Bethesda (North)

Bacchus	7945 Norfolk Ave	301-657-1722	$$$$	10:30 pm	Lebanese menu with lots of twists and turns.
BlackFinn Restaurant & Saloon	4901 Fairmont Ave	301-951-5681	$	10 pm	Do you like sports, beer, and not much else?
The Burger Joint	4827 Fairmont Ave	301-358-6137	$$	10 pm	Gigantic burgers for gigantic people.
Cafe Prezzo	4867 Cordell Ave	301-654-0001	$$		Tel Aviv Cafe reopens, reserving Middle Eastern and Med faves.
Delicias Carry Out	4708 Highland Ave	301-654-7887	$	6 pm	Mom-and-pop burritos in a land of Chipotles.
Faryab	4917 Cordell Ave	301-951-3484	$$$	10:30 pm	Premier DC metro area Afghan stop.
Grapeseed	4865 Cordell Ave	301-986-9592	$$$$	11 pm	Spanish cuisine to go with wine list al grande.
Haandi	4904 Fairmont Ave	301-718-0121	$$$	10:30 pm	Super-tasty Indian.
Javan	7710 Wisconsin Ave	301-656-4040	$$	11 pm	Persian-recommended and Persian-approved.
La Miche	7905 Norfolk Ave	301-986-0707	$$$$	10 pm	Provence cooking with all your French favorites
Louisiana Kitchen & Bayou Bar	4907 Cordell Ave	301-652-6945	$$	10 pm	Get your Muffuletta fix here.
Matuba	4918 Cordell Ave	301-652-7449	$$$	10 pm	Basic sushi and buffet.
Mia's Pizzas	4926 Cordell Ave	301-718-6427	$$	10:30 pm	Pizza pies from a wood-burning oven.
Olazzo	7921 Norfolk Ave	301-654-9496	$$$	10:30 pm	Italian with a brick oven (and yet no pizza!).
The Original Pancake House	7700 Wisconsin Ave	301-986-0285	$	3 pm	Oh, go ahead. Bring back a few childhood memories.
Passage to India	4931 Cordell Ave	301-656-3373	$		Sudhir Seth's top-notch culinary aromatherapy.
Peter's Carry Out	8017 Wisconsin Ave	301-656-2242	$	4:30 pm	Best greasy spoon according to some people.
Tako Grill	7756 Wisconsin Ave	301-652-7030	$$$	10:30 pm	Traditional and nontraditional Japanese for the enthusiast.
Tastee Diner	7731 Woodmont Ave	301-652-3970	$	24 hrs	Surly waitresses, free refills, clogging arteries, and a whole lotta pies
Tia Queta	4839 Del Ray Ave	301-654-4443	$$	10 pm	Margaritas on a rooftop. Need we say more?
Tragara	4935 Cordell Ave	301-951-4935	$$$$	10:30 pm	Traditional Italian with elegant surroundings.

Map 23 • Chevy Chase (North)

Tavira	8401 Connecticut Ave	301-652-8684	$		Wonderful Portuguese in subterraneon Chevy Chase MD.

Map 24 • Upper Rock Creek Park

Parkway Deli	8317 Grubb Rd	301-587-1427	$$	9:30 pm	Another rare high-quality Jewish deli.

Map 25 • Silver Spring

8407 Kitchen and Bar	8407 Ramsey Ave	301-587-8407	$		"Organic-Modern" American from ex-Nicaro.
A Taste of Jerusalem	8123 Georgia Ave	301-495-3067	$		Family-run restaurant of mezza amidst Silver Sprung chains.
Addis Ababa	8233 Fenton St	301-589-1400	$$	1 am	Authentic Ethiopian. Ask to sit on the rooftop.
Austin Grill	919 Ellsworth Dr	240-247-8969	$$	1 am	Down-home grub at down-home prices. Yee-haw.
Ceviche	921 Ellsworth Dr	301-608-0081	$$$	11 pm	Latin Concepts delivers again in this swank lounge.
Cubano's	1201 Fidler Ln	301-563-4020	$$$	10:30 pm	Fountain and foliage make the décor cheessisimo.
Eggspectation	923 Ellsworth Dr	301-585-1700	$$	10 pm	So many eggs you wonder where they hide their hens.
El Aguila	8649 16th St	301-588-9063	$$	2 am	Better than its location would have you believe.
Fractured Prune	8512 Fenton St	301-565-8007	$		Fresh, hand-dipped donuts, made to order.
Gallery	1115 E West Hwy	301-589-2555	$		Nuevo Latino by day, flashy dance lounge by night.
Jackie's	8081 Georgia Ave	301-565-9700	$$	10:30 pm	Wine and food at your neighborhood hot spot

Lebanese Taverna	933 Ellsworth Dr	301-588-1192	$$	10 pm	Fast, decent Middle Eastern food.
Mandalay	930 Bonifant St	301-585-0500	$$	10:30 pm	Addictive Burmese food next door to a gun shop.
Mi Rancho	8701 Ramsey Ave	301-588-4872	$$	11 pm	Quite cheap Mexican/Salvadorean.
Mrs. K's Toll House	9201 Colesville Rd	301-589-3500	$$$$	9:30 pm	Quaint country inn
Nicaro	8229 Georgia Ave	(301) 588-2867	$$$$	11 pm	Independent, fresh, local, seasonal, and stylish
Ray's The Classics	8606 Colesville Rd	301-588-7297		10 pm	Need a steak in your life?
Roger Miller Restaurant	941 Bonifant St	301-650-2495	$$	12 am	Unique Cameroonian fare, named after a soccer star. Try the goat.
Romano's Macaroni Grill	931 Ellsworth Dr	301-562-2806	$$$	11 pm	Good standard Italian.

Map 26 • Takoma Park

Capital City Cheesecake	7071 Carroll Ave	202-821-8251	$		Cheesecakes and so much more!
Mark's Kitchen	7006 Carroll Ave	301-270-1884	$$	9 pm	Green-friendly American and Korean fare.
Olive Lounge	7006 Carroll Ave	301-270-5154	$$		Middle Eastern cuisine.
Summer Delights	6939 Laurel Ave	301-891-2880	$		Frozen treats.

Map 27 • Walter Reed

Blair Mansion Inn/ Murder Mystery Dinner Theatre	7711 Eastern Ave	301-588-6646	$$$$	9 pm	What's better than finding a hair in your soup? Finding a dead body during mystery dinner theater!
Cedar Crossing Tavern	341 Cedar St NW	202-882-8999	$$		Bistro and bar on the other side of the Takoma tracks.
El Tamarindo	7331 Georgia Ave NW	202-291-0525	$		Pupusas y tamales for Shepard Park.
Teddy's Roti Shop	7304 Georgia Ave NW	202-882-6488	$		West Indian curries with ginger drink… mmm…

Map 28 • Chevy Chase

American City Diner & Cinema Cafe	5532 Connecticut Ave NW	202-244-1949	$	24-hrs	1950s drive-in themed diner, complete with movies.
Arucola	5534 Connecticut Ave NW	202-244-1555	$$$$	10:30 pm	Straightforward Italian.
Bread & Chocolate	5542 Connecticut Ave NW	202-966-7413	$	9 pm	Can't go wrong with this combination.
La Ferme	7101 Brookville Rd	301-986-5255	$$$$	10 pm	Charming (if bizarre) French bistro in a residential area.
Pumpernickel's Bagelry & Delicatessen	5504 Connecticut Ave NW	202-244-9505	$		Top-notch local bagels, sandwiches, and attitude.
Senor Pepper	5507 Connecticut Ave NW	202-244-7774	$		Chicken enchilada with a signature Senor Pepper margarita, anyone?

Map 29 • Bethesda (South)

Bethesda Crab House	4958 Bethesda Ave	301-652-3382	$$	11 pm	More like "basement" than "house" with excellent crabs year-round and little else
Brownbag	7272 Wisconsin Ave	301-654-4600	$$	3:30 pm	Outstanding sandwiches
Clyde's of Chevy Chase	5441 Wisconsin Ave NW	301-951-9600	$		All-American fare amidst Orient Express décor.
Georgetown Cupcake	4834 Bethesda Ave	301-907-8900	$	9 pm	From Georgetown to Bethesda Row, these are the fanciest cupcakes in town.
Gifford's	7237 Woodmont Ave	800-708-1938	$††	11 pm	Next to movie theater—deals for cones + tickets.
Green Papaya	4922 Elm St	301-654-8241	$$$$	10 pm	Tasty but ridiculously inauthentic Vietnamese.
Hinode	4914 Hampden Ln	301-654-0908	$$$	11 pm	No-surprises Japanese.
Indique Heights	2 Wisconsin Cir	301-656-4822	$$	10:30pm	Fusion Indian.
Jaleo	7271 Woodmont Ave	301-913-0003	$$$$	12 am	Good, if overpriced, tapas.
Levante's	7262 Woodmont Ave	301-657-2441	$$	11 pm	Sleek Turkish eatery with a decent Sunday brunch buffet.
Louisiana Express Company	4921 Bethesda Ave	301-652-6945	$$	10 pm	Get your Muffuletta fix here.
M Café & Bar	5471 Wisconsin Ave	301-986-4818	$		Bellinis and insalate after you shop til you drop.
Moby Dick House of Kabob	7027 Wisconsin Ave	301-654-1838	$	11 pm	Mind your manners or "No kebob for you!"
Mon Ami Gabi	7239 Woodmont Ave	301-654-1234	$$$$	11 pm	Authentic French atmosphere: expensive and snooty. Half-price wines on Wednesday evenings.
Persimmon	7003 Wisconsin Ave	301-654-9860	$$$$	10:30 pm	Superlative Bethesda continental experience.
Potomac Pizza	19 Wisconsin Cir	301-951-1127	$		Much-loved pizza parlor for 30+ years.
Raku	7240 Woodmont Ave	301-718-8680	$$$	10:30 pm	Pan-Asian delight with lovely outdoor patio.
Redwood	7121 Bethesda Ln	301-656-5515	$$$$	11 pm	Seasonal, new American food from the Sonoma folks.

Key: $: Under $10 / $$: $10–$20 / $$$: $20–$30 / $$$$: $30–40 / $$$$$: $40+
* : Does not accept credit cards. / † : Accepts only American Express. / †† : Accepts only Visa and Mastercard.
Time refers to weekend night closing time.

Ri-Ra Irish Restaurant Pub	4931 Elm St	301-657-1122	$$$	12:45 pm	Irish pub; utterly American grub.
Rio Grande	4870 Bethesda Ave	301-656-2981	$$$	11:30 pm	Great free chips and salsa—good Tex Mex.
Rock Creek Restaurant	4917 Elm St	301-907-7625	$$$$	11pm	Super serene ambience. Nutritional facts on each dish listed on back of menu.
Sushi Ko Chevy Chase	5455 Wisconsin Ave	301-961-1644	$$$	11 pm	Sexy second edition of DC's first sushi spot includes a room just for sake swilling
Sweetgreen	4831 Bethesda Ave	301-65-GREEN	$		Baby arugula, "guac deconstructed," and yogurt dressings on the go.
Tara Thai	4828 Bethesda Ave	301-657-0488	$$	11 pm	Well-known for bold Thai.
Vace	4705 Miller Ave	301-654-6367	$	8 pm	Queue up for the best pizza in town..

Map 30 • Westmoreland Circle

Dahlia	4849 Massachusetts Ave NW	202-364-1004	$$$$	9:30 pm	Fine dining with Spring Valley socialites.
DeCarlo's	4822 Yuma St NW	202-363-4220	$$$	10 pm	The geriatric crowds feasts on tasty Italian here, the definition of a neighborhood joint.
Le Pain Quotidien	4874 Massachusetts Ave NW	202-459-9141	$$$	10 pm	Delicious French-y café, with French-y food and French-y portions.

Map 31 • Chesterbrook

Amoo's House of Kabob	6271 Old Dominion Dr	703-448-8500	$$	10 pm	Go for the great kabobs; ignore the bland décor.
Café China	6271 Old Dominion Dr	703-821-8666	$	10 pm	Pick up little white boxes on the way home from work.
China Kingdom	6222 Old Dominion Dr	703-532-1088	$$	10:30 pm	Basic neighborhood storefront Chinese.
Dominion Restaurant	6238 Old Dominion Dr	703-533-5880	$$	9 pm	Casual, family-friendly, and one of the only options in Chesterbrook.
Pizza Hut	6263 Old Dominion Dr	703-448-3535	$	12 am	You get what you pay for.
Subway	6216 Old Dominion Dr	703-532-3700	$		If it's good enough for Jared, it's good enough for me.

Map 32 • Cherrydale / Palisades

Bambu	5101 MacArthur Blvd NW	202-364-3088	$$$	10 pm	Reliable Asian fusion.
DC Boathouse	5441 MacArthur Blvd NW	202-362-2628	$$$$	11 pm	Don't crack your skull on the skull.
Listrani's Italian Gourmet	5100 MacArthur Blvd NW	202-363-0620	$$$	10 pm	A real neighborhood-y pizza & pasta place.

Map 33 • Falls Church

Huong Viet	6785 Wilson Blvd	703-538-7110	$$	11 pm	Over 163 items! All Vietnamese!
Joe's Pizza	5555 Lee Hwy	703-532-0990	$	10 pm	Pizza by New York transplants is a team/school favorite.
Lebanese Taverna	5900 Washington Blvd	703-241-8681	$$$	10:30 pm	Family-style Lebanese.
Lost Dog Café	5876 Washington Blvd	703-237-1552	$*	11 pm	Monster sandwiches, gourmet pizza, and cute puppy pics.
Peking Pavilion Chinese Restaurant	2912 N Sycamore St	703-237-6868			Hidden Chinese gem in strip mall Arlington hell.
Pie Tanza	2503 N Harrison St	703-237-0200	$$	10 pm	Thin crust, toppings galore, and wallet-friendly.
Restaurant Vero and Wine Bar	5723 Lee Hwy	703-538-4600	$$$	9:30 pm	Elegant, cultured jewel tucked in a strip mall setting
Stray Cat Café	5866 N Washington Blvd	703-237-7775	$	10 pm	Kitty kat décor with great sandwiches, burgers, and salads.
Sushi Zen	2457 N Harrison St	703-534-6000	$$$	10 pm	Sushi and sashimi served in hand-carved wooden boats draw families—lots of them.
Taqueria Poblano	2503 N Harrison St	703-237-8250	$$	10 pm	As predictable as it cheap.
Thai Noy	5880 N Washington Blvd	703-534-7474	$$	10 pm	Above-average Thai in arty, Buddha-filled space

Map 34 • Cherrydale / Ballston

Big Buns Gourmet Grill	4401 Wilson Blvd	703-276-3032	$$	9 pm	Step by step ordering plus lots of choices equals brain overload.
Buffalo D's	4213 Fairfax Dr	703-465-8888	$$		Bar and grille of the sporty/dive variety.
Café Parisien Express	4520 Lee Hwy	703-525-3332	$$††	9:30 pm	French dining on the cheap.
Café Tirolo	4001 N Fairfax Dr	703-528-7809	$$	2:30 pm	Hidden European treasure with modest prices.

Cassatt's	4536 Lee Hwy	703-527-3330	$$	9 pm	Head over on Kiwi Mondays for interesting dinner fare and an art lesson downstairs.
Crisp & Juicy	4540 Lee Hwy	703-243-4222	$$*	9:30 pm	Latino-barbecued chicken.
Grand Cru Wine Bar and Bistro	4401 Wilson Blvd	703-243-7900	$		If you like to pretend you're a wine snob. Food—not so grand cru.
Heidelberg Pastry Shoppe	2150 N Culpeper St	703-527-8394	$		A tasty German bakery "Shoppe" fit for a president. Move over, cupcakes.
Hunan Gate	4233 Fairfax Dr	703-243-5678	$	11 pm	Cheap Chinese. Good.
Layalina	5216 Wilson Blvd	703-525-1170	$$$	10:30 pm	Middle Eastern rugs adorn walls. Straight out of *Aladdin*.
The Melting Pot	1110 N Glebe Rd	703-243-4490	$$$	11 pm	Mmmm overpriced melted cheese.
Metro 29 Diner	4711 Lee Hwy	703-528-2464	$$	1 am	Diner breakfast with some Greek touches.
PF Chang's	901 N Glebe Rd	703-527-0955	$$$	11:30 pm	Tasty posh Chinese; lettuce wraps are a crowd pleaser.
Rio Grande Café	4301 N Fairfax Dr	703-528-3131	$$$	11:30 pm	We don't know what café means anymore.
Ted's Montana Grill	4300 Wilson Blvd	703-741-0661	$$	11 pm	Upscale, red-state buffalo meat chain.
Tutto Bene	501 N Randolph St	703-522-1005	$$$	11 pm	Italian cuisine, when not Bolivian. We love America.
Vapiano	4401 Wilson Blvd	703-528-3113	$$	11 pm	Dining hall setup, fancy restaurant food and feel but on the cheap.
Willow	4301 N Fairfax Dr	703-465-8800	$$$$	10:30 pm	Snazzy spot helmed by Kinkhead's ex-head chef.

Map 35 • Cherrydale / Clarendon

Aladdin's Eatery	4245 N Fairfax Dr	703-528-0078	$	10 pm	Cheap Middle Eastern eats guaranteed to give you your 8 servings of veggies for the day.
Boulevard Woodgrill	2901 Wilson Blvd	703-875-9663	$$$	11:30 pm	Classy American comfort food with worthwhile weekend brunch.
Delhi Club	1135 N Highland St	703-527-5666	$$	10 pm	Good Indian. Try the salmon tandoori.
Delhi Dhaba & Carryout	2424 Wilson Blvd	703-524-0008	$$	11 pm	Indian curries make delicious cafeteria-style dishes.
Faccia Luna Trattoria	2909 Wilson Blvd	703-276-3099	$$	12 am	Good pizza for a low-key night out or in.
Hard Times Café	3028 Wilson Blvd	703-528-2233	$$	3 am	Chili-making is a science. Home-brewed root beer a bonus.
Harry's Tap Room	2800 Clarendon Blvd	703-778-7788	$$$$	11 pm	Nearly a dozen filet mignon options.
La Tasca	2900 Wilson Blvd	703-812-9120	$$$	2 am	Great Tapas and Paellas.
Liberty Tavern	3195 Wilson Blvd	703-465-9360	$$$	11 pm	Make a reservation. One of Washingtonian's 100 best.
Lyon Hall	3100 N Washington Blvd		$$		Bohemian sausages and beers for the bourgeoisie of Arlington.
Mexicali Blues	2933 Wilson Blvd	703-812-9352	$$	11 pm	Most colorful restaurant in Arlington. First time? Order a burro.
Minh's Restaurant	2500 Wilson Blvd	703-525-2828	$$	11 pm	Ten bucks goes a long way at this Vietnamese establishment.
Northside Social	3211 Wilson Blvd		$$		Coffee/wine bar... kinda like a bourgie speedball.
Pasha Café	3911 Lee Hwy	703-528-1111	$$††	10 pm	Casual storefront café serves Middle Eastern favorites, and pizza too.
Portabellos	2109 N Pollard St	703-528-1557	$$	10 pm	Contemporary American.
Restaurant 3	2950 Clarendon Blvd	703-524-4440	$$$	11 pm	Clever name for the owner's third restaurant.
Rocklands Barbeque and Grilling Company	3471 Washington Blvd	703-528-9663	$$	10 pm	Barbeque! What ho! It doesn't take long. Mercy me!
Sette Bello	3101 Wilson Blvd	703-351-1004	$$$$	12 am	Sister spot of DC faves Café Milano and Sette Osteria.
Silver Diner	3200 Wilson Blvd	703-812-8600	$$	4 am	Good place for a date, or to end a relationship.

Map 36 • Rosslyn

Café Tivoli	1700 N Moore St	703-524-8900	$	9:30 pm	Gourmet sandwiches and pastries.
Choupi	1218 19th St N		$		Where crepe-making is a form of art. Fantastique!
Gua-Rapo	2039 Wilson Blvd	703-528-6500	$$$	12:30 am	Chi-Cha Lounge flavor in NoVA.
Guajillo	1727 Wilson Blvd	703-807-0840	$$	11 pm	Don't let the strip mall fool you. It's what's inside that counts.
Il Radicchio	1801 Clarendon Blvd	703-276-2627	$$$	11 pm	Quiet outdoor dining evokes *Lady and the Tramp*'s aura.
Ireland's Four Courts	2051 Wilson Blvd	703-525-3600	$$$	2 am	Makes you forget that Ireland ever had a famine.

Key: $: Under $10 / $$: $10–$20 / $$$: $20–$30 / $$$$: $30–$40 / $$$$$: $40+
*: Does not accept credit cards. / † : Accepts only American Express. / †† : Accepts only Visa and Mastercard.
Time refers to weekend night closing time.

Jerry's Subs and Pizza	1500 N Court House Rd	703-312-9026	$	11 pm	Thin, small and tasteless.
Quarter Deck Restaurant	1200 Fort Myer Dr	703-528-2722	$$$	10 pm	Cold beer, hot crabs, familiar faces.
Ray's the Steaks	1725 Wilson Blvd	703-841-7297	$$$$	10 pm	Beef. It's what's for dinner.
Red, Hot, and Blue	1600 Wilson Blvd	703-276-7427	$$	11 pm	Slightly depressing atmosphere, but tasty bbq makes up for it.
Rhodeside Grill	1836 Wilson Blvd	703-243-0145	$$$	1 am	Hot plates on dinner tables, live music in the basement.
Village Bistro	1723 Wilson Blvd	703-522-0284	$$$	11 pm	Surprisingly quaint for part of a shopping strip.

Map 37 • Fort Myer

Astor Mediterranean	2300 N Pershing Dr	703-465-2306	$		Decent falafel and typical Greek fare. Free delivery!
Atilla's	2705 Columbia Pike	703-920-8100	$$	10 pm	Savory gyros, kabobs, salads, and more.
Bakeshop	1025 N Fillmore St	571-970-6460	$$		Home-baked cookies, cupcakes, and cakes from Justin.
Bangkok 54	2919 Columbia Pike	703-521-4070	$$$	11 pm	Upscale Thai at downscale prices.
Bob and Edith's Diner	2310 Columbia Pike	703-920-6103	$$	24-hrs	Probably the most charming all-night diner in Virginia.
Broiler	3601 Columbia Pike	703-920-5944	$$	11 pm	Blue collar subs and Ms. Pac-Man.
El Charrito Caminante	2710 N Washington Blvd	703-351-1177	$*	10 pm	Papusas worthy of the gods.
El Paso Café	4235 N Pershing Dr	703-243-9811	$$	11:30pm	Kick-ass margarita hidden gem known for George Bush sightings.
El Pollo Rico	932 N Kenmore St	703-522-3220	$*	10 pm	Eating this chicken is a sacramental experience.
LA Bar and Grille	2530 Columbia Pike	703-685-1560	$		Grub and booze, dive-style.
Manee Thai	2500 Columbia Pike	703-920-2033	$	11 pm	True Thai treasure.
Mario's Pizza House	3322 Wilson Blvd	703-525-7827	$$	4 am	Late night tradition for the bleary-eyed.
Matuba	2915 Columbia Pike	703-521-2811	$$$	10 pm	Unlike the Bethesda location, no buffet.
Mrs Chen's Kitchen	3101 Columbia Pike	703-920-3199	$	12 am	Chinese food before competition from Thai.
Pan American Bakery	4113 Columbia Pike	703-271-1113	$	8:30 pm	Saltenas and glistening pastries from South America.
Pike Grill	3902 Wilson Blvd	703-243-0279	$††	2 am	Bolivian bliss.
Ragtime	1345 N Courthouse Rd	703-243-4003	$		Come for the sandwiches, stay for the sports.
Ravi Kabob	305 N Glebe Rd	703-522-6666	$*	2 am	Top kabobs. Cash only. Long lines but worth it.
Rincome Thai Cuisine	3030 Columbia Pike	703-979-0144	$$	11 pm	Friendly owners, sumptuous food, neighborhood atmosphere.
Tallula	2761 Washington Blvd	703-778-5051	$$$	11 pm	The wine bar craze has officially hit Arlington.

Map 38 • Columbia Pike

Andy's Carry-Out	5033 Columbia Pike	703-671-1616	$$	12 am	Oily food cooked in woks.
Athens Restaurant	3541 Carlin Springs Rd	703-931-3300	$$	10:45 pm	Greek menu for everyone, even Greeks.
Atlacatl and Pupuseria	4701 Columbia Pike	703-920-3680	$$$	12 am	Laid-back, delicious Salvadorian and Mexican cuisine with attentive staff.
Brick's Pizza	4809 1st St N	703-243-6600	$	10 pm	Order "The Ballston" for pizza with a mediterranean flair.
The Chicken Place	5519 Leesburg Pike	703-931-3090	$	10 pm	Ask for extra white sauce, and say gracias
Crystal Thai	4819 Arlington Blvd	703-522-1311	$$$	10:30 pm	Moderate prices will allow you to order extra Singha.
Five Guys	4626 King St	703-671-1606	$*	10 pm	THE Alexandria burger joint.

Map 39 • Shirlington

Aladdin's Eatery	4044 S 28th St	703-894-4401		11 pm	Take-out recommended.
Best Buns Bread Co	4010 Campbell Ave	703-578-1500	$	7 pm	The name says it all. The best buns in town!
Bonsai	4040 Campbell Ave	703-824-8828	$$	10:30 pm	Reliable sushi joint.
Capitol City Brewing Company	4001 Campbell Ave	703-578-3888		11 pm	Pool, beer, and really good food.
Carlyle Grande Café	4000 Campbell Ave	703-931-0777	$$$	12 am	Popular for Friday and Saturday dinner, arrive early.
Extra Virgin	4053 28th St S	703-998-8474	$$$$	11 pm	SOPHISTICATED! "CONTEMPORARY!" Yawn, it's Italian in the suburbs.
Great Harvest	1711 Centre Plaza	703-671-8678	$††	6 pm	A wholesome neighborhood bakery.
Guapo's	4038 S 28th St	703-671-1701	$$$	11 pm	Everyone's favorite Mexican–great margarita's.

Luna Grill & Diner	4024 28th St S	703-379-7173	$$	11:30 pm	Homey comfort food and breakfast served all day.
PING by Charlie Chiang's	4060 28th St S	703-671-4900	$$$	10:30 pm	A definite step up from your local hole-in-the wall Chinese.
Rampart's	1700 Fern St	703-998-6616	$$	11 pm	Family restaurant with true dive sports bar on the side.
THAI Shirlington	4029 28th St S	703-931-3203	$$$	11 pm	Modern setting and Thai food with a twist.
Weenie Beanie	2680 S Shirlington Rd	703-671-6661	$	6 pm	Old-school half-smokes and burgers stand.

Map 40 • Pentagon City / Crystal City

Bonsai Grill	553 23rd St S	703-553-7723	$$$	11 pm	Nowhere in the area is the white tuna as good as it is here.
Crystal City Restaurant	422 S 23rd St	703-892-0726	$$	1:45 am	Kegs and legs at this diner/strip club.
Crystal City Sports Pub	529 23rd St S	703-521-8215	$$	2 am	Rated a top ten sports bar nationwide by *Sports Illustrated*. Dozens of TVs.
Kabob Palace	2333 S Eads St	703-979-3000	$		Kabobs fit for a king.
Legal Seafood	2301 Jefferson Davis Hwy	703-415-1200	$$$$	11 pm	A Boston institution. Here, it feels more... Institutional.
Morton's of Arlington	1750 Crystal Dr	703-418-1444	$$$$$	11 pm	Gluttony with valet parking.
Noodles & Company	1201 S Joyce St	703-418-0001	$	10:30 pm	Ultra-fusion noodle chain.

Map 41 • Landmark

Akasaka	514 S Van Dorn St	703-751-3133	$$$	10:30 pm	Decent sushi at decent prices.
American Café	5801 Duke St	703-658-0004	$$$	11 pm	You can't do Ruby Tuesday all the time.
Clyde's	1700 N Beauregard St	703-820-8300	$$$	12 am	Take to the seas in this nautical-themed favorite.
Edgardo's Trattoria	281 S Van Dorn St	703-751-6700	$$	10:45 pm	Authentic wood-fired pizzas and flat breads.
El Paraiso	516 S Van Dorn St	703-212-9200	$$	1 am	A slice of El Salvador on Van Dorn.
Finn & Porter	5000 Seminary Rd	703-379-2346	$$$$	11:30 pm	Yes, it's in a hotel, but it's still nice.
Mediterranean Bakery	352 S Pickett St	703-751-0030	$		More market and lunch than bakery, but still a Turkish delight.
Sakulthai Restaurant	408 S Van Dorn St	703-823-5357	$	10:30 pm	Wallet-friendly Thai.
Thai Lemon Grass	506 S Van Dorn St	703-751-4627	$$	11 pm	Thai for surburbanites.

Map 42 • Alexandria (West)

Café Monti	3250 Duke St	703-370-3632	$$	9 pm	Diamond in the very rough, serving Austrian and Italian.
Rocklands	25 S Quaker Ln	703-778-9663	$$	8 pm	DC BBQ in NoVA.
Tempo Restaurant	4231 Duke St	703-370-7900	$$$	10 pm	French-Italian fusion.

Map 43 • Four Mile Run / Del Ray

Afghan Restaurant	2700 Jefferson Davis Hwy	703-548-0022	$$	11 pm	Bountiful $7.95 lunch buffet; reportedly a good place for spook-spotting.
Al's Steak House	1504 Mt Vernon Ave	703-836-9443	$	7 pm	Cheesesteaks worthy of Philly.
Bombay Curry Company	3110 Mt Vernon Ave	703-836-6363	$$$	9:30 pm	Curry that fulfills with understated authenticity.
Chez Andree	10 E Glebe Rd	703-836-1404	$$$	9:30 pm	When you feel like eating a different part of the pig.
The Dairy Godmother	2310 Mt Vernon Ave	703-683-7767	$††	10 pm	This homemade custard cuts the mustard.
Del Merei Grill	3106 Mt Vernon Ave	703-739-4335	$$$$	11 pm	Swanky steaks with sumptuous sauces.
Evening Star Café	2000 Mt Vernon Ave	703-549-5051	$$$$	11 pm	Streaky service, hip but grounded atmosphere.
Huascaran	3606 Mt Vernon Ave	703-684-0494	$$$	9 pm	Platefuls of Peruvian perfection.
Lilian's Restaurant	3901 Mt Vernon Ave	703-837-8494	$††	12 am	Plump pupusas and Spanish-language karaoke.
Los Tios Grill	2615 Mt Vernon Ave	703-299-9290	$$	11 pm	Monster margaritas in a cozy, family-friendly space.
Mancini's	1508 Mt Vernon Ave	703-838-3663	$$††	9 pm	Café, carryout and catering.
Monroe's Trattoria	1603 Commonwealth Ave	703-548-5792	$$	10:30 pm	Great wines and brunch.
RT's Restaurant	3804 Mt Vernon Ave	703-684-6010	$$	11 pm	Creole and cajun before the Birchmere.
Taqueria Poblano	2400 Mt Vernon Ave	703-548-8226	$$	10 pm	The real deal, amigo.
Thai Peppers	2018 Mt Vernon Ave	703-739-7627	$$	10 pm	Let "peppers" be a warning!
Waffle Shop	3864 Mt Vernon Ave	703-836-8851	$*	24-hrs	24-hour grease and caffeine.

Map 44 • Alexandria Downtown

Name	Address	Phone	$	Close	Description
Café Old Towne	2111 Eisenhower Ave	703-683-3116	$††	4 pm	Variety of coffee/pastries, worth traveling off the beaten path.
Café Salsa	808 King St	703-684-4100	$$$	11 pm	THE hottest salsa club in DC.
FireFlies	1501 Mt Vernon Ave	703-548-7200	$$$	10 pm	Affordable eclecticism; try it at happy hour.
Joe Theismann's Restaurant	1800 Diagonal Rd	703-739-0777	$$$	12 am	Former Redskins QB's bar and grill draws visitors and locals alike.
The Perfect Pita	1640 King St	703-683-4330	$	5 pm	Pitas and pizza, perfect for lunch on the cheap.
Pops Old Fashion Ice Cream	109 King St	703-518-5374	$		The way ice cream was meant to be— homemade and creamy.
Quattro Formaggi	1725 Duke St	703-548-8111	$	11 pm	Gourmet pizza options you've never dreamed of, and other Italian fare.
Table Talk	1623 Duke St	703-548-3989	$	3 pm	Terrific breakfast/lunch. Often jammed, always good.
Ted's Montana Grill	2451 Eisenhower Ave	703-960-0500	$$$	11 pm	Home, home on the chain er, range.

Map 45 • Old Town (North)

Name	Address	Phone	$	Close	Description
Buzz Bakery	901 Slaters Ln	703-600-2899	$	12 am	Cheerful and colorful bakery/coffee spot open surprisingly late.
Esmeralda Restaurant	728 N Henry St	703-739-7774	$$	2 am	Tasty Salvadoran fare.
La Piazza	535 E Braddock Rd	703-519-7711	$$	9:30 pm	Solid Italian cuisine in a curious locale.
Rustico	827 Slaters Ln	703-224-5051	$$$	11 pm	Largest beer selection in NoVa (~300) and hearth-fired pizzas to boot.
Stardust	608 Montgomery St	703-548-9864	$$		Fun and funky decor, great seafood.

Map 46 • Old Town (South)

Name	Address	Phone	$	Close	Description
219 Restaurant	219 King St	703-549-1141	$$$	11 pm	Interior looks like the swankiest hotel in New Orleans.
Bilbo Baggins	208 Queen St	703-683-0300	$$$	10:30 pm	Coziest tavern this side of Middle Earth. Health-conscious options.
Casablanca Restaurant	1504 King St	703-549-6464	$$$	2 am	Good deals on multi-course meals.
Chart House	1 Cameron St	703-684-5080	$$$$	11 pm	Chain steak and seafood restaurant.
Eamonn's: A Dublin Chipper	728 King St	703-299-8384	$$$	11 pm	Their motto: Thanks be to cod.
Faccia Luna Trattoria	823 S Washington St	703-838-5998	$$	12 am	The best pizza around, locals love it.
Fish Market	105 King St	703-836-5676	$$$	12 am	Just follow your nose!
Five Guys	107 N Fayette St	703-549-7991	$	9 pm	Best burgers in Old Town (and maybe in all of the East Coast).
Grape + Bean	118 S Royal St	703-664-0214	$		It's wine! It's coffee! It's…the best of both worlds, done well.
The Grille	116 S Alfred St	703-838-8000	$$$$	10 pm	Where luxury and Alexandria collide.
Hard Times Café	1404 King St	703-837-0050	$$	12 am	Nothing but chili, but plenty of it.
Il Porto	121 King St	703-836-8833	$$$$	12 am	Best Italian around. Make reservations.
King Street Blues	112 N St Asaph St	703-836-8800	$$$	11 pm	Not quite on King St., but great BBQ.
La Bergerie	218 N Lee St	703-683-1007	$$$$$	10:30 pm	Pay the tab if you can-can.
La Tasca	607 King St	703-299-9810	$$$	11 pm	Great Tapas and Paellas.
Las Tapas	710 King St	703-836-4000	$$$	12 am	As almost always with tapas, hit and miss.
Masaya	1019 King St	703-548-3736	$$	10 pm	No fusion here, just dependable Thai.
The Pita House	407 Cameron St	703-684-9194	$	10 pm	Intimate Middle Eastern.
Restaurant Eve	110 S Pitt St	703-706-0450	$$$$	10 pm	Reservations a must.
Southside 815	815 S Washington St	703-836-6222	$$	1:30 am	New Orleanean fare.
The Warehouse	214 King St	703-683-6868	$$$	11 pm	A bit forgotten but excellent food. Plan to eat hearty.

Baltimore

Bertha's	734 S Broadway	410-327-5795	$$	12 am	Seafood. Dark, dank, and famous for its mussels.
Brass Elephant	924 N Charles St	410-547-8480	$$$	10:30 pm	American. Gorgeous townhouse, fancy food, and expense account prices.
Café Hon	1002 W 36th St	410-243-1230	$$$	10 pm	Kitsch central. If not for the meatloaf or the beehive 'dos on the wait staff, come to see John Waters's Baltimore.
The Daily Grind	1720 Thames St	410-558-0399	$††	10 pm	Laid-back Fells Point coffee house.
Faidley's Seafood	203 N Paca St	410-727-4898	$$	5 pm	Seafood. Stand up and rub elbows while chowing down some of the city's best crab cakes.
Helen's Garden	2908 O'Donnell St	410-276-2233	$$$††	9:30 pm	Feel like a local at this Canton outpost. Good food, nice owners, wine flows.
Helmand	806 N Charles St	410-752-0311	$$	11pm	An elegant local favorite beyond kebabs
Ikaros	4805 Eastern Ave	410-633-3750	$$$	11 pm	Greek. Cheap, big portions, and Greektown neighborhood staple.
Jimmy's	801 S Broadway	410-327-3273	$$††	8 pm	Classic Bawlmer greasy spoon. Check your attitude at the door.
John Steven Ltd	1800 Thames St	410-327-5561	$$$	12 am	Seafood. Outdoor patio, steamer bar, crab cakes, and stocked bar.
Obrycki's Crab House	1727 E Pratt St	410-732-6399	$$$	11 pm	The king of the many local crab houses.
Pete's Grille	3130 Greenmount Ave	410-467-7698	$$*	1 am	Cure your hungryover.
Rusty Scupper	402 Key Hwy	410-727-3678	$$$	11 pm	Enjoy a Bloody Mary at their Sunday Jazz Brunch.
Tapas Teatro	1711 N Charles St	410-332-0110	$$$	12 am	Tapas. Before and after a movie at The Charles, check out this neighborhood favorite.
Wyman Park Restaurant	138 W 25th St	410-235-5100	$*	3 pm	Mobtown diner cuture at its finest.
Ze Mean Bean	1739 Fleet St	410-675-5999	$$$	11 pm	Eastern European. More than a coffeehouse, with meaty dishes and live music.

DC has erected an endless amount of chic boutiques, high-end stores, and outdoor markets to cure your shopping addiction (if by cure, you mean yield). What used to be solely a city of stiff suits, pearls, and loafers has transformed into high-end Italian footwear with Louis Vuitton bags to match, or peculiar work-fashion choices that would land a candidate on *What Not To Wear* or a visit to the HR. Not that a trip on the Metro at rush hour won't reveal the traditional Brooks Brothers signature look of khakis with a blue blazer. DC is a big city with big wallets and there's no shortage of wealthy folks and new stores. But you don't have to have a fat bank account to look good in this city; there are diamonds in the rough, if you know where to look.

Clothing/Beauty

Georgetown is DC's best-known shopping destination. There's something for everyone, from designer stores like **Kate Spade (Map 8)** to mainstream mainstay **Banana Republic (Map 8)** to trendy boutiques like **Sherman Pickey (Map 8)** and **Commander Salamander (Map 8)**—if you can handle pushing your way through the mobs of flip-flop-wearing college students and Europeans preying on the weak dollar. For the best of the chains, try the palatial three-story **Anthropologie (Map 8)**. For boutiques, try **Sassanova (Map 8)** for shoes and the ultra-feminine **Sugar (Map 8)** for your next party dress.

If you prefer to avoid the crowds of Georgetown but want a similar mix of chains and boutiques, you can make a day of shopping in the Dupont Circle area. **Proper Topper (Maps 8, 9)** is the place to go when you need a Kentucky Derby (or Preakness) hat, but they also offer gifts and trendy clothing. Despite the fact that you have to be buzzed in, **Betsy Fisher (Map 9)** is a surprisingly friendly boutique geared toward (expensive) unique shoes and fashions from labels you maybe never heard of. If you've had a rough week, slip into **Blue Mercury (Maps 8, 9)** and treat yourself to one of their luxurious beauty products.

For those in search of the fresh and funky, the U Street Corridor is a great place to shop and is refreshingly chain-free. **Nana (Map 9)** is a sweet little clothing boutique that's not too hard on the wallet. For truly sophisticated fashionistas, **Muleh (Map 10)** offers men's and women's über-hip designer clothing (by the likes of Rozae Nichols, Nicole Farhi, and 3.1 by Phillip Lim) as well as fabulously modern furniture, all in a NY-loft-style space. And if youre looking for something "different" (i.e. used), **Treasury Vintage Boutique (Map 10)** offers some nifty vintage picks for the hopelessly trendy.

Rivaling Georgetown in volume, space and parking is the continuously-developing Friendship Heights, or the East's response to Rodeo Drive. There's a selection of favorite department stores like **Saks Fifth Avenue (Map 29)** and a smattering of other high-end and luxury designer shops lining Wisconsin Avenue and the corner of Wisconsin and Western, like **Barney's Co-Op (Map 29)** and **Cartier (Map 29)** that will set you back $1,000 by the bracelet. Friendship Heights keeps unveiling construction sites that then burst with new, expensive and fancy shops every month to keep your mouth watering and your paycheck in, well, check. If you've got label-whore tendencies, but no money to spare, there are plenty of consignment shops like **Secondi (Map 9)** to get your fix. Though not for the faint of heart, **Filene's Basement (Maps 1, 9)** is hands-down the best spot for designer bargains—amidst the disorganized racks, deodorant stains, and the occasional broken zipper, there are treasures to be plundered.

Housewares and Furniture

Like most major cities, DC has all the major furniture and houseware chains: **Target (Maps 15, 38, 43)**, **Crate & Barrel (Map 30)**, **Pottery Barn (Maps 8, 19, 35)**, etc. DC boasts three locations of **Design Within Reach (Maps 8, 16, 22)** (or more appropriately, "Design Just Out Of Reach"). For those who don't think anything should cost that much, there's the **Crate & Barrel Outlet (Map 44)** in Alexandria.

If you want your living space to have a bit more character, don't lose hope, there are more options out there. **Tabletop (Map 9)** in Dupont Circle is packed with cool home décor and modern housewares. **Millennium Decorative Arts (Map 9)** will more than satisfy Danish Modern aesthetes and furnishers. Turn to **Home Rule (Map 10)** for kitschy kitchen fun. If you like a little adventure when you shop, don't miss **Ruff & Ready (Map 10)**. From the outside it looks like a decrepit old house in a horror movie. Inside it's crammed with so much used furniture, junk, and antiques that you can barely squeeze through the aisles. Perhaps the most unique furniture store in the district is **Reincarnations Furnishings (Map 10)** where you can get couches and chairs in more than 600 fabrics that no one else in DC will have in their digs. If vintage floats your boat, check out the **Hunted House (Map 10)**, which features more than a few quirky mid-century modern and art deco pieces. And for the eco-minded among us, **Greater Goods (Map 9)**, can provide a wide range of things to help you live green. And by everything, we mean everying, from herbal bug spray to eco-friendly razor blades to your own personal compost bin.

Electronics

Superstores like **Best Buy (Map 43)** and the requisite picked-on little sibling **Radio Shack (Map 9, 16)** can be found across the region. Die hard Mac-heads will love the gorgeous, high-tech **Apple Store (Map 40)** in the Pentagon City mall in Arlington. If you're desperate and car-less, Staples (Map 43) offers a small collection of computers and software.

Food

Some will quibble, but many DC residents just love **Trader Joe's (Map 29)** and will voluntarily wait on the very long check-out line that wraps around the store, twice, on weekends. The location in DC sells wine and beer, too. The food stores your parents would like are also plentiful. You can't swing an empty shopping basket without hitting a **Safeway (Map 6)**, **Giant (Maps 10, 11)**, or **Harris Teeter (Map 40)**.

If you live in Dupont or Logan Circle, likely you visit **Whole Foods (Maps 10, 44)** for free-ranging, organic and expensive apples and eggs. There's also **Dean & DeLuca (Map 8)** for gourmet prepared foods and coffee. If you love cheese, and who doesn't, check out **Cheesetique (Map 43)** in Del Ray or **Cowgirl Creamery (Map 1)** in Chinatown. And if you're looking to impress your date, take him or her to **Sabores (Map 17)**, an eclectic eatery with Latin vibes that serves a mean sangria. Just make sure you bring your own bags to stores selling food in DC, or you will be charged 5 cents a bag for trying to pollute the Anacostia River.

Last but certainly not least, the DC area is ripe with wonderful farmer's markets—almost every neighborhood has one. The most famous can be found at **Eastern Market (Map 5)**. Although the historic main building was gutted by fire a few years back, it has since been rebuilt, reopened, and is open for business.

Bookstores and Music Stores

There are plenty of **Borders (Maps 1, 9, 19, 25)** and **Barnes & Noble (Maps 1, 8, 29, 35, 43)** stores in the area, but smaller independent bookstores also abound. **Kramerbooks & Afterwords (Map 9)** is the local favorite, where only in DC, people hang out checking out latest reads like a nearby watering hole. There is a bar with a wine list where you can hang out 7:30 am until well past midnight (all night Fridays and Saturday). Music nerds have a good chance of finding that hard-to-find album at **Crooked Beat Records (Map 16)**, a small shop that specializes in rare and independent label music. For more specialized finds, drop into DC's oldest independent bookstore, **Reiter's Books (Map 9)**. It's known for scientific, medical, and technical books, but also carries a host of games and puzzles for the less serious-minded.

Wine, Beer, Liquor

Laws regarding alcohol vary throughout the region, but as a general rule, only Virginia supermarkets and drug stores sell wine. Also, Maryland has a few grocery stores and a ton of liquor stores, especially in Silver Spring, that sell wine. In DC, your best bet is to check out **Georgetown Wine and Spirits (Map 8)**, as well as **Best**

Cellars (Map 9) in Dupont. Both stores stock a wide variety of wine and employ knowledgeable staff. The bourgie demographic of the District ensures for plenty of gourmet alcoholic shops in most affluent neighborhoods. In Virginia, wine lovers frequent **The Curious Grape (Map 39)**. Not only is the selection great, but the staff often hosts informative—and free—classes with wine experts from France, Chile, and beyond! There's also a tasting bar, open daily. For those who like their alcohol hoppy, here's a tip: **Rustico (Map 45)**, an Alexandria restaurant with beer list of heavenly proportion (nearly 300), has a note on their menu encouraging patrons to ask about purchasing a six-pack to take home of any beer they happen to like.

Late-night revelers should keep in mind that you can't buy anything alcoholic in DC stores after 10 pm. Most liquor stores close at 9 pm on weekdays and 10 pm on Fridays and Saturdays. On Sundays, it's beer and wine only, so make sure to stock up early if you're having people over for the Redskins game.

Map 1 • National Mall

American Apparel	1090 F St NW	202-628-0438	Clothes that make your skin, wallet, and conscience feel good.
Barnes & Noble	555 12th St NW	202-347-0176	Mega bookstore.
Café Mozart	1331 H St NW	202-347-5732	Germanic treats.
Celadon Spa	1180 F St NW	202-347-3333	Great haircuts.
Chapters Literary Bookstore	445 11th St NW	202-737-5553	Lunch-hour reads.
Coup de Foudre Lingerie	1001 Pennsylvania Ave NW	202-393-0878	New high-end lingerie store.
Cowgirl Creamery	919 F St NW	202-393-6800	Cheese delights from all over the world
Fahrney's	1317 F St NW	202-628-9525	Fussy pens.
Filene's Basement	529 14th St NW	202-638-4110	Incredible discounts on designer clothes.
H&M	1025 F St NW	202-347-3306	New downtown outlet of European clothing giant.
International Spy Museum Gift Shop	800 F St NW	202-654-0950	James Bond would be jealous.
Macy's	1201 G St NW	202-628-6661	Only full-service department store in downtown Washington.
Mia Gemma	933 F St NW	202-393-4367	High-end, trendy baubles.
Penn Camera	840 E St NW	202-347-5777	Say cheese.
Political Americana	1331 Pennsylvania Ave NW	202-737-7730	Souvenirs for back home.
Utrecht Art & Drafting Supplies	1250 I St NW	202-898-0555	Channel Picasso.
West Elm	1020 G St NW	n/a	Modern, colorful furniture and home décor for the younger crowd.

Map 2 • Chinatown / Union Station

Alamo Flags	50 Massachusetts Ave NW	202-842-3524	Don't bring matches.
Apartment Zero	406 7th St NW	202-628-4067	Gorgeous, if overpriced, modern furniture.
Appalachian Spring	50 Massachusetts Ave NE	202-682-0505	Pottery, jewelry, and other unique knick-knacks.
Aveda Institute	713 7th St NW	202-824-1610	Beauty on a budget for the willing guinea pig.
Bed, Bath and Beyond	709 7th St NW	202-628-0002	Moderately priced home furnishings.
Comfort One Shoes	50 Massachusetts Ave NE	202-408-4947	Beyond Birkenstocks.
Godiva Chocolatier	50 Massachusetts Ave NE	202-289-3662	Indulge.
National Air and Space Museum Shop kids	Independence Ave SW & 4th St SW	202-357-1387	Great plane-related stuff for the (or for you).
Pua Naturally	701 Pennsylvania Ave NW	202-347-4543	Locally designed women's clothing.
Urban Outfitters Downtown	737 7th St NW	202-737-0259	Slightly hipper than its Georgetown cousin.

Map 3 • The Hill

George's Place Limited	1001 H St NE	202-397-4113	On-the-spot alternation and all size menswear from regular to 8X.
Pulp on the Hill	303 Pennsylvania Ave SE	202-543-1924	Dirty birthday cards.
S&S Shoe Repair	1126 H St NE	202-397-2676	Save your soles.
Stella Bleu	1208 H St NE	202-396-3528	Salon specializing in African-American hair care.

Map 5 • Southeast / Anacostia

Backstage	545 8th St SE	202-544-5744	A store with theatrics.
Capitol Hill Bikes	709 8th St SE	202-544-4234	Pedal away from politics.
Capitol Hill Books	657 C St SE	202-544-1621	Plenty of page-turners.
Eastern Market	225 7th St SE	202-544-0083	Open-air stalls and weekend flea market. Back in business after '07 fire.
Ipso Crafto	733 8th St SE	202-546-4329	DC's only arts & crafts store is an urban haven of glue sticks, pipe cleaners, and stamp pads
Marvelous Market	303 7th St SE	202-544-7127	Prepared (but fresh) salads and wraps. Other goodies to go as well.
The Remix	645 Pennsylvania Ave SE	703-549-4110	Classic vintage clothing.
Uncle Brutha's Hot Sauce Emporium	323 7th St NE	202-546-FIRE	Light your mouth on fire.
Woven History & Silk Road	311 7th St SE	202-543-1705	Visit Afghanistan without the war hassle.

Map 6 • Waterfront

Maine Avenue Fish Market	Maine Ave SW & Potomac River	202-484-2722	Fresh off the boat.
Safeway	401 M St SW	202-554-9155	Grim, but in a pinch it will have what you need.

Map 7 • Foggy Bottom

Saks Jandel	2522 Virginia Ave NW	202-337-4200	For the well-dressed socialite.

Map 8 • Georgetown

Abercrombie & Fitch	1208 Wisconsin Ave NW	202-333-1566	Quintessemtial college kids' clothes.
Ann Sacks	3328 M St NW	202-339-0840	Bury yourself in tile.
Anthropologie	3222 M St NW	202-337-1363	Pretty, super-feminine women's clothing.
Banana Republic	3200 M St NW	202-333-2554	It is what it is.
BCBG	3210 M St NW	202-333-2224	B well-dressed.
Betsey Johnson	1319 Wisconsin Ave NW	202-338-4090	Mix girlie and insane.
Blue Mercury	3059 M St NW	202-965-1300	Spa on premises.
Bo Concepts	3342 M St NW	202-333-5656	Modern décor.
Commander Salamander	1420 Wisconsin Ave NW	202-337-2265	Teenage funk.
CUSP	3030 M St NW	202-625-0893	Max out your credit card with one dress.
Dean & DeLuca	3276 M St NW	202-342-2500	Dean and delicious.
Design Within Reach	3307 Cady's Alley NW	202-339-9480	Furniture showroom.
Diesel	1249 Wisconsin Ave NW	202-625-2780	Hip designer jeans.
Dolcezza	1560 Wisconsin Ave NW	202-333-4646	Sleek Argentinian gelato nook.
Express	3276 M St NW	202-338-6626	Sexy, fashionable women's clothes.
Georgetown Running Company	3401 M St NW	202-337-8626	Gear up for a race.
Georgetown Tobacco	3144 M St NW	202-338-5100	Celebrate smoke.
Georgetown Wine & Spirits	2701 P St NW	202-338-5500	Gorgeous wine store; great selection, friendly owners.
H&M	3222 M St NW	202-298-6792	Cheap Euro clothes for the college crowd.
The Hattery	3222 M St NW	202-364-4287	Gorgeous vintage hats for men and women.
Illuminations	3323 Cady's Aly NW	202-965-4888	Hot flashes.
Intermix	3222 M St NW	202-298-8000	Cutting-edge women's designer fashions.
J Crew	3222 M St NW	202-965-4090	Inoffensive yuppie casual gear.
J Mclaughlin	3278 M St NW	202-333-4333	Jet-setting to the Hamptons?
Jaryam	1631 Wisconsin Ave NW	202-333-6886	Lacy lingerie.
Jinx Proof Tattoo	3289 M St NW	202-337-5469	The best place in town to get inked.
Kate Spade	3061 M St NW	202-333-8302	Preppy polish.
The Keith Lipert Gallery	2922 M St NW	202-965-9736	Unique global gifts.
Ligne Roset	3306 M St NW	202-333-6390	Check out the caterpillar couch.
lil' thingamajigs	3222 M St NW	202-944-8449	Japanese pop-art trinkets.
Lush	3066 M St NW	202-333-6950	Handmade soap and cosmetics; stratospheric prices.
MAC	3067 M St NW	202-944-9771	Sephora's main rival in the cosmetics biz.
Marvelous Market	3217 P St NW	202-333-2591	Try their blueberry muffins.
Old Print Gallery	1220 31st St NW	202-965-1818	The name says it all.
Patisserie Poupon	1645 Wisconsin Ave NW	202-342-3248	Old-world-style bonbons.
Pottery Barn	3077 M St NW	202-337-8900	Yuppie interior style.
Proper Topper	3213 P St NW	202-333-6200	Cutesy hats and gifts.
Puma	1237 Wisconsin Ave NW	202-944-9870	Cool athletic gear.
Ralph Lauren Polo Shop	1245 Wisconsin Ave NW	202-965-0905	Where Dad should shop, but probably doesn't.
Relish	3312 Cady's Aly NW	202-333-5343	For your bod, not your hot dog.
Restoration Hardware	1222 Wisconsin Ave NW	202-625-2771	High-end home goods.
Revolution Cycles	3411 M St NW	202-965-3601	Replace stolen bikes here!
Sassanova	1641 Wisconsin Ave NW	202-471-4400	The latest and greatest in shoes.

Secret Garden	3230 M St NW	202-337-0833	Romantic flowers and plants store.
See	1261 Wisconsin Ave NW	202-337-5988	Fashionable, cheap eyewear.
Sephora	3065 M St NW	202-338-5644	Popular high-end cosmetics chain.
The Sharper Image	3222 M St NW	202-337-9361	Gifts for gadget-hounds.
Sherman Pickey	1647 Wisconsin Ave NW	202-333-4212	Pet-friendly attire.
Smith & Hawken	1209 31st St NW	202-965-2680	Pricey garden gloves.
Sugar	1633 Wisconsin Ave NW	202-333-5331	Overly sweet concoctions.
Talbots	3222 M St NW	202-338-3510	Shop for Mom, buy clothes for work.
Thomas Sweet Ice Cream	3214 P St NW	202-337-0616	Known to provide the White House with desserts.
Toka Salon	3251 Prospect St NW	202-333-5133	Relax.
Up Against the Wall	3219 M St NW	202-337-9316	Urban designer labels.
Urban Chic	1626 Wisconsin Ave NW	202-338-5398	Super chic if you have serious cash
Urban Outfitters	3111 M St NW	202-342-1012	More like dorm outfitters.
Victoria's Secret	3222 M St NW	202-965-5457	The J Crew of lingerie.
The White House/Black Market	3222 M St NW	202-965-4419	Monochromatic women's clothing.
Zara	1234 Wisconsin Ave NW	202-944-9797	A step up from H&M.

Map 9 • Dupont Circle / Adams Morgan

Andre Chreky, the Salon Spa	1604 K St NW	202-293-9393	Fancy trims.
Ann Taylor	1140 Connecticut Ave NW	202-659-0120	Corporate duds that are budget-friendly.
Ann Taylor Loft	1611 Connecticut Ave NW	202-299-9845	Last year's corporate duds.
Bang Salon	1612 U St NW	202-299-0925	Cool trims.
Bedazzled	1507 Connecticut Ave NW	202-265-2323	Make your own jewelry.
Best Cellars	1643 Connecticut Ave NW	202-387-3146	Non-snobby wines.
Betsy Fisher	1224 Connecticut Ave NW	202-785-1975	Expensive casual Fridays.
Blink	1776 18th St NW	202-776-0999	Wear your sunglasses at night.
Blue Mercury	1619 Connecticut Ave NW	202-462-1300	Cosmetics for maidens and metrosexuals alike.
Books-A-Million	11 Dupont Cir NW	202-319-1374	If you just can't hold out until you get to Borders.
Borders	1801 K St NW	202-466-4999	General.
Brooks Brothers	1201 Connecticut Ave NW	202-659-4650	DC's uniform supply shop.
Burberry	1155 Connecticut Ave NW	202-463-3000	Fashionistas and foreign correspondents.
Cake Love	1506 U St NW	202-588-7100	Lust-worthy cupcakes.
Chocolate Moose	1743 L St NW	202-463-0992	Great candies and cards.
Comfort One Shoes	1630 Connecticut Ave NW	202-328-3141	Beyond Birkenstocks.
Comfort One Shoes	1621 Connecticut Ave NW	202-232-2480	Beyond Birkenstocks.
Custom Shop Clothiers	1033 Connecticut Ave NW	202-659-8250	Design your own button-down.
DeVino's	2001 18th St NW	202-986-5002	A yuppie wine shop.
Doggie Style	1825 18th St NW	202-667-0595	Irreverent pet gifts.
Downs Engravers & Stationers	1746 L St NW	202-223-7776	When the occasion calls for uptight.
Drilling Tennis & Golf	1040 17th St NW	202-737-1100	Big Bertha lives here.
Dupont Market	1807 18th St NW	202-797-0222	Upscale stuff you won't find at Safeway.
Filene's Basement	1133 Connecticut Ave NW	202-872-8430	No annual bridal dress sale, but good bargains abound.
The Gap	1120 Connecticut Ave NW	202-429-0691	Affordable, inoffensive, basic gear.
Ginza	1721 Connecticut Ave NW	202-332-7000	Japanica.
Godiva Chocolatier	1143 Connecticut Ave NW	202-638-7421	Indulge.
The Grooming Lounge	1745 L St NW	202-466-8900	Feed your inner metrosexual.
The Guitar Shop	1216 Connecticut Ave NW	202-331-7333	Self-explanatory.
Habitat Home Accents & Jewelry	1510 U St NW	202-518-7222	Hip knick-knacks for home and body.
Human Rights Campaign	1640 Rhode Island Ave NW	202-232-8621	Gifts and cards for a cause.
J Press	1801 L St NW	202-857-0120	Conservative conservative.
Jos A Bank	1200 19th St NW	202-466-2282	For professional types who can't afford Brooks Brothers.
The Kid's Closet	1226 Connecticut Ave NW	202-429-9247	Buy your niece an Easter dress.
Kramerbooks & Afterwords Café	1517 Connecticut Ave NW	202-387-1400	Scope for books and dates.
Lambda Rising	1625 Connecticut Ave NW	202-462-6969	Center of gay culture.
Leather Rack	1723 Connecticut Ave NW	202-797-7401	Hint: don't go here looking for a nice jacket.
Lucky Brand Dungarees	1739 Connecticut Ave NW	202-265-8285	Sexy jeans, shirts, and more.
Marvelous Market	1511 Connecticut Ave NW	202-332-3690	Bread and brownies.
Meeps and Aunt Neensie's	2104 18th St NW	202-265-6546	Vintage clothes.
Melody Records	1623 Connecticut Ave NW	202-232-4002	Best record store in town.
Millennium Decorative Arts	1528 U St NW	202-483-1218	Cool stuff for your crib.
Nana	1528 U St NW	202-667-6955	Chic boutique.
National Geographic Shop	1145 17th St NW	202-857-7591	Travel the world in a shop.
Newsroom	1803 Connecticut Ave NW	202-332-1489	Café with foreign papers.
Pasargad Antique and Fine Persian	1217 Connecticut Ave NW	202-659-3888	Beautiful rugs.
Pleasure Place	1710 Connecticut Ave NW	202-483-3297	Sex toys and gear.
Proper Topper	1350 Connecticut Ave NW	202-842-3055	Cutesy hats and gifts.
Red Onion Records	1901 18th St NW	202-986-2718	Great vinyl selection.
Rizik's	1100 Connecticut Ave NW	202-223-4050	Designer department store.
Salon Cielo	1741 Connecticut Ave NW	202-518-9620	Early morning karaoke with your clip. Ask for Jamie.

Map 9 • Dupont Circle / Adams Morgan—*continued*

Second Story Books & Antiques	2000 P St NW	202-659-8884	Largest outlet of this used and antiquarian book operation.
Secondi	1702 Connecticut Ave NW	202-667-1122	Consignment shop so chic you forget the clothes are used.
Skynear and Co	2122 18th St NW	202-797-7160	Funky décor.
Tabletop	1608 20th St NW	202-387-7117	Dress up your dinner table.
Thomas Pink	1127 Connecticut Ave NW	202-223-5390	The perfect dress shirt.
Tiny Jewel Box	1147 Connecticut Ave NW	202-393-2747	Ready to pop the question?
United Colors of Benetton	1666 Connecticut Ave NW	202-232-1770	Generic clothing.
Video Americain	2104 18th St NW	202-588-0117	Great indie film rentals, but beware the snobby clerks.
Wild Women Wear Red	1512 U St NW	202-387-5700	Pay dearly for shoe art.
Wine Specialists	2115 M St NW	202-833-0707	Bone up on your grapes.

Map 10 • Logan Circle / U Street

13th & U Street Flea Market	13th St NW & U St NW	N/A	Find a gem and make an offer.
Blink	1431 P St NW	202-234-1051	Wear your sunglasses at night.
Candida's World of Books	1541 14th St NW	202-667-4811	International bookstore with travel guides, lit, and more.
Garden District	1801 14th St NW	202-797-9005	Urban gardeners dig it here.
Giant Food	1414 8th St NW	202-234-0215	Washington DC's first supermarket.
Go Mama Go!	1809 14th St NW	202-299-0850	Whacked-out décor.
Good Wood	1428 U St NW	202-986-3640	Antique furniture built from, you guessed it.
Home Rule	1807 14th St NW	202-797-5544	Kitchen treasures.
Logan Hardware	1416 P St NW	202-265-8900	Super-friendly, sort-of-hipster hardware joint.
Muleh	1831 14th St NW	202-667-3440	Javanese furniture.
Pink November	1231 U St NW	202-232-3113	Small, artsy women's boutique.
Pop	1803 14th St NW	202-332-3312	Trendy wendys.
Pulp	1803 14th St NW	202-462-7857	Dirty birthday cards.
Reincarnations Furnishings	1401 14th St NW	202-319-1606	Furniture that would make Liberace cringe; great window-shopping.
Ruff & Ready Furnishings	1908 14th St NW	202-667-7833	Find a diamond in the ruff.
Storehouse	1526 14th St NW	202-462-7891	A chain store on 14th Street?!
Universal Gear	1529 14th St NW	202-319-0136	Trendy threads for 20-somethings.
Urban Essentials	1330 U St NW	202-337-4462	Lust-worthy décor.
Vastu	1829 14th St NW	202-234-8344	Upscale contemporary furnishings.
Whole Foods Market	1440 P St NW	202-332-4300	Expensive organic food chain store.
The Written Word	1427 P St NW	202-223-1400	Invites and cards.

Map 11 • Near Northeast

Anna's Linen	1060 Brentwood Road, NE	202-529-3402	Nicely priced linens and curtains
The Brass Knob Back Door Warehouse, Inc	57 N St NW	202-265-0587	Outfit your row house with authentic, turn-of-the-century fixtures while trying not to giggle over the name.
Giant Food	1050 Brentwood Rd NE	202-281-3900	Washington DC's first supermarket.
Home Depot	901 Rhode Island Ave NE	202-526-8760	You know, Home Depot.
Windows Café & Market	101 Rhode Island Ave NW	202-462-6585	Ethiopian/IKEA furnished café with sit-down sandwiches and bottled wine.

Map 15 • Columbia Heights

Carvel	3307 14th St NW	202-797-0654	Custom ice cream cakes, as well as the usual cups, cones, etc.
Mom & Pop's Antiques	3534 Georgia Ave NW	202-722-0719	Perhaps the last affordable antique store in DC.
Rita's	3237 14th St NW	202-582-1177	Gelato, italian ice, frozen custard.
Sticky Fingers Bakery	1370 Park Rd NW	202-299-9700	Vegan bakery.
Target	3100 14th St NW	202-777-3773	DC's first. Is that bull's eye aimed at small and local business?

Map 16 • Adams Morgan (North) / Mt Pleasant

Antiques Anonymous	2627 Connecticut Ave NW	202-332-5555	Classy boutique of little treasures.
Brass Knob	2311 18th St NW	202-332-3370	Architectural antiques from doors to knobs.
CD/Game Exchange	2475 18th St NW	202-588-5070	Great selection of cheap CDs and video games.
City Bikes	2501 Champlain St NW	202-265-1564	Where the couriers shop.
Crooked Beat Records	2318 18th St NW	202-483-2328	Off-beat, hard to find selections.
Demian	2427 18th St NW	202-234-8050	Cult classic for the edgy hipster.
Design Within Reach	1838 Columbia Rd NW	202-265-5640	Trendy furniture in a trendy part of town.
Fleet Feet	1841 Columbia Rd NW	202-387-3888	No referee uniforms here and maybe you'll see Mayor Fenty.

Idle Time Books	2467 18th St NW	202-232-4774	Disorganized lit.
Little Shop of Flowers	2421 18th St NW	202-387-7255	Great name, good flowers.
Miss Pixie's Furnishing and What-Not	2473 18th St NW	202-232-8171	Second-chance finds.
Radio Shack	1767 Columbia Rd NW	202-986-5008	Great for headphones, batteries, and that special connection.
Shake Your Booty	2439 18th St NW	202-518-8205	Watch for their kick-ass sales.
Smash	2314 18th St NW	202-337-6274	Vintage punk vinyl, new punk clothes.
So's Your Mom	1831 Columbia Rd NW	202-462-3666	Über-deli with great sandwiches, imported NY bagels.
Trim	2700 Ontario Rd NW	202-462-6080	If you need hip bangs.
Yes! Natural Gourmet	1825 Columbia Rd NW	202-462-5150	Yes! Wheat germ!

Map 17 · Woodley Park / Cleveland Park

All Fired Up	3413 Connecticut Ave NW	202-363-9590	Local version of Color Me Mine.
Allan Woods Flowers	2645 Connecticut Ave NW	202-332-3334	Gorgeous buds and blossoms.
Bombe Chest	2629 Connecticut Ave NW	202-387-7293	Fancy a curio, perchance?
Guitar Gallery	3400 Connecticut Ave NW	202-244-4200	Flamenco and classical guitars, plus lessons.
Manhattan Market	2647 Connecticut Ave NW	202-986-4774	Upscale cornerstore.
Transcendence-Perfection-Bliss of the Beyond	3428 Connecticut Ave NW	202-363-4797	Children's toys and gift cards with inexplicable name.
Vace	3315 Connecticut Ave NW	202-363-1999	Best pizza in town.
Wake Up Little Suzie	3409 Connecticut Ave NW	202-244-0700	Wacky gifts and knick-knacks for the home.
Yes! Organic Market	3425 Connecticut Ave NW	202-363-1559	A healthy lifestyle will cost you.

Map 18 · Glover Park / Foxhall

Ann Hand Collection	4885 MacArthur Blvd NW	202-333-2979	Top-notch jewelry boutique.
Encore Resale Dress Shop	3715 Macomb St NW	202-966-8122	Second-hand glitzy gowns.
Inga's Once Is Not Enough	4830 MacArthur Blvd NW	202-337-3072	Chanel, Valentino, and Prada, for example.
The Kellogg Collection	3424 Wisconsin Ave NW	202-363-6879	Local chain of upscale home furnishings.
Marvelous Market	4885 MacArthur Blvd NW	202-625-5110	Treat yourself to gourmet cheeses, breads, and olives.
Sullivan's Toy Store	3412 Wisconsin Ave NW	202-362-1343	Trove of toys, costumes, and art supplies.
Theodore's	2233 Wisconsin Ave NW	202-333-2300	Funky décor.
Tree Top Kids	3301 New Mexico Ave NW	202-244-3500	Independent and fun.
Vespa Washington	2233 Wisconsin Ave NW	202-333-8212	Both new and vintage Vespa scooters here.

Map 19 · Tenleytown / Friendship Heights

Borders	5333 Wisconsin Ave NW	202-686-8270	Books and music.
The Container Store	4500 Wisconsin Ave NW	202-478-4000	Buckets, shelves, hangers.
Elizabeth Arden Red Door Salon & Spa	5225 Wisconsin Ave NW	202-362-9890	Serious pampering.
Hudson Trail Outfitters	4530 Wisconsin Ave NW	202-363-9810	Tents and Tevas.
Johnson's Florist & Garden Centers	4200 Wisconsin Ave NW	202-244-6100	For those of you with a yard.
Loehmann's	5333 Wisconsin Ave NW	202-362-4733	An exciting melange of trash and treasures.
Neiman Marcus	5300 Wisconsin Ave NW	202-966-9700	Ultra-upscale department store.
Pottery Barn	5345 Wisconsin Ave NW	202-244-9330	Yuppie interior style.
Roche Bobois	5301 Wisconsin Ave NW	202-686-5667	African traditions.
Rodman's	5100 Wisconsin Ave NW	202-363-3466	Luggage, wine, scented soaps, and other necessities.
Serenity Day Spa	4000 Wisconsin Ave NW	202-362-2560	Name says it all.

Map 20 · Cleveland Park / Upper Connecticut

Calvert Woodley Liquors	4339 Connecticut Ave NW	202-966-4400	Paradise for the snooty but cheap booze hound.
Marvelous Market	5035 Connecticut Ave NW	202-686-4040	Try their blueberry muffins.
Politics & Prose	5015 Connecticut Ave NW	202-364-1919	Bookstore mecca, great readings too!

Map 21 · 16th St. Heights / Petworth

Flip It	4530 Georgia Ave NW	202-291-3605	Chef Rodriguez bakes up donuts, mini cupcakes, and Salvadoran turnovers.

Map 22 · Bethesda (North)

Big Planet Comics	4908 Fairmont Ave	301-654-6856	Superhero genealogy experts on hand.
Daisy Too	4940 St Elmo Ave	301-656-2280	Unique and girly.
Design Within Reach	4828 St Elmo Ave	301-215-7200	IKEA's expensive older brother.
Promise For the Savvy Bride	4931 St Elmo Ave	301-215-9232	Not your typical bridal shop.
The Purse Store	8211 Wisconsin Ave	410-653-5002	Not just purses.

Map 22 • Bethesda (North)—*continued*

Ranger Surplus	8008 Wisconsin Ave	301-656-2302	Smaller than the Fairfax branch but worth a look.
Wiggle Room	4914 Del Ray Ave	301-656-5995	Consignment shop for kids' clothes. Why spend more?

Map 25 • Silver Spring

CakeLove	935 Ellsworth Dr	301-565-2253	High-end and tasty.
Color Me Mine	823 Ellsworth Dr	301-565-5105	Do-it-yourself pottery.
Dale Music	8240 Georgia Ave	301-589-1459	Amazing collection of sheet music. Open since 1950.

Map 26 • Takoma Park

House of Musical Traditions	7040 Carroll Ave	301-270-9090	Looking for a new skakuhachi or hurdy-gurdy? They've got it.
Polly Sue's	6915 Laurel Ave	301-270-5511	Vintage heaven.
Takoma Park/Silver Spring Co-op	201 Ethan Allen Ave	301-891-2667	Natural foods store for the people.
Video Americain	6937 Laurel Ave	301-270-4464	Where people cooler than you rent movies.

Map 27 • Walter Reed

Georgia Avenue Super Thrift	6101 Georgia Ave NW	202-291-4013	A landmark DC thrift store.
KB News Emporium	7898 Georgia Ave	301-565-4248	Catch up on the headlines.

Map 28 • Chevy Chase

Chevy Chase Wine & Spirits	5544 Connecticut Ave NW	202-363-4000	Charming, expert boozologists.

Map 29 • Bethesda (South)

Barney's New York Co-op	5471 Wisconsin Ave	301-634-4061	Fresh-off-the-runway fashions without schlepping to Neiman's.
Bethesda Tattoo Company	4711 Montgomery Blvd	301-652-0494	It wouldn't hurt you to commit to something.
Brooks Brothers	5504 Wisconsin Ave	301-654-8202	DC's uniform supply shop.
Chicos	5418 Wisconsin Ave	301-986-1122	Clothing for stylish women with professional bank accounts.
Luna	7232 Woodmont Ave	301-656-1111	Small boutique carrying expensive designer labels.
Marvelous Market	4832 Bethesda Ave	301-986-0555	Try their blueberry muffins.
Mustard Seed	7349 Wisconsin Ave	301-907-4699	Not your typical resale store.
Parvizian Masterpieces	7034 Wisconsin Ave	301-654-8989	Serious rugs.
Saks Fifth Avenue	5555 Wisconsin Ave	301-657-9000	Where rich people shop.
Saks Jandel	5510 Wisconsin Ave	301-652-2250	For the well-dressed socialite.
Knit and Stitch=Bliss	4706 Bethesda Ave	301-652-8688	Knit and crochet supplies.
Strosnider's Hardware	6930 Arlington Rd	301-654-5688	Serious hardware store with an irascible and knowledgeable staff.
Sylene	4407 S Park Ave	301-654-4200	Fine lingerie.
Tickled Pink	7259 Woodmont Ave	301-913-9191	Palm beach chic.
Tiffany & Co	5481 Wisconsin Ave	301-657-8777	Pop the question.
Trader Joe's	6831 Wisconsin Ave	301-907-0982	If only the folks shopping there were as laid back as the décor.
Writer's Center	4508 Walsh St	301-654-8664	Funky bookstore with literary journals

Map 30 • Westmoreland Circle

Crate & Barrel	4820 Massachusetts Ave NW	202-364-6100	Wedding registry HQ.
Ski Center	4300 Fordham Rd NW	202-966-4474	Umm, skis.
Spring Valley Patio	4300 Fordham Rd NW	202-966-9088	Furniture for your expansive, green, upper NW lawn.
Wagshal's Market	4845 Massachusetts Ave NW	202-363-0777	Gourmet foodstuffs.
Western Market	4840 Western Ave	301-229-7222	Lonesome general store.

Map 33 • Falls Church

Calico Corners	6400 Williamsburg Blvd	703-536-5488	Reams of fabric and helpful guidance
Westover Shopping Center	Washington Blvd	N/A	Old-timey village feel, almost everything you need

Map 34 • Cherrydale / Ballston

Arrowine	4508 Lee Hwy	703-525-0990	Eclectic wine, gourmet cheese, and tastings of both.

Lebanese Taverna Market	4400 Old Dominion Dr	703-276-8681	Area's favorite shawarma and tabouleh to go.
Pastries by Randolph	4500 Lee Hwy	703-243-0070	Bustling, no-nonsense bakery with killer cheesecake and pies.

Map 35 • Cherrydale / Clarendon

Barnes & Noble	2800 Clarendon Blvd	703-248-8244	Borders, but with a different name.
CD Cellar	2614 Wilson Blvd	703-248-0635	If you missed the Internet music revolution.
Company Flowers	2107 N Pollard St	703-525-3063	Crafted bouquets, assorted gifts, cards, and tchotchkes
The Container Store	2800 Clarendon Blvd	703-469-1560	Buckets, shelves, hangers.
The Italian Store	3123 Lee Hwy	703-528-6266	The best Italian heros.
Kinder Haus Toys	1220 N Fillmore St	703-527-5929	Hooray for puppet shows.
Orpheus Records	3173 Wilson Blvd	703-294-6774	Stacks of dusty LPs await for music geeks to delve through.
Orvis Company Store	2879 Clarendon Blvd	703-465-0004	Practical clothes to match the rhino guard on your SUV.
Pottery Barn	2700 Clarendon Blvd	703-465-9425	Yuppie interior style.
South Moon Under	2700 Clarendon Blvd	703-807-4083	Cool casuals and stuff for the home.

Map 36 • Rosslyn

Café Tivoli	1700 N Moore St	703-524-8900	Gorgeous Continental sweets in the Rosslyn metro.

Map 37 • Fort Myer

Ski Chalet	2704 Columbia Pike	703-521-1700	For all the snow elsewhere.

Map 38 • Columbia Pike

REI	3509 Carlin Springs Rd	703-379-9400	Sports emporium.
Target	5115 Leesburg Pike	703-253-0021	Wal-Mart in drag.

Map 39 • Shirlington

Books-A-Million	4017 28th St S	703-931-6949	Top titles and some old faves too.
CakeLove	4150 Campbell Ave	703-933-0099	High-end and tasty.
The Curious Grape	4056 28th St S	703-671-8700	Many wines, free tastings, great spot to stop on a date.
Diversions Cards and Gifts	1721 Centre Plaza	703-578-3237	Nice alternative to blah greeting cards you get at the supermarket.
Unwined	3690 King St	703-820-8600	One-stop shop if you're throwing a cocktail party.
Washington Golf Centers	2625 Shirlington Rd	703-979-1235	Gear up for the links.

Map 40 • Pentagon City / Crystal City

Abercrombie & Fitch	1100 S Hayes St	703-415-4210	Quintessential college kids' clothes.
Actors Center	601 S Clark St	703-413-3270	Do your best Pacino impression.
Apple Store	1100 S Hayes St	703-418-1092	Don't come looking for produce.
BCBG	1100 S Hayes St	703-415-3690	Cheap, trendy women's clothing.
bebe	1100 S Hayes St	703-415-2323	Sexy clothing for twentysomething women.
Costco	1200 S Fern St	703-413-2324	Exactly what you'd expect, but this one's the busiest in the country - beware!
Denim Bar	1101 S Joyce St	703-414-8202	When your butt is too good for $200 jeans.
Elizabeth Arden Red Door Salon & Spa	1101 S Joyce St	703-373-5888	Pampered facials.
Fashion Center-Pentagon City	1100 S Hayes St	703-415-2400	DC's best metro-accessible mall. Popular with tourists.
Harris Teeter	900 Army Navy Dr	703-413-7112	Pricey food mecca with a great selection.
Jean Machine	1100 S Hayes St	703-415-3815	Inexpensive jeans from a variety of lines.
Kenneth Cole	1100 S Hayes St	703-415-3522	Metrosexual heaven, great guys' shoes and accessories.
Macy's	1000 S Hayes St	703-418-4488	Yes, DC, department stores still exist.
Williams-Sonoma	1100 S Hayes St	703-416-6700	High-end cooking supplies.
World Market	1301 S Joyce St	703-415-7575	Wine, beer, furniture, and that British candy bar you've been craving.

Map 41 • Landmark

Authentically Amish Fine Furnishings	4609 Duke St	703-212-9890	Quality furniture for your barn.
BJ's Wholesale Club	101 S Van Dorn St	703-212-8700	If you need a 24-pack of anything.

Map 43 • Four Mile Run / Del Ray

A Show of Hands	2204 Mt Vernon Ave	703-683-2905	Local arts, crafts, jewelry; less highbrow than the Torpedo Factory.
Artfully Chocolate	116 E Del Ray Ave	703-635-7917	All you need to know: artisinal chocolate.
Barnes & Noble	3651 Jefferson Davis Hwy	703-299-9124	Mega bookstore.
Best Buy	3401 Jefferson Davis Hwy	703-519-0940	All sorts of electronics.
Cheesetique	2411 Mt Vernon Ave	703-706-5300	The ultimate neighborhood cheese shop.
The Clay Queen Pottery	2303 Mt Vernon Ave	703-549-7775	Throw it yourself.
The Dairy Godmother	2310 Mt Vernon Ave	703-683-7767	Make yourself comfy with homemade marshmallows and custard.
Eight Hands Round	2301 Mt Vernon Ave	703-518-3058	Great mix of home crafts and antiques.
Five Oaks Antiques	2413 Mt Vernon Ave	703-519-7006	Classic 19th and 20th century furniture; over 40 dealers.
Old Navy	3621 Jefferson Davis Hwy	703-739-6240	Super-cheap, super-basic clothes.
Potomac West Antiques	1517 Mt Vernon Ave	703-519-1911	Kin to Five Oaks; new and garden items, too.
The Purple Goose	2005 Mt Vernon Ave	703-683-2918	Consignments for the kiddies.
Sports Authority	3701 Jefferson Davis Hwy	703-684-3204	The authority on sports.
Staples	3301 Jefferson Davis Hwy	703-836-9485	Everything you need for your home (or work) office.
Target	3101 Jefferson Davis Hwy	703-706-3840	Tar-zhay offers housewares, furniture and more.

Map 44 • Alexandria Downtown

Crate & Barrel Outlet	1700 Prince St	703-739-8800	Perfectly complements hyper-inflated real estate.
Whole Foods Market	1700 Duke St	703-706-0891	Expensive organic food chain store.

Map 46 • Old Town (South)

ArtCraft	132 King St	703-299-6616	Unique gifts and furnishings that are oh-so-not Old Town.
Arts Afire	1117 King St	703-548-1197	American and alternative crafts.
Banana Republic	628 King St	703-739-0888	It is what it is.
Big Wheel Bikes	2 Prince St	703-739-2300	Rent one and do the Mt. Vernon Trail.
Books-a-Million	503 King St	703-548-3432	If you just can't hold out until you get to Borders.
Chinoiserie	1024 King St	703-838-0520	A sure shot for unique home décor or a gift for a hip friend.
Comfort One Shoes	201 King St	703-549-4441	Beyond Birkenstocks.
Hysteria	125 S Fairfax St	703-548-1615	Wearable art at museum prices.
Irish Walk	415 King St	703-548-0118	Every day is St. Patrick's Day.
Jos A Bank	728 S Washington St	703-837-8201	For professional types who can't afford Brooks Brothers.
Kingsbury Chocolates	1017 King St	703-548-2800	Mmmmmm.
Kosmos Design & Ideas	1010 King St	703-837-1955	Creative tchotchkes.
La Cuisine	323 Cameron St	703-836-4435	Upscale cookware.
The Lamplighter	1207 King St	703-549-4040	Get plugged in.
Montague & Son	115 S Union St	703-548-5656	Birkenstocks on cobblestone streets?
My Place in Tuscany	1127 King St	703-683-8882	Hand-painted ceramics.
Notting Hill Gardens	815 King St	703-518-0215	A delightful urban nursery.
P&C Art	212 King St	703-549-2525	Original art.
Pacers	1301 King St	703-836-1463	Running wear, if you insist on it.
Paper Source	118 King St	703-299-9950	Heaven for scrapbookers and greeting card seekers alike.
Papyrus	721 King St	571-721-0070	Cards, gifts, and wrap.
Tickled Pink	103 S Asaph St	703-518-5459	Palm beach chic.
Torpedo Factory Art Center	105 N Union St	703-838-4565	Giant artist compound; most of it's pretty touristy stuff.
Williams-Sonoma	825 S Washington St	703-836-1904	Great cooking stuff if you know how.
The Winery Inc	317 S Washington St	703-535-5765	Because you shouldn't buy wine in Safeway.

Baltimore

The Antique Man	1806 Fleet St	410-732-0932	The most eclectic of the string of antique/junk shops around Fells Point.
Cook's Table	1036 Light St	410-625-5757	For the perfectly-appointed mogul kitchen.
Di Pasquale's Italian Marketplace	3700 Gough St	410-276-6787	Italian grocer.
Karmic Connection	508 S Broadway	410-558-0428	Get Good Karma Goods.
Mystery Loves Company	1730 Fleet St	410-276-6708	No mystery to the genre of books here.
Sound Garden	1616 Thames St	410-563-9011	Independent music store worthy of *High Fidelity*. Also hosts impromptu performances.
Stikky Fingers	802 S Broadway	410-675-7588	Dress like it's halloween every night.
Vaccaro's Italian Pastry Shop	2000 Pennsylvania Ave NW	410-685-4905	A Baltimore institution.

There's a two-tiered theater scene here: flashy, national traveling productions; and edgy, organic gems. Count on **The Kennedy Center (Map 7)** and **National Theatre (Map 1)**—members of the former group—schedule a lineup of touring productions that appeal largely to those under 12 or over 55. Look for several other playhouses, some tucked away in neighborhoods, that give new playwrights, innovative ideas, and local actors a chance. Perhaps further still, consider all the DC-based companies that don't have a theater of their own, and follow their season—not their space (…because they don't have one).

If you're interested in the uniqueness of DC's theater scene, you'll find it on the high quality, smaller stages. **Arena Stage (Map 6)** on the SW waterfront (www.arena-stage.com; 202-488-3300) has earned its reputation as a well-respected local from decades of fine productions. The **Studio Theatre (Map 10)** in Logan Circle (www.studiotheatre.org; 202-332-3300), in addition to its larger productions, is also known for developing some of Washington's best actors and directors on its **2ndStage**. But perhaps the most successful yet cutting edge club in the city is **Woolly Mammoth (Map 2)**, a company that is constantly trying to redefine the relationship between theater and the DC community. In addition to stages with their own companies, remember that this city has a thriving number of theater companies without spaces to call home—including Didactic, Catalyst, and Rorschach.

For modern takes on the classics, visit the **Folger (Map 3)** and **Shakespeare Theatres (Map 2)**. The Folger Theatre, part of the Folger Shakespeare Library, stages three plays per year in its intimate Elizabethan-style theater (www.folger.edu; 202-544-7077), The Shakespeare Theatre recently expanded, making tickets easier to come by (www.shakespearedc.org; 202-547-1122).

The theater scene changes in the summer, with most playhouses taking a break. But for real buffs, there's the popular Contemporary American Theater festival in nearby Shepardstown, West Virginia, in July. Closer to home, there's a run of free shows at the outdoor **Carter Barron Amphitheatre (Map 21)** in Rock Creek Park; 202-426-0486.

Remember: one must never have to pay full-price for a night at the theater. Whether it's a pay-what-you-can night, 25 & under, residents only, student prices, or standing room only—there's always a cheapo culture vulture solution. DC theater is not just for thespians, and the thespians like it that way.

Theater	Address	Phone	Map
The American Century Theater and the Gunston Arts Center	2700 S Lang St	703-553-7782	40
Arena Stage	1101 6th St SW	202-488-3300	6
Atlas Performing Arts Center	1333 H St NE	202-399-7993	3
Blair Mansion Inn/Murder Mystery Dinner Theatre	7711 Eastern Ave	301-588-6646	27
Capitol Hill Arts Workshop	545 7th St SE	202-547-6839	5
Carter Barron Amphitheatre	16th & Colorado Ave NW	202-426-0486	21
Casa de la Luna	4020 Georgia Ave	202-882-6227	21
Dance Place	3225 8th St NE	202-269-1600	14
Discovery Theater	1100 Jefferson Dr SW	202-357-1500	1
District of Columbia Arts Center	2438 18th St NW	202-462-7833	16
Flashpoint	916 G St NW	202-315-1305	1
Folger Shakespeare Theatre	201 E Capitol St SE	202-544-7077	3
Ford's Theatre	511 10th St NW	202-426-6924	1
GALA-Tivoli Theater	3333 14th St NW	202-234-7174	15
H Street Playhouse	1365 H St NE	202-396-2125	3
Hartke Theatre	3801 Harewood Rd NE	202-319-4000	14
Imagination Stage	4908 Auburn Ave	301-280-1660	22
Kennedy Center	2700 F St NW	202-467-4600	7
Lincoln Theatre	1215 U St NW	202-397-7328	10
Little Theatre of Alexandria	600 Wolfe St	703-683-0496	46
Metro Stage	1201 N Royal St	703-548-9044	45
Mount Vernon Players Theater	900 Massachusetts Ave NW	202-783-7600	10
National Theatre	1321 Pennsylvania Ave NW	202-628-6161	1
Rosslyn Spectrum Theatre	1611 N Kent St	703-228-1843	36
Round House Theatre	4545 East West Hwy	240-644-1100	29
Round House Theatre	8641 Colesville Rd	240-644-1100	25
Shakespeare Theatre	450 7th St NW	202-547-1122	2
Signature Theater	4200 Campbell Ave	703-820-9771	39
St Mark's Players/St Mark's Church	118 3rd St SE	202-546-9670	3
Studio Theatre	1501 14th St NW	202-332-3300	10
Theatre on the Run	3700 S Four Mile Run Dr	703-228-1850	39
The Warehouse	1017 7th St NW	202-783-3933	10
Warner Theatre	513 13th St NW	202-783-4000	1
Washington Shakespeare Co	601 S Clark St	703-418-4808	40
Washington Stage Guild	1901 14th St NW	240-582-0050	10
Woolly Mammoth Theatre	641 D St NW	202-393-3939	2

Washington, DC

Street	Range	Page	Grid
1st Ave		6	B2/C2
1st Ave SW		2	C2
1st Pl NE	(2100-2121)	11	B1
	(4400-5924)	14	A1/B1
1st Pl NW	(1100-1199)	11	C1
	(5400-5649)	14	A1
1st St NE	(1-5510)	14	A1/B1
	(51-832)	2	A2/B2
	(833-1999)	11	B1/C1
1st St NW	(100-849)	2	A2/B2
	(850-2812)	11	A1/B1/C1
	(2813-5549)	14	A1/C1
	(5758-6699)	26	C1
1st St SE	(1-249)	2	C2
	(250-599)	5	A1
	(900-4550)	6	A2/B2
1st St SW		6	A2/B2/C2
1st Ter NW		11	C1
2nd Ave		6	C2
2nd Ave SW	(100-257)	2	C1
	(258-499)	6	A2
2nd Pl NW		27	C2
2nd Pl SE		5	A1/B1
2nd St NE	(1-849)	3	A1/B1/C1
	(850-2599)	11	A1/B1/C1
	(4200-5649)	14	B1
2nd St NW	(200-2341)	11	A1/B1/C1
	(550-849)	2	A1/B2
	(4200-5549)	14	A1/B1
	(5650-6399)	27	C2
	(6600-6754)	26	C1
2nd St SE	(200-1199)	5	A1/B1
		3	C1
2nd St SW		6	B2/C2
3rd Ave		6	B2/C2
3rd Ave SW	(100-249)	2	C1
	(250-399)	6	A2
3rd Pl NW		14	A1
3rd St NE	(1-849)	3	A1/B1/C1
	(850-2699)	11	A2/B2/C2
	(5200-5635)	14	A2
3rd St NW	(1-849)	2	A1/B1
	(850-2099)	11	B1/C1
	(3900-5506)	14	A1/B1
	(5850-6799)	27	B2/C2
3rd St SE	(1-249)	3	C1
	(250-1199)	5	A1/B1
3rd St SW	(400-1499)	2	C1
		6	A2/B2
4th Ave		6	B2/C2
4th Pl SW		6	A2
4th St NE	(1-849)	3	A1/B1/C1
	(850-2849)	11	A2/B2/C2
	(2850-5522)	14	A2/C2
4th St NW	(1-849)	2	A1/B1
	(850-2149)	11	B1/C1
	(2213-2499)	15	C2
	(3800-5549)	14	A1/B1
	(5550-5849)	21	A2
	(5850-6999)	27	B2/C2
4th St SE	(1-261)	3	C1
	(262-3955)	5	A1/B1
4th St SW	(200-1499)	2	C1
		6	A2/B2
5th Ave		6	B2/C2
5th St NE	(1-849)	3	A1/B1/C1
	(850-2849)	11	A2/B2/C2
5th St NW	(243-2899)	15	B2/C2
	(400-899)	2	A1/B1
	(900-2574)	10	A2/B2/C2
	(3700-5849)	21	A2/B2/C2
	(5850-7099)	27	B2/C2
5th St SE	(1-299)	3	C1
	(300-1199)	5	A1/B1
6th Pl NE		14	A2/B2
6th Pl SW		6	A2
6th St NE	(1-849)	3	A1/B1/C1
	(850-2817)	11	A2/B2/C2
	(2818-4850)	14	C2
6th St NW	(200-899)	2	A1/B1
	(456-5849)	21	A2
	(901-2219)	10	A2/B2/C2
	(2220-3599)	15	A2/B2/C2
	(5850-7099)	27	B2/C2
6th St SE	(1-299)	3	C1
	(150-799)	5	A1
6th St SW	(200-275)	2	C1
	(276-1399)	6	A2/B2
7th Pl NE		14	A2
7th Pl NW	(5000-5099)	21	B2
	(6000-6699)	27	B2/C2
7th St NE	(1-849)	3	A1/B1/C1
	(850-2849)	11	A2/C2
	(2850-5199)	14	A2/B2/C2
7th St NW	(30-1999)	10	A2/B2/C2
	(65-915)	2	A1/B1
	(3700-5849)	21	A2/B2/C2
	(5850-7499)	27	A2/B2/C2
7th St SE	(1-249)	3	C1
	(250-1199)	5	A1/B1
7th St SW	(1-299)	2	C1
	(288-899)	6	A1
8th Pl NE		11	A2
8th St NE	(1-849)	3	A2/B2/C2
	(850-2899)	11	C2
	(2900-5449)	14	A2/B2/C2
8th St NW	(200-949)	1	A2/B2
	(950-2199)	10	A2/B2/C2
	(2200-5849)	21	A2/B2/C2
	(5806-7599)	27	A2/B2/C2
8th St SE	(1-249)	3	C2
	(250-1199)	5	A1/B1
9½ St NW		10	A2
9th Pl NW	(1000-1048)	21	C2
	(1950-1999)	11	B2
9th St NE	(1-849)	3	A2/B2/C2
	(850-1999)	11	B2/C2
	(2900-4099)	14	B2/C2
9th St NW	(100-2168)	10	A2/B2/C2
	(150-949)	1	A2/B2
	(2169-2999)	15	C2
	(3700-5899)	21	A2/B2/C2
	(5900-7699)	27	A2/B2/C2
9th St SE	(1-249)	3	C2
	(250-1199)	5	A1/B1
9th St SW		6	A1
10th St NE	(1-849)	3	A2/B2/C2
	(850-2849)	11	A2/C2
	(2850-5099)	14	A2/B2/C2
10th St NW	(300-949)	1	A2/B2
	(950-2249)	10	A2/B2/C2
	(2250-3724)	15	A1
	(3725-3899)	21	C2
10th St SE	(1-249)	3	C2
	(250-1299)	5	A1/B1
10th St SW		6	A1
11th Pl NE		14	B2
11th St NE	(127-849)	3	A2/B2
	(850-1099)	11	C2
	(4900-5299)	14	A2
11th St NW	(400-949)	1	A2/B2
	(950-2149)	10	A1/B1/C1
	(2150-3649)	15	A1/B1/C1
11th St SE	(1-262)	3	C2
	(263-1399)	5	A2/B2
11th St SW		6	A1
11th Street Brg		5	B2
12th Pl NE	(200-299)	3	B2
	(4200-4399)	14	B2
12th St NE	(100-2849)	11	A2/C2
	(127-860)	3	A2/B2
	(2850-5299)	14	A2/B2/C2
12th St NW	(200-2249)	10	A1/B1/C1
	(250-949)	1	A2/B2
	(2250-2599)	15	C1
	(6200-7899)	27	A1/B1/C1
12th St SE	(100-241)	3	C2
	(242-1499)	5	A2/B2
12th St SW	(100-249)	1	C2
	(250-699)	6	A1
12th Street Tunl		1	C2
13 1/2 St NW		1	B2
13th Pl NE		13	A1
13th Pl NW		27	B1/C1
13th St NE	(1-4515)	3	A2/B2/C2
	(2250-2849)	11	A2/C2
	(2850-4949)	14	B2/C2
13th St NW	(401-949)	1	A2/B2
	(950-2249)	10	A1/B1/C1
	(2250-3649)	15	A1/B1/C1
	(3650-5851)	21	A2/B2/C2
	(5852-7949)	27	A1/B1/C1
	(7909-8098)	25	C1
13th St SE	(1-227)	3	C2
	(228-2299)	5	A2/B2/C2
13th St SW		6	A1
14th Pl NE		4	C2
14th Pl NW		27	B1
14th St NE	(1-2708)	4	A1/B1
	(2200-4759)	13	A1/B1/C1
14th St NW	(1-949)	1	A1/B1/C1
	(950-2249)	10	A1/B1/C1
	(2250-3573)	15	A1/B1/C1
	(3574-5849)	21	A2/B2/C2
	(5819-7852)	27	A1/B1/C1
	(7853-8099)	25	C1
14th St SE	(1-265)	4	C1
	(266-2299)	5	A2/B2/C2
14th St SW	(100-265)	1	C1
	(266-499)	6	A1
15th St NE	(51-799)	4	A1/B1
	(1700-1799)	12	A1
	(2200-3799)	13	A1/B1/C1
15th St NW	(1-949)	1	A1/B1/C1
	(332-599)	6	A1
	(950-2265)	9	A2/B2/C2
	(2266-4349)	16	B2/C2
	(4350-4899)	21	B1
	(6900-6999)	27	B1
15th St SE	(1-266)	4	C1
	(267-2399)	5	A2/B2/C2
15th St SW		1	C1
16th Pl NE		13	B1

Street Index

Street Index

Street	Page	Grid
Groff Ct NE	3	B1
Guetlet Ct SE	5	A2
H Pl NE	4	A2
H St NE		
(1-149)	2	A2
(150-1366)	3	A1/A2
(1367-2399)	4	A1/A2
H St NW		
(1-749)	2	A1/A2
(750-1749)	1	A1/A2
(1750-2499)	7	A1/A2
H St SE	5	A1/A2
H St SW	6	A2
Hadfield Ln NW	18	C2
Half St SE	6	A2/B2
Half St SW	6	A2/B2
Hall Pl NW	18	B2
Hamilton St NE	14	A1/A2
Hamilton St NW		
(1-449)	14	A1
(450-1499)	21	B2
Hamlin Pl NE	13	B2
Hamlin St NE		
(500-1349)	14	C2
(1350-2799)	13	B1/B2
Hanover Pl NW	11	B1
Harewood Rd NE	14	B2/C2
Harewood Rd NW	14	B1
Harlan Pl NW	26	C1
Harrison St NW		
(3000-3749)	20	A1
(3750-4599)	19	A1/A2
Harvard Ct NW	15	B1
Harvard St NW		
(500-1456)	15	B1/B2
(1457-1899)	16	B1/B2
Hawaii Ave NE	14	B1/B2
Hawthorne Ct NE	14	C1
Hawthorne Dr NE	14	C1
Hawthorne Dr NW	18	A2
Hawthorne Ln NW	18	A1
Hawthorne Pl NW	32	A2
Hawthorne St NW		
(2300-3149)	17	B2
(3150-4599)	18	A1/A2
Hemlock St NW	27	A1/A2
Henry Bacon Dr NW	7	B2
High St SE	5	
Highland Ave NW	27	B2
Highland Pl NW	17	A1
Highwood Ct NW	18	B2
Hillandale Ct NW	18	B2
Hillandale Dr NW	18	B2
Hillbrook Ln NW	30	C2
Hillyer Ct NW	9	B1
Hillyer Pl NW	9	B1
Hoban Rd NW	18	C2
Hobart Pl NW	14	C1
(400-799)	15	B2
Hobart St NW	16	B2
Holbrook St NE	12	B1/C1
Holbrook Ter NE		
(1100-1154)	11	B2
(1155-1299)	12	B1
Holly St NW	27	A1
Holmead Pl NW	15	A1
Hoover Rd NE	13	B2
Hopkins St NW	9	B1
Hospital Cent Ser Rd	14	C1
Howard Pl NW	15	C2
Howard Rd SE	5	C1/C2
Howard St NW	19	B2
Howison Pl SW	6	B2
Hughes Mews St NW	7	A1
Huidekoper Pl NW	18	B2
Huntington St NW	19	A2
Hurst Ter NW	32	A2
Hutchins Pl NW	18	B1
I St NE		
(1-1749)	11	C1/C2
(1750-2399)	12	C2
I St NW		
(1-449)	11	C1
(450-2298)	2	A1
(750-1749)	1	A1/A2
(1750-2699)	7	A1/A2
I St SE		
(1-150)	6	A2
(151-1299)	5	A1/A2
I St SW	6	A2
Idaho Ave NW		
(3000-3499)	18	A2
(3501-3999)	19	C2
Illinois Ave NW		
(3800-4049)	14	B1
(4050-5599)	21	A2/B2/C2
Independence Ave SE		
(1-149)	2	C2
(150-1349)	3	C1/C2
(1350-2649)	4	C1/C2
Independence Ave SW		
(1-799)	2	C1/C2
(800-1299)	1	C1/C2
Indian Ln NW	32	A2
Indian Rock Ter NW	18	C1
Indiana Ave NW	2	B1/B2
Ingomar Pl NW	20	A1
Ingomar St NW	19	A1/A2
Ingraham St NE	14	A1/A2
Ingraham St NW		
(1-449)	14	A1
(450-1449)	21	B2
International Ct NW	20	B1
International Dr NW	20	B1
Iowa Ave NW	21	B1/B2
Iris St NW	27	A1
Irving St NE		
(700-1349)	14	C1/C2
(1350-2699)	13	B1/B2
Irving St NW		
(1-405)	14	C1
(406-1432)	15	B1/B2
(1433-1856)	16	B2
Isaac Hull Ave	5	B1
Isherwood St NE	4	B1
Ives Pl SE	5	A2
Ivy Terrace Ct NW	18	B2
Jackson Pl NW	1	A1
Jackson St NE		
(600-1349)	14	C2
(1350-2099)	13	B1
James Creek Pky SW	6	B2
Jefferson Dr SW		
(600-949)	2	C1
(1300-1450)	1	C1
Jefferson Pl NW	9	C2
Jefferson St NE	14	A1/A2
Jefferson St NW		
(100-449)	14	A1
(450-1399)	21	A2
Jenifer St NW		
(2700-3849)	20	A1/A2
(3850-4499)	19	A1/A2
Jocelyn St NW		
(3100-3849)	20	A1
(3850-3999)	19	A2
John Phillip Sousa Brg	5	B2
Jones Ct NW	8	B1
Jonquil St NW	27	A1
Jordan Aly SE	5	A2
Joyce Rd NW	21	A1
	20	A2
	27	C1
Juniper St NW	27	A1/A2
Justice Ct NE	3	B1
K St NE		
(1-1299)	11	C1/C2
(1600-1849)	12	C1
K St NW		
(1-449)	11	C1
(450-1464)	10	C1/C2
(1465-2430)	9	C1/C2
(2420-3799)	8	C1/C2
K St SE		
(1-105)	6	A2
(106-1699)	5	A1/A2
K St SW	6	A2
K Ter NW	11	C1
Kabrawa Sq	9	A1
Kalmia Rd NW		
(1100-1620)	27	A1
(1713-1799)	24	C2
Kalorama Cir NW	8	A2
Kalorama Rd NW		
(1600-1949)	16	C1/C2
(1950-2349)	9	A1
(2350-2499)	8	A2
Kanawha St NW		
(2800-2999)	28	C2
(3600-3849)	20	A1
Kansas Ave NE	26	C1
Kansas Ave NW		
(3600-5149)	21	B2/C2
(5150-5524)	14	A1
Kearney St NE		
(600-1349)	14	C2
(1350-2299)	13	B1/B2
Keefer Pl NW	15	B2
Kendall St NE	11	B2
Kenmore Dr NW	18	C1
Kennedy Pl NW	21	A1
Kennedy St NE	14	A1/A2
Kennedy St NW		
(1-449)	14	A1
(450-1699)	21	A1/A2
Kent Pl NE	11	C2
Kentucky Ave SE		
(100-274)	3	C2
(275-899)	5	A2
Kenyon St NW		
(421-16354)	15	B1/B2
(1600-1909)	16	B2
Key Brg	8	C1
Kilbourne Pl NW	16	B2
King Pl NE	13	B2
King Pl NW	18	B1
Kingman Pl NW	10	B1
Kings Ct SE	4	C1
Kirby St NW	11	C1
Klingle Pl NW	18	A2
Klingle Rd NW		
(2000-2099)	16	A1
(2603-3299)	17	A2/B1
Klingle St NW		
(4350-4599)	18	A1
(4900-5299)	32	A2
Kramer St NE	4	A1
L Pl NW	11	C1
L St NE		
(1-999)	11	C1/C2
(1600-1850)	12	C1
L St NW		
(1-449)	11	C1
(512-1459)	10	C1/C2
(1460-2499)	9	C1/C2
(2450-2599)	8	C1/C2
L St SE		
(1-114)	6	B2
(115-1499)	5	B1/B2
L St SW	6	B1/B2
Lafayette Ave NE	13	C2
Lamont St NW		
(400-1299)	15	A2/B1
(1500-2099)	16	A1/A2/B2
Lang Pl NE	12	C1
Langley Ct NW	19	C2
Langston Ter NE	4	A2
Lanier Pl NW	16	B2
Laurel St NW	27	B2
Laverock Pl NW	18	C2
Lawrence Ave NE	13	C1
Lawrence St NE		
(700-1349)	14	C2
(1350-2499)	13	B1/B2
Leegate Rd NW	25	C1
Lees Ct SE	9	C1
Legation St NW	28	C1/C2
Lenfant Plz	6	A1
Lenfant Plz SW	6	A1
Lenore Ln NW	20	B2
Leroy Pl NW	9	A1
Levis St NE	12	C1
Lexington Pl NE	3	B1
Library Ct SE	3	C1
Ligman Rd	18	C2
Lincoln Memorial Cir	7	B1/C1
Lincoln Rd NE	11	A1/B1
Linden Ct NE	3	A2
Linden Pl NE	3	A2
Lindsey Dr NW	28	B2
Lingan Rd NW	18	C2
Linnean Ave NW	20	

Street Index

Street	Page	Grid
Okie St NE		
(1100-1349)	11	B2
(1350-1599)	12	A1
Oklahoma Ave NE	4	B2
Olive Ave NW	8	C2
Oliver St NW	28	C1/C2
Oneida Pl NW	27	C2
Ontario Rd NW	16	B1/B2/C2
Orchard Ln NW	8	B2
Orchid St NW	25	C1
Ordway St NW		
(2700-2999)	17	A2
(2989-3550)	20	C1
(3551-3699)	19	C2
Oregon Ave NW	28	A2/B2/C2
Oregon Knolls Dr NW	28	B2
Orleans Pl NE	11	C2
Orren St NE	12	B1/C1
Otis Pl NE	13	A1
Otis Pl NW	15	A1/A2
Otis St NE		
(900-1349)	14	C2
(1350-3099)	13	A1/A2
Overlook Ln NW	30	C2
Overlook Rd NW		
(5001-5063)	32	A2
(5046-5099)	30	C2
Owen Pl NE	11	C2
P St NE	11	B1
P St NW		
(1-449)	11	B1
(450-1449)	10	B1/B2
(1450-2457)	9	B1/B2
(2458-3649)	8	B1/B2
(3650-4499)	18	C2
P St SE		
(1-99)	6	B2
(1800-1949)	5	B2
P St SW	6	B2
Palisade Ln NW	32	A2
Paper Mill Ct NW	8	C1
Park Pl	14	C1
Park Pl NW		
(3645-3698)	21	C2
(2900-3049)	14	C1
(3050-3646)	15	A2/B2
Park Rd NW		
(400-1449)	15	A1/A2/B1
(1450-2107)	16	A1/A2
(2108-2199)	21	C1
Park St NE	3	B2
Parkglen Ct NW	18	B2
Parkside Dr NW	24	C2
Parkside Ln NW	24	C2
Parkwood Pl NW	15	A1
Parsons Ave	5	B1
Partridge Ln NW	32	A2
Patterson Ave SE	5	B1
Patterson Pl NW	28	B2
Patterson St NE	11	C1
Patterson St NW	28	C1/C2
Paulding Ave	5	B1
Paulding St	5	B1
Payne Ter SE	5	C2
Peabody St NW	27	C1/C2
Penn St NE	11	B2
Pennsylvania Ave NW		
(200-749)	2	B1/B2
(750-1749)	1	A1/B1/B2
(1750-2149)	7	A2
(2150-2450)	9	C1
(2451-2899)	8	C2
Pennsylvania Ave SE		
(200-449)	3	C1
(450-2259)	5	A1/A2/B2
Perry Pl NE	14	B2
Perry Pl NW	21	C1
Perry St	13	A2
Perry St NE		
(1000-1349)	14	B2
(1350-3099)	13	A1/A2
Phelps Pl NW	9	A1
Pickford Pl NE	3	A2
Pierce Mill Rd NW	16	A1
Pierce St NE	11	C1
Pierce St NW	11	C1
Pinehurst Cir NW	28	B1
Piney Branch Pky NW	21	C1
	16	A1
Piney Branch Rd NW		
(4600-5099)	21	B1
(5900-7399)	27	A2/B2/C1
Pitts Pl SE	5	C2
Plattsburg Ct NW	19	C2
Pleasant St SE	5	C2
Plymouth Cir NW	24	C2
Plymouth St NW	24	C2
Pomander Walk NW	8	B1
Pomeroy Rd SE	5	C2
Poplar St NW	8	B2
Portal Dr NW		
(1500-1684)	25	C1
N Portal Dr NW		
(1600-1682)	25	C1
(1683-1799)	24	C2
(1685-1799)	24	C2
Porter St NE	11	B1
Porter St NW		
(2300-2370)	16	A1
(2353-2649)	17	A2
(2962-3549)	20	C1
(3550-3899)	19	C2
Portner Pl NW	10	A1
Potomac Ave NW		
(4501-5349)	18	B1/C1
(5450-5899)	32	A1
Potomac Ave SE		
(1-99)	6	B2
(800-1899)	5	A2/B1
Potomac Ave SW	6	B2
Potomac St NW	8	C1
Powhatan Pl NW	27	C2
Primrose Rd NW		
(1400-1661)	25	C1
(1662-1899)	24	C2
Princeton Pl NW	15	A2
Proctor Aly NW	10	C1
Prospect St	18	C2
Prospect St NW	8	C1
Providence St NE	12	A1
Puerto Rico Ave NE	14	B2
Q Ln NW	18	C1
Q Pl NW	18	C1
Q St NE	11	B1
Q St NW		
(1-454)	11	B1
(455-1449)	10	B1/B2
(1450-2499)	9	B1/B2
(2500-3499)	8	B1/B2
(4401-4699)	18	C1/C2
Q St SE	5	B2
Q St SW	6	B2
Quackenbos St NW	27	C1/C2
Quarry Rd NW	16	B2
Quebec Pl NW		
(62-1299)	21	C2
(3100-3399)	20	C1
Quebec St NW		
(2600-3549)	20	C1/C2
(3550-3799)	19	C2
(4700-4999)	30	C2
Queen Annes Ln NW	7	A1
Queen St NE		
(1100-1229)	11	B2
(1230-1599)	12	B1/C1
Queens Chapel Rd NE	13	C2
Quesada St NW	28	B1/B2
Quincy Pl NE	11	B1
Quincy Pl NW	11	B1
Quincy St NE		
(700-1399)	14	B2
(1400-2299)	13	A1/A2
Quincy St NW	21	C1/C2
Quintana Pl NW	27	C2
R St NE		
(1-399)	11	B1/B2
(2100-2499)	12	A2
R St NW		
(1-460)	11	B1
(461-1462)	10	B1/B2
(1463-2299)	9	B1/B2
(2500-3549)	8	B1/B2
(3550-3799)	18	C2
R St SE	5	B2
R St SW	6	B2
Railroad Ave SE	5	A1/C2
Rand Pl NE	12	A2
Randolph Pl NE	11	B1/B2
Randolph Pl NW	11	B1
Randolph St NE		
(700-1349)	14	B2
(1350-2699)	13	A1/A2
Randolph St NW		
(300-456)	14	B1
(457-1899)	21	C1/C2
Raoul Wallenberg Pl SW		
(50-199)	1	C1
(262-331)	6	A1
Raum St NE	12	B1
Red Bud Ln NW	24	C2
Redwood Ter NW	24	C2
Reed Ct NW	7	A2
Reed St NE	11	A2
Reno Rd NW		
(3700-4261)	20	B1/C1
(4262-5399)	19	A2/B2
Reservoir Rd NW		
(3200-3549)	8	B1
(3550-4998)	18	B1/C1/C2
Rhode Island Ave NE		
(1-1314)	11	A2/B1
(1315-3199)	13	
Rhode Island Ave NW		
(1-459)	11	B1
(460-1449)	10	B1/B2
(1450-1799)	9	B2/C2
Richardson Pl NW	11	B1
Ridge Pl SE	5	B2
Ridge Rd NW	20	A2/B2
Riggs Ct NW	9	B1
Riggs Pl NW		
(1300-1399)	10	B1
(1600-1849)	9	B2
Riggs Rd NE	14	A1/A2
Rittenhouse St NW		
(150-1499)	27	C1/C2
(2600-3699)	28	B1/B2
River Rd NW	19	A1/B1
Rock Creek	14	A1
Church Rd NE		
Rock Creek Church Rd NW		
(1-499)	14	B1
(500-3621)	21	C2
Rock Creek Dr NW	8	A2
(2401-2899)	17	C2
Rock Creek	27	C1
Ford Rd NW		
Rock Creek Pky NW	16	A1/B1/C1
Rock Crk and Potomac Pky NW		
	7	A1/B1
	16	A1/B1
	8	A2/B2/C2
(2400-2499)	9	B1
Rockwood Pky NW		
(4701-4975)	32	A2
(4976-5174)	30	C2
Rodman St NW		
(3000-3577)	20	C1
(3578-3899)	19	C2
(4600-5199)	30	C2
Rosedale St NE	4	A1/B2
Rosemont Ave NW	16	A1
Ross Pl NW	17	A2
Rowland Pl NW	20	C1
Roxanna Rd NW	25	C1
Roxboro Pl NW	27	C2
Rumsey Ct SE	5	A1
S Rumsey Ct SE	5	A1
Runnymede Pl NW	28	B1
S St NE		
(1-399)	11	B1/B2
(2100-2499)	12	A2
S St NW		
(1-459)	11	B1
(460-1457)	10	A1/A2
(1458-2349)	9	A1/A2
(2350-3549)	8	A1/A2
(3550-3899)	18	B2
S St SE	5	B2
S St SW	6	B2
Saint Mathews Ct NW	9	C2
Salem Ln NW	18	C1

Street Index

Street	Page	Grid
Waterside Dr N	8	A2
(2000-2549)	16	C1
Watson Pl NW	18	A2
Watson St NW	32	A2
Waverly Ter NW	10	A1
Weaver Ter NW	32	A2
Webster St NE		
(1-249)	14	B1/B2
(1311-1999)	13	A1
Webster St NW		
(100-404)	14	B1
(405-1799)	21	B1/B2
Wesley Cir NW	19	C1
Wesley Pl SW	6	A2
West Beach Dr NW	24	C2
West Beach Ter NW	24	C2
West Lane Ky NW	8	B2
West St SE	5	C2
West Virginia Ave NE		
(700-1749)	11	B2/C2
(1750-2199)	12	A1/B1
Westminster St NW	10	A2
Westmoreland Cir NW	30	B2
Whitehaven Pky NW		
(3500-3555)	8	A1
(3531-4799)	18	B1/B2
Whitehaven St	8	A1
Whittier Pl NW	27	B1
Whittier St NW		
(1-225)	26	C1
(226-1599)	27	B1/B2
Willard St NW	9	A2
Williamsburg Ln NW	16	A1
Willow St NW	27	B2
Wiltberger St NW	10	A2
Windom Pl NW		
(3600-4649)	19	B1/B2
(4650-4799)	30	B2
Window Pl NW	20	B1
Windy Ct SE	5	A2
Wisconsin Ave NW		
(900-2149)	8	A1/B1/C1
(2150-3549)	18	A2/B2
(3550-5399)	19	A1/B2/C2
Woodland Dr NW	17	B1/C2
Woodley Rd NW		
(2500-2559)	16	B1
(2560-3549)	17	A1/B1/B2
(3550-3899)	18	A2
Woodridge St NE	13	B2
Woodway Ln NW	30	C2
Worthington St NW	28	B2
Wylie St NE	3	A2
Wyndale St NW	28	A2
Wyoming Ave NW		
(1800-2349)	9	A1
(2350-2499)	8	A2
Yorktown Rd NW	24	C2
Yost Pl NE	13	B2
Yuma Ct NW	30	B2
Yuma Pl NW	30	B2
Yuma St NW		
(3400-3649)	20	B1
(3648-4649)	19	B1/B2
(4650-5199)	30	B2
Zei Aly NW	1	A1

Maryland

Bethesda

Street	Page	Grid
Abingdon Rd	30	B1
Acacia Ave	22	A1/A2/B1
Albemarle St	30	B1/B2
Allan Pl	30	B2
Allan Rd	30	A2
Allan Ter	30	A2
Allandale Rd		
(5300-5328)	30	A2
(5329-5399)	29	C1
Alta Vista Ct	22	A2
Alta Vista Rd	22	A1/A2
Alta Vista Ter	22	A1
Arlington Rd	29	A1/B1
Asbury Ln	22	A2
Ashfield Rd	30	B1
Auburn Ave	22	C2
Avamere St	22	A2
Avondale St	29	A2
Baccarat Ct	22	C2
Balfour Ct	22	A1
Balfour Dr	22	A1
Baltimore Ave	30	A1/A2
Barrister Ct	22	A1
Bates Rd	22	B2
Battery Ln	22	C1/C2
Battery Pl	22	C1
Bayard Blvd	30	A2/B2
Beech Ave	22	A1
Bellevue Dr	29	A2
Benton Ave	22	A1/A2
Berkley St	30	B2
Bethesda Ave	29	A1/A2
Beverly Rd	29	A1
Blackistone Rd	30	B1
Blakeford Ct	30	A1
Boxwood Ct	30	B1
Boxwood Rd	30	B1
Bradley Blvd	29	B1/B2
Brandt Pl	22	B2
Bristol Square Ln	22	A1
Broad Brook Ct	22	A2
Broad Brook Dr	22	A2
Broad St	30	C1
N Brook Ln	22	C1
S Brook Ln	22	C1
Brookdale Rd	30	A2
Brookview Dr	30	A1
Butler Rd	29	C1
Bywood Ln	22	B2
Camberley Ave	22	B1
Cammack Dr	30	A1
Cardinal Ct	30	A1
Carvel Cir	30	B1
Carvel Rd	30	B1
Cedar Ln	22	A2
W Cedar Ln	22	B1/B2
Cedar Way	22	A2
Cedarcrest Dr	22	A2
Center Dr	22	B1/B2
Chalfont Ct	30	B1
Chalfont Pl	30	B1
Chandler St	22	A1

Street	Page	Grid
Chanute Dr	22	A2/B2
Charlcote Rd	22	C1
Charles St	22	A1
Chase Ave	22	C2
N Chelsea Ln	22	C2
S Chelsea Ln	22	C2
Cheltenham Dr	22	C2
Chelton Rd		
(7600-7749)	29	A2
(7750-7999)	22	C2
Chestnut St		
(4300-4354)	23	C1
(4355-4799)	22	C2
Clara Barton Pky	30	C1
Clarden Rd	29	A1
Clarendon Rd	29	A1/B1
Clipper Ln	29	C1
Cloister Ct	22	B1
Convent Dr	22	B1
Cooper Ln	30	A2
Cordell Ave	22	C2
Corsica Dr	22	A2
Crescent St	30	A2
Danbury Ct	22	A2
Danbury Rd	22	A1
Del Ray Ave	22	C2
Denton Rd	29	A1
Dorsey Ln	29	C1
Dover Rd	30	A2
Dudley Ct	22	A1
Dudley Ln	22	A1/A2
Dudley Ter	22	A1
Duvall Dr	30	B1
Earlston Dr	30	A2
East Dr	22	B2
East Ln	29	A1
East Rixey	22	B2
East West Hwy	29	A2
Edgemoor Ln	29	A1
Elliott Rd	30	B1
Elm St	29	A1/A2
Elmhirst Dr	22	A2
Elmhirst Ln	22	A2
Elsmere Ave	22	A1/A2
Elsmere Ct	22	A1
Elsmere Pl	22	A2
Enfield Rd	22	A2
Exeter Rd		
(7000-7699)	29	A1
(7700-7899)	22	C1
Exfair Rd	29	A1
Fairfax Ct	29	B1
Fairfax Rd		
(6649-7699)	29	A1/B1
(7700-7899)	22	C1
Fairfield Dr	22	B2
Fairmont Ave	22	C2
Falmouth Ct	30	B1
Falmouth Rd	30	A1/B1
Farrington Rd	30	B1
Flint Dr	30	A2
Fordyce Pl	22	A1
Forest Rd	22	A1
Fresno Rd	22	A2
Garden Ln	22	B2
Garfield St	22	B1/C1
Gladwyne Ct	22	B2

Street	Page	Grid
Gladwyne Dr	22	B2
Glen Cove Pky	30	A2
Glenbrook Pky	22	B2
Glenbrook Rd		
(6601-7649)	29	A1/B1
(7650-8199)	22	C1/C2
Glenwood Rd	22	C1
Goddard Rd	22	C1
Grant St	22	B1
Greentree Rd	22	B1
Greenway Dr		
(4900-5018)	30	A2
(5015-5098)	29	C1
Gretna St	22	A2
Grier Rd	22	B2
Grounds Rd	22	B2
Hagar Ln	29	A1
Hampden Ln		
(4700-7649)	29	A1/A2
(7650-8299)	22	C1
Harling Ln	22	C2
Harwood Rd	22	C1
Hempstead Ave	22	B1
Highland Ave	22	C2
Holland Ave	22	A1
Holland Ct	22	A1
Hoover St	22	B1
Huntington Pky	22	C1
Jamestown Ct	30	A2
Jamestown Rd	30	A2/B1/B2
Jefferson St	22	B1/C1
Jesup Ln	22	A1
Johnson Ave	22	B1
Jones Bridge Rd	22	B2
Kentbury Dr	23	C1
Kentbury Way	23	C1
Kentucky Ave	22	C2
Keokuk St	30	A2
Keystone Ave	22	C1
Kingsley Ave	22	A1
Lambeth Rd	22	C1
Lancaster Dr	22	B2
Landy Ln	29	C1
Leroy Pl	30	A2
Lincoln Dr	22	B1
Lincoln St	22	B1
Linden Ave	22	A1
Linden Ct	22	A1
Little Falls Dr	30	A2
Little Falls Pky	30	A1
	29	B1
Locust Ave	22	A1
Locust Hill Ct	22	A2
Locust Hill Rd	22	A2
Lucas Ln	22	C1
Lynbrook Dr	22	B2/C2
Mac Arthur Blvd	30	C1
Malden Dr	30	A2
Manning Dr	29	B1
Maple Ave	22	C2
Maplewood Park Dr	22	A1
Marion Ln	22	C1
Maryland Ave	22	B2/C2
Massachusetts Ave	30	A1/B2
McKinley St	22	B1
Meldar Dr	22	B2
Memorial Rd	22	B1

Silver Spring

Street Index

Street Index

Street Index

Street Index

Street Index